ECUADOR &
THE GALÁPAGOS ISLANDS

BETHANY PITTS

Contents

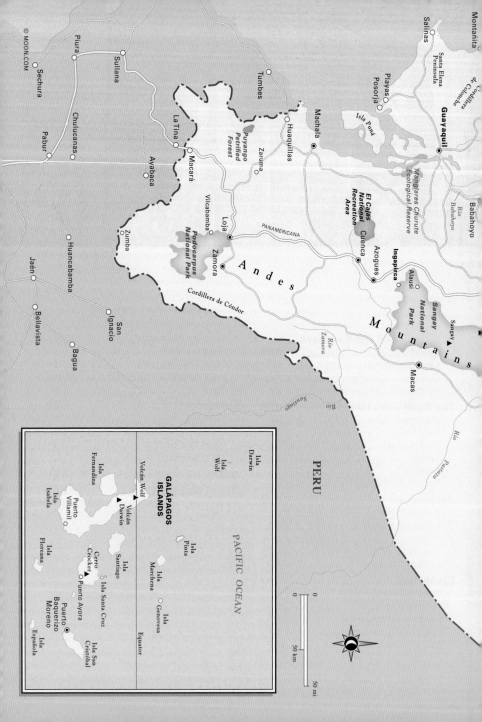

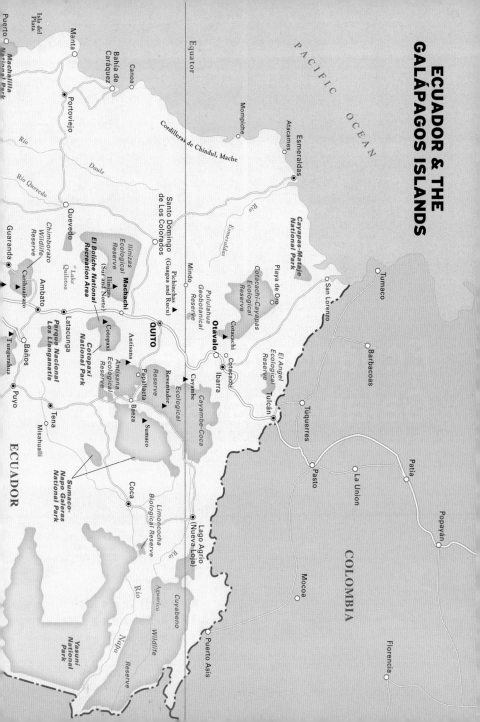

ECUADOR & THE GALÁPAGOS ISLANDS

Ecuador & the Galápagos Islands

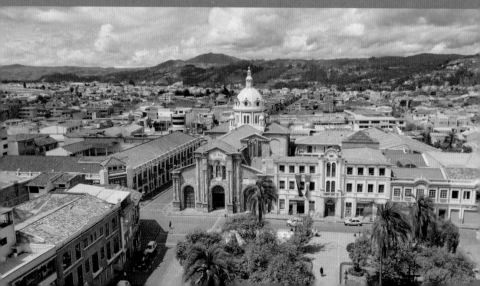

The people are as varied as the landscape. The Amazon alone is home to 11 indigenous nationalities, including two uncontacted tribes, each with its own language and ancestral traditions. This is a country where shamans invoke jungle spirits in ancient ceremonies and Kichwa farmers gather at the top of a gorilla-shaped hill to conduct rituals asking for rain.

Despite its astonishing wealth of attractions, much of Ecuador's potential remains largely untapped, offering perhaps its best hope for a sustainable future. This book highlights destinations and projects that help conserve its natural eco-systems and benefit its warm, welcoming people, while providing visitors with authentic experiences.

Be prepared, though. A holiday romance with Ecuador might just turn into the love of your life.

Clockwise from top left: sword-billed hummingbird; Volcán Cotopaxi; marine iguanas in Tortuga Bay on Santa Cruz island; La Basílica del Voto Nacional's clock tower.

During my first visit to Ecuador, I wandered the colonial streets of Quito; marveled at the luminous water of the Quilotoa crater lake; and watched jewel-bright hummingbirds from a cloud forest lodge. It was all unimaginably exotic and beautiful. But it was my Amazon experience that forever stamped this country into my heart. On a moonlit canoe journey under the Milky Way, I glided silently across a lagoon amid giant lily pads illuminated by fireflies, accompanied by an orchestra of insects and frogs. Upon returning home, I promised myself that I would return one day.

I fulfilled my promise. That was 10 years ago; since then I have fallen more in love with Ecuador every day. Formerly a restless traveler, I have found my place in the world.

I have spent the last decade discovering the treasures within the borders of this diminutive nation. From my home, I can walk to beaches, mangroves, and tropical forests, where I have spotted whales, iguanas, howler monkeys, hummingbirds, and blue-footed boobies. In less than a day, I can be in the Amazon, Andes, or Galápagos Islands. It is no surprise to anyone who has spent time in Ecuador that this is the most biodiverse country in the world per unit area.

Clockwise from top left: the *coraza*, representing the Spanish invaders, at the Peguche waterfall; textiles on display at the Otavalo textile market; a Salasaca woman spins wool; blue-footed boobies on the Galápagos; bromeliad; the historical center of Cuenca and church in Plaza San Blas.

10 TOP
EXPERIENCES

1 **Hike and Bike the Waterfall Route:** The 17km **Ruta de las Cascadas** takes intrepid cyclists past a series of spectacular waterfalls set amid lush mountain scenery (page 171).

2 **Wander Amid Colonial Architecture:** Gaze up at cathedral spires and get lost along cobblestone streets. The best place to revisit the colonial past is in charming **Cuenca,** nestled amid the stunning Andes (page 200).

3 **Wake Up at an Amazon Jungle Lodge:** Experience nature's impressive orchestration of life like you can nowhere else. You might glimpse caimans, monkeys, or pink river dolphins (page 271).

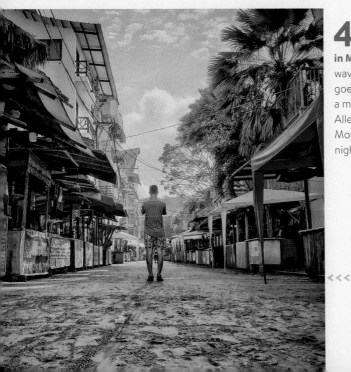

4 **Soak Up the Surf Scene in Montañita:** Ride waves 'til the sun goes down, then sip a mojito on Cocktail Alley, the epicenter of Montañita's legendary nightlife (page 334).

5 **Watch the Sun Rise or Set Over the Vilcabamba Valley:** The light shifts dramatically, illuminating lush green slopes and craggy peaks (page 236).

6 **Dive and Snorkel:** Swim alongside marine marvels like sea turtles, sea lion pups, and whale sharks (page 322, page 346, and page 384).

7 **Get a Condor's Eye View of Quito:** The climb up the tower of **La Basílica del Voto Nacional** isn't for the faint of heart, but those that dare are rewarded with a spectacular view of the Old City (page 44).

8 **Explore Volcanic Landscapes:** Laguna Cuicocha (page 112), Laguna Quilotoa (page 156), and the blackened lava trails in Sierra Negra (page 426) offer a chance to wander through otherworldly terrain.

9 **See Evolution in Action in the Galápagos:** Learn about the science and history of this unique ecosystem at the Charles Darwin Research Station (page 386), San Cristobal's Interpretation Center (page 405), and the Tortoise Reserves on Santa Cruz (page 398).

10 **Go Bird-watching:** Admire hundreds of species of birds—from Mindo's Andean cocks-of-the-rock and colorful toucans to the Galápagos' blue-footed boobies (page 80 and page 402).

Planning Your Trip

Where to Go

Quito

A dramatic backdrop of Andean peaks and snow-capped volcanoes adds to the delight of exploring the cobblestone streets and elegant plazas of Quito's Old Town, one of the best preserved colonial cities in Latin America and a UNESCO World Heritage Site. For a condor's-eye view, brave the climb to the top of the basilica's tower. The capital also hosts the country's best restaurants, museums, and nightlife, with a vibrant cultural scene. North of Quito, the village of Mindo, set amid lush cloud forest, is paradise for birders and nature lovers, while Maquipucuna is the best place in the world to see spectacled bears.

Northern Sierra

The northern Sierra's most famous attraction is the Otavalo textile market, one of the oldest and largest on the continent. Throughout the region, indigenous artisans practice traditional crafts such as weaving and embroidery, and villages such as San Clemente offer the chance to share the Andean Kichwa way of life. The cloud-forested slopes of Intag provide some of the richest biodiversity on the planet and the opportunity to support local conservation efforts. Farther north, the eerily beautiful El Ángel Ecological Reserve protects some of the country's most pristine high-altitude *páramo* (grassland).

In rural parts of the Central Sierra, life has remained unchanged for decades.

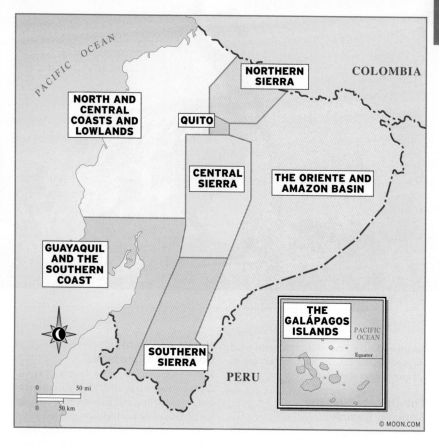

© MOON.COM

Central Sierra

The Avenue of the Volcanoes is a jaw-dropping procession of some of the world's highest peaks, with the snowy flanks of picture-perfect Cotopaxi and colossal Chimborazo easily accessible as day trips. The volcanic crater lake Quilotoa, with its luminous turquoise water, is one of Ecuador's most iconic sights. Baños is a hub for spa treatments and adventure sports, including a downhill bike ride past a series of impressive waterfalls. The idyllic colonial town of Alausí is a charming jumping-off point for some truly spectacular hikes, including to the Ozogoche lakes and to a viewpoint overlooking the Devil's Nose railway line. Much of the region is steeped in myth and legend, hosting unique celebrations fusing ancient indigenous and Catholic traditions.

Southern Sierra

Forget itineraries and wander the colonial streets of Cuenca, Ecuador's most charming city, gazing up at spires, cupolas, and geranium-covered wrought-iron balconies. Explore the country's most important Inca ruins at Ingapirca, where the sun temple still stands. Be as active or decadent as you like in picturesque Vilcabamba, hiking and biking in the dramatic scenery or taking it in from a hammock after a relaxing massage. Visit rural villages for traditional crafts such as woven shawls, handmade guitars, filigree jewelry, and

brown pelican in Tortuga Bay on Santa Cruz island

beaded necklaces. Find wilderness in the wind-swept *páramos* of El Cajas National Park and the untamed forests of Podocarpus.

The Oriente and the Amazon Basin

These mystical forests host nature's most intricate and impressive orchestration of life, where 1 hectare (2.5 acres) can contain as many tree species as all of North America. In a single river journey, a visitor might spot pink river dolphins swimming alongside the canoe, gigantic iridescent blue morpho butterflies flitting overhead, monkeys peering down from the branches, and macaws screeching in the treetops. The Oriente is also home to several indigenous peoples, including two uncontacted tribes, many of whom still live by hunting and gathering. Powerful shamans communicate between the living forest and its human inhabitants and, it is rumored, can shape-shift into jaguars.

North and Central Coasts and Lowlands

The north coast is more lush and tropical than the south, with Afro-Ecuadorian-influenced music and cuisine. The crescent bay of Mompiche is a highlight and one of the region's many good surf breaks. Inland, Playa de Oro is a community-run ecotourism project where wildcats are released into primary rainforest. Farther south, near-deserted beaches can be found in the province of Manabí. Machalilla National Park protects many Galápagos species, such as blue-footed boobies, and is the best place to see humpback whales. The small town of Montecristi is the birthplace of the misnamed "Panama" hat, which has been made there since pre-Columbian times. The indigenous Tsáchila people near Santo Domingo keep their unique ancestral traditions alive and hold shamanic ceremonies in a candlelit underground chamber.

Guayaquil and the Southern Coast

Ecuador's largest city has begun to stand up as a tourist destination, undergoing a major redevelopment in recent years. To the west, Montañita is the star attraction of Santa Elena province, with a world-class point break, legendary nightlife, and hallucinatory sunsets. The neighboring beaches all have their own character and charm, and most have good surf breaks. Inland is a jungly interior dotted with waterfalls. South of Guayaquil, the infrequently visited province of El Oro includes the charming mountain town of Zaruma, the petrified forest at Puyango, the dramatic labyrinthine rock formations rising from the *páramo* at Cerro de Arcos, and the lush green birding paradise of Buenaventura.

The Galápagos Islands

The legendary Galápagos Islands, located about 1,000 kilometers (620 mi) west of Ecuador's mainland, are in fact the peaks of underwater volcanoes. Because the islands developed in complete isolation, their flora and fauna are found nowhere else on earth. Visitors will encounter land iguanas and giant tortoises fearlessly roving the lunar scenery, with blue-footed boobies and frigate birds soaring overhead. Snorkelers can play with curious seal pups and admire the sunlight dappling on the shells of sea turtles, while marine iguanas graze seaweed from the rocks below. Those who venture farther underwater will discover some of the world's best dive sites, with giant manta rays, hammerheads, and whale sharks.

Know Before You Go

When to Go

Ecuador's climate is so varied that it's impossible to make sweeping generalizations. The Sierra, Amazon, and coast all have their own climate, and within these are countless microclimates, often depending on altitude. The good news is that there is no bad time to visit.

Broadly speaking, the coast is sunny and hot (around 30°C/86°F) from December to May, with occasional torrential downpours. It's cooler (20-25°C/68-77°F) and grayer the rest of the year, especially August to November. The climate in the Galápagos more or less mirrors the mainland coast. In the Sierra, it's often sunny during the day and chilly at night. Daytime temperatures average 15-20°C (59-68°F), occasionally peaking at 25°C (77°F), with nights falling to 7-8°C (45-46°F) and sometimes dropping to freezing. The driest, warmest months are June to September, with December to May the wettest. Whatever the season, Andean weather can change very quickly. In the Amazon, the wettest period is April to May and the driest is August to October. Year-round, daily highs average 30°C (86°F), with nighttime lows around 20°C (68°F). Rainstorms tend to be torrential and brief.

There are no national high or low tourism seasons, but accommodations are likely to be booked up—and may be double in price—around New Year's Day, Carnival, and Easter.

Passports, Visas, and Entry Requirements

Travelers from the vast majority of countries do not require a visa to enter Ecuador and will be given a 90-day permit stamp upon arrival. This permit can only be issued once per year (i.e., if you are granted one on April 1, 2019, you cannot request another until April 1, 2020). A passport with validity of at least six months is required. You may be asked for proof of onward travel (a reservation for a bus ticket to Peru or Colombia is sufficient). If you are traveling from a country with a risk of yellow fever transmission, including Peru, Colombia, Brazil, Argentina, and Bolivia, you may be asked for a vaccination certificate, which is valid for life. Check with the

World Health Organization for the current list of affected countries.

To enter the Galápagos, it is necessary to show a reservation for a Galápagos hotel or cruise boat, or a letter of invitation from a local resident of the islands. A health insurance requirement may be introduced. Check with your tour operator or hotel for the latest information.

If you know beforehand that you would like to stay in Ecuador beyond 90 days, consider applying for a longer visa with your local Ecuadorian embassy before your trip, to avoid formalities in Ecuador. Alternatively, the 90-day visa can be extended once, by paying a fee. After that, it's possible to apply for various longer-term tourist and resident visas. Since February 2018, overstaying involves a fine.

See the *Visas and Officialdom* section of the *Essentials* chapter for more details.

Vaccinations

All visitors should make sure their routine immunizations are up to date, along with hepatitis A and tetanus. Those whose activities may put them at extra risk should also consider hepatitis B, rabies, typhoid, and tuberculosis vaccinations. Yellow fever immunization is recommended for those traveling to the Amazon region and Esmeraldas province. A yellow fever vaccination certificate is required when entering Ecuador from a country where it is present and is valid for life. There is a low risk of malaria in the Amazon basin; bite avoidance is advised, rather than antimalarial medication.

Ecuador is considered high risk for the Zika virus, which is usually mosquito-borne. The official advice is that pregnant women should postpone non-essential travel to Ecuador. Women should avoid becoming pregnant while in Ecuador and for eight weeks after leaving.

Transportation

Ecuador has two international airports, both modern and efficient: the Mariscal Sucre International Airport, located near the town of Tababela, about 12 kilometers (7.5 mi) east of Quito, and José Joaquín de Olmedo International Airport in Guayaquil. A network of domestic airports across the country can be accessed in under an hour by plane from Quito. Guayaquil has direct domestic connections to Quito and the Galápagos. With some exceptions, mainland flights are generally economical (from $40 one way). Flying to the Galápagos is much more expensive (at least $400 round-trip).

Ecuador's bus system is comprehensive and economical, and the roads are generally good. For short journeys, taxis are readily available and affordable. For longer journeys, hiring a driver is an option, but it's not cheap. Car rental is more budget friendly, but driving in urban areas can be quite alarming and tough to avoid, as rental companies are only present in the largest cities.

The Best of Ecuador

Ecuador is so compact that, if you plan it right and are prepared to move around, you can see a decent chunk of the country in just two weeks, traveling by bus. If you have an extra week and the available budget, consider adding a visit to the Galápagos Islands, easily accessible from Quito or Guayaquil.

Days 1 & 2
QUITO

Arrive in Quito, check into your hotel, and then explore **Old Town,** taking in the churches, plazas, and museums of the historical center, before heading to the **Museo Fundación Guayasamín** and **Capilla del Hombre,** just north of New Town. While in Quito, dine on the beautifully preserved colonial street of **La Ronda.**

Days 3-5
OPTION 1: MINDO

Take an early morning bus northwest from Quito to **Mindo,** where you can visit a **butterfly farm** and **hummingbird garden,** or go hiking, birding, or biking in the cloud forest. In the evenings, choose one of the excellent restaurants on Gourmet Avenue. When you're done exploring Mindo, head back to Quito early enough to continue to Machachi in the Central Sierra.

OPTION 2: OTAVALO

Take an early morning bus from Quito to Otavalo, and spend time exploring the surrounding countryside or visiting a **Kichwa village.** If you're in Otavalo on a Saturday, don't miss the **textile market.** Head back to Quito and continue to Machachi.

Days 6-9
CENTRAL SIERRA

From Machachi, spend three days in the Central Sierra. Start your exploration with a tour of the **Cotopaxi National Park,** including the walk to

Plaza Grande and Catedral Metropolitana de Quito

the **José Rivas Refuge** at 4,800 meters (15,750 ft.). Continue south from the park to **Latacunga** and visit the historical center, or head to the **Brazales neighborhood** to see the traditional **barley toasting furnaces.**

From Latacunga, take a day trip to the volcanic **crater lake Quilotoa** and the nearby village of Tigua, famous for traditional **paintings of Andean scenes.**

Travel from Latacunga to Baños and get active (hiking, rafting, climbing, or bridge jumping) or take it easy at the thermal baths, followed by a massage. From Baños, rent a mountain bike and enjoy the **Ruta de las Cascadas,** a downhill bike ride past a series of spectacular waterfalls.

Days 10-13
OPTION 1: COCA
For a rainforest immersion, travel from Baños to Quito, then on to Coca by air or overnight bus.

From Coca, either visit a **jungle lodge** in the **Yasuní National Park** for a three-day/two-night package or take a three-day/two-night combined tour to Yasuní and Limoncocha (both options should be reserved in advance).

Arrive back in Coca and return to Quito by air or bus.

OPTION 2: SANTA ELENA
Take a one-day **"rainforest lite" tour** from Baños to Puyo before heading to the coast on the overnight bus to Santa Elena.

While on the coast, you have several options. You can head to Montañita for **surf lessons,** swim in the horseshoe bay of Ayangue, take a tour to Isla de la Plata for **wildlife viewing,** or simply **relax on the sand.** Pick your favorite activities before returning to Quito.

Day 14
On your final day in day in Quito, get your last glimpses of the city before heading home.

tablecloths at the Otavalo textile market

Sani Lodge in Yasuní National Park

Explore Indigenous Cultures

Throughout Ecuador, direct descendants of pre-Inca civilizations still maintain their traditional ways of life, including ancestral rituals, language, agriculture, handicrafts, and medicines. Visiting indigenous communities will not only enrich your visit to Ecuador, but provides them with a sustainable source of income and helps preserve their rich cultural heritage.

Tigua paintings often depict traditional celebrations.

- In the northern Sierra, villages near **Otavalo** offer weaving demonstrations, Andean cooking classes, and energy-cleansing rituals. This is perhaps the best region to participate in the celebrations of Inti Raymi and Pawkar Raymi.

- Near Ibarra, a community ecotourism project in **San Clemente** shares the **Caranqui** way of life and Andean cosmovision, including a path of medicinal plants.

- In the central Sierra, there are several **Panzaleo** villages near Quilotoa, such as **Sasquili,** known for its indigenous market; **Tigua,** where artists paint Andean scenes on sheepskin; and **Pujilí,** famous for its traditional Corpus Christi celebrations.

- On the flanks of Chimborazo, **Purahá** guides take visitors to a sacred cave where their ancestors performed rituals asking the volcano for blessings.

- Near Baños, the **Salasacas** still weave in the ancestral way, using sheep wool and plant dyes. Women can be seen spinning yarn as they walk.

- In the southern Sierra, Cuenca provides easy access to the **Cañari** community tourism projects at **Jima** and **Kushi Waira.** The Cañari are famous for their fierce resistance to the Inca invasion.

- Between Cuenca and Loja, five **Saraguro** villages have formed a community tourism network, where visitors can participate in handicrafts workshops, traditional agriculture, ancestral medicines, music, and dance.

- In the northern Amazon region, the **A'i Kofán** and **Siekopai** people are known for their skilled shamans and can be visited from Lago Agrio.

- There are several lodges run by Amazonian **Kichwa** communities in **Yasuní National Park.** Other Kichwa community tourism projects include **Shayari** near Lago Agrio, **Sinchi Warmi** near Misahuallí, **Cabañas Rayukindi** at Limoncocha, and **Sarayaku** in Pastaza.

- The **Tsáchila** community of **Chigüilpe** near Santo Domingo holds ayahuasca ceremonies in a subterranean shamanic chamber. To represent the knowledge of their shamans, the men wear a *mushily,* a cotton doughnut perched on top of their head.

- In coastal Manabí, the ancestral community of **Agua Blanca** offers hikes in the tropical dry forest and to a lake of therapeutic water and healing mud. An archaeological museum includes pieces of the famous U-shaped shamanic stone chairs made by their forebears, the Manteños.

14 Days of Ecoadventures

This two-week itinerary includes some of the country's best examples of eco- and community led tourism in the cloud forest, rainforest, and Sierra. You'll see a side of Ecuador rarely seen by visitors, while directly supporting environmental conservation and the preservation of indigenous cultures.

Day 1

Arrive in Quito and spend the day exploring the churches, plazas, and museums of the historical district, before dining at Tandana, a nonprofit ecological restaurant with wonderful views.

Days 2 & 3
OPTION 1: MAQUIPUCUNA RESERVE & BEAR LODGE

From Quito, head north to **Maquipucuna Reserve & Bear Lodge,** the best place in the world to see **spectacled bears.**

OPTION 2: YUNGUILLA

From Quito, head northwest to the cloud forest reserve and community ecotourism project at **Yunguilla.** The community project produces organic cheeses and jams.

Days 4-6
INTAG

Return to Quito from the Bear Lodge or Yunguilla and then continue to **Intag,** where the rugged cloud forested slopes and crystalline streams host some of the highest biodiversity on the planet. Every visit helps the local people in their struggle against mega-mining.

Hike in the **Intag Cloud Forest Reserve,** known for its orchids, hummingbirds, and the Andean cock-of-the rock; or nearby **Junín,** where a community ecotourism project offers horseback riding and a guided hike to a waterfall.

Visit one of the projects that provide Intag residents with sustainable sources of income,

hummingbird nest in the garden of El Refugio de Intag

Surf's Up!

Montañita local and Latin American champion Dominic "Mimi" Barona

Ecuador is a warm-water paradise for surfers of all levels. Peak season is from December to May, though there are rideable waves year-round. There is a wide variety of breaks, many of them uncrowded and some world class.

- **Montañita** is Ecuador's main surf destination. The world-class right-hand point break at the Point (La Punta) is for advanced surfers only, with waves up to 3 meters (10 ft), but the long beach break is suitable for all levels. Classes and board rental are readily available.

- The beaches north of Montañita (**Olón, Curia, San José,** and **Ayampe**) all have long, uncrowded beach breaks for all levels of surfer. Olón is perhaps the best place in the country to learn.

- Farther north, **Puerto Cayo** is a world-class barreling beach break. **San Lorenzo** is another beach break with some of the country's biggest waves.

- Often considered Ecuador's second surf destination after Montañita, **Canoa** has a long, quality beach break suitable for all levels, with board rental and classes available. The town isn't without its safety issues, however.

- In Esmeraldas province on the northern coast, **Mompiche** is one of Ecuador's best waves: a world-class, epically long left point break that can be flat out of season. Board rental and classes are available.

- South of Montañita, there are a number of breaks around **Salinas,** mostly for advanced surfers, such as **La Chocolatera** and **Lobería. Chulluype** is a left-hand point break suitable for intermediates. Board rental and classes are available in Salinas.

- Just 90 minutes from Guayaquil, **Playas** has a series of beach breaks for surfers of all levels. It's not the most picturesque of destinations, but there are often waves and sun here in low season, when both are lacking in the Montañita area. Nearby, the small village of **Engabao** has a consistent right-hand point break and adjoining beach break.

- Surf on the **Galápagos Islands** is focused on the island of **San Cristóbal,** which has world-class, fickle waves and uncrowded lineups for advanced surfers only. Reef breaks are sharp, rocky, and shallow, with colder water than on the mainland. **Tortuga Bay** on **Santa Cruz** is the only Galápagos beach break that is suitable for learning.

There are plenty of thrills to be had in a country that boasts such dramatically changing terrain. Whether you want to zoom downhill on a bike, raft through river rapids, or scale a peak, you'll find what you're looking for in Ecuador.

QUITO

- In **Mindo,** adventure seekers will enjoy **zip-lining** through the forest canopy, **tubing** down pristine rivers, or exploring the area on two wheels.

- Quito tour operators offer **rafting** in the **Toachi** and **Blanco Rivers,** which provide some of the longest navigable sections of white water in Ecuador.

- Peaks such as **Pasochoa** and **Guagua Pichincha** are good training for **mountaineers** looking to acclimatize and get into shape.

NORTHERN SIERRA

- The countryside around **Otavalo** offers wonderful **hiking, biking,** and **horseback riding,** including spectacular descents into the Intag Valley. Tour agencies offer **climbing, rafting,** and **kayaking.**

- For **mountaineering,** "starter peak" **Fuya Fuya** is a popular climb as acclimatization practice for higher peaks.

- Near **Ibarra,** tandem **paragliding** rides and courses are available on the slopes of the volcán Imbabura.

CENTRAL SIERRA

- The three big peaks for **mountaineering** are **Cotopaxi, Chimborazo,** and **Cayambe.** **Rumiñahui** and **Iliniza Sur** are less challenging. Chimborazo and Cayambe offer thrilling **downhill biking.**

- Spectacular **hiking, horseback riding,** and **biking** are available around the volcanic crater lake **Quilotoa,** which can also be explored by kayak.

- **Baños** is Ecuador's **adventure sports capital,** with vast range of activities including hiking, biking, horseback riding, rafting, kayaking, rock climbing, canyoneering, zip-lining, bridge jumping, and paragliding. A highlight is the **Ruta de las Cascadas,** a downhill bike ride past a series of waterfalls.

- **Riobamba** is a hub for **mountaineers, trekkers,** and **mountain bikers.** Biking excursions include the descent of **Chimborazo** and longer tours to the **Lagunas de Ozogoche** and **El Altar.**

SOUTHERN SIERRA

- The stunning scenery around **Vilcabamba** offers wonderful **hiking, biking,** and **horseback riding.** Downhill bike tours are available in **Podocarpus National Park.**

THE ORIENTE AND THE AMAZON BASIN

- **Tena** has developed into Ecuador's **watersports** capital, and there is excellent **whitewater rafting** and **kayaking** nearby, along with **caving, canyoneering,** and **tubing.**

- There is excellent **rafting** and **kayaking** near **Baeza** on the **Río Quijos** and other local rivers. Also near Baeza is **Peña Pivico,** a 75-meter (245-ft) natural rock wall with 39 **rock climbing** routes.

NORTH AND CENTRAL COASTS AND LOWLANDS

- On the coast near Manta, **Santa Marianita** is a kitesurfers' mecca, and nearby **Crucita** is the place for **paragliding.** Just outside the village of **Libertador Bolívar** in Santa Elena province, **Playa de Bruja** also has excellent paragliding (known locally as parapenting).

- Outside the Galápagos, the best **scuba diving** can be found at **Isla de la Plata** off the coast of Manabí, known for its population of giant manta rays.

THE GALÁPAGOS ISLANDS

- The Galápagos Islands rank among the world's best **diving** and **snorkeling** destinations. **Santa Cruz** has the most dive sites, while **San Cristóbal** has relatively fewer. **Isabela** has Isla Tortuga and the more advanced sites La Viuda and Cuatro Hermanos.

- The center of **surfing** in the archipelago is **San Cristóbal,** which has a few good sites within easy access of Baquerizo Moreno. **Santa Cruz** and **Isabela** have popular surf sites, too.

The Siekopai people paint their faces with paste from the achiote fruit.

including organic coffee grown in the shade of native trees, artisanal natural toiletry products, and handicrafts made from woven sisal.

Days 7 & 8
SAN CLEMENTE
Travel from Intag to **San Clemente,** a small village just outside Ibarra where a community ecotourism project shares the indigenous **Kichwa Caranqui** way of life with visitors.

Hike the path of **medicinal plants** before helping to harvest and cook a **traditional Andean meal** straight from the organic gardens.

Days 9-12
From San Clemente, head back to Quito to continue to either Lago Agrio or Puyo.

OPTION 1: LAGO AGRIO TO THE AMAZON
From Quito travel to Lago Agrio by air or bus. Stay overnight at **Amisacho,** a regenerative permaculture project.

The following day, continue into the Amazon to visit either the **A'i Kofán Avie** or **Siekopai**

Remolino community, both of which have ecotourism projects and are known for their skilled shamans. Spend the next days in the rainforest, hiking, birding, learning about ancestral medicines, and sharing community life.

OPTION 2: PUYO TO THE SARAYAKU COMMUNITY
From Quito, take the bus to Puyo and stay overnight at **Los Yapas,** a sister project to Amisacho.

The following day, travel by canoe or plane to the **Sarayaku community,** known for their defense of the rainforest against oil exploitation (tour should be booked well in advance). Spend the next days in the rainforest, sharing community life.

Day 13
Return to Quito via Lago Agrio or Puyo.

Day 14
This is your last day in Quito. Head to the **Mindalae Ethnic Museum** to learn about Ecuador's indigenous cultures and pick up some souvenirs at the attached fair trade store.

Beach and Mountain Getaway

Conveniently located between the coast and the Andean foothills, the up-and-coming city of Guayaquil is a good jumping-off point for exploring Southern Ecuador. Fly into its efficient international airport for your two-week getaway. Marvel at Ecuador's mind-blowing diversity with this itinerary, which takes in the best of the coast, the colonial delights of Cuenca, the idyllic town of Vilcabamba, and the highlights of El Oro province, including a petrified forest and a natural rock fortress.

Days 1 & 2

Arrive in Guayaquil and take the 3-hour trip straight to the coast: **Montañita** or **Olón** for surfing, or **Ayangue** for calmer seas. Check into your beachside hotel, enjoy some of the local cuisine, and spend your time taking surfing, yoga, or salsa lessons during the day, followed by nights out in Montañita.

Day 3

Head to Isla de la Plata to see **blue-footed boobies** and **humpback whales** (June to Oct.), or explore the coast's lush green interior with a **hike or horseback ride** to the tropical forest near Dos Mangas.

Days 4 & 5

Head back to Guayaquil and on to the colonial city of Cuenca. Wander the **colonial streets** and elegant plazas of **Cuenca's historical district**, gazing up at spires, cupolas and geranium-covered wrought iron balconies.

Day 6

Take a day trip from Cuenca to the pristine windswept *páramo* of **El Cajas National Park,** or the country's most important **Inca ruins** at **Ingapirca**.

The Point and the long beach breaks at Montañita and Olón provide waves for surfers of all levels.

Ingapirca Ruins

Day 7

Spend the morning in **Cuenca,** taking in a couple of **museums** or heading to the **Mirador de Turi and Aventuri Extreme Park** for the swing that flies you out over the city. Take a shuttle to **Vilcabamba** in the afternoon and arrive in time for dinner.

Days 8 & 9

Spend the days **hiking, biking, or horseback riding** in Vilcabamba. You can also tour an **organic coffee growers association** (APECAEL) in nearby San Pedro de Vilcabamba. While in town, treat yourself to a massage.

Day 10

From Vilcabamba, take an early bus to Loja and take an organized day tour to **Bosque Petrificado de Puyango,** the largest petrified forest in South America.

Day 11

From Loja, head to the charming mountain town of **Zaruma** and spend the afternoon enjoying the beautiful scenery, wooden architecture and great coffee.

Days 12 & 13

Stay and explore Zaruma, or head to the natural **rock fortress** at **Cerro de Arcos** with its labyrinth of caves and spend the night in the refuge there.

Day 14

Head back to Guayaquil on the 5-hour bus ride from Zaruma.

WITH MORE TIME

Guayaquil provides tourists with a convenient departure point for the **Galápagos Islands.** Via land tour or cruise, admire nature's fragile beauty seen in the stunning landscape and diverse wildlife of this fascinating archipelago.

Quito

At 2,850 meters (9,350 ft) above sea level, Ecuador's dramatic capital city is the second highest in the world after Bolivia's La Paz. Built on the ashes of the northern Inca capital following the 1533 Spanish conquest, Quito is nestled in a valley surrounded by majestic Andean peaks, among them the restless Volcán Pichincha.

This spectacular backdrop adds to the joy of exploring the cobblestone streets, stately plazas, and lavish churches of Quito's Old Town, one of the best-preserved colonial cities in Latin America and a UNESCO World Heritage Site. Amid the spires and cupolas, rows of pastel-colored houses with flower-decked wrought-iron balconies sit beside lovingly restored mansions with tranquil inner courtyards. Looking further back in time, museums provide fascinating insights

Highlights

Look for ★ to find recommended sights, activities, dining, and lodging.

★ **Plaza Grande:** Find a quiet bench alongside Quiteño elders in the heart of Old Town to watch city life swirl past, surrounded by lily-filled flower beds, elegant colonial architecture, and magnificent mountain scenery (page 39).

★ **La Compañía:** The epitome of golden grandeur, this extravagant chapel is the most dazzling of Quito's many beautiful churches (page 42).

★ **La Casa de Alabado:** Learn about Ecuador's ancient indigenous cultures at this museum, with beautifully arranged exhibits of pre-Columbian artifacts and fascinating displays on the underworld and shamanism (page 43).

★ **La Basílica del Voto Nacional:** With its mystical animal gargoyles, the country's tallest church is a striking sight. Even more spectacular is the condor's-eye view of the historical district from the spire, for those who dare to make the climb (page 44).

★ **Mindo:** A world-class birding and ecotourism destination, this village nestled in the cloud forest is heaven for nature lovers and adventure seekers (page 80).

★ **Maquipucuna Biological Reserve:** Protecting over 6,000 hectares (14,800 acres) of pristine rainforest in the heart of one of the

earth's top five biodiversity hot spots, this is the best place in the world to see the Andean or spectacled bear (page 87).

into Ecuador's pre-Columbian ancestral cultures, some dating back to 4000 BC. The vibrant, living city is as intriguing as its rich history. Stop at a sidewalk café and watch formally dressed Quiteños hurrying to work alongside shoe shiners, street vendors, and indigenous women in traditional dress.

A short hop from Old Town are the modern streets and shining office blocks of New Town, where some of the country's best hotels, restaurants, and nightlife are found. Historically known for its conservative values, these days Quito is home to Ecuador's most vibrant alternative music, art, and theater scene. Relief from the city noise can be found in the welcome green spaces of the capital's well-kept parks.

Despite its proximity to the equator, Quito is spared the oppressive heat of the lowlands by its altitude. Locals are fond of saying that their city gives you four seasons in one day—a statement supported by the spring-like mornings, summery afternoons, autumnal evenings, and wintry nights. The Quiteños themselves are welcoming, helpful, and speak a beautifully clear Spanish, great for visitors who are practicing their language skills.

For many tourists, Quito is simply a convenient launching point for travel to the Galápagos Islands or the Amazon, but it's worth devoting at least a couple of days to exploring this captivating city in its own right.

PLANNING YOUR TIME

Quito extends over 50 kilometers (31 mi) north-south, and about 8 kilometers (5 mi) across. Fortunately, it's easily divided into zones: one for historical sights (**Old Town**); one for the majority of restaurants, accommodations, nightlife, and visitor services (**New Town**); and then everything else. Its long, narrow geography and abundance of transport options make the capital quite easy to get around.

In Old Town, El Centro Histórico, most of the plazas, churches, and other religious buildings are situated within a few blocks of the original heart of the city, Plaza de la Independencia or **Plaza Grande**. This is also where most of the museums and theaters are located. You may choose to head straight for the sights that are of most interest or to forget itineraries and simply wander the cobbled streets. There are several spectacular viewpoints to admire Old Town from a bird's eye view, from the gothic spires of the *basílica* to the even loftier heights of the **TelefériQo** (cable car).

Old Town is cleaner, safer, and a joy to explore following a multimillion-dollar regeneration. The blue-uniformed Metropolitan Police have a visible presence and are generally friendly, helpful, and happy to give directions. The municipality of Quito has put together an excellent map of themed historical walks, available at the Plaza Grande tourist office, where it is also possible to book **multilingual tours** given by municipal police.

Northeast of the historical center, **La Alameda** and **El Ejido** parks form a buffer between Old and New Town. Linking the two districts are the major thoroughfares **Avenida América** and **Avenida 10 de Agosto.**

The hub of New Town is Plaza Quinde, commonly known as **Plaza Foch,** and the surrounding area, Mariscal Sucre, or simply **La Mariscal.** Here you'll find most of the visitor amenities: hotels, restaurants, bars, Internet cafés, banks, shops, and tour agencies. The nightlife is particularly raucous Thursday-Saturday. The contrast with Old Town is striking; this sector has a decidedly modern, international feel. North of New Town is **Parque La Carolina,** a popular park with impressive facilities and a botanical garden. To the east of the park, the **Museo Fundación Guayasamín,** formerly the home of master painter and sculptor Oswaldo Guayasamín, is also the location of

---

Previous: Plaza San Francisco; hummingbird in Mindo; the ornate ceiling of La Compañía.

his unfinished masterpiece, the **Capilla del Hombre (Chapel of Man).**

North and east of La Mariscal are quieter neighborhoods such as arty, bohemian **La Floresta** and **Guápulo,** worth a visit for the spectacular views and lovely park.

Most visitors, especially backpackers, stay in New Town, mainly because there are so many amenities. However, following the regeneration, there is an increasing number of good accommodation and dining options in Old Town, offering a more authentic and picturesque experience. Wherever you stay, it's only a short cab or bus ride between the two districts. Traffic is overwhelming everywhere, though it's noticeably lighter on the weekends, when the lack of commuter traffic makes taxi journeys quicker and cheaper.

If you only have a couple of days in Quito, spend most of it in Old Town and perhaps half a day in New Town. Four days is a good amount of time to take in the key sights of both areas, by which time you may be ready to head out of the city for the welcome tranquility of **Mindo.**

CLIMATE

Quito is famed for its spring-like climate, with daytime temperatures usually 10-22°C (50-72°F), though a sunny day can feel hotter. Mornings tend to be chilly, but it can heat up considerably around midday. Temperatures drop quickly on rainy afternoons and in the evenings, with nighttime as low as 7°C (45°F). There is generally more sun in the mornings, so sightseeing early is a good idea. Locals say that the city can experience all four seasons in a single day, and that isn't far off the mark. The two rainy seasons are February-April and, to a lesser extent, October-November.

Even on a sunny day, Andean people are much more formal in dress than their coastal counterparts. Long shorts with a T-shirt is fine, but skimpy clothes should be avoided. The weather can change suddenly, so bring lots of layers and a light waterproof jacket. Jeans, a T-shirt, and a light sweater are usually fine for the daytime, but you'll want to add a jacket for the evening. Closed shoes rather than sandals are recommended. Don't underestimate the strength of the equatorial sun, and wear sunscreen, even on a cloudy day.

Bear in mind that the elevation may leave you breathless and lightheaded. Dizzy spells, stomach upsets, insomnia, headaches, and fatigue can also occur. It is best not to overexert yourself and to minimize caffeine and alcohol in favor of plenty of water and light food, at least for the first couple of days.

SAFETY

The majority of visitors to Quito experience no difficulties with security. However, as with most countries, extra precaution is needed in Ecuador's big cities. The high concentration of foreigners in the capital has led to an increased number of criminals targeting them, but if you stay alert and take some commonsense precautions, your visit will likely be incident-free.

If you feel unsafe or are lost, Quito's Metropolitan Police are the most friendly and helpful in the country. They wear blue uniforms and are out in force in the main tourist areas.

Watch out for pickpockets and bag-slashers in crowded areas, at tourist spots, and on public transport. The trolley bus services (Trole, Ecovia, and Metrobus) are perhaps the worst for pickpockets. Don't go into any parks after dark. It is a good idea to seek current advice from your hotel about places to go and places to avoid.

La Mariscal in New Town is the most risky area for foreign visitors. Walk just a couple of blocks from the main drag and the police presence is replaced by groups of thieves or drug dealers. Unlike in the rest of the country, drunken street violence is common. Always use a prebooked taxi to get to and from La Mariscal after dark, even if your hotel is only a few blocks away. Drink spiking is prevalent, so don't leave your beverage unattended. Don't accept flyers from anyone on the street, as they may be dusted with scopolamine, a

Quito

© MOON.COM

Map labels:

TELEFERICO

SEE "OLD TOWN QUITO" MAP

SEE "NEW TOWN QUITO" MAP

OCCIDENTAL/ SUCRE

BAHÍA DE CARÁQUEZ

24 DE MAYO

LA CASA DE ALABADO

LA COMPAÑÍA

PLAZA GRANDE

El Panecillo

Cumandá

Recoleta

MALDONADO

Santo Domingo

Qmandá Urban Park

Qmandá

Marín

GUAYAQUIL

PICHINCHA

Plaza del Teatro

LA BASÍLICA DEL VOTO NACIONAL

Santa Prisca

Consejo Provincial

Marín Central

MOSAICO

COLOMBIA

Parque La Alameda

NUCANCHI PEÑA

UNIVERSITARIA

UNIVERSIDAD CENTRAL

LA GASCA

Seminario Mayor

HOSPITAL CARLOS ANDRADE MARÍN

AMERICA

Espejo

Perez Guerrero

10 DE AGOSTO

El Ejido

Parque

TARQUI

PATRIA

ORELLANA

ELOY

AMAZONAS

POST OFFICE

PLAZA FOCH

COLÓN

LIBERTADOR

EL TREBOL

SIMÓN

GRAL

ITCHIMBIA PARK AND CULTURAL CENTER

BOLÍVAR

INSTITUTO GEOGRAFICO MILITAR

LADRON

DE

12 DE OCTUBRE

COLISEO RUMIÑAHUI

RUMIÑAHUI

AVE CUMANDÁ

To Quitumbe Terminal and Chimbacalle Train Station

To Machachi Latacunga and South

To Los Chillos

GUEVARA

Río Machángara

IGLESIA GUAPULO

Guapulo

Legend:

- TROLÉ LINE
- ECOVÍA LINE
- TROLÉ/METROBUS
- ECOVÍA STOP
- METROBÚS

Scale:

0 — 0.5 mi

0 — 0.5 km

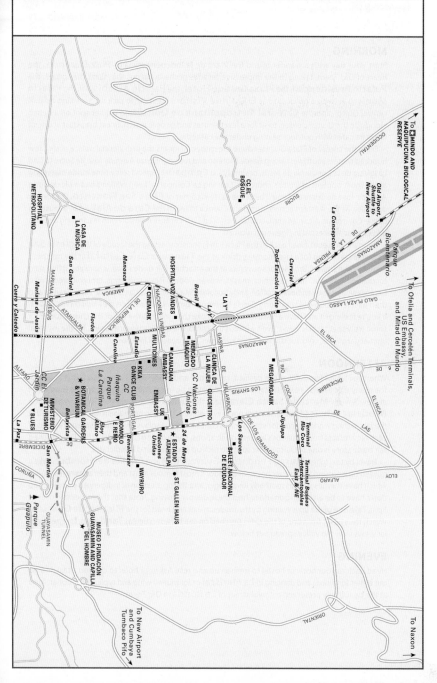

One Day in Quito

MORNING

Start your day with a wander round the Plaza de la Independencia or **Plaza Grande,** the heart of Old Town, taking in the impressive facades of the buildings that flank the square: the **Palacio Presidencial,** the **Plaza Grande Hotel,** the **Palacio Arzobispal,** the **Palacio Municipal** (with a quick stop at **El Quinde Visitors Center** to pick up a walking map of central Quito), and the **Catedral Metropolitana de Quito.** Find a quiet spot on a bench alongside the Quiteño elders to sit for a few minutes and people watch, or eat breakfast at one of the little cafés with outdoor seating under the cathedral.

From the corner of Plaza Grande where the cathedral meets the presidential palace, walk a few hundred meters southwest along García Moreno and turn right onto Avenida José de Sucre to find La Iglesia de la Compañía de Jesús, or simply **La Compañía.** Spend some time inside marveling at the most opulent of Quito's churches. Leaving La Compañía, keep walking half a block along Avenida José de Sucre and you'll be at the eastern corner of **Plaza San Francisco.** Diagonally opposite, at the western corner, turn onto Cuenca to reach the **Casa de Alabado,** a museum of pre-Columbian art, in an immaculately restored 17th-century mansion with fascinating displays on Ecuador's ancestral indigenous cultures.

From the museum, head back to the Plaza San Francisco, passing the facade of the **Iglesia San Francisco** to stop for a late-morning drink at the **Tianguez Café Cultural** at the northern corner of the square. Browse for souvenirs at the attached fair trade store, where you'll find *paja toquilla* or "Panama" hats, ceramics, masks, woven goods, Tigua paintings, embroidered shirts, *tagua* jewelry, wooden bowls, coffee, and chocolate. Make your way back to the Plaza Grande and then past it for seven blocks along García Moreno to get to **La Basílica del Voto Nacional.** If you're feeling fit and have a head for heights, make the ascent to the top of the church tower for some truly spectacular views. Even without the climb, the basilica is worth a visit, for the mystical animal gargoyles, colorful stained-glass windows, and peaceful interior.

AFTERNOON

When you've had your fill at the basilica, take a taxi and enjoy a well-deserved lunch at one of the many **excellent restaurants in New Town** or, to eat with the locals, try the food court at New Town's **Mercado Santa Clara,** near the Central University. After lunch, walk to the **Mindalae Ethnic Museum** at the north end of New Town, to once again immerse yourself in the fascinating world of Ecuador's indigenous cultures, with displays on shamanism and replicas of ceramic artifacts from Ecuador's ancient civilizations, some dating back to 4000 BC. The attached fair trade store is one of Quito's best spots to pick up souvenirs and handicrafts.

Travel by taxi to the **Museo Fundación Guayasamín** and **Capilla del Hombre.** Take a guided tour around the former house of Ecuador's most famous artist and then admire his works, which have themes such as motherly love, anger, and the oppression of indigenous peoples. You don't have to be an art aficionado to find these deeply moving. Note that the museum closes at 5pm. Take one of the taxis waiting by the museum exit and head for the **Mirador de Guápulo.** Watch the sunset from one of the cafés perched on the hillside (such as **Tandana**), for spectacular views over the valley spread out below.

EVENING

Head back to your hotel or hostel to freshen up and rest. Ask your hotel to call you a taxi and go out either for dinner and dancing in **La Mariscal** or for mulled wine and typical Ecuadorian food at the beautifully preserved colonial street of **La Ronda** in Old Town.

substance that leaves victims in a docile state, vulnerable to robbery or assault.

The area around El Panecillo (the hill with the Virgin Mary on top) is not safe, so take a taxi there and back. If walking to La Tola neighborhood from Old Town, take Manabí rather than Esmeraldas, as the latter street is the red-light district and can feel pretty sketchy even during the day. At the *teleférico* (cable car), assaults and muggings have been reported on the hike to Rucu Pichincha, although there are now police patrols on the weekend. Do not attempt this climb alone, and ideally don't take valuables.

Rather than flagging taxis down on the street, especially at night, ask your hotel, restaurant, or bar to call you a radio (pre-booked) taxi. If you have a phone, save the number of a reliable taxi company and call one yourself (see the *Getting Around* section for some numbers). It might seem like an inconvenience to wait the few extra minutes for it to arrive, but it's a sure way to avoid "express kidnappings," where shady drivers relieve passengers of cash, valuables, and PIN numbers. Victims are usually released unharmed, but these incidents are terrifying and can turn violent. After Guayaquil, this type of crime is most common in Quito, especially in La Mariscal. See the *Crime* section of the *Essentials* chapter for more information on how to travel safely by taxi in these cities.

Sights

OLD TOWN
Keep in mind that opening hours fluctuate regularly; those provided here are the latest available.

★ Plaza Grande and Vicinity
The ornate 16th-century **Plaza Grande** (Venezuela y Chile) is the focal point of colonial Quito. Officially called the Plaza de la Independencia, it features a winged statue to independence atop a high pillar. The surrounding park is a great place for people watching; it's bustling with activity but there is always a quiet bench from which to take in the city life and beautiful surroundings. Join the locals in getting your shoes expertly shined under the arches on the northeastern side of the square.

On the plaza's southwest side, the **Catedral Metropolitana de Quito,** or simply **La Catedral** (Venezuela y Espejo 715, tel. 2/257-0371, www.catedraldequito.org/en, mass 7am and 8:30am daily), is actually the third to stand on this site since the founding of the city in 1534. Buried here is hero of independence Antonio José de Sucre, along with Ecuador's first president, Juan José Flores, and President Gabriel García, who died on August 6, 1875, after being attacked with machetes outside the presidential palace. The adjoining **Museo de la Catedral** (9am-5pm Mon.-Sat., $3) houses religious artifacts and paintings.

Next door, the **Iglesia El Sagrario** (tel. 2/228-4398, 7:30am-6pm Mon.-Fri., 7:30am-noon Sat., 8am-1pm and 4pm-6pm Sun.) was begun in 1657 and completed half a century later. Originally built as the cathedral's chapel, it is considered one of the city's most beautiful churches. Unlike at La Compañía, photography is allowed inside.

The northwest side of the plaza is taken up by the long, columned facade of the seat of government, the **Palacio Presidencial** (9am-5pm Tues.-Sat., 9am-4pm Sun.), also known as El Carondelet. Entrance is only possible with a free tour and upon presentation of ID. Tours leave every 15-20 minutes and last 80 minutes.

The **Palacio Arzobispal** (Archbishop's Palace) on the northeast side of the plaza leads to a three-story atrium housing a number of small shops and eateries. The cobbled courtyard, thick whitewashed walls, and wooden balconies make it worth a look.

Old Town Quito

© MOON.COM

MARISCAL SUCRE

CHIMBORAZO

LOJA

ROCAFUERTE

LÓPEZ

BAHIA

DE

CARAQUEZ

BOLIVAR

IMBABURA

MIDEROS

LA CONCEPCIÓN ★

CHILE

TIANGUEZ CAFÉ & FAIR TRADE STORE

PORTAL DE CANTUÑA ●

CASA DE ALABADO ☩

MERCADO
CENTRAL ■

IGLESIA SAN
FRANCISCO ▲

CAPILLA DE
CATUÑA

MUSEO FRAY
PEDRO GOCIAL ★

*Plaza San
Francisco* ★

CENTRO CULTURAL
METROPOLITANO

PALACIO PRESIDENCIAL ★

MONASTERIO EL
CARMEN ALTO ●

HOSTAL SUCRE ●

AMBATO

El Panecillo ▲

MUSEO
DE LA CIUDAD ★

SUCRE

CASA MARIA
AUGUSTA
URRUTIA ★

LA COMPAÑÍA ★

MUSEO
NUMISMÁTICO ★

IGLESIA EL
SAGRARIO ★

CATHEDRAL ★

PLAZA
GRANDE ☩

Plaza Grande

ARCHBISHOP'S
PALACE ★

LA
RONDA

LOJA

24
DE
MAYO

LEÑA QUITEÑA ▲

Santo Domingo

CASA DE SUCRE ★

HOTEL SAN FRANCISCO DE QUITO ●

ESPEJO

TOURIST
OFFICE

IGLESIA
SAN AGUSTIN ★

▼ EL CAFÉTO

5 DE

Cumanda ■

*Plaza
Santo Domingo*

HOTEL BOUTIQUE
PLAZA SUCRE ●

TEATRO
BOLIVAR ★

SANTA
CATALINA ★

MAMACUCHARA

IGLESIA
SANTO DOMINGO ●

La Recoleta ■

MALDONADO

TEXEIRA

JUNIN

Marin Terminal ●

PICHINCHA

← To Trole Estacion Sur

24
DE
MAYO

Cumandá

Urban

Park

To Playón, el Trébol,
and el Censo

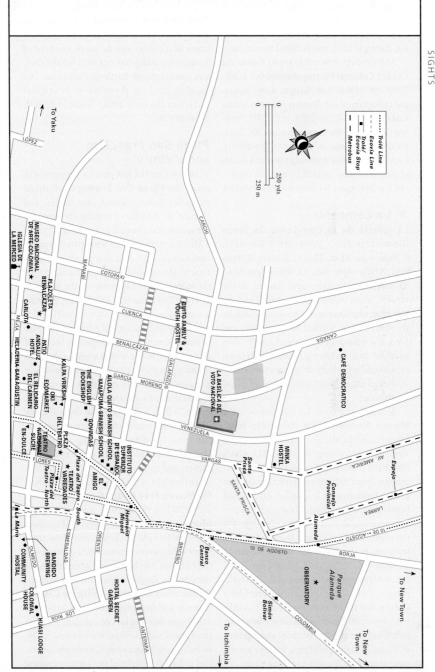

To Yaku

LÓPEZ

Trolé Line
Ecovia Line
Trolé/
Ecovia Stop
Metrobus

0   250 yds
0   250 m

IGLESIA DE
LA MERCED ■
MUSEO NACIONAL
DE ARTE COLONIAL ★

CARCHI

To New Town

MANABI
COTOPAXI

PLAZOLETA
BENALCÁZAR ★
CARLOTA

QUITO FAMILY &
YOUTH HOSTEL ●

CUENCA

HELADERIA SAN AGUSTIN
MEJIA

CANADA

LA BASÍLICA DEL
VOTO NACIONAL ✚

BENALCÁZAR

PATIO
ANDALUZ
HOTEL
EL RELICARIO
DEL CARMEN

KALPA VRIKSHA ★
OKI
ECOMARKET
THE ENGLISH
BOOKSHOP ■
YANAPUMA SPANISH SCHOOL ▼
AILOLA QUITO SPANISH SCHOOL ▼
GOVINDAS ▼

GARCÍA
MORENO
GALÁPAGOS

CAFÉ DEMOCRÁTICO ●

VENEZUELA

MINKA
HOSTEL ●

EN-DULCE ▼
TEATRO
NACIONAL
SUCRE ★
PLAZA
DEL TEATRO ★
DEL TEATRO ▼

FLORES

INSTITUTO
SUPERIOR
DE ESPAÑOL
EL
AMIGO ▼

VARGAS

Santa
Prisca ●

Consejo
Provincial ■

AV AMÉRICA

Espejo
LARREA

TEATRO
VARIEDADES ★
Plaza del
Teatro - North

Plaza del Teatro - South

SANTA PRISCA

Alameda

10 DE AGOSTO

La Marín

OLMEDO

ESMERALDAS

ORIENTE

Hermano
Miguel

BRICEÑO

Banco
Central ●

BORJA

To New Town

BANDIDO
BREWING

COMMUNITY
HOSTAL ●

HOSTAL SECRET
GARDEN ●

LOS RIOS

COLONIAL
HOUSE ●

HUASI LODGE ●

ANTEPARA

10 DE AGOSTO

Parque
Alameda
OBSERVATORY ★

Simón
Bolívar ●

COLOMBIA

To New
Town

To Itchimbia

The church of **La Concepción** (7am-11am daily) stands at the corner of Chile and García Moreno. The attached convent is Quito's oldest, dating to 1577, and is closed to visitors.

At the corner of Benalcázar and Espejo, the **Centro Cultural Metropolitano** (tel. 2/395-2300, ext. 15508, 9am-4:30pm daily) houses the collection of the **Museo Alberto Mena Caamaño** (tel. 2/395-2300, ext. 15535, 9am-5pm Tues.-Sat., 10am-4pm Sun., $1.50). There are displays of colonial and contemporary art, a set of wax figures depicting the death throes of patriots killed in 1810 by royalist troops, and a gallery space for temporary art exhibits.

★ La Compañía

La Iglesia de la Compañía de Jesús (Benalcázar 562 y Sucre, tel. 2/258-4175, 9:30am-6pm Mon.-Thurs., 9:30am-5:30pm Fri., 9:30am-4pm Sat., 12:30pm-4pm Sun., $5, free visits 12:30pm-4pm 1st Sun. of the month) is one of the most beautiful and extravagant churches in the Americas. Built by the wealthy Jesuit order between 1605 and 1765, it is a glorious example of both human endeavor and opulence gone mad, with seven tons of gold reportedly decorating the ceiling, walls, and altars. Night visits can be arranged in advance.

Across Sucre from La Compañía is the **Museo Numismático** (tel. 2/393-8600, https://numismatico.bce.fin.ec, 9am-5pm Tues.-Fri., 10am-4pm Sat.-Sun., $1), which traces the history of Ecuador's various currencies, from indigenous bartering systems to the adoption of the U.S. dollar. Also housed here is the national music library, where there are often free concerts in the evenings. On the opposite side of García Moreno from the museum is the **Casa de María Augusta Urrutia** (tel. 2/258-0103, 10am-6pm Tues.-Fri., 9:30am-5:30pm Sat.-Sun., $2). This well-preserved 19th-century mansion provides a glimpse into the life of one of the city's wealthiest former inhabitants, with luxurious accoutrements from all over the globe and a gallery of Victor Mideros paintings. Visitors are accompanied by a Spanish-speaking guide.

Heading east on Sucre brings you to the **Casa de Sucre** (Venezuela 573 y Sucre, tel. 2/295-2860, 9am-5:30pm daily, free), former home of Antonio José de Sucre, the hero of Ecuadorian independence who led the decisive victory of the Battle of Pichincha. The building has been preserved in its original state from the early 1800s. Tours in English are available.

Plaza San Francisco and Vicinity

Turn right up the hill past La Compañía to reach the **Plaza San Francisco,** flanked by Calles Bolívar, Benalcazár, Sucre, and Cuenca. At the time of writing, the center of the square was closed for the construction of a Metro station with an anticipated completion date of 2019. It is still possible to walk around the outside of the plaza and to visit the **Iglesia San Francisco** (on the west side of Plaza San Francisco on Cuenca, 6:30am-6:45pm Mon.-Sat.), the oldest colonial edifice in the city and the largest religious complex in South America. It was begun on the site of an Inca royal house within weeks of the city's founding in 1534. The first wheat grown in Ecuador sprouted in one of its courtyards, and Atahualpa's children received their education in its school. Inside the church, many of the design motifs come from indigenous cultures, including the smiling and frowning faces of sun gods, and harvest symbols of flowers and fruit.

To the right of the church's main entrance, the **Museo Fray Pedro Gocial** (Sucre, tel. 2/295-2911 or 98/729-9479, www.museofraypedrogocial.com, 9am-5:30pm Mon.-Sat., 9am-1pm Sun., $2.50) houses one of the city's finest collections of colonial art, dating from the 17th and 18th centuries. Guided tours are included in English, Spanish, and French. On the other side, the **Capilla de Catuña** (Cuenca y Bolívar, 8am-noon and 3pm-6pm daily) also has displays of colonial art. The story goes that this chapel was constructed by an indigenous man named Catuña who promised to have it completed in a certain amount of time. When it became obvious that he wasn't going to meet his deadline, he offered his soul to the devil in exchange for help getting the job done. Catuña finished the chapel but had a sudden change of heart, begging the Virgin Mary to save him from his hasty agreement. Sure enough, a foundation stone was found to be missing during the inauguration, negating his deal with the devil.

Under the church on the plaza is the **Tianguez Café Cultural** (tel. 2/257-0233, www.tianguez.org, 9:30am-6:30pm Mon.-Tues., 9:30am-11:30pm Wed.-Sun.), a great place to sample Ecuadorian cuisine from the coast, Amazon, and Andes. The attached Tianguez fair trade store is one of Quito's best spots to pick up souvenirs and handicrafts. Both the café and the shop are run by the Sinchi Sacha Foundation, a nonprofit set up to support indigenous Amazon communities.

★ La Casa de Alabado

Just off the Plaza San Francisco is the **Casa de Alabado** (Cuenca y Bolívar, tel. 2/228-0940, www.alabado.org, 9am-5:30pm daily, $4), a museum of pre-Columbian Ecuadorian art in an immaculately restored 17th-century house. The exhibition is organized with the aim of communicating the indigenous cosmovision or world view. Rather than being arranged by chronology or region, the artifacts are grouped by themes such as "Underworld," "Spiritual World of the Shaman," and "World of the Ancestors." Some ceramic sculptures are from civilizations as ancient as 4000 BC. The exhibits are exquisitely presented and the museum is an oasis of tranquility. All signage is in Spanish and English. Guided tours and audio guides are available. The café in the courtyard by the entrance is a pleasant spot to take a break from museum hopping and doesn't require an entrance fee.

Plaza Santo Domingo and Vicinity

Down the hill southeast of Plaza San Francisco, bounded by Bolívar, Guayaquil, and Rocafuerte, is the elegant **Plaza Santo Domingo,** decorated with a statue of Sucre pointing to the site of his victory on the slopes of Pichincha. Built between 1581 and 1650, the interior of the **Iglesia Santo Domingo** (7am-6:45pm daily), on the west side of the plaza, is an ornate and atmospheric mix of styles, including colonial and Moorish. It is possible to quietly enter the church during the daily services (7am-1pm and 5pm-6:45pm), but tours are only possible between 1pm and 5pm. The attached **Museo Fray Pedro Bedon** (tel. 2/228-0518, 9am-1:30pm and 2:30pm-5pm Mon.-Fri., 9am-2pm Sat., $3) allows entry to the church cupolas and terraces.

From the western corner of Plaza Santo Domingo, turn onto Guayaquil to reach one of the best-preserved colonial streets in Old Town. Also called Calle Juan de Dios Morales, **La Ronda** was nicknamed for the evening serenades (*rondas*) that once floated through the air. The narrow lane is lined with painted balconies, craft shops, tiny art galleries, and cafés. During the day, it's a charming place to wander and relish the lack of traffic (it's a pedestrian-only zone). At night, it's a popular and safe spot for Quiteños and visitors to soak up the atmosphere with a drink of *canelazo* and some traditional music.

Directly below La Ronda, the urban park **Cumandá** (Av. 24 de Mayo, tel. 2/257-3645, Facebook @quitocumanda, 7am-8pm Mon.-Fri., 8am-6pm Sat.-Sun., $1-5) is a masterpiece of urban renewal. Located in a refurbished former bus station, the park has green spaces and gardens, six swimming pools, a climbing wall, cycling and jogging paths, covered indoor soccer and *ecuavolley* courts, exhibition spaces, children's areas, exercise studios, a gym, a table tennis area, and a chess area. The three-story complex also acts as a cultural center. Check Facebook for event listings. Art and photography exhibits are displayed on the lower levels alongside a sprawling satellite map of Ecuador and a 3-D sculpture of Quito.

Museo de la Ciudad and Monasterio El Carmen Alto

Just up from La Ronda is **Museo de la**

Ciudad (García Moreno y Rocafuerte, tel. 2/228-3883, www.museociudadquito.gob.ec, 9:30am-4:30pm Tues.-Sun., $3), which traces Quito's history from precolonial times to the beginning of the 20th century, with scale models of the city at different periods. Tours in English can be arranged for $1.

Opposite the Museo de la Ciudad, the **Monasterio y Museo del Carmen Alto** (tel. 2/281-513, 9:30am-5:30pm Wed.-Sun., $3), was the home of Santa Mariana de Jesús from 1618 to 1645. Abandoned children were once passed through a small window in the patio to be raised by the nuns. Exhibitions focus on religious art, the history of the monastery, and the life of Santa Mariana de Jesús. A small adjacent shop sells cookies, chocolate, honey, creams, and herbs. The **Arco de la Reina** (Queen's Arch) over García Moreno marks the original southern entrance to Quito's center.

Iglesia de la Merced and Vicinity

The entrance to one of Quito's most modern churches, **Iglesia de la Merced,** completed in 1742, is on Chile, just up from the corner of Cuenca. The 47-meter (154-ft) tower contains the city's largest bell. The church is dedicated to Our Lady of Mercy, whose statue inside is said to have saved the city from an eruption of Pichincha in 1575. To the left of the altar is the entrance to the **Monasterio de la Merced,** housing Quito's oldest clock, built in London in 1817. There are many paintings by Victor Mideros depicting the catastrophes of 1575.

Across Mejía is the **Museo Nacional de Arte Colonial** (Cuenca y Mejía, tel. 2/228-2297, 9am-5pm Tues.-Sat., $2), home to Quito's finest collection of colonial art, including works by Miguel de Santiago, Caspicara, and Bernardo de Legarda.

TOP EXPERIENCE

★ La Basílica del Voto Nacional

Walk eight blocks northeast from Plaza Grande on Venezuela to reach **La Basílica del**

Voto Nacional (Carchi 122 y Venezuela, tel. 2/228-9428, 8am-6pm daily, $2). Even though construction began in 1892, the church is still officially unfinished. Inside, the gray interior is illuminated by dappled colored light from the stained-glass windows, making a peaceful change from the gaudiness of many other churches. The basilica is famous for its mystical gargoyles in the form of pumas, monkeys, penguins, tortoises, and condors, and for the spectacular views from the spire. Its two imposing 115-meter (377-ft) towers make this the tallest church in Ecuador, and the climb to the top isn't for the faint of heart, but those that dare are rewarded with a wonderful panorama of the Old City. A separate ticket, available from the window labeled "Administración General Boletería" in the square in front of the church, is required to enter the tower (9am-4pm daily, $2). An elevator goes as far as a café and gift shop; those wishing to go higher must rely on their legs and nerves. If you're feeling brave, head through the gift shop, then across a narrow wooden bridge over the nave of the church and up a series of metal ladders. It's also possible to climb a small metal staircase to look inside the clock tower.

Iglesia San Agustín and Vicinity

If you've seen enough ornate gold to last a lifetime, the **Iglesia San Agustín** (Chile y Guayaquil, 7:30am-noon and 2pm-5pm Tues.-Fri., 8am-noon Sat.-Sun.) offers something different, with its pastel frescoes and elegant chandeliers. The adjoining **Convento y Museo de San Agustín** (tel. 2/295-1001, 9am-12:30pm and 2pm-5pm Mon.-Fri., 9am-1pm Sat., $2) features a feast of colonial artwork on the walls and surrounds a palm-filled cloister. Ecuador's declaration of independence was signed in the *sala capitular* on August 10, 1809. Many of the heroes who battled for independence are buried in the crypt.

1: pastel frescoes in the Iglesia San Agustín; 2: La Basílica del Voto Nacional; 3: pre-Columbian pottery at La Casa de Alabado; 4: Plaza Grande in Old Town

Plaza del Teatro and Vicinity

This small plaza at Guayaquil and Manabí is surrounded by restored colonial buildings, including the **Teatro Nacional Sucre** (tel. 2/295-1661, www.teatrosucre.com, Facebook @TeatroSucreQ). Erected in 1878, it's one of the country's finest theaters, hosting frequent plays and concerts, including opera, jazz, ballet, and international traveling groups. Tucked in the far corner is the renovated **Teatro Variedades** (tel. 2/295-1661, ext. 125, Facebook @TeatroVariedadesQuito), part of the same organization as the Teatro Sucre. Check Facebook for listings. Next door is the popular **Café Teatro**.

Teatro Bolívar

Built in 1933, the 2,200-seat **Teatro Bolívar** (Pasaje Espejo 847 *y* Guayaquil, tel. 2/228-5278, www.teatrobolivar.org) was designed by the famous American theater architects Hoffman and Henon in a lavish eclectic style, combining art deco, Spanish, and classical motifs. Sadly, the theater was scorched by a fire in 1999, only two years after an extensive restoration. After appearing on the World Monuments Watch's "100 Most Endangered Sites" list in 2004, funds were raised for another restoration, which was 85 percent complete at the time of writing. The theater reopened to the public in early 2016, and ticket prices help to fund the remaining work.

Santa Catalina

The **Convent Museo Santa Catalina** (Espejo *y* Flores, tel. 2/228-4000, 1pm-5pm Mon.-Fri., 9am-1pm Sat., $2.50) is attached to the church of the same name. The remains of assassinated president Gabriel García Moreno rested here secretly for many years before being buried under the cathedral. His heart is still buried in the private chapel. There is also an extensive display of religious art and artifacts. A guided tour is included.

ABOVE OLD TOWN
El Panecillo

Old Town's skyline is dominated by a 30-meter (98-ft) statue of the **Virgen del Panecillo** (Calle Palestina, tel. 2/317-1985, www.virgendelpanecillo.com) on the hill at the southern end. The Virgin Mary is depicted preparing to take flight, with a chained dragon at her feet. You can climb up inside the base (9am-5pm Mon.-Wed., 9am-9pm Thurs.-Sun., $1) to an observation platform for views of the city from an altitude of 3,027 meters (9,931 ft) above sea level. The neighborhood at the foot of the hill and on the way up is dangerous, so take a taxi and ask the driver to wait. A round-trip taxi ride from Old Town is $5-8, including a short wait.

Itchimbía Park and Cultural Center

The old Santa Clara market building—imported from Hamburg in 1899 and brought to the highlands by mule, in sections—has been transported from Old Town and rebuilt in all its glory on top of a hill to the east. The glass structure, known as the Palacio de Cristal (Crystal Palace), is now the **Itchimbía Cultural Center** (José María Aguirre, tel. 2/322-6363, Facebook @ItchimbiaCentroCultural). It hosts occasional exhibitions and events, but the more common reason to come here is the view. The vicinity is more pleasant than around El Panecillo, and it's not as hair-raising as climbing the basilica. The center is surrounded by 34-hectare (84-acre) **Itchimbía Park** (*entre* Av. Velasco Ibarra *y* José María Aguirre), which is being reforested and laced with footpaths. Just below on Samaniego is the restaurant **Mosaico** (www.cafemosaicoecuador.com), along with other bars and cafés offering wonderful views. A taxi from Old Town costs $3.

BETWEEN OLD TOWN AND NEW TOWN
Parque La Alameda

Ornamental lakes and a monument to Simón Bolívar sit at opposite ends of this triangular park. Parque La Alameda is bounded by Avenidas Gran Colombia, 10 de Agosto, and Luis Sodiro. Many of the large trees were planted in 1887, when it was a botanical garden. In the center stands South America's oldest astronomical observatory, **Observatorio Astronómico de Quito** (tel. 2/257-0765, http://oaq.epn.edu.ec, 9am-5pm Mon.-Sat., $2), inaugurated in 1864. Night visits can be arranged Tuesday-Thursday via the website. The beautiful old building also houses a **museum** (9am-5pm Mon.-Sat.) filled with books, photos, and antique astronomical tools.

Parque El Ejido

Quito's most popular central park is all that remains of the common grazing lands that once stretched for more than 10 kilometers (6.2 mi) to the north. **El Ejido** (bounded by Avenidas 6 de Diciembre, Patria, 10 Agosto, and Tarqui) played its part in one of the most infamous moments in Ecuador's history, when liberal president Eloy Alfaro's body was dragged here and burned following his assassination. These days, it's a great spot for people watching. Courts for *ecuavolley* (the local version of volleyball) occupy the northwest corner of the park, and there is often a game to watch. A children's playground takes up the northeast corner. On weekends, the area near the arch at Amazonas and Patria becomes an outdoor arts and crafts market. At the time of writing, a section of the park was closed for the construction of a Metro station, anticipated to be finished in 2019.

Casa de la Cultura

On the northern edge of Parque El Ejido, the **Casa de la Cultura** (Av. 6 de Diciembre *y* Av. Patria, www.casadelacultura.gob.ec) may look like a convention center but in fact houses some of Ecuador's most well-known museums. At the time of writing, the main museums were closed for refurbishment and no reopening date had been set. This affects the **Museo del Banco Central**, the **Sala de Arqueología**, and the **Sala de Arte Colonial**.

Still open are the **Museo Etnográfico** (Ethnographic Museum, Facebook @ museoetnograficocce) and the **Museo de Arte Moderno e Instrumentos Musicales** (Museum of Modern Art & Musical Instruments) (both 9am-4:45pm Mon.-Fri., free). The **Agora**, a huge concert arena in the center of the building, still hosts concerts, and the Casa de la Cultura exhibition space is open. Check the website for upcoming events and exhibits. There's also a cinema showing art and cultural films most evenings.

NEW TOWN
Museo Abya-Yala

The small **Abya Yala** complex (12 de Octubre *y* Wilson, tel. 2/396-2899, www.abyayala.org) contains a bookstore with the city's best selection of works on the indigenous cultures of Ecuador. Shops downstairs sell snacks, crafts, and natural medicines, while the second floor is taken up by the small but well-organized **Museo Abya-Yala** (previously Museo Amazónico, 8:30am-1pm and 2pm-5:30pm Mon.-Fri., $2). The museum has two areas: archaeological and ethnographic. The latter is the most interesting, focusing entirely on Amazonian cultures. Two rooms exhibit instruments, clothing, and ceramics from various indigenous nationalities; the third is dedicated to the Shuar people and is the only exhibition in Quito with permission to display real *tsantsas* (shrunken heads). One impactful display contrasts photos of rainforest flora and fauna with images of oil spills to raise awareness of the biggest threat faced by the Ecuadorian Amazon: oil exploitation.

Mindalae Ethnic Museum

Run by the Sinchi Sacha Foundation, which promotes indigenous cultures, fair trade, and responsible tourism, the **Mindalae Ethnic Museum** (Reina Victoria *y* La Niña, tel. 2/223-0609, www.mindalae.com.ec, 9am-5:30pm Mon.-Sat., $3) has five floors with comprehensive collections of ethnic clothing, artifacts, and pottery from all regions, with signage in English. The shamanic-themed room on the top floor is especially interesting, with displays showing the ceremonial altars

New Town Quito

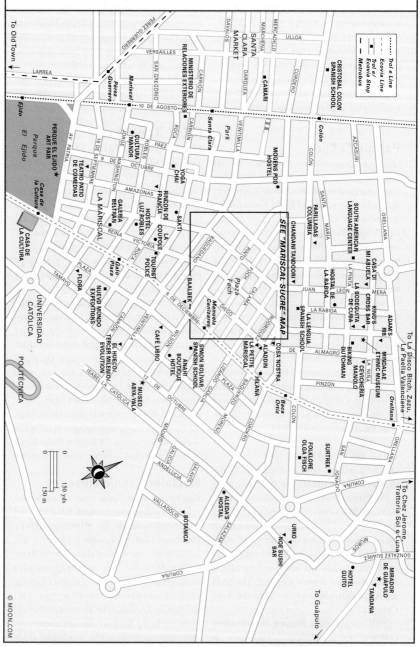

Trol e Line
Ecovia Line
Trol e/
Ecovia Stop
Metrobus

To Old Town ←

CRISTOBAL COLON SPANISH SCHOOL

MINISTERIO DE RELACIONES EXTERIORES

SANTA CLARA MARKET

CAMARI

Park

Colón

MOGENS POD HOSTEL

Santa Clara

PARQUE EL EJIDO ★ ART FAIR
Parque El Ejido

Casa de la Cultura

CASA DE LA CULTURA

TEATRO PATIO DE COMEDIAS

CULTURA MANOR

YOGA CHAI

RINCON DE LA FRANCIA

HOSTEL LUZ ROBLES

GALERIA BELTRAN

LA COUPOLE

SAKTI

TOURIST POLICE

Galo Plaza

PLAZA FLORA

NUEVO MUNDO EXPEDITIONS

EL HUECO/ TERCER MILENIO/ EVOLUTION

SOUTH AMERICAN LANGUAGE CENTER

PARILLADAS COLUMBIA

CHANDANI TANDOORI

BAALBEK

Plaza Foch

Manuela Cañizares

CASA DE MI ABUELA

KING'S CROSS BAR

LA BODEGUITA DE CUBA

HOSTAL DE LA RABIDA

LA RABIDA

LA LENGUA SPANISH SCHOOL

ADAM'S RIB

MINDALAE ETHNIC MUSEUM

BIKING DUTCHMAN

CEVICHERIA MANOLO

ALADDIN

COSA NOSTRA

LA PETITE MARISCAL

HILANA

Baca Ortiz

FOLKLORE OLGA FISCH

SURTREK

To Lá Disco Bitch, Zazu, La Paella Valenciana →

To Chez Jerome, Trattoria Sol e Luna →

CAFE LIBRO

ANAHI BOUTIQUE HOTEL

SIMON BOLIVAR SPANISH SCHOOL

MUSEO ABYA-YALA

UNIVERSIDAD CATOLICA

POLITECNICA

ALEIDA'S HOSTAL

BOTANICA

URKO

MOE SUSHI BAR

HOTEL QUITO

MIRADOR DE GUAPULO ★

TANDANA

To Guápulo →

SEE "MARISCAL SUCRE" MAP

0   150 yds
0   150 m

© MOON.COM

of contemporary shamans from the coast, Andes, and Amazon. The ceramics are replicas of ancient pieces, lovingly recreated by the descendants of the original cultures. The attached fair trade store, beautifully arranged by region, is one of the best places in Quito to pick up souvenirs and crafts, with items such as coffee, chocolate, "Panama" hats, ceramics, woven goods, embroidered shirts, jewelry, and wooden bowls. There is also a restaurant.

NORTH OF NEW TOWN
Parque La Carolina

To escape the concrete of New Town without actually leaving the city, head for Quito's largest park, **Parque La Carolina,** bounded by Avenidas de los Shyris, Naciones Unidas, Amazonas, de la República, and Eloy Alfaro. Popular with early morning joggers and families, it's a great spot for people watching and sampling typical street food. The impressive facilities include courts for tennis, basketball, football, and *ecuavolley*; athletics and cycle tracks; a skate park; a children's play area; a lake with paddleboats; and a gym. Like most of Quito's parks, it's not safe after dark.

Three museums are located on Rumipamba, one of the two boulevards that bisect the park. The **Vivarium** (tel. 2/227-1820, www.vivarium.org.ec, 9:30am-1pm and 1:30pm-5:30pm Tues.-Sun., $3.75) houses more than 100 reptiles and amphibians, including boa constrictors, in relatively spacious tanks with plenty of vegetation. To retreat farther from the city bustle and get your nature fix, visit the **Jardín Botánico** (tel. 3/332-516, www.jardinbotanicoquito. com, 8am-4:45pm daily, $3.50), which showcases Ecuador's vast array of flora, including a bonsai exhibition and 500 species of orchid. Natural history is the focus of the recently refurbished **Instituto Nacional de Biodiversidad** (tel. 2/244-9824, 8am-4:45pm Mon. and Fri., 9am-4:45pm Tues.-Thurs., 10am-4pm Sat.), next to the botanical gardens.

Museo Fundación Guayasamín and Capilla del Hombre

East of Parque La Carolina, up a steep hill in the Bellavista neighborhood, the former home of Ecuador's most famous artist has been converted into the **Museo Fundación Guayasamín** (Mariano Calvache y Lorenzo Chávez, tel. 2/244-6455, www.guayasamin. org, 10am-5pm daily, $8). Guayasamín designed the house himself and filled it with pre-Columbian, colonial, and contemporary art. His own large-scale paintings are alternately

replicas of pre-Columbian ceramic masks at Mindalae Ethnic Museum

tender and tortured, but always deeply emotive. The artist is buried beneath the Tree of Life in the garden just above the museum.

Completed three years after his death in 1999 by the Guayasamín Foundation, the **Capilla del Hombre (Chapel of Man)** is dedicated to the struggles endured by the indigenous peoples of the Americas. Huge paintings fill the open two-story building. In the center is a circular space beneath an unfinished dome mural portraying the workers who died in the silver mines of Potosí, Bolivia. Other works cover topics both heartwarming and wrenching, from the tenderness of a mother and child's embrace in *La Ternura* to the gigantic *Bull and Condor,* symbolizing the struggle between Spanish and Andean identities.

A guided tour in Spanish or English is obligatory in the museum, but visitors are free to wander the Chapel of Man unattended. Entrance to both is included in the ticket. To get there, take a bus bound for Bellavista from Parque La Carolina (marked "Batan-Colmena") or hail a taxi ($2-3). Taxis wait by the main entrance for the return journey.

OTHER AREAS
Guápulo
Just behind Hotel Quito is the **Mirador de Guápulo,** a viewing platform looking down over the charming hillside neighborhood of Guápulo, where the cobblestone streets and lush green park provide a welcome break from the noise and bustle of the city. Take the precipitous Camino de Orellana down the hill to reach the beautiful **Iglesia de Guápulo,** built between 1644 and 1693.

A 15-minute walk up the road behind the church is **Parque Guápulo** (Av. de los Conquistadores, 6am-6:30pm daily)

Previously a wealthy banker's estate, the park has attractive running and walking paths, a lake, an exhibition area, a camping ground, and a children's play area. There is an exit near the lake and parking lot where it is possible to flag down a bus or taxi.

TelefériQo Cable Car
Completed in 2005, the **TelefériQo** (tel. 2/222-2996 or 99/736-0360, www.teleferico.com.ec, 8am-8pm daily, $8.50) ascends the slope of the Pichincha volcano. It departs from above Avenida Occidental, where a tourist center with restaurants, go-karting, and a small theme park has been built. The 2.5-kilometer (1.6-mi) ride to the top takes about 10 minutes, and the views over the city and the Andes from 4,050 meters (13,285 ft) make it worth the entrance fee. On a clear day, it is possible to see an impressive chain of volcanoes, including Cayambe, Chimborazo, and Cotopaxi. Adrenaline seekers can bring a mountain bike and make the return descent on two wheels, or hike to the volcano Rucu Pichincha. Those making the hike should bring an experienced guide, start early, and allow five hours for the round-trip. Assaults and muggings have been reported on the way, although there are now police patrols on the weekend. Do not attempt this climb alone, and don't take valuables. See the *Sports and Recreation* section of this chapter for recommended guides.

There are no public transport options for the TelefériQo. Take a taxi ($3) from the closest trolley station at Mariana de Jesús to Avenida Occidental at the bottom of the hill, then continue on foot, by taxi (another $2), or on the free shuttle bus for the VulQano Park theme park, which is next to the TelefériQo. It's cold at the top so bring warm clothes.

Entertainment and Events

NIGHTLIFE

Quito has a thriving nightlife scene centered around Plaza Foch, Reina Victoria, and Calama in the **Mariscal Sucre** neighborhood. These blocks heave with locals and visitors on Thursday, Friday, and Saturday evenings. The party doesn't really get going until after 11pm, but live music usually starts earlier, between 9pm and 10:30pm. Although the sale of alcohol is officially illegal after midnight Monday-Thursday and after 2am Friday-Saturday, almost no drinking establishments respect this law, though most close before 3am. Many bars and clubs (and even some restaurants) are closed on Sunday and/or Monday. Remember to take your ID, whatever your age, as many places won't let you in without it. Clubs usually have a small cover charge ($3-5), which includes a drink. Bars often have happy hours 5pm-8pm to bring in the early crowds, and several have ladies' nights with free drinks before 10pm. The opening hours listed here were correct at the time of writing; check Facebook pages for updates before venturing out.

As well as the most popular nightlife spot, Mariscal Sucre is the most risky area for foreign visitors. Walk just a couple of blocks from the main drag and the police presence is replaced by groups of thieves or drug dealers. After dark, it's recommended to take a pre-booked taxi from your hotel to your destination, even if it's only a few blocks away. Ask a hotel or bar in La Mariscal to call you a taxi for the return journey, rather than flagging one down in the street. This is a hotspot for "express kidnappings," where shady taxi drivers rob passengers and leave them by the side of the road, usually unharmed. Don't take valuables, credit cards, or more cash than necessary. Drink spiking is common, so don't leave your beverage unattended. Don't accept flyers from anyone on the street, as they may be dusted with scopolamine, a substance which leaves victims in a docile state, vulnerable to robbery or assault.

BARS, PUBS, AND LATE-NIGHT CAFÉS

A block from Plaza Foch, Irish-run **Finn McCool's** (Diego de Almagro y Joaquín Pinto, tel. 2/252-1780, www.irishpubquito. com, noon-1am Mon.-Wed., noon-3am Thurs., 11am-3am Fri.-Sat., 11am-7pm Sun.) is an eternal favorite with visitors and locals alike. It has friendly staff, a warm fire, filling Irish pub food, pool, darts, foosball, and live sports on the TV. It's a good spot to meet people in the early evening, and the party gets lively as the night goes on. **Dirty Sanchez** (Joaquín Pinto y Reina Victoria, tel. 2/255-1810, www.dirtysanchezbar.com, 5pm-12:30am Mon., 3pm-12:30am Tues.-Thurs., 3pm-2:30am Fri.-Sat.) has an eclectic, alternative vibe with live music and DJs. The "We Love Mondays" DJs nights are popular, when many other places are closed. Another café/bar with live music is **Garúa** (Joaquín Pinto y Reina Victoria, tel. 99/713-2286, www.garua-cafe.com, 5pm-9:30pm Tues., 5pm-11:45pm Wed.-Fri., 5:30pm-11:45pm Sat.).

Poetry, tango, art, and salsa nights attract an arty crowd to **Café Libro** (Leonidas Plaza y Wilson, tel. 2/250-3214, www.cafelibro. com, noon-2pm Mon., noon-2pm and 5pm-11:30pm Tues.-Thurs., noon-2pm and 5pm-2am Fri.-Sat.), one of Quito's most established cultural cafés, opened in 1992.

La Mariscal is not the only option in New Town. If you want a quieter evening, head to the neighborhood of Guápulo, where the stunning view makes any night out special. Perched on a steep hillside, **Ananké** (Camino de Orellana 781, tel. 2/255-1421, 6pm-midnight Mon.-Thurs., 6pm-1am Fri.-Sat., www.anankeguapulo.com) is a bohemian pizzeria and bar with regular live music ranging from jazz to funk, dancehall to blues. On

Mariscal Sucre

CORDERO

EL CAFECITO

EL PATIO

MILE TIME

CALAMA

LIZARDO GARCÍA

GALERÍA ECUADOR
AND TOURIST OFFICE

ACHIOTE

NO BAR

TOUCH
UIO

CAYMAN
HOTEL

AMAZONAS

FOCH

MERA

RED HOT
CHILI PEPPERS

LEON

VICTORIA

CAFÉ
DEMOCRATICO

HOSTAL
NEW BASK

CASA JOAQUÍN
BOUTIQUE HOTEL

Plaza del
Quindé

BUNGALOW 6

KALLARI
CAFÉ

JUAN

MISKAY

REINA

GULLIVER
EXPEDITIONS

UNCLE
HO'S

MARISCAL
ARTISANAL
MARKET

ATM BANCO
PICHINCHA

ALMAGRO

GUAYASAMÍN
SPANISH
SCHOOL

GALERÍA
LATINA

DULCE ALBAHACA

GARÚA

PINTO

DIEGO DE

CASA
MARISCAL

DIRTY
SANCHEZ

EL MAPLE

FINN
MCCOOL'S

MEXICALI
BAJA GRILL

WILSON

HOSTAL
HUAKI

Manuela
Canizares

To
Tourist Police

0   100 yds

0   100 m

BAALBEK

© MOON.COM

the same street is **Café Arte Guápulo** (tel. 2/513-2424, Facebook @CafeArteGuápulo, 6pm-midnight Mon.-Thurs., 6pm-2am Fri.-Sat.). With good food, hot wine, and *canelazo* (spiced hot fruit punch with *aguardiente*), it's a good place to warm up on chilly nights. There is often live music on weekends and the venue has hosted some big names in the past, including Manu Chao.

Founded over three decades ago, **Ñucanchi Peña** (Av. Universitaria y Armero, tel. 2/254-0967, Facebook @Niucanchi, 7:45pm-2:45am Fri.-Sat.) is Quito's most famous *peña*, or traditional music club, where live acts from around Ecuador play every weekend. It's not exactly the hippest scene, though Ecuadorian roots music fans can catch everything from Pacific coast *amorfino* songs to *pasillo* waltzes and Andean panpipes. The interior is small, informal, and often crowded, with blacked-out decor and folk art on the walls.

In Old Town, there are a few good cafés and bars along the regenerated **La Ronda,** several of which offer live music at the weekends. The cobbled street's many small establishments serve empanadas, hot mulled wine, hot chocolate, and *canelazo*. **Leña Quiteña** (tel. 2/228-9416, noon-midnight daily) has wonderful views of the Panecillo from the top floor—a great spot for a romantic evening. Thanks to police presence, La Ronda is safe to walk around at night. **Bandido Brewing** (Olmedo y Pedro Fermín Cevallos, tel. 2/228-6504, www.bandidobrewing.com, 4pm-11pm

Mon.-Thurs., 4pm-midnight Fri., 2pm-midnight Sat.) is Old Town's first microbrewery, with a rotating variety of craft beers served in a converted chapel by its three friendly, expat owners. There is regular live music.

Wherever you go out, you cannot help but notice that Ecuadorians' salsa-dancing skills leave the rest of us looking like we have two left feet. You can do something about this; take the plunge and get some classes at one of these **dancing schools: Ritmo Tropical Dance Academy** (Amazonas y Calama, tel. 2/255-7094, www.ritmotropicalsalsa.com), **Tropical Dancing School** (Veracruz y Villalengua, tel. 2/245-9991, and Plaza Kendo, República del Salvador y Portugal, tel. 2/226-8999, www.tropicaldance.com.ec), and **Son Latino** (Reina Victoria N24-211 y Lizardo García, tel. 2/223-4340). Prices start at around $10 pp per hour for one-on-one or couples' lessons.

NIGHTCLUBS

Clubbing in La Mariscal tends to be aimed at the mass market, with a herd mentality. It's noisy and hectic, and you'll either love it or hate it. By far the most popular spot is the American- and British-run **Bungalow 6** (Diego de Almagro y Calama, tel. 99/751-0835, www.bungalow6ecuador.com, 8pm-3am Wed.-Sat.), playing mostly electronic and pop. Local students mix with backpackers on three dance floors. Another option is the **No Bar** (Calama y Juan León Mera, tel. 2/245-5145, 8pm-3am Wed.-Sat.), one of La Mariscal's most well established clubs. Open since 1994, it plays commercial music over two floors. **Blues** (República 476 y Pradera, tel. 99/985-1138, Facebook @ClubBlues, 9pm-3am Wed. and Fri.-Sat.) plays a mix of electronic and rock.

With one location in La Mariscal and another on the edge of Old Town just north of the basilica, **Café Democrático** (www.cafedemocratico.wordpress.com, Facebook @DemocraQuito) offers a different late-night experience, catering to Quito's alternative crowd. There are cultural events, DJs,

and live music several times a week. The La Mariscal location (Lizardo García y Diego de Almagro, tel. 2/603-4775, 6pm-3am Tues.-Sat.) has a café menu, and the Old Town location (in the Centro de Arte Contemporáneo, Montevideo y Luis Dávila, tel. 2/315-0008, 10am-1am Tues.-Sat., 10am-9pm Sun.) has a full restaurant menu.

There are a few **gay bars and clubs** in Quito. One of the best known confusingly has three names: **El Hueco / Tercer Milenio / Evolution** (Veintemilla y Av. 12 de Octubre, tel. 98/729-9228, Facebook @discotecatercermilenio, 10pm-3am Fri.-Sat.) and mostly plays pop music. **TOUCH Uio** (Joaquín Pinto y Juan León Mera, tel. 98/304-6843, 6pm-2am Tues.-Wed., 6pm-3am Thurs., 8am-3am Fri.-Sat.) is primarily a lesbian club. By Parque La Carolina is **Kika Dance Club** (Japón E569 y Av. Amazonas, tel. 99/750-8228, Facebook @fedearguellok, Thurs.-Sat. 9pm-4am). It's smaller than El Hueco and more trendy. It has an open bar with $10 entry before midnight and then turns into a disco playing Latino pop music, as does **La Disco Bitch** (Av. 6 de Diciembre y Av. República, tel. 99/966-4311, Facebook @EsLaDiscoB, 10pm-2:30am Fri.-Sat.).

THEATER, DANCE AND MUSIC

The municipality's website **Quito Culture** (www.quitocultura.info) is the best place to find cultural events, including music, theater, exhibitions, cinema, and festivals.

The **Casa de la Cultura** (6 de Diciembre y La Patria, tel. 5/352-8014, www.casadelacultura.gob.ec) is the city's leading venue for theater, dance, and classical music. The colorful, indigenous-themed **Jacchigua Ecuadorian Folklore Ballet** (tel. 2/295-2025, www.eng.jacchigua.org) performs here at 7:30pm every Wednesday ($35, $82 with dinner). **Casa de la Música** (Valderrama y Av. Mariana de Jesús, tel. 2/226-7093, www.casadelamusica.ec) is an excellent venue for classical music, jazz, and ballet, hosting regular concerts for as little as $5-10.

The **Ballet Nacional de Ecuador** (Manuel Abascal N40-63 *y* Gaspar de Villarroel, Facebook @balletnacionalecuador) puts on shows in a variety of styles, from urban to traditional ballet. Shows are often at their own theater, at Casa de la Música or Casa de la Cultura.

Quito has several excellent theaters. The 19th-century **Teatro Sucre** (Plaza del Teatro, tel. 2/295-1661, www.teatrosucre.com, Facebook @TeatroSucreQ) is Ecuador's national theater and one of the best. Also on Plaza del Teatro and part of the same organization is **Teatro Variedades** (tel. 2/295-1661, ext. 125, Facebook @TeatroVariedadesQuito). Check Facebook for listings. The iconic **Teatro Bolívar** (Pasaje Espejo *y* Guayaquil, tel. 2/228-5278, www.teatrobolivar.org) has been reopened following a devastating fire, and ticket prices help fund the remaining refurbishment work. The

Patio de Comedias (18 de Septiembre *entre* 9 de Octubre *y* Av. Amazonas, tel. 2/256-1902, www.patiodecomedias.org) is a good spot to catch a play Thursday-Sunday in a more intimate atmosphere with dinner options available.

Quito's biggest rock and pop concerts take place at the **Coliseo Rumiñahui** and **Estadio Olímpico.** A good website for tickets to upcoming events is Ecutickets (www.ecutickets.ec).

FESTIVALS

The annual week-long **Fiestas de Quito** celebrate the founding of the city, culminating on December 6. The festivities include parades, fireworks, street parties, and concerts.

The **Verano de las Artes Quito** (Summer of Arts) is an annual cultural program that takes place in August, incorporating musical and theater events and light shows.

Sports and Recreation

CLIMBING AND MOUNTAINEERING
Climbing Companies

A few of Quito's tour companies specialize in climbing, with the experience to get you back down in one piece should anything go wrong. Prices vary from $70 per person for easier climbs, such as the Pichinchas, to $220-350 per person for a two-day ascent of Cotopaxi.

The **Ecuadorian Association of Mountain Guides** (tel. 2/254-0599, www.aseguim.org) is a guide and mountain rescue cooperative that trains and certifies mountain guides. On its Members page are listed the contact details of guides who speak English, German, French, and Italian. **Andean Face** (Luis Coloma *y* Av. El Inca, tel. 2/245-6135, www.andeanface.com) is a Dutch-Ecuadorian company specializing in climbing and trekking in Ecuador. They can arrange anything from a Cotopaxi trek to a weeks-long tour of all the country's peaks. Andean Face

supports the Daniëlle Children's Fund, an NGO working with Ecuador's street children. **Ecuadorian Alpine Institute** (Ramírez Dávalos *y* Amazonas, 1st floor, Oficina 102, tel. 2/256-5465, www.volcanoclimbing.com) has well-organized, professionally run climbs and treks in English, German, French, and Spanish.

Climbing and Camping Equipment

Quito has by far the best selection of outdoor gear stores in the country. Everything from plastic climbing boots and harnesses to tents, sleeping bags, and stoves is readily available, although not always of the highest quality. Large-size footgear (U.S. size 12 and up) may be hard to find. Be aware that imported items will come at a high markup.

Equipos Cotopaxi (6 de Diciembre *y* Jorge Washington, tel. 2/225-0038, www.equiposcotopaxi.com) sells equipment for mountaineering, fishing, camping, trekking, cycling, swimming, astronomy, birdwatching, and canoeing. The company makes its own sleeping bags, backpacks, and tents for less than you'd pay for imported items. Equipos Cotopaxi also owns the following stores, which sell a similar range of products: **Antisana Sport** (tel. 2/246-7433, www.antisana.com.ec) in the El Bosque Shopping Center; **Camping Sport** (Av. Colón y Reina Victoria, tel. 2/252-1626, Facebook @ CampingSport); and **Aventura Sport** (tel. 2/292-4372, Facebook @AventuraSportEc) in the Quicentro mall. The various **Marathon Sports** outlets in the malls stock light-use sportswear.

CYCLING & MOUNTAIN BIKING

The **Aries Bike Company** (Av. Interoceanica km 22.5, Vía Pifo, La Libertad, tel. 2/389-5712, www.ariesbikecompany.com) near the airport offers 1- to 14-day biking and hiking tours all over Ecuador. Popular options include the cloud forest near Quito, Papallacta hot springs, Otavalo, Pichincha, Cotopaxi National Park, Chimborazo, and Quilotoa. The guides speak English, Dutch, and Spanish.

Biking Dutchman (La Pinta y Reina Victoria, tel. 2/254-2806, www.bikingdutchman.com) runs well-reviewed day trips to Cotopaxi, Papallacta, and the Tandayapa-Mindo area. The 30-kilometer (19-mi) descent of Cotopaxi is thrilling! Longer trips range 2-8 days.

Every Sunday 8am-2pm, a 30-kilometer (19-mi) north-south section of road through Quito is closed to motorized vehicles and open only to cyclists, skateboarders, skaters, runners, and walkers. For a map·of the **CicloPaseo** route, which includes Parque La Carolina, Parque Ejido, and Plaza Grande, see www.ciclopoliisecuador.wixsite.com/ciclopolis/ciclopaseo-quito. **Ciclopolis** (tel. 2/604-2079) rents bicycles from one hour ($2.50) to a morning ($8). Their rental locations at Tribuna del Sur and the Bicentennial Park

are marked on the map. Two forms of ID are required. Another option is the **Quito Bike Rental Network** (tel. 98/401-4852, Facebook @QuitoBikeRentalNetwork), which has 3 locations: Dulce Albahaca (Juan León Mera y Wilson); El Cafecito (La Reina Victoria y Cordero); and Lord Guau (Cumbayá, one block from the Chaquiñan entrance).

RAFTING AND KAYAKING

The **Río Blanco** and **Río Toachi** provide the nearest year-round white water to Quito, 3 hours from the capital. The Toachi (Class III-III+) is closest to the city and is therefore Ecuador's most rafted river, though not its most pristine. It's navigable all year and is particularly good during the high water season from January to the end of May. Much cleaner and more beautiful is the Upper Río Blanco (Class III), though the water can be too low to navigate June-December. Kayakers can take on **Río Mindo** (Class III-IV), **Río Saloya** (IV-V), **Río Pilatón** (V-V), and the upper **Río Toachi** (IV-V), depending on the time of year and their ability. A highly recommended company is **Torrent Duck** (Gonzáles Suárez y Eloy Alfaro, Tumbaco, tel. 99/867-9933, www.torrent-duck.com), for their excellent customer service and environmental responsibility. **Rios Ecuador** (www.riosecuador.com) is the most well-established operator of white-water trips out of Quito, charging $87 for a rafting day trip to Ríos Toachi and Blanco, $299 for 2 days. Customized itineraries are possible, as are kayak rentals and courses.

Only a 90-minute drive from the capital, but more seasonal, is **Baeza** on the **Río Quijos** (Class III-IV), where there is excellent rafting and kayaking between October and February. Class III-V kayaking is also available on the nearby **Ríos Oyacachi** and **Cosanga,** with the Cosanga Gorge a highlight. Local family-run **Baeza Tours** (Facebook @BaezaToursEcuador) offers rafting and kayaking for $65-75 pp per day and kayaking courses ranging from two days/one

Ethical Tour Agencies

Quito has many excellent tour agencies that offer expertise, local knowledge, and the peace of mind that comes with knowing that accommodations, food, and logistics are taken care of. The following companies are recommended for their quality, professionalism, and policies of **environmental** and/or **social responsibility.** Please note that most are closed on weekends. Don't be surprised if you're asked to pay in advance by Western Union or PayPal.

- **Neotropical Nature & Birding Trips** is based at El Quinde Visitors Center on the corner of the Plaza Grande (Palacio Municipal, Venezuela y Espejo, tel. 99/252-5251, www.neotropicalecuador.com). Tours include Quito day trips, Amazon lodges, Galápagos cruises, and the Avenue of the Volcanoes. This Ecuadorian-owned, family-run ecotourism agency supports sustainable development in fragile and threatened ecosystems throughout Ecuador, working with locally managed ecotourism projects.

- **GreenGo Travel** (Española 161 y Rumiñahui, tel. 2/603-4262, www.greengotravel.com) is an Ecuadorian-owned ecotour agency offering a broad range of experiences, from city day tours to extensive two-week programs all over mainland Ecuador and the Galápagos.

- **Enchanted Expeditions** (De las Alondras N45-102 y Los Lirios, tel. 2/334-0525, www.enchantedexpeditions.com) covers the entire country, with a focus on the Galápagos—the boats *Cachalote* and *Beluga* receive frequent praise.

- **Gulliver Expeditions** (Juan León Mera N24-156 y José Calama, tel. 2/252-8030, www.gulliver.com.ec) offers a huge range of climbing, biking, horseback riding, and sightseeing tours nationwide, including many one-day options. Gulliver's supports a day-care center for Ecuadorian children.

- **Nuevo Mundo Expeditions** (Vicente Ramón Roca N21-293 y Leonidas Plaza, tel. 2/450-5412, www.nuevomundoexpeditions.com) was started in 1979 by a founder and former president of the Ecuadorian Ecotourism Association. Among the offerings are an Amazon cruise and a Shamanism & Natural Healing Tour.

- **Happy Gringo Travel** (Oficina 207, Edificio Catalina Plaza, Aldaz N34-155 y Portugal, tel. 2/512-3486, www.happygringo.com) offers a wide variety of tours all over Ecuador. Best known for their Cuyabeno trips, they have also designed an eight-day Responsible Traveler tour of the Andes that includes several eco- and community tourism destinations. The agency was given the UNESCO-recognized Smart Voyager award for its ecological practices.

- **Surtrek** (Calle San Ignacio E10-114 y Plácido Caamaño, tel. 2/250-0660, www.surtrek-adventures.com) offers a wide range of high-end ecotourism and adventures tours. The agency is Rainforest Alliance Certified.

- **Destination Ecuador** (U.S. tel. 888/207-8615, https://destinationecuador.com) is an ecotourism company specializing in responsible, community-based tourism. Bestsellers include Galápagos land-based tours and cruises, a Cotopaxi hiking tour, and an Andes to Amazon wildlife adventure. Headed by Andy Drumm of the Ecuadorian Ecotourism Association, their trips have won awards for socially responsible tourism.

---

night ($180 pp) to four days/three nights ($360 pp), including accommodations. Companies in Quito also offer tours in the Baeza area.

HORSEBACK RIDING

Ride Andes (tel. 9/973-8221, www.rideandes.com) offers top-quality riding tours through the highlands, using local horse wranglers, support vehicles, and healthy animals. Options range from $110 pp for a one-day tour for two people to 7- to 10-day trips staying in some of the country's plushest haciendas.

Green Horse Ranch (tel. 8/612-5433, www.horseranch.de) offers riding trips starting from the Pululahua Crater for people of all experience levels. Prices range from $95 pp for one day, to $250 pp for two days, and up to $1,550 pp for the eight-day Secrets of the Andes tour. Multilingual guides accompany all trips.

SPECTATOR SPORTS

Soccer (*fútbol*) is by far the most popular sport in Ecuador. The best place to see a game in Quito is the **Estadio Atahualpa** (6 de Diciembre *y* Naciones Unidas) when the national team plays. Check www.elnacional. ec for details of the next match. Tickets can be bought at the stadium. Take the Ecovia to the Naciones Unidas stop to get there. The **Casa Blanca,** which is the stadium of **Liga de Quito,** the city's most successful club, has home games several times per month. Buy tickets ahead of time at the stadium, which is a few minutes' walk from the Ofelia bus terminal.

YOGA

Yoga Chai (9 de Octubre *y* Jerónimo Carrión, tel. 99/452-9962, http://yogachaivegan.com) is a yoga and dance studio and vegan café in La Mariscal.

CITY TOURS

The municipality of Quito has put together an excellent map of themed historic walks through Old Town, available at the Plaza Grande tourist office, where it is also possible to book **multilingual tours** given by municipal police.

Carpe Diem Adventures offers a free **Old Town Walking Tour** (Antepara *y* Los Ríos, tel. 2/295-4713, www.carpedm.ca, 10:30am Mon.-Fri.) that explores plazas, churches, and other colonial sights. Tours leave from the Secret Garden hostel. **Quito Street Tours** (Guipuzcoa *y* Coruña, tel. 99/886-0539, www.quitostreettours.com) focuses on local food and street art on their walking tours of La Floresta and Guápulo (free, but donations of $5-10 are appreciated).

The **Quito Tour Bus** (tel. 2/245-8010, www.quitotourbus.com, 8:30am-4pm daily, 7pm Fri.-Sat., $15) provides a hop-on hop-off bus service with 12 stops across the city, including Plaza Grande, La Compañía, El Panecillo, La Basílica, the TelefériQo, and the major parks. The nighttime tour includes a one-hour stop at La Ronda. Audio is available in English, Spanish, French, and German. Tickets can be bought online or at various points across the city, including Plaza Foch and Plaza Grande. There are also daily tours to Otavalo, Papallacta, Cotopaxi, and Quilotoa.

Ecuador Freedom Bike Rentals (Finlandia *y* Suecia, tel. 98/176-2340, www.freedombikerental.com, 10am-6pm daily) offers self-guided GPS tours of the city and surrounding area by motorbike, scooter, or bicycle, plus longer guided or self-guided tours that go farther afield.

Shopping

CRAFTS, SOUVENIRS, ART, JEWELRY, AND ACCESSORIES

In Old Town, one of the best options for souvenirs is **Tianguez** (underneath the Iglesia San Francisco, Plaza San Francisco, tel. 2/257-0233, www.tianguez.org, 9:30am-6:30pm daily). The fair trade store has an excellent selection of high-quality products and handicrafts from around the country, including *paja toquilla* or "Panama" hats, ceramics, masks, woven goods, Tigua paintings, embroidered shirts, *tagua* jewelry, wooden bowls, coffee, and chocolate. An outdoor café serves good Ecuadorian food. Tianguez is run by the Sinchi Sacha Foundation, a nonprofit supporting sustainable development in Ecuador, specializing in ecotourism, fair trade, the restoration of natural and cultural heritage, and the generation of income for populations with scarce resources. In New Town, **Mindalae Ethnic Museum** (Reina Victoria y La Niña, tel. 2/223-0609, www.mindalae.com/ec, 9am-5:30pm Mon.-Sat.) is also operated by the Sinchi Sacha Foundation. The museum houses a large fair trade store selling an even more extensive range of products than Tianguez, beautifully arranged by region.

Another fair trade store in New Town is the **Camari Cooperative** (Antonio de Marchena y Versalles, tel. 2/252-3613, www.camari.org), offering a wide selection of handicrafts, clothing, jewelry, and food. Camari is dedicated to providing high-quality Ecuadorian products while helping to better the living conditions of small-scale producers.

A couple of blocks from Plaza Foch, **Galería Ecuador** (Reina Victoria y Lizardo García, tel. 2/223-9469, www.galeriaecuador. com, 9am-9pm Mon.-Sat., 10am-8pm Sun.) sells chocolate, coffee, perfumes, handicrafts, clothes, jewelry, books, and music. An official tourist information office and an organic bistro are attached. Another branch of Galería Ecuador can be found in Old Town at El Quinde Visitors Center on the Plaza Grande. The organization works with over a hundred indigenous communities, associations of small-scale producers, and entrepreneurs with organic and fair trade certifications.

Hungarian-born Olga Fisch came to Ecuador to escape the war in Europe in 1939, becoming a world-renowned expert on South American crafts and folklore. **Folklore Olga Fisch** (Av. Colón y Caamaño, tel. 2/254-1315, www.olgafisch.com, 9am-7pm Mon.-Fri., 10am-6pm Sat.), which was her house until her death in 1991, is now a fair trade store selling handmade products, including *paja toquilla* or "Panama" hats, handbags, home decor items, jewelry, and woven goods.

Beautiful, high-quality Andean wool textiles with *tagua* nut buttons can be found at **Hilana** (6 de Diciembre y Veintimilla, tel. 2/254-0714, www.hilana.ec, 9am-7pm Mon.-Fri., 10am-1pm Sun.), with designs inspired by pre-Columbian art.

There is a cluster of art galleries and stores selling handicrafts and antiques on Juan León Mera and Veintimilla. Try **Galería Latina** (Juan León Mera y Veintimilla, tel. 2/222-1098, www.galerialatina-quito.com, 10am-7pm Mon.-Sat., 11am-6pm Sun.) for alpaca clothing, ceramics, and jewelry. **Casa Mariscal** (Juan León Mera y Baquedano, tel. 2/515-3800, @Facebook CasaMariscalQuito, 10am-7pm Mon.-Sat.) is a fair trade store for hand-made decorative items and fine crafts, including a wide range of jewelry. **La Mariscal Artisanal Market** (Jorge Washington *entre* Juan León Mera y Reina Victoria, tel. 2/512-4716, www.mercadoartesanal.com.ec, 8am-7pm Mon.-Sat., 8am-6pm Sun.) sells just about every souvenir and handicraft available in Ecuador, plus artisanal food items. Quality is variable, and haggling is obligatory.

Hugo Chiliquinga (Huachi y Av. Bernardo de Legarda, tel. 2/259-8822, www. guitarrashugochiliquinga.com, 9am-6pm daily) is considered by many to be the best guitar maker in Ecuador. He may have a waiting list.

For exclusive jewelry designs, stop by the **Museo Fundación Guayasamín** (Mariano Calvache y Lorenzo Chávez, tel. 2/244-6455, www.guayasamin.org, 10am-5pm daily).

A popular place to buy paintings is the **Parque El Ejido Art Fair** (Patria y Amazonas), open all day Saturday-Sunday. Many pieces are imitations of famous works, but you may find some original gems. Haggling is advised. Just north of the park, **Galería Beltrán** (Reina Victoria y Jorge Washington, tel. 2/222-1732, www.galeria-beltran.jimdo.com) has a good selection of paintings by Ecuadorian artists.

On Saturday, dozens of artisans and artists gather in Plaza Foch from 10:30am to 8pm to sell work in wood, *tagua*, glass, fabric, leather, and recycled paper. Organic products such as jams, chocolate, and honey-based cosmetics are also available.

MALLS

Remember that if you want your visit to benefit Ecuadorians, it's much better to shop at locally owned businesses, but if you're looking for big supermarkets, international chain stores, and movie theaters, you'll find them in Quito's many *centros comerciales* (malls). Major malls include **El Bosque** (Al Parque *y* Alonso de Torres), **El Jardín** (República and Amazonas), **CCI (Centro Comercial Iñaquito)** (Amazonas *y* Naciones Unidas), **Multicentro** (6 de Diciembre *y* La Niña),

CC Nu (Naciones Unidas *y* Amazonas), and **Quicentro** (6 de Diciembre *y* Naciones Unidas).

BOOKS

For great deals on secondhand books in English and other languages, have a free cup of tea at the friendly English-run **English Bookshop** (Venezuela *y* Manabi, tel. 98/424-1707, Facebook @The English Bookshop, 10am-6:30pm daily). Mark, the owner, is a great source of information on Ecuador.

Food

Quito has the widest range of international restaurants in Ecuador as well as many excellent local eateries. A lot of restaurants outside New Town close by 9 or 10pm, and throughout the city many are closed on Sunday.

OLD TOWN
Bakeries, Cafés, and Snacks

There is a row of nice little cafés with outdoor seating under the cathedral on the Plaza Grande. At the entrance of San Agustín monastery is Ecuadorian-owned **El Cafeto** (Chile *y* Guayaquil, tel. 2/257-2921, Facebook @ CafetoQuito, 8am-8pm Mon.-Sat., 8am-4pm Sun.), specializing in coffee and hot chocolate served with *humitas* (ground corn mashed with cheese, onion, garlic, eggs, and cream and steamed in corn leaves), tamales, empanadas, and cakes. **En-Dulce** (Guayaquil N6-56 *y* Olmedo, tel. 2/228-8000, http://endulce.com. ec, 7:30am-7:30pm Mon.-Fri., 8:30am-7:30pm Sat., 8:30am-5pm Sun.) has excellent cakes, pastries, and desserts, as well as breakfasts and sandwiches.

Ecuadorian

For cheap, good quality Ecuadorian food, eat with the locals at the food courts of Quito's markets, where you'll find Andean specialties such as *hornado* (roasted pork) and *fritada* (crispy fried pork) served with *mote* (white corn), *llapingachos* (fried potato cakes), and avocado. Set lunches are also available. Meals cost $2.50-3.50 with a fresh juice for $1. In Old Town, the best food court is found at the ★ **Mercado Central** (Av. Pichincha, 6am-5pm daily), a few blocks from Plaza Grande.

Heladería San Agustín (Guayaquil 1053 *y* Mejia, tel. 2/228-5082, http://heladeriasanagustin.net, 10am-3:30pm Mon.-Fri., $8.50-12.50) serves a wide range of typical Ecuadorian dishes. The attached ice cream parlor (10am-5:30pm Mon.-Fri.) is the oldest in the city, having made *helados de paila* sorbets in copper bowls for 150 years.

On Plaza San Francisco, ★ **Tianguez Café Cultural** (tel. 2/257-0233, www.tianguez.org, 9:30am-6:30pm Mon.-Tues., 9:30am-11:30pm Wed.-Sun., $6-12) serves good quality Ecuadorian cuisine from the coast, Amazon, and Andes. The café is run by the Sinchi Sacha Foundation, a nonprofit set up to support indigenous Amazon communities.

Inside the Teatro Bolívar is **La Purísima** (Espejo *y* Guayaquil, tel. 98/301-1740, Facebook @lapurisimaec, noon-10pm Mon.-Sat., noon-5pm Sun., $12-15), a very well-reviewed restaurant serving innovative takes on traditional Ecuadorian dishes. Vegetarian options are available. The complimentary infused spirits at the end of the meal will put hairs on your chest!

International

On the hill beneath the Itchimbía Cultural Center is ★ **Mosaico** (Samaniego N8-95 y Antepara, tel. 2/254-2871, 4pm-11pm Mon.-Wed., 1pm-11pm Thurs.-Sat., 1pm-10:30pm Sun., www.cafemosaicoecuador.com, $10-18). Start with pre-dinner drinks at sunset, when the views of Old Town from the terrace are wonderful. Arrive early to secure a table. The menu is a mix of Ecuadorian and international, with vegetarians and vegans catered for. Pets are welcome and there are even a couple of dishes for your four-legged companions! The house band is live every Friday and Saturday 8:30pm-11:30pm, playing music from the 1940s to the 1990s. A taxi from Old Town is $2.

Vegetarian

Vegetarian food is harder to come by in Old Town than in La Mariscal, but there are three places clustered together a few blocks from Plaza Grande toward the basilica. All three adhere to Hare Krishna principles. **Govindas** (Esmeraldas Oe3-119 y Venezuela, tel. 2/295-7849, Facebook @GovindasQuito, 8am-4pm Mon.-Sat., $2-3) has a wide range of lunches, including a filling set menu. Part of the same complex is the **Oki Ecomarket** (tel. 2/295-7849, Facebook @okiecomarket.ecuador, 9am-7pm Mon.-Sat., 8am-3pm Sun.), a shop selling fresh produce, health supplements, snacks, and light meals. The desserts and sweets are yummy. Next door is the ★ **Restaurant Kalpa Vriksha / Tree of Desire** (tel. 2/258-1280, 11am-3pm Mon.-Sat., $2.80), a small, friendly place serving imaginative, healthy set lunches that include soup, main course, drink, and dessert.

NEW TOWN
Asian

Noe Sushi Bar (Isabel La Católica N24-6274 y Coruña, tel. 2/322-7378, 12:30pm-11:30pm Mon.-Thurs., 12:30pm-midnight Fri.-Sat., 12:30pm-10pm Sun., $10-20) has excellent combination platters and sashimi. For curries, you can't beat ★ **Chandani Tandoori** (Juan León Mera y Cordero, tel. 2/222-1053, 11am-11pm Mon.-Thurs., 11am-2am Fri., 1pm-2am Sat., $4-8). Everything from *dopiaza* to korma, tikka masala, and *balti* is done well here, with some great veggie options. For Vietnamese, Thai, and Asian fusion specialties, head to **Uncle Ho's** (Calama y Almagro, tel. 2/511-4030, 11am-11pm Mon.-Sat., $5-14). Choose from a wide range of tasty rolls, soups, and curries.

Cafés, Bakeries, and Snacks

El Cafecito (Luis Cordero y Reina Victoria, tel. 2/223-0922, www.cafecito.net, $3-8) is a long-standing Mariscal favorite for breakfasts, Sunday brunches, coffee, and cakes. Service is friendly, it's peaceful during the day, and the Wi-Fi works well, so it's a good spot for digital nomads. Chocoholics should head to **Kallari Café** (Wilson E4-266 y Juan León Mera, tel. 2/223-6009, www.kallari.com. ec, 9am-6pm Mon.-Fri., $3-8), run by a cooperative of 850 Kichwa families from the Ecuadorian Amazon who cultivate heirloom organic cacao trees to create their award-winning chocolate. Not surprisingly, the hot chocolate is wonderful. In La Floresta, family-run **Botánica** (Guipúzcoa E14-125 y Coruña, tel. 2/222-6512, www.botanicaquito.com, 12:30pm-9pm, Tues.-Fri., 2pm-9pm Sat.) is a treat, offering a small but freshly prepared organic menu of Ecuadorian coffee, sandwiches ($6), desserts ($4), and great cocktails. The interior decor is artsy recycled chic, and there is a plant-filled outdoor patio.

Burgers and Steaks

Burgers, grilled plates, and barbecue are the specialties at **Adam's Rib** (La Niña y Reina Victoria, tel. 2/222-3086, noon-11pm Mon.-Fri., noon-5pm Sat.-Sun., $7-18). For Argentinian steak try **La Casa de Mi Abuela** (Juan León Mera 1649 y La Niña, tel. 2/256-5667, noon-11pm Mon.-Sat., $8-12), a Quito institution in the renovated house of the owner's grandmother. For beer, burgers, and wings, head to **King's Cross Bar** (La Niña y Reina Victoria, tel. 2/252-3597, 6pm-midnight Mon.-Thurs., 5:30pm till late Fri.-Sat., $5-8), where the Ecuadorian/Canadian owner dishes up her two menu items and tends bar.

Cuban

La Bodeguita de Cuba (Reina Victoria 1721 y La Pinta, tel. 2/254-2476, noon-10pm Sun.-Tues., noon-midnight Wed., noon-1am Thurs., noon-2am Fri.-Sat., $8-10) is popular for its *bocaditos* (appetizers) as well as the live Cuban music.

Ecuadorian

For cheap, good quality Ecuadorian food, eat with the locals at the food courts of Quito's **markets** ($2.50-3.50). In New Town, try ★ **Mercado Santa Clara** (Antonio de Ulloa, near the Central University, 7am-5pm Mon.-Fri., 8am-2pm Sat.-Sun.) or **Mercado Iñaquito** (Iñaquito Bajo, 6am-5pm daily), north of Carolina Park.

★ **La Petite Mariscal** (Diego de Almagro N24-304 y Juan Rodríguez, tel. 2/604-3303, www.lapetitemariscal.com, noon-3pm and 6pm-9:30pm Mon.-Fri., $12-22) serves excellent Ecuadorian cuisine with service to match. There is also an international menu with a couple of vegetarian options. The ambience is cozy with a fireplace. ★ **Miskay** (Joaquín Pinto 312 y Reina Victoria, 3rd Fl., tel. 2/255-2872, https://miskayrestaurant.wordpress. com, noon-10:30pm daily, $8-19) consistently receives rave reviews for its top quality national cuisine and service. Vegetarians are catered to. Another consistently well-reviewed option is family-run **Achiote** (Juan Rodríguez 282 y Reina Victoria, tel. 2/250-1743, Facebook @AchioteEcuador, noon-10pm daily, $15-28), which offers organic, gourmet Ecuadorian cuisine with vegetarian options.

At the top end of the scale, both **Urko** (Isabel La Católica N24-862 y Julio Zaldumbide, tel. 2/256-3180, www.urko. rest) and **Zazu** (Mariano Aguilera 331 y La Pradera, tel. 2/254-3559, http://zazuquito.

com) offer exquisite tasting menus (each $75 not including drinks). Vegetarian menus are available.

French

Chez Jérôme (Whymper 3096 y Coruña, tel. 2/223-4067, www.chezjeromerestaurante. com, 12:30pm-3pm and 7:30pm-11pm Mon.-Fri., $10-33) offers top-notch food, decor, ambience, and service. A six-course tasting menu is available. Vegetarians are accommodated. **Rincón de Francia** (Vicente Ramón Roca N21-182 y Av. 9 de Octubre, tel. 2/222-5053, www.rincondefrancia.com, noon-3pm and 7pm-11pm Mon.-Fri., 7pm-11pm Sat., $20-25), has been in business for over 40 years.

Italian

Sol y Luna (Whymper N31-29 y Coruña, tel. 2/223-5865, www.trattoriasoleeluna.com, 12:30pm-3:30pm and 7pm-11pm Mon.-Fri., 12:30pm-4:30pm Sat., $14-20), offers tradiional dishes, including carpaccio, pasta, and gnocchi. Good service and generous portions make the prices more bearable, as does the delicious tiramisu. **Cosa Nostra Trattoria Pizzería** (Moreno and Almagro, tel. 2/252-7145, http://pizzeriacosanostra.ec, 12:30pm-11pm Mon.-Sat., 12:30pm-10pm Sun., $12-18) has a wide selection of pizza, spaghetti, ravioli, and gnocchi. All the vegetables are organic. The owner, Simone, is from Italy and brought not only his family recipes to Quito but their hospitality as well. Home delivery is available. Close to Parque La Carolina, **Romolo e Remo** (República de El Salvador y Portugal, Edificio Rosanía, tel. 2/600-0683, 9am-8pm Mon.-Fri., 10am-5pm Sat.-Sun., $8-10) is friendly and has a small, inexpensive menu of pizzas, pastas, and focaccia. There is a three-course set menu with a glass of wine for $14.

Mexican

A plate of fajitas at **Red Hot Chili Peppers** (Foch y Juan León Mera, tel. 2/255-7575, Facebook @red.hot.mexican.food, noon-11pm Mon.-Sat., $6-10) will easily fill two people. A tiny place with a big TV and graffiti covering the walls, it serves top-notch Tex-Mex food and margaritas. Nearby is the ★ **Mexicali Baja Grill** (Reina Victoria N23-69 *y* Wilson, tel. 2/290-8277, Facebook @mexicalibajagrill, 2pm-midnight Mon.-Sat., noon-8pm Sun.), which uses fresh, locally sourced ingredients for their expansive menu, from fish tacos to two-for-one frozen margaritas.

Middle Eastern

Shawarma (grilled meat in warm pita bread with yogurt sauce and vegetables) is increasingly popular in Ecuador. The patio at **Aladdin** (Almagro *y* Baquerizo Moreno, tel. 2/222-9435, 10:30am-midnight daily, $2-4) can get packed at night. The shisha pipes and 16 kinds of flavored tobacco probably have something to do with it, along with the cheap falafel and *shawarma*. **Baalbek** (Av. 6 de Diciembre N23-103 *y* Wilson, tel. 2/255-2766, http://restaurantbaalbek.com, noon-5pm Sun.-Tues., noon-10:30pm Wed.-Sat., $6-14) stands out for its hummus, *mansafh, fatush,* and other Lebanese favorites. There are plenty of veggie options and a belly-dancing show on Thursday at 8:30pm.

Seafood

Cevichería Manolo (Diego de Almagro 1170 *y* La Niña, tel. 2/256-9254, Facebook @CevicheriaManolosQuito, 8am-6pm Mon.-Sat., $7-15) is popular, with a wide selection of Ecuadorian and Peruvian ceviches.

Spanish

La Paella Valenciana (Alpallana E7-294 *y* Diego de Almagro, tel. 2/250-1018, noon-3pm and 7pm-9pm Mon.-Sat., noon-3pm Sun., $10-20) has a wide range of Spanish entrées and tapas.

Vegetarian

New Town has the best selection of meat-free restaurants in the country (alongside Cuenca). Veggies and vegans are advised to make the most of this cornucopia of excellent options! **Sakti** (Jerónimo Carrión E4-144 *y* Amazonas, tel. 2/252-0466, http://sakti-quito.

com, 9am-6pm Mon.-Fri., $4-6) is a vegetarian restaurant, bakery, and hostel with decent set lunches. **Dulce Albahaca** (Juan León Mera N23-66 *entre* Baquedano *y* Wilson, tel. 2/510-3881, Facebook @dulcealbahacaec, 8am-8pm Mon.-Fri., 10am-6pm Sat.-Sun., $7-9) has great food, ambience, and service. The fruit tea infusion is such a work of art, it is a shame to drink it. There is also a health food store and deli selling fair trade and organic products. **El Maple** (Joaquín Pinto *y* Diego de Almagro, tel. 2/290-0000, Facebook @elmaplerestaurante, noon-10pm Mon.-Wed., noon-midnight Thurs.-Sat., noon-6pm Sun.) has a wide-ranging menu of national and international dishes. Especially recommended is the *sustento de altiplano,* a plate of meat-free versions of Andean specialties. **Mile Time** (Baquerizo Moreno *y* Reina Victoria, tel. 2/604-1475, Facebook @miletimeecuador, 9am-11am and noon-4:30pm Mon.-Sat.) has good set lunches ($3.75), breakfasts, and Chinese food. **Yoga Chai** (9 de Octubre *y* Jerónimo Carrión, tel. 99/452-9962, http://yogachaivegan.com, $3-6) is a vegan café and yoga studio open daily for breakfast, lunch, and dinner.

★ **Flora** (Leonidas Plaza N21-22 *y* Jorge Washington, tel. 2/603-5008, noon-9pm Mon.-Fri., noon-4pm Sat., $6.50-10) is a vegan, organic, non-GMO restaurant that uses local products from farmers that practice permaculture, agro-ecology, and fair trade. The decor is stylish and the service friendly. The set menu is imaginative, delicious, and beautifully presented. Flora is also a community center that aims to establish an urban example for conscious, regenerative, and harmonic living, with regular workshops on permaculture, natural medicines, and vegan cooking.

★ **Tandana** (Mirador de Guápulo, tel. 2/323-8234, www.tandanaecuador.com, 12:45pm-7pm Wed.-Thurs., 12:45pm-10pm Fri.-Sat., 10am-4pm Sun., $5-9) is an excellent vegan restaurant with spectacular views

1: the cobbled streets of La Ronda; 2: vegan food at Tandana

over Guápulo. All proceeds go to Fundación Libera Ecuador, an organization working for the rights of nature and vulnerable local people. Chairs, tables, and glasses are made from reclaimed and recycled materials. There is a good selection of locally produced craft beer.

ORGANIC PRODUCE

There is an agro-ecological market, the **Feria Agroecológica La Carolina** (Pasaje Rumipamba *y* Av. Shyris, tel. 98/063-0519, Facebook @carolina.feria.71, 8am-2pm Sun.) every Sunday next to the botanical garden in Parque La Carolina. A few blocks north of the park, **Mega Organik** (Av. Río Coca E 6-90 *y* Isla Genovesa, tel. 2/243-6864, http:// megaorganik.com, 9:30am-5:30pm Mon.-Sat., 10am-2:30pm Sun.) stocks fruit, vegetables, eggs, and chicken, alongside coconut oil, *guayusa* tea, *kombucha* tea, and natural toiletry products. Home deliveries are available every Wednesday. East of Carolina Park, **Wayruro Orgánico** (Juan de Dios Martínez N35-120 *y* Portugal, tel. 2/224-4855, Facebook @wayruro.organico, 10am-6pm Tues.-Sat.) sells organic Ecuadorian products that contribute to the sustainable development of communities. West of La Mariscal, near the Santa Clara Market, is **Camari** (Marchena Oe-2 38 *y* Versalles, tel. 2/254-9407, www. camari.org, 8am-6pm Mon.-Fri., 8:30am-4:30pm Sat.), a fair trade store with a wide range of products, listed in their online catalog.

MARKETS

Markets are great places to pick up fresh fruit and vegetables (including many never-seen-before varieties), flowers, meat, and other items, with the income going straight to local people. Every produce market has a food court, where you can sample cheap, typical Ecuadorian dishes alongside the locals. Quito's best markets include New Town's **Mercado Santa Clara** (Antonio de Ulloa, near the Central University, 7am-5pm Mon.-Fri., 8am-2pm Sat.-Sun.); **Mercado Iñaquito** (Iñaquito Bajo, 6am-5pm daily), located north of Carolina Park; and, a few blocks from Plaza Grande in Old Town, **Mercado Central** (Av. Pichincha, 6am-5pm daily).

You will find large supermarkets, either **Supermaxi, Megamaxi,** or **Mi Comisariato,** at all the major malls.

Accommodations

Quito has an enormous range of hostels and hotels, from bargain basement to lavish luxury. Most are found in New Town, although Old Town has a growing number of good options, many in renovated colonial mansions. There are several accommodations near the airport in Tababela.

OLD TOWN
Under $10

There are few budget options in Old Town, but **Hostal Sucre** (Bolívar 615 *y* Cuenca, tel. 2/295-4025, Facebook @hostel.sucre, $5-7 pp) bucks the trend. It's astonishing that such a cheap place is right on Plaza San Francisco with views of the square (it's worth paying the extra dollar for a room with a window). Rooms are basic, all bathrooms are shared, and there is no breakfast, but guests can use the communal kitchen. The hostel entrance is not easy to find; look for a double wooden door with a square hole and stairs leading up to the second floor.

$10-25

Quito Family & Youth Hostel (Galápagos *y* Benalcázar, tel. 99/549-8055, Facebook @ Quito Family & Youth Hostel, $12 s, $13 d) is up a steep hill in a residential apartment block, but it's a good option for the price and location near the basilica. All bathrooms are shared and there is a communal kitchen.

Breakfast is available at additional cost. Book in advance as it gets busy.

There are several hostels in the La Tola neighborhood on a steep hill to the east of Avenida Pichincha. If walking from Old Town, take Manabí rather than Esmeraldas, as the latter is the red-light district. **Colonial House** (Olmedo *y* Los Ríos, tel. 2/316-1810, www.colonialhousequito.com, $10 dorm, $25 s/d) is a spacious, friendly, colorful place with a big garden and communal area with pool and foosball. Spanish and salsa classes and tours are available. Breakfast costs $3.50. Family-owned ★ **Huasi Lodge** (Olmedo *y* Los Ríos, tel. 2/316-1644, www.huasilodge. com, $10 dorm, $25 s, $40 d, including breakfast) is an absolute gem. Situated in a historical house with wooden floors and a courtyard, the rooms are large, bright, stylish, and spotlessly clean. Service is top-notch. Rooms are cheaper without breakfast or with shared bathroom.

$25-50

Also in the La Tola neighborhood is family-owned ★ **Community Hostel** (Pedro Fermín Cevallos *y* Olmedo, tel. 95/904-9658, www.communityhostel.com, $10 dorm, $30 s/d). Immaculate, modern, and stylish, the hostel has wooden floors throughout, and the famously comfortable beds are made by a local artisan carpenter. Dorms have double-width bunk beds and plenty of showers. Staff are English-speaking trained chefs and food is a focus. Gourmet breakfast is available at additional cost. Communal dinners are offered nightly with vegetarian and vegan options. The hostel offers a free walking tour, free yoga on the rooftop terrace, and daily evening activities. It's a great place to meet fellow travelers. Ten percent of the proceeds support local community efforts in education. There are sister hotels in Alausí and Baños.

Bright, stylish, and friendly, **Minka Hostal** (Matovelle *entre* Venezuela *y* Vargas, tel. 98/024-3729, www.minkahostel.com, $9-11.50 dorm, $30 s/d) is an excellent option near the basilica. Services include a free

walking tour, daily activities, a tour agency, Spanish classes, a pool table, and a communal kitchen. The hostel makes efforts to compost organic waste and supports the Camino a Casa Foundation, which rescues and seeks homes for stray dogs. Reception is on the second floor. A good breakfast is available at additional cost.

A former colonial home, the **Hotel San Francisco de Quito** (Sucre *y* Guayaquil, tel. 2/228-7758, www.sanfranciscodequito.com. ec, $46 s, $73 d) is a wonderful upper mid-range option, with a fountain and ferns filling the courtyard and a rooftop patio with great views.

$50-100

All the Old Town hotels listed in the categories below include breakfast in the price, unless stated otherwise.

The **Hotel Boutique Plaza Sucre** (Sucre *entre* Guayaquil *y* Flores, tel. 2/295-4926, www.hotelplazasucre.com, $57 s, $65 d) has a lovely courtyard lobby. Rooms are clean and spacious. The included buffet breakfast is good, with views overlooking the Panecillo.

★ **Portal de Cantuña** (Bolívar *y* Cuenca, tel. 2/228-2276, www.portaldecantunaquito. com, $79 s, $79 d) is an absolute gem. The lovingly restored 200-year-old convent tucked away on a side street, run by the same family that has owned it for generations, is an oasis of calm. The service is friendly and top-notch. Solar panels provide some of the hotel's energy. There is a restaurant, and tours can be arranged.

A former family home dating back to 1705, **El Relicario del Carmen** (Venezuela *y* Olmedo, tel. 2/228-9120, www.hotelreli-cariodelcarmen.com, $86 s, $112 d) has been meticulously renovated and turned into an 18-room hotel. The abundant artwork, handmade furniture, and stained-glass windows are particular highlights.

$100-200

Patio Andaluz (García Moreno *y* Olmedo, tel. 2/228-0830, www.hotelpatioandaluz.com,

$200 s/d) is a restored 16th-century colonial home. Rooms are luxurious and service is excellent. The hotel is part of the Rainforest Alliance's Sustainable Tourism Program, audited in areas such as clean technologies, waste management and recycling, carbon offsets, biodiversity conservation, cultural preservation, and gender equality.

★ **Carlota** (Benalcázar y Mejía, tel. 2/380-1410, www.carlota.ec/en, $200 s, $250 d) is a stylish 12-room boutique hotel in the renovated home of the owner's grandmother. Facilities include a bistro and a rooftop bar overlooking Old Town. Rates include a one-way transfer to or from the airport. Carlota is the first hotel in Ecuador to be LEED Certified (Leadership in Energy & Environmental Design) by the U.S. Green Building Council, with all operations and services Green Globe certified. Their sustainable and environmentally responsible practices include solar panels; gray water re-usage with an advanced water filtration system; biodegradable toiletry products; high efficiency water and lighting fixtures; use of recycled and upcycled materials in construction and finishes; and an urban garden growing organic ingredients for the menu.

NEW TOWN
Under $10

Those looking for rock-bottom dorm prices will find a couple of options in New Town, though it's worth bearing in mind that you get what you pay for. If you have the few extra dollars for one of the pod hostels, it's worth the extra investment. **Hostel Luz Robles** (Calle General Robles y Juan León Mera, tel. 2/255-5604, cdc_2466@outlook.com, $6 dorm, $10 s, $18 d) is shabby with a shared kitchen. **Hostal New Bask** (Lizardo García y Diego de Almagro, tel. 2/256-7153, www.newhostalbask.com, $6 dorm, $16-20 s/d) has a café and shared kitchen.

$10-25

★ **Mogens Pod Hostel**, (9 de Octubre y Luis Cordero, tel. 2/601-6913, www.

mogenspodhostel.com, $10 s, $25 d) is a budget traveler's dream. Opened in 2016, the hostel is stylish, modern, and immaculately clean. Rather than standard bunk beds in the dormitories, there are 2-6 "pods" (single or double), each with curtains, electrical sockets, a reading lamp, and a locker. The hostel has an excellent 24-hour café with vegetarian options, a bakery, a bar, laundry, and parking. The beds are comfortable, the Wi-Fi is good, the showers have great pressure, and the bilingual staff are friendly and helpful.

Another excellent hostel with pod beds is **El Patio** (Luis Cordero y Reina Victoria, tel. 2/252-6342, www.elpatiohostels.com, $12 pp). Run by two friendly local sisters who converted their family home into the hostel, El Patio has 12 pods in dormitories and three double rooms ($25). The pods are wide enough to comfortably sleep couples. The hostel is bright, modern, colorful, and welcoming. There is a rooftop food garden, and the hostel recycles, composts, and uses biodegradable cleaning products. Yoga classes are offered several times a week. On the edge of La Mariscal, it's quieter than many other New Town hostels. Emphasis is on community; it's a great place to meet other travelers.

$25-50

All hotels in this category and up include breakfast in the price unless otherwise indicated.

Sakti (Jerónimo Carrión y Amazonas, tel. 2/252-0466, www.sakti-quito.com, $22-28 s, $45-60 d) is a newly renovated, family-run B&B with an excellent vegetarian restaurant attached.

A few blocks uphill from La Mariscal in the quiet, bohemian neighborhood of La Floresta is **Aleida's Hostal** (Andalucia y Francisco Salazar, tel. 2/223-4570, www.aleidashostal.com.ec, $33 s, 45 d), a friendly family-run guesthouse with large guest rooms. The owner, Elena, is a wonderful host.

Bright, modern, and spotlessly clean with friendly service, **Cayman Hotel** (Juan Rodríguez y Reina Victoria, tel. 2/256-7616, www.hotelcaymanquito.com, $39 s, $61 d) has 11 rooms, a huge fireplace, a lush garden, and a terrace. The hotel is certified by the Ministry of the Environment, audited in its energy- and water-saving measures, waste disposal, and use of biodegradable products.

$50-100

Casa Joaquín Boutique Hotel (Joaquín Pinto *y* Juan León Mera, tel. 2/222-4791, www.hotelcasajoaquin.com, $85 s, $110 d) features 13 stylish, spotless rooms in a restored colonial house with a rooftop terrace and bar. Service is top-notch.

The bright and clean **Hostal de La Rábida** (La Rábida 227 *y* Santa María, tel. 2/222-2169, www.hostalrabida.com, $61 s, $61-95 d) has 11 rooms, an immaculate white interior, and dark wood floors. Amenities include a fireplace in the living room and a peaceful garden. The vegetables for the restaurant are grown organically in a greenhouse. A pet-friendly room is available.

Over $100

Boutique hotel ★ **Cultura Manor** (Jorge Washington *y* Ulpiano Páez, tel. 2/222-4271, www.culturamanor.com, $250 s/d) is the spectacular result of a seven-year project to restore a colonial mansion with exquisite attention to detail. Each room is uniquely decorated with frescoes inspired by Renaissance masters. Some have private balconies. The excellent restaurant has vegetarian and vegan options. Every Thursday evening, a different Latin American writer joins the guests for dinner after making an appearance at the Centro Cultural Benjamín Carrión across the street. Cultura Manor is part of a group of luxury eco-hotels, haciendas, lodges, and yachts across Ecuador. The hotel re-uses gray water; harvests and uses rainwater; grows organic produce for the restaurant in an on-site greenhouse; and is in the process of building 14 off-the-grid rooms.

La Coupole (Vicente Ramón Roca *y* Reina Victoria, tel. 2/515-4960, info@hotel-lacoupole.com, $112 s/d) is a renovated family mansion from 1800 with distinctive Moorish blue tiled cupolas. The interior is light and airy with wooden floors. Each room has a balcony. Service is friendly.

★ **Anahi Boutique Hotel** (Tamayo *y* Wilson, tel. 2/250-1421, www.anahihotelquito.com/en, $130 s/d) has 16 uniquely decorated, elegantly themed suites within a restored colonial mansion. Price includes buffet breakfast and access to the Jacuzzi. Staff are friendly and attentive. The hotel is LGBTQ friendly and certified by the Rainforest Alliance and the International Ecotourism Society. The hotel is part of a group that works with a Kichwa community and has invested to protect 280 hectares (690 acres) of Ecuadorian Amazon.

CLOSE TO THE AIRPORT

All hotels in this category include private bathroom and breakfast. All offer airport transfers for $8-10 each way.

$25-50

Hostal El Parque (29 de Abril Oe1-125 *y* 24 de Septiembre, Tababela, tel. 2/239-1280 or 99/272-0615, www.hostalelparqueaeropuerto.com, $25 s, $40 d) uses solar power for the hot water and lights. All rooms have satellite TV and overlook the attractive gardens, which feature avocado, lime, and orange trees. Nonalcoholic drinks are complimentary, and there is a free airline ticket printing service. **Hotel-Residential El Viajero** (Nicolas Baquero S1-125 *y* 29 de Abril, Tababela, tel. 2/359-9054 or 98/440-3800, hotelviajeroquito@hotmail.com, $25 s, $40 d) offers clean, basic rooms and friendly service.

Set in beautiful gardens with views of Cotopaxi and Cayambe, ★ **Zaysant Ecolodge** (Calle Manuel Burbano, Puembo, tel. 98/248-7487, https://zaysant.com, $45 s, $90 d, including breakfast) is owned by a welcoming local family. Just 15 minutes from the airport, it's a peaceful spot. Built with local materials, the rooms are comfortable and stylish. There is a small gym and a spa with Turkish bath, sauna, and massages. Organic gardens supply the kitchen, where decent pasta dishes are rustled up.

$100-200

Owned by an Ecuadorian family, ★ **Hacienda La Jimenita** (Barrio Andrango via Pifo, Pifo, tel. 2/38-0253 or 99/875-0972, www.jimenita.com, $99 s, $130 d) is an absolute gem and well worth a visit in its own right. The hacienda sits on a 7.3-hectare (18-acre) eco-reserve with beautiful gardens and plenty of places to sit and enjoy the mountain scenery. Sunsets are spectacular, as are the early morning views of Cotopaxi. Guests can explore ancient Inca trails and a mysterious 300-meter (980-ft) archaeological tunnel, the origins of which are unknown. All food served in the restaurant is GMO free, organic, and grown either on-site or by local families as part of a fair trade program. Meals can be enjoyed outside with the hummingbirds or inside by a cozy fire. The menu includes vegetarian and vegan options. Half of all income from the hacienda goes to the sustainable protection of 30 hectares (74 acres) of local forest and 700 hectares (1,730 acres) of primary forest in Santa Clara in the province of Pastaza. The owners work with the local community to provide sustainable sources of income, offering training in hospitality, language, organic agriculture, construction, nutrition, water conservation, and alternative energies. Accommodations are luxurious and the service is bilingual and friendly.

OUTSIDE TOWN
$50-100

San Jorge Eco-lodge Quito (km 4 Vía Cotocollao-Nono, tel. 2/224-7549, http://sanjorgeecolodges.com, $77 s, $85 d) is an 18th-century Spanish hacienda 30 minutes from central Quito. Set on an 80-hectare (200-acre) bird reserve in one of the last remnants of pristine Andean forest around the city, the house was once owned by former Ecuadorian president Eloy Alfaro. There are beautiful gardens, a lake, a spring-fed swimming pool, and wonderful views from 3,000 meters (9,800 ft) up in the Pichincha foothills. You can get here by taxi or arrange transport with the lodge. San Jorge is part of a group of eight private reserves and four ecolodges in birding hot spots around the country, including the Tandayapa Cloud Forest Reserve and Mindo.

Hacienda La Jimenita

LONGER STAYS

Most hotels will arrange a discount for stays of a few weeks or more. **St. Gallen Haus** (Guanguiltagua N37-04 y Diego Noboa, tel. 2/225-3699, www.stgallenhaus.com) specializes in longer-term rentals and is in the scenic El Batan neighborhood, north of New Town and away from the fray. The modern complex has a wide variety of accommodations, ranging from a single room with shared bathroom ($88 weekly/$280 monthly) to a double room with private bathroom ($189 weekly/$450 monthly) and an apartment with three bedrooms ($440 weekly/$1,000 monthly).

For a more authentic cultural experience and a chance to practice your Spanish, consider a **homestay** with a local family for $17-25 per day, including some meals. It is often just as affordable as a budget hotel. Check with Spanish schools for their recommendations as they often have a list of families they trust with their students.

Information and Services

VISITOR INFORMATION

There are state **tourist offices** (www.quito-turismo.gob.ec) in various locations around the city, where English-speaking staff can provide information, maps, and brochures. The walking map, with themed historical and cultural routes, is excellent. The main office, **El Quinde Visitors Center,** on the corner of the Plaza Grande (Palacio Municipal, Venezuela y Espejo, tel. 2/257-2445, 9am-6pm Mon.-Fri., 9am-8pm Sat., 10am-5pm Sun.) also has public restrooms, lockers, free Internet, a bookstore, a café, a chocolate store, and a handicrafts store. There are other offices in La Mariscal (Galería Ecuador, Reina Victoria y Lizardo García, tel. 2/223-9469, www.galeriaecuador.com, 9am-9pm Mon.-Sat., 10am-8pm Sun.), the Mariscal Sucre International Airport (tel. 2/255-1566), and at Quitumbe bus terminal (Av. Cóndor Ñan y Av. Mariscal Sucre, tel. 2/382-4815, 8:30am-5:30pm daily).

The tourist office works with the Tourism Unit of the Metropolitan Police to provide two **guided tours** of Old Town: *patrimonio,* focusing on religious art and history (2 hours, $17), and *fachadas* (facades, 1.5 hours, $8.50).

VISAS

For anything visa related, head to the **Ministerio de Relaciones Exteriores** (Carrión E1-76 at 10 de Agosto, tel. 2/299-3200, 8:30am-5pm Mon.-Fri.). See the *Essentials* chapter for more information about visas.

EMBASSIES AND CONSULATES

Several nations have embassies or consulates in Quito, including: **Canada** (Av. Amazonas 3729 y Unión Nacional de Periodistas, tel. 2/245-5499, 9am-noon Mon.-Fri., www.canadainternational.gc.ca, Australians also welcome; the Australian consulate is in Guayaquil), **United Kingdom** (Ed. Citiplaza, 14th Fl., Naciones Unidas y República de El Salvador, tel. 2/297-0800, www.gov.uk, 9am-11am Mon.-Fri.), and the **United States** (Av. Avigiras y Av. Eloy Alfaro, tel. 2/398-5000, https://ec.usembassy.gov, 8am-12:30pm and 1:30pm-5pm Mon.-Fri.). For details of other embassies and consulates, see www.embassypages.com.

MAPS

The **Instituto Geográfico Militar** (IGM, Seniergues y Gral. Telmo Paz y Miño, Sector El Dorado, tel. 2/397-5100, www.igm.gob.ec, 7:30am-4pm Mon.-Thurs., 7am-3pm Fri., 10am-3pm Sat.-Sun.) provides general tourist maps of Ecuador, as well as topographical maps for hiking. Maps can be requested in person at the office (visitors must surrender their passport at the gate) or online (see *Servicios* on the IGM website).

The main state tourism office on the corner of the Plaza Grande (Palacio Municipal, Venezuela y Espejo, tel. 2/257-2445, 9am-6pm Mon.-Fri., 9am-8pm Sat., 10am-5pm Sun.) can supply maps with themed routes for self-guided walking tours.

POST OFFICES AND COURIERS

Quito's main **post office (Correos del Ecuador)** is in New Town (Eloy Alfaro 354 y 9 de Octubre, tel. 2/256-1962, 8am-6pm Mon.-Fri., 9am-1pm Sat.), including the Express Mail Service (tracked national and international deliveries). There are several branch offices, including in the commercial center at the Palacio Arzobispal on the Plaza Grande (tel. 2/295-9875, 8am-1pm and 2pm-5pm Mon.-Fri.).

For national courier deliveries, **Servientrega** has several offices in Quito, including New Town (Av. Amazonas N24-31 y Pinto, tel. 2/254-0372, 9am-1pm and 2pm-6pm Mon.-Fri.) and Old Town (Plaza del Teatro, tel. 2/295-5860, 9am-1pm and 2pm-5:30pm Mon.-Fri.). If you're sending something important, urgent or internationally, using **DHL** is the best option. There are several offices throughout the city, including on Eloy Alfaro y Avenida de Los Juncos (8am-6pm Mon.-Fri.) and Colón 1333 at Foch (8:15am-7pm Mon.-Fri., 9am-5pm Sat.).

MONEY
Banks and ATMs

Bank branches and ATMs are located all over the city. Most reliable for foreign cards are **Banco Pichincha** (www.pichincha.com), **Banco Bolivariano** (www.bolivariano.com), and **Banco Internacional** (www.bancointernacional.com.ec). For locations, see the bank websites or Google Maps.

Exchange Houses

Since the introduction of the U.S. dollar, exchanging other currencies has become more difficult, and many exchange houses have closed, though there is one at the airport.

HEALTH
Hospitals and Clinics

A centrally located public hospital is **Hospital Carlos Andrade Marín** (Av. 18 de Septiembre y Ayacucho, tel. 2/256-4939, emergency tel. 2/256-2206, http://hcam.iess.gob.ec/).

Private hospitals are likely to have shorter waiting times and a higher level of care, especially for more complicated medical issues. **Hospital Metropolitano** (Av. Mariana de Jesús y Nicolás Arteta, tel. 2/399-8000, http://hospitalmetropolitano.org) is the best hospital in Quito, priced accordingly. The emergency room is on the east side of the building. The American-run **Hospital Voz Andes** (Villalengua 267 y 10 de Agosto, tel. 2/397-1000, http://hospitalvozandes.com) is cheaper and receives the most business from Quito's foreign residents. It's described as fast, competent, and inexpensive, with an emergency room and outpatient services. To get there, take the trolley bus north along 10 de Agosto just past Naciones Unidas.

Medicentro (Veracruz N35-100 y Av. República, tel. 2/394-9490, www.medicentro.ec) has a laboratory that can perform analysis for internal parasites, plus blood and urine tests. **Clínica de la Mujer** (Amazonas N39-216 y Gaspar de Villarroel, tel. 2/245-8000, www.clinicadelamujer.com.ec) is a 24-hour women's health clinic.

OTHER SERVICES
Laundry

Laundries (*lavanderías*) are not hard to find, especially in La Mariscal (head for Wilson, Pinto, and Foch). Some places offer collection and delivery to nearby accommodations. Dry cleaners (*lavado en seco* or *lavaseco*) also exist. Both **Clean & Clean** (www.cleanclean.ec) and **La Química** (www.laquimica.ec) have several locations around the city.

Spanish Lessons

Quito is an especially good place to learn Spanish because the people tend to speak clear, fairly textbook Spanish. Dozens of schools offer intensive Spanish instruction, and it's worth your while to shop around for one that fits your needs. Tuition usually includes 2-6 hours of instruction per day, either in groups ($5.50-6.50 per hour) or one-on-one ($7-13). Four hours daily are usually plenty. An initial registration fee may be required ($20-35), and discounts are often possible for long-term commitments. Make sure to get a receipt when you pay, and check to see if any extras are not included in the hourly rate.

Many schools offer extras such as sports facilities and activities such as cooking, dancing, cultural experiences, and group trips. Some will house you in private or shared accommodations (prices vary) or arrange for a homestay with a local family (typically $20-25 per day for full board, $17-20 for board plus 2 meals per day). Don't sign any long-term arrangements until you're sure of both the school and the family.

The following schools have received many positive reviews:

- **Yanapuma Spanish School** (Guayaquil N9-59 *y* Oriente, tel. 2/228-0843, www.yanapumaspanish.org) is part of a nonprofit organization that promotes sustainable development in indigenous and marginalized communities.

- **Simon Bolivar Spanish School** (Mariscal Foch E9-20 *y* Av. 6 de Diciembre, tel. 2/254-4558, www.simon-bolivar.com)

- **Ailola Quito Spanish School** (Guayaquil N9-77 *y* Oriente, tel. 2/228-5657, www.ailolaquito.com)

- **Cristóbal Colón Spanish School** (Colón 2088 *y* Versalles, tel./fax 2/250-6508, www.colonspanishschool.com) is the most economical for one-on-one classes at $7 per hour.

- **Guayasamín Spanish School** (Calama E8-54 *cerca* 6 de Diciembre, tel. 2/254-4210, www.guayasaminschool.com)

- **Instituto Superior de Español** (Guayaquil N9-77 *y* Oriente, tel. 2/228-5657, www.superiorspanishschool.com)

- **La Lengua** (Av. Cristóbal Colón E6-12 *y* Rábida, Building Ave María, tel. 2/250-1271, www.la-lengua.com)

- **South American Language Center** (Amazonas N26-59 *y* Santa María, tel. 99/520-2158, http://spanishschoolsouth-american.com)

Getting There and Around

GETTING THERE AND AWAY
Air
The award-winning **Mariscal Sucre International Airport** (tel. 2/395-4200, www.aeropuertoquito.aero) opened in February 2013, replacing the old airport of the same name. The impressive new facility serves all airlines flying in and out of Quito and is located in the suburb of Tababela, 12 kilometers (7.5 mi) east of the city center.

Airport services include tourist information, a post office, restaurants, a money exchange, luggage storage, ATMs, telephone and Internet booths, airport shuttles, car rental,

duty-free shops, Wi-Fi, a children's area, and a VIP lounge (domestic $19, international $31). Personalized arrival and departure assistance can be arranged at the collection desks located on Level 1 of the Passenger Terminal, next to the Administration entry door and the Amazonia Café. Customer Services can be contacted at supervisor.sac@quiport.com or tel. 99/831-4152. **The Quito Airport Center** (http://quitoairportcenter.com), across the road from the airport's main exit, has restaurants, a pharmacy, ATMs, and a room where you can rest between flights. You can buy an Ecuadorian SIM card at the Claro center.

The following airlines serve Quito to/from

domestic destinations: **TAME** (tel. 2/396-6300, www.tame.com.ec) flies to/from Coca, Cuenca, Esmeraldas, Galápagos (Baltra and San Cristóbal), Guayaquil, Lago Agrio, Loja, Manta, and Santa Rosa. **Avianca** (tel. 2/294-3100, www.avianca.com) and **LATAM** (tel. 2/299-2300, www.latam.com) fly to Coca, Galápagos (Baltra and San Cristóbal), Guayaquil, and Manta. LATAM also flies to Cuenca. Good deals (e.g., $60 return tickets) are sometimes available on domestic flights if you book online, in advance, and can be flexible with your dates and departure times.

The following airlines serve Quito to/from international destinations: **AeroMexico** (tel. 3/332-212, www.aeromexico.com, to/from Mexico City); **AirEuropa** (www.aireuropa.com, to/from Madrid); **American Airlines** (tel. 2/299-5000, www.aa.com, to/from Dallas and Miami); **Avianca** (tel. 2/294-3100, www.avianca.com, to/from San Salvador, Bogota, and Lima); **Condor** (www.condor.com, to/from Munich, Frankfurt, and Dusseldorf); **Copa Airlines** (tel. 2/394-6680, www.copaair.com, to/from Panama); **Delta Airlines** (tel. 2/333-1691, ext. 92, www.delta.com, to/from Atlanta); **Iberia** (tel. 2/256-6121, www.iberia.com, to/from Madrid); **JetBlue** (U.S. tel. 801/449-2525, www.jetblue.com, to/from Fort Lauderdale); **KLM** (tel. 2/298-6820, www.klm.com.ec, to/from Amsterdam); **LATAM** (tel. 2/299-2300, www.latam.com, to/from Lima); **TAME** (tel. 2/396-6300, www.tame.com.ec, to/from Bogota, Cali, Caracas, Lima, Fort Lauderdale, and New York); **United** (tel. 2/255-7290, www.united.com, to/from Houston); and **Wingo** (1800/400-423, www.wingo.com, to/from Bogota).

Getting To and From the Airport

Aeroservicios (tel. 2/604-3500, www.aeroservicios.com.ec) offers an airport shuttle running between the new airport and the Parque Bicentenario (the site of the old airport) in the north of Quito for $8. The buses depart every half hour (every hour in off-peak times), and the journey takes around 45 minutes. From the city center to the airport, buses run 3:30am-11pm Monday-Friday, 4am-9:30pm Saturday, 4am-11:30pm Sunday. From the airport to the city center, buses run 4:30am-11pm Monday-Friday, 5am-10:30pm Saturday, 5am-11:30pm Sunday). Passengers are allowed one bag up to 50 pounds (23 kg) and a small carry-on bag. A $2 fee is charged for each additional bag. Tickets can be bought online or at the departure points with cash or credit card.

Cheaper and just as quick are the **public transportation buses** that run between the airport and three of Quito's bus terminals for $2. Buses to Quitumbe run every 15 minutes (5:40am-9pm daily), and the journey takes an hour. Buses to Río Coco run every 20 minutes (6:20am-10pm daily), and the journey takes 40 minutes. Buses to Carcelén run every 30 minutes (6:20am-8pm daily), and the journey takes an hour.

In the airport, there is a **taxi** desk next to the car rental booths. Taxis to and from the airport have set rates, mostly between $22 and $33, though the fare may be as high as $47.50 for some peripheral areas. The normal rate for either La Mariscal or Old Town is $26. **Car rental** is available with Thrifty, Hertz, Avis, Budget, and Localiza.

International Buses

See the *Essentials* chapter for information on international buses to/from Quito.

National Buses

Quito has three major bus terminals. The biggest, **Quitumbe,** in the far south of the city, mostly serves long-distance routes traveling west, east, and south. The other interprovincial terminal, **Carcelén,** in the north of Quito, historically served northern destinations, though it also has buses to the coast (Manta and Salinas) and the Oriente (Coca, Tena, Puyo), among other destinations. The other northern terminal, **Ofelia,** is only for county buses (including Mindo and Otavalo). The trolley bus serves all three terminals. A shuttle bus service connects the Ofelia and

Carcelén terminals. From the city center, a taxi to the Carcelén or Ofelia bus terminal might cost $5; to Quitumbe it's $8.

Rental Cars and Motorcycles

Few visitors rent vehicles in Ecuador (see the *Getting Around* section of the *Essentials* chapter for more information). If you do decide to hire a car, several major rental companies operate in Quito, including **Avis** (at the airport, tel. 2/281-8160, www.avis.com.ec); **Thrifty** (at the airport, tel. 2/222-8688, www.thrifty.com.ec); **Budget** (at the airport, tel. 2/281-8040, Av. Eloy Alfaro S40-153 *y* José Queri, tel. 2/224-4095, www.budget-ec.com); and **Hertz** (at the airport, tel. 2/281-8410, and via Inka's Rent A Car, República del Salvador 35-126 *y* Suecia, tel. 2/333-3207, www.hertz.com).

For motorcycles, U.S.-owned **Ecuador Freedom Bike Rentals** (Finlandia *y* Suecia, tel. 98/176-2340, www.freedombikerental.com, 10am-6pm daily) offers various options for exploring the country on their fleet of high-end motorcycles and scooters. These include guided tours and self-guided GPS tours through the Andes, the coast, and the jungle using relatively unknown routes.

Trains

These days Ecuador's railway, **Tren Ecuador** (tel. 1800/873-637, http://trenecuador.com/en) operates as a scenic tourist attraction, rather than a functional means of transport. Quito's historic **Chimbacalle train station** (Sincholagua y Maldonado) is a few kilometers south of Old Town and can be accessed easily on the trolley bus. Three round-trip services are available. Quito to El Boliche to Machachi to Quito (8:30am-5:30pm Fri.-Sun., $53) is a day trip. Quito to Ambato to Quito (departs once a month, see website for dates, $63 single, $100 round-trip) takes one day each way. There is also a three-day/four-night route from Quito to Durán outside of Guayaquil (departs once a month, see website for dates, $1,650). Tickets can be bought online, by phone, or at El Quinde Visitors Center on Plaza Grande.

GETTING AROUND

Local Buses

Local bus routes are rather complicated, so it's best to stick to simple, short journeys along the major roads, especially Amazonas and 10 de Agosto. It's a good idea to ask a local person at the bus stop which bus number goes to your destination. For more complex journeys, you're better off taking the trolley systems or a taxi.

Any of 10 de Agosto's major crossroads, including Patria, Orellana, and Naciones Unidas, are good places to find a bus heading south to Old Town or north as far as the turn to Mitad del Mundo. "La Y," the meeting of 10 de Agosto with América and De la Prensa, is a major bus intersection. Have the fare ($0.25) ready and take care with your belongings.

Trolley Systems

Quito's network of three electric trolley buses is the best of its kind in Ecuador; it is cheap, clean, fast, and well-organized. The trolleys have their own lane, so they can be much faster than traveling by car, especially in heavy traffic. Flat fare for all services is $0.25, payable at machines on entry. There are manned kiosks at every station to give change. Trolleys arrive every 5-10 minutes.

There are a few downsides. Pickpockets are rife, so stay alert, strap your bag to the front of your body, and keep valuables well hidden. At peak times, the buses can be full, and it may sometimes be necessary to wait until the next one comes, as it's simply impossible to squeeze on. There are route maps at all the trolley stations, though not all the buses have them onboard and some don't announce the next stop. It helps to take a digital photo of the trolley map for reference and to keep count of the number of stops. The central stops are shown on the maps in this chapter. Your fellow passengers will be happy to help if you're not sure where to get off. If you miss your stop, it's usually not far until the next one. Don't be put off; if you master the trolley system, you will save an enormous amount of money

Buses from Quito Terminals

FROM QUITUMBE

Alausí	$7	6 hours
Ambato	$4	3 hours
Baños	$4.25	3.5 hours
Coca	$12.50	9 hours
Cuenca	$12	9 hours
Esmeraldas	$10	7 hours
Guayaquil	$10	9 hours
Latacunga	$2.35	1.5 hours
Manta	$11	8 hours
Puerto López	$14	10 hours
Puyo	$7	5 hours
Riobamba	$5	4 hours
Santa Elena	$13	10 hours
Tena	$7.5	5 hours
Tulcán	$6	5 hours

FROM CARCELÉN

Baños	$4.25	3.5 hours
Cuenca	$13	10 hours
Esmeraldas	$8	7 hours
Guayaquil	$10	9 hours
Los Bancos	$3	2 hours (indirect to Mindo)
Manta	$13.20	8 hours
Otavalo	$2.70	2 hours
Riobamba	$5	4.5 hours
Santa Elena	$13	10 hours
Tulcán	$5	5 hours

FROM OFELIA

Mindo (direct)	$3.10	2.5 hours
Mitad del Mundo	$0.40	1.5 hours (via the Metrobus line)
Otavalo	$2.50	2 hours

compared to using taxis and will have the satisfaction of being one of the few foreigners to be traveling like a local.

El Trolébus runs north-south from Carcelén station to the Quitumbe station. En route it passes Estación Norte (La Y) and the major tourist areas (Mariscal, Parque Ejido, Plaza del Teatro, and Plaza Chica (the stop for Plaza Grande). The main Trolébus thoroughfare is the 10 de Agosto.

The **Ecovia** is similar, but without the overhead wires. It also runs north-south, from Río Coca terminal to Quitumbe terminal. Notable stops are the Casa de Cultura and the Naciones Unidas (for the Olympic Stadium). The third line, **Sur Occidental,** runs between Quitumbe terminal and Ofelia terminal.

Note that different trolley numbers service different sections of each line. This isn't clear from the maps at the stations and can cause confusion, but makes more sense if you look at the online map: www.trolebus.gob.ec. For example, on the Trolébus line, C1 buses run from El Recreo to Estación Norte, whereas C5 buses run from Ejido to Carcelén. Ask at the change kiosk at the station if you are unsure which bus number to take. Different buses have different operating hours, so check the website if you need to travel early, late, or on a Sunday.

Metro

At the time of writing, the **Quito Metro** (www.metrodequito.gob.ec) was under construction and is projected to be operational by July 2019 (delays not withstanding). Extending from Quitumbe in the south to El Labrador in the north, the line's 15 stations will include San Francisco, La Alameda, El Ejido, Universidad Central, La Carolina, and Iñaquito.

Taxis

Taxi meters in Quito start at $0.50, with a $1.45 minimum charge ($1.75 after 7pm). Rides within and between Old Town and New Town shouldn't be more than $3 during the day or $4 in heavy traffic. Prices increase at night but shouldn't be more than double. From the city center, a taxi to the Carcelén or Ofelia bus terminal might cost $5; to Quitumbe $8.

After Guayaquil, Quito (especially La Mariscal) is the worst place in the country for "express kidnappings," where criminal taxi drivers relieve passengers of their valuables and PIN numbers. Victims are usually released unharmed, but these incidents are terrifying and can turn violent. See the Crime section of the *Essentials* chapter for more information on how to travel safely by taxi in the city.

The surest way to avoid this kind of crime is to ask your hotel, restaurant, or bar to call you a radio (prebooked) taxi, rather than flagging one down on the street, especially at night. If you have a phone, save the number of a reliable taxi firm and call one yourself. In Quito, recommended companies are **Quito Sur** (tel. 99/501-1230) or **Taxi Amigo** (tel. 2/222-2222 or 2/222-2220). Both are reliable and available at any hour.

Bicycles

The **Quito Bike Rental Network** (tel. 98/401-4852, Facebook @QuitoBikeRentalNetwork) has 3 locations: Dulce Albahaca (Juan León Mera *y* Wilson); El Cafecito (Reina Victoria *y* Cordero); and Lord Guau (Cumbayá, one block from the Chaquiñán entrance).

Vicinity of Quito

CALDERÓN

Nine kilometers (5.6 mi) from Quito's northern suburbs, this small town is famous for its artisans, who make varnished figures out of a type of bread dough called *masapan*. This craft originated with the creation of bread babies for the annual Day of the Dead in November. Craftspeople in Calderón gradually developed more elaborate and lasting figures, adding salt, carpenter's glue, and aniline dyes. In stores all over town, tiny indigenous dolls called *cholas* stand in formation next to brightly painted parrots, llamas, fish, and flowers. They make unusual, inexpensive gifts and are popular as Christmas ornaments. Buses for Calderón leave regularly from the Ofelia terminal.

LA MITAD DEL MUNDO

The main reason to come to the Middle of the World complex is to stand with a foot in each hemisphere. **La Mitad del Mundo** (tel. 2/239-4803, 9am-6pm daily, www.mitaddelmundo.com, $7.50) lies just beyond the village of **Pomasqui,** 14 kilometers (8.7 mi) north of the city. The centerpiece is a 30-meter-high (98-ft-high) monument topped by a brass globe; a bright red line bisecting it provides the backdrop for the obligatory photo. However—whisper it quietly—the real equator is actually a few hundred meters away. Inside the monument are interactive, equator-themed **science exhibits** and an **ethnographic museum** with displays on Ecuador's diverse indigenous cultures. Tours are available in English and Spanish.

The rest of the complex has an assortment of attractions and feels somewhat like a theme park. The **France building** tells the story of the expedition to plot the equator in the mid-18th century. The **Fundación Quito Colonial** features an intricate model of colonial Quito that took almost seven years to build. There are several restaurants and craft shops. At the weekends and public holidays, the central square hosts music and dance performances.

To get to the Mitad del Mundo, take the Metrobus on Avenida América to the Ofelia

boulevard leading to the La Mitad del Mundo

Vicinity of Quito

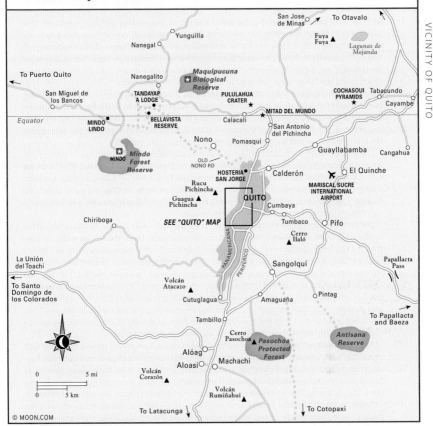

To Otavalo
San Jose de Minas
Fuya Fuya ▲
Lagunas de Mojanda
Yunguilla
Nanegal
To Puerto Quito
Nanegalito
Maquipucuna
★ Biological Reserve
COCHASOUI PYRAMIDS ★ Tabacundo
San Miguel de los Bancos
TANDAYAP A LODGE
PULULAHUA CRATER
Cayambe
MITAD DEL MUNDO
Calacalí
Equator
MINDO LINDO
BELLAVISTA RESERVE
San Antonio del Pichincha
Guayllabamba
Cangahua
MINDO
Mindo Forest Reserve
Nono
Pomasqui
OLD NONO RD
Calderón
El Quinche
Chiriboga
Rucu Pichincha
HOSTERIA SAN JORGE
MARISCAL SUCRE INTERNATIONAL AIRPORT
Guagua Pichincha ▲
QUITO
Cumbaya
SEE "QUITO" MAP
Tumbaco
Pifo
La Unión del Toachi
Cerro Ilaló ▲
To Santo Domingo de los Colorados
Sangolquí
Papallacta Pass
Volcán Atacazo ▲
PANAMERICANA
PERIFERICO
Cutuglagua
Amaguaña
Pintag
To Papallacta and Baeza
Tambillo
Cerro Pasochoa ▲
Pasochoa Protected Forest
Antisana Reserve
Alóag
Machachi
Aloasí
0   5 mi
0   5 km
Volcán Corazón ▲
Volcán Rumiñahui ▲
To Latacunga
To Cotopaxi

© MOON.COM

terminal and catch the connecting Mitad del Mundo bus, or join a tour organized by a hotel or tour operator in Quito. The **Quito Tour Bus** (tel. 2/245-8010, www.quitotourbus.com) organizes a daily tour leaving Quito at noon ($30).

Museo de Sitio Intiñan

Located about 300 meters (980 ft) east of the Mitad del Mundo complex on the real equatorial line, the **Museo de Sitio Intiñan** (tel. 2/239-5122, www.museointinan.com.ec/en, 9:30am-5pm daily, $4) features displays on local plants and indigenous cultures. Visitors are able to participate in equator-themed experiments: flushing water in opposite directions on either side of the line; walking along the line and feeling the strong gravitational pull; and the nearly impossible task of balancing an egg on the equator (you get a certificate if you can do it).

Museo Templo del Sol Pintor Ortega Maila

Past the Museo de Sitio Intiñan, toward Calacalí by the Mirador Pululahua, is the **Museo Templo del Sol Pintor Ortega Maila** (Calle Eduardo Kingman y Av. Manuel Córdova Galarza, tel. 98/484-1851, Facebook @PintorOrtegaMaila, 9am-6pm daily). The

Measuring the Earth

By 1735, most people agreed that the world was round, but another question remained: *How round was it?* **Isaac Newton** had theorized that the rotation of the earth caused it to bulge outward slightly in the middle and flatten at the poles, while others disagreed. With explorers setting out frequently to the far corners of the globe, it became increasingly important to determine how much, if any, the earth bulged in the middle, since even a few degrees of error on navigational charts could send ships hundreds of kilometers in the wrong direction.

To resolve the debate, the **French Academy of Sciences** organized two **expeditions**: one to **Lapland,** as close to the Arctic pole as possible; the other to **Ecuador** on the equator. Each party was tasked with measuring one degree of latitude, about 110 kilometers (68 mi), in its respective region. If the length of the degree at the equator proved longer than the degree near the Arctic, then the earth bulged. If they were the same length, it didn't.

The **expedition to Ecuador,** which was then part of the Spanish territory of Upper Peru, was led by academy members **Louis Godin, Pierre Bouguer,** and **Charles Marie de La Condamine.** They were accompanied by seven other Frenchmen, including a doctor-botanist, a surgeon, a naval engineer, and a draftsman, and two Spaniards. In 1736, the party sailed into Ecuador's port of Manta and then traveled to Quito, where Ecuadorian mapmaker and mathematician Pedro Vicente Maldonado joined the expedition.

The party decided to take the measurements in the flat plains near Yaruquí, 19 kilometers (12 mi) northeast of Quito. As the work progressed, troubles mounted. Unused to the elevation and the cold, the Europeans began to fall ill and suffered their first death—the nephew of the academy's treasurer, one of the youngest team members. As they continued to wander the plains with their strange instruments, local residents grew suspicious. Rumors began circulating that they had come to dig up and steal buried treasure, maybe even Inca gold. The situation became so tense that La Condamine was forced to travel to Lima to obtain official papers from the viceroy to support their story. By 1739, the goal of determining the true shape of the earth was in sight. Then disastrous news arrived from the academy: The verdict was already in. The Lapland expedition had succeeded in determining that the earth was flattened at the poles.

As La Condamine tried to keep the Ecuadorian expedition from disintegrating, more bad luck struck. The party surgeon, Juan Seniergues, was stabbed to death in a dispute over a woman, forcing the rest of the group to seek refuge in a monastery. In the confusion, Joseph de Jussieu, lost his entire collection of plants, representing five years' work; the loss eventually cost him his sanity as well. The draftsman was then killed in a fall from a church steeple near Riobamba.

Finally, in March 1743, the remaining scientists made the last measurements, confirming the Lapland expedition's findings and, in the process, laying the foundation for the entire modern metric system. Upon completion of their task, most of the party went back to Europe. French cartographer Jean Godin des Odonais stayed on in what is now Ecuador, settling in Riobamba after marrying a local woman. In 1749, after a visit to French Guiana, he was barred from re-entering the country, thus becoming separated from his wife, Isabel. They were to be reunited two decades later, in 1770, after she became famous for being the only survivor of a 42-person, 4,800-kilometer (3,000-mi) expedition through the Amazon Basin to look for him.

La Condamine, accompanied by Maldonado, also completed an epic Amazon journey, traveling by raft for four months to reach the Atlantic Ocean. From there, the pair sailed to Paris, where they brought the first samples of rubber seen in Europe and were welcomed as heroes. Maldonado died of measles in 1748, while La Condamine enjoyed the high life in Paris until his death in 1774.

In 1936, on the 200th anniversary of the earth measurers' arrival in Ecuador, the Ecuadorian government built a stone pyramid on the equator in their honor. This pyramid was eventually replaced by the **30-meter-tall (100-ft-tall) monument** that stands today at **Mitad del Mundo.** Busts along the path leading to the monument commemorate the 10 Frenchmen, two Spaniards, and one Ecuadorian who risked their lives—and sanity—for science.

studio and art gallery of the artist Ortega Maila was designed to replicate an Inca temple. If you're lucky, the artist might be there working.

Pululahua Crater and Geobotanical Reserve

About 6 kilometers (3.7 mi) north of Mitad del Mundo, the 3,200-hectare (7,900-acre) **Pululahua Reserve** ($5 pp) sits inside one of the largest inhabited volcanic craters in the world. The volcano bubbled with lava thousands of years ago, but these days the main activity is that of the hundred farming families who reside in the flat, fertile bottom.

Buses and taxis take the road from the base of Mitad del Mundo's pedestrian avenue toward the village of Calacalí. Ask to be let off just after the gas station in Caspigasi, where a dirt lane leaves the road to the right and climbs 1.2 kilometers (0.7 mi) to the lip of the crater at the Ventanilla viewpoint; this becomes a path that continues down into the crater. It's a 90-minute hike to the bottom and back. Alternatively, to go directly to Pululahua from Quito, there are buses from the Ofelia terminal.

With an office inside the Mitad del Mundo complex, **Calimatours** (tel. 2/239-4796, www.mitaddelmundotour.com) offers bilingual tours to Pululahua ($8, 1.5 hours).

Located in the crater, **Pululahua Hostal** (tel. 99/946-6636, www.pululahuahostal.com, $20-40 s, $30-50 d) is an eco-hostel and restaurant that serves food largely grown on its organic farm. Lunch and dinner (soup, main course, salad, dessert, and coffee) both cost $12. The hostel has a variety of rooms and bamboo cabins, two with their own wood-burning stove. It generates its own power with a combination of solar, wind, and biogas. The water for showers and the Jacuzzi is heated by a thermo-solar system. Guided or self-guided tours on foot, bike, or horseback are available on several trails within the reserve, where there is good birding. The hostel accepts volunteers.

THE PICHINCHAS

Towering over Quito, the twin peaks for which the province was named dominate the city's history as well as its landscape. It was on the flanks of these volcanoes that Ecuador won its independence in 1822. Both are named Pichincha, which is thought to come from indigenous words meaning "the weeper of good water." **Rucu** (Elder) is actually shorter (4,700 m/15,420 ft) and nearer to the city, while **Guagua** (Baby) stands 4,794 meters (15,728 ft) high and has always been the more active of the two. After erupting in 1660, Guagua sat quietly until October 1999, when it blew out a huge mushroom cloud that blotted out the sun over Quito for a day and covered the capital in ash.

Climbing Rucu is easier and more accessible, requiring no special equipment. Unfortunately, the trail has been plagued by robberies. The opening of the TelefériQo (cable car) has led to increased security, especially on weekends, but it is wise to inquire locally about the current situation. It is highly recommended to hire a local guide from the **Ecuadorian Association of Mountain Guides** (tel. 2/254-0599, www.aseguim.org). To make the hike, take the TelefériQo to Cruz Loma and allow 5 hours for the round-trip. Start early and wear suitable footwear and warm clothes. Bring a waterproof jacket, water, and energy snacks; the weather can change suddenly and it's a demanding hike at high altitude.

Private transportation—preferably a four-wheel-drive vehicle—is essential to reach Guagua. The starting point is the village of **Lloa,** southwest of Quito. A dirt road leaves the main plaza and heads up the valley between the Pichinchas, ending in a shelter maintained by the national civil defense directorate. Park here, pay the entry fee ($1), which goes toward the guardian's salary, and don't leave anything of value in the car. A three-hour hike will take you to the summit, where the west-facing crater is pocked by smoking fumaroles, active domes, and collapsed craters. Hire a guide through the

Ecuadorian Association of Mountain Guides (tel. 2/254-0599, www.aseguim.org) or go with a climbing-tour operator, such as Andean Face (www.andeanface.com, tel. 2/245-6135).

★ MINDO

Set in a tranquil valley northwest of Quito, Mindo is known for the astonishing biodiversity of its surrounding cloud forest. Since being recognized as South America's first Important Bird Area by Birdlife International in 1997, this small peaceful town has gradually blossomed into a world-class birding and ecotourism destination. There are over 500 bird species here, many of them endemic, including antpittas, toucans, and the famous Andean cock-of-the-rock. In fact, Mindo has won the international Christmas Bird Count six times, meaning that more bird species were counted here in a 24-hour period than in any other location in the world. Even non-birders will love watching countless jewel-bright hummingbirds flit around the feeders that many hotels and restaurants have in their gardens.

Aside from birds, the 19,200-hectare (47,400-acre) Mindo-Nambillo Protected Forest is home to 250 species of butterfly, 80 species of orchid, and a great variety of reptiles and amphibians, including tree frogs and glass frogs. Mammal species, harder to spot, include armadillos, anteaters, monkeys, ocelots, sloths, and deer. It's relatively easy to explore parts of the forest alone, but for a more informative experience, particularly for bird-watchers, it's recommended to hire a local guide. Adventure seekers will enjoy zip-lining through the forest canopy, tubing down the pristine rivers, hiking to waterfalls, or exploring the area on two wheels.

The daytime temperature in Mindo can reach 26°C (79°F), with nighttime lows of 10°C (50°F). Mornings tend to be clear and sunny, the afternoons cloudy or rainy. It's wetter from January to May, though rain is common year-round. Mindo fills up on the weekend with day-trippers from Quito, so consider coming during the week for a quieter experience.

Recreation and Tours
WILDLIFE

While Mindo is not difficult to navigate, many businesses don't have addresses. At the center of the village is the Parque Central, where a taxi rank, two ATMs, and a pharmacy can be found. Bird of Paradise Tours (http://mindobirdparadisetours.com) has put together an excellent map of Mindo's main attractions, available in many of the tourist establishments and downloadable on their website.

Mindo is filled with knowledgeable bird-watching guides. Dawn is the best time to go. The most popular trip is to see the spectacular mating display of the brilliant crimson-colored Andean cock-of-the-rock ($10 pp plus $25 for transport). For other tours, most guides charge small groups $60 for a half day and $100 for a full day. Three highly recommended English-speaking guides, all Mindo locals, are Julia Patiño (tel. 98/616-2816, juliaguideofbirds@gmail.com), Danny Jumbo (tel. 99/328-0769, mindobirding@gmail.com), and Irman Arias (www.mindobirdguide.com).

For customized, private bird-watching and nature tours in and around Mindo, contact SabinaTour (tel. 98/659-4965, U.S. tel. 650/855-4077, www.mindosabinatour.com). Co-founded by Mindeño Efrain Toapanta, the company has unrivaled knowledge of the area and is at the forefront of local conservation efforts. All the SabinaTour guides are bilingual and native to the region.

The Yellow House & Trails / Hacienda San Vicente (no address, located near the south end of the main park, tel. 2/217-0124, www.ecuadormindobirds.com) is a privately owned 200-hectare (500-acre) forest reserve at the north end of Mindo. It has a main trail and five side trails, for which maps are provided. Trail 3 leads to a viewing platform

Mindo

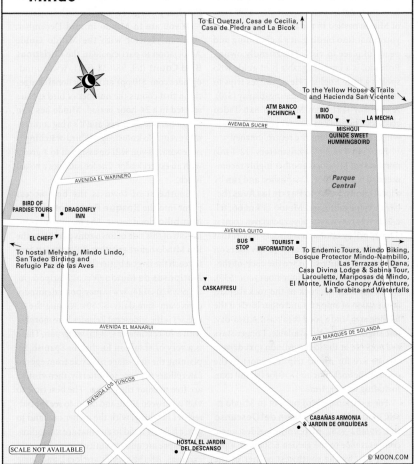

To El Quetzal, Casa de Cecilia,
Casa de Piedra and La Bicok

To the Yellow House & Trails
and Hacienda San Vicente

ATM BANCO
PICHINCHA

BIO
MINDO
LA MECHA

AVENIDA SUCRE

MISHQUI
QUINDE SWEET
HUMMINGBOIRD

AVENIDA EL WARINERO

Parque
Central

BIRD OF
PARDISE TOURS

DRAGONFLY
INN

EL CHEFF

AVENIDA QUITO

To hostal Melyang, Mindo Lindo,
San Tadeo Birding and
Refugio Paz de las Aves

BUS
STOP

TOURIST
INFORMATION

To Endemic Tours, Mindo Biking,
Bosque Protector Mindo-Nambillo,
Las Terrazas de Dana,
Casa Divina Lodge & Sabina Tour,
Laroulette, Mariposas de Mindo,
El Monte, Mindo Canopy Adventure,
La Tarabita and Waterfalls

CASKAFFESU

AVENIDA EL MANARUI

AVE MARQUES DE SOLANDA

AVENIDA LOS YUNCOS

CABAÑAS ARMONIA
& JARDIN DE ORQUÍDEAS

SCALE NOT AVAILABLE

HOSTAL EL JARDIN
DEL DESCANSO

© MOON.COM

from where you can see the entire Mindo valley. Aside from birds, butterflies, and orchids, lucky visitors might glimpse armadillos, porcupines, and monkeys. There is a $6 entrance fee for day visitors, which includes juice from fruit grown at the hacienda.

A German-Ecuadorian couple owns a section of 7 hectares (17 acres) of land 7 kilometers (4.3 mi) uphill from Mindo called **Mindo Lindo** (tel. 99/807-5177, www.mindolindo.de/en), which offers easy access to the cloud forest. The couple have been involved in the conservation of Mindo for many years, working in the areas of forest conservation, environmental education, reforestation, and scientific research. They charge $5 per person to use the trails and $30 per person for accommodations.

Near Mindo Lindo is **San Tadeo Birding** (6am-6pm daily, tel. 98/089-9882, Rolando-garcia62@hotmail.com, $5), a beautiful spot for stationary birding, ideal for those who want to see birds without having to hike. The first garden, with comfortable seats where hot drinks are served, is for viewing birds that feed on bananas. The second garden is for hummingbirds and has an incredible view of Mindo nestled in the valley below. Even if you're not into birding, it's a charming and peaceful place to visit. The friendly owner, Rolando, is a knowledgeable bird guide who speaks a little English. He organizes trips to see the cock-of-the-rock mating display ($10). A one-way taxi from Mindo to San Tadeo costs $5. The taxi can wait for you, or Rolando will call you a taxi for the return journey.

Past San Tadeo, 20 kilometers (12.4 mi) northeast of Mindo, is another highly recommended birding spot. Established and run by a local family, **Refugio Paz de las Aves** (between Nanegalito and Mindo at km 66, tel. 2/211-6124, www.refugiopazdelasaves.com) is a fairly pricey option, but birders report that it is well worth it. There are two day tours on offer: a one-hour visit to see the cock-of-the-rock ($10) or a three- to four-hour tour ($35), which includes the cock-of-the-rock display, observation of antpittas and other birds at the feeding area, and a good breakfast. A two-day, one-night tour is also available. Longer stays are possible at the lodge. Mindo taxi drivers charge $20 for round-trip transport to the cock-of-the-rock tour and $30 for the full tour, including waiting time.

For a stationary birding spot in Mindo itself, head to **Hostal El Jardín del Descanso** (tel. 99/482-9587, http://mindoeldescanso. com, entrance to the garden 6:30am-5:30pm daily, $4), by the southwest corner of the sports courts. The hostel's back garden is filled with hummingbirds flitting around the many feeders. Toucans, armadillos, and monkeys are also occasionally spotted. There is seating on the covered patio, where food and drinks are available.

By the southeast corner of the sports courts, **Cabañas Armonía & Jardín de Orquídeas** (Lluvia de Oro y Sixto Durán Ballén, tel. 2/217-0131, www.birdingmindo. com, $3) is a friendly, family-run hostel that allows visitors into the orchid garden, which features 250 species, as well as bromeliads and

hummingbirds. The garden was established by the father 25 years ago, and a member of the family will give a tour (English available).

If you are in Mindo in mid-December, you can register with the Mindo Guide Association to participate in the **Christmas Bird Count** (tel. 98/634-0341, www.mindoguides.com, $10 pp), an international competition that counts the number of bird species spotted in a 24-hour period. Mindo has won the global title six times, and it's a big community event. No knowledge of bird-watching is necessary, as you will be assigned to a group with an expert leader. The fee includes a boxed lunch.

Southeast of town is the best access point into the **Bosque Protector Mindo-Nambillo** cloud forest. The main road coming out of this side of town runs parallel to the Río Mindo before splitting. Take the left fork to reach the largest butterfly farm in Ecuador, **Mariposas de Mindo** (Vía al Mariposario, tel. 99/920-2124, www.mariposasdemindo. com, 9am-4pm daily, $7.50). Among the 25 species is the iridescent Peleides blue morpho, with a 20-centimeter (7.9-in) wingspan. There is a very brief talk in English or Spanish explaining the four-stage life cycle from eggs to caterpillars to pupae to butterfly, then visitors are free to enjoy the garden. The best time to visit is between 10am and noon, to see the butterflies hatching, with the owner on hand to give a helping hand to any that are struggling. The pupae are quite beautiful, some like gold earrings. All the species are local, and some are released daily into the wild as part of a conservation program, simply by opening the door. A restaurant overlooks tropical gardens full of birds (vegetarian options are available). The staff are friendly and helpful.

CHOCOLATE TOURS

Two blocks north of the park is **El Quetzal** (9 de Octubre, tel. 2/217-0034, www.elquetzaldemindo.com), an organic, fair trade,

---

1: chrysalises waiting to hatch at Mariposas de Mindo; **2:** garden at San Tadeo Birding

bean-to-bar chocolate factory offering one-hour tours in English or Spanish (10am-5pm daily, $10). The tour includes a tasting of the factory's seven chocolate varieties, a cup of cacao tea, and a truly delicious brownie. The on-site shop sells a wide range of chocolate products. An additional tour, The Legend of Chocolate (6pm daily, book in advance, $10) allows visitors to participate in making a chocolate drink from a 5,000-year-old recipe, accompanied by live drumming. El Quetzal also has a hotel and restaurant.

ADVENTURE SPORTS

The right fork of the main road (away from the butterfly farm) leads to the canopy tour. **Mindo Canopy Adventure** (km 2.5 Vía las Cascadas, tel. 98/542-8758, www.mindocanopy.com, 9:30am-4:15pm daily, $20) has 13 zip lines and a 40-meter (130-ft) Tarzan swing, suitable for adults and children over 6 years old. The company's safety record is excellent and there are guides to assist throughout. A coffee tour is also available.

About 1 kilometer (0.6 mi) up the hill from Mindo Canopy Adventure is a more relaxed way to travel across the treetops. **La Tarabita** (tel. 99/949-5044, Facebook @ MindoTarabita, $5) is a cable car that cruises 150 meters (500 feet) above a river basin. On the far side trails lead to several **waterfalls.** Although the paths are not well marked, you're unlikely to get lost because the route is circular. The entire loop takes 2-3 hours and gets muddy in places. A basic level of fitness is required. Wear hiking boots and bring waterproof clothing, food, and water, as there is nowhere to buy anything. There is another waterfall on the opposite side, **Tambillo** (entrance $5 pp), where you can swim or slide downstream. It's about an hour's walk uphill from Mindo to reach La Tarabita and the entrance to the waterfalls, so consider taking a taxi for $7.

Another fun activity is **tubing**—tumbling down the river rapids in an inflatable tube. This can be arranged with any of the agencies in Mindo ($10 pp) or directly with the **Mindo Tubing Association** (tel. 99/544-9292 or 98/733-3813).

A highly recommended tour operator for a wide range of Mindo tours and activities, including hiking, zip-lining, tubing, horseback riding, and canyoneering, is **SabinaTour** (tel. 98/659-4965, U.S. tel. 650/855-4077, www.mindosabinatour.com). SabinaTour offers a high standard of English-speaking customer service and is at the forefront of local conservation efforts.

Take any road out of town to discover the incredible scenery of the cloud forest on two wheels. **Endemic Tours** (Av. Quito y Gallo de la Peña, tel. 2/217-0265) rents bicycles for 90 minutes ($5), four hours ($10), and all day ($15). If you're not too confident about striking out on your own, **Mindo Biking** (Vicente Aguirre y Av. Quito, tel. 2/217-0350, www.mindobiking.com) offers English-speaking bike tours led by local guides.

Bucketpass (www.bucketpass.com) offers discounted rates on Mindo activities. You can choose four of the following activities for $38 (a discount of $12): chocolate tour, butterfly house, zip-lining, cable car with waterfall tour, biking.

Food

Mindo might be small, but there are some great restaurants to choose from. Most people will find something to their taste on Gourmet Avenue, off the main road near the park, where three of Mindo's best restaurants are clustered. ★ **Bio Mindo** (tel. 98/372-4955, $3-10) serves nutritious soups, salads, burgers, steaks, and ceviches, made with flair and freshly prepared from scratch. Veggies and non-veggies are equally well catered to, and the service is excellent. Next door, **Mishqui Quinde / Sweet Hummingbird** (tel. 98/489-9234, Facebook @MishquiMindo, 10am-5pm Wed.-Mon.) is a vegetarian restaurant specializing in quinoa burgers and quinoa desserts with fruit and home-made ice cream. Even non-veggies give it rave reviews. Across the road is Italian restaurant **La Mecha** (tel. 98/057-4817, Facebook @

restauranteit.lamecha, noon-8pm Mon.-Wed., noon-10pm Thurs., noon-11:15pm Fri., noon-2am Sat., noon-5pm Sun.), which serves pizza and pasta freshly made to order. The eggplant and vegetable pizza is the house specialty. On the main road, carnivores will appreciate **El Cheff** (Av. Quito, tel. 2/217-0478, 9am-8pm daily, $4-10), where the set lunch is great value at $3.50 and the specialty is steak. On a side street off the main road, opposite the church, is **Caskaffesu** (Sixto Durán Ballén y Quito, tel. 2/217-0100), which serves chili con carne (or *sin carne* for the veggies, $7.50), coffee from their own plantation, and desserts. There is live music (Tues.-Sat., $3 cover) and a bar. Two blocks north of the park is **El Quetzal** (9 de Octubre, tel. 2/217-0034, www.elquetzaldemindo.com, 8am-9pm daily), offering a fusion of Ecuadorian and North American cuisine made from fresh, local ingredients, some grown in the restaurant's two-acre organic garden. The restaurant specializes in chocolate dishes and cocktails. The brownie is squidgy heaven.

Just before the butterfly farm, Swiss/Ecuadorian-owned **La Roulotte** (Vía al Mariposario km 2, tel. 99/014-2921, www.hosterialaroulottemindo.com) serves cheese fondue, *rösti* (potato fritters), and wood-fired pizza in a large, airy dining area. A small organic vegetable garden provides the salad. The butterfly farm, **Mariposas de Mindo** (Vía al Mariposario, tel. 99/920-2124, www.mariposasdemindo.com, 9am-4pm daily, $7.50-18), has a restaurant with an extensive menu and lots of vegetarian options. Open after 4pm for reservations.

Accommodations
UNDER $10
On the northwest edge of town on the main road is **Hostal Melyang** (Vía a Mindo y Bijao, tel. 99/388-8125, Facebook @Hostal.Melyang.Mindo, $6 dorm, $10 s, $16 d), the lowest-priced place in town. It's basic but the service is friendly. Dorms are single sex with three bunk beds in each. All private rooms have private bathrooms and hot water. There

is a shared kitchen and a common area on the third floor with a nice view.

$10-25
On the northern edge of town, **Casa de Cecilia** (north of 9 de Octubre, tel. 2/217-0243, $10 dorm, $11-25 pp private room) is a decent budget option with rooms in rustic cabins on the edge of a rushing stream. Breakfast is available at extra cost. Casa de Cecilia works with the nature reserve Mindo Lindo.

Cabañas Armonía & Jardín de Orquídeas (Lluvia de Oro y Sixto Durán Ballén, tel. 2/217-0131, www.birdingmindo.com, $12.50-25 pp, including breakfast) is run by a local family. Comfortable, clean rooms and cabins are available with shared or private bathrooms. What sets the hostel apart is the friendly service and the beautiful orchid garden, which hostel guests can access for free. Breakfast is served in the garden by the hummingbird feeders.

Nearby **Hostal El Jardín del Descanso** (tel. 99/482-9587, rodny_garrido@hotmail.com, Facebook @Hostal El Descanso, $15 dorm, $22 pp private room, including breakfast) has a garden full of hummingbirds.

The Yellow House & Trails / Hacienda San Vicente (no address, located near the south end of the main park, tel. 2/217-0124, www.ecuadormindobirds.com, $20 pp without breakfast, $25 pp with breakfast) is a privately owned reserve at the north end of Mindo. The lodge is family-owned and run by three sisters, who are very kind hosts. Breakfast is made with organic produce from the hacienda (including the coffee) and nearby farms. Guests have free access to the six walking trails, which costs $6 for nonguests.

On a quiet street on the other side of the stream to Casa de Cecilia, ★ **Casa de Piedra** (Calle Julio Goethche, Barrio Magdalena, tel. 2/217-0436, www.casadelpiedramindo.com, $15 dorm, from $25 pp s/d) is an absolute gem and excellent value. Set in large gardens, the rooms are very stylish and the service is exceptionally friendly and helpful. A wide range of accommodation options are available, from a mixed dorm to a three-bedroom apartment. It has a restaurant, games room, and an outdoor pool. Massage and bike hire are available. Pet friendly.

$25-50

All the rates in this category and up include breakfast.

On the main road as you arrive in town, **The Dragonfly Inn** (Av. Quito *y* Río Canchupí, tel. 2/217-0319, $30 s, $50 d) is a popular midrange choice. Rooms are wooden, each with a balcony and hammock. A good but pricey restaurant with fresh, often organic ingredients overlooks the river (vegetarian options available). On the main road, it's not the most peaceful spot, but it's a good option for those who like to be near all the amenities of town.

At **El Quetzal** (9 de Octubre, tel. 2/217-0034, www.elquetzaldemindo.com, $35 s, $68 d), each room features a balcony with a hammock and includes a tour of the chocolate factory. The staff speak English.

At the north end of town, tucked away on a side street just past Casa de Piedra, **La Bicok** (tel. 99/942-1945, $9 camping, $45 s, $70 d) was designed by a bioclimatic architect to have a low environmental impact. The construction is 100 percent natural materials, there is a gray water system to reduce water consumption, and the restaurant serves local organic produce (for guests only, upon request). The rooms are stylish and excellent value. One room has a wheelchair-accessible shower. There is a swimming pool with sun loungers. A fire is lit every night for guests.

Part of the butterfly farm, ★ **Hostería Mariposas de Mindo** (Vía al Mariposario, tel. 99/920-2124, www.mariposasdemindo.com, $43 pp) has eight attractive wood-paneled cabins set in tropical gardens. Staff are helpful and friendly. Guests have free, unlimited access to the butterfly garden ($7.50 for nonguests). There is a good on-site restaurant.

$50-75

Halfway to the butterfly farm is the Swiss/Ecuadorian-owned **La Roulotte** (Vía al Mariposario km 2, tel. 99/014-2921, www.hosterialaroulottemindo.com, $50 s, $75 d). Five charming gypsy wagons (two with wood-burning stoves) serve as sleeping accommodations surrounding an expansive central restaurant that doubles as a bird-watching station. Toucans and hummingbirds are frequent visitors. It's a quiet, peaceful spot. Additional amenities and services are quirky: an impressive bamboo maze and a *petanque* court. There is a small organic vegetable garden and a filtration system for the output from the toilets, which fertilizes the massive stands of bamboo.

$100-200

Just outside town to the east are three excellent ecolodges that deserve special mention. All include breakfast.

Las Terrazas de Dana (Vía a Las Cascadas, km 1.2, tel. 98/409-9146, www.lasterrazasdedana.com, $130 s, $140 d) offers six immaculate modern cabins, each with a two-person hot tub and private terrace with spectacular views. All three meals can be brought to your room and enjoyed on the terrace, surrounded by butterflies and hummingbirds attracted to the specially chosen flowering plants. You can also book an in-room massage with organic Ecuadorian chocolate and coffee products. The lodge's owner, David, and all the staff go out of their way to make sure their guests have a wonderful stay. The lodge was the first in Mindo to receive an Environmental Certificate from the provincial government. The sister tour company, Dana Tours, offers local birding and adventure trips and Galápagos cruises.

Next to Terrazas de Dana, ★ **Casa Divina Lodge** (tel. 98/659-4965, www.mindocasadivina.com, $145 s, $250 d) is owned and managed by Mindo local Efrain Toapanta and his Californian wife, Molly Brown. With a warm, welcoming main lodge and hospitality to match, Casa Divina is set in bird-filled gardens on 2.7 hectares (6.7 acres) of cloud forest. The property features two self-guided forest trails and a bird observation deck. The four thoughtfully appointed wooden guest cabins, each with a private balcony and hammock, were hand-built by Efrain, along with most of the furniture. Efrain was instrumental in establishing Mindo as an ecotourism destination from the very beginning, over 30 years ago. He and Molly have purchased a 100-hectare (250-acre) protected reserve and are at the forefront of local conservation efforts. The lodge is an internationally certified community-based green business, built and operated for minimum environmental impact. The restaurant uses locally produced, organic ingredients. All the staff, guides, and drivers are local. Molly and Efrain also own SabinaTour, an excellent tour operator for a wide range of Mindo tours and activities (www.mindosabinatour.com).

To really get away from it all, head to **El Monte Sustainable Lodge** (tel. 99/308-4675, www.ecuadorcloudforest.com, $140 pp, reservation only), just past the butterfly farm. The entrance to the lodge is via a hand-pulled cable car over a rushing river. Upon arrival, either telephone or shout loudly and someone will appear to pull you across. It's a fun and novel experience that only serves to heighten the feeling of isolation, as does the lack of Internet (although Wi-Fi connection is available in the office upon request). The six guest cabins and large, open-sided central lodge are a perfect mix of rustic and luxury. Guests eat a delicious candle-lit dinner together in the evenings, with vegetarians beautifully catered for. Rates include all meals and a Spanish-speaking naturalist guide. Solar panels and a micro-hydro system generate part of the electricity; an organic garden supplies some of the fruit and vegetables for the restaurant; and there is a biological sewage system. To facilitate cloud forest research, El Monte founded the Mindo Biological Station, which protects 6,500 hectares (16,100 acres) of land within the Mindo-Nambillo Protected Forest.

Information

There's a **Centro de Información** on Avenida Quito near the plaza.

Getting There

The road from Quito to Mindo runs west from Mitad del Mundo. The direct service by **Cooperativa Flor del Valle** takes around 2.5 hours and leaves from the Ofelia terminal. Note that the buses leave from a separate concourse just outside the main terminal. Exit the terminal just left of the row of snack stalls and cross the road to find it. Buses leave Monday-Friday at 8:30am, 9am, 11am, 1pm, and 4pm; Saturday at 7:40am, 8:20am, 9:20am, 11am, 1pm, 2pm, and 4pm; and Sunday at 7:40am, 8:20am, 9:20am, 11am, 1pm, 2pm, and 5pm. Coming back from Mindo, direct buses to Quito leave from the town center Monday-Friday at 6:30am, 11am, 1:45pm, 3:30pm, and 5pm; on Saturday at 6:30am, 11am, 1pm, 2pm, 4pm, and 5pm; and Sunday at 6:30am, 11am, 1pm, 2pm, 4pm, and 5pm. For up-to-date bus schedules check www.lasterrazasdedana.com/the-lodge/how-to-get-the-lodge.

If you miss the bus from Ofelia, head for the Carcelén terminal and take the first bus to Los Bancos, which leaves you on the main road at the top of the hill above Mindo, where you can catch a taxi (around $3). Leaving Mindo, take a taxi to the main road and flag down any Quito-bound bus.

★ MAQUIPUCUNA BIOLOGICAL RESERVE

Just two hours north of Quito, the **Maquipucuna Reserve & Bear Lodge** (tel. 99/421-8033, www.maquipucuna.org, $95-208 s, $185-337 d) protects over 6,000 hectares (14,800 acres) of pristine rainforest in the heart of the Chocó Andean Corridor, one of the earth's top five biodiversity hot spots. The reserve's wide range of eco-zones between 900 and 2,785 meters (3,000-9,000 ft) has led to an astonishing diversity of flora and fauna. A whopping 25 percent of Ecuador's bird species and 10 percent of its mammal species

The Andean Bear

If you spend any time in the center of Quito, you will probably see a government poster campaign promoting the city as the Tierra de Osos, or Land of Bears (www.quitotierradeosos.org). The bears in the posters are Andean bears, which are in danger of extinction due to hunting and habitat loss.

The only bear species in South America, it is also known as the "spectacled bear" for the markings on its face, which are unique to each individual. The males are larger than the females, reaching 1.8 meters (5.9 ft) in height and 175 kilograms (385 lb) in weight. Despite their size, the bears are 90 percent vegetarian, which is fortunate because they can run at up to 50 kph (30 mph). These clever, arboreal animals build platforms and nests in trees for eating and sleeping. They are so shy and secretive that little is known about their habits. In fact, they are so good at hiding that it can hard to spot one up a tree, even if you know it is there.

a spectacled bear in the Maquipucuna Biological Reserve

The story of how these elusive creatures were adopted as mascots of the city is a fascinating one. It started in 1985 when an Ecuadorian couple, Rebeca Justicia and Rodrigo Ontaneda, first decided to protect a section of cloud forest north of Quito. After establishing the 6,500-hectare (16,100-acre) Maquipucuna Reserve in 1988, the couple spent the following decades restoring degraded pasturelands and working with local communities and the government to protect the surrounding forests. Their work was instrumental in creating a safe haven for at least 60 Andean bears, dozens of which congregate annually to feed on their favorite fruit—the small, wild avocados that are now only abundant on the northern end of the reserve. Maquipucuna is now the best place in the world to see the Andean bear in the wild.

After three decades of conservation work, the government of Quito declared Maquipucuna and the surrounding area a protected bear corridor, preserving a total area of 65,000 hectares (161,000 acres). In July 2018, it was declared a UNESCO Biosphere Reserve.

The ecotourism opportunities presented by the congregation of Andean bears may be the key to finding sustainable economic alternatives to destructive logging and mining practices. Thus, the couple's efforts are not about saving just bears, but the Ecuadorian cloud forest itself, one of the earth's top five biodiversity hot spots, and all the species that call it home. For more information, see www.maquipucuna.org.

call Maquipucuna home, among them the reserve's most famous resident, the Andean or spectacled bear. In fact, this is the best place in the world to see these shy endangered creatures, which come to the forest to feed on a type of wild avocado that is only abundant at Maquipucuna. As well as watching bears, visitors can go on guided walks, explore self-guided trails, bird-watch, go on night hikes, and bathe in waterfalls and swimming holes. A less vigorous activity is harvesting and

processing cacao and then enjoying a chocolate massage with the results!

Maquipucuna is managed by Rebeca and Rodrigo Ontaneda, the Ecuadorian couple who first established the area as a reserve in 1988. Both speak English and are on hand to share their fascinating stories and knowledge with visitors. Accommodation prices include three meals (vegetarians catered for) and daily guided walks with a bilingual guide. Camping is also available. The reserve accepts volunteers. Note that the bears are not present year-round and their annual migration to the reserve can happen anytime between July and February. Check the reserve's Facebook page for updates. Also be aware that afternoons at Maquipucuna tend to be rainy.

To get to the reserve, take a bus from Quito's Ofelia station to Nanegalito, the nearest village to Maquipucuna. From there, hire a taxi to the reserve ($15). The reserve can arrange transport from the airport ($142 for 2 people) or from Quito ($87 for 2 people). A taxi from Mindo to the reserve should be around $35.

YUNGUILLA

An hour north of Quito, **Yunguilla** (tel. 98/021-5476, www.yunguilla.org.ec) is a cloud forest reserve of 2,600 hectares (6,400 acres) that borders Maquipucuna to the west. Until the late 1990s, the 60 families that inhabit the reserve were forced to traffic moonshine and fell their forests for charcoal production to make ends meet. When the Maquipucuna Foundation realized the extent of the threat posed by their neighbors' unsustainable land-use practices, they assisted the Yunguilla community to find alternative sources of income. Funds were raised for the purchase of the Tahuallullo farm, which has a central building that serves as a hostel and the headquarters of a community enterprise that produces orchids, handicrafts, and organic cheeses and jams. Other projects included reforestation, soil conservation, and the creation of organic gardens. Now completely financially independent and flourishing, Yunguilla is a shining example of eco- and community tourism. Visitors can sleep and eat at the lodge or with local families, all of whom have guest rooms

in their homes. To get to Yunguilla, take a bus to Calacali from the Ofelia terminal, then take a taxi or pickup truck from Calacali's central park ($4).

PASOCHOA PROTECTED FOREST

The most untouched stretch of forest close to Quito is the **Pasochoa Protected Forest** (open daily, $5 pp), 30 kilometers (19 mi) southeast of the city. The reserve ranges 2,700-4,200 meters (8,900-13,800 ft) in elevation, the highest point being Cerro Pasochoa, an extinct volcano. The forest and *páramo* ecosystems are home to 126 species of birds, including many hummingbirds and a family of condors.

Loop paths of varying lengths and difficulty lead higher and higher into the hills, ranging from 30 minutes to eight hours in duration. A guide and a good level of fitness are required for the longer hikes. It's possible to climb to the lip of Cerro Pasochoa's blasted volcanic crater in six hours. Take food, water, and waterproof clothes. Campsites and a few dorm rooms with showers and cooking facilities are available near the bottom.

From Quito, take a bus marked Playón from the south end of the Plaza La Marín below Old Town to the village of Amaguaña (30-40 minutes, $0.60). Hire a taxi or pickup ($5-8) from the village plaza to the turnoff for the reserve. From there, a dirt road leads 7 kilometers (4.3 mi) up a rough, cobbled road to the reserve. Ask the driver to come back for you, or take a phone and call a taxi for the return journey. Some tour operators in Quito offer day trips to hike Cerro Pasochoa, including **Gulliver's** (tel. 2/252-8030, www.gulliver.com.ec).

Northern Sierra

Like much of the country, Ecuador's most northerly region, which stretches from Quito to the Colombian border, is astonishingly diverse. Its most famous attractions, the Otavalo textile market and the iconic Laguna Cuicocha, are most definitely worth a visit, but even more captivating experiences lie in the surrounding countryside and rural villages.

Just west of Otavalo, Intag is located at the confluence of two of the world's biological hot spots, the Tumbes-Chocó-Magdalena and the Tropical Andes. The rugged, cloud-forested peaks and valleys are home to several idyllic villages, where community ecotourism projects provide sustainable sources of income. Also inspiring and picturesque is the small village of San Clemente near Ibarra, where visitors are

Highlights

Look for ★ to find recommended sights, activities, dining, and lodging.

★ **Textile Market:** Even non-shoppers will enjoy browsing the incredible range of textiles and handicrafts at Otavalo's Saturday market—or just soaking in the festival atmosphere (page 95).

★ **Laguna Cuicocha:** This stunning crater lake in the shadow of Volcán Cotacachi is one of Ecuador's most iconic sights. Hike around it or take a boat trip between two volcanic cones rising from the azure waters (page 112).

★ **Intag:** These cloud-forested slopes, alive with rushing rivers and dotted with picturesque villages, provide some of the richest biodiversity on earth. Every visit helps the local people in their struggle against mega-mining (page 113).

★ **San Clemente:** Stay with a Kichwa family and experience their typical way of life. Learn about the Andean cosmovision and cook traditional meals with ingredients straight from the organic gardens. This is eco- and community tourism at its best (page 124).

★ **El Ángel Ecological Reserve:** An eerily beautiful place with giant *frailejón* plants standing like silent sentries watching over the misty *páramo*. Nearby is a rare and ancient polylepis forest, with 4,000-year-old trees (page 129).

Northern Sierra

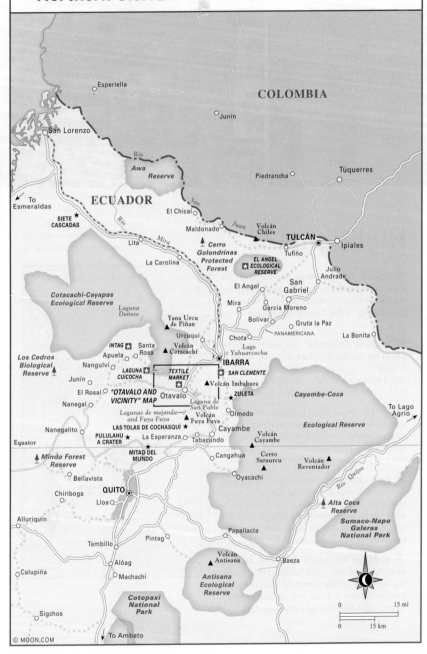

COLOMBIA

Esperiella

Junín

San Lorenzo

Río
Awa
Reserve

Piedrancha

Túquerres

ECUADOR

Río San

El Chical

Maldonado

Volcán
Chiles

TULCÁN

Ipiales

To
Esmeraldas

SIETE
CASCADAS

Lita

Río Mira

Cerro
Golondrinas
Protected
Forest

Tufiño

Julio
Andrade

La Carolina

EL ANGEL
ECOLOGICAL
RESERVE

El Angel

San
Gabriel

*Cotacachi-Cayapas
Ecological Reserve*

*Laguna
Doñoso*

Yana Urcu
de Piñan

Mira

García Moreno

Bolívar

Gruta la Paz

La Bonita

Urcuquí

Chota

PANAMERICANA

*Los Cedros
Biological
Reserve*

INTAG

Santa
Rosa

Volcán
Cotacachi

*Lago
Yahuarcocha*

IBARRA

Apuela

Nangulví

LAGUNA
CUICOCHA

TEXTILE
MARKET

SAN CLEMENTE

Volcán Imbabura

Junín

El Rosal

"OTAVALO AND
VICINITY" MAP

Otavalo

ZULETA

Cayambe-Coca

Nanegal

*Lagunas de mojanda—
and Fuya Fuya*

*Laguna de
San Pablo*

Volcán
Fuya Fuya

Olmedo

To Lago
Agrio

LAS TOLAS DE COCHASQUÍ

Cayambe

Ecological Reserve

Nanegalito

Equator

PULULAHU
A CRATER

La Esperanza

Tabacundo

Volcán
Cayambe

*Mindo Forest
Reserve*

MITAD DEL
MUNDO

Cangahua

Cerro
Saraurcu

Volcán
Reventador

Bellavista

Oyacachi

Río Quijos

Chiriboga

QUITO

Lloa

*Alta Coca
Reserve*

Alluriquín

*Sumaco-Napo
Galeras
National Park*

Calupiña

Tambillo

Pintag

Papallacta

Baeza

Alóag

Machachi

Volcán
Antisana

Sigchos

*Cotopaxi
National
Park*

*Antisana
Ecological
Reserve*

0   15 mi

0   15 km

To Ambato

© MOON.COM

invited to experience life in a rural Kichwa community, sharing the people's way of life and helping to keep ancient traditions alive.

The Cotacachi-Cayapas and Cayambe-Coca Ecological Reserves encompass an almost unbelievable number of ecosystems, including wildflower-strewn *páramo*, orchid-filled cloud forest, and steamy Amazon rainforest. Farther north are the haunting, windswept wilds of the El Ángel Ecological Reserve, protecting some of the most pristine high-altitude country in Ecuador. These three reserves are home to many threatened and endangered animals, including Andean bears and foxes, jaguars, pumas, ocelots, and Andean tapirs.

Many of the northern Sierra's residents are direct descendants of the region's pre-Columbian inhabitants, from the Otavalos to the Caranquis and Pastos. Alongside this strong indigenous presence is an Afro-Ecuadorian influence, mostly in Ibarra and the Chota Valley.

PLANNING YOUR TIME

The northern Sierra is the most compact Andean region. Even the remote El Ángel reserve is only four hours by bus from Quito. Otavalo is a good base for exploring much of the region. The textile market and town itself can be seen in a day, with the surrounding villages, lakes, waterfalls, and hikes worth at least another two to three days. Laguna Cuicocha is also an easy day trip from Otavalo, though it's closer to Cotacachi. Intag merits at least three or four days, though it's so idyllic that you might be tempted to stay for much longer.

You can spend an enjoyable day wandering the wide cobbled streets and colonial architecture of Ibarra, and another two or three days in the nearby villages of San Clemente and Zuleta. El Ángel Ecological Reserve, the polylepis forest, and the highlights of the surrounding area can be seen in three days.

A good approach is to travel north from Quito, exploring the region using Otavalo, Ibarra, and El Ángel as bases. Most of the area is well served by buses and taxis, though the roads in some of the more remote destinations are in poor condition and it may be necessary to hire a *camioneta* (white pickup truck taxi), rather than a yellow cab. These are usually easy to find.

There are so many microclimates in the northern Sierra that it's impossible to plan a visit around the weather. Aside from the Otavalo textile market, crowds of tourists are not generally present in this region and there is no busy season.

Quito to Otavalo

LAS TOLAS DE COCHASQUÍ

On the road from Quito to Otavalo, west of Cayambe, are the ruins of 15 flat-topped pre-Inca pyramids and 21 burial mounds. At 3,100 meters (10,170 ft) elevation, **Cochasquí** (tel. 2/399-4524, 8am-4pm daily, $3) is one of Ecuador's most important archaeological sites, built by the Cara and/or Caranqui people between AD 950 and the Spanish conquest in the 1530s.

Cochasquí is thought to have been a military, ceremonial, and astronomical center. Excavations have revealed what appears to be a calendar atop one pyramid, with stones casting shadows to indicate the solstices and the best times to plant and harvest. Festivals are still held here at the solstices and equinoxes.

Previous: Mirador El Lechero; El Ángel Ecological Reserve's *frailejón* plants; textiles for sale at the market in Otavalo.

The site's setting is dramatic, with spectacular views over Quito, Cotopaxi, the Ilinizas mountains, and Antisana on clear days.

Visitors must be accompanied by a guide, and a tour is included in the ticket price (English-speaking available), which is payable at the clearly marked entrance. As well as a scale model of the site, there are small archaeological and ethnographic museums, and replicas of traditional buildings with medicinal gardens. Local cuisine is available at a small restaurant. **Camping Cochasquí** (tel. 99/491-9008, campingcochasqui@pichincha. gob.ec) offers cabins ($10 pp), rented tents ($10 for 2 people), and camping spaces ($3 pp).

Getting There

Take a bus from Quito's Ofelia terminal to the small village of Malchingui with a bus company of the same name (approx. 1 hour). In Malchingui, take another bus headed for Cayambe and ask the driver to let you off after 6 kilometers (3.7 mi) at Cochasquí ($0.50), or hire a *camioneta* ($3-5 one way). *Camionetas* can also be hired in Tabacundo or Cayambe ($15 one way). Ask the staff at Cochasquí to call a driver for your return journey.

CAYAMBE-COCA ECOLOGICAL RESERVE

Home to the snowcapped volcano Cayambe and the headwaters of the Coca River, the 4,000 square kilometers (1,500 sq mi) of the **Cayambe-Coca Ecological Reserve** (http://areasprotegidas.ambiente.gob.ec) range in elevation from 600 to 5,790 meters (2,000-19,000 ft). Encompassing windswept *páramo*, Amazon rainforest, and everything in between, the park boasts some 900 species of birds, from condors to toucans and macaws. Among the 200 mammal species are spectacled bear, mountain tapir, howler monkey, and spider monkey.

The reserve spans four provinces, divided according to altitude. The parts of the park that fall within Pichincha and Imbabura are known as the *zona alta*, or high zone; those within Napo and Sucumbíos are the *zona baja*, or low zone. The key attractions of the high zone are the **Oyacachi hot springs** and the **Cayambe volcano.** The attractions of the low zone, including the San Rafael waterfall and the Papallacta hot springs, are covered in the *Oriente and the Amazon Basin* chapter of this book.

Oyacachi

The Kichwa community of **Oyacachi** (tel. 6/238-6019 or 95/891-8101, http://oyacachi. org) is known for the woodcarving skills of its inhabitants and its **hot springs** (8am-5pm daily, $5), which are popular with locals on weekends and less busy on midweek days. Accommodations are available at the **Cabañas Oyacachi** (tel. 99/370-0529, www.cabanasoyacachi.com, $15 pp, including breakfast). As well as taking visitors on hikes and horseback rides to nearby rivers and waterfalls, local guides offer a strenuous but spectacular two- to three-day trek from Oyacachi to El Chaco in the Amazon. The best season for this adventure is November to February; it may be too rainy the rest of the year, but ask locally for current conditions. Local guides can be found at the information office next to the entrance to the hot springs. For an English- and French-speaking guide, contact Ivan Suarez (tel. 99/993-3148, http://www.all-about-ecuador.com).

Volcán Cayambe

The summit of Ecuador's third-tallest peak (5,790 m/18,996 ft) is not only the highest point in the world on the equator, but also the coldest—and the only place where temperature and latitude reach zero simultaneously. Suitable for advanced climbers only, **Cayambe** is a seven-hour climb from the refuge to the summit, and there are many obstacles—an ever-changing network of crevasses, unusually high winds, strong snowstorms, and occasional avalanches. At 4,600 meters (15,090 ft), the **Bergé-Oleas-Ruales refuge,** named for three mountaineers killed in an avalanche in 1974, offers a mattress, dinner, and breakfast ($32 pp, bring your own sleeping bag). See the **Ecuadorian Association of Mountain Guides** (tel. 2/254-0599, https://aseguim.org/miembros) to find a guide, or contact **Andean Face** (www.andeanface.com) in Quito. In Otavalo, all the tour operators listed offer the climb, including a night at the refuge (approx. $280).

Getting There

The Cayambe-Coca reserve is accessed via the town of Cayambe. To get there, take a bus with **Flor de Valle** (http://coopflordelvalle.com) from Quito's Ofelia terminal (1.5 hours). From Otavalo, there are frequent buses to Cayambe.

Buses from Cayambe to Oyacachi take 1.5 hours, leaving Cayambe at 8am and 3pm, returning at 10am and 5pm. A *camioneta* to Oyacachi from Cayambe costs $35 one way. To drive to Oyacachi, you'll need four-wheel drive. Take the road from Cayambe to Cangahua and drive for 40 kilometers (25 mi) until you reach a checkpoint, from where Oyacachi is another 15 minutes.

A *camioneta* to the Bergé-Oleas-Ruales refuge from Cayambe is $35 one way (1 hour). To drive there from Cayambe, take the Juan Montalvo-El Hato-PieMonte road in a four-wheel-drive vehicle.

Otavalo

Otavalo is one of the oldest towns in Imbabura Province and was a market town long before the Incas arrived. Today, the textile market is the biggest in Ecuador and one of the most renowned in South America. Textile and handicrafts stalls are a permanent fixture in the Plaza de Ponchos, but the biggest day is Saturday, when the streets near the square are pedestrianized to make room for the additional vendors who flock into town and there is a festival atmosphere.

The town has a dramatic setting, nestled at 2,530 meters (8,300 ft) in the verdant Valle del Amanecer (Valley of the Sunrise) between two dormant volcanoes: Cotacachi to the northwest and Imbabura to the east. There is great hiking around several stunning lakes and waterfalls close to town, and adventure sports such as climbing, rafting, and biking in the surrounding mountains and rivers. Traditional crafts are still practiced in the neighboring indigenous villages, where there are several community tourism projects.

On the whole, the streets of Otavalo are safe, even at night. Sadly, however, the large number of visitors has led to occasional robberies, and there are bag-slashers and pickpockets in the crowded Saturday market. Take care with your belongings on the bus between Otavalo and Quito. When exploring the area's trails and more remote locations, it's best not to go alone, as robberies of lone hikers are not unheard of.

ORIENTATION

Otavalo is easy to navigate, with most hotels, restaurants, and amenities near the two main squares, Plaza de Ponchos (to the northeast of the center) and Parque Simón Bolívar (less than a kilometer to the southwest). The main avenue between the two squares is Antonio José de Sucre. The Pan-American Highway skirts the town to the west.

SIGHTS
★ Textile Market

The town's biggest draw is the Saturday **textile market** (7am-6pm). By 9am, the Plaza de Ponchos is packed with a brightly colored, murmuring throng of vendors and visitors haggling over every imaginable type of textile and craft. Although there is a wide range of goods available throughout the week, the largest market is on Saturday, and it's worth a visit even if you don't intend to buy anything. Wednesday is the second-biggest day.

Otavalo

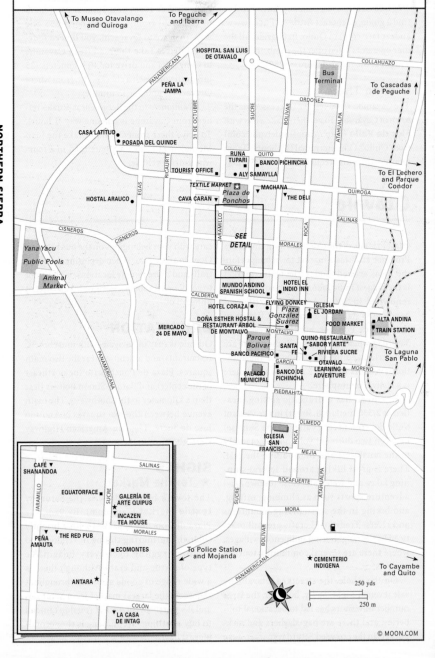

To Museo Otavalango and Quiroga
To Peguche and Ibarra

PANAMERICANA

HOSPITAL SAN LUIS DE OTAVALO

Bus Terminal

COLLAHUAZO

To Cascadas de Peguche

PEÑA LA JAMPA

ORDONEZ

31 DE OCTUBRE

SUCRE

BOLIVAR

ATAHUALPA

CASA LATITUD
POSADA DEL QUINDE

QUITO

RUNA TUPARI
BANCO PICHINCHA
ALY SAMAYLLA

RICAURTE

TOURIST OFFICE

EGAS

TEXTILE MARKET
Plaza de Ponchos

CAVA CARAN

MACHANA
THE DELI

To El Lechero and Parque Condor

QUIROGA

HOSTAL ARAUCO

SALINAS

JARAMILLO

SEE DETAIL

ROCA

MORALES

CISNEROS

CISNEROS

COLÓN

Yana Yacu Public Pools

Animal Market

CALDERÓN

MUNDO ANDINO SPANISH SCHOOL

HOTEL EL INDIO INN

HOTEL CORAZA

FLYING DONKEY
Plaza González Suárez

IGLESIA EL JORDAN

DOÑA ESTHER HOSTAL & RESTAURANT ARBOL DE MONTALVO

MERCADO 24 DE MAYO

MONTALVO

FOOD MARKET

ALTA ANDINA
TRAIN STATION

Parque Bolivar

QUINO RESTAURANT "SABOR Y ARTE"

To Laguna San Pablo

BANCO PACIFICO

SANTA FE

RIVIERA SUCRE

PANAMERICANA

GARCIA

PALACIO MUNICIPAL

BANCO DE PICHINCHA

OTAVALO LEARNING & ADVENTURE

MORENO

PIEDRAHITA

OLMEDO

IGLESIA SAN FRANCISCO

ROCA

MEJIA

ROCAFUERTE

SUCRE

MORA

ATAHUALPA

To Police Station and Mojanda

BOLIVAR

PANAMERICANA

★ CEMENTERIO INDIGENA

To Cayambe and Quito

0   250 yds
0   250 m

Detail

CAFÉ SHANANDOA

SALINAS

JARAMILLO

EQUATORFACE

SUCRE

GALERÍA DE ARTE QUIPUS

INCAZEN TEA HOUSE

MORALES

PEÑA AMAUTA
THE RED PUB

ECOMONTES

ANTARA ★

COLÓN

LA CASA DE INTAG

© MOON.COM

Weaving the History of the Kichwas of Otavalo

Alongside Otavalo's white and mestizo residents, more than 40,000 indigenous Otavalos of Kichwa nationality live in the town and surrounding villages. Thanks to their famous weaving skills, the Kichwas of Otavalo are a special case among indigenous groups; their unusual financial success and cultural stability allow them to travel internationally and educate their children abroad while still keeping a firm hold on their traditions at home.

When the Incans arrived, the Otavalos had already been using the backstrap weaving loom for centuries. The Incas, appreciating the fine work, collected the weavings as tributes. Specially chosen women dedicated their lives to creating fine textiles, some of which were burned in ritual offerings to the sun. After the Spanish conquest, exploitation of the local craftspeople pervaded, and they were forced to work in sweatshops, or *obrajes*, in terrible conditions. In the 19th century, mass production switched to factories, where the oppression continued. In the early 20th century, Otavalo's weavers caught the world's attention with a popular and inexpensive imitation of cashmere, a fine woven cloth from Asia, but their virtual slavery continued until the Agrarian Reform Law of 1964. This law granted indigenous people land and control over their choice of work, enabling them to weave in their own homes on a self-employed basis.

Although traditional weaving is still practiced in a few of the surrounding villages, these days most Otavalos have adapted their processes to keep up with the global economy, using electric machines or cheaper material bought in other countries. Others work as merchants or in the tourism industry. The Kichwas of Otavalo own most of the businesses in the town, as well as many stores throughout Ecuador and in other countries in South America. They travel extensively abroad in the Americas, Europe, and Asia to sell their products.

While some Otavalos still wear the traditional poncho, particularly on special occasions, others prefer western clothes. However they dress, the Otavalos of Kichwa take great pride in their cultural identity, and the election of Otavalo's first indigenous mayor in 2000 reflects the strength of their presence in the region.

Traditional wares include wool and alpaca sweaters, blankets, wall hangings, and ponchos; embroidered shirts; and long cloth strips called *fajas*, used by Sierra Kichwas to tie back their hair. There is a wide range of hats, from felt to Panama to woolly with bobbles; lots of jewelry made from beads, *tagua* nut, and silver; and handbags of every variety. Other items include paintings, wooden ornaments, hand-painted wooden plates and dishes, musical instruments, dream catchers, leather goods, fake shrunken heads, and spices.

While there are some true treasures to be found in the market, as the city has become more of a tourist attraction, some of the goods have started to be mass-produced in nearby factories; many are actually made in China or Peru. Some blankets and ponchos are advertised as "alpaca" but may be synthetic. Unless you're a textile expert, there is really no way to know what you're buying. A good general rule is, if you like it, buy it, regardless of its claimed origin or pedigree. The only items likely to be handmade locally are the traditional wall hangings, or *tapices*, which have pre-Columbian geometric motifs or depict a row of indigenous people in hats, seen from behind (these figures are known as the *chismosas* or "the gossipers"). *Tapices* are still made in the surrounding villages using traditional methods.

For the Saturday market, it's best to spend Friday night in town, but make a reservation because hotels fill up fast. Alternatively, get a Saturday morning bus from Quito. Bargaining is expected, even in the textiles and handicrafts stores in town. Foreigners are naturally offered rather inflated prices, so haggle away, but don't be too pushy; if you get 30 percent off the starting price, you're doing well. Linger toward the end of the day for the best deals.

Parque Bolívar

The most attractive and historic part of Otavalo is at the south end of town. **Parque Bolívar** is dominated by the statue of Inca general Rumiñahui, who valiantly resisted the Spanish invaders and remains a symbol of indigenous resistance. The park often hosts events and live music on weekends. On the west side of the park is the main church, **San Luis,** built in the late 19th century with a single octagonal tower. Two blocks southeast on Calderón and Roca is a more attractive church, **El Jordán,** which has impressively carved wooden doors.

Museo Otavalango

It's worth making the trip a couple of kilometers northwest of town to visit the **Museo Otavalango** (Antigua Fábrica San Pedro, Pedro Perez, Vía Antigua a Quiroga, tel. 6/290-3879, https://otavalango.wordpress.com, 9am-5pm Mon.-Sat., free). The museum was once the home of Ecuador's first president, José Féliz Valdivieso, before being converted into the northern Sierra's first factory in 1858, where indigenous Otavalos were forced to work in slave-like conditions. Although working life improved, the factory continued to operate until the late 1990s before closing its doors. Years later, an ex-worker at the factory, René Zambrano, visited his former workplace to find it derelict. He and his wife, Ludmilla, organized a group of ex-factory workers to raise the funds needed to buy the site and turn it into a museum, which opened in 2011. As well as housing exhibits on the history of the factory, the museum is a living community space, dedicated to the preservation of Kichwa culture, encouraging local youngsters to maintain their ancestral traditions. A visit here is not a highly polished experience, but that is its charm; you may have to wander around a bit before finding someone to show you around. Call ahead of time to make a reservation for a tour in English or to request special demonstrations of traditional weaving, music, and dance.

Cementerio Indígena

On Mondays and Thursdays between 7am and 10am, many indigenous Otavalos gather to pay their respects to the dead at the **Cementerio Indígena,** which is just across the Pan-American Highway south of town. They bring the favorite dishes of the deceased, socialize, and share food with one another. It is perfectly acceptable for non-indigenous people to visit the cemetery, but be respectful; don't go in a big group or take photos near visiting families. The best day to visit is November 2, the Day of the Dead.

Mirador El Lechero

Four kilometers (2.5 mi) outside town, the **Mirador El Lechero** is a hill offering 360-degree views of Otavalo, Laguna de San Pablo, and Imbabura. The mirador's name, which means "the milkman," comes from a tree with milky white sap that is renowned for its healing powers. The tree has been used as a ceremony site for shamanic rituals and, along with 12 others planted in the area over a century ago, is where the umbilical cords of newly born babies were buried to connect local communities with the land. The mirador is a one-hour uphill walk from Otavalo. Head southeast out of town on Piedrahita and follow the signs as the road quickly steepens into a series of switchbacks. Alternatively, take a taxi from Otavalo for $3.5-4 (one way). Ask the driver to wait, or make the return journey on foot.

Parque Cóndor

Parque Cóndor (tel. 98/431-1769, www.parquecondor.com, 9:30am-5pm Wed.-Sun., $4.75), 2.5 kilometers (1.6 mi) north of the mirador, is a sanctuary for condors, hawks, eagles, owls, and other birds of prey, which are

---

1: Parque Bolívar; **2:** colorful indigenous wood carvings for sale at the Saturday textile market; **3:** spices; **4:** barn owl at Parque Cóndor

well cared for after being rescued or donated. There are shows at 11:30am and 3:30pm (in Spanish), where visitors can see the birds flying up close. The center has a strong focus on environmental education. Walk there via El Lechero, or take a $4 taxi from Otavalo. Ask the driver to come back at an allotted time (2 hours is plenty, including the show).

ENTERTAINMENT AND EVENTS
Nightlife

Nightlife is low-key in Otavalo during the week but gets going on weekends, particularly Saturdays. Recommended bars include ★ **Cava Caran** (Modesto Jaramillo y Salinas, tel. 99/189-7959, Facebook @ CavaCaran, 5pm-midnight Tues.-Fri., 10am-midnight Sat.), a basement bar on Plaza de Ponchos serving locally brewed craft beer and whisky made with a still that belonged to the friendly owner's grandfather. The food menu includes burgers, burritos, pizzas, and sandwiches, with veggie options available. Also right on the plaza, **Machana** (Sucre, tel. 99/258-5316, Facebook @Machana Lounge) is a café, bar, live music venue, and gallery that is hopping with an arty, alternative crowd on weekends. Another option is **The Red Pub** (Morales y Sucre, tel. 98/762-7666, Facebook @TheRedPub, 3pm-midnight Sun.-Wed., 3pm-3am Thurs.-Sat.). Despite its name, it's frequented by as many locals as gringos. It has an alternative vibe and plays rock music.

For dancing, try **Peña Amauta** (Morales 5-11 y Modesto Jaramillo, tel. 2/924-435, Facebook @amautabar, 8pm-3am Fri.-Sat.), an intimate spot with live traditional Andean music every Friday and Saturday at 10pm; or **La Jampa** (31 de Octubre y Panamericana Norte, tel. 99/818-8976, Facebook @lajampa, 9pm-2am Fri.-Sat.), which has live music every Saturday, often folkloric or salsa. Three dance floors play a mix of dance, salsa, reggaetón, merengue, and rumba.

Festivals

These festivals can fall on different days from year to year, so check with the tourist office on the Plaza de Ponchos (http://otavalo.travel) for specific dates.

Pawkar Raymi (Blossoming Festival) is the Quechua equivalent of Carnival, usually held in February, to celebrate the fertility of the earth. Celebrations last for 11 days and include fireworks, parades, musical events, an indigenous football competition, and various rituals involving water and flowers.

The **Fiesta del Coraza,** a local festival dating back to the early 18th century, is celebrated in and around Laguna San Pablo between June 9 and 15. Two personages on horseback appear during the event: the *coraza*, his skin painted white to represent the Spanish and his face covered in silver chains to symbolize greed; and the *pendonero*, who represents resistance to the Spanish invasion, dressed as a warrior waving a blood-red flag. Another highlight of the festival is a race on the lake between floating horses made of reeds.

Inti Raymi (Quechua for Sun Festival) is the Inca festival of the northern solstice and the most important Andean celebration. Every indigenous group has its own specific dates and traditions for Inti Raymi, but the main event starts on June 21 and continues for several days. In the Otavalo area, people gather to bathe in sacred rivers and waterfalls on June 22 to eliminate negative energies accumulated during the previous year, to purify themselves and kick off the festivities. The Peguche waterfall is the best spot to participate in this cleansing ritual, known as Armay Chishi. Throughout the celebrations, there is live music and dancing in the Plaza de Ponchos as well as the streets and houses of the surrounding villages.

The **Yamor** festival, held from the end of August until the first week of September, dates back to pre-Incan times and centers around a drink, a type of *chicha*, which is made from seven varieties of corn and represents the unity of the people, coming together like grains of corn. This is a local festival that originated in the village of Monserrat, home

The Language of the Incas

Indigenous peoples in the Sierra speak various dialects of Kichwa that are very different from those spoken by the Kichwas in the Amazon. The language evolved from Quechua, which pre-dates the Incas and was enforced by them as the official tongue of the empire. Many Kichwa words are commonly used in English, including "condor," "jerky," "llama," "puma," and "quinine." South American Spanish is also full of Kichwa words, including *"papa"* (potato), *"choclo"* (corn), *"chompa"* (sweater), and, more amusingly, *"chuchaqui"* (hangover). Some other basic phrases are:

- *Ama shua, ama llulla, ama killa*—Don't steal, don't lie, don't be lazy

- *Napaykuna*—Greetings

- *Alli puncha*—Good morning

- *Alli chishi*—Good afternoon

- *Alli tuta*—Good evening

- *Yupaychani*—Thank you/Thanks for everything

- *Alli shamushka*—You are welcome

- *Ima shinalla?/allillachu kanki?*—How are you?

- *Allilla, kan ka?*—Fine, and you?

- *Ima shuti kanki?*—What's your name?

- *Ñuka _____ shutimi kani*—My name is _____.

- *Maymanta shamunki?*—Where are you from?

- *Ñukaka _____ mantami kani*—I am from _____.

- *Rikunakushun*—See you later

- *Kayakama*—See you tomorrow

- *Tayta*—Sir, gentleman

- *Mama*—Madam, lady

- *Mashi*—Friend

- *-pay* (verb suffix)—Please

- *Mikupay*—Eat, please

- *Shamupay*—Come on, please

- *Apapay*—Bring it, please

- *Imamanta*—Why?

to the Virgin of Monserrat, the patron saint of Otavalo. The festival includes parades, musical events, and a swimming competition in the Laguna San Pablo.

RECREATION AND TOURS

Hiking

The **Mirador El Lechero** and **Parque Cóndor** make a good combined hike from Otavalo. It's also possible to add the waterfalls and town of **Peguche** for a total 10-kilometer (6.2-mi) walk, which will take most of a day. The path is signposted. There are cafés at the Condor Park and in Peguche, but take plenty of water, snacks, and sunblock. There may be some unfriendly dogs en route to Peguche, so it's a good idea to carry a stick. The tourist office on the Plaza de Ponchos has hiking maps, which are also available on their website: http://otavalo.travel/en/.

Tour Operators

Although many of the areas around Otavalo can be explored independently, several agencies in town organize English-speaking tours. Most offer day trips to see weavers and other artisans in the surrounding villages ($50 pp); hikes around Cuicocha ($40 pp); trips to Lagunas de Mojanda and Fuya Fuya ($40 pp); and ascents of the region's peaks. See their websites for the full range of tours.

The most ecologically minded tour agency in Otavalo is **All About EQ** (tel. 99/993-3148, www.all-about-ecuador.com), owned by friendly Otavaleño Ivan Suarez, who speaks fluent English and French. As well as all the usual local activities, Ivan is a skilled mountain guide for the whole northern Sierra region. He has a special interest in community tourism and offers a spectacular multi-day trekking and/or horseback-riding adventure, starting in the remote mountain village of Piñan and ending in Intag.

Runa Tupari (Calle Sucre y Quiroga, tel. 6/292-2320, www.runatupari.com) provides the most authentic indigenous experiences. The company can set up homestays ($35 pp including meals and transportation) with 25 families in five nearby small communities. Also available is a shamanic medicine tour ($55 pp), horseback-riding in Cotacachi-Cayapas National Park ($45 pp), and a downhill bike ride into the Intag Valley ($85 pp).

Half a block from Plaza de Ponchos, locally owned **EquatorFace** (Sucre *entre* Salinas y Morales, tel. 6/292-2665, www.equatorface.com) is a new, friendly, and professional outfit. As well as all the local activities, a variety of national tours are offered, up to 15 days in length.

Another reputable agency in town is family-run **Ecomontes Tour** (Sucre y Morales, tel. 6/292-6244, http://otavaloguide.com), where the friendly staff specialize in adventure tours (climbing, mountain biking, rafting, kayaking). Mountain-bike rental is also available.

Tren Ecuador offers a scenic round-trip train ride ($39) is available from Otavalo to the Afro-Ecuadorian community of Salinas, leaving on Fridays, Saturdays, Sundays, and public holidays at 8am and getting back into Otavalo at 5:55pm. During the stop in Salinas, visitors can learn about Afro-Ecuadorian history and culture, and sample the cuisine. See http://trenecuador.com for more information.

SHOPPING

In addition to the market, throughout Otavalo are stores where you can browse huge selections of woven goods and other textile products such as clothes, bags, and hammocks. **La Casa de Intag** (Colón y Sucre, tel. 6/292-0608, Facebook @LaCasadeIntag) is a café and fair trade store opened by grassroots organizations in the Intag region, offering local organic coffee and honey, bags and handicrafts made from cloud forest sisal, and handmade aloe toiletry products. Proceeds go toward local communities and environmental conservation.

Sisa Morales (Facebook @coloressisa) is an Otavalo Kichwa fashion designer who makes beautiful, hand-embroidered traditional indigenous clothing with a

Tourism Micro-Enterprises

The following projects have been set up by local people to share their traditions with visitors. Supporting them is an excellent way to boost the local economy and help keep ancestral customs alive. Most are not of sufficient size to have someone manning the operation at all times, so it's necessary to make reservations a few days in advance. Be aware that almost no English is spoken in rural communities. The tourist office on the corner of the Plaza de Ponchos has more information about these micro-enterprises on its website under Tourism Projects (http://otavalo.travel). They can also help to set up visits and advise on transport.

Near Otavalo there are many opportunities to experience traditional Andean music and gastronomy.

- **Sumak Pacha** (turismopijal@hotmail.com or sumakpacha@hotmail.com, tel. 6/261-8150 or 99/758-7263): The Community Tourism Center in the village of Kayambi offers family homestays and activities including organic agriculture, music, dance, traditional cuisine, hikes, and horseback riding. Location: Pijal community, San Pablo Lake parish, $6 taxi from Otavalo.

- **Asociacíon Pachamama** (pachamama@hotmail.com, tel. 98/253-0105 or 98/501-0112) offers talks on Andean cosmovision and medicinal plants, traditional energy cleansing and purification rituals ($6), traditional gastronomy (tortillas made with quinoa, amaranth leaves, nettle, beets, Swiss chard, and zambo squash), pomades of medicinal plants, totems against bad energy, and embroidery. Location: Angla community, $6-8 taxi from Otavalo or $4 from Laguna San Pablo.

- **Totora Sisa** (www.totorasisa.blogspot.com, totorasisa@yahoo.coman) is an association of communities near the Laguna San Pablo that make mats, furniture, and decorative items from reeds that grow in the lake. The workshop is open to the public and they give demonstrations. Location: San Rafael, Laguna San Pablo, $0.30 by bus from Otavalo or $3 by taxi.

- **Inka Tambo** (inkatamboecuador@gmail.com, tel. 6/269-0798 or 99/362-2058) offers indigenous plant-based medicine, organic agriculture, traditional gastronomy, and handicrafts. Location: Peguche, $0.30 by bus or $3 by taxi from Otavalo.

- **Jatary** (asojatary@outlook.com, tel. 98/911-2465 or 6/269-0512) is an association of Kichwa female entrepreneurs that promote *"sumak kawsay"* (good living in harmony with nature and community). They provide lodging, local gastronomy, hiking, and textile demonstrations. Location: Peguche, $0.30 by bus or $3 by taxi from Otavalo.

- **Kawsaymi** (www.kawsaymi.com, kawsaymi@gmail.com, tel. 98/768-4914) is a Kichwa family offering Andean cooking classes, local gastronomy, homestays, music, dance, and long-term volunteering. *"Kawsaymi"* means "our daily living" in Kichwa. Location: Parroquia San José de Quichinche, Comunidad Kichwa Panecillo, Vía Andaviejo; $0.30 by bus from Otavalo to Panecillo, or $3 by taxi.

- **Ayllukunapak** (Facebook @ayllukunapak, tel. 93/916-1458 or 99/298-2433) is an agro-ecological association that holds a twice-weekly organic farmers market (7am-2pm Wed. and Sat.). The community also offers a homestay package ($100 pp), where guests help to harvest the ingredients for traditional meals, which are then cooked together with the hosts, accompanied by an Andean band. Location: San Vicente de Cotama, $0.30 on the bus heading to Los Lagos or $2 by taxi.

contemporary twist. She employs local single mothers as embroiderers. **Alta Andina** (www.altaandina.com), based at the train station on Calle Guayaquil with a stall at the Saturday market, offers lovingly handcrafted leather products, including bags, belts, and wallets, that are made to order and come with a lifetime guarantee. All materials are ethically sourced. **Antara** (Morales *y* Sucre, tel. 6/292-6107, Facebook @casamusicalantara) sells handmade Andean musical instruments, such as guitars, flutes, and panpipes. For work by local artists, try the **Galería de Arte Quipus** (Sucre *y* Morales), which specializes in oil paintings and watercolors. At the west end of town on Morales, just before the Panamericana, the **Municipal Market 24 de Mayo** is the best place to pick up fresh produce.

FOOD

On the south side of the Plaza de Ponchos, the legendary **Café Shenandoah** (Salinas 5-15, 11am-9pm daily, $2-3) has been serving homemade fruit pies for decades. Choose from 10 flavors, including lemon, passion fruit, and blackberry. One block from the market, ★ **IncaZen Tea House & Gallery** (Sucre *y* Morales, Facebook @incazentea, 11am-8pm Thurs.-Sun., noon-2pm Mon.) offers Ecuadorian teas, *kombucha*, cocktails, cupcakes, and vegan food. The friendly Californian owner supports local producers and artists. ★ **La Casa de Intag** (Colón *y* Sucre, tel. 6/292-0608, Facebook @ LaCasadeIntag) is a café and fair trade store opened by grassroots organizations in the biodiverse Intag region, serving great organic coffee, fried yucca, pancakes, breakfasts, and sandwiches.

The best place to sample Andean cuisine alongside local people is the **Municipal Market 24 de Mayo**, at the west end of town on Morales, just before the Panamericana. The food court on the upper floor serves local specialties, including *hornado* (slow roasted pork), *llapingachos* (potato patties), and *mote con fritado* (hominy with fried pork).

A good place for Ecuadorian seafood dishes is **Quino Restaurant Sabor y Arte** (Roca near Montalvo, tel. 6/292-4994, 10am-11pm daily, $6-13).

A couple of places offer a mix of national and international dishes. Half a block from Parque Bolívar, Dutch-owned **Restaurant Árbol de Montalvo** (Montalvo *y* Roca, inside Hostal Doña Esther, tel. 6/292-0739, www.otavalohotel.com, 6pm-9pm Tues.-Thurs., 7am-10pm Fri.-Sun., $8-11) offers typical Ecuadorian specialties such as *cazuela* (a fish and shrimp dish with plantain and peanuts) alongside its famous wood-fired pizza. ★ **The Deli** (Quiroga *y* Bolívar, tel. 6/292-1558, www.delicaferestaurant.com, 10am-8pm Mon.-Sat., $5-8) is a cozy little gem of a café a block from the market. The menu includes *mote con fritado* (hominy with fried pork), *humitas* (ground corn mashed with cheese, onion, garlic, eggs, and cream and steamed in corn leaves), Tex-Mex, pasta, and pizza, with vegetarian options.

ACCOMMODATIONS

Otavalo has lots of locally owned budget and midrange accommodations, with some top-end haciendas outside town. During the week there is usually plenty of availability, but the best hotels fill up fast on Friday and Saturday nights, so consider booking ahead.

$10-25

Right on the Plaza de Ponchos, **Hostal Aly Samaylla** (Quiroga *y* Modesto Jaramillo, tel. 6/292-6865, $10 s, $15 d) is one of the cheapest options. Simple rooms with private bathrooms, hot water, Wi-Fi, and cable TV overlook the market.

Slightly to the west of the town center near the Mercado 24 Mayo, ★ **Hostal Arauco** (Calle Miguel Egas *y* Calle Salinas, tel. 99/911-5019, Facebook @arauco.hs, $15 s, $20-40 d) offers amazing value. Light, airy, and stylish, the individually decorated guest rooms are immaculate and quiet at night. Beds are comfortable and the showers are excellent.

Many of the best accommodations are located toward Parque Bolívar. **Hostal Flying Donkey** (Abdón Calderón y Simón Bolívar, tel. 6/292-8122, Facebook @flyingdonkeyotavalo, $9.50 dorm, $12-17 pp private room) is a friendly, family-run hostel with clean rooms, a shared kitchen, fast Wi-Fi, and a terrace with wonderful views. Mountain bike hire is available. The rooms at nearby **Hotel Coraza** (Calderón y Sucre, tel. 6/292-1225, https://hotelcoraza.wixsite.com/otavalo, $18.50 pp, including breakfast) are very clean and comfortable. **Hostal Santa Fe** (Roca y García Moreno, tel. 6/292-3640, www.hotelsantafeotavalo.com, $16 pp or $19 pp including breakfast) is warm and inviting, with excellent service and a good restaurant.

Over $25

The renovated colonial **Doña Esther** (Montalvo 444 y Bolívar, tel. 6/292-0739, www.otavalohotel.com, $45 s, $65 d, including breakfast) is the best value in this range, with 12 attractive rooms around a central, plant-filled courtyard and a great restaurant. The Dutch couple who owns it are welcoming hosts, happy to share information about the area.

The ★ **Hotel Riviera Sucre** (Moreno y Roca, tel. 6/292-0241, $25 s, $40 d) is an excellent option, with a courtyard, flower-filled garden, lounge area, and spacious, colorful rooms. Breakfast is available for $2.50-4.

The **Hotel El Indio Inn** (Bolívar y Abdón Calderón, tel. 6/292-0325, www.hotelelindioinn.com, $43 s, $64 d, including breakfast) has comfortable guest rooms arranged around two inner courtyards. Service is friendly and helpful. Massages are available ($40/hour).

For longer stays and group bookings, email Maggie Reniers (maggie@latitudefoundation.org), owner of the beautiful **Casa Latitud** (previously Posada del Quinde, Av. Quito y Miguel Egas, tel. 6/292-0750, www.casalatitud.org). Home to Fundación Latitud, the hotel shares space with Maggie's scholarship program, local acupuncture clinic, and English-language school, all nonprofit

ventures. Availability can be limited when groups are lodging.

INFORMATION AND SERVICES

The **tourist office** (Quiroga y Jaramillo, tel. 6/292-7230, http://otavalo.travel, 8am-5:30pm Mon.-Fri., 8am-5pm Sat.) is at the corner of Plaza de Ponchos. It has helpful English-speaking staff, good maps on attractions and hikes, and free storage lockers. The website, available in English, is a good source of information and downloadable maps.

Banco Pichincha has ATMs near Plaza de Ponchos and Simón Bolívar Park. The local **hospital** (tel. 6/292-0444) is northeast of town on Sucre, and the **police station** (tel. 101) is at the southwest edge of town on the Panamericana.

Spanish Lessons

Mundo Andino Spanish School (Bolívar y Abdón Calderón, 3rd floor, tel. 6/292-1864, www.mandinospanishschool.com) and **Otavalo Learning & Adventure** (García Moreno y Atahualpa, tel. 99/700-8542) are recommended.

GETTING THERE AND AROUND

There are frequent buses (2 hours, $2.50) to/from Quito's Carcelén terminal with Cooperativa Otavalo (tel. 6/292-0405 Facebook @cooperativatransotavalo) and Cooperativa Los Lagos (tel. 6/292-0382).

Otavalo's **bus terminal** (Atahualpa and Ordoñez) is on the northeast corner of town, where you can catch buses to Quito, Ibarra (40 minutes, $0.55), Cayambe, Cotacachi, and local villages such as Ilumán and Peguche.

Taxis charge $1.25 for short journeys around town and $3 for attractions on the edge of town (e.g., Peguche waterfall and El Lechero).

LAGUNA DE SAN PABLO

The nearest lake to Otavalo is the huge **Laguna de San Pablo** that you pass on the way from Quito. At the foot of **Volcán Imbabura,** it's a pleasant spot with impressive views of the volcano. Although the area around the lake is increasingly developed, the small shoreline villages still specialize in making traditional woven reed mats (see Tourism Micro-Enterprises in the Otavalo section). The road surrounding the lake makes a nice hike (3-4 hours) or bike ride.

The southwestern side of the lake is less developed than the north side, with less infrastructure and more greenery. Just off the Panamericana, near the community of San Rafael, there is a floating dock, the **Muelle Flotante Cachiviro,** with expansive views and a community tourism project which takes visitors around the lake by boat (8am-5pm, $20 for a 30-minute boat ride, 2 person minimum). The turnoff for dock is clearly signposted on the highway, from where it's a short drive or walk. On this side of the lake is the **Hostería Puertolago** (tel. 6/263-5400, www.puertolago.com, $65-135 s, $80-135 d), which has individual cabins with fireplaces set in beautiful grounds. The restaurant (7:30am-9pm Mon.-Thurs., 7:30am-9:30pm Fri.-Sun.) serves good quality national and international dishes with all vegetables grown in the organic gardens.

The northeastern side of the lake is very popular with local families on weekends. The **Parque Acuático Araque** (tel. 98/728-8158 Facebook @parqueacuaticoaraque) is a community tourism project offering boat trips, horseback riding and local cuisine. Nearby, the comfortable **Hostería Cabañas del Lago** (tel. 6/291-8108, www.cabanasdellago.com.ec, $115-160 s/d), has cabins with fireplaces and a lakeside restaurant (8am-10:30am and noon-8pm daily) serving Ecuadorian food with a contemporary twist.

A taxi from Otavalo to the lake costs $3. The 4-kilometer (2.5-mi) hike from Otavalo takes about an hour, or go via El Lechero and Parque Cóndor for a longer walk. For the south side of the lake, take any bus heading to Quito and ask the driver to let you off. For the north side, take the bus heading to Araque.

Ecuadorian-owned **My Sachaji** (tel. 9/845-65012, www.mysachaji.com, $290-380 pp, including breakfast) is a luxury hotel and wellness retreat a few kilometers east of the lake. Rooms with views of the lake or volcano are designed for ultimate coziness, with fireplaces, thermal windows, blackout curtains, and a poncho to wear. Various treatments and therapies are available and the staff includes a shaman, a yoga teacher, a massage therapist, and an indigenous traditional medicine practitioner. Among the facilities are a hydro-massage pool, a polar plunge pool and a trampoline. The hotel was built using sustainable and environmentally-friendly methods, including bricks made from earth excavated on-site, and used tires as below-floor insulation. Green roofs reduce CO_2 emissions and solar panels are installed above the rooms. For each wooden door, a tree of the same species was planted on site. Water for bathing is sun-heated and comes from rainwater and nearby waterfalls. Organic gardens supply fruit, vegetables and herbs for the restaurant. The hotel is LGBTQ friendly.

LAGUNAS DE MOJANDA AND FUYA FUYA

South of Otavalo, the cobbled Vía a Lagos de Mojanda winds up into the *páramo* to three beautiful lagoons in the shadow of dark, jagged mountains. The **Laguna Grande** (also known as Caricocha), **Laguna Negra** (Huarmicocha), and **Laguna Chiquita** (Yanacocha) are 3,700 meters (12,100 ft) above sea level. At 2 kilometers (1.2 mi) wide, Laguna Grande is the biggest, with a dirt road extending part of the way around it to simple cabins, accessible by four-wheel drive or on foot, where it is possible to stay ($20) or camp ($2, bring your own tent). Only breakfast is available, so bring food with you. Be aware that the *páramo* is very cold at night, with sudden rains. An overnight stay is especially recommended on clear, full moon nights, when the sky is spectacularly reflected in the lake's surface. Trails also lead east and south from Laguna Grande to the two smaller lakes.

Otavalo and Vicinity

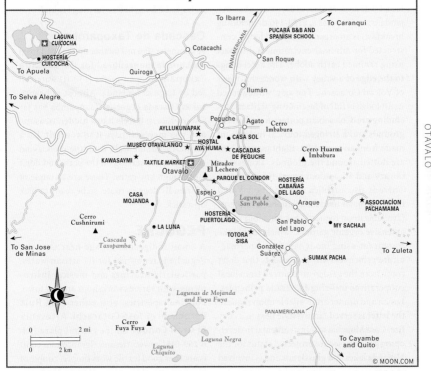

The peak of **Fuya Fuya** (4,262 m/13,983 ft), the highest point to the west, is a popular climb as acclimatization practice for higher peaks. Paths lead up the mountainside from Laguna Grande and can be climbed without a guide for a four-hour round-trip.

The lakes are 15 kilometers (9.3 mi) from Otavalo, a 30-minute taxi ride ($15 each way). To have a quick look around and take some photos, ask the taxi driver to wait. If you are planning on hiking for a few hours, arrange a pickup time. For a more informed experience, go with a tour agency from Otavalo ($40 pp).

Until the new highway was built in 1900, the road to the lakes was the main thoroughfare from Otavalo to Quito for people on their way to the capital to sell goods. Since the trek took 2-3 days, there were a couple of simple lodgings en route for travelers to sleep.

Legend has it that the owners of one such place, the Remache family, used to kidnap and kill some of their guests and serve them up as *fritada* to other unsuspecting customers. Once a year, on the last Saturday of October, the municipal government organizes a walk to commemorate the old road and the people who used it. It's a popular event, leaving from the Parque Bolívar in Otavalo at 4am. Participants are transported to a spot 52 kilometers (32 mi) up the Vía a Lagos de Mojanda and return to Otavalo on foot, via the lakes. To join the walk, register with the tourist office in Otavalo (Quiroga *y* Jaramillo, tel. 6/292-7230, http://otavalo.travel) a couple of days in advance.

Casa Mojanda

Four kilometers (2.5 mi) from Otavalo on the

road to the Mojanda lakes, the American/ Ecuadorian-owned ★ **Casa Mojanda** (tel. 6/304-9253 or 98/033-5108, www.casamojanda.com, $116-122 s, $134-146 d, including breakfast) is an organic farm and lodge, constructed for minimal environmental impact using rammed earth adobe. The hotel clings to the edge of a valley with wonderful views of Volcán Cotacachi. The airy, whitewashed main lodge is full of fascinating artifacts, including pre-Columbian pottery found on the grounds and a stringed musical instrument made from an armadillo. Eight guest cabins are dotted around the grounds, alongside a library and an outdoor wood-fired hot tub. There is also a replica of a traditional mud dwelling that is used for shamanic treatments (available upon request). Ask for a tour of the extensive organic gardens, which supply the restaurant using biodynamic and permaculture principles. Any ingredients that don't come from the garden are sourced from local cooperatives utilizing fair trade principles. Lunch and dinner are available upon request; the latter is served family-style next to a cozy fire. Casa Mojanda was instrumental in developing a plan to secure protected status for the Mojanda lakes and grasslands and is involved in a program to sterilize local dogs. The lodge employs local people, and service is absolutely top-notch.

La Luna

A kilometer (0.6 mi) farther up the road from Casa Mojanda is English/Ecuadorian-owned ★ **La Luna Mountain Lodge** (tel. 99/315-6082, www.lalunaecuador.info, camping $8, dorm $14 pp, $22-30 s, $38-47 d), an excellent option for travelers of all budgets. Rooms are rustic and charming, with fresh flowers, hammocks, and wonderful views. Some have their own fireplace. Breakfast is included in the small restaurant, which also offers lunch and dinner, with plenty of vegetarian options. A small organic garden partially supplies the restaurant.

Casa Mojanda and La Luna are a 90-minute walk or $4-5 taxi ride from Otavalo. Buses operated by Cooperativa Imbaburapak leave the terminal every 40 minutes ($0.40) and go as far as La Luna before turning around.

Cascada de Taxopamba

A kilometer (0.6 mi) farther up the road from La Luna is the trailhead for the **Cascada Taxopamba,** a 40-meter (130-ft) waterfall fed by Laguna Mojanda. Almost as beautiful as Cascada Peguche, Taxopamba has far fewer visitors; it feels like a hidden treasure, and you may well have it to yourself. It's a scenic 15-minute walk from the road; avoid getting lost by staying on the path, and don't go through any gates. There are a couple of unfriendly dogs en route, so be ready to pick up a stick.

PEGUCHE

A small indigenous village near Otavalo, Peguche is renowned for its artisan wares, particularly weavings and musical instruments, with various workshops around town. For fine tapestries, visit either **José Ruiz Perugachi** or **José Cotacachi. Artesanía El Gran Condor** on the central plaza (tel. 6/269-0161, www.artesaniaelgrancondor.com) is another good textile workshop. A couple of blocks north of the plaza, **Ñanda Mañachi** (tel. 6/269-0076, open daily) makes a variety of traditional instruments, including *flautas* (reed flutes) and *rondadores* (Andean panpipes). See *Tourism Micro-Enterprises* in the *Otavalo* section for other local ventures.

Cascadas de Peguche

Surrounded by lush, green vegetation, the **Peguche waterfall** plunges 30 meters (100 ft) into a large pool, before the waters continue down the valley into Laguna de San Pablo. The entrance is 1.5 kilometers (0.9 mi) south of Peguche, where there is a small visitors center (8:30am-5pm daily). There is no entrance fee, but you are asked to give

---

1: the Peguche waterfall; 2: hikers ascending Fuya Fuya; 3: the Volcán Cotacachi seen from Casa Mojanda

The Shamans of Ilumán

Ilumán shamans work with candles and medicinal plants.

Ilumán is known for its *curanderos or yachaks* (native healers or shamans), who have passed down natural remedies and spiritual cures through the generations for centuries, treating everything from back problems to cancer. Most older people in the region have sought their services at one time or another, though the younger generation often prefers Western medicine.

The shamans, who usually wear white to represent purification, work with a blend of indigenous and Christian rituals and herbal medicines. In a traditional cleansing session, invocations in Kichwa to Mama Cotacachi and Taita Imbabura are sent up alongside prayers in Spanish to the Virgin Mary and the saints. Diagnoses are made by passing a guinea pig or candle over the patient, then watching for the reaction in the animal or flame. The shaman will then recommend a cure for any ailment discovered, which may take the form of prayers or medicinal herbs like wild fuchsia, nettle, and red and white carnation petals.

Even for those who speak some Spanish, a visit to an Ilumán shaman can be a bewildering and intense experience, as they often don't explain what they are doing or why. Patients may get whipped with plants and will very likely be covered in spittle.

There are about 30 shamans in the **Asociacíon de Yachaks de Ilumán** (tel. 96/967-3924), which is recognized by the Public Health Ministry. A cleansing ritual may cost $20-40. Alternatively, a recommended shaman is Yuru Parayaku, who speaks a little English and is in Natabuela, between Ilumán and Ibarra (tel. 99/945-1682).

a small donation, which goes toward the upkeep of the forest. From the center, it's a short, pleasant walk through the trees to the waterfall.

The *cascadas* are perfectly safe if you arrive via the main entrance and stick to the main paths leading to the biggest waterfall and the mirador. There is a secondary fall, higher up, where occasional robberies have been reported, so it's advisable to go with a guide or a group.

Rustic but charming wooden cabins are available for rent in a forest clearing ($5 pp) near the visitors center. They have electricity and access to toilets and a barbecue area, but nothing else. Bring an inflatable mattress if you don't want to sleep on the floor, plus a sleeping bag. Food is available in the village.

Camping is available for $1 (bring your own tent).

A taxi from Otavalo to Peguche or the waterfall costs $3. There are buses from the Otavalo terminal to the village of Peguche or Las Cascadas, and it's a short walk between the two. To make the 45-minute hike from Otavalo, follow the railroad tracks north out of town at Quito and Guayaquil. Follow the road right when it leaves the tracks at the police station, and look for the sign at the waterfall entrance. Keep heading north to reach the village.

Food and Accommodations

Peguche offers a few options for those who want to stay outside of Otavalo but close to town. Just up the hill from the entrance to the waterfall is **La Casa Sol** (tel. 6/269-0500, www.lacasasol.com, $49 s, $59 d, including breakfast). Eight cozy, colorful rooms and two suites were built using traditional materials and methods. Each is equipped with a private bathroom, a fireplace, and a balcony with great views over Peguche and the Otavalo Valley. The restaurant is good and the staff are friendly.

Straddling the railroad tracks farther into town is **Hostal Aya Huma** (tel. 6/269-0333, www.ayahuma.com, $23 s, $37 d), which has fireplaces, hammocks, and a beautiful garden. There is live Andean music most Saturday nights. Among the many services offered are Spanish classes, massage, reiki, and personal coaching (in English). There is a sweat lodge on the first Saturday of every month, and various ceremonies and shamanic rituals are also available. Staff can help organize hikes, bike trips, horseback riding, and tours to several villages. The restaurant, open for breakfast and dinner, offers vegetarian options. The hostel is pet-friendly and camping is available. To get there, follow the signs through town, or ask directions.

Northwest of Otavalo

COTACACHI

Cotacachi (pop. 8,500) is somewhat neater and tidier than many other small towns, with a more affluent feel. It's best known for its leather goods, with stores on the main street offering belts, bags, saddles, jackets, boots, wallets, and purses.

Sights

The **crafts market,** in the Parque San Francisco at 10 de Agosto and Rocafuerte, two blocks south of Bolívar, is modest during the week but larger on Saturday and Sunday. As well as leather goods, vendors sell woven textiles, alpaca blankets, and artisanal food items such as chocolate, coffee, honey, and liquor.

Food and Accommodations

On Parque San Francisco, **Cafe Rio Intag** (tel. 6/256-6029) is a café, bar, and fair trade store that supports grassroots organizations in the Intag region. The café offers great organic coffee, pastries, desserts, sandwiches, and empanadas. **Especiales Carnes Coloradas Esther Morenode Unda** (Bolívar 16-70 y Modesto Peñaherrera, tel. 6/291-6802, Facebook @Especiales Carnes Coloradas Esther Morenode Unda) is the original and best place to get Cotacachi's most famous dish, carnes coloradas (smoked pork with achiote), invented by the restaurant's original owner in 1930. Surprisingly, it's a pretty good place for vegetarians, as the sides (potatoes, hominy, avocado, and an empanada filled with plantain) make a decent meal by themselves.

A block from Parque Abdón Calderón, locally owned **Ananda** (Sucre 860, $20 s, $27 d) is clean, with good, hot water, a shared kitchen, and a rooftop terrace. Breakfast is $3.75. Also in the town center is the **Land of the Sun Inn** (García Moreno 13-67 y Sucre, tel. 6/291-6009, http://landofthesunhotel.com, $49 s, $59 d, breakfast included). Inside a spacious colonial building, there's a bright, three-story courtyard with flowers spilling over the edges. There is a spa with a massage therapist on call. The restaurant serves Ecuadorian food with vegetarian options.

Just outside Cotacachi on the way to Ibarra, the excellent **Pucará B&B & Spanish School** (tel. 99/521- 6665, www.pucaraspanishschool.com) is in a beautiful rural setting in the village of Pucará. It's owned by a Swiss/Ecuadorian couple, who are wonderful hosts and also grow organic quinoa. Classes are available one on one or in a group ($360/week for accommodations and 20 hours of one-on-one lessons). For the full range of accommodations and class prices, see the website. The B&B is just off the Pan-American Highway 4 kilometers (2.5 mi) after Ilumán.

Getting There

Frequent buses run from Cotacachi bus station (Sucre *y* 10 de Agosto) to Otavalo (25 minutes, $0.25) and Ibarra (40 minutes, $0.50). *Camionetas* run to Laguna Cuicocha ($5), and you can arrange to have them pick you up later.

COTACACHI-CAYAPAS ECOLOGICAL RESERVE

The **Cotacachi-Cayapas Ecological Reserve** (tel. 6/304-9110, http://areasprotegidas.ambiente.gob.ec) stretches over 2,000 square kilometers (770 sq mi), ranging from 4,939 meters (16,204 ft) above sea level at the top of Volcán Cotacachi to just 30 meters (100 ft) in the lowlands. Due to this altitudinal variety, like the Cayambe-Coca reserve, Cotacachi-Cayapas encompasses an astonishing number of ecosystems. Descending through the park, the rocky, sometimes snow-capped summit of the volcano gives way to the wildflower-strewn grasses of the *páramo*, followed by orchid-filled cloud forests and finally tropical rainforest at the shoreline of the Cayapas River.

Access

The reserve is best accessed via the entrance near Laguna Cuicocha. It's also possible to enter via San Lorenzo in Esmeraldas province, but security is a problem in that area, so that route is best avoided.

★ Laguna Cuicocha

This stunning crater lake is one of the most beautiful and frequently visited in Ecuador. At the foot of Volcán Cotacachi, 3,070 meters (10,070 ft) up in the *páramo*, the azure waters of **Laguna Cuicocha** are 200 meters (655 ft) deep. Considered sacred by many locals, the lake is a popular spot for purification baths at summer solstice. Boat trips are available (20-25 minutes, $3.50 pp), during which volcanic bubbles can be seen rising from the depths. It can get chilly, but warming *canelazo* (hot fruit punch with aguardiente) is for sale at the café for $0.75.

The visitors center and pier, with handicrafts stalls, a café, and a restaurant, are fairly touristy, especially on weekends, but it's easy to escape the crowds by hiking the four- to six-hour trail around the crater, with wonderful views of Cotacachi, Imbabura, and Cayambe. Bring water, snacks, sunscreen, and sturdy boots.

The Laguna Cuicocha entrance to the Cotacachi-Cayapas Ecological Reserve is manned 8am-5pm daily, and visitors must present ID and register. It's possible to stay right next to the lake at **Hostería Cuicocha** (tel. 6/301-7219 or 99/147-4172, http://cuicocha.org, $55 pp); accommodations include breakfast, dinner, and a boat tour.

Buses run regularly from Otavalo to Cotacachi and Quiroga, where taxis and *camionetas* wait to take visitors to the lake ($5-6 one way). On weekends, there may be taxis waiting at the lake for the return journey. Alternatively, consider taking the driver's number or arranging a pickup time. If driving from Cotacachi, take a left at the last traffic light in town on 31 de Octubre, and follow the road west through the town of Quiroga to the park entrance gate near the Laguna Cuicocha. On foot, it's a two-hour uphill hike. Note that occasional robberies have been reported, so it's probably best not to hike alone midweek.

Volcán Cotacachi

On a clear day, the six-hour climb up **Cotacachi** (4,939 m/16,204 ft) offers wonderful views of the Avenue of the Volcanoes. The last 50-100 meters (165-300 ft) of the ascent is particularly tricky, and it's necessary to go with an experienced guide. See the **Ecuadorian Association of Mountain Guides** (tel. 2/254-0599, https://aseguim. org) to find a guide. In Otavalo, all the tour operators listed in this book offer the climb (approx. $120).

LOS CEDROS BIOLOGICAL RESERVE

Founded in 1988, **Los Cedros Biological Reserve** (tel. 6/301-6550 or 99/277-8878, jose@reservaloscedros.org, www. reservaloscedros.org) protects nearly 7,000 hectares (17,300 acres) of tropical forest and cloud forest and four major watersheds. The reserve is a southern buffer zone for the Cotacachi-Cayapas park; both are part of the Choco region, one of the planet's most biologically diverse endemic habitats. Like the neighboring Intag region, most of the Los Cedros protected area has been concessioned to mining interests. The journey to the reserve takes the best part of a day, so it's only possible to visit with at least one overnight stay.

Among the reserve's 240 bird species are hummingbirds, toucan barbetts, umbrella birds, motmots, quetzals, and Andean cock-of-the-rocks. Mammals include spider monkeys, capuchin monkeys, howler monkeys, kinkajous, spectacled bears, deer, jaguars, and pumas.

Although most of the reserve remains untracked and rarely visited by humans, there is a network of trails ranging 2-7 hours in duration, including one to a waterfall. The reserve

receives a lot of rainfall, but the driest months are generally July to October.

Accommodations ($65 pp) are rustic but comfortable, with private and dorm rooms, hot showers, compost toilets, social areas, and hammocks. Electricity comes from a micro-hydroelectric plant and a solar panel. There is no Wi-Fi, but dial-up Internet can be arranged if required. Volunteering ($300/2 weeks or $500/month) is an option, as are research opportunities. When contacting the reserve, email is preferred due to unreliable telephone service. Rates include all food (vegetarian available), with meals cooked by the staff midweek and by guests on weekends. Ingredients are sourced locally. All fees go to maintenance, staff wages, and conservation and education projects.

To get to Los Cedros in one day, travel to Chontal on the 6am bus from Quito's Ofelia terminal with Transportes Minas (3.5 hours, $2.50), or on the 8am Trans Otavalo bus from Otavalo (4 hours, $3.75). Previously, guests had to walk the 17-kilometer (10.6-mi) trail from Chontal to the reserve (which is still an option for the intrepid), but now it's possible to travel two-thirds of the way by truck, to Brilla Sol ($10), then walk the remaining 90 minutes. The reserve provides mule transport for you and/or your luggage. If you take later buses from Quito/Otavalo, you will need to spend the night in Chontal.

★ INTAG

Located at the confluence of two of the world's biological hot spots, the Tumbes-Chocó-Magdalena and the Tropical Andes, this beautiful mountainous region provides some of the richest biodiversity on earth. Named for the river that runs through it, **Intag** occupies the western part of Imbabura province and is bordered to the north by the Cotacachi-Cayapas Ecological Reserve. Its rugged, cloud-forested peaks and valleys, alive with rushing streams and waterfalls, are home to many rare mammals, including Andean bears, jaguars, pumas, ocelots, Andean tapirs, and the critically endangered brown-headed spider monkey. There is a great diversity of flora, especially orchids, and it's a bird-watching paradise, with famous residents including the plate-billed mountain toucan, the giant antpitta, and the cock-of-the-rock. Amazingly, 40 percent of Intag's bird and plant species are found nowhere else on the planet.

While easily reached from Otavalo and Quito, Intag is remote enough for visitors to really get away from it all. Amid the lush greenery, often the only sounds are rushing water and birdsong, and with much of the area lacking cell phone signal and Internet, even a day spent here leaves the visitor with a profound sense of peace.

Intag is home to several farming communities living in picturesque villages and hamlets dotted throughout the region. Since 1995, these residents have been battling to conserve the area from mega-mining. Every visit is a direct support of their conservation efforts. For more information, see the *Background* chapter.

July to September is the driest time to visit Intag, though the wetter months bring their own joys in the form of more orchids, birds, fruit, and greenery. For further information on the Intag valley, contact **Red Ecoturistica Intag** (tel. 98/631-3812, www.intagturismo. org).

Apuela

Apuela is Intag's main village and its transportation hub. On Sunday, people from all over the region take a day off from farming to gather in the village to buy and sell goods, play *ecuavolley,* and socialize.

Asociacíon Río Intag or **AACRI** (tel. 6/256-6029, www.aacri.com) is an association of 120 local **coffee farms,** mostly small, family-run places growing organically in the shade of native trees. AACRI offers **guided tours** of its processing plant ($5), showing how the beans are shelled, sorted, roasted, ground, and packaged. Tours should be reserved a week in advance. A Ruta del Café tour with accommodations and food is being planned.

AACRI works with several **local families** who offer **accommodations** in their homes for $8-10 per person, with meals available for $2.50. Alternatively, rooms with shared bathrooms are available at **Residencial Don Luis** (20 de Julio, tel. 6/256-6055, $10 pp).

Nangulví

The mineral-rich hot springs at **Piscinas Nangulví** (tel. 6/301-5892, $3) include six pools of varying temperatures. A riverside restaurant serves gigantic portions next to the rushing rapids ($3.50 lunch/dinner, vegetarian options available).

Just down the road from the hot springs, ★ **Pacheco** (tel. 6/301-5655, Facebook @ PachecoIntagValley, www.pachecofarmhouse. com) is a small B&B with picturesque whitewashed wooden cabins next to the river. The friendly Argentinian owner speaks perfect English and can arrange local transport. Breakfast consists of bread, jam, butter, and peanut butter, all homemade, supplemented with produce from the on-site permaculture garden and organic local suppliers. A map of self-guided trails is available. The B&B is pet-friendly.

Nangulví is 15 minutes by bus or *camioneta* from Apuela.

Santa Rosa

The village of **Santa Rosa** is the access point for Intag's first protected forest, the 505-hectare (1,250-acre) **Intag Cloud Forest Reserve** (tel. 6/299-0001, www. intagcloudforest.com, $10 pp entrance), owned and operated by conservationists and anti-mining activists Carlos Zorrilla and Sandy Statz. Their mission is not only to preserve the area's ecosystem, but also to involve local communities and foreign students through educational programs and projects, including talks on activism. For more information, contact **DECOIN** (Organization for the Defense and Conservation of the

1: The cloud forests of Intag are alive with rushing rivers. **2:** Laguna Cuicocha

Ecology of Intag, www.decoin.org, Facebook @decoinorg), an organization co-founded by Carlos in 1995.

The reserve has several hiking trails ranging 1-4 hours in length, including to a nearby waterfall. The bird-watching is outstanding, with a cock-of-the-rock lek, more than 20 species of hummingbirds, and dozens of tanagers. You might even spot the plate-billed mountain toucan or the elusive white-faced nunbird.

FOOD AND ACCOMMODATIONS

Cabins on the reserve ($55 pp including all meals) are rustic but comfortable, the largest having three bedrooms. There are plenty of hammocks. Managed by Carlos Zorrilla, the cabins have solar-heated water, clean-composting latrines, and solar lamps. If you must use it, Wi-Fi is available. A small part of the reserve is dedicated to sustainable agriculture, which supplies guests with organic, vegetarian food. Coffee is also grown and roasted on-site.

Another option within the reserve is **Colibrí Cabins** (https://intagcolibri.com, $45 per cabin), run by Sandy Statz. Cabins have electricity, solar-heated water, balconies, hammocks, and beautiful views. A kitchen is available for guests to use. Sandy was instrumental in setting up a group of 43 women artisans who weave bags, hats, table mats, and other items out of fibers from the *cabuya* plant (see https://intagsisal.com for more information).

Reservations are needed for both Carlos's and Sandy's cabins. No walk-ins please; remember the reserve is also their home. By prior arrangement, they will come and meet guests at the school in Santa Rosa. Both speak English. The accommodations are a 60-minute walk from the road.

The most easily accessible and upscale accommodation option, located by the reserve entrance, is ★ **El Refugio de Intag** (tel. 6/301-5842 or WhatsApp 99/717-5208, www.elrefugiocloudforest.com, $45 pp, including breakfast). Owned by birder Peter Joost, who works closely with Carlos and Sandy,

the attractive wooden rooms are right next to a rushing river, with 4 kilometers (2.5 mi) of private forest trails to explore. Lunch and dinner are available for $12 each, or at the village's two restaurants.

The most economical option is the **San Antonio Organic Farm** (Facebook @Finca San Antonio Marisol, tel. 95/976-3721, $15 pp), which has 4 hectares (10 acres) of sugarcane, fruit trees, coffee, and food gardens along with 160 hectares (395 acres) of forest with rivers, waterfalls, and trails. A campsite for tents ($6 with own tent, $8 tent hire) and camping vehicles ($8) has composting toilets and showers. Organic, vegetarian meals are available ($3 breakfast, $5 lunch/dinner). Day visits cost $5. The friendly owners speak English.

Near Santa Rosa is the small village of **Pucará,** location of an experimental **"eco-pueblo,"** a new model for rural, low-income housing using **sustainable energy technology,** ecological design, and permaculture concepts. Volunteers are welcomed. For more information, see http://casainteram.org/pucara. The **Intag Spanish School** (tel. 98/684-9950 or 6/301-5638, https://intagspanishschool.wordpress.com) provides the community with a source of income. The **school** offers one-on-one and group lessons with certified teachers, homestays, and volunteer opportunities.

GETTING THERE

Santa Rosa is 1.5 hours from Otavalo. Transportes Otavalo and 6 Julio leave from Otavalo, and Valle de Intag buses leave from Cotacachi and will stop in Santa Rosa before they reach Apuela.

El Rosal

With panoramic views, the idyllic hamlet of **El Rosal** is the location of a women's association, **ASOFEPAR** (tel. 6/305-1026, http://asociacionelrosal.org, Facebook @naturaloe.intag), that makes natural soaps, shampoos, and body creams by hand using locally grown extracts, including aloe, papaya, lemongrass, and *sangre de drago*. Products are sold internationally and in shops nationwide, and are available for delivery throughout Ecuador. The friendly, welcoming women also offer a two-night community tourism package ($45), which includes all meals, a tour of the soap factory, a visit to an organic coffee farm, and a class in baking yucca bread. Massages are available for $15. Reservations should be made two weeks in advance.

To get to El Rosal, take the bus from Otavalo to García Moreno with Transportes Otavalo (leaving at 7:30am, 10am, or 2pm), or from Cotacachi with Valle de Intag. Cooperativa Minas also operates twice-daily buses to García Moreno from Quito's Ofelia terminal. From García Moreno, hire a *camioneta* ($5) or take the student bus to El Rosal at 1pm.

Junín

At the very heart of the struggle, the residents of **Junín** have been resisting mining since 1995. During that time, the community tourism project **Cabañas EcoJunín** (tel. 98/887-1860, www.ecocabanas-junin.com, $40 pp including 3 meals) has provided the principal economic alternative. Rustic cabins with shared bathrooms are located in the cloud forest 1 km (0.6 mi) from the village. Activities include a hummingbird garden, horseback riding, waterfall walks, visits to local coffee and sugarcane farms, and thermal pools. Volunteers and research students are welcomed.

Visiting Junín is by reservation only. To get there, take the bus to Cielo Verde or Magdalena and ask to be let off at the Junín turnoff. Cabañas EcoJunín will arrange for a pickup truck to meet you there.

Cuellaje

Of all the Intag communities, **Cuellaje** is the worst affected by the planned mining projects, with 95 percent of the territory concessioned.

Fifteen minutes' walk from the village center is the **Río Lindo Coffee Lodge** (www.

intagcoffeelodge.com, $40 pp, including 3 meals), an organic farm growing coffee in the shade of native trees. Activities include bathing in a nearby waterfall, a coffee tour, participating in the coffee-making process, or just soaking in the peace from a hammock. The farm mostly hosts groups of young foreign students, who carry out solidarity work in the community (rebuilding houses, repainting communal buildings, etc.), but also welcomes individuals. Breakfast is accompanied by home-grown coffee that is brewed in an Italian espresso machine. The lodge's owner claims it is the best coffee in the country, and it's certainly a contender!

To get even further off the beaten track, check out **Finca San Antonio** (tel. 6/301-7543, https://cloudforestadventure.com/en, $20 pp, including 3 organic meals and farm tours), 15 kilometers (9.3 mi) from Cuellaje. Owned by an English/Ecuadorian couple, the **farm** is an **ecotourism project** aiming to provide local people with a sustainable source of income. Local tours are available. Volunteers are welcomed.

Cuellaje is also the location of a remarkable **special education center** for 35 people with disabilities and special needs, where the attendees work on various projects to generate a community fund to meet their needs. At the time of writing, they were making photo frames from recycled paper.

Cuellaje is three hours from Otavalo, with one direct bus a day (5pm) with Transportes Otavalo.

Getting There

Bus tickets to Intag should be bought in person the day before. **Valle de Intag** (tel. 6/256-6079, Facebook @TransValleIntag) has five buses daily to Apuela and five to Cielo Verde from Cotacachi. Tickets are available at their office half a block from the park in Quiroga. From Otavalo, buses leave the terminal at 7:30am, 10am, 1pm, 2pm, and 5pm with **Transportes Otavalo** (tel. 6/292-0405, Facebook @cooperativatransotavalo) and at 9am, 11am, and 3pm with **6 Julio** (tel.

6/292-3677). **Imbaburapak** also has buses to Apuela, though they go the long way, via Selva Alegre.

All buses stop in Apuela, then continue on to various destinations within Intag. Check the route and schedule with the bus company when you book your ticket; if necessary, get off in Apuela and then take a *camioneta* or *ranchero* (an open-sided local bus) to your destination. Valle de Intag operates *rancheros* from Apuela to Peñaherrera, El Cristal, Plaza Gutiérrez, and Cuellaje. During term time, school buses leave Apuela to ferry students to various villages in Intag at noon or 1pm. Local people are also often happy to help with transport for a dollar or two.

Cooperativa Minas operates twice-daily buses to García Moreno from Quito's Ofelia terminal.

If you are driving from Otavalo, take the road that goes past Lake Cuicocha. Instead of going through the gates into the park, take the road to the left and continue for 1.5 hours to Santa Rosa or two hours to Apuela.

In Otavalo, tour operators **Runa Tupari** (tel. 6/292-2320, www.runatupari.com) and **Ecomontes** (tel. 6/292-6244, http://otavaloguide.com) organize bike tours to Intag. For a truly adventurous way to arrive, ask English-speaking ecotourism guide **Ivan Suarez** (tel. 99/993-3148, http://www.all-about-ecuador.com) about making the spectacular two- to three-day trek from the mountaintop community of Piñan.

Ibarra and Vicinity

Founded in 1606 on land donated by the granddaughter of the legendary Inca leader Atahualpa, the capital of Imbabura province is known as "La Ciudad Blanca" (The White City) for its wealth of whitewashed colonial buildings. Ibarra served as the administrative center for the textile *obrajes* of the Otavalo region until an earthquake destroyed the city in August 1868, killing 5,000 of its 7,200 inhabitants. It took a long time to recover, but today Ibarra is a thriving, attractive city with wide, easily navigable streets. The inactive Volcán Imbabura provides a dramatic backdrop, and on clear days the towering snowcapped peak of Cayambe is clearly visible beyond.

Only half an hour northeast of Otavalo, Ibarra is culturally very different from its neighbor, with far less indigenous influence and a sizable Afro-Ecuadorian population from the nearby Chota Valley. At a slightly lower elevation of 2,225 meters (7,300 ft), it's warmer than both Quito and Otavalo, with a pleasant sunny climate.

Ibarra's main draw is the historic center, where elegant squares are shaded by flowering trees and flanked by spired churches and arched colonnades. A very enjoyable half day can be spent wandering the cobbled streets, including a visit to the most famous and historical ice-cream café in the country. Nearby parishes have set up community tourism projects to share their ancestral ways of life and traditional crafts, including saddle-making and embroidery.

The city center is safe during the day, but at night it's best to stick to well-lit, populated streets. During the week, even the central streets are fairly deserted by 9pm, so it's not advisable to walk alone, but there are more people out enjoying themselves until later on the weekends. Avoid wandering the Amazonas market area at night, especially the Monseñor Leonidas Proaño Park, where robbers are known to lurk, and the neighboring streets (the triangle formed by Avenidas Alfredo Perez Guerrero, Mariano Acosta, and Luis Cabezas Borja).

SIGHTS

At the heart of the historic center, the **Parque Pedro Moncayo** and the **Parque La Merced** (two blocks west) are Ibarra's two

Ibarra

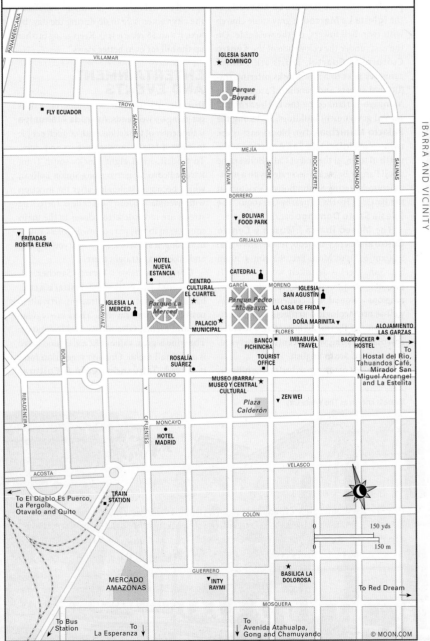

VILLAMAR

IGLESIA SANTO ★ DOMINGO

Parque Boyacá

TROYA

■ FLY ECUADOR

SANCHEZ

OLMEDO

BOLIVAR

MEJÍA

SUCRE

ROCAFUERTE

MALDONADO

SALINAS

BORRERO

▼ BOLIVAR FOOD PARK

GRIJALVA

▼ FRITADAS ROSITA ELENA

HOTEL NUEVA ESTANCIA ●

CATEDRAL ✝

NARVAEZ

IGLESIA LA MERCED ✝

CENTRO CULTURAL EL CUARTEL ★

GARCÍA

MORENO

IGLESIA SAN AGUSTÍN ♦

Parque La Merced

Parque Pedro Moncayo

LA CASA DE FRIDA ▼

DOÑA MARINITA ▼

PALACIO MUNICIPAL ★

FLORES

ALOJAMIENTO LAS GARZAS ●

BORJA

ROSALÍA SUÁREZ ●

BANCO PICHINCHA ■

IMBABURA ■ TRAVEL

BACKPACKER ● HOSTEL

TOURIST OFFICE ●

To Hostal del Rio, Tahuandos Café, Mirador San Miguel Arcangel and La Estelita

RIBADENEIRA

OVIEDO

Y

MUSEO IBARRA/ MUSEO Y CENTRAL CULTURAL ★

ZEN WEI ●

C FUENTES

MONCAYO

Plaza Calderón

HOTEL MADRID ●

VELASCO

ACOSTA

To El Diablo Es Puerco, La Pergola, Otavalo and Quito

TRAIN STATION

COLÓN

0   150 yds
0   150 m

GUERRERO

★ BASILICA LA DOLOROSA

MERCADO AMAZONAS

▼ INTY RAYMI

To Red Dream

MOSQUERA

To Bus Station

To La Esperanza ↓

To Avenida Atahualpa, Gong and Chamuyando ↓

© MOON.COM

main squares. Both are leafy and well-kept—attractive spots to find a shady bench and people watch. The **Parque La Merced** has the **Iglesia La Merced,** a gray stone church with twin bell towers, on the west side. On the east, under the colonnade of the **Centro Cultural El Cuartel,** artists sell painted canvases next to a row kiosks offering traditional sweets and candies. Parque Pedro Moncayo is flanked by the **cathedral** and several government buildings, including the **Palacio Municipal.** Two blocks east is the twin-spired **Iglesia de San Agustín.** At the north of town, at the end of Calle Bolívar, the small Parque Boyacá is decorated with a monument celebrating Simón Bolívar's victory at the Battle of Ibarra in nearby Caranqui. The **Iglesia Santo Domingo** backs the square.

The **Museo Ibarra / Museo y Centro Cultural** (Sucre *y* Oviedo, tel. 99/969-7976, 9:30am-6:30pm Mon.-Fri., 9:30am-4:30pm Sat.-Sun., free) is definitely worth a look. It has interesting, well-arranged collections of religious, colonial, and contemporary art, as well as archaeological artifacts and historical photos of Ibarra, all housed in a restored colonial building with a central courtyard. Descriptions are in English.

To the east of town, perched on the hillside, is the **Mirador San Miguel Arcangel,** with impressive views of Imbabura and the city spread out below. It's a 40-minute walk from the city center, safe to do during the day. By taxi, it's an $8 return trip. Keep going farther up the hill for even better views.

ENTERTAINMENT AND EVENTS

Ibarra is not known for its nightlife, but it does get going on weekends. **Avenida Atahualpa** is the center of the action, with enough people to make it safe to browse the bars and clubs. To find it, head eight blocks south from Parque Pedro Moncayo along Simón Bolívar, which becomes Atahualpa after the junction with Avenida Teodoro Goméz de la Torre. The streets are more deserted closer to the main squares, so in this part of town, unless you're in a group, it's best to know where you're going and take a taxi straight there.

Gong (Atahualpa *y* Ricardo Sanchez, tel. 6/264-0100, Facebook @gongibarra) is a café, bar, and cultural center attracting arty, alternative locals and travelers. There are regular cultural events, salsa nights, and live music. The wine is great value at $2 a glass and there is a cocktail menu. Organic vegetarian food is served. **Tahuandos Café & Cultural**

Ibarra is known as The White City.

Center (Salinas 543 y Oviedo, tel. 6/260-9929 or 97/871-3164, Facebook @centrocultural-tahuandos and @cafetahuandos, 6pm-9pm Tues., 6pm-10pm Wed.-Thurs., 6pm-11:45pm Sat.-Sun.) was originally Café Arte, opened by local painter Olmedo Moncayo in 1996. It's now run by the artist's son under a new name. It has a friendly vibe and hosts events every couple of nights, such as open mic, live bands, jam sessions, micro-theater, and DJs.

Local annual events include El Retorno, which celebrates the homecoming of the 550 Ibarreños who fled to neighboring La Esperanza following the 1868 earthquake and remained there for four years. Around 2,000 people participate in a walk on April 28 to commemorate the return of the people, alongside concerts, parades, and sporting events. July 17 sees the commemoration of Simón Bolívar's victory at the Battle of Ibarra in 1823. The founding of the city is marked every year on September 28.

RECREATION

Imbabura Travel (Rocafuerte 608 y Flores, tel. 6/295-7766, http://imbaburatravel.com, 9am-6:30pm Mon.-Fri.) is the only tour agency in Ibarra offering experiences within the city and the northern Sierra. Half- and one-day trips include embroidery villages; a city tour; the polylepis forest; Las Tolas de Cochasquí; ancestral Cotacachi (including a visit to a shaman); rappelling, and zip-lining. Two- to eight-day tours are also available.

To see Ibarra and its dramatic surroundings from above, contact Fly Ecuador (Rafael Troya y José Vinueza, tel. 6/295-3297, www.flyecuador.com.ec) for a tandem paragliding ride from the slopes of Imbabura ($67 pp). Paragliding courses are also available.

Tren Ecuador (http://trenecuador.com) offers a scenic round-trip train journey from Ibarra to Salinas (departures Thurs., Fri., and Sun., $39), a small town with a warm climate and a strong Afro-Ecuadorian influence. During the stop in Salinas, visitors can learn about Afro-Ecuadorian history and culture, and sample the cuisine. The train leaves Ibarra at 11:25am and returns at 4:40pm. Be at the station at least half an hour early to buy your ticket.

SHOPPING

A few blocks west of the town center near the bus terminal, the Mercado Amazonas sells clothing, electronics, fresh produce, and pretty much everything else, but take care with your belongings and avoid wandering here at night.

On Friday mornings there is a farmers market, the Feria Esperanza, outside the Iglesia San Agustín on Rocafuerte and Flores, where campesinos from neighboring communities sell fresh vegetables, homemade bread, and local cuisine.

FOOD

Ibarra definitely has a sweet tooth and is known for its *arrope de mora* (blackberry syrup) and *nogadas* (nougat candies). Numerous kiosks selling these and other sweets line the southeast side of Parque La Merced. The most famous indulgences in Ibarra are the delicious *helados de paila*. Several *heladerías* sell these in town, but the best is ★ Heladería Rosalía Suárez (Olmedo y Oviedo, tel. 6/295-8722, Facebook @HeladosRosaliaSuarez, 7am-6:30pm daily, $1-5), run by Rosalía's grandchildren, where you can watch the ice cream being made. Many flavors are vegan, some are not; the staff will be happy to advise. Also available are fruit salads (with ice cream, of course) and savory items such as empanadas. Be aware that there are two cafés bearing the name Rosalía Suárez; the original has a plaque on the wall to that effect.

Fritadas Rosita Elena (Eloy Alfaro 2-12, Facebook @fritadasdecajon, from 5pm, $2.75-3) has been offering *fritada seca* (fried pork with potatoes, toasted corn, and hot sauce) since 1958. The current owner, who has been making the traditional dish for 40 years, grinds the ingredients for the sauce with a stone, the way her mother taught her, and swears this gives the sauce its unique flavor.

Helados de Paila

helado de paila at Heladería Rosalía Suárez

Ibarra's most delicious treat is *helado de paila,* a sorbet invented by Rosalía Suárez in her Ibarra kitchen in 1896. Since her death in 1985 at age 105, her descendants have continued to follow her recipes in her original café **Heladería Rosalía Suárez.** Traditionally, the only ingredients were ice, sugar, and fruit. (These days, milk and/or eggs are added to a few of the flavors, but many are still made without.) The mixture is blended by hand with a large wooden paddle in a *paila* (a large bronze pan) that sits on ice sprinkled with salt to maintain the temperature. Now *helados de paila* are sold all over Ecuador, but Rosalía's are the original and the best.

The restaurant is open until the *fritada* runs out, usually between 7pm and 8:30pm. **Doña Marinita** (Rocafuerte *y* Flores, 8am-7pm daily, $0.60) has been selling *empanadas de morocho* (corn empanadas filled with chicken) for 100 years. The current owner learned the recipe from her grandmother. The food court in the **Mercado Amazonas** is another good option for local dishes at low prices.

Owned by a friendly Ibarreña, ★ **La Casa de Frida** (Rocafuerte *y* Flores, tel. 98/833-0353, 8am-10pm Mon.-Thurs., 11am-midnight Fri., noon-midnight Sat.) is a charming café near the Iglesia San Agustín. The Frida Kahlo-themed decor is quirky and fun, and the coffees, sandwiches, cakes, and cocktails are delicious and beautifully presented. The café collects $2 donations from customers, which go toward either feeding local people with low economic resources (you get to write a message to the recipient that will accompany their free meal) or to a program to sterilize local dogs. Old clothes are collected and recycled into bags for dog food donations.

There are a few veggie options in Ibarra, including **Zen Wei** (José Antonio de Sucre *y* Pedro Moncayo, tel. 98/206-6985, 8:30am-3:30pm Mon.-Sat., $2.50) and **Inty Raymi** (Av. Pérez Guerrero 6-39 *y* Bolívar, tel. 6/258-5359, $3), both of which serve decent set lunches. **Gong** (Atahualpa *y* Ricardo Sanchez, tel. 6/264-0100, Facebook @gongibarra, 5:30pm-11:45pm Wed.-Thurs., 5:30pm-2am Fri.-Sat.) offers organic vegetarian food, including burgers and falafels.

Recommended international options include **El Diablo es Puerco** (Av. Mariano Acosta 24-40, tel. 6/265-8500, 10am-5pm

Wed. and Sun., 10am-10pm Thurs.-Sat.), which serves Peruvian food; **La Pergola** (Dr Cristóbal Tobar y Av. Cristóbal de Troya, tel. 95/981-4896, Facebook @chefmarcoc, 6pm-11pm Tues.-Fri., 1pm-11pm Sat., 1pm-6pm Sun.), an Italian place; and **Chamuyando** (Río Cenepa 4-18, tel. 6/264-3847, 7pm-10pm Thurs.-Sat., 12:30pm-4pm Sun.), an Argentinian steak house.

Many town center restaurants are closed on Sundays, but **Bolívar Food Park** (Bolívar 3-64 y Grijalva, tel. 99/870-6537, Facebook @ foodparkdelabolivar), which has various establishments on-site, is an exception.

ACCOMMODATIONS
In Ibarra
The center of Ibarra has mostly budget accommodations. Unless stated otherwise, all the options below have hot water, Wi-Fi, and private bathrooms. None include breakfast.

UNDER $25
★ **Hostal del Rio** (Juan Montalvo y Flores, tel. 6/261-1885, Facebook @hostaldelrioibarra, $12 s, $15 d) is great value, with an attractive, airy reception area. A wooden spiral staircase leads to the upper floors, where rooms have beautiful views, small balconies, and cable TV. Parking is available. One block west is another great budget option, the locally owned **Alojamiento Las Garzas** (Flores y Salinas, tel. 6/295-0985, $13-15 s, $18-20 d), which has friendly service and six clean, simple rooms with cable TV and DVD players. Just down the street is the friendly Ecuadorian-owned **Backpacker Hostal** (tel. 99/959-0868, Facebook @backpackerhostal, $8 dorm, $12 s, $18 d), in a restored colonial building with rooms around an attractive plant-filled central courtyard. There is a shared kitchen and a washing machine that is free for guests to use. Breakfast is available for $2.50.

OVER $25
One of the only midrange hotels in town, with a prime location on the north side of Parque La Merced, is **Hotel Nueva Estancia** (García

Moreno 7-58, tel. 6/295-1444, $25 s, $40 d), with spacious, comfortable rooms.

Vicinity of Ibarra
The more expensive accommodations are found outside the city. All include breakfast. **Hacienda Chorlaví** (tel. 6/293-2222, www. haciendachorlavi.com, $105 s, $115 d), dating back to 1620, sits 4 kilometers (2.5 mi) south on the Panamericana. It has all the facilities one might expect of a luxury hotel. The pool is heated with solar panels.

Three kilometers (1.9 mi) past the Mirador San Miguel Arcangel, **La Estelita** (tel. 6/304-7079, www.laestelitahosteria.com, $120 pp) has dramatic views of Imbabura and the city spread out below, especially enjoyable from the heated outdoor pool. Owned by a local family, the hotel was designed as a place for guests to recharge their batteries. An organic garden and a series of nature trails are open to the public free of charge.

Ten minutes west of Ibarra, ★ **Hostería Cananvalle** (tel. 98/260-9132, http://hosteria-cananvalle.com, $62 s, $78 d) is a family-owned hotel on a 1.6-hectare (4-acre) organic farm that includes an avocado orchard, fruit trees, seasonal crops, and flowering and herbal gardens that attract many butterflies and birds, especially hummingbirds. The farm provides a significant proportion of the restaurant's food. The hostería uses soil, water, and energy conservation techniques and takes measures to minimize waste and contamination. It's only a $5 taxi ride from Ibarra, but it feels a world away from the city noise, with beautiful views of a river canyon. The friendly, helpful hosts can organize a variety of day trips.

INFORMATION AND SERVICES
The **municipal tourist office** (Sucre y Oviedo, tel. 6/260-8489, https:// ibarraesturismoeng.wordpress.com, Facebook @IbarraPuroEncanto, 9am-12:30pm and 2pm-5pm Mon.-Fri.) is very helpful. Their website, in English, is also very informative.

GETTING THERE AND AROUND

Midway between Quito and the Colombian border, Ibarra is a travel hub of the northern Sierra. The bus terminal is near the Mercado Amazonas. There are frequent buses to/from Cotacachi (40 minutes, $0.50), Otavalo (40 minutes, $0.55), Quito's Carcelen terminal (3 hours, $3), and Tulcán (3 hours, $3.50). Other destinations include Guayaquil, Manta (both 10 hours, $14), and Cuenca (10 hours, $17). A timetable of all buses from Ibarra's terminal is downloadable on the tourist office website (https://ibarraesturismoeng.wordpress.com).

SOUTH OF IBARRA
★ San Clemente

At nearly 3,000 meters (9,800 ft), with views of Ibarra spread out below, this small Kichwa village is a shining example of eco- and community tourism. Twenty years ago, the inhabitants of **San Clemente,** descendants of the Caranqui people, were struggling to make a living by growing traditional Andean crops, such as corn, potatoes, and quinoa. Then, in 2000, a small group of locals had the idea of opening up family homes in the village to guests, with the income going back into the community. The project has been a huge success and there are now 24 families participating, each offering guest room(s) with a separate bathroom and hot water. One of the requirements of joining the project is that no chemicals are used in the cultivation of produce, so the whole community now eats fresh, organic food. Since the project began, local people have diversified their crops, which now include a wide variety of salad leaves, vegetables, and fruits, among them blackberries, peaches, and strawberries. In fact, the agriculture is so diverse that the community is now pretty much self-sufficient, only needing to purchase cooking oil, salt, and—for now—sugar from outside (they are working on growing sugarcane).

Guests are invited to share their hosts' daily life, discovering the Caranqui people's culture and traditions. Meals, often prepared together, are eaten with the families. Activities include exploring a path of medicinal plants; feeding the llamas, guinea pigs, and rabbits; plowing with bulls; and participating in *mingas,* where the community comes together to work on a specific building or agricultural project. Additional activities include bike and horse rental and guided tours, shamanic healing, and Andean music nights. Some of the young local people have been trained as guides, offering trips to Imbabura and Cubilche ($45 per group of up to 12 people plus $30 transport).

As well as sharing the Andean cosmovision with guests, the project also involves local indigenous youth, aiming to keep Kichwa traditions alive.

It's possible to stay with project cofounders Manuel and Laura Guatemal, who have expanded their house to include several guest cabins, some with their own organic garden encircled by flowering hedge, as idyllic as The Shire from Tolkien. As organizers, the Guatemals can put visitors in touch with other community members who offer guest rooms within the family home itself, for a more integrated, authentic experience. Accommodation costs $50 per person, including all meals. Be aware that there is no Internet in San Clemente (though there is cell phone signal) and that very few local people speak English. Volunteers are welcomed, especially to work at the local school.

GETTING THERE

San Clemente is 15-20 minutes from Ibarra, $5 or $6 by taxi. Direct the driver to *"Avenida Atahualpa, dirección La Esperanza."* When you climb the hill and reach the San Clemente church, turn right at the sign saying "Pukya Pamba" and follow the road until the last house, which is Manuel and Laura's. For more information, see www.sclemente.com or contact Manuel Guatemal (tel. 99/916-1095 or manuel_guatemal@hotmail.com).

La Esperanza and Imbabura

Many Ibarrans relocated to **La Esperanza**

de Ibarra (Hope of Ibarra), 9 kilometers (5.6 mi) south of the original city, after the 1868 earthquake. In the hopes of avoiding future catastrophes, La Esperanza's new residents dedicated their town to Santa Marianita, the patron saint of earthquakes. At 2,505 meters (8,220 ft), La Esperanza sits at the foot of the inactive **Volcán Imbabura** (4,630 m/15,190 ft), making it a good departure point for climbs of the volcano or its smaller sibling, **Cubilche** (3,802 m/12,474 ft). The climb up Cubilche takes about four hours from La Esperanza, and you can descend the other side to Laguna San Pablo in another three hours or retrace your steps. Climbing Imbabura is a bit more of an undertaking, but it's still possible to reach the summit and get back in one long day with no special equipment. You will, however, need hiking shoes with good grip, a waterproof jacket, and warm clothes. Even if it's hot and sunny when you set out, conditions can change quickly, and you may be very glad that you carried your woolly hat, scarf, and gloves. It's also highly recommended to go with an experienced guide, for the same reason. Plan on leaving at or before dawn and making a solid 8- to 10-hour round-trip from La Esperanza. The IGM *San Pablo del Lago* 1:50,000 map covers the mountain.

FOOD AND ACCOMMODATIONS

A recommended **guide** for climbing Imbabura can be found at **Refugio Terra Esperanza** (tel. 6/266-0228 or 9/99-687-577, www.hostelterraesperanza.com, $13 dorm, $28 d, including breakfast), a chilled-out hostel aimed at mountaineers, run by a friendly Ecuadorian, Emerson Obanda, and his mother. Rooms are basic with shared bathrooms. The hostel has a bar and shared kitchen. Lunch and dinner are available at extra cost. The family lives on-site but is sometimes working out back, so you may need to ring the bell a few times upon arrival. Emerson is a mountain guide and leads trips to the nearby peaks and other adventure tours, including rock climbing; the Inca Trek to Ingapirca; hikes to hot springs, rivers,

waterfalls; and an overnight stay in a local cave. Climbing Imbabura costs $120 for up to three people, including car transport to and from the trailhead. The hostel organizes a monthly "plogging" event, which is a mixture of a fitness walk and litter picking.

Señora Aida Buitrón has run the rustic, tranquil **Casa Aida** (tel. 6/266-0221, www.casaaida.com, $10 pp, camping $6 with your own tent) since the 1970s. She'll reminisce about visits from Bob Dylan and Pink Floyd back in the day when famous musicians used to search for magic mushrooms in the fields after rains. Aida still runs the hostel with her daughter and grandson. Rooms are basic with shared bathrooms and Wi-Fi. Breakfast, lunch, and dinner are offered at additional cost, with vegetarian options available.

Both hostels are on the main road that passes through La Esperanza.

GETTING THERE

Cooperativa La Esperanza buses run from the terminal in Ibarra (30 minutes, $0.50). A taxi from Ibarra costs $5.

Zuleta

The tiny, picturesque village of **Zuleta** is best known for the Zuleteño embroidery, in which intricate, colorful designs are sewn onto white cloth shirts, napkins, table cloths, and wall hangings. Introduced by the Spanish, the embroidery method was blended with traditional indigenous motifs to create the signature style. On Saturdays, Sundays, and public holidays there is a *feria* from 10am, where local people sell artisanal items including embroidery, alpaca goods, soap, jam, honey, and honey liqueur. Local specialty cuisine is also available. The biggest *ferias* are at Carnival, Independence Day in August, and All Souls' Day on November 2. Zuleta is easy to navigate; everything is located on the main road through the village.

On any day of the week, there are three **embroidery workshops** in the village that can be visited with no reservation. For groups of over 10 people, book 2-3 days ahead and the locals can arrange a small *feria*, with food. Also in the village is a small *talabartería* (**saddle workshop**), opened by the current owner's father in the 1940s. Jaime Sarzosa still makes saddles for the local people in the traditional way. Each saddle takes three months to make and will last for 40-60 years. He now also makes items for tourists, including bags, belts, wallets, and notebooks.

For more information about tourism in Zuleta, contact the saddle maker, Jaime Sarzosa (tel. 6/266-2014 or 97/977-0909, talabarteriajszuleta@gmail.com), who is also the president of the well-organized local tourism association.

FOOD AND ACCOMMODATIONS

La Estancia de Antonio (Barrio Santa Marianita, via San Pablo, *frente al estadio,* tel. 6/266-2194 or 96/862-7426, is one of the few restaurants in the village and the only bar. Specialties include *caldo de gallo* (chicken soup). The friendly owner can whip up an omelet and a good salad for vegetarians.

Hospedaje Carmita (tel. 6/266-2176 or 98/015-4751, $20 pp, including breakfast) has warm, comfortable rooms decorated with local *artesanía.* Lunch and dinner are available for $7.50 each. The owner offers classes in

cooking traditional cuisine and can organize guided hikes.

Zuleta is also the location of one of Ecuador's most historic haciendas, **Hacienda Zuleta** (tel. 6/266-2182, www.zuleta.com, $283-458 pp, plus 30 percent single supplement, including all meals). Dating back to 1691, the hacienda has been owned by the family of Galo Plaza Lasso, a former president of Ecuador, for more than 100 years. As well as a luxury hotel, it's also a working **farm** and **cheese factory** that employs more than 100 local people. There are extensive organic gardens. A small percentage of income from the hotel goes toward the Galo Plaza Lasso Foundation, which works in the areas of conservation and education. The foundation oversees the hacienda's **condor rehabilitation project,** which bred the only specimen born in captivity to be released into the wild, and monitors the local condor population. The foundation also finances the local library, summer school, and scholarships for local children. Day visits to the hacienda cost $94, including lunch, plus $7 to visit the condor project. Reservations are required for day visits and accommodations; the hacienda does not allow walk-ins. German, French, English, and Spanish are spoken.

samples of Zuleteño embroidery

GETTING THERE

To get to Zuleta, take a bus with La Esperanza Cooperativa from the bus terminal in Ibarra (40 minutes, $0.60), or a bus from Cayambe (1 hour).

IBARRA TO THE COAST

Traveling from Ibarra to San Lorenzo in Esmeraldas is a four- to five-hour journey, and many buses ply this spectacular route daily. Bear in mind that only the first half of the journey, from Ibarra to Lita, is considered safe. Guerrilla groups, drug traffickers, and criminal gangs are active in the northern part of Esmeraldas province.

La Carolina

Also known as El Limonal or Guallupe, **La Carolina** is 1.5 hours northwest of Ibarra on the road to San Lorenzo. The climate is subtropical, and there is lots of lush, green vegetation. Coffee, cacao, and various fruits are all grown in the area. The village itself is very small, with a couple of shops and restaurants.

PARQUE BAMBÚ

A few minutes' walk from the village center, **Parque Bambú** (tel. 6/301-6606, www. bospas.org, $15 dorm, $22 pp private room, including breakfast) is a permaculture farm owned by Belgian Piet Sabbe. Short-term guests are welcomed, especially those with an interest in sustainable farming techniques, but the place is really geared toward providing courses in **permaculture** and **volunteering opportunities** ($18/day first two weeks, then $15/day, or $260/month). Prices include accommodations, meals, and permaculture instruction. After the first month, volunteers are paid $4.30/day. Accommodations are rustic. Before exploring the 45-minute self-guided trail, ask Piet to show you the photos of the 15-hectare (37-acre) plot when he bought it in 1995, to fully appreciate the contrast between the then barren, wasted scrubland and today's verdant jungle. What he has achieved is quite remarkable, including an increase in bird species from 12 to 79. Piet is currently implementing the 4 per 1,000 initiative (www.4p1000.org), a bold and fascinating proposal on how permaculture techniques could not only stabilize food production in the face of a warming planet, but could also solve the problem of climate change. Parque Bambú is LGBTQ friendly.

HACIENDA PRIMAVERA WILDERNESS ECOLODGE

There is also access from La Carolina to the **Hacienda Primavera Wilderness Ecolodge** (tel. 6/301-1231, www.haciendaprimavera.com, $120 pp, including all meals), set deep in the cloud forest at 1,200 meters (3,900 ft) elevation. Gorgeous, whitewashed, wooden-beamed rooms are individually themed, each dedicated to a different local bird, with beautiful views of jungly slopes and a rushing river. There is an excellent **restaurant** and a **pool** nestled in the lush green vegetation. Service is friendly and top-notch. Activities include **bird-watching, horseback riding, mountain biking,** and **hiking** with an English-speaking guide. **Rafting** is also available ($85 pp, minimum 3 people). The hacienda owns and protects 3 hectares (7.4 acres) of primary forest. It also has an organic **coffee plantation** and **fruit farm** that employs local women and supplies the restaurant. Staff are happy to collect guests from La Carolina. Transport can also be arranged from Quito or Otavalo ($120).

SAN JERÓNIMO

Ten kilometers (6.2 mi) from La Carolina on the way to Buenos Aires is the small community of **San Jerónimo,** where community members offer guided walks in primary cloud forest, bird-watching, horseback riding, camping, and tours of local fruit farms. Accommodations are available at the **Tienda del Descanso** (tel. 98/458-0482, Facebook @latiendadeldescanso.ec), where guests can participate in artisanal cheese and coffee making or just chill in a riverside hammock.

Farther down the San Lorenzo road, near Lita, the **Siete Cascadas** (Seven Waterfalls,

$10) live up to their name, with **waterfalls** set in luxurious vegetation. There's a **police checkpoint** here, where you need to show your ID.

GETTING THERE

Cooperativa Valle de Chota, Cooperativa Espejo, and Pullman Carchi all operate buses from Ibarra to La Carolina (1.5 hours) and Lita (2 hours).

IBARRA TO TULCÁN

The Pan-American Highway stretches 125 kilometers (78 mi) north from Ibarra to the border with Colombia, crossing some beautiful and remote high altitude terrain. Most travelers only bypass this area en route to or from the border crossing town of Tulcán, but they are missing out, because the town of El Ángel and the nearby attractions are a true highlight of the region.

The U.K. Foreign Office advises against all travel within 20 kilometers (13 mi) of the Colombian border, except the town of Tulcán, which is the only safe place to cross into Colombia, and the area either side of the Pan-American Highway (for a map showing the exclusion zone and current security information, see www.gov.uk/foreign-travel-advice). Guerrilla groups, drug traffickers, and criminal gangs are active in this area.

El Ángel

By the time your bus finally chugs all the way up to **El Ángel** (pop. 6,000), the town's motto—"Paradise Closer to the Sky"—doesn't seem so far from the truth. At 3,000 meters (9,800 ft), on clear days there are wonderful views of volcanoes Cayambe, Imbabura, Pichincha, and Cotacachi. As well as beautiful scenery, El Ángel is culturally interesting, as many of the area's indigenous inhabitants are direct descendants of the Pastos, who lived here in pre-Columbian times.

The topiary works in the **Parque Libertad** were begun by José Franco, the creator of Tulcán's famous topiary cemetery. Also on the square is a tourist office, where helpful staff can provide information about the attractions of the region or put visitors in touch with a guide (Spanish-speaking only). On the opposite side of the square, a small collection of pottery is displayed in the **Museo Arqueológico Municipal.** There is also a Banco Pichincha ATM. Two blocks west from the Parque Libertad is the church and the Parque de los Animales, with statues of various animals.

At the north edge of town, at the exit to the El Ángel reserve, is a monument of the globe surrounded by 20 *frailejón* plants, representing the community's commitment to protecting its natural resources. Built to mark the millennium, each of the 20 plants represents 100 years. The clock is a reminder of the urgency of the task.

FOOD

On the Parque de los Animales, **Rincón del Ángel** (tel. 6/297-8049, noon-10pm daily, $1.50-5) is a friendly café, awarded a prize by the local government for its excellent traditional local food. Specialties include *chuleta* (fried pork chop) and *alitas asadas* (barbecued chicken wings with hominy, potatoes, and toasted corn). On the corner of Parque Libertad, **Doña Mary** (tel. 6/297-8054 or 92/034-391, $2.50-4) is open for all three meals, serving chicken, burgers, and trout with fries. El Ángel has slim pickings for vegetarians. Cheese empanadas are available in a few places, and there is a fruit and vegetable market opposite the college on a side street off Espejo, the main entrance road into town.

ACCOMMODATIONS

There aren't many accommodation options in El Ángel. A block up from the gas station, **Paisajes Andinos** (Calle Río Frio, tel. 6/297-7307 or 98/613-0892, $10 pp) is somewhat ramshackle but charming, run by a friendly elderly couple. A couple of blocks west of Parque Libertad, **El Andarín** (Calle José Benigno Grijalva y Av. Espejo, tel. 96/909-4274, Facebook @TurismoElAndarin, $60 s/d, including breakfast) is a more upmarket option, with a garden and terrace. Some rooms have a kitchenette.

GETTING THERE
Cooperative Trans Espejo (tel. 6/297-7216) has an office on the Parque Libertad. Buses go to Ibarra (2 hours, $1.60) and on to Quito (4 hours, $4) every hour 3am-7pm; and to Tulcán (7am and 1:15pm, 1.5 hours, $2). **Cooperative Mira** (tel. 6/228-0193) also operates several buses daily to Tulcán and Ibarra leaving from the Parque de los Animales. If you miss the last bus of the day, hire a taxi to the Panamericana at Bolívar, where it's easy to flag down a bus passing in either direction.

Vicinity of El Ángel
The **Piedra Pintada Ingüeza** is a large mushroom-shaped rock with 1,000-year old petroglyphs carved into it by the Pastos, who used the site for rituals. Sadly, the rock has been vandalized and only the carvings on the left (a monkey, some human faces and figures, and concentric circles) are genuinely old; those to the right are much more modern additions. Despite this, the original carvings are intriguing and the setting is beautiful, amid rolling hills. To get there, take a taxi from El Ángel ($3 one way, or $5 round-trip with a short wait) or a bus to San Isidro (20 minutes with Cooperative Espejo, $0.50) and then walk for half an hour on the Vía Ingüeza until you reach a sign for the Piedra Pintada. From there, it's a couple of hundred yards up a steep cobbled road until you reach a barbed wire fence on the right that is actually a gate. The rock is just across the field, which is state property with public access.

With almost permanently hot and sunny weather, the thermal baths at **Balneario La Calera** (tel. 99/314-8058, 6am-5pm daily, $2) are the perfect place to warm up after a hike in the chilly El Ángel reserve. Surrounded by forested hills are two clean pools: a larger, cooler one for swimming and a smaller, warmer one for lounging and absorbing the minerals in the water, which give it a yellow color. Amenities include a sauna, a deck for sunbathing, and a café. The baths are quiet midweek and fill up with local families on weekends. To get there, take a taxi from El Ángel ($6). To walk or bike, head out of the town on the Vía Calera near the exit for San Isidro. Turn off after 3 kilometers (1.9 mi) at the sign for the baths, after which it's a 5-kilometer (3.1 mi) downhill bumpy ride. It's a steep walk/bike back, so consider calling a taxi/pickup truck for the return journey.

★ El Ángel Ecological Reserve
High above El Ángel is Ecuador's premier *páramo* reserve. Created in 1992, **El Ángel Ecological Reserve** protects 15,700 hectares (38,800 acres) of some of the most pristine high-altitude country in Ecuador, ranging 3,650-4,770 meters (11,975-15,650 ft). The reserve is famous for the abundance of giant, spiky-headed *frailejón* plants which, despite only growing 1 centimeter (0.4 in) every year, can reach several meters in height. The reserve is an eerie, otherworldly place, with the *frailejones* standing like mute sentries watching over the misty *páramo*, as they have for time immemorial. The silence is profound, broken only by the occasional sounds of running water and birdcalls. Hawks and *curiquingues* (a bird of prey sacred to the Incas) soar overhead. Also present, though less often spotted, are condors, Andean bears, Andean foxes, and deer.

Starting at the main entrance of the reserve, a 2.5-kilometer (1.6-mi) trail leads to the **Laguna Voladero,** where, legend has it, a Pasto chief disappeared in 1634 after being pursued by the Spanish. According to the locals, he reappears at the solstice. From the lake, head back on the same trail to the visitors center, or climb the stairs to the Mirador Corazones Sanos for a shorter, steeper, circular route back. Wherever in the reserve you go, stick to the path; the fragile vegetation can take months to recover from a careless footstep.

The biggest threat to this pristine and unique environment is land clearance for cattle grazing and potato farming. The surrounding patchwork quilt of rolling fields dotted with cows might look picturesque, but much of it was once *páramo*. Efforts are being made to protect the belt of land that surrounds the reserve and prevent the advance of agricultural lands, but without an alternative source of income, support from local farmers is limited. Responsible tourism is their best option, although currently the majority of tourists just visit the reserve and leave. A Pasto community in La Libertad, direct descendants of the area's pre-Columbian inhabitants, is trying to set up a community tourism project, with trails and accommodations, to protect the reserve and transform it into a source of sustainable income—a unique community fighting to protect a unique ecosystem. For more information, contact the tourist office in Parque Libertad in El Ángel.

Be aware that temperatures in El Ángel can drop below freezing. Rain is common, though it's slightly drier May-October. Also be aware that the reserve technically falls within the 20-kilometer (12-mi) exclusion zone that runs along the border with Colombia. Being close to Tulcán and the Pan-American Highway, however, it is generally considered safe to visit, although the road that borders the reserve to the north should be avoided.

GETTING THERE

To get to the reserve, hire a *camioneta* in Parque Libertad in El Ángel. It's a $30 round-trip, including a 90-minute wait for the walk to the lake. Lone travelers may be able to find other people in the park to share the ride. It's a one-hour, bumpy journey to the reserve, though, sadly, there are plans to asphalt the road.

To make your own way, you will need a four-wheel-drive vehicle. To reach the main entrance, follow the old road to Tulcán, past the guard post at La Esperanza, and keep going. For Laguna Crespo, near the Cerro El Pelado (4,149 m/13,612 ft), pass through La Libertad to the north by car, then walk for an hour to reach the lake. On the western side

of the reserve are the Colorado guard post, the Cerro Negro (3,674 m/12,054 ft), and the Laguna Negra. Volcán Chiles and the Lagunas Verdes are accessed via the road from Tufiño to Maldonado, which traverses the northern part of the reserve, though this is not recommended for safety reasons.

INFORMATION AND SERVICES

For information on the El Ángel reserve, stop by the **tourist office** (on the main park in El Ángel) or the **Ministerio del Ambiente** (Ministry of the Environment, Calle Río Frio, tel. 6/297-7597). The office isn't obvious; look for the sign in a third-floor window and walk up the stairs.

Polylepis Lodge

Adjoining the southwestern edge of the El Ángel Ecological Reserve, **Polylepis Lodge** (tel. 6/263-1819, www.polylepis.com, $138-160 pp, all meals and guided tours included) is a luxury ecolodge and private reserve, named for the ancient forest that lies within its grounds. Some of the trees are 3,500-4,000 years old, making this the oldest forest of its kind. This species of polylepis is endemic to Ecuador, only growing in a handful of places, and there are just 12 hectares (30 acres) of forest left. Its growth rate is astonishingly slow, at 1 millimeter (0.04 in) in diameter every decade. Laying a hand gently on one of these millennial beings, so cold to the touch, one can't help but wonder what stories they would tell, if only they could communicate with us.

A guided walk through the polylepis forest is an unforgettable experience (free for hotel guests and $38 for nonguests, by reservation only, including lunch). The forest is flooded in parts, and sometimes the trails are more like streams (rubber boots are provided). The short hike passes a peaceful lake, La Laguna de Deseos, where visitors are invited to make a wish. In such a magical place, it's easy to believe one's wish might be granted! Available for hotel guests is a nighttime "Legends and Goblins" tour of the forest by torchlight. The reserve also includes an expanse of *páramo*, where the value of ecotourism can clearly be seen at its boundary, with *frailejones* and wildflowers safely protected on one side of the fence, contrasting starkly with potato fields and cattle grazing pastures on the other.

The winner of several luxury travel and responsible tourism awards, the lodge is an experience in itself. Formerly a trout farm, it makes features of the pools left over from its previous incarnation, with one running the length of the dining room floor, covered in glass. Some cabins have their own Jacuzzis in glass-walled rooms overlooking rushing streams, almost part of the forest. It gets cold at night, but each room has a gas heater and an electric blanket. Attached to the dining area is the **Museo Pastos,** housing a fascinating collection of ancient pottery found in the area, some pieces dating back to AD 500.

The lodge is heavily involved in conservation education programs and has created a cutting-edge **research station,** the **PolylepisLab.** The bedroom heaters use biodegradable alcohol and methanol, and biodigesters process gray and black water to produce organic compost. The majority of the ingredients for the restaurant come from organic local farms. The lodge has also set up a project involving 50 local women of low economic means in micro-enterprises, such as weaving and making souvenirs.

GETTING THERE

Polylepis Lodge is 25 minutes north of El Ángel. *Camionetas* charge $15 one-way, or $30 for round-trip with a 90-minute wait for the guided walk.

Bolívar and Gruta La Paz

An initiative of a local women's association, the **Museo Paleontológico** (tel. 6/228-7733, www.museopaleontologicodebolivar. wordpress.com, 8am-5pm daily, $2) in the village of Bolívar houses a collection of 205 fossils found by visiting Italian scientists, including mammoth and sabertooth tiger bones. It has a café and a shop selling local handicrafts.

Just to the north, one of the region's most famous religious icons sits in a huge natural cave just outside the village of La Paz. The **Gruta La Paz** (Peace Grotto), also called Rumichaca, contains a chapel dedicated to the Virgen de Nuestra Señora de la Paz. Stalactites and stalagmites lend the site a gothic atmosphere that is amplified by the fluttering bats and dark waters of the Río Apaquí. At the entrance to the cave are hundreds of plaques, erected in gratitude by pilgrims for whom the Virgin has granted miracles. In addition to the subterranean chapel, there is a **restaurant** and a set of **thermal baths** (7am-4pm daily, tickets available at the shop next to the white church, $2). The cave is busy on weekends, holidays, and during the **Fiesta del Virgen de la Paz** on July 8. At other times, you may have it almost completely to yourself.

GETTING THERE

Bolívar and La Paz are just off the Panamericana, midway between Tulcán and Ibarra. In La Paz, Cristóbal Colón buses wait in the village to ferry visitors to the grotto. The journey is actually more stunning than the cave, with the narrow road making a series of hair-raising switchbacks with a vertiginous drop on one side.

Tulcán and the Colombian Border

At 3,000 meters (9,800 ft), Tulcán (pop. 63,000) is the highest provincial capital in the country, considerably colder than Ibarra and Otavalo. Apart from the topiary-filled municipal cemetery, there is little of interest in the town itself. The main reason for coming is the border crossing located 7 kilometers (4.3 mi) to the north—the only recommended place to enter Colombia overland from Ecuador. The city has its rough edges, so take care walking around at night, and don't stray from the center. Wherever you go, make sure you carry your passport, as police checks are common.

The road west from Tulcán follows the Río San Juan (called the Mayasquer in Colombia), which serves as the international border, much of the way to the ocean. As the road passes through Tufiño and Maldonado to El Chical, where it becomes impassable, the vegetation changes from pristine *páramo* to untouched cloud forest and tropical forest. Sadly, for the fledging tourist industry in this area, it's not considered safe. Coca plantations are visible just across the border, and guerrilla groups, drug traffickers, and criminal gangs are present.

SIGHTS

Tulcán's Municipal Cemetery

Located at the northwestern edge of town, Tulcán's **municipal cemetery** (Cotopaxi *y* Ambato) is its principal attraction. Local resident José Franco started the famous topiary works decades ago and is now buried here under an epitaph that calls his creation "a cemetery so beautiful, it invites one to die." Monumental cypresses have been trained and trimmed into figures from Roman, Greek, Inca, and Aztec mythology, interspersed with arches, passageways, and geometric shapes. The cemetery has a security presence during the day and is safe to visit. Needless to say, exercise discretion if a burial procession is in progress. The **municipal tourist office** (tel. 6/298-5760, 8am-6pm Mon.-Fri.) is at the entrance to the cemetery.

FOOD

For Ecuadorian fare, especially fried pork, try **Mama Rosita** (Av. Coral *y* Roberto Grijalva, tel. 6/296-1192, 9am-3pm daily, $2-3). Another good option is ★ **The Forest Coffee** (Cuenca *y* Guayaquil, tel. 98/239-3721, Facebook @Forest.Coffee.Tulcan, 10am-8pm Mon.-Thurs., 10am-11pm Fri.). This charming, friendly café is an oasis of light and color, with a giant mural of a forest on one wall and live music Thursday and Friday evenings. The menu includes sandwiches, Ecuadorian snacks, and set lunches ($2.75).

For vegetarian food, head to ★ **Govinda's** (Calle Sucre *entre* Rocafuerte *y* 9 de Octubre, tel. 99/830-5489), a cozy restaurant serving tasty, healthy, imaginative breakfasts and set lunches ($2.50). Yoga classes are available on-site. Beneath Palacio Imperio Hotel, **Chifa Pack Choy** (Sucre *y* Pichincha, tel. 6/298-0638, 10:30am-10:30pm daily, $5-8) serves up decent Chinese.

ACCOMMODATIONS

Family-owned ★ **Hotel Lumar** (Sucre *entre* Rocafuerte *y* Pichincha, tel. 6/298-0402 or 99/303-6350, www.hotellumar.com, Facebook @HotelLumar, $22 pp, breakfast included until 9am) is the best place in town and excellent value. The 140 clean, modern rooms have very comfortable beds and excellent hot showers. The on-site restaurant is decent (and great for digital nomads, with plug sockets at most tables), though it lacks meat-free options (there is a veggie restaurant just down the street). **Flor de los Andes** (Sucre *y* Junín, tel. 6/296-2390 www.flordelosandes.com, $36 s, $62 d, breakfast included until 9am) is another good option, with helpful service and comfortable rooms. Both hotels have Wi-Fi, cable TV, and parking.

INFORMATION AND SERVICES

The **tourist information office** (Cotopaxi y Ambato, tel. 6/298-5760, 8am-6pm Mon.-Fri.) is at the entrance to the municipal cemetery. **Sumak Ecuador** (Calle Bolívar y Ayacucho, Edificio Muñoz Oficina 504, tel. 6/298-2999 or 99/823-3798, Facebook @sumakecuadortouroperador, sumakecuadortour@ hotmail.com) is a professional, friendly tour operator offering trips in the area, including to nearby lakes and waterfalls, and to Chilmá Bajo and Maldonado west of Tulcán. With a three-day notice, transport and an English-speaking guide can be arranged for those who would like to explore the surrounding area (it is not advisable to do this alone, due to security concerns near the Colombian border and in Esmeraldas province).

Money changers in Parque Ayora are happy to transform your dollars into pesos. Rates are better in Tulcán than at the border or in Colombia. There is a **Banco Pichincha** ATM on Parque de la Independencia. The **police station** is on Avenida Manabí and Guatemala (tel. 6/298-5911).

GETTING THERE AND AROUND
Bus

The *terminal terrestre* (bus terminal) is on Bolívar 1.5 kilometers (0.9 mi) south of the center of Tulcán—a $1 taxi ride, $0.20 bus ride, or 30-minute walk from the main plaza. Being the only northern border town, Tulcán has buses leaving for just about every major city in the country, including Ibarra (3 hours, $3), Quito (5 hours, $7), Guayaquil (16 hours, $23), Ambato (8 hours, $10), Lago Agrio (7 hours, $9), Coca (9 hours, $12), and even an *ejecutivo* bus to Huaquillas (17 hours, $24) if you want to bypass Ecuador altogether and go straight to Peru! More locally, Cooperativa Espejo has buses to El Ángel at 1pm and 4:45pm (1.5 hours, $2).

THE COLOMBIAN BORDER

Seven kilometers (4.3 mi) north of Tulcán, a bridge over the Río Carchi at **Rumichaca** marks the only recommended border crossing with Colombia, open 24 hours. It's necessary to clear both countries' immigration stations, no matter which direction you're crossing, and there is just one line at each immigration station. At the time of writing, the influx of Venezuelans entering Ecuador has increased queues at the border from 15 minutes to several hours, so be prepared to wait. Direct any questions to the **Ecuadorian immigration office** (open 24 hours) located in the CENAF buildings at the bridge.

If you need pesos, it's best to change your money in Parque Ayora in Tulcán, where the money changers are more trustworthy than at the border, with better rates. Official Ecuadorian changers should have photo IDs. Most stores in Ipiales accept dollars and will give change in pesos. There's also an ATM in Ipiales.

Private hire taxis from Tulcán to the border cost $4 one-way. There are also yellow taxis and microbuses waiting in Parque Ayora to take passengers to the border, when full. Taxis ($1 pp) only require four passengers, whereas the microbuses need 16 ($0.75 pp). On the Colombian side, the transport arrangements are the same, with private taxis, shared taxis, and microbuses waiting to make the 13-kilometer (8-mi) trip to Ipiales.

Central Sierra

South of Quito, the central highlands contain

Ecuador's most dramatic Andean scenery and its legendary volcanoes. Stars of the show include the colossal Chimborazo, picture-perfect Cotopaxi, and the tempestuous duo of Sangay and Tungurahua. Much of the time, you'd be forgiven for not realizing that you were in the famous Avenue of the Volcanoes, as the peaks are often wreathed in cloud. However, when one of these giants does choose to reveal its magnificent face, it's a jaw-dropping sight that will likely stop you in your tracks.

Steeped in tradition, myth, and legend, life in parts of the central Sierra continues much as it has for centuries. Near Machachi, *chagras*, or Andean cowboys, still ride the highlands dressed in poncho

Highlights

Look for ★ to find recommended sights, activities, dining, and lodging.

★ **Cotopaxi National Park:** Llamas graze and wild horses gallop on grasslands strewn with wildflowers, overlooked by the picture-perfect cone of the country's most beautiful volcano (page 142).

★ **Laguna Quilotoa:** The luminous turquoise water of this volcanic crater lake is one of Ecuador's most spectacular sights, and the Quilotoa Loop around nearby indigenous villages is an unbeatable hike (page 156).

★ **Ruta de las Cascadas:** Freewheel past a series of waterfalls on the Baños-Puyo road, stopping to zip-line and ride a cable car across the Río Pastaza Gorge, ending with exhilarating close-up views of the thundering Pailón del Diablo waterfall (page 171).

★ **Chimborazo Fauna Reserve:** Hike through the snow to 5,000 meters (16,400 ft), visit a sacred cave, or mine for ice on the flanks of Ecuador's highest peak (page 184).

★ **Alausí:** This charming town and the surrounding countryside have more spectacular experiences to offer than the **Devil's Nose train ride** for which it is famous (page 188).

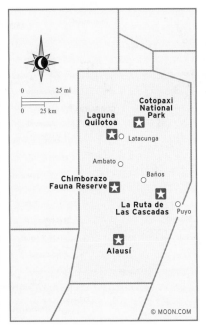

© MOON.COM

Central Sierra

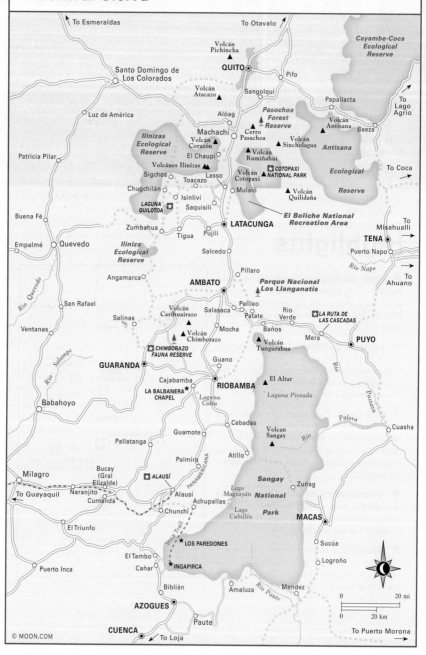

To Esmeraldas

To Otavalo

Cayambe-Coca
Ecological
Reserve

Volcán
Pichincha ▲

QUITO ◉

Pifo

Santo Domingo de
Los Colorados

Sangolquí

To
Lago
Agrio

Luz de América

Volcán
Atacazo ▲

Alóag

Papallacta

Volcán
Antisana ▲

Baeza

Patricia Pilar

*Ilinizas
Ecological
Reserve*

Machachi

Volcán
Corazón ▲

El Chaupí

Volcánes Ilinizas ▲▲

Sigchos

Toacazo

Lasso

Chugchilán

Isinliví

Saquisilí

*Pasochoa
Forest
Reserve* ▲

Cerro
Pasachoa ▲

Volcán
Sincholagua ▲

Antisana

Volcán
Rumiñahui ▲

Volcán
Cotopaxi ▲

✚ **COTOPAXI
NATIONAL PARK**

Ecological

Volcán
Quilidaña ▲

Reserve

To Coca

*LAGUNA
QUILOTOA* ✚

Zumbahua

Tigua

Pujilí

Mulaló

*El Boliche National
Recreation Area*

LATACUNGA ◉

To
Misahualli

*Iliniza
Ecological
Reserve*

Salcedo

TENA ◉

Puerto Napo

Río Napo

Buena Fé

Empalmé

Quevedo

Angamarca

Pillaro

*Parque Nacional
Los Llanganatis* ▲

To
Ahuano

San Rafael

AMBATO ◉

Salinas

Volcán
Carihuairazo ▲

Salasaca

Peliléo

Patate

Río
Verde

✚ *LA RUTA DE
LAS CASCADAS*

Ventanas

Mocha

Baños

Mera

PUYO ◉

Volcán
Chimborazo ▲

✚ *CHIMBORAZO
FAUNA RESERVE*

Guano

Volcán
Tungurahua ▲

Río

GUARANDA ◉

Cajabamba

★ *LA BALBANERA
CHAPEL*

RIOBAMBA ◉

*Laguna
Colta*

El Altar ▲

Laguna Pintada

Pastaza

Palora

Cuasha

Babahoyo

Guamote

Cebadas

Volcan
Sangay ▲

Río

Pallatanga

Palmira

Atillo

Sangay

Zuñag

Milagro

Bucay
(Gral
Elizalde)

✚ *ALAUSÍ*

Naranjito

Cumandá

Alausí

*Lago
Magtayán*

National

MACAS ◉

Chunchi

Achupallas

*Lago
Cubillín*

Park

El Triunfo

Inca Trail

Puerto Inca

★ *LOS PAREDONES*

Sucúa

El Tambo

★ **INGAPIRCA**

Cañar

Logroño

Biblián

Amaluza

Río Paute

Mendez

0   20 mi

0   20 km

AZOGUES ◉

Paute

CUENCA ◉ To Loja

To Puerto Morona

© MOON.COM

and chaps, rounding up bulls. The women of Salasaca can be seen spinning wool as they walk, wearing black felt hats and shawls, their necks strung with beads. Just outside Alausí, shepherds live in mud huts on the windswept *páramo*, walking miles every day with their sheep, faces bronzed by the sun. On the flanks of Chimborazo, the last ice merchant, the *ultimo hielero*, still mines ice by hand before hauling it by mule to Riobamba and selling it to the juice stalls in the market. Not far from the Quilotoa Lake, Kichwa farmers gather at the top of a gorilla-shaped hill to conduct rituals asking for rain. This love of tradition extends to festivals, meaning that this is one of the best regions to participate in authentic Andean celebrations, such as Corpus Christi in Pujilí, La Fiesta de la Mama Negra in Latacunga, and Carnival in Guaranda.

Offering more modern forms of entertainment is Baños, the country's premier adventure sports destination and its best spot for spa treatments. Riobamba is another good base for adventure seekers, and it's the access point for the El Altar volcanic lake, considered one of the most beautiful treks in the country. The colonial town of Alausí is a charming jumping-off point for some truly spectacular hikes, including to the Lagunas de Ozogoche and a viewpoint overlooking the Devil's Nose railway line. The region contains some of the country's most, and least, accessible national parks. Anyone can make the breathless 40-minute walks to the snowy refuges of Cotopaxi and Chimborazo, whereas the fortnight-long expedition looking for Atahualpa's lost treasure in the wilds of Llanganates National Park is for serious outdoor enthusiasts only.

PLANNING YOUR TIME

It's worth spending at least three days in **Baños,** to make the most of the hiking, adventure sports, and spa treatments. It's also a good place from which to organize one- to two-day trips into the Amazon near Puyo, especially for those short on time and/or budget for longer jungle trips.

Both the **Cotopaxi** and **Chimborazo National Parks** can easily be visited as day trips, for hiking, biking, or horseback riding. Latacunga is the best access point for Cotopaxi, with Machachi an alternative. Riobamba is best for accessing Chimborazo, with Guaranda an alternative. Allow 3-4 days for climbing each volcano. Bear in mind that climbers of any glaciated mountain must be accompanied by an accredited, specialized guide and be registered in the Biodiversity Information System (SIB), which was introduced in 2015. Any reputable agency will take care of this formality, so make sure that yours does.

Laguna Quilotoa can be visited on a day trip from Latacunga, a charming city worth an overnight stay. To hike the **Quilotoa Loop,** you'll need 3-5 nights. Latacunga also makes a good jumping-off point for the **Cunucyacu waterfall,** the **Sacharuna hot springs,** and the nearby **polylepis forest,** which can be seen in a day or two.

While there isn't much to see in **Guaranda,** the journey there is stunning, and it's worth passing through to spend a night in **Salinas,** a small town that has become a model for self-sufficiency and community development through a number of successful cooperatives.

It's worth devoting at least three days to **Alausí** and the hikes in the surrounding countryside. There are also several wonderful two- to three-day treks that depart from **Riobamba.**

Previous: Tungurahua is one of Ecuador's most temperamental volcanoes; Cunucyacu waterfall; Laguna Quilotoa.

Machachi

Located in the Valley of the Nine Volcanoes, **Machachi** (elevation 2,950 m/9,680 ft) is a small town an hour south of Quito along the Panamericana. There isn't much to see in the town itself, but, surrounded by majestic peaks, it's a good base for popular climbs, including Cotopaxi, Rumiñahui, the Ilinizas, and Corazón, and for accessing Cotopaxi National Park as a day trip.

This is agricultural country, known for being home to the Andean cowboy, or *chagra*. These skilled horsemen still ride the highlands dressed in poncho, chaps, scarf, and hat, rounding up bulls and driving them into corrals for branding and vaccinating.

SIGHTS

Machachi's central plaza is flanked by an ornate painted **church**, the **Teatro Municipal,** and the **tourist office** (9am-1pm and 2pm-5pm Mon.-Fri.), which can provide maps and information on exploring the surrounding area on horse, foot, and bike. On Sundays, Machachi hosts one of the region's largest **markets,** with people flocking from the surrounding rural communities to sell their fruit, vegetables, eggs, cheeses, and yogurts.

The town comes alive on the third Saturday of July for the **Processional Parade of the Chagra,** where 2,000 cowboys ride through the streets with bands and dancers.

Outside Machachi, 8 kilometers (5 mi) to the southwest is **Bee Farm Shunku** (Rieles del Tren, La Moya, tel. 98/461-7156, www.beefarmecuador.com), a working bee farm that offers tours on weekends with apiculture activities ($25, including breakfast or lunch, reserve one day ahead), honey and pollen products, and honey massages. Intensive, 48-hour apiculture workshops are also available.

FOOD AND ACCOMMODATIONS

The **Central Market** (Amazonas *y* Cordero, 7am-7pm daily) is the place to sample local dishes. ★ **Steak House El Rincón del Valle** (Av. Amazonas *y* Kennedy, tel. 2/231-5908, Facebook @steakvalle) is one of the best restaurants in town and can put together a surprisingly good vegetarian plate. South of town on the Panamericana, **El Café de la Vaca** (Panamericana Sur km 41, 0.5 km/0.3 mi *al norte del* Peaje, tel. 2/231-5012, www.elcafedelavaca.com, 8am-5:30pm daily, $7-16) offers traditional Ecuadorian dishes, with vegetarian options. All to-go packaging is biodegradable, made from sugarcane, and the restaurant doesn't use straws.

By far the best place to stay is ★ **Casa Sakiwa** (Los Quishuares *y* Los Mortiños, tel. 99/266-8619, www.casasakiwa.com, $27.50 s, $40 d, including breakfast). The 20 rooms are clean, modern, and comfortable, with excellent Wi-Fi, breakfast, and hot water, but what really sets the hotel apart is the local family that owns it, who are outstandingly kind, efficient, and helpful. They are an excellent source of information about activities in the area and can book guides and tours, with the most popular being to Cotopaxi National Park.

A full-day **basic tour** ($120 pp for 1 person, $50 pp for 4 people) includes transport from the hotel, a visit to the Limpiopungo Lake, and a walk to the refuge at 4,800 meters (15,750 ft) elevation, from the car park at 4,500 meters (14,750 ft). If conditions are good, it may also be possible to walk beyond the refuge to the glaciers at 5,000 meters (16,400 ft). Another tour includes the same elements but with horseback riding with a local cowboy to the base of Rumiñahui ($140 for 1 person, $180 for 2 people, $220 for 3 people, including lunch). A third option is a tour with Biking Dutchman, where participants descend from the Cotopaxi refuge by bike ($65 pp including lunch). A full-day tour from the hotel to the Quilotoa Lake costs $90-120 per person. It's also possible to book transport and guides for climbing any of the surrounding peaks, including the Ilinizas. The family is equally happy to provide details on how to explore the area independently. Casa Sakiwa gets busy, so it's advisable to book accommodations and tours ahead of time, especially in high season (late May to mid-September).

If Casa Sakiwa is full, a decent alternative is **Hostería Chiguac** (Calle Los Caras y Cristóbal Colón, tel. 2/231-0396, www.hosteriachiguac.com, $16.50 pp, including breakfast).

GETTING THERE AND AROUND

From Quito, the **Cooperatives Carlos Brito** (tel. 2/231-5192) and **Mejía** (tel. 2/231-5014) operate direct buses from Quitumbe and Trebol (near Old Town) 5am-9pm weekdays and until 6:30pm on weekends ($0.75, 55 minutes). Alternatively, any bus running north or south along the Panamericana can drop you on the western edge of Machachi, leaving a 1-kilometer (0.6-mi) walk or taxi ride into the center. Buses back to Quito leave Machachi from two blocks west of the plaza.

ILINIZA ECOLOGICAL RESERVE

The 149,900-hectare (370,400-acre) **Iliniza Ecological Reserve** (http://areasprotegidas. ambiente.gob.ec) encompasses an incredible variety of ecosystems, from Andean *páramo* to subtropical forests. Established in 1996, the reserve spans the provinces of Cotopaxi, Los Ríos, Pichincha, and Santo Domingo de los Tsáchilas and is home to pumas, Andean bears, and highland wolves. Its main attractions are **Laguna Quilotoa** (see *Latacunga and Vicinity*), the twin peaks of **Iliniza Norte** and **Iliniza Sur,** the **Corazón volcano,** the **Cunucyacu waterfall,** and **Sacharuna thermal waters.**

Climbing the Ilinizas

According to indigenous tradition, **Iliniza Norte** (5,126 m/16,818 ft, also known as **Tioniza**) and **Iliniza Sur** (5,263 m/17,267 ft), the country's eighth and sixth highest peaks, respectively, were once young lovers. Tioniza, the beautiful daughter of the Zarabullo tribe's chief, fled with her forbidden love from the enemy Insilivies tribe to live in hiding on the *páramo*. When her father discovered their whereabouts, he sent his sorcerers after the couple, and they were turned into mountains.

Iliniza Norte is known for being less difficult to climb and, in good conditions, can be tackled by anyone with decent hiking and scrambling skills. In snow/ice conditions, however, it can be challenging, even for experienced climbers. While it is not compulsory to climb with an accredited guide, it is highly recommended, as is wearing a helmet. Iliniza Sur has permanent snow cover, as it receives greater humidity from clouds coming in from the coast. Climbers must be accompanied by an accredited, specialized guide and be registered in the Biodiversity Information System (SIB), which was introduced in 2015 to log the identities of all climbers on glaciated mountains. Any reputable agency will take care of this formality.

The Ilinizas are accessed via the village of **El Chaupi,** 15 kilometers (9.3 mi) south of Machachi. Buses leave Machachi every half hour from outside the TIA supermarket (45 minutes) by the Central Market. From El Chaupi, it's 9 kilometers (5.6 mi) to the Ilinizas parking lot, **La Virgen,** at 3,900 meters (12,800 ft), where camping is available (bring everything with you). From La Virgen, it's a three-hour signposted hike to the **Nuevos Horizontes refuge** (tel. 98/133-3483, www.ilinizasclimbing.com, $15 pp) at 4,700 meters (15,420 ft). Built right on the saddle between the two peaks, it's well located for climbing either. Facilities include bunk beds and mattresses (bring your own sleeping bag), a kitchen, living room, fireplace, electricity, outdoor toilets, and running water. Meals are available for $7.50. For a $5 fee (per tent) campers are allowed to use the refuge's facilities.

In El Chaupi, head to the **Refugio Los**

Ilinizas Office (tel. 98/133-3483, www.ilinizasclimbing.com), at the north side of the park, to organize two-day climbs of Iliniza Sur ($150 pp) or Iliniza Norte ($120 pp); a one-day climb of Norte ($80); transport to La Virgen ($15); horseback riding ($35/day); and horses to carry luggage. The office is managed by the same people as the Nuevos Horizontes refuge. The telephone number stated is for Fernando Isa, who speaks English. A good place to stay in El Chaupi is **La Llovizna Lodge** (tel. 9/969-9068, https://lalloviznalodge.weebly.com, $12-19 pp), just past the church, which has warm bedrooms, fireplaces, and a shared kitchen. The owner, Vladimir Gallo, can arrange guided hikes, climbs, and horses.

Climbing Volcán Corazón

A short distance west of Machachi across the Panamericana sits this extinct volcano, first climbed in 1738 by Charles Marie de La Condamine while on a break from measuring the planet. At 4,788 meters (15,709 ft), **Corazón** is a challenging day climb, consisting mostly of uphill hiking through grassy fields, with some moderate but exposed rock scrambling for the last 500 meters (1,640 ft). There are two ways to summit Corazón. Starting from Andes Alpes hostel in El Chaupi, it's a tough 8- to 10-hour round-trip hike. The alternative is to get a *camioneta* to the entrance of the reserve, from where it is a 4- to 6-hour round-trip hike. There is minimal signage. For peace of mind, go with a guide.

Recommended agencies for climbing the Ilinizas or Corazón are **Ecuador Eco Adventure** (tel. 99/831-1282, www.ecuadorecoadventures.com) and **Ilinizas Climbing** (tel. 2/367-4125, https://ilinizasclimbing.com).

Cunucyacu and Sacharuna

Adjoining the Iliniza Ecological Reserve on the slopes of Iliniza Sur is a 500-hectare

(1,235-acre) section of privately owned, pristine *páramo*. It has three stellar attractions: a millennial **polylepis forest,** the **Cunucyacu waterfall,** and the **Sacharuna hot springs.**

Covered in lichen and moss, the ancient trees of the polylepis forest are worthy of Tolkien. Nearby, the crystalline waters of the Sacharuna hot springs are steaming as they rush out from fern-covered rocks into a natural pool, perfect for bathing at 27°C (81°F). The hot spring feeds the Cunucyacu waterfall, which has cut a deep gully into the rocks, coloring them gold with minerals.

The family that has owned this land for generations has recently converted part of their home into a guest lodge, ★ **Sacharuna Lodge** (tel. 99/247-0691, Facebook @Casa DeCampo sacharuna Hacienda LaVaqueria, $60 s/d, including breakfast). The lodge offers guided tours of the polylepis forest, waterfalls, and hot springs on foot, horseback, or mountain bike.

With views of Tungurahua, Cotopaxi, and the Ilinizas on clear days, the lodge has four guest bedrooms and a living room with a fireplace. The decor is rustic, stylish, and comfortable, with all furniture made by local artisans. Amenities include Wi-Fi and solar-powered hot water (with gas/electric backup). A biodigester is planned, to cook with gas from animal waste. The hacienda is a working farm, with cattle, organic Andean crops, and beehives. In addition to visiting the forest, waterfall, and hot springs, guests can participate in farming activities; hike to a nearby lake; and enjoy nighttime torch-lit walks and bonfires. Lunch and dinner are available for $5-12, with vegetarian options. The lodge makes tea made from wild herbs as well as jam and wine from native fruits, including the endemic *rundubelines*.

To get to the Sacharuna Lodge, take a bus from Latacunga to Pastocalle (40-50 minutes), then hire a *camioneta* ($5), or contact the owner, David Larrea (tel. 99/247-0691) to request a map or help with transport.

1: Andean cowboys, or *chagras,* in Machachi;
2: Iliniza Sur and Iliniza Norte

Machachi to Latacunga

★ COTOPAXI NATIONAL PARK

Spanning the provinces of Cotopaxi, Napo, and Pichincha, Ecuador's top mainland national park is second only to the Galápagos in the annual number of visitors, and it's easy to see why. Just 50 kilometers (31 mi) south of Quito, 32,255 hectares (79,700 acres) of *páramo* enclose one of the most beautiful volcanoes in the Americas, with its picture-perfect cone and permanent mantle of snow. Llamas graze and wild horses gallop on grasslands strewn with wildflowers, including clouds of purple lupines. Higher up, the landscape is barren and lunar, a stark canvas from which to marvel at the colossus that is **Volcán Cotopaxi,** whose name means "Neck of the Moon."

At 5,897 meters (19,347 ft), this is Ecuador's second tallest peak after Chimborazo, and one of the world's highest active volcanoes. It's often shrouded in cloud, but the weather is ever-shifting and, when Cotopaxi does choose to show her face, it's an awe-inspiring sight. July to September tends to be the clearest time of year to visit but can be windy. Since the beginning of the Spanish conquest, Cotopaxi has presented five major eruptive periods: 1532-1534, 1742-1744, 1766-1768, 1853-1854, and 1877-1880. Most recently, it rumbled into life in April 2015 by emitting a 10-kilometer (6.2-mi) ash plume, culminating in an eruption in August 2015 that caused earth tremors in the nearby towns. Gas and steam were released over the next several weeks, along with thousands of tons of ash that covered the surrounding countryside and even reached Quito.

There are several ways to explore **Cotopaxi National Park** (tel. 3/305-3596, http://areasprotegidas.ambiente.gob.ec, Facebook @ Parque Nacional Cotopaxi, free). Entrance is permitted 8am-3pm daily, although visitors can remain within the park until 6pm. ID is required to enter. If you have your own four-wheel-drive vehicle, you can drive around the signposted tracks that lead to the various attractions. From the main entrance (**Control Sur**), the road through the park curves in a semicircle north around Volcán Cotopaxi. As it heads northeast, 10 kilometers (6.2 mi) from the entrance is a small **museum** (8am-3pm daily, free) with an exhibition on the geology, history, flora, and fauna of the park.

Shortly beyond the museum, there's a path leading to **Laguna Limpiopungo,** a shallow lake at 3,800 meters (12,470 ft) elevation whose reeds provide a habitat for several species of birds. The volcano is sometimes spectacularly reflected in the lake's surface. From the lake there is a signposted 90-minute easy **hike** past a **natural spring** and a **viewing point** to the **Control Norte,** as well as two circular **cycle routes,** one to the natural spring (3 hours), the other to the **Santo Domingo Lake** (4-5 hours). A trail leads around the lake to the northwest for access to **Rumiñahui.**

Shortly beyond that trail, another track heads 9 kilometers (5.6 mi) south to the parking lot for the **José Rivas Refuge** (tel. 3/223-3129 or 98/790-8704, Facebook @refugiocotopaxijoseribas) at 4,800 meters (15,750 ft), which is open to climbers and non-climbers alike. Although the walk from the parking lot to the refuge is only 1 kilometer (0.6 mi), it takes most people 45 minutes to an hour, due to the altitude and level of difficulty. It's a steep walk on rocky paths surrounded by snow. If conditions are good, it's possible to walk beyond the refuge for another hour to the glaciers at 5,000 meters (16,400 ft). If you're planning on doing the walk, bring water, snacks (especially chocolate, which is an excellent source of energy at high altitude), sunglasses, warm clothes, and sunblock. Built in 1971 and remodeled in 2009, the refuge is warm and welcoming, with hot drinks and

Cotopaxi's Dark Secret

Once upon a time, an old woman called María Juana Veracruz sought a wealthy wife for her son. Upon finding a suitable candidate, the marriage was quickly arranged, but the woman and her son mysteriously disappeared during the celebrations, and the bride was not seen again. A few months later in a different village, the residents were invited to celebrate the nuptials of the same young man whose mother had, it seems, found an even wealthier wife for her offspring. Once again, however, the duo fled following the ceremony. Upon the man's third wedding, the local *yachaks* (shamans, or wise men) went looking for the suspicious pair before the wedding feast and discovered a horrifying sight: María Juana Veracruz chopping up her son's new bride and cooking the pieces in a cauldron. In unison, the *yachaks* cast a spell on the old woman—"If you cook a woman in a cauldron, you shall be a cauldron!"—and they turned her into a vessel of such boiling fury that even to this day, she hurls torrential rain and freezing temperatures on everyone around her. Though most refer to her as Cotopaxi, older residents can still be heard entreating with her, "Mama Juana, please don't be angry!" "Mama Juana, we'll be good!" "Mama Juana, please don't destroy our crops!"

This story was compiled over three years by a young Latacungan historian, Carlos Sandoval, who collected oral testimonies from several older residents in various parts of the province, who all told the same dark tale.

food available. Be aware that prices are high because all supplies are carried in on foot. A hot chocolate costs $2 (worth it after the walk) and a corn cob with cheese is $5.

On the eastern edge of the park, 15 kilometers (9.3 mi) beyond the lake, are the oval ruins of **El Salitre,** formerly an Inca *pucara* (fortress), abandoned soon after the arrival of the Spanish.

Tours and Guides

Those without their own transport can take a tour offered by the local guides who wait with trucks by the two main access points to the park. The standard three-hour tour ($50 1 person, may be negotiable to $40; $25 pp for 2 people; and $20 pp for 3 people) includes three stops: the museum; the refuge parking lot (your guide might accompany you while you walk to the refuge or glacier and back, or may wait with the car); and the Limpiopungo Lake. Just driving around the park is an experience, especially when the volcano shows its face, and the guides are happy to stop for you to take photos. Be aware that they speak little English.

For a tour that includes transport to and from the park, or additional activities such as downhill mountain biking or horseback riding, go with an organized tour. From Machachi, the best option is **Casa Sakiwa** (tel. 99/266-8619, www.casasakiwa.com), which offers the same standard tour plus return transport from Machachi ($120 pp for 1 person, $50 pp for 4 people). Another option includes the same elements but with horseback riding with a local cowboy to the base of Rumiñahui ($140 for 1 person, $180 for 2 people, $220 for 3 people, including lunch). **Biking Dutchman** (http://www.bikingdutchman.com) in Quito offers a tour of the park plus a downhill bike ride from the refuge, which can be booked directly with them or via Casa Sakiwa in Machachi ($65 pp including lunch and transport from Quito or Machachi).

In Latacunga, **Cotopaxi Travel** (Guayaquil 6-4 y Sánchez de Orellana, tel. 98/133-3483, www.cotopaxi-travel.com); **Neiges** (Sánchez de Orellana 17-38 & Guayaquil, tel. 3/281-1199 or 99/826-5567, http://neigestours.wixsite.com/neiges); and **Greivag Turismo** (Plaza Comercial Santo Domingo, Calles Guayaquil y Sánchez de Orellana, tel. 3/281-0510 or 99/864-7308, www.greivagturismo.com) all offer the standard tour, with transport and lunch, for $35-100 per person, depending on the number of people.

Climbing Volcán Cotopaxi

Cotopaxi is Ecuador's most popular high-altitude climb because of its relative simplicity. Crevasses are usually large and obvious, making it mostly an uphill slog. However, less than half of those who attempt the summit actually reach it. You need to be in good physical condition, be fully acclimatized, be accompanied by an accredited guide, and have a certain amount of luck with the conditions. Technical equipment is necessary: ice axes, crampons, ropes, marker wands, and crevasse rescue gear.

As with any peak over 5,000 meters (16,400 ft), acclimatization is essential. If you've been staying in Quito at 2,850 meters (9,350 ft), this is unlikely to be sufficient preparation (although you may be lucky). Ideally you should trek and sleep at around 4,000 meters (13,000 ft) for a couple of days or, even better, do a practice climb of a smaller peak such as Iliniza Norte or Rumiñahui before attempting Cotopaxi. All mountaineering tour agencies offer acclimatization climbs.

Although Cotopaxi can be climbed year-round, the best months are usually December and January. The February-April period is often clear and dry as well. August and September are also good but windy.

Most climbers make their bid for the summit from the **José Rivas Refuge** (tel. 3/223-3129 or 98/790-8704, Facebook @ refugiocotopaxijoseribas, $32 pp, including breakfast and dinner). The refuge has bunk beds, toilets, running water, a fireplace, a café, and lockers for your gear while you climb. A night's stay is usually included in the price of a tour booked with an agency. Camping outside the refuge is not permitted, and neither is use of the kitchen. Lunch is available for $7.

Catch a few hours of sleep before starting to climb around midnight or 1am. It takes 6-10 hours to reach the summit from the refuge, and the route contains smoking fumaroles reeking of sulfur. The views over the neighboring volcanoes are spectacular. The summit is actually the northern rim of the crater, which is rounded and measures approximately 480 meters (1,575 ft) wide. The descent takes 3-6 hours.

The park has issued the following requirements for those wishing to summit Cotopaxi. Any reputable agency will fulfill these criteria, so make sure that yours has. A reservation is required at one of the three accommodation options within the park: the José Rivas Refuge, the Hostería Tambopaxi Lodge (www. tambopaxi.com), or La Rinconada Camping Area (tel. 98/424-9333). Those climbing with a tour operator must be registered in the Biodiversity Information System (SIB), which was introduced in 2015 to log the identities of all climbers on glaciated mountains. Climbers must be accompanied by an accredited, specialized guide. Members of mountaineering clubs and qualified individuals must apply for permission to enter the protected area at least 15 days in advance by emailing gregorio. nunez@ambiente.gob.ec. Mountaineering clubs must submit a copy of the membership card of each climber and a certificate to show that the club is legally recognized and registered. Entry to the park for climbers is permitted 8am-5pm daily.

Ecuador Eco Adventure (tel. 99/831-1282, www.ecuadorecoadventure.com, ecuadorecoadventure@gmail.com) in Riobamba offers a four-day Cotopaxi climb including acclimatization hikes (4 days, $495 1 person, $375 pp 2 people), as well as a combined Cotopaxi and Chimborazo climbing tour (5 days, $960 1 person, $750 pp 2 people). Prices include a night in Riobamba the night before departure, all equipment, permits, accommodations, and most meals. In Latacunga, contact **Cotopaxi Travel** (Guayaquil 6-4 y Sánchez de Orellana, tel. 98/133-3483, www.cotopaxi-travel.com).

1: wild horses and lupines in the Cotopaxi National Park; 2: climbers descending the red sand towards José Rivas Refuge; 3: mountain biking in Cotopaxi National Park

Climbing Volcán Rumiñahui

This peak, 13 kilometers (8 mi) northwest of Cotopaxi, was named after Atahualpa's bravest general, who famously hid the huge Inca ransom after Atahualpa's death and refused to give up its whereabouts when tortured by the Spanish. **Rumiñahui** (4,712 m/15,459 ft), officially dormant but most probably extinct, actually has three peaks. It's a relatively straightforward climb, combining an uphill hike with a bit of scrambling, but because the quality of rock can be poor, a rope and climbing protection are recommended for the more exposed stretches. While it is not compulsory to climb with an accredited guide, it is highly recommended. Contact the same agencies as for the Cotopaxi climb.

The east side of Rumiñahui is reached through Cotopaxi National Park along tracks that skirt Laguna Limpiopungo to the north or south. A path toward the central peak is clearly visible along a well-defined ridge. From the lake to the base is about a two-hour hike, and it's possible to camp along the way. The south peak involves some moderately technical rock climbing (class 5.5). The IGM *Machachi* and *Sincholagua* 1:50,000 maps cover this area.

Food and Accommodations

Located 6 kilometers (3.7 mi) from the main park entrance, **Cuello de Luna** (El Chasqui, Panamericana Sur km 44, tel. 3/330-53898 or 99/970-0330, www.cuellodeluna.com, dorm $20 pp, $54-75 s, $66-94 d, including breakfast) has rooms with private bathrooms and fireplaces. The hotel can arrange transport, tours, and horseback riding.

The only hotel within the national park, with great views of Cotopaxi, is **Tambopaxi** (tel. 2/600-0365, www.tambopaxi.com, camping $16 pp, dorm $20 pp, $91 s, $115 d, including breakfast). Rooms have wood-burning stoves, and there is a decent restaurant using organic ingredients with vegetarian options. Horseback riding and hiking tours are available. The hotel is certified by Smart Voyager,

a UNESCO- recognized program for environmental sustainability.

Four kilometers (2.5 mi) from the northern entrance of the park is **Hacienda El Porvenir** (tel. 2/600-9533, www.tierradelvolcan.com, $43-113 s, $54-170 d, including breakfast). Accommodation ranges from thatched huts with shared bathrooms to suites. Tours are offered on foot, mountain bike, and horseback. Camping is available for $6 per person (not including breakfast). The hacienda was a finalist for Ecuador's Leading Green Hotel in the 2017 World Travel Awards.

Off the beaten path is the ★ **Secret Garden Cotopaxi** (tel. 9/357-2714, www.secretgardencotopaxi.com, dorm $40 pp, $60-80 s, $80-125 d), sister hotel of the backpacker favorite in Quito. This ecolodge is set in the foothills of Pasochoa, near the village of Pedregal, overlooking the national park. Rooms range from mixed dorms to hobbit houses and private cabins. Rates include three meals, snacks, drinks, a tour to a waterfall, and use of the Jacuzzi. Daily shuttles ($5) are available from Quito (2 hours) and Machachi (1 hour), as are treks and trips to the nearby peaks.

Getting There and Around

There are two ways to enter the park. The South Entrance or **Control Sur** is the main gate, located 25 minutes south of Machachi along the Panamericana. The North Entrance or **Control Norte,** accessed via the village of El Pedregal to the north of the park, is lesser used, but the route is more scenic. Those planning on arranging a tour with a local guide upon arrival at the park are advised to use the main entrance, especially if hoping to meet fellow travelers to share the cost.

To get to the South Entrance from Quito, take a bus from the Quitumbe terminal heading to Latacunga (or any destination south of the park along the Panamericana) and ask the driver to let you off at the park, after about a 90-minute drive. From any destination south of the park, flag down any bus heading north to Quito along the Panamericana and ask the driver to let you off.

To get to the South Entrance from Machachi, head to the Panamericana on foot, by taxi, or by bus (it's 1 km/0.6 mi from the town center), then flag down any bus going south. Ask the driver to let you off at the park ($0.75).

Local guides with *camionetas* wait at the Panamericana offering tours of the park and transport to the South Entrance, which is another 10 minutes' drive.

To get to the North Entrance, first take a bus to Machachi. From Quito, the **Cooperatives Carlos Brito** (tel. 2/231-5192) and **Mejía** (tel. 2/231-5014) operate buses from Quitumbe and Trebol (near Old Town) 5am-9pm weekdays and until 6:30pm on weekends ($0.75, 55 minutes). Alternatively, any bus running south or north along the Panamericana can drop you at the entrance to Machachi, marked by a statue of a rider on a horse, leaving a 1-kilometer (0.6-mi) walk/taxi into town. A block north of the main square in Machachi, take a bus to Pedregal with **Transportes Machachenas.** Buses leave at 7am, 11am, and 4pm and take 45 minutes. Alternatively, take a *camioneta* from Machachi to El Pedregal ($15) or onwards into the park. Guides wait in El Pedregal to offer tours of the park and transport to the entrance, which is another 25 minutes' drive.

Latacunga and Vicinity

Just 30 kilometers (19 mi) from Volcán Cotopaxi, **Latacunga** (2,750 m/9,020 ft) is the capital of Cotopaxi Province. It's an attractive, pleasant destination with sufficient historical, architectural, and cultural assets to justify its status as a Patrimonial City of the Nation. Traditionally, Latacunga is known for producing ground barley, or *máchica*, and its inhabitants are affectionately known as *mashca pupos*, literally *ground barley navels*. The joke is that they eat so much *máchica* that it's even found in their belly buttons.

Many visitors just use Latacunga as a jumping off point for Cotopaxi or Quilotoa, but it's worth spending a day exploring the historical district and taking a tour of the barley-toasting furnaces and mills in the neighborhood of Brazales.

Latacunga was founded in 1584 when three Spanish *marqueses* (Villa Orellana, Maenza, and Miraflores) oversaw the colonization of the city's 30,000 indigenous inhabitants and built extensive estates, funded by a brutal system of forced labor. Aside from the well-preserved colonial squares, villas, and churches, the historical district is notable for its wide cobbled streets, which are paved with volcanic rock from Cotopaxi. In contrast, the sidewalks are extremely narrow, which dates back to the days when indigenous people had to walk in single file to be counted by the Spanish.

Latacunga is a safe city and a good transport hub due to its central location.

SIGHTS

Latacunga's attractive main square, **Parque Vicente León,** is flanked on the south side by a whitewashed **cathedral** with carved wooden doors and the elegant **town hall** on the east side. A couple of blocks north is another impressive church, **Iglesia Santo Domingo,** overlooking the square of the same name. Another block north is the **Iglesia La Merced**, home of the Virgin who is said to have saved the city from volcanic destruction, and in whose honor the Mama Negra festival is held. Near La Merced is the **Casa de los Marqueses de Maenza,** with a central courtyard garden. A few blocks southwest of the center, **Parque La Filantrópia** is flanked by the grand old **Hospital General.**

Just north of Parque Vicente León, **Calle Luis Fernando Vivero** and **Calle Padre Salcedo** are two charming cobbled

Latacunga

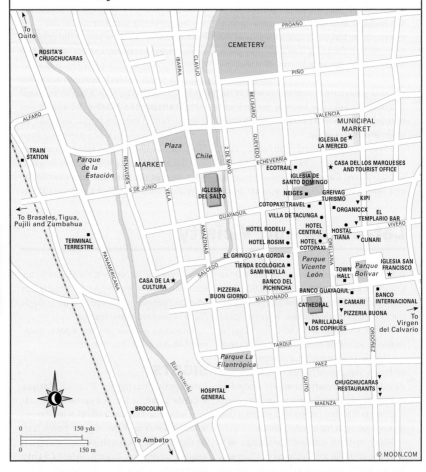

To Quito
ROSITA'S CHUGCHUCARAS
CEMETERY
PROAÑO
PIÑO
IBARRA
CLAVIJO
BELISARIO
QUEVEDO
2 DE MAYO
VALENCIA
MUNICIPAL MARKET
IGLESIA DE LA MERCED ★
ALFARO
ECHEVERRÍA
CASA DEL LOS MARQUESES AND TOURIST OFFICE ★
ECOTRAIL ■
Plaza Chile
TRAIN STATION
Parque de la Estación
MARKET
BENAVIDES
5 DE JUNIO
VELA
IGLESIA DEL SALTO
IGLESIA DE SANTO DOMINGO
NEIGES ■
GREIVAG TURISMO
KIPI
COTOPAXI TRAVEL ■
ORGANICCX ■
EL TEMPLARIO BAR
VILLA DE TACUNGA ■
VIVERO
GUAYAQUIL
AMAZONAS
HOTEL RODELU ■
HOTEL CENTRAL ■
HOSTAL TIANA
CUNARI
To Brasales, Tigua, Pujili and Zumbahua
TERMINAL TERRESTRE
PANAMERICANA
HOTEL ROSIM ■
HOTEL COTOPAXI ■
ORELLANA
EL GRINGO Y LA GORDA ■
Parque Vicente León
Parque Bolivar
IGLESIA SAN FRANCISCO ★
TIENDA ECOLÓGICA SAMI WAYLLA ■
TOWN HALL
SALCEDO
CASA DE LA CULTURA ★
BANCO DEL PICHINCHA ■
PIZZERIA BUON GIORNO
BANCO GUAYAQUIL ■
CAMARI ■
BANCO INTERNACIONAL ■
MALDONADO
CATHEDRAL
PIZZERIA BUONA ■
To Virgen del Calvario
PARILLADAS LOS COPIHUES ■
ORDÓÑEZ
TARQUI
Río Cutuchi
Parque La Filantrópica
PAEZ
QUITO
CHUGCHUCARAS RESTAURANTS
HOSPITAL GENERAL ■
MAENZA
BROCOLINI ■
0   150 yds
0   150 m
To Ambato

© MOON.COM

pedestrian streets lined with well-kept colonial buildings, some of which are now little cafés and shops.

For the best views of the town and surrounding valley, head to the **Mirador de la Virgen del Calvario.** To get here, go east on Maldonado, climb the steps, and walk to the left, up Oriente.

Markets

Plaza Chile, better known as El Salto, a couple of blocks northwest of the center, hosts Latacunga's **market,** which spills down almost to the river on the busiest days, Tuesday and Sunday. To the east, the daily **municipal market** borders the Iglesia La Merced between Valencia and Echeverría.

For organic and fair trade products head to **Camari** (Sánchez de Orellana 14-49 *y* General Maldonado, www.camari.org), **Tienda Ecológica Sami Waylla** (Padre Salcedo *y* Quito), or **Organiccx** (Calle Sánchez de Orellana *y* Pasaje Luis Fernando Vivero, tel. 96/824-2343, Facebook @OrganicCotopaxi).

Museums

Built on the site of an old Jesuit flour mill along the river, the **Casa de la Cultura** (Maldonado *y* Antonio Vela, 8am-noon and 2pm-6pm Tues.-Fri., free) contains part of the old water mill as well as an ethnographic collection of ceramics, paintings, dolls in indigenous festival costumes, and colonial artifacts.

ENTERTAINMENT AND EVENTS

Latacunga hosts one of the biggest and most colorful festivals in the Sierra, the Fiesta de la Santísima Virgen de la Merced (Sept. 23-24), known familiarly as **Fiesta de La Mama Negra.** This unique and flamboyant celebration combines not only Spanish and indigenous traditions, but also African elements, following the importation of slaves in the 14th century.

During the festivities, a number of key personages (a Spanish captain, a Moorish king, a standard bearer, the Archangel Gabriel, and, finally, La Mama Negra herself) parade through the streets, each accompanied by his or her own entourage of musicians, dancers in traditional indigenous dress, and other colorful characters. Among these are verse tellers, who recite comical limericks, and whip-wielding *camisonas* (men dressed as women). *Huacos* (healers), dressed in masks and white robes, act out cleansing rituals by blowing smoke and aguardiente on the spectators while invoking the spirits of the nearby volcanoes. The celebration culminates in the arrival on horseback of La Mama Negra, a blackened man dressed as a gaudy woman, who bears dolls to represent her children and sprays the crowd with donkey milk and water.

While the roots of many of its elements are unknown, the festival itself originated in 1742 following the eruption of Cotopaxi, when Latacungans carried a statue of the Virgen de la Merced on their shoulders to the place where the Mirador de la Virgen del Calvario now lies, praying and asking for her help. According to legend, the Virgin raised her hand and held back the fury of the volcano,

thus saving the city from destruction. The grateful residents swore to commemorate the event annually. The statue resides in the Iglesia La Merced.

There are actually two Mama Negra celebrations: the more authentic, raucous people's festival, held September 23-24, and the state-sponsored version, held on the Saturday prior to November 11.

There isn't much nightlife in Latacunga, but one of the few late-night weekend hangouts is **El Templario** (Pasaje Luis Fernando Vivero, tel. 99/737-9154, Facebook @eltemplariolatacunga, noon-midnight Mon.-Thurs., noon-2am Fri., and 4pm-2am Sat.), which serves craft beer, snacks, and sandwiches.

RECREATION AND TOURS

Carlos Sandoval (tel. 99/843-8530, Facebook @la.tacungahistorytours) is a historian and guide who offers English-speaking tours of the city and nearby attractions. Part of a group of young people keen to show visitors that Latacunga is more than a jumping-off point for Cotopaxi and Quilotoa, his passion for the city and its legends is contagious. His one-hour tour of the historical center ($10) and 90-minute tour of church cupolas and museums ($20) include an ice cream and a cocktail or drink of *máchica*. He also offers a tour to Tilipulo, a 400-year-old hacienda 12 kilometers (7.5 mi) from Latacunga ($25 including transport). Upon request, Carlos can give the tours in the costume of a marquis and can even provide costumes for visitors! Book at least a day in advance. Guests at the Villa Tacvunga hotel receive a discount.

Brazales is a neighborhood of Latacunga that traditionally produces the city's signature product, *máchica,* or ground barley. Before being ground, the barley or *cebada* is toasted on a giant flat metal pan over a wood furnace, known as a *tiesto.* Where there were previously 24 *tiestos de cebada* in Brazales, now there are just 5. The **Ruta de la Máchica** (tel. 99/289-9824, Facebook @Harika, Fri.-Sun., $12 including transport) is a tour of two of these, plus a tasting session. By offering these tours, founder Adrian Cruz, whose family has had their furnace for generations, is hoping to keep this most Latacungan of traditions alive. Indeed a visit to his grandparents' *tiesto* is a special experience, with the roaring flames, the crackling of the barley as it is stirred, and the smell of the toasting grains. Once toasted, the barley is ground and bagged for sale. As well as traditional *máchica* products, including a comforting drink made with milk, raw sugar, and cinnamon, the tour includes a tasting of El Mashcazo, a delicious *máchica* liquor made with local aguardiente and sold in recycled wine bottles. Adrian hopes to revitalize the whole neighborhood with this project. He offers the tour to locals, especially youngsters; distributes barley seeds to the community and buys their crops; and is starting a program to collect local organic waste and use it to create compost.

There are four recommended tour agencies in Latacunga. **Ecotrail** (Calle Quito 17-44 *y* Juan Abel Echeverría, tel. 3/223-3125 or 99/945-1401, https://ecotrail.com.ec) offers kayaking in Quilotoa Lake ($25); biking trips from Quilotoa ($30); hiking around Quilotoa with camping at Shalala ($29); horseback riding on various routes near Quilotoa ($27); a full-day trip in an open-sided bus to La Maná, with a hike to a waterfall and visits to small-scale local producers; and a day visit to Posada del Tigua ($40). They work with local eco- and community tourism projects, and also offer tours farther afield, in the rest of the Sierra, the coast, the Amazon, and the Galápagos.

Cotopaxi Travel (Guayaquil 6-4 *y* Sánchez de Orellana, tel. 98/133-3483, www.cotopaxi-travel.com) is owned by mountain guide Fernando Isa, who also manages the Nuevos Horizontes climbing refuge in the Ilinizas. He offers climbing, hiking, and trekking in the central Sierra, as well as tours to other parts of the country and South America. A page on the website allows visitors to join popular local climbs and hikes, great for lone travelers.

Locally owned and operated, **Neiges** (Sánchez de Orellana 17-38 *y* Guayaquil, tel. 3/281-1199 or 99/826-5567, http://neigestours.wixsite.com/neiges) offers hiking and climbing tours to Quilotoa, the Ilinizas, Cayambe, Cotopaxi, and Chimborazo. **Greivag Turismo** (Plaza Comercial Santo Domingo, Calles Guayaquil *y* Sánchez de Orellana, tel. 3/281- 0510 or 99/864-7308, www.greivagturismo.com) offers hiking tours to Quilotoa, Iliniza Norte, and Cotopaxi, plus coastal tours to Montañita.

FOOD

The best-known local specialties are *chugchucara*, a fried dish with chunks of pork, crispy skins, potatoes, plantains, and corn; and *allullas* (ah-YU-yahs), doughy cookies made with cheese and pork fat. The best places to find these are on Quijano *y* Ordoñez, also known as **Calle de los Chugchucaras,** or at **Chugchucaras Rosita** (Eloy Alfaro *y* General Montero, tel. 3/281-3468 or 99/565-0873, Facebook @ChugchucarasRosita, 9:30am-7:30pm daily, $8.50). For other local cuisine, try the **Mercado El Salto,** a couple of blocks northwest of Parque Vicente León.

Owned by a friendly local woman who speaks fluent English, **Cunani** (Pasaje Luis Fernando Vivero, tel. 93/280-9214, http://cunani.weebly.com, 8:30am-1pm and 5pm-9pm Mon.-Fri., $1-7) is a delightful place offering local specialties such as *empanadas de morocho* (filled corn pastry), *humita* (a steamed savory corn bun), and *quimbolito* (a steamed cake, wrapped in a leaf), alongside fresh salad straight from the garden, homemade ravioli, and waffles. There are plenty of vegetarian options. Drinks include *canelazo*, mulled wine, and hot chocolate made from Ecuador's famous Pacari brand, with optional *máchica* (ground barley) for a really Latacungan drink. Cunani uses organic ingredients, supports small-scale producers, and

1: barley toasted on a furnace in Latacunga's Brazales neighborhood; **2:** local youths dressed as healers during Fiesta de La Mama Negra

showcases handicrafts made by local and traveling artisans.

★ **El Gringo y la Gorda** (Padre Salcedo *y* Quito, tel. 3/223-3043, Facebook @CafeElGringoyLaGorda, 2pm-10pm Tues.-Sat., $4.50-15) occupies one side of the courtyard of the Casa de los Marqueses de Maenza, which was renovated by the restaurant's owner, a friendly local who spent time in the United States and speaks fluent English (hence the name). The restaurant offers traditional Ecuadorian dishes alongside sandwiches made with artisanal bread. There is a separate vegetarian menu, available upon request. The ingredients are sourced locally.

★ **Kipi** (Quijano Ordóñez 6-73 *y* Guayaquil, tel. 99/813-7160, Facebook @ KipiNatural, 7am-8pm Mon.-Fri., 8am-7pm Sun., $4-6) is a charming café offering healthy organic food. Veggie and vegan options are available, including a version of the local specialty, *chugchucara*, and some tasty meat substitutes made with *zambo* (squash) seeds. Another specialty is chicken cooked in chicha. The chef is happy to accommodate special requests. He works with local youth to keep Kichwa traditions alive and can advise on ancestral Andean medicines.

The one vegetarian restaurant in town is **Brocolini** (Quito *y* Manuel Maldonado, tel. 98/381-6486, Facebook @Restaurante. Cafeteria.Vegetariano.Vegano.Brocolini, 10am-5pm Mon.-Fri., $3), which serves set lunches, soy meat burgers, and empanadas.

It can be hard to find somewhere to eat on a Sunday, but **Pizzeria Buona** (Sánchez de Orellana 1408 *y* Gral. Maldonado, tel. 99/920-8261), half a block south of Parque Vicente León, is a good option any day of the week.

ACCOMMODATIONS

Latacunga has a decent selection of accommodations, both budget and midrange.

$10-25

The best value place in town is ★ **Villa de Tacunga** (Sánchez de Orellana *y* Guayaquil, tel. 3/281-2352 or 98/798-7391, https://villadetacvnga.com, $10 pp, including breakfast, or $8 not including breakfast), a midrange hotel that has rooms with shared bathrooms in the basement.

Hostal Tiana (Luis F. Vivero N1-31 *y* Sánchez de Orellana, tel. 3/281-0147, www. hostaltiana.com, dorm $9.50-11.50 pp, $16-25 s, $25-32 d, breakfast included) offers good-quality guest rooms with private or shared baths as well as dorms. It's a good spot for meeting fellow travelers for the Quilotoa Loop or Cotopaxi.

Hotel Cotopaxi (tel. 3/280-1310, $15 s, $25 d) and **Hotel Central** (tel. 3/280-2912, $14.50 dorm, $19 s, $30 d) occupy the same building overlooking the main square, Parque Vicente León, and both offer comfortable guest rooms with private baths. Slightly quieter is **Hotel Rosim,** just off the square (Quito *y* Salcedo, tel. 3/280-0853, www.hotelrosim.com.ec, $8 dorm, $15 s, $30 d, including breakfast).

$25-50

Hotel Rodelu (Quito 1631 *y* Salcedo, tel. 3/280-0956, fax 3/281-2341, www.rodelu.com. ec, $22-73 s, $42-73 d, including breakfast) has comfortable guest rooms, helpful service, and a good restaurant with room service.

Once part of the estate of the Marqués de Miraflores, ★ **Villa de Tacunga** (Sánchez de Orellana *y* Guayaquil, tel. 3/281-2352 or 98/798-7391, https://villadetacvnga.com, $50 s, $70 d, including breakfast) is steeped in history. The building had fallen into disrepair before being bought and restored by a local family. The walls and cobbled floor are built with volcanic pumice stone from Cotopaxi, and there are still many original features, including a wood-fired oven, a cow-bone mosaic in the courtyard, and a water well. Guests can pull up water from the well and filter it using a porous stone bucket filled with sand and carbon, as was done in the past. The rooftop terrace has wonderful views of the city's churches and, on a clear day, the volcanoes Cotopaxi, Tungurahua, and Chimborazo. The guest rooms are located in a new part of the hotel, built to blend in with the old part.

The bedrooms have been soundproofed, and the beds are comfortable. The owner speaks English and is a great source of tourist information. The hotel works with a local tour guide and historian, Carlos Sandoval, who is absolutely the best person to speak to if you'd like to explore the city or discover the lesser known attractions in the surrounding area. Guests of the hotel receive a discount on his tours.

INFORMATION AND SERVICES

Banco Pichincha has an ATM on Parque Vicente León. **Banco Internacional** and **Banco Guayaquil** both have ATMs half a block east on Calle General Maldonado. The **hospital** is on Hermanas Páez near 2 de Mayo. The **tourist office** is in the **Casa de los Marqueses de Maenza** (Sánchez de Orellana y Juan Abel Echeverría, tel. 3/370-0440, ext. 1303, www.amalatacunga.com).

GETTING THERE AND AROUND

Latacunga's **bus terminal** is right on the Panamericana at the west end of town. There are buses every 10 minutes from/to Saquisilí (20 minutes, $0.50), Salcedo (25 minutes, $0.50), Ambato (1 hour, $1.50), and Quito (1.5 hours, $2.50). Quevedo departures are generally hourly, and there are a few daily departures to Santo Domingo. A few early morning direct buses leave for Baños 6am-8am; otherwise you must go via Ambato.

There are more or less hourly departures to Laguna Quilotoa 6:30am-6pm (2.5 hours, $2). For information on buses to Sigchos, Isinliví, Chugchilán, Zumbahua, Angamarca, Tigua, and Pujilí, see the *Quilotoa Loop* section of this chapter.

SALCEDO

This small village 13 kilometers (8 mi) south of Latacunga is the birthplace of the famous *helados de Salcedo*, layered fruit ice creams that are imitated and sold nationwide. The original **Helados Salcedo** (Facebook @

heladossalcedo1956, tel. 98/338-8685) is on the central park, owned and managed by the granddaughter of the founder, who started selling the ice creams in 1956. The original recipe has multicolored layers of ice cream in coconut, blackberry, mango, *taxo* (banana passion fruit), naranjilla, and milk flavors.

Five kilometers (3 mi) south of Salcedo is ★ **Hostería Los Molinos de Yanayacu** (tel. 98/767-2017, www.losmolinosdeyanayacu.com, $35 pp, including breakfast), Ecuador's first watermill. Built in 1539, the mill was operational until 50 years ago, before being abandoned and falling into disrepair. Now lovingly restored by the friendly local owners, it's been open as a hotel and restaurant since 2010. As well as the original mill buildings, the site includes a 1700s Jesuit chapel, beautiful guest rooms built in the 1800s, and extensive riverside gardens with lilies, figs, peaches, pears, avocados, and grapes. The hotel protects 8 hectares (20 acres) of natural vegetation, with many native medicinal plant species, including *molle*, small hallucinogenic berries that are used by local shamans in ceremonies. The owner, Isabel Fonseca, does a cleansing ritual with guests using some of the plants gathered from the walking trails by the river. She can also arrange for a local shaman to visit for a healing session using native plants, liquor, and tobacco. From the hotel, it's possible to walk to a nearby Incan cemetery, also owned by Isabel and her husband, to find fragments of ancient ceramic pots, used to bury the belongings of the dead. Trips to Llanganates National Park can also be arranged. Other amenities include an on-site pool, sauna, and steam room. Prior reservations are needed at the hotel and restaurant, which specializes in trout and has vegetarian options.

To get to Salcedo, take a bus from the terminal in Latacunga (25 minutes). In Salcedo, hire a *camioneta* for the 10-minute drive to the Molinos de Yanayacu ($2.50-3). From Latacunga to the Molinos is $7-8 in a *camioneta*.

SAQUISILÍ

Saquisilí, a 20-minute bus ride northwest of Latacunga, is known for its bustling Thursday market, which is gaining popularity as a more authentic indigenous market than Otavalo. On market day, seven plazas in the town center flood with traders selling animals, grains, vegetables, woolen clothes, and handicrafts. You can buy Tigua paintings, herbal remedies, and squealing piglets (if you want to adopt one), and the smells of roasted pork and guinea pig are never far away.

There is a bus to Saquisilí every 10 minutes from Latacunga's bus terminal (20 minutes, $0.50).

THE QUILOTOA LOOP

The spectacular scenery and remote Kichwa villages to the northwest of Latacunga can be explored on a self-guided, multi-day hike known as the **Quilotoa Loop.** You'll need between three and five nights, staying in hostels along the way, though with additional stops you could spend over a week. Most days you'll be walking for around 4-6 hours.

If that sounds like too much of a commitment, hike just part of the loop by taking a bus from Latacunga to the village of **Chugchilán,** spending a night there, and walking 6-8 hours to the Quilotoa volcanic crater lake the following day. (It's also possible to visit the lake as a day trip with no hiking whatsoever. For details, see the *Laguna Quilotoa* section).

The loop can be tackled clockwise or counterclockwise. The advantage of the clockwise direction is that you finish at the lake, a fitting reward for your efforts; the advantage of the counterclockwise direction is that there are fewer challenging ascents.

The basic counterclockwise route is as follows: Latacunga to Isinliví to Chugchilán to Quilotoa and back to Latacunga, which can be completed in four days and three nights. Additional stops can be added, as follows: Latacunga to Sigchos to Isinliví to Chugchilán to Quilotoa to Zumbahua to Angamarca to Zumbahua to Tigua to Pujilí and then back to Latacunga.

The hike could start in **Sigchos,** or in **Isinliví,** both of which are accessible by bus from Latacunga. There isn't much in Sigchos, except for the Sunday market, but you could spend a night there if you choose, or take an early morning bus from Latacunga to Sigchos before hiking to Isinliví and spending the night there. Alternatively, skip Sigchos altogether and start the hike in Isinliví.

After a night in Isinliví, walk to Chugchilán and spend the night there. The following day's hike, from Chugchilán to Laguna Quilotoa, is the toughest and may take 6-8 hours. After a night at a hostel near the lake, make your way to **Zumbuaha** on foot, by *camioneta*, or by bus. From Zumbuaha, you can take a bus back to Latacunga.

Additional stops can be made from Zumbuaha, all accessible via bus. A detour can be made to **Angamarca,** a new destination on the route, and/or stops can be made in **Tigua** and **Pujilí** en route back to Latacunga. On the sections of the loop with roads, it's common for local people to offer rides for a couple of dollars.

Generally, the trails on the loop are pretty well marked, but there are sections where this is not the case. Make sure to ask for maps and directions from each hostel before you embark on that day's hike. Swap information with fellow hikers at the hostels and en route.

It's advisable to leave your big backpacks in Latacunga and only take your day packs. Hostal Tiana offers secure storage facilities (the first day is free for guests, after that its $1.50 pp/day), plus information and maps; it's also a great place to meet fellow hikers. It gets very cold at night on the loop, so make sure to bring warm clothes in layers (you might even consider thermal underclothes, gloves, and a woolly hat). You'll also need comfortable hiking shoes and a waterproof jacket. Hostels along the way can prepare packed lunches. Carry drinking water and snacks with you. Note that there are no banks or ATMs on the route.

Sigchos

Sigchos's main attraction is its Sunday market. Most people just pass through en route to Isinliví, but accommodations are available a block east of the main square, at **Hostal Dinos** (Plaza 24 de Mayo *e* Ilinizas, tel. 3/271-4237, $15 pp, including breakfast) or **Hostal Jardín De Los Andes** (Ilinizas *y* Tungurahua, tel. 3/271-4114 or 99/287-7968, Facebook @jardinsigchos).

There are almost hourly bus departures to Sigchos from Latacunga between 6am and 6pm daily, with 3:30am departures on Saturday and Sunday ($2, 2 hours). If you're planning on hiking to Isinliví the same day, take one of the early departures (6am, 9:30am, 10am, 10:30am), as the hike takes 4-5 hours. Heading back to Latacunga, there are daily buses at 4am, 8:30am, 1:30pm, 2:30pm, and 4pm.

Isinliví

Isinliví has a beautiful setting and, at 2,700 meters (8,860 ft), it's greener and warmer than the higher altitude villages of Chugchilán and Quilotoa. Horseback riding and tours of a local cheese factory are available.

Almost universally considered the best place to stay on the whole loop, ★ **Llullu Llama Hostal** (two blocks west of the main square on General Morales, tel. 99/292-8559, www.llullullama.com, $19 dorm $28-55 s, $46-78 d) has rooms in a restored farmhouse and cottages in the garden. There are fireplaces in the common areas and a terrace with beautiful views. Rates include an excellent dinner and breakfast (vegetarians are catered for), hot drinks, and hiking maps. Additional costs include a packed lunch ($5) and use of the solar-power-heated Jacuzzi, dry sauna, and Turkish bath ($7.50). The hostel donates 3 percent of all profit to local causes. Book ahead because it gets busy. The hostel is an excellent source of information about exploring the loop area.

A great option is the ★ **Hotel Taita Cristóbal** (tel. 99/137-6542, www. hostaltaitacristobal.com, $15 pp, including breakfast and dinner), a block west of the main square on General Morales. Vegetarian meals are available and the hotel uses organic vegetables. There is space for camping, and volunteer opportunities are available in the local community.

Arrive on foot from Sigchos (4-5 hours), or by bus from Latacunga (2.5 hours, $3). Buses depart daily at 12:15pm and 1pm, except Thursdays and Saturdays, when the departures are at 11am and 12:15pm. The 12:15pm Thursday bus doesn't actually leave from Latacunga but from Sasquili, 20 minutes from Latacunga. Thursday is market day in Sasquili, giving you the opportunity to visit the market in the morning and then take the bus to Isinliví. Going back to Latacunga, buses leave at 2:30am (daily except Wed. and Sun.) and 5am (Mon., Tues., Thurs., Fri.). There are also departures on Wednesday (6:30am and 7am), Saturday (4am), and Sunday (6:45am and 1pm).

Chugchilán

Activities in Chugchilán include visiting a cheese factory and taking hikes and horseback rides in the cloud forest and to the Pailacocha waterfall.

There are excellent accommodation options on a 1.5-kilometer (0.9-mi) stretch of the Vía Sigchos Quilotoa, the main road that runs through the village. At ★ **Hostal Cloud Forest** (tel. 3/270-8016, www.cloudforest-hostal.com, $15 dorm, $20 pp private room, breakfast and dinner included), all rooms have a terrace, hammocks, and a mountain view. A packed lunch can be prepared for $3. Gluten-free, vegetarian, and vegan options are available for all meals. **El Vaquero** (tel. 3/270-8003 or 99/372-7298, www.hostalelvaquero.com, $20-30 pp, breakfast and dinner included) is at the trailhead to Laguna Quilotoa.

The town's most famous accommodation is community-operated **Black Sheep Inn** (tel. 3/270-8077, www.blacksheepinn.com, $35-100 pp including 3 meals, unlimited tea, coffee, and purified water). The inn is a model of ecological sustainability and self-sufficiency, with composting toilets, alternative energy installations, permaculture gardens, recycling and reforestation programs, and water collection facilities. Amenities include a gym, a yoga studio, a sauna, and a hot tub. Food is all vegetarian, made with ingredients from the organic gardens.

Arrive on foot from Isinliví (4-6 hours) or Laguna Quilotoa (6-8 hours). The trailhead from Quilotoa to Chugchilán is signposted at the lake. Alternatively, take a bus from Latacunga to Chugchilán and walk to the lake, though this direction involves more uphill hiking.

Cooperativa Transportes Iliniza operates daily buses from Latacunga ($3), leaving at 11:30am, 11:45am (both via Zumbahua), and 3:15pm (via Sigchos). Buy your ticket 30 minutes in advance. From Chugchilán to Latacunga, daily buses depart at 5am, 6am, and 1pm. There are also departures on Sunday at 9am, 11am, and 2pm.

TOP EXPERIENCE

★ Laguna Quilotoa

The luminous turquoise water of this lake in a dormant volcano is perhaps the most breathtaking sight in Ecuador. On a clear day, the spectacle of the sky reflected in its surface, with the snowcapped peaks of the Ilinizas and Cotopaxi in the distance, is jaw-droppingly beautiful. At 3,900 meters (12,800 ft) elevation, **Laguna Quilotoa** (entrance free, $2 to park) was formed about 800 years ago after a massive eruption led to the collapse of the volcano. According to local legend, it is bottomless, but geologists estimate its depth at 250 meters (820 ft).

Part of the Iliniza Ecological Reserve, the lake is sometimes shrouded in mist (most commonly in the afternoon), so it's best to come in the morning. In recent years, there has been a spate of development by the entrance to the lake, with accommodations, stores, and cafés, but persevere through this somewhat ramshackle area to reach a series of walkways and viewing platforms to appreciate the stunning views. The hike around the rim (4-5 hours) is the best way to escape the infrastructure and the crowds. The walk down to the lake (around 2 hours round-trip) is shorter, though the return journey is tough at this altitude. Donkeys ($10) are available to carry you back up (make sure you choose a well-cared-for animal), and canoes ($5 pp) can be rented on the lake. Rental fees are paid to the donkey and boat owners at the water's edge.

TOURS AND GUIDES

Agencies all over the Sierra offer tours to Quilotoa. Check the agency listings in Latacunga, Riobamba, Baños, and Quito for details. Recommended in Latacunga is **Ecotrail** (tel. 3/223-3125 or 99/945-1401, https://ecotrail.com.ec), which offers kayaking in Quilotoa Lake ($25); biking trips from the lake to Shalala and Zumbahua ($30); hiking around the crater with camping at Shalala ($29); and horseback riding on various nearby routes ($27).

FOOD AND ACCOMMODATIONS

The accommodations at the lake are quite expensive, and not of the highest standard, but there are a couple of decent options. Next to the viewing platform is **Chukirawa** (tel. 3/305-5808, www.hostalchukirawa.com, $34 s, $54 d, breakfast and dinner included). Some 250 meters (820 ft) from the lake is **Princesa Toa** (tel. 9/455-6944, Facebook @ HotelPrincesaToa, $56 pp, breakfast and dinner included).

The best place to stay is ★ **Shalala** (tel. 98/813-0143, www.quilotoashalala.com, $35 pp, including breakfast and dinner), a community-run enterprise on the eastern side of the crater, a 30-minute walk heading right from the main viewing platform. Be aware that the crater-side path is steep and narrow in places. The lodge offers accommodations in the main house or in cabins, a restaurant, gardens, and local handicrafts. A five-minute trail leads to the crater's edge, where there is a glass-fronted viewing platform.

GETTING THERE

From Latacunga, the lake is an easy day trip and the bus passes some beautiful scenery. **Cooperativa Vivero** operates buses from the terminal more or less hourly between 6:30am and 6pm (2 hours, $2). There are direct buses from Quilotoa to Latacunga more or less hourly between 5:30am and 5pm.

If you're hiking the loop, arrive on foot from Chugchilán (6-8 hours). To continue the loop and reach Zumbahua, you can either walk the 12 kilometers (7.5 mi) along the main road, wait for a bus, or hitch a ride in one of the *colectivo* trucks shuttling people between the towns for a dollar or two.

Zumbahua

Zumbahua becomes the weekend hub of the region during its busy Saturday market, when people from surrounding communities flock to town with livestock and various wares carried by llama. Most travelers just pass through without spending the night, but you could stay at **Mirador Oro Verde** (Av. Zumbagua Quilotoa *y* Calle Angel Maria Umajinga, tel. 99/598-0047, http://mirador-oro-verde-ec. book.direct/en-gb, $16.20-22.50 $27-35 d, including breakfast) which has basic, clean rooms and a restaurant.

Arrive on foot, bus, or *camioneta* from Laguna Quilotoa. From Latacunga, there are hourly departures from 6am to 6pm.

Angamarca

Nearly 20 kilometers (12.5 mi) from Zumbahua, Angamarca is a new destination on the loop, home to ★ **Barro Lodge** (tel. 99/565-2475, Facebook @BarroLodge), an eco-hostel owned by the same people as Hostal Tiana in Latacunga. Ten minutes before arriving in Angamarca, the road passes a cave and a Virgin statue on the right-hand side, with a sign for Barro Lodge signaling a turn-off. Follow that road for 1 kilometer (0.6 mi) to find the lodge. Built using bio-construction methods with bricks made from earth and straw, the lodge reuses water and has a recycling program and organic gardens. The oven is wood-fired. Activities include horseback riding, hiking, rappelling, and visits to local caves, rock formations, and an Incan fortress.

From Latacunga, buses ($3.50) leave at 9:30am (Tues.-Sun.), 11am (Sun.-Tues.), 11:30am (Wed.), 1:30pm (Tues. and Thurs.-Sun.), 1pm (Mon.), and 4:30pm (daily). The journey takes three hours. Buses from Zumbahua leave one hour later than those from Latacunga.

Tigua

Fourteen kilometers (8.7 mi) east of Zumbahua, the village of **Tigua** is famous for its bright paintings on sheepskin canvases. The best gallery in town is on the main road, owned by renowned artist **Alfredo Toaquiza,** whose father pioneered the art form. His daughter is now one of the gallery's foremost painters. Prices range $5-550.

Alongside the artwork, which is really wonderful, the gallery also sells traditional wooden festival masks of devils, lions, monkeys, and other characters.

A great place stay is the idyllic ★ **La Posada de Tigua** (Vía Latacunga-Zumbahua km 49, tel. 99/161-2391, Facebook @PosadadeTigua, $42 pp, breakfast and dinner included), a working hacienda that has been in the same family for six generations. The 12 rooms are stylish and comfortable, the food is healthy and organic with ingredients from the farm, and the drinking water comes from a spring. Lunch is available for $9-10. Camping is possible for $5. There is no TV or Wi-Fi here, rather guests are invited to participate in farming activities, such as milking the cows, churning butter, and making cheese. A guided walk to Laguna Quilotoa costs $30 per group and takes six hours. Horseback riding is also available. Accommodations are available by prior reservation only. The farm is an 800-meter (0.5 mi) walk from the main road.

Buses between Quilotoa/Zumbahua and Latacunga pass Tigua; just ask the driver to let you off in Tigua. A private taxi from Laguna Quilotoa costs $25.

Tigua Hide Paintings

a Tigua painting by Alfonso Toaquiza at the Galeria Arte de Tigua Alfredo Toaquiza

The origins of Tigua art lie in the Corpus Christi festival, where brightly painted sheepskin drums are traditionally used as part of the musical accompaniment. In the 1970s, Hungarian collector and art dealer Olga Fisch, admiring the drums, made the suggestion that the same painting method could be used to paint sheepskin "canvases," and, thus, the art form evolved into its current incarnation. At first, artists painted with the same aniline dyes used to color wool, but they soon began to use enamels and acrylic paint.

Tigua paintings reflect the Kichwa culture and world view, with common themes including religious festivals and daily agricultural activities. Crops of barley, potatoes, and beans are often depicted, alongside grazing llamas and sheep. Worship of the Pachamama, or Mother Earth, is another popular subject.

The Cotopaxi volcano is present in the majority of the work. Other local landmarks also appear, such as the Quilotoa Lake, the Tungurahua volcano, and the Amina hill. This last, which resembles a gorilla lying down, is sacred to the inhabitants of the area, who perform ceremonies at the top to ask for rain. Mountains and hills, or *urku*, are especially important to these rural communities, as they control the rain and, therefore, the fertility of the fields and the prosperity of the people. They are painted with human faces in some works, thus expressing the Kichwa world view, where they are seen as living beings. Other paintings are political, depicting national historical events and the indigenous struggle.

Pujilí

Twelve kilometers (7.5 mi) west of Latacunga, this bustling little market town springs to life on Sundays and Wednesdays when Plaza Sucre, a couple of blocks north of the main square, fills with market stalls.

Pujilí is the best place in the country to celebrate **Corpus Christi** in early June, 60 days after Easter Sunday. Blending pre-Incan and Catholic traditions, the festival has been declared Intangible Cultural Heritage by UNESCO. A key character, the "priest of the rain," dances through the streets in an elaborate costume with high plumes, wide lace pants, bells, and espadrilles. Adorned with mirrors, shells, religious figures, necklaces, beads, and colored coins, the plumes alone weigh more than 11 kilograms (25 lb). The dancer, carrying a cane and a bottle of liquor, moves to the beat of a drum and flutes and is accompanied by a colorful cast of characters.

Buses between Quilotoa/Zumbahua and Latacunga pass the entrance to Pujilí; just ask the driver to let you off. Buses run every 15 minutes between Latacunga and Pujilí (30 minutes, $0.45).

Ambato and Vicinity

The sprawling city of **Ambato** (pop. 180,000, elevation 2,580 m/8,460 ft) is more of a commercial hub than a tourist town, and most travelers will just see the inside of the bus terminal en route to other destinations, such as Riobamba or Baños. Unless you're a fan of Ecuadorian history, there is little reason to make a special stop, though it's possible to entertain yourself for an afternoon if you find yourself here.

History buffs will be interested to visit the estates, now museums, of two of Ambato's most famous sons: **Juan Montalvo,** one of Ecuador's foremost writers and liberals, and **Juan León Mera,** composer of Ecuador's rousing national anthem. Both have streets named after them in just about every town in the country.

Although Ambateños (affectionately nick-named Guaytambos, after a type of local fruit) are friendly and helpful, Ambato is not the safest of cities, so avoid wandering around at night. The area around the Mercado Modelo, especially, should be avoided, even during the day, when pickpocketing and muggings are fairly common.

SIGHTS

Parque Montalvo, graced by a statue of the city's most famous son, Juan Montalvo, is backed by Ambato's brash, modern, white-domed **cathedral.** On the corner of Montalvo and Bolívar is the **Casa de Montalvo** (tel. 3/282-4248, www.casademontalvo.gob.ec, 9:30am-5pm Mon.-Fri., 10am-3pm Sat., $2), where the author was born and laid to rest. A noted liberal, he was forced into exile by conservative president Gabriel García Moreno in 1869. As well as collections of photos,

manuscripts, and clothing, Montalvo's body is on display in the mausoleum, his face covered by a death mask. Also on Parque Montalvo, **Museo Provincial Casa del Portal** (9am-1pm and 2pm-6pm Mon.-Fri., 10am-4pm Sat.-Sun., free) has rooms of photography, archaeology, and art, including an exhibition by Ambateño Oswaldo Viteri.

The **Museo de Ciencias Naturales** (tel. 3/282-7395, Facebook @crissross1964, 8am-noon and 2:30pm-5:30pm Mon.-Fri., free, ID required) in the **Colegio Nacional Bolívar** on the elegant **Parque Cevallos** is worth a visit. As well as an impressive collection of stuffed mammals and birds, including condors, there are two fascinating and grisly display cases of deformed animals. Some are in jars, including a two-headed dog and a no-legged guinea pig. Most memorable is the three-horned, three-eyed bull. One can't help but wonder what the third eye could see; another dimension perhaps?

Both famous Juans had estates outside the city center. Juan Montalvo's summer home, **La Quinta de Montalvo** (tel. 3/246-0643, 9am-5pm Wed.-Sun., $1) is in the Ficoa suburb. Head west on Miraflores and across the river onto Avenida Los Guaytambos, or take a taxi ($1.50).

More impressive is the home of Juan León Mera, **La Quinta de Mera** (Av. Rodrigo Pachana Lalama, 9am-5pm Wed.-Sun., $1), a short trip north over the Río Ambato. The grand old 19th-century building houses a museum with period furnishings and artifacts from Mera's family. The ticket includes entrance to the **Jardín Botánico La Liria,** 13 hectares (32 acres) of well-maintained botanical gardens. To get there, take a taxi ($1.50) or

The Inca's Lost Ransom

One of the most famous mysteries—and treasure hunts—in the Americas began in 1532 when Inca leader Atahualpa was captured by the Spanish at Cajamarca in Peru. When conquistador Francisco Pizarro threatened to execute Atahualpa unless he bought his freedom, Atahualpa responded by claiming he could fill the room with gold and silver. The Inca, who revered their leader as a god, set about collecting the largest ransom ever assembled from all corners of his conquered empire.

Pizarro became fearful of Atahualpa's power, however, and went back on his word, staging a trial and sentencing the Inca chief to death. Just before his execution, Atahualpa converted to Christianity to avoid being burned at the stake as a heathen, as he believed this would prevent his body from reaching the afterlife. In accordance with his request, he was strangled in July 1533. When this news reached Atahualpa's general, Rumiñahui, he quickly hid the largest part of the ransom, which was being transported from Ecuador. The fortune was estimated at 15,000 kilograms (33,000 lb) of gold and silver, including an 82-kilogram (181-lb) throne of solid gold. The entire ransom was spirited away almost overnight on the shoulders of porters who were ordered to commit suicide to avoid interrogation. The Spanish began a frantic campaign of torture and killing but failed to find any answers. Even as they were burned alive, Inca nobles taunted the invaders, saying that the treasure would never be found.

Over the years, accounts of the treasure's size, location, and very existence have drifted like clouds over the Andes, with the wild, inhospitable Llanganati Mountains emerging as its most probable location. Rumiñahui could hardly have found a more forbidding spot in the entire Inca empire, where wind, rain, and fog make it all too easy to get lost. Rumors about the treasure's exact whereabouts have included deep caves and the bottom of an icy lake.

Years after Atahualpa's death, one of Pizarro's soldiers, a man named Valverde, who had married an indigenous woman in Latacunga, claimed that his wife's father, the chief of Pillaro, the closest town to the Llanganatis, had told him where the ransom was hidden. On his deathbed, Valverde dictated a map named the *Derrotero* (Path) that contained detailed directions through the Llanganati Mountains to a lake where the treasure lay. Infuriatingly, it contained some vague,

walk north on Montalvo to the bridge over the river. From there, take a bus labeled "Atocha" or go on foot, taking a right on Capulíes. The walk should take about 45 minutes.

SHOPPING

The **Mercado Central,** east of Parque 12 de Noviembre, is open daily. Flowers grown on farms throughout the central Sierra are sold in bright, fragrant bunches along a whole row of stalls.

The small village of **Quisapincha,** 10 kilometers (6.2 mi) to the west of Ambato, is known for its leather craft. Avoid the row of stalls at the entrance of the village (these are boutiques, not workshops) and head to the central square, where an association of artisans sell their wares, including shoes, belts, wallets, and jackets (these start at $55). Items from sheep leather are more economical. The leather market is open 7am-5pm Saturday, Sunday, and public holidays. To get to Quisapincha, take a bus from Plaza Rodó, or go by taxi.

FOOD

The **Mercado Central** is the best place for local cuisine. Ambato's most famous local specialty is *llapingachos,* crispy potato patties with cheese and onion, fried in pork fat, and accompanied by sausage, avocado, lettuce, and a fried egg ($2). Other stalls sell bags of *mote de ñata* (hominy with pork, cilantro, and onion), though these are usually sold out by late morning. The *mercado* is also known for its juices, especially health drink concoctions. Most popular is the *bebida divertida* (fun drink), made with aloe, alfalfa, blackberry, carrot, coconut, and various mystery ingredients. The best juice stall is **Tutti Frutti.**

confusing instructions. The king of Spain sent the map to the authorities in Latacunga, where various expeditions were organized, but no treasure was found. Many explorers never returned, fueling the rumor that both the area and the treasure were cursed.

The trail went cold until British botanist Richard Spruce came across a copy of the map in the 1850s. He also uncovered a map drawn by Anastasio Guzmán, a Spanish botanist and farmer who had lived in Píllaro. Building on the knowledge of many trips into the Llanganatis, Guzmán's 1800 map roughly corresponded with Valverde's guide. Seven years after drawing the map, Guzmán walked off a cliff in his sleep. The story of the treasure, along with a copy of the *Derrotero,* appeared as the final chapter in Spruce's *Notes of a Botanist on the Amazon and Andes,* published in 1908.

Spruce's writings inspired Nova Scotian explorer Barth Blake to travel to Ecuador. According to letters written to a friend, Blake did indeed strike gold after an expedition into Llanganati. In one letter he wrote: "There are thousands of gold and silver pieces of Inca and pre-Inca handicraft, the most beautiful goldsmith works you are not able to imagine." He took as much gold as he could but claimed, "I could not remove it alone, nor could thousands of men." Blake's best friend, who accompanied him on the expedition, died in the mountains, and Blake reportedly journeyed to North America to organize an expedition to remove the rest of the gold, but he mysteriously disappeared on the way.

In the early 20th century, many treasure hunters followed in Blake's footsteps and shared similarly mysterious fates, including Scotsman Erskine Loch, who shot himself after a failed expedition, and American Colonel Brooks, who ended up in a mental institution after his wife died of pneumonia in the mountains.

British author Mark Honigsbaum is the most recent writer to investigate the story in his 2004 book, *Valverde's Gold.* He concluded: "My own feeling is that this gold was probably taken out centuries ago. If not, and it's still there, I think it's lost forever, because those mountains are so vast and inaccessible that you're looking for a needle in a haystack." It remains to be seen whether his words will dampen the gold lust of future treasure hunters.

Colada morada is a thick, sweet drink made from ground purple corn and fruit, including pineapple. In the rest of the country, it's only available for the Day of the Dead celebrations on November 2, but on the **Avenida Rodrigo Pachano** in the Atocha neighborhood, near La Quinta de Mera, it is sold daily, accompanied by *empanadas de viento* filled with meat, chicken, or cheese. It's $1.50 by taxi.

For local cuisine in a restaurant environment, take a $3 taxi from the center to **Cocina al Horno** (Av. Indoamerica *frente a* CNT, *cerca del* Redondel de Izamba, tel. 3/285-6264, Facebook @c.alhorno, 11:30am-10:30pm Tues.-Fri., 7am-10:30pm Sat., 7am-5:30pm Sun.).

For decent Italian food in the center, head to **La Fornace** (Av. Cevallos Mariano Castillo, tel. 3/282-3244, Facebook @ LaFornacePizzeriaGelateria).

There is one vegetarian restaurant in town, ★ **Govinda's** (Juan Benigno Vela *y* Montalvo, tel. 3/242-0966), offering delicious, filling set lunches ($2.50).

ACCOMMODATIONS

The best budget option by far is ★ **Pakari** (Av. Indoamerica *y* Buenos Aires, tel. 98/240-0750, Facebook @HotelPakari, $15-17 s, $25 d). It's a 15-minute drive from the center, but buses pass every couple of minutes ($0.30), or it's a $2 taxi ride. What sets the hotel apart is the young family who run it, who are outstandingly kind and helpful.

In the center, the beautiful **Hotel Roka Plaza** (Bolívar *entre* Quito *y* Guayaquil, tel. 3/242-3845, www.hotelrokaplaza. com, $44 s, $69 d, including breakfast in your room) is set in a restored colonial house with a good restaurant in the central courtyard. On the corner of Parque Cevallos, ★ **Mary Carmen** (tel. 3/244-2451, www. hotelboutiquemc.com, $55 s, $95 d, including breakfast) offers something a bit different, with three stylish animal-themed floors (rhino, zebra, and tiger) with lots of chandeliers. The suites ($150-180) are quite spectacular. Amenities include a spa, a hairdresser, parking, and a restaurant with national and international dishes. Service is friendly and professional.

For a good night's sleep, head to **Quinta Loren** (Calle Los Taxos y Guaytambos, tel. 3/246-0699, www.quintalorenhosteria.com, $58 s, $100 d, including breakfast). Perched on a hill overlooking the city, it's quiet at night, and on clear days there are views of Tungurahua. The bedrooms are plush and comfortable.

INFORMATION AND SERVICES

The Tungurahua province's **tourist information office** (Bolívar y Castillo, tel. 3/242-6290, 8am-4:30pm Mon.-Fri.) is extremely helpful and can provide information, maps, and leaflets on the city and the province, including rural community tourism projects.

Banco Pichincha and **Banco Guayaquil** both have ATMs near Parque Cevallos.

GETTING THERE AND AROUND

Ambato's **bus station,** 2 kilometers (1.2 mi) north of town, can be reached by taxi ($1.50) or local bus from Parque Cevallos. It's necessary to buy a $0.20 ticket to access the platforms. Buses run daily every few minutes to Quito between 2:15am and 7:50pm (2.5 hours, $3.35) and to Riobamba between 5:20am and 7:20pm (1.5 hours, $2). For these destinations, rather than buying a ticket at one of the windows, head straight to the platforms and someone will point you in the direction of the next departing bus.

Flota Pelileo runs buses to Baños at 6:10am, 9:20am, 10:20am, 1:20pm, 7:20pm, and 8:20pm. There are also departures to Guayaquil (frequent between 1:15am and 10:45pm, 6 hours, $8); Cuenca (every 1-2 hours from 6am to midnight); Coca (7pm with Flota Pelileo and 10:30pm with El Dorado, $12.50); Puyo (10am and 1pm with Flota Pelileo, $3.65); Tena (regular morning departures and then at 9pm, 10pm, and midnight, $6.25); and Huaquillas (12:50pm and regular evening departures).

PARQUE NACIONAL LLANGANATES

Cloaked in mystery and clouds, **Llanganates National Park** is wild, rugged, unspoiled country. Filled with mountains, lakes, waterfalls, *páramo,* and forest, it's the birthplace of the waters that form the mighty Pastaza and Napo rivers. With often inhospitable weather and some fairly impenetrable terrain, this is truly the road less traveled.

The parks 2,190 square kilometers (845 sq mi) span the provinces of Cotopaxi, Tungurahua, Napo, and Pastaza. With an altitudinal range of 1,200-4,638 meters (3,937-15,217 ft) and temperatures between 3-24°C (37-75°F), the park is extremely biodiverse, known for its orchids, tapirs, and the pudu, the world's smallest deer.

The Llanganates were sacred sites to the region's pre-Incan indigenous people. After the occupation, the Incas mined the area for gold, creating a road infrastructure that can still be seen today.

For a true adventure, take a **15-day trek** within the park, following **Valverde's treasure map** (with Sachayacu Explorer). Shorter excursions include the **Pisayambo, Patojapina,** and **Anteojos lakes;** a **valley of endemic** *frailejón* **plants;** and the nonvolcanic peak of **Cerro Hermoso.**

If you have your own four-wheel-drive vehicle, you can enter the national park near Píllaro and drive to the Pisayambo lake, 10-15 kilometers (6-9 mi) from the entrance. While it is possible to camp here and explore the park independently, it is not recommended. The weather makes it easy to get lost, and there are feral bulls in the grasslands.

The best option for exploring the central Sierran part of the park is a tour with **Sachayacu Explorer** (Bolívar 229 y Urbina, Píllaro, tel. 3/287-5316, 3/287-3292, or 98/740-3376, juanllanganati@gmail.com, Facebook @jmedinaduenas). The company is based in Píllaro, 20 kilometers (12.4 mi) east of Ambato, which is the access point for this part of the park. Tours, available in English, range 1-15 days and include the treasure route and climbing Cerro Hermoso. Costs vary $50-150 per person per day, depending on the number of people and the tour, including transport, food, tents, local guides, porters, and all equipment. Owner Juan Medina comes highly recommended and is also a guide in the Oriente, including the Yasuní Biosphere Reserve, the Huaorani reserve, and the Francisco de Orellana route along the Amazon River into Peru.

The lowland, more tropical part of Llanganates National Park can be visited with tour agencies in Tena, Napo province. See the *Oriente and the Amazon Basin* chapter for more details.

SALASACA

The people of **Salasaca,** 14 kilometers (8.7 mi) southeast of Ambato, are known for their weaving skills and traditional way of life. According to legend, a condor fell in love with a woman centuries ago and kept her in a cave for years, and the Salasacas are their offspring. Thus, condors are sacred to the local people and often feature in their tapestries. The people still weave in the ancestral way, using sheep wool and plant dyes, with the women spinning and the men sitting at the looms. Indeed, the women can be seen spinning as they sit outside their stalls in the craft market, or even as they walk along the street. As well as tapestries, it's possible to buy beautifully soft woolen items, including shawls.

For an authentic experience of the rich Kichwa culture, stay for a couple of days at **Hostal Runa Huasi** (tel. 9/984-0125, www.hostalrunahuasi.com, $18 pp, breakfast included), owned by local weaver Alonso Pilla and his friendly, welcoming family. To get there from the center of Salasaca, head north on Avenida Rosario, which meets the Panamericana next to the pedestrian bridge. After about one kilometer (0.6 mi), turn left at the sign for the hostel and keep going for about 500 meters (1,640 ft). The views are beautiful, and the rooms are comfortable and clean with shared bathrooms. Lunch and dinner are available. As well as weaving

women of Salasaca spinning wool while walking along the street

workshops (where you can make your own small rug or scarf), Alonso offers half-day visits to local communities ($15 pp) and various other tours ($65 pp). These include a walk to a sacred mountain, where locals still perform rituals; hikes to learn about medicinal plants and natural dyes; and a horseback ride through the trail of the Huacas, the route taken by Rumiñahui to hide his legendary gold (1-week notice required). A visit to a local shaman, who uses a guinea pig to diagnose illness, can also be arranged through the hostel.

PATATE

This quiet town filled with evacuees when the Tungurahua volcano woke up in 1999 and has become a popular spot for volcano-watchers to see the sporadic fireworks that continue to shoot out of the "throat of fire." More predictable sources of enjoyment are the town's famous sweet *arepas*, *chicha de uva* (a sweet, fizzy non-alcoholic drink made with fermented grapes), and *vino de uva*, a sweet grape wine.

The best place for these local specialties is **Mama Lucha,** just off the main square. The owner, who is over 90 years old, learned the *arepa* recipe (said to be pre-Incan) from her grandmother and has passed it on to her grandkids. Made with pumpkin, cinnamon, raw sugar, and (veggies beware) lard, the *arepas* are baked in a wood-fired oven and served in a leaf. As well as *chicha de uva*, Mama Lucha also sells bottles of absolutely delicious local wine, Llanganates ($6).

A block east of the square, the church, or **Santuario del Señor del Terremoto,** houses the Señor del Terremoto (Lord of the Earthquake), a ceramic religious figurine that was found intact amid the rubble following the 1797 earthquake. This miracle is celebrated annually on February 4 in the **Fiesta del Señor,** the town's biggest event. As well as the usual bands and parades, there is a *castillo* (firework tower) competition. A painting inside the church recounts the miracle performed by the Señor when a builder fell from the spire and survived unharmed. Locals claim that when the neighboring town of Pelileo tried to steal the Señor, he suddenly became so heavy that the would-be robbers were unable to lift him. The church also houses an archaeological museum with artifacts from the Panzaleo and Puruhá cultures.

There is only one hostel in Patate, **Hotel Casa Del Valle Patate** (Av. Juan Montalvo, tel. 98/150-1062, $12 s, $20 d).

Just outside Patate, **La Montaña** (Ruta Mundug, tel. 99/332-9704, Facebook @lamontanamundug) is a family-owned enterprise with a restaurant, guest cabins ($35 pp, including breakfast, reservation required), and a viewing platform from which to admire Tungurahua, Chimborazo, and El Altar. The restaurant (noon-6pm Sat.-Sun.) offers organic local brunches and buffets. To get there, follow the sign from the roundabout at the entrance of Patate. The Munduj waterfall, great for bathing, can be visited on foot in half a day, with a guide ($20) or without (the family will provide a map).

Buses for Patate leave Ambato every 10 minutes with Cooperative Patate or Trans Valle ($0.90). From Baños, there is a daily bus at 1pm that takes 45 minutes, or hire a taxi ($10).

Ten kilometers (6.2 mi) outside Patate, the luxury **Hacienda Manteles** (tel. 98/821-9095, www.haciendamanteles.com, $112 s, $162 d) is well known for its ecological practices, with organic gardens and 200 hectares (490 acres) of cloud forest. Rates include a walk to the Payacucho waterfall on the edge of Llanganates National Park. Other activities include horseback riding, bird-watching, cooking classes, and massages. The hacienda was named Ecuador's Best Green Hotel in the 2017 World Travel Awards.

Baños and Vicinity

Baños (pop. 20,000) is one of Ecuador's most popular tourist hubs, and with good reason. While the town itself is not particularly beautiful, its dramatic setting more than makes up for it. Nestled in a valley near the active Tungurahua volcano, the buildings are dwarfed by the verdant peaks of the Andean foothills rising up on all sides. The **Cascada Cabellera de la Virgen** (Virgin's Hair Waterfall) adds to the backdrop, tumbling down the mountainside like a long strip of fine lace.

This small town is the country's premier adventure sports destination and its best spot for spa treatments. Here, you can hike, cycle, raft, climb, and bungee-jump to your heart's content amid the lush slopes and waterfalls of the Pastaza Valley, then treat your aching muscles with a massage or a relaxing soak in the volcanic baths. Baños also has an excellent range of accommodations, some of the best restaurants in Ecuador, and good nightlife on weekends. At 1,820 meters (5,970 ft) above sea level, there is a pleasant spring-like climate year-round. Many days have a mix of sunshine and brief showers, with the most rain between June and September.

According to local legend, the Virgin Mary blessed the town with holy water containing healing properties—hence the town's full name: Baños de Agua Santa (Holy Water Baths). Fittingly, and unusually for Ecuador, here the water is drinkable straight from the faucet. Baños is generally a safe town, though it's not recommended to stray from the city center alone at night, especially on the trails at the edges of town.

SIGHTS
Iglesia de Nuestra Señora de Agua Santa
The center of town is dominated by the twin white-topped towers of an enormous church,

La Basílica de Nuestra Señora de Agua Santa, erected in the Virgin Mary's honor. Inside, 10 huge paintings record incidents when the Virgin saved the faithful from various disasters, including Tungurahua's eruptions, car wrecks, and plunges into the Río Pastaza. The statue of the Virgin sits to the left of the main body of the church, accessible via a separate entrance.

Museo de Mi Pueblo
The **Museo de Mi Pueblo** (12 de Noviembre y Juan Montalvo, tel. 3/274-2909, www. huillacuna.com, 8am-9pm daily, $2) is housed in the Huillacuna Hostal & Gallery. The friendly owner, who can give tours in English, has spent 33 years collecting items of local historical interest, from pre-Incan relics to much more recent antiques, including items from Baños's first hair salon and photography studio, and a collection of photos of the town from 100 years ago. There are also some beautiful wooden boxes and pieces of furniture made by local craftspeople, a tradition that is dying out. The gallery sells items from local artists and sculptors. Entry is free for hostel guests.

Thermal Baths
Baños gets its name from the **thermal springs** that are heated by the Tungurahua volcano to around 55°C (131°F). Varying amounts of cold water are added to create pools in a range of temperatures, which are recommended for the curative properties of their dissolved minerals, including sulfur and iron. The water's brownish-yellow color isn't immediately appealing, but there's no denying the therapeutic effects of soaking in it, especially while enjoying the views of the surrounding mountains. There are four sets of public baths around town, which get very busy with families on weekends and with an

Baños

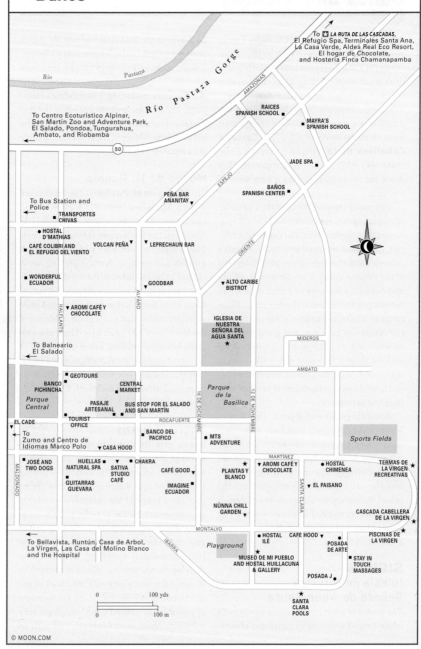

To ⊞ *LA RUTA DE LAS CASCADAS*,
El Refugio Spa, Terminales Santa Ana,
La Casa Verde, Aldea Real Eco Resort,
El hogar de Chocolate,
and Hostería Finca Chamanapamba

Río   *Pastaza*

Río Pastaza Gorge

AMAZONAS

To Centro Ecoturistico Alpinar,
San Martín Zoo and Adventure Park,
El Salado, Pondoa, Tungurahua,
Ambato, and Riobamba

50

RAICES
SPANISH SCHOOL ■

MAYRA'S
■ SPANISH SCHOOL

ESPEJO

JADE SPA ■

PEÑA BAR
AÑANITAY ▼

BAÑOS ■
SPANISH CENTER

To Bus Station and
Police

ORIENTE

■ TRANSPORTES
CHIVAS

● HOSTAL
D'MATHIAS

CAFÉ COLIBRI AND
EL REFUGIO DEL VIENTO ■

VOLCAN PEÑA ▼

▼ LEPRECHAUN BAR

■ WONDERFUL
ECUADOR

▼ GOODBAR

▼ ALTO CARIBE
BISTROT

ALFARO

▼ AROMI CAFÉ Y
CHOCOLATE

HALFLANTS

IGLESIA DE
NUESTRA
SEÑORA DEL
AGUA SANTA
★

MIDEROS

To Balneario
El Salado

AMBATO

■ GEOTOURS

BANCO
PICHINCHA

CENTRAL
MARKET

*Parque
de la
Basílica*

16 DE DICIEMBRE

12 DE NOVIEMBRE

*Parque
Central*

PASAJE
ARTESANAL

BUS STOP FOR EL SALADO
AND SAN MARTÍN

■ TOURIST
OFFICE

ROCAFUERTE

Sports Fields

EL CADE
▼
To
Zumo and Centro de
Idiomas Marco Polo

BANCO DEL
PACIFICO

▼ CASA HOOD

■ MTS
ADVENTURE

MARTÍNEZ

MALDONADO

● JOSÉ AND
TWO DOGS

HUELLAS ■
NATURAL SPA

▼

■ CHAKRA

SATIVA
STUDIO
CAFÉ

CAFÉ GOOD ▼

PLANTAS Y
BLANCO

▼ AROMI CAFÉ Y
CHOCOLATE

● HOSTAL
CHIMENEA

TERMAS DE
LA VIRGEN ★
RECREATIVAS

GUITARRAS
GUEVARA

IMAGINE
ECUADOR ■

SANTA CLARA

● EL PAISANO

CASCADA CABELLERA
DE LA VIRGEN ★

NÚNNA CHILL
GARDEN ▼

MONTALVO

● HOSTAL   CAFÉ HOOD ▼
ILÉ

PISCINAS DE
LA VIRGEN ★

To Bellavista, Runtún, Casa de Arbol,
La Virgen, Las Casa del Molino Blanco
and the Hospital

IBARRA

Playground

POSADA
DE ARTE

■ STAY IN
TOUCH
MASSAGES

■ MUSEO DE MI PUEBLO
AND HOSTAL HUILLACUNA
& GALLERY

POSADA J ●

★ SANTA
CLARA
POOLS

0   100 yds

0   100 m

© MOON.COM

after-work crowd in the evenings. Swimming caps are needed to enter most of the public baths and are available to purchase ($0.50-1).

Termas de la Virgen has two separate complexes on the eastern edge of town near the Virgin's Hair Waterfall. **Termas de la Virgen Recreativas** (Luis Martínez y Montalvo, 2pm-9pm Wed.-Fri., 10am-9pm Sat.-Sun., $6) is much newer, opened in 2017, and more expensive. Eight immaculate pools range 18-42°C (64-108°F). Of these, two are filled with volcanic, mineral-rich water; the others hold regular chlorinated water. Other attractions include a Jacuzzi, a sauna, a steam room, a wave pool, children's pools with play areas, and water slides. Lockers provide secure storage, and there is a café and bar. Across the road, at the very foot of the waterfall, are the original **Termas de la Virgen** (5am-4pm and 6pm-9:30pm daily, $2 daytime, $3 evening), which are cheaper and shabbier. The three volcanic-water pools are cold (18°C/64°F), warm (35°C/95°F), and hot (45°C/113°F). At the back of the complex you can see the steaming volcanic water gushing from the rocks. Although thefts from the locker rooms are rare, it's best to avoid bringing valuables.

Outside town to the southwest, **Balneario El Salado** (Av. El Salado, 5am-8pm daily, $3 pp) is another good option, with five pools ranging from cold (16°C/61°F) to hot (42°C/108/°F). Buses from the terminal and the market run to the springs every half hour throughout the day, or take a taxi ($1.50). On foot, it's a 25-minute walk from the town center: Follow Ambato west out of town, cross the Río Bascún, and turn left onto the Avenida El Salado. Alternatively, follow Martínez through the cemetery and keep going.

There are two other sets of baths in town, but they are mainly used by local families as swimming pools. On the southeastern edge of town, **Complejo Recreacional Santa Clara** (Calle Velazco Ibarra, 2pm-9pm Fri., Mon., and Tues., 10am-9pm Sat.-Sun., $1) features a semi-Olympic cold pool, a heated pool (though not volcanic), a sauna, Jacuzzi, and steam room. A couple of kilometers outside

the town to the east, on the Panamericana, **Termales Santa Ana** (9am-4:30pm Fri.-Sun., $2) has two thermal volcanic pools and two cold chlorinated pools.

Volcán Tungurahua

Just 8 kilometers (5 mi) from Baños within Sangay National Park, Tungurahua, which means "throat of fire" in Kichwa, is the 5,016-meter (16,457-foot) volcano for which the province is named. The fate of the town is inextricably linked to the volatile peak, which not only threatens its potential destruction but supplies the thermal waters that have made it famous.

This comparatively young volcano is one of Ecuador's more temperamental, having erupted violently in 1773, 1877, and 1916. During its most recent awakening in 1999, the town was covered in ash and the government took the precaution of ordering a complete evacuation. Residents protested but were forcibly removed by the army. Four months later, about half the city's inhabitants returned, finding Baños still in one piece but many of their homes and businesses looted. Since then, the volcano has remained in an eruptive phase that shows no sign of abating. The 2006 eruptions caused pyroclastic flows on the volcano's western slopes (fortunately Baños lies to the south), and ashfall reached Guayaquil, nearly 300 kilometers (185 mi) away. Further eruptions occurred in 2010, 2012, and 2013. An ash plume in 2014 reached 10 kilometers (6.2 mi) into the sky.

Some of the more devoutly Catholic locals believe that the town's continued survival in the face of such volcanic activity is the work of the Virgin Mary, who, according to legend, appeared on the hill when Tungurahua erupted in 1773 and diverted the lava flow away from the town.

Despite its looming influence over Baños, it's not possible to see the volcano from the town center. Often wreathed in cloud, it is only visible on a clear day from the hills and viewpoints above town, such as the Virgin statue and the Casa del Arbol. To get close enough to see plumes of steam or fire, night tours are available to the Bellavista viewpoint, but on most occasions very little action is seen.

The best source for the latest news on Tungurahua (in Spanish) is the **Ecuadorian Geophysical Institute** (http://www.igepn.edu.ec/tungurahua).

Climbing Tungurahua can be complicated and dangerous. Without a guide, it's possible to hike as far as Pondoa, 12 kilometers (7.5 mi) southwest of town, where a community tourism project offers accommodations, local cuisine, horseback riding, and hikes to the summit. On the flanks of the volcano, the **Centro de Turismo Comunitario Pondoa** (tel. 99/839-1072, Miguel_perez87@hotmail.com, Facebook @Centro de Turismo Comunitario Pondoa, $25 pp, including breakfast and dinner) offers clean, comfortable brick cabins with private bathrooms and hot water. Camping is available for $5 with tent provided; dorm beds with no meals are $7. Lunch is available for $8-12. The restaurant serves local cuisine such as guinea pig, trout, and quinoa soup (vegetarians have options). A day-visit package includes visits to family farms, lunch, and a guided walk ($20) or horseback ride ($25). Reservations are required for all services. Contact details given are for Miguel Perez, who speaks English.

There are mountain guides in Pondoa for the walk to the Tungurahua refuge or the climb to the summit. Porters and horses are also available. A guide from Pondoa to the refuge costs $25, or $40 from Baños with transport and lunch. On horseback from Pondoa, it's $50. Anyone can walk to the refuge, but a decent level of fitness is required to summit the volcano. The cabins in Pondoa are a good place to acclimatize the night before. The hike from Pondoa to the refuge takes two hours and should be started before 4pm. After a night in the refuge ($10 pp), the climb starts between 3am and 5am and takes 3-4 hours. A recommended guide in Pondoa is Gonzalo (tel. 98/717-3573), who charges $160 for 1-4 people. Contact him directly or via Miguel Perez. A recommended guide in Baños is

mountain rescue expert Milton Muñoz (tel. 99/582-9078), known locally as El Ñato, who speaks some English.

It's not possible to proceed beyond Pondoa without an experienced guide, as all visible paths were destroyed in a previous eruption, and the weather can change rapidly. Explosions of gases, ash, and lava can occur. People have died on the mountain, and several tourists have had to be rescued after getting lost and contracting hypothermia.

Casa del Arbol

For magnificent views of Tungurahua and the surrounding scenery, head to the **Casa del Arbol** (6:30am-7pm daily, $1) on a clear day. This viewpoint and seismic monitoring station is most famous for the "Swing at the End of the World," which sits at the edge of a cliff! Anyone can take a turn at swinging over the abyss, but bear in mind that safety measures are nonexistent. There is also a café and a small zip-lining course.

There are several ways to get to the Casa del Arbol. Bear in mind that late afternoons often have the clearest weather. A blue bus leaves from Pastaza and Vicente Rocafuerte at 6am, 11am, 2pm, and 4pm ($1). It's a good idea to arrive 20 minutes ahead of departure time. Located one block from the bus terminal, **Transportes Chiva** (Espejo *entre* Halflants *y* Maldonado, tel. 97/904-2194) offers daily tours at noon and 4:30pm (2 hours, $5, does not include entry). **Chebas Tours** (Calle Ambato *y* Thomas Halflants, tel. 3/274-3450, www.chebastour.com) offers a $10 tour that also stops at Café del Cielo, part of the luxury hotel Luna Runtún. The 4pm departure arrives at the café at dusk, in time to see the city lights come on. A taxi to the Casa del Arbol costs $10 one-way, or $20-25 with a 45-minute wait.

Those who wish to drive themselves can hire quad bikes in town, but take care, as accidents have been reported and the vehicles

1: Casa del Arbol; 2: Balneario El Salado; 3: Pailón del Diablo waterfall along the Ruta de las Cascadas

are not always in the best state of repair. On foot, it's a steep 2.5-hour climb from the town center. Follow Calle Maldonado south until you get to the trailhead and follow the signs.

Eco Zoológico San Martín

Two kilometers (1.2 mi) west of town, the **San Martín Zoo** (tel. 3/274-1966, 8am-5pm daily, http://ecozoosanmartin.com, $3) houses 48 species of animals, most of which were rescued from traffickers or surrendered by people who kept them as pets. The most impressive inhabitants include a condor, jaguar, ocelot, *páramo* wolf, puma, and spectacled bear. There are also several types of monkey. The zoo has successfully bred some species, including tapirs, spider monkeys, pumas, and capybaras. The animals are well cared for, although some of the enclosures are rather small. An aquarium and serpentarium (8am-5pm daily, $1) opposite the zoo has tropical fish as well as reptiles and birds. To get there, take the Panamericana east out of town and turn off at the sign.

Parque Aventura San Martín

Next to the zoo is the **San Martín Adventure Park** (tel. 99/971-5445 or 98/791-4616, Facebook @parquedeaventurasanmartin, 9am-5pm daily), which offers activities for adrenaline seekers. A four-activity package ($20) includes two zip lines, a suspension bridge, and a 90-meter (300-ft) rock climb. The Extreme Adventure Circuit ($25) includes dry rappelling into a cave, two suspension bridges, a rock climb, and a cable car. Safety standards are high and the staff are friendly and professional.

ENTERTAINMENT AND EVENTS
Nightlife

Baños has good nightlife on weekends, mostly concentrated on Alfaro between Oriente and Espejo. ID is required to enter some of the clubs. A perennial favorite with locals and visitors alike, the **Leprechaun Bar** (Alfaro *y* Oriente, tel. 98/459-3829, http://leprechaunbar.net, Facebook @ LeprechaunBarBanios, 8:30pm-2am Mon.-Thurs., 8:30pm-3am Fri.-Sat.) has an outdoor area with a fire pit and a couple of dance floors playing different music. As well as the club, there is a Leprechaun pub/restaurant farther down Alfaro, between Oriente and Ambato (tel. 98/761-6540, www.leprechaun-pub.com, open daily until midnight). Opposite the Leprechaun Bar, the dance floor at the **Volcán Peña Bar** (Alfaro *y* Oriente, tel. 3/274-2379 or 99/778-9628, Facebook @ Volcan Bar Disc, 8pm-2am Mon.-Thurs., 8pm-3am Fri.-Sat.) attracts a more local crowd. On the same street is **Goodbar** (tel. 98/479-0938, Facebook @ Goodbar.Banos, 8pm-2am Wed.-Thurs., 8pm-3am Fri.-Sat.), popular for its good cocktails and service.

The stylish and friendly **Nünna Chill Garden** (12 de Noviembre *y* Montalvo, tel. 98/443-0710, Facebook @nunnagarden, 5pm-noon Mon.-Thurs., 5pm-2am Fri.-Sat., 2pm-10pm Sun.) has a large open-air space, a mezzanine floor, hammocks, and furniture made from recycled oil drums. There are DJs, live music, and a menu offering craft beer, burgers, and snacks, with vegetarian options.

For a more authentic Andean experience, head to the **Peña Bar Amanitay** (16 de Diciembre *y* Espejo, tel. 3/274-2396, 9pm-midnight daily), which has folkloric music from 9:30pm on weekends.

Festivals

Baños's **Canonization Festival** is celebrated at the end of November or beginning of December with bands, processions, kart racing, and the election of the Queen of Baños. The **Fiestas de la Virgen** are celebrated in October and November. Contact the tourist office or your hotel for exact dates.

RECREATION AND TOURS

★ Ruta de las Cascadas

The 61-kilometer (38-mi) road heading east from Baños to Puyo follows the spectacular Río Pastaza gorge, dropping nearly 1,000 meters (3,280 ft) in elevation through rapidly changing terrain that becomes increasingly tropical as it approaches the Amazon. There is a series of waterfalls along the first half of the road, known as the **Ruta de las Cascadas,** including the **Pailón del Diablo,** the star of the show and Ecuador's second biggest waterfall. Along the *ruta,* adrenaline seekers can whiz across the gorge via cable cars and zip lines, or jump from the San Francisco bridge.

There are several ways to explore the Ruta de las Cascadas. **Transportes Chiva** (Espejo *entre* Halflants *y* Maldonado, tel. 97/904-2194) offers a daily tour in an open-sided bus (10am-2pm, $6). A private taxi costs $25 for four people. A public bus goes directly to the Pailón del Diablo every half hour from outside the Supermercado 99 (Alfaro *y* Martínez).

By far the most popular and fun way is by bicycle, especially as nearly the whole route is downhill, with trucks waiting at Río Verde and Machay for the return trip to Baños. Most hotels and tour agencies in town rent bikes ($6-10 pp) and provide maps. Check the state of your bike carefully before setting out, and make sure it comes with a lock, so you can leave it at the various stops along the way.

The first part of the route is on the main road and can feel a little hair-raising, especially as it passes through a tunnel. Be aware that buses are no longer prepared to ferry stranded cyclists back to Baños with bikes on top, so if you run into trouble, flag down a *camioneta.* Take the number of the bike company with you so you can contact them if necessary.

Leaving Baños, the first waterfall you come to is Agoyán, at around 3 kilometers (1.9 mi). At around 7 kilometers (4.3 mi), you'll pass one of the most impressive waterfalls on the route, the **Manto de la Novia** (Bride's Veil). **Río Verde,** 15 kilometers (9.3 mi) from Baños, is the access point for the **Pailón del Diablo** (Devil's Cauldron, $2 entry), well worth the steep 20-minute hike into the forest. A series of paths and viewing platforms allow close-up encounters of the thundering water. It's an exhilarating experience, but be prepared to get soaked with spray.

Río Verde has several cafés, restaurants, hostels, and shops selling local crafts. Of the accommodation options, one of the best is **Miramelindo** (Vía Baños-Puyo km 15, tel. 3/249-3004, www.miramelindo.com, $80 s/d, buffet breakfast included), which has beautiful guest rooms beside the river, an orchid garden, a heated pool, and a spa.

Many people turn back at Río Verde, and trucks wait here to take cyclists and bikes back to the bus terminal in Baños ($2). Those who continue for another 2.5 kilometers (1.6 mi) will reach the village of **Machay,** where trails lead up into the hills to a series of small waterfalls. The most impressive, **Manantial del Dorado,** is at the end of the trail, but this is quite a hike; over four hours there and back. A good place to stay is the friendly **Camping Paraíso** (Vía Baños-Puyo, tel. 3/249-3049, Facebook @paraisocampingecua, $5 pp camping, $8 pp dorm, $15 s, $25 d), which has a café, pool, volleyball court, and weekend barbecues with live music. *Camionetas* are available in Machay for the return journey to Baños.

After Machay, there isn't much more to see, and the road starts to take some uphill turns. There are also no more chances to stow your bike in a vehicle for the return journey to Baños, until Puyo. If you do keep going, the scenery becomes noticeably more tropical as you reach **Río Negro,** 30 kilometers (19 mi) from Baños. The towns of **Mera** and **Shell** are next, before you hit **Puyo,** 60 kilometers (37 mi) from Baños.

Hiking Around Baños

There are several good self-guided hikes around Baños. These are fairly well signposted, but it's a good idea to ask your hostel or the tourist office for a map. One of the best is to the south of town, with spectacular views of Tungurahua and the Pastaza Valley. Start on Maldonado and walk for 1-1.5 hours up to the **Bellavista** viewing platform, where there is a white cross. Continue for 40 minutes to reach the village of **Runtún,** and another 40 minutes to the **Casa del Arbol.** From there, you can pass **La Virgen del Agua Santa** and be back on the west edge of town in two hours. With stops, it will take three-quarters of a day. Shorter there-and-back hikes can be made to Bellavista (3-hour round-trip, start on Maldonado), La Virgen (1-hour round-trip, start at Montalvo and Mera), and the Casa del Arbol (5-hour round-trip, keep going past La Virgen).

The **Ruta de las Sauces** is a circular, two-hour hike to the north of town. Start on Oscar Efrén Reyes and take the San Francisco bridge over the river. Take the second right to reach the village of Illuchi Bajo. Keep following the Río Pastaza on a path that crosses a stream and ends up crossing a wooden suspension bridge, Puente Los Sauces, back into the San Vicente neighborhood at the eastern edge of Baños.

To hike west of town, follow the Panamericana over the San Martín bridge and turn off at the sign for the San Martín Zoo, from where the **Inés María** waterfall is another 90 minutes on foot. Either walk back from there, or keep going for another two hours to the village of Ligua, from where there are buses back to the market in central Baños.

Adventure Sports and Tour Operators

Baños has an enormous number of tour agencies, and quality varies. Many tours can be booked through hotels and hostels. Activities (with some approximate prices) include hiking, cycling ($8 half-day rental), horseback riding ($28-38, 2 hours), rafting ($30/half day), kayaking ($90/full day), canyoneering ($30/half day), swing-jumping ($20), rock climbing ($45/half day), ziplining ($25), and paragliding ($70/half day). Different agencies have different specialties. Renting all-terrain vehicles is another popular craze around Baños, but be careful, particularly on hilly terrain, as accidents have been reported, and not all vehicles are in a good state of repair.

Rainforest trips can also be arranged. The shorter and more economical tours visit reserves and communities near Puyo, but bear in mind that this is secondary rainforest. A popular day trip is to the Hola Vida protected area and the waterfall of the same name. It's worth a visit, especially if it's your only chance to visit the jungle, but for primary rainforest you'll need to head farther east—to Yasuní, for example.

Geotours (Ambato *y* Halflants, tel./fax 3/274-1344, www.geotoursbanios.com) was the first adventure operator to open in Baños, in 1991, and is still one of the best, offering canyoneering, rafting, paragliding, bungee jumping, jungle tours, rock climbing, and more. **José and Two Dogs** (Maldonado *y* Martínez, tel. 98/420-6966, Facebook @JoseTwoDogsBanos) has a reputation for being respectful to people and the environment. They offer all the usual tours but are best known for horseback riding and hiking (including to the Llanganates). **MTS Adventure** (16 de Diciembre *y* Martínez, tel. 3/274-3283 www.mtsadventure.com) is best for canyoneering and also offers caving. **Starline** (Molitones *y* Oriente, tel. 3/274-3149, Facebook @starlineexpeditions) has specialists in rafting, kayaking, and canyoneering. Owned by a rainforest guide, not surprisingly **Imagine Ecuador** (16 de Diciembre *entre* Montalvo *y* Luis A. Martínez, tel. 98/523-8214, www.imagineecuador.com) is best for one- to five-day jungle trips. They also offer Galápagos tours, plus the usual local activities. Helpfully, all their prices are listed on their website. **Wonderful Ecuador** (Oriente *y* Maldonado, tel. 3/274-1580, www.

wonderfulecuador.org) is known for having the best-quality mountain bikes.

A block from the bus terminal, **Transportes Chivas** (Espejo *y* Halflants, tel. 97/904-2194) offers daily tours in colourful open-sided buses known as *chivas*. Departures include: Ruta de las Cascadas (10am, 1pm, and 4pm, 3 hours, $5, does not include entry to the Pailón del Diablo, $2, or any adventure activities); Casa del Arbol (noon and 4:30pm, 2 hours, $5, does not include $1 entry); and Bellavista (7pm and 9pm, 2 hours, $3, includes a *canelazo* and entry to the Buenavista disco, does not include $0.50 entry to Bellavista). Most agencies and hostels can book tickets for the *chiva* tours.

Massage and Spa Therapies

Baños has plenty of places offering a wide range of spa therapies, but be careful which place you choose, or you may be subjected to a comedy of errors. As a general guide, a one-hour massage costs around $25. One of the best options is outside the town center, $2 in a taxi. **El Refugio Spa** (Camino Real, Barrio San Vicente, tel. 3/274-0482, www.elrefugiospa.com) offers massages, facials, mud baths, and other treatments. The grounds have fruit orchards, flowering gardens, and walking trails. In the center, the following are recommended: **Jade Spa** (Oriente *y* Pablo Arturo Suarez, tel. 99/858-4553, http://jadespabanos.wixsite.com/home), **Huellas Natural Spa** (Luis A. Martínez *y* Halflants, tel. 3/274-0425, www.huellasnaturalspa.com), and **Stay in Touch** (Velasco Ibarra *y* Montalvo, tel. 98/885-9078, Facebook @StayInTouchMassage).

SHOPPING

On the **Pasaje Artesanal,** which leads along the side of the market between Ambato and Rocafuerte, there are stalls selling handicrafts, woven textiles, ponchos, and jewelry. The **Huillacuna Hostal & Gallery** (12 de Noviembre *y* Juan Montalvo, tel. 3/274-2909, www.huillacuna.com, 8am-9pm daily) sells work by local artists and sculptors. For handmade guitars, visit **Guitarras Guevara** (Halflants *y* Martínez, tel. 3/274-0866, 10am-10pm daily), which has instruments starting from $100. Opened in 1945 on the corner of the central square, **El Cade** (tel. 3/274-2933, Facebook @ArtesElCade, 8:30am-7pm daily) sells items made from *tagua*. The craft was passed down the generations by the owner's grandfather.

FOOD

Like its hotel offerings, Baños has an amazing range of food options for such a small town, with restaurants that rival those in Quito and Cuenca. It's also a joy of a destination for vegetarians and vegans.

Ecuadorian

Baños most famous specialty is *milcocha*, chewy sugarcane bars that you can watch being made all over the town center, swung over wooden pegs. It's not great food for conversation, as it does tend to stick your teeth together. For a typically local drink, try the freshly squeezed sugarcane juice at the stalls near the bus terminal.

The *patio de comidas* in the **Central Market** (Eloy Alfaro *y* Ambato) is the best place to try local cuisine. Most dishes are regional, rather than specific to Baños, such as *hornado* (roast pork), *caldo de gallina* (chicken soup), *locro de papa* (potato soup), and *llapingachos* (potato patties). Outside the market on Ambato is a row of stalls selling *cuyes,* roasted guinea pigs. One of the most popular juices in the market is *borojó*, a fruit with energizing properties, laughingly referred to by the locals as the natural Viagra.

Ambato between Halflants and 12 Noviembre is lined with *almuerzo* restaurants, colloquially known as *huecos* (holes), where the locals eat set lunches.

With two locations, ★ **Aromi Café y Chocolate** (Oriente *y* Halflants and 16 Diciembre *y* Martínez, tel. 98/445-9988, Facebook @Aromi Café y Chocolate) is a real find, serving fair trade, organic coffee from Ecuador's best high-altitude Arabica-growing regions, including Loja, Zaruma, and Intag. The menu also offers hot chocolate made from Pacari, a fair trade organic chocolate bar known as the country's finest, alongside sandwiches and desserts.

Attached to the **El Refugio del Viento** art gallery and set in beautiful gardens, ★ **Café Colibrí** (Calle Maldonado *entre* Espejo *y* Oriente, tel. 98/468-7581, Facebook @Café Colibrí, 7am-9pm Fri.-Wed.) is run by a young local family. The menu offers a mixture of Ecuadorian and international breakfasts, snacks, and desserts.

International

There are three restaurants in Baños with similar names, causing much confusion with taxi drivers. Fortunately, all three are good, but if you have a specific place in mind, give the full address to make sure you end up at the right spot. By the foot of the Virgin's Hair Waterfall, ★ **Café Hood** (Montalvo, tel. 3/250-5097, http://cafehoodecuador.com, noon-10pm daily, $3.50-9) was opened in 1993 by local chef Karina Sanchez and her then-husband, Ray Hood. The healthy, eclectic menu includes Asian, Mexican, and Italian dishes, with lots of vegetarian and vegan options. The decor is colorful and welcoming, as is the service. **Casa Hood** (Martínez *y* Halflants, tel. 3/274-2668, https://casahood. wixsite.com/casahood, noon-10:15pm daily, $3-8) was opened subsequently by Ray Hood when the couple split. The menu is similarly international, with vegetarian and vegan options. ★ **Café Good** (16 de Diciembre *y* Luis A. Martínez, tel. 3/274-0592, Facebook @cafe-goodbooksandfood, 8am-10pm daily, $4-9) is an excellent option, offering healthy international dishes with lots of vegetarian specialties, cooked on the spot.

★ **Alto Caribe Bistrot** (Oriente *y* 16 de Deciembre, tel. 96/887-6078, noon-10pm Mon. and Wed.-Sat., 3pm-10pm Sun., $3-11) is an absolute gem. The food is delicious, fresh, and healthy, with *arepas* the specialty. The chef is happy to accommodate preferences

and dietary requests. Service is top-notch and friendly.

Zumo (Rocafuerte *entre* Pastaza *y* Reyes, tel. 99/337-3964, https://zumobanos.jimdo. com, noon-5pm and 6pm-10pm daily, $4-10) serves Ecuadorian-Asian fusion, including sushi, curry, and noodles, using local ingredients, many from the garden. Also available are brunches, salads, wraps, sandwiches, and wings, with plenty of vegetarian and vegan options.

Family-run **Sativa Studio Café** (Luis A. Martínez *y* Eloy Alfaro, tel. 99/530-4432, 11am-11pm Mon.-Sat., $8) offers 100 percent vegan meals in a café made from 100 percent recycled materials. The Afro Caribbean menu is imaginative, with big portions, including tamales, burgers, and salad straight from the garden. There is a tantalizing array of health elixirs, including *kombucha*, and Caribbean drinks made with honey, coconut, hibiscus flowers, and spices.

ACCOMMODATIONS
Under $10

D'Mathias (Espejo *y* Maldonado, tel. 3/274-3203, www.hostaldmathias.com/en, $6 dorm, $10 pp private room) is great value, with clean comfortable rooms, two kitchens, pool table, garden, and rooftop terrace. The staff are helpful and offer great deals on tours.

$10-25

Run by a friendly local family, ★ **Centro Ecoturístico Alpinar** (Vía a Caserio Illuchi, tel. 98/553-3117, 98/093-3110, or 3/274-1027, www.ecoturismoalpinar.com, $15 pp, including breakfast) is a $2 taxi ride north of town, perched on a hill with wonderful views, nature trails, organic gardens, and viewpoints. There are bonfires in the evenings, and dinner is available upon reservation (vegetarian options). Camping is available for $5, or $8 with breakfast.

Family-run **Hostal Chimenea** (Luis A. Martínez *y* Rafael Vieira, tel. 3/274-2725, www.hostelchimenea.com, $7.50-8.50 dorm,

$17 s, $20 d) has a rooftop terrace with a café and waterfall views, a pool, hot tub, and massage rooms. Some guest rooms have balconies. Breakfast is available ($2.50-3.75) and there is a shared kitchen.

Backpacker institution **Hostal Plantas y Blanco** (Martínez *y* 12 de Noviembre, tel. 3/274-0044, https://plantasyblanco.com, $8 dorm, $13 pp private) is a great meeting spot for kindred spirits, with group dinners and free tours of the city and local attractions. There's a rooftop terrace with a café; a shared kitchen; a garden with a fire pit, pool table, foosball, and Ping Pong; and a movie room with Playstation and Netflix. Healthy, organic breakfasts are available with homemade bread, jam, and yogurt ($4-6). The restaurant specializes in bruschetta.

★ **La Casa del Molino Blanco** (Barrio San José, Subida a la Virgen, tel. 3/274-1138, www.casamolinoblanco.com, $11 dorm, $17 s, $27-34 d, including breakfast) is named for the windmill on the roof, which provides 90 percent of the property's lighting energy, along with a solar panel. Rooms are clean, comfortable, and thoughtfully equipped, most with shared bathrooms. Amenities include a massage room, movie room, and shared kitchen with free tea and coffee. Breakfast includes homemade bread and jam. The helpful staff speak English and German and are happy to organize tours or order pizza for those recovering from the day's adventures.

On a quiet street near the Virgin's Hair Waterfall is **Posada J** (Pasaje V. Ibarra *y* Av. Montalvo, tel. 3/274-0053, http://www.posada-j.com, $25 s, $50-60 d, including breakfast). There is an in-house spa, and some rooms have balconies overlooking the waterfall.

$25-50

★ **Hostal Ilé** (12 de Noviembre *y* Montalvo, tel. 3/274-2699, Facebook @HostalIle, $30 pp, including breakfast) is an undiscovered treasure and amazing value. With dark wood floors, whitewashed walls, and jungle-themed

original art throughout, it's a beautiful hotel. The service is excellent and there's a good Mexican restaurant downstairs.

La Posada del Arte (Pasaje Ibarra *y* Montalvo, tel. 3/274-0083, www.posadadelarte.com, $42.50 s, $80 d) is a special place, with walls adorned with work by Ecuadorian artists. Some rooms have waterfall views, Jacuzzi, fireplace, or private balcony. The breakfast is wonderful, with good coffee, fruit salads, pancakes, omelets, and homemade passion fruit honey. The excellent restaurant offers a mix of Ecuadorian and international dishes, with vegetarian options. The owners were involved in founding the of Fundación Arte del Mundo (www.artedelmundoecuador.org), a not-for-profit that provides a children's library and a free arts-based afterschool program for children aged 6 to 12.

$50-100

A couple of kilometers east of the center is the wonderful ★ **La Casa Verde** (Calle Camino Real, Barrio Santa Ana, tel. 8/659-4189, www.lacasaverde.com.ec, $33-60 s, $55-72 d, including breakfast). Big, airy rooms have enormous, comfortable beds, some with balconies overlooking the Río Pastaza. The gigantic breakfast is nothing short of spectacular, with everything homemade. The hotel uses black and gray water systems to create compost and irrigate the organic gardens; collects rainwater for drinking; supports small-scale local producers; and offers discounts to guests who arrive on foot or by bicycle. It's run by a kind local woman who makes all the hotel's toiletry products from natural ingredients, plus truly delicious brownies. She manages the hotel with her son, and they treat guests like family. Vegetarian dinners from the gardens are available upon request. Tours are available, including to the Amazon. A taxi from the town center to the hotel is only $1.50, but many taxi drivers don't know it, so make sure yours does. Another eco-friendly place, a neighbor to La Casa Verde on the banks of the

Río Pastaza, is **Aldea Real Eco Resort** (tel. 3/274-3514, www.aldearealresort.com, $60-80 s/d, including breakfast). The rooms are light, airy, and stylish. There is a black water system and organic gardens. Guests can participate in toasting and grinding their own coffee. The owner is friendly and helpful.

Outside town 4 kilometers (2.5 mi) to the east are a couple of eco-friendly options in lush countryside, where bears and pumas roam amid the waterfalls of the Chamana reserve. It's a world away from Baños, and yet only $3 by taxi. ★ **El Hogar de Chocolate** (Cascadas de Chamana, Parroquia Ulba, tel. 99/710-4844, www. elhogardechocolatebanos.com, $80 s, $120 d, including vegetarian breakfast and dinner) is simply beautiful. Immaculate guest rooms with balconies are set in extensive grounds with treehouses and a pool. Energy comes from hydroelectric turbines, water from a natural spring, and fruit and vegetables from the organic gardens. As well as minimizing environmental impact as far as possible, the friendly local owner, Malu, is involved in several projects that actively benefit local wildlife and domestic animals, including environmental education and reforestation. Income from the hotel goes to support her dog shelter, and she spearheads sterilization and adoption programs (see www.ministeriodebienestarcanino.com). Accommodation is by prior reservation only.

A few minutes' walk from three waterfalls, the 30-hectare (74-acre) grounds of the **Hostería Finca Chamanapamba** (Caserio Chamana, Ulba, tel. 3/277-6241, www.chamanapamba.com, $92 s, $126 d) have trails with views of the Tungurahua and Sangay volcanoes and Llanganates National Park. Made using 100 percent natural materials and ecological building methods, it feels like a luxury treehouse. The German owners built the place by hand with their young family, and now, over 20 years later, their children help to run it with them. The restaurant is excellent.

INFORMATION AND SERVICES

Head to the **Departamento de Turismo del Municipio** (tel. 3/274-0483) on the Parque Central for maps and information on places to stay, places to eat, and things to do. **Banco Pichincha** has an ATM on the same park. The **police station** is by the bus terminal on Espejo and Óscar Efrén Reyes. The **hospital** is on Montalvo near Pastaza (tel. 3/296-1891, Facebook @hospitalbasicodebanos).

Spanish Lessons

Most schools offer individual and group instruction, starting at $8 per hour, and can arrange homestays, hostel accommodations, and additional activities. Recommended are **Centro de Idiomas Marco Polo** (Rocafuerte *y* Maldonado, tel. 9/499-5161, http://languageschool-marcopolo.squarespace.com), **Baños Spanish Center** (Oriente *y* Cañar, tel. 8/704-5072, www.bspanishcenter.com), **Mayra's Spanish School** (Eduardo Tapia *y* Oriente, tel. 3/274-3019, www.mayraspanishschool.com), and **Raices Spanish School** (16 de Diciembre *y* Suárez, tel. 3/274-1921, www. spanishlessons.org).

The **Yanapuma Spanish School** (www. yanapumaspanish.org) offers one-week study and adventure packages to Baños from Quito, including transport, classes, accommodations, and activities. Income from the school supports the Yanapuma Foundation, which promotes sustainable development in indigenous and marginalized communities in Ecuador and Peru.

GETTING THERE AND AROUND

The **bus terminal** is bordered by Reyes and Maldonado, along the main road at the north end of Baños. There are frequent departures to Puyo, Ambato, and Riobamba. **Transportes Baños** (www.cooperativabanos.com.ec) has more or less hourly departures to Quito's Quitumbe station 4am-6:40pm and to Carcelén at 2pm, 3:50pm, and 5:20pm. There are overnight departures to Santa Elena (for access to Montañita) at 5pm, 7:30pm, and 10pm. From Santa Elena, buses run to Baños at 8pm, 9pm, and 10pm. From Baños to Guayaquil, there are buses at 12:20pm, 2:30pm, 5:30pm, 7:30pm, 10pm, 11pm, midnight, and 1am. Buses run to Baños from Guayaquil at 8:10am, 12:10pm, 4:45pm, and 7:30pm. If you miss the direct buses between Baños and Guayaquil, go via Ambato. **Transportes Amazonas** has buses going to Cuenca at 8:45am, 4pm, and 10pm. **Coop Sangay** has departures to Tena at 8:15am, 12:15pm, and 3:15pm.

Guaranda and Vicinity

Despite being the capital of Bolívar province, **Guaranda** is a peaceful town with a small-town feel. With steep, cobbled streets and colonial architecture, it's surrounded by dramatic Andean scenery. Whichever road you take, the journey to Guaranda is beautiful and one of the main reasons to come. The road from Ambato, in particular, is truly spectacular, passing through misty, rolling *páramo* and the Chimborazo reserve, offering awe-inspiring close-ups of Ecuador's highest mountain. With sections at over 4,000 meters (13,000 ft), it's one of the highest paved roads in the world.

Most famous for its week-long Carnival celebrations, Guaranda is considered the most traditional, festive place in the country to join in the fun. The rest of the year, it's a pleasant place to spend a day soaking up the tranquil atmosphere of a traditional agricultural town with a strong indigenous influence. It's not touristy, and that is part of its charm.

Guaranda is the access point for Salinas de Guaranda and an alternative to Riobamba for day trips to the Chimborazo reserve.

Sights

The city's **cathedral** sits on the edge of **Parque El Libertador,** the town's most attractive square. Overlooking the town, 3 kilometers (1.9 mi) to the west, is **El Indio Guaranga,** a statue of a warrior from the indigenous nationality that gave the town its name. The views from the small plaza surrounding the statue are worth the hike, and there is a small museum of historical and cultural exhibits. A taxi from the center costs $1.50.

Entertainment and Events

Carnival in Guaranda is one of the most festive and traditional in the highlands. Expect plenty of water fights, drinking, street dancing, parades, live music, and sprayed foam. Ask the locals about Carnival and they will talk about unity, solidarity, and families coming together. Ancestral call-and-response songs called *coplas* are sung, about love and gratitude for the harvest.

Nightlife is low-key the rest of the year, but try **Los 7 Santos** (Olmedo *y* Convención de 1884, tel. 3/298-0612, Facebook @los7santosgda, 10am-midnight Mon.-Sat.), an arty café and bar that sometimes has live music. The local tipple is *pájaro azul,* a faintly blue, aniseedy liqueur made with local herbs ($2.50/shot).

Shopping

The city's two daily **markets,** biggest on Wednesday, Friday, and Saturday, are in the Plaza 15 de Mayo at the north end of town and in the Mercado 10 de Noviembre at the south end.

On Plaza Roja, **Salinerito** (Gral. Enrique *y* Mons. Cándido Rada, tel. 3/298-2205, www. salinerito.com) sells products from the cooperatives in Salinas de Guaranda, including cheese, chocolate, dried fruit and mushrooms, and jam.

Food

Head to the *patio de comidas* in the Mercado 10 de Noviembre for local food. Most of the dishes are regional, rather than specifically Guarandan, including *hornado* (roast pork—Doña Marina has the best), *llapingachos* (fried potato patties), and *mote* (hominy). The market is also known for frozen drinks called *rompanucas*, literally "break necks," the colloquial term for brain freeze. A bit like liquid ice cream, the most popular flavor is *rosa y lecha*, which is a violent shade of pink.

The neighborhood of Chimbo is known for having the best *cuy*, or roast guinea pig.

The best restaurants are on the Parque El Libertador. **Pizzeria Buon Giorno** (tel. 3/255-0813, Facebook @buongiornogda, noon-10pm Tues.-Sun., noon-5pm Mon., $5-10) serves good pizza and does deliveries. **La Bohemia** (Convención de 1884 and 10 de Agosto, tel. 3/298-4368, 8am-9pm Mon.-Sat., $6-10) serves decent local fare with a set lunch ($4). The menu includes a vegetarian pasta dish. **La Estancia** (García Moreno, tel. 99/961-3407, 7am-7pm Mon.-Sat., $3-5) has set lunches and national and international dishes including chicken, steak, and pasta.

Accommodations

By far the best place to stay is ★ **La Rústica Hotel** (El La Merced Baja, Vía a Chimbo, tel. 3/298-1506 or 99/562-5862, rosma_vinueza@hotmail.com, $24.50, including breakfast). Owned by a friendly local retired teacher, the rooms are stylish and immaculate, with very comfortable beds and original local art and antiques on the walls. There are also some luxurious suites. To combat the chilly nights, the hot water is excellent and each room has its own fan heater. Transport can be arranged to Chimborazo ($25), and the owner works with **Salinas Andes Tour** in Salinas de Guaranda, which offers community and adventure tours (see http://salinasandes.com.ec)

A couple of blocks from the main square, **Hotel Bolívar** (Sucre *entre* Olmedo *y* Rocafuerte, tel. 3/298-0547, https://hotelbolivar.wordpress.com, $20 s, $35 d) has pleasant guest rooms set around a plant-filled courtyard and a restaurant. **Hotel Palacio Real** (7 de Mayo *y* García Moreno, tel. 98/828-1063, Facebook @GerentePR, $25 s, $37 d) is another good option.

Getting There and Around

Guaranda's **bus station** is a 20-minute walk east of the city center on Moreno. There are several buses each hour to Ambato (2 hours, $2) and Riobamba (2 hours, $2), plus hourly service to Guayaquil (2:45am-4:45pm, 4.5 hours, $4) and Quito (3am-5pm, 5 hours, $6). There are also daily departures for Esmeraldas and Lago Agrio.

SALINAS

With 10,000 inhabitants, 85 percent of them indigenous, this small town in the hills above Guaranda has become a model for self-sufficiency and community development through a number of successful cooperatives. In the 1970s, the people of **Salinas** lived in poverty, with homes made from mud and hay; the only source of income was a nearby salt mine. Then, with the help of a visiting Italian Salesian monk and some Swiss technology, the first cooperative was born, a cheese factory. It was so successful that the community branched out into other products, including chocolate, nougat, dried fruit and mushrooms, jam, herbal teas, woolen yarn, and clothes. Under the brand **Salinerito** (tel. 3/221-0185, www.salinerito.com), it has several stores throughout the country and exports internationally. Profits are reinvested back into the cooperatives and used for the development of the community, including initiatives in social support, education, permaculture, and agro-ecological farming.

The **Community Tourism Office** (tel. 3/221-0197 or 9/924-8312, www.salinerito.com) is on the central square, next to the church. As well as tours of the various cooperatives, the office can organize hikes, visits to the salt mines, biking, horseback riding, and climbing. **Salinas Andes Tour** (Calle

Tibospungo y Los Pinos, tel. 96/928-0482, http://salinasandes.com.ec) offers a variety of community and adventure tours, including biking and hiking.

Food and Accommodations

The community-owned hotel **El Refugio** (Salinas y Samilagua, tel. 3/221-0197 or 99/248-3126, hrefugiotour@gmail.com, www.salinerito.com, $22.40 pp, including breakfast) is a good option. Rooms with shared bathroom and no breakfast are also available ($10 pp). ★ **La Minga** (El Salinerito y Guayamas, tel. 3/221-0255, http://lamingahostal.com) is colorful and friendly, with very kind and helpful owners. The hostel supports the WELTHAUS Bielefeld Foundation, a German social justice and sustainable development NGO.

If you're not full of cheese and chocolate, there is good pizza, including some with local llama cheese, at **Pizzeria Casa Nostra** (Facebook @Pizzeria Casa Nostra, 5:30pm-9pm Tues.-Fri., 12:30pm-9pm Sat.-Sun.), which is attached to La Minga.

Getting There

Shared *camionetas* with **Cooperativa Antonio Polo** leave Guaranda every few minutes (or when they are full) from Plaza Roja and also from Parada de Cuatro Esquinas ($1). A private taxi costs $7-10. Red tourist buses leave from Plaza Roja on weekends. The journey takes around 40 minutes.

Riobamba and Vicinity

The capital of Chimborazo province, **Riobamba** (elevation 2,750 m/9,020 ft) has wide avenues, elegant squares, and a peaceful feel. Parts of the city are almost deserted in the early morning and evening, and there is comparatively little traffic. The city's mixed heritage is best exemplified by its name, which combines the Spanish word for river with the Kichwa word for valley.

Tourism has dropped significantly since the Devil's Nose train stopped running from Riobamba in 2007, which is a great shame, because there are other reasons to visit. The historical district is a charming place to spend an afternoon, and the scenic Ice Train still departs from the station. Riobamba is the main access point for hiking, biking, horseback riding, and climbing in Chimborazo National Park, and the surrounding countryside also offers plenty of opportunities for nature and adventure enthusiasts. The trek to El Altar, an extinct volcano in Sangay National Park, is considered one of the most beautiful in the country.

SIGHTS

Most of the city's sights can be seen in the 1-kilometer (0.6-mi) stretch between the stately **Parque Maldonado** and **Parque 21 de Abril**. The former, named for local scientist Pedro Vicente Maldonado, is flanked by the city's **cathedral;** the **Museo de la Ciudad,** which has a free art museum; and the **government offices.** Walk two blocks northwest along the main thoroughfare, **Primera Constituyente,** to reach **Parque Sucre**, with its central **Neptune fountain** and the impressive **Colegio Maldonado.**

Three blocks northeast of Parque Sucre is the **Convento de la Concepción** (Argentinos y Larrea, tel. 3/296-5212, 9am-12:30pm and 3pm-5:30pm Tues.-Sat., $3), one of Ecuador's foremost religious art museums.

Five blocks northwest of Parque Sucre is the renovated **train station** (Av. Daniel León Borja y Carabobo), which has a tourist information office and a shop selling Andean handicrafts, jewelry, and clothes. There is a

Central Riobamba

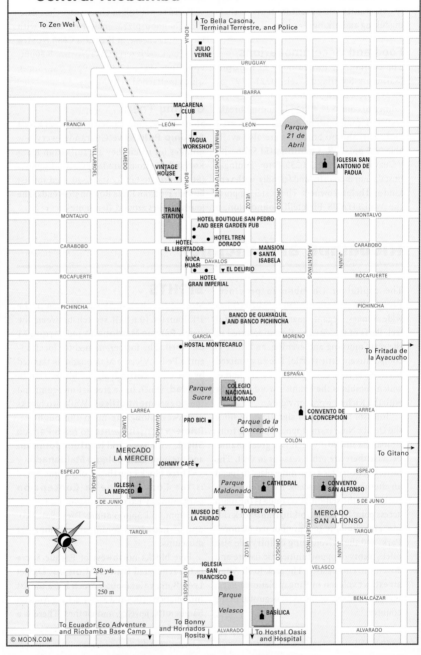

To Zen Wei

BORJA

To Bella Casona,
Terminal Terrestre, and Police

JULIO
VERNE

URUGUAY

ÍBARRA

MACARENA
CLUB

FRANCIA

LEÓN

LEÓN

Parque
21 de
Abril

TAGUA
WORKSHOP

PRIMERA CONSTITUYENTE

IGLESIA SAN
ANTONIO DE
PADUA

VINTAGE
HOUSE

BORJA

VELOZ

OROZCO

MONTALVO

MONTALVO

VILLARROEL

OLMEDO

TRAIN
STATION

HOTEL BOUTIQUE SAN PEDRO
AND BEER GARDEN PUB

HOTEL TREN
DORADO

MANSION
SANTA
ISABELA

ARGENTINOS

JUNÍN

CARABOBO

CARABOBO

HOTEL
EL LIBERTADOR

NUCA
HUASI

DAVALOS

EL DELIRIO

ROCAFUERTE

ROCAFUERTE

HOTEL
GRAN IMPERIAL

PICHINCHA

PICHINCHA

BANCO DE GUAYAQUIL
AND BANCO PICHINCHA

GARCÍA

MORENO

To Fritada de
la Ayacucho

HOSTAL MONTECARLO

ESPAÑA

Parque
Sucre

COLEGIO
NACIONAL
MALDONADO

LARREA

OLMEDO

GUAYAQUIL

LARREA

CONVENTO DE
LA CONCEPCIÓN

PRO BICI

Parque de la
Concepción

COLÓN

To Gitano

MERCADO
LA MERCED

JOHNNY CAFÉ

ESPEJO

ESPEJO

VILLARROEL

IGLESIA
LA MERCED

Parque
Maldonado

CATHEDRAL

CONVENTO
SAN ALFONSO

5 DE JUNIO

5 DE JUNIO

MUSEO DE
LA CIUDAD

TOURIST OFFICE

MERCADO
SAN ALFONSO

ARGENTINOS

JUNÍN

TARQUI

TARQUI

VELOZ

OROZCO

VELASCO

0   250 yds

0   250 m

IGLESIA
SAN
FRANCISCO

10 DE AGOSTO

Parque
Velasco

BASÍLICA

BENALCÁZAR

To Ecuador Eco Adventure
and Riobamba Base Camp

To Bonny
and Hornados
Rosita

ALVARADO

To Hostal Oasis
and Hospital

ALVARADO

© MOON.COM

large pedestrianized area in front, surrounded by pleasant cafés and hotels.

A few blocks northeast of the station, the **Parque 21 de Abril** (Argentinos *y* León) occupies a small hill called **La Loma de Quito.** It offers a great view of the city, but keep your valuables out of sight and avoid the park at night. On the north side of the park sits the small **Iglesia San Antonio de Padua.**

ENTERTAINMENT AND EVENTS

Riobamba's Independence is celebrated the whole month of April. The celebrations culminate on April 21, commemorating victory at the Battle of Tapi, with parades, musical and sporting events, and the election of the Queen of Riobamba.

The best area for nightlife is along **Avenida Borja** near the train station, which comes alive on weekends, with plenty of bars and clubs to browse. For local craft beer, head to the **Beer Garden Pub** (Av. Daniel León Borja 29-50 *entre* Carabobo *y* Juan Montalvo, tel. 3/294-0586, Facebook @beergardenpub). There are concerts at the **Macarena Club** (tel. 99/796-5009, Facebook @MacarenaConcertClubRio).

RECREATION AND TOURS

Ecuador Eco Adventure (tel. 99/831-1282, www.ecuadorecoadventure.com) is Riobamba's best one-stop-shop for mountain climbing and trekking. As well as offering tours to all the nearby peaks, the friendly local owner, Wlady Ortiz, who speaks perfect English, has opened the **Riobamba Base Camp** (Vienna *y* Varsovia, www. riobambabasecamp.com, $15 pp), a hostel designed exclusively for hikers and climbers. It's a great place to spend the night before or after a climb, and to meet up with fellow enthusiasts to socialize or share tours. Wlady is also happy to provide information, maps, GPS coordinates, and equipment to those looking to undertake self-guided hikes or treks. He makes efforts to minimize environmental impact; hires local and indigenous guides from rural communities; and founded a volunteer work agency, Ecuador Volunteer (www. ecuadorecovolunteer.org).

Popular climbs include Chimborazo (2 days, $430 1 person, $295 pp for 2 people, for those already acclimatized; or 4 days, $495 for 1 person, $375 pp for 2); El Altar and Chimborazo (5 days, $550 for 1 person, $430 pp for 2); Carihuairazo and Chimborazo (5 days, $860 for 1 person, $675 pp for 2); Cotopaxi (4 days, $495 1 person, $375 pp 2 people); and Cotopaxi and Chimborazo (5 days, $960 1 person, $750 pp 2 people). Prices include a night at the Riobamba Base Camp the night before departure, all equipment, permits, accommodations, and most meals. Contact the agency for information on other climbs. Popular treks include Ingapirca (3 days, $325); the Condor Trek from Antisana to Cotopaxi (3-5 days, from $550); the lagoons of El Altar Sangay National Park (2-3 days, from $325); and the Pyramid Puñay Archaeological Ruins (2 days, $180). Amazon and Galápagos trips are also available.

Ecuador Eco Adventure also offers one-day "Ecuador Hopping" tours across the country, such as Quito to Baños, stopping at Cotopaxi and Quilotoa Lake en route ($55); and Baños to Cuenca, stopping at Chimborazo Urbina Station, Alausí, and Ingapirca en route ($55). Contact them for full itineraries.

Dutch/Ecuadorian-run **Julio Verne** (Brasil *entre* Primera Constituyente *y* Daniel León Borja, tel. 3/296-3436 or 99/416-7350, www.julioverne-travel.com) is a highly recommended and professional agency offering a wide range of local and national tours including biking, trekking, climbing, Amazon trips, and Galápagos cruises and diving. Staff speak English and Dutch.

Pro Bici (Primera Constituyente 23-51 *y* Larrea, tel. 3/294-1880, www.probici.com) offers mountain-biking excursions from one-day descents of Chimborazo to two- to three-day tours to Ozogoche lakes and El Altar. The bikes are good quality, and support vehicles are provided. **Biking Spirit** (tel. 99/415-6348, www.bikingspirit.com) is another recommended biking tour operator, with prices ranging $45-75 per person per day depending on the tour and the number of people.

Puruha Razurku (tel. 3/260-6744, https://puruharazurku.wordpress.com) is a community tourism agency offering tours to local agricultural villages, cycling, horseback riding and hiking. It's owned by the Corporation for the Development of Community Tourism in Chimborazo (CORDTUCH), which is formed by 11 indigenous communities in the province, descendants of the pre-Incan Purahá people. One-day tours include a hike to the Templo Machay, a sacred cave on the flanks of Chimborazo where the Purahá performed rituals asking the volcano for blessings; and ice-mining with the legendary "last ice merchant of Chimborazo," who extracts and transports ice from the volcano to the market in Riobamba. Also available is a 15-day national tour of various community tourism projects. Tours should be booked at least 48 hours in advance. Ninety percent of profits are invested back into the communities, providing a sustainable source of income for rural people.

Hotel Tren Dorado (Carabobo 22-35 y 10 de Agosto, tel. 97/943-5244, www.hoteltrendorado.com) has its own tour agency, **SoulTrain** (www.soultraintours.es.tl), offering several one-day hikes, bike and horseback rides, plus longer treks to Ingapirca and El Altar. The owner, Pablo, speaks fluent English and is able to coordinate any of the CORDTUCH tours.

SHOPPING
Arts and Crafts

Several shops on or near Borja sell *tagua* nut carvings. **Tagua Workshop** (Borja y León, tel. 99/736-6374, www.taguavegetalivory.com) is one of the best, as is **The Tagua Shop** (Av. Manuel Elicio Flor y Autachi, tel. 99/582-9579, Facebook @ArtesaniasTagua).

Markets

Saturday is the main trading day, when indigenous people come from all over the province and stalls overflow the markets into the surrounding streets. Wednesday is the second biggest day. The stalls in the **Plaza de la Concepción** or Plaza Roja are the best place to buy handicrafts, textiles, and alpaca clothing; **San Alfonso** is the main produce market and **La Merced** is the place to eat typical food alongside the locals. All three markets are within a couple of blocks of Parque Maldonado.

FOOD

For the best *hornado* (roast pork), head a couple of kilometers southwest of the town center to **Hornados Rosita** (Rotonda de San Luis, Av. 9 de Octubre y Juan Féliz Proaño, daily from 9am until it runs out). Served with hominy, potatoes, lettuce, and peanut sauce, it's cheaper and fresher than in the **Mercado Central**, with bigger portions, though the market is the second-best option. The best fritada (fried pork) is found at **Fritada de la Ayacucho** (Ayacucho y Moreno, 5pm-9pm daily). For other traditional meat dishes, try **Gitano** (Ayacucho y Cristóbal Colón and Venezuela y Puruhá, tel. 99/831-3524, Facebook @GitanoRestoBarGrill), which has two locations in Riobamba.

The **Mercado La Merced,** two blocks west of Parque Maldonado on Espejo, is known for its fresh juices and frozen drinks, made with ice mined from Chimborazo by the last ice merchant. The frozen drinks are called *rompanucas*, literally "break necks," the colloquial term for brain freeze.

Owned by a friendly local family, **Bonny** (Primera Constituyente y Darquea, tel. 3/296-6460, www.bonnyrestaurant.com, 11am-10pm Tues.-Sun.) is one of the best restaurants in town, offering national and international dishes, including a vegan soup and pasta. The specialty is snapper. Organic ingredients are used where possible, some from local small-scale farmers.

El Delirio (Primera Constituyente y Rocafuerte, tel. 3/296-6441, 11am-10pm Tues.-Sun.) is steeped in history, located in the house where Simón Bolívar wrote his poem

"My Delirium on Chimborazo" and met with his lover, Manuela Sáenz, herself a revolutionary hero. There are meat, chicken, fish, and seafood dishes, but not much for vegetarians.

Avenida Daniel León Borja near the train station is a good place to browse for eateries, especially cafés, bakeries, *gelaterias*, and *crêperies.* ★ **Vintage House** (Daniel León Borja *y* Juan Lavalles, tel. 99/641-5087, Facebook @Vintagehouse Riobamba) is a stylish café where delicious breakfasts, sandwiches, *arepas*, and *crêpes* are cooked fresh by the friendly owner. The coffee is good and there are lots of veggie options, including a burrito, a burger, and lasagna. **The Beer Garden Pub** (Av. Daniel León Borja 29-50 *entre* Carabobo *y* Juan Montalvo, tel. 3/294-0586, Facebook @beergardenpub) also has a good veggie option, an organic polenta dish with organic vegetables and cheese.

The only vegetarian restaurant in town is ★ **Zen Wei** (Princesa Toa 43-29 *y* Calicuchima, tel. 3/296-4015, Facebook @ Restaurant Vegetariano Zen Wei, noon-3pm Mon.-Sat.), which serves Chinese dishes and an excellent set lunch.

ACCOMMODATIONS
Under $10

Most of the budget hotels are clustered near the train station. The **Hotel Gran Imperial** (Rocafuerte *y* 10 de Agosto, tel. 3/294-3195, Facebook @hotelgranimperial, $6-9 pp) has rooms with shared or private bathrooms. **Ñuca Huasi** (Magdalena Dávalos 22-24 *y* 10 de Agosto, tel. 98/113-8830, Facebook @hotelnucahuasi, $10 pp) has private bathrooms, Wi-Fi, cable TV, and parking.

$10-25

Riobamba Base Camp (Vienna *y* Varsovia, tel. 99/831-1282, www.riobambabasecamp.com, $15 pp) is a hostel designed exclusively for hikers and climbers. It's a great place to spend the night before or after a climb, and to meet up with fellow enthusiasts to socialize or share tours. It's also home to **Ecuador Eco Adventure** (www.ecuadorecoadventure.

com), a tour agency specializing in climbing and trekking.

On a quiet street just outside the center, **Hostal Oasis** (Veloz 15-32 *y* Almagro, tel. 3/296-1210, www.oasishostelriobamba.com, $18 s, $30 d) is run by a lovely local family. Colorful guest rooms are arranged around a flower-filled courtyard, some with their own small kitchen. No breakfast is offered, but there is a shared kitchen. RVs/camper vans can use the facilities ($6 per vehicle).

Closer to the station, **Hotel Tren Dorado** (Carabobo 22-35 *y* 10 de Agosto, tel. 97/943-5244, www.hoteltrendorado.com, $20 s, $34 d) is another friendly family-run hotel, with clean comfortable guest rooms. Breakfast is available for $4. Pablo, the owner, is a great source of tourist information, and the hotel has its own tour agency, **SoulTrain** (www.soultraintours.es.tl), offering several one-day hikes, bike and horseback rides, plus longer treks to Ingapirca and El Altar. **Hotel El Libertador** (Av. Daniel León Borja *y* Carabobo, tel. 3/296-4116, $20 s, $30 d) is excellent value with clean, modern guest rooms in a colonial-style building overlooking the train station.

$25-50

A kilometer northwest of the train station is **Hotel Bella Casona** (Duchicela *y* Monterrey, tel. 3/296-0073, www.hotelbellacasona.com, $36 pp, including breakfast), which has stylish rooms with cream and dark wood decor, comfortable beds, a good breakfast, and great service.

More central is the beautiful ★ **Hotel Boutique San Pedro** (Av. Daniel León Borja *entre* Carabobo *y* Juan Montalvo, tel. 3/294-1359, $50 s, $80 d, including breakfast), an oasis of tranquility in a lovingly restored colonial building. Owned by an environmentally and community-minded local couple, the rooms are luxurious, and the bar serves organic food and local craft beer. Also highly recommended is **Mansión Santa Isabela** (Veloz 28-48 *y* Magdalena Dávalos, tel. 3/296-2947, www.hotelesriobamba.com, $66 s, $86 d, including breakfast), with guest rooms around a fern-filled central courtyard and an excellent restaurant.

SERVICES

There are **tourist information** offices in the municipal building on **Parque Maldonado** and in the **train station**. **Banco Pichincha** and **Banco Guayaquil** have ATMs a block northeast of Parque Sucre at García Moreno and Primera Constituyente. There is a **police station** outside the bus station at La Prensa and Borja. The **hospital** is south of the city center on Juan Félix Proaño and Chile.

GETTING THERE AND AROUND

Bus

Riobamba's main **bus terminal** (La Prensa y Borja) is about 2 kilometers (1.2 mi) west of the center. There are buses to/from Quito's Quitumbe terminal (every 15 minutes 4am-10pm, 4 hours, $5); Guayaquil (every half hour 5am-9pm, 5 hours, $6); Cuenca (every 2 hours 5:30am-4pm, 6 hours, $6); Baños (every half hour 5am-4pm, 1.5 hours, $2); Ambato (every few minutes 5:20am-7:20pm, 1.5 hours, $2); and Alausí (every 30-60 minutes 5am-8pm, 2.5 hours, $2.35).

Train

Currently there is one scenic round-trip train ride from Riobamba, the **Tren de Hielo I** (Ice Train I, http://trenecuador.com) with two stops: one in Urbina, to meet the legendary last ice merchant, Baltazar Ushca, and another to La Moya, to visit a Puruhá community for a traditional lunch in the *páramo* of Chimborazo. The train departs at 8am Saturday-Sunday, returning at 2pm. Tickets cost $28 and can be bought online (http://trenecuador.com), by phone (1800-873-637), or in person at the station.

★ CHIMBORAZO FAUNA RESERVE

The 58,560-hectare (144,700-acre) **Chimborazo Fauna Reserve** (8am-4pm daily, http://areasprotegidas.ambiente.gob.

ec, free) spans three provinces: Cotopaxi, Tungurahua, and Bolívar. Its main attraction is Ecuador's highest mountain, **Chimborazo** (6,310 m/20,702 ft), which is the planet's closest point to the sun. Even though it is 2,500 meters (8,200 ft) shorter than Everest when measured from sea level, Chimborazo's peak is actually farther from the center of the earth because of the earth's equatorial bulge. The reserve is also home to a smaller peak, **Carihuairazo** (5,020 m/16,470 ft).

At the reserve's higher altitudes, the landscape is barren and lunar, with snow near the summits. Lower down, the *páramo* is home to thousands of **llamas, alpacas,** and **vicuñas.** The last, having been hunted to extinction and reintroduced from Chile and Bolivia in the 1980s, now number over 12,000. The padded hooves of these camelids are perfectly adapted to their environment, allowing the animals to graze on the fragile moors without causing damage, unlike domesticated animals. There is also a forest of **polylepis trees** in the park, some hundreds of years old.

As well as summiting the peaks, several activities are available in the reserve. It's worth driving through just to gaze upon the mighty Chimborazo. There are two refuges on the volcano's flanks, both open to non-climbers: **Carrel Brothers Refuge** (4,800 m/15,750 ft) and **Edward Whymper Refuge** (5,000 m/16,400 ft), where empanadas, sandwiches, and hot drinks are available Sunday-Tuesday. It's possible to drive almost to the former and climb a cold, breathless 40 minutes through the snow to the latter. The path between the two is clearly marked and can be completed without a guide, though visitors must not stray from the path. Bring sunblock, sunglasses, warm clothes, and a waterproof jacket. It is not possible to proceed beyond the Whymper refuge without a specialist guide and technical equipment.

It's a cold 8-kilometer (5-mi) walk from the park's main entrance to the first refuge,

1: the Edward Whymper Refuge; **2:** Colegio Maldonado and the Neptune fountain on Parque Sucre in Riobamba

but local guides and drivers wait at the gate with trucks, offering transport and tours. Descendants of the pre-Incan Puruhá people, they are part of a community tourism organization that provides alternative sources of income for rural people since sheep and horses were banned from the park to protect the fragile ecosystem. Return transport to the first refuge costs $20 per group of up to three people, plus $35 for a guided walk to the second refuge (or $50 with an additional hike to the polylepis forest). These tours can be undertaken without prior reservation. After the hikes, to avoid a long, cold wait for a bus at the entrance, the drivers offer transport to Riobamba, Ambato, and Guaranda for $20-30.

Other guided hikes are available in the park, including to the **Templo de Machay** (5 hours, $50 for group of up to 6), a sacred cave at 4,560 meters (14,960 ft) altitude, where the pre-Incan Puruhá people conducted rituals asking Chimborazo for blessings, a practice still carried out by their descendants today. Another unforgettable experience is ice mining with the *ultimo hielero*, the last ice merchant. At over 70 years old, Baltazar Ushca is the only person who still maintains the tradition of mining ice by hand from Chimborazo and then hauling the blocks down from 4,800 meters (15,750 ft) by mule and selling them to the juice stalls in the Riobamba market. Accompanying him is a six- to seven-hour round-trip. The Templo de Machay and polylepis forest can be visited on horseback. These tours should be booked 2-3 days in advance with **Puruha Razurku** (tel. 3/260-6744, https://puruharazurku.wordpress.com). The local guides speak little English. Pablo Manzano at **Hotel Tren Dorado** (tel. 97/943-5244, www.soultraintours.es.tl) in Riobamba speaks fluent English and is able to coordinate the Templo de Machay and Last Ice Merchant tours.

In Riobamba, **Pro Bici** (tel. 3/294-1880, www.probici.com) and **Biking Spirit** (tel. 3/261-2263, www.bikingspirit.com) offer descents of Chimborazo by mountain bike (approx. $65 pp).

If you're considering **summiting Chimborazo,** bear in mind that it's a challenging climb that requires acclimatization, a good level of physical fitness, a specialist guide, technical equipment, and permits. The ascent takes 7-10 hours, usually starting around 10pm and arriving at the summit in the early morning. The descent takes 3-4 hours. The climb is possible year-round, but the best months are December-January. February-April brings rain and heavy snowfall; by June you can expect high winds, clear sky, and good snow.

Climbers must be accompanied by an accredited, specialized guide and be registered in the Biodiversity Information System (SIB), which was introduced in 2015 to log the identities of all climbers on glaciated mountains. Any reputable agency will take care of this formality. Agencies all over the country offer the Chimborazo climb, but choose carefully, because it can be dangerous.

A recommended agency in Riobamba is **Ecuador Eco Adventure** (tel. 99/831-1282, www.ecuadorecoadventure.com), which offers a two-day Chimborazo climb for those already acclimatized ($400 1 person, $420 for 2 people) or four-day tours including acclimatization hikes ($495 for 1 person, $375 for 2).

Carihuairazo (5,020 m/16,470 ft) is usually climbed as practice for scaling its taller neighbor, with a new refuge at 4,600 meters (15,090 ft) as the base. Ecuador Eco Adventure offers the climb for $375 for one person or $250 per person for two people. Also available is a five-day Carihuairazo and Chimborazo tour ($860 for 1 person, $675 pp for 2), plus the following other combinations: El Altar and Chimborazo (5 days, $550 for 1 person, $430 pp for 2); and Cotopaxi and Chimborazo (5 days, $960 1 person, $750 pp 2 people). Prices include a night in Riobamba the night before departure, all equipment, permits, accommodations, and most meals.

Accommodations

The following accommodation options are available in or near the park. All are open to climbers and non-climbers. (Note that accommodations are included in most climbing tours).

The **Carrel Brothers Refuge** (4,800 m/15,750 ft) and **Edward Whymper Refuge** (5,000 m/16,400 ft) both offer basic food, hot drinks, a shared kitchen, toilets, and bunk beds (bring your own sleeping bag). Both cost $15/night, or $30 with meals. Day visitors are common at both refuges, but overnight guests are almost exclusively climbers.

Ten minutes from the park entrance at 4,000 meters (13,000 ft) is **Casa Cóndor** ($15 with no meals, $28 including two meals), which has hot showers and a shared kitchen. Owned by the same organization as the community tourism operator **Puruha Razurku** (tel. 3/260-6744, https://puruharazurku.wordpress.com), it makes a good base for undertaking any of their tours, and reservations should be made in advance. If you just turn up, you may find no one there and no food. The nearby **Chakana Lodge** (tel. 96/829-6999, $30 with meals) is new and better organized.

At the base of the volcano, **Chimborazo Lodge** (tel. 3/302-2284 or 99/886-8112, http://chimborazolodge.com, $100 s, $141 d) is a luxury option frequented by climbers and non-climbers alike. Owned by famous Riobambeño mountaineer Marco Cruz, it has a good quality restaurant.

Twenty minutes from the park entrance on the road from Riobamba is **Dream Garden Lodge** (Vía al Chimborazo, San Juan, tel. 3/293-3340, www.dreamgardenlodge.com, $35 s, $60 d, including breakfast), a new hotel owned by the same local family as Tren Dorado in Riobamba. Set in beautiful gardens with a restaurant, it's a very pleasant place to acclimatize.

To travel to the Chimborazo Fauna Reserve, take a bus from Riobamba to Guaranda, or vice versa, and ask to be let off at the entrance to the park. A taxi from Riobamba costs $35 one-way; from Guaranda it's $25.

GUANO

Eight kilometers (5 mi) north of Riobamba, artisans in the craft village of **Guano** sell distinctive wool rugs and wall hangings featuring pre-Columbian motifs and typical Andean scenes. Also on and around the main square are a number of leather artisans. Saturday is market day, but the shopping is good any day of the week. The village is also known for its sweet bread rolls called *cholas,* which are filled with molasses and baked in a wood-fired oven.

Frequent buses to Guano with the 20 de Diciembre bus company (20 minutes, $1.50) leave from Plaza de Toros Raúl Dávalos in Riobamba, a couple of blocks north of the train station.

GUAMOTE

The main reason to come to **Guamote,** 50 kilometers (31 mi) south of Riobamba, is for the Thursday market, which is one of the largest and most authentic in the region. There are a few handicrafts stalls, but the focal point is the chaotic animal market. You're not likely to buy anything, but it is an interesting experience, if hardly an advertisement for animal rights.

To see the market at its best, spend the night here and get up early. The best place to stay is the Belgian- and Ecuadorian-run **Inti Sisa Guesthouse** (Calle Vargas Torres y García Moreno, tel. 3/291-6529, www.intisisa.org, $25 dorm, $50 s, $65 d, including breakfast), which has 23 guest rooms with private bathrooms, a spacious dormitory, and a lounge with a fireplace. Lunch and dinner are available, as are tours to a local community, the Ozogoche lakes, and horseback riding. The guesthouse funds a foundation that offers educational support to underprivileged local people, especially young girls and women, by providing free classes in IT, sewing, music, and English, and daily homework support to children.

Buses for Guamote have their own bus terminal a block from main terminal in Riobamba and leave frequently.

★ ALAUSÍ

This charming town has more far more spectacular experiences to offer than the **Devil's Nose** train for which it is most famous. In fact, those who only come for the train ride are doing themselves, and Alausí, a great disservice. Perched on the edge of a dramatic gorge and surrounded by mountains, the setting is magnificent. In the town center, presided over by a giant statue of Saint Peter on a hill, the railway tracks are flanked by pastel colonial houses on cobbled streets. Every Sunday, indigenous people in traditional colorful clothing come from the surrounding rural communities to trade their handicrafts and fresh produce in the lively market.

On other days, visitors can climb the Lluglli hill to gaze upon the panoramic views from the **Saint Peter statue,** or follow the railway tracks to the northern end of town to admire the impressive **Puente Negro,** a bridge spanning the river gorge. There's not much else to do in Alausí itself, apart from wandering the picturesque streets or watching the light change on the surrounding peaks and valleys, but this very tranquility is part of its charm. In many ways, a trip to Alausí is like taking a trip back in time and, if you're anything like this travel writer, you may not want to leave.

While the cobbled streets might tempt one to amble, the surrounding countryside is an invitation to get active. Alausí is the jumping-off point for some of the **most spectacular hikes in the country,** with April and May the best months to visit, for the clear skies and wildflowers.

Nariz del Diablo

The **Devil's Nose** was one of the most incredible feats of railroad engineering when it was completed in the early 1900s as part of the train line linking the Andes with the coast. To descend the almost perpendicular slopes of the Cóndor Puñuna or Sacred Condor Nest mountain, the tracks make a series of switchbacks that are so tight the entire train has to back up to fit through, descending over 500 meters (1,640 ft) in just 12 kilometers (7.5 mi). A high price was paid for this wonder of the steam age; over 4,000 people lost their lives during construction, most of them indigenous locals and Jamaican slaves—hence the name, Nariz del Diablo.

When it opened, the train line was used to transport goods and passengers between the coast and the Sierra. Suddenly, trade between the two regions was possible in hours, rather than days, and, with three classes of ticket, rail travel was affordable for local people, boosting the economy along the whole route. In the 1990s, following years of neglect and some devastating landslides, the train line was closed and fell into disrepair, before the Devil's Nose section was renovated and opened as a tourist attraction. Sadly, the ticket prices are out of reach for most locals these days.

During the 45-minute journey, there is a guided tour in English and Spanish. Just after the switchbacks, the train stops for an hour near **Sibambe** before turning around and climbing back through the entire route to Alausí. During the stop, passengers can spend time in the museum, the café, or the shop, which sells handicrafts made by local communities, including bags woven from the *cabuya* cactus. Dancers from the nearby village of Tolte perform a traditional folk dance.

Alausí's **train station** sits behind the small plaza at the north end of the main street, 5 de Junio. The train departs twice daily (except Mon.) at 8am and 11am ($33). The return journey takes 2.5 hours. Tickets should be bought in advance, especially on weekends, and are available online (http://trenecuador.com), by phone (800/873-637), or at the train station in Alausí or Riobamba. For the best views, sit on the right-hand side of the train.

Hiking

While the famous train ride is somewhat of a tourist trap, it's possible to hike from Alausí into the nearby mountains, where a **mirador** overlooks the dramatic zigzagging tracks of **Devil's Nose,** providing a much better view than from inside the carriages. If you time it right, you can see the train going past. Best of all, you'll probably have the whole scene to yourself, or perhaps share it with a local farmer. Here, people live much as they have for centuries, wearing brightly colored woolen ponchos as they ride on donkeys or walk miles every day with their sheep, faces bronzed and lined by the sun. The hike also takes in the small village of **Nisag,** a traditional Kichwa agricultural community where the people weave bracelets, hats, and bags out of the sisal plant. The hike takes half a day.

Alausí is also an excellent jumping-off point for the **Lagunas de Ozogoche,** a beautiful series of lakes high in the pristine *páramo* of Sangay National Park. The lakes are best known for a mysterious phenomenon that takes place annually in mid-September, when hundreds of migrating plovers, *cuvives,* appear to commit suicide by diving into the water. The Kichwa people see this as a tribute to the Pachamama (Mother Earth) and organize a festival, with rituals, music, and dancing. The entrance to the lakes is less than hour's drive from Alausí, and on a clear day (more likely May-November) the journey is a joy, with views of Chimborazo in the distance. The road also passes some traditional indigenous dwellings made of mud and straw. Although it's becoming less common, some people continue to live an astonishingly hard life on the windswept *páramo* with their livestock, without running water or electricity, and with only the icy river to bathe in. The lakes can be visited in half to three-quarters of a day from Alausí.

Both of these hikes can be undertaken with **Marco Tulio Fiallo,** the owner of **Community Hostel** (tel. 98/563-7714, www.communityalausi.com). Don Marco offers the half-day Devil's Nose/Nisag hike free to hostel guests. The Lagunas de Ozogoche tour costs $50 for one person or $25 per person for 2-4 people.

Half an hour from Alausí, **Achupallas** is the starting point for the three-day **Inca Trail to Ingapirca,** the largest known Inca ruins in Ecuador (see the *Southern Sierra* chapter for more information). Achupallas also has **waterfalls, lakes,** and some **giant petrified shells.** A round-trip by *camioneta* costs $12. Community Hostel can organize the Inca Trek for $250 per person, including tents, meals, and rubber boots.

Food and Accommodations

At the north end of town next to the railway track, the best place to stay is ★ **Community Hostel** (Eloy Alfaro Casa 172, tel. 98/563-7714, www.communityalausi.com, Facebook @CommunityAlausi, $12.50 dorm, $30 s, $50 d). It's owned by local septuagenarian legend Marco Tulio Fiallo, who converted his childhood home into the hostel. It's immaculate, offering luxury accommodations and gourmet breakfasts at backpacker prices. A great spot for digital nomads, with fast Wi-Fi and lots of plug sockets, it's a sister establishment to the excellent hostel of the same name in Quito. Don Marco, who speaks fluent English, takes guests on free hikes to the Devil's Nose mirador and Nisag; leads tours to the Ozogoche lakes ($50 for 1 person, $25 pp for 2-4 people); and can organize the Inca Trek. He founded a free annual 12-kilometer (7.5-mi) race, in which around 2,000 local people participate, and is a great person to speak to about local history.

Most other accommodations are on the main drag, the 5 de Junio. **Hotel Europa** (5 de Junio y Esteban Orozco, tel. 3/293-0200, www.hoteleuropa.com.ec, $10-25 s, $18-44 d) has friendly service and rooms to suit different budgets, with private or shared bathrooms. Breakfast is available for $3.50. Family-owned **Hotel Noris** (5 de Junio 122 y Pedro de Loza, tel. 3/293-1111, Facebook @ Hotel Noris, $25 s, $40 d, including breakfast) has attractive guest rooms and a third-floor mirador overlooking the Saint Peter statue. The restaurant serves traditional food.

Just southwest of town, 1.5 kilometers (0.9 mi) from the center is **Killa Wasi** (La Quinta de la Familia Rivadeneira, Barrio Mullenquiz, tel. 9/886-03535, www.hostelalausi.com, $5 camping, $10 dorm, $15-20 s/d). Set on an organic farm, the hostel is run by a friendly local mother-and-son team. Guest rooms are clean with comfortable beds, and the common area walls are painted with motifs from Inca and Kichwa mythology. Meals are available at additional cost, with vegetarian options.

The **municipal market** (García Moreno *entre* Pedro Loza *y* Chile) has fresh produce and a food court with local dishes, including *hornado*, pork roasted in a wood-fired oven.

One of the best places to eat is ★ **Estación del Tren** (Calle Ricaurte *entre* Av. 5 de Junio *y* Antonio Mora, tel. 3/293-0952, 8am-10pm daily), opposite the train station. Owned by a friendly local family, the restaurant uses organic produce, with vegetables from small-scale farmers in Nisag, fruit from the owner's brother's farm, and coffee from Loja. Many of the recipes come from a 90-year-old nun's grandmother's secret recipe book. The chef can whip up a wonderful vegetarian meal upon request. The dessert specialty is passionfruit mousse.

Right next to the station, **El Mesón de Tren** (Ricaurte *y* Eloy Alfaro, tel. 99/343-4081, Facebook @elmesondeltrenalausi) offers filling local specialties such as roast pork and *llapingachos*. Set lunch is $5 and entrées around $9.

Information and Services

There is a Banco Pichincha ATM at the north end of the main street, 5 de Junio.

Buses depart from the Alausí terminal with **Coop Patria** (tel. 3/293-0189) to Cuenca (7:15am, 9:30am, 11:30am, 1pm, 3pm, and 5:30pm, 4 hours, $6) and Quito (8am, 9:30am, noon, 1:30pm, 3:30pm, and 6pm, 5 hours, $7).

Coop Alausí runs buses to Riobamba (every 30-60 minutes 5:10am-6:30pm, 2.5 hours, $2.35); Cuenca (6:15am and 10:30am, $6.25); Quito (4am, 8:10am, 10am, and 11am, $7); Guayaquil (4am, 9am, 1pm, and 3pm, 5 hours, $6.25). More buses pass on the highway up the hill ($1 by taxi), picking up passengers at the gas station on the Panamericana.

Buses to Alausí run from Riobamba (every 30-60 minutes 5:10am-8pm); Cuenca (5am, 2:45pm); Quito (7:25am, 9:25am, 12:25pm, and 5:25pm); and Guayaquil (6:15am, 9:25am, 1pm, and 4pm) with **Coop Alausí.**

SANGAY NATIONAL PARK

A UNESCO World Heritage Site, **Sangay National Park** (http://areasprotegidas. ambiente.gob.ec) features two of Ecuador's most active volcanoes, **Tungurahua** (5,016 m/16,457 ft) and **Sangay** (5,230 m/17,159 ft), as well as the extinct **El Altar** (5,319 m/17,451 ft). Spanning over 500,000 hectares (1.2 million acres), the park connects the provinces of Cañar, Chimborazo, Morona-Santiago, and Tungurahua. Although there are a few accessible attractions, most of the reserve receives few visitors and contains some of the wildest terrain in the central highlands.

Aside from the volcanoes, the park is known for its beautiful lakes and staggering level of biodiversity. With elevations ranging 900-5,319 meters (2,953-17,451 ft), the geography includes moors, high-Andean forests, and subtropical forests. The area near Volcán Sangay protects one of the last sizable refuges of the highly endangered Andean tapir. Another threatened species, the pudu, can also be found. This nocturnal deer is one of the world's smallest, weighing just 10 kilograms (22 lb) and standing 40 centimeters (16 in) tall. Other mammal species include Andean bears, pumas, and *páramo* wolves in the upper regions, and ocelots, spider and woolly monkeys, anteaters, and giant armadillos in the lower regions. There are over 400 types of birds and over 3,000 species of plants, of which 586 are unique to the area.

The most accessible Sierran parts of Sangay National Park are covered elsewhere in this chapter. **Volcán Tungurahua** can be visited via Pondoa just outside Baños; the **Inca Trail** is accessed via Achupallas near Alausí; and the **Lagunas de Ozogoche** can be visited on tours from Guamote and Alausí. The mountainous parts of the park are inhabited by descendants of the Cañari and Puruhá peoples.

The lower altitude section of the park is covered in rainforest and falls within the territory of the Shuar. This part of the park can be visited on tours from Macas in the province of Morona-Santiago. See the *Oriente and the Amazon Basin* chapter for more details.

With your own transport, you can drive through the park on the Riobamba-Macas road.

Volcán El Altar

Unlike its neighbors, **El Altar** (5,319 m/17,451 ft) is long since extinct, but it went out in spectacular style. It must have been an incredible cataclysm as one of the highest mountains in the world blew apart, leaving nine jagged peaks around a crater lake 3,000 meters (9,800 ft) in diameter. It may be a shell of its former self, but El Altar is still the fifth-highest mountain in Ecuador. The trek to the crater lake, the **Altar Yellow Lagoon,** is one of the most beautiful in the country, and can be undertaken in two days, either independently or with a tour agency.

Start by taking a bus from Riobamba to Candelaria (elevation 3,100 m/10,170 ft). Buses leave at 6:30am and 10am and take 1.5 hours. Take the early bus to arrive in daylight. Two kilometers (1.2 mi) past the center of Candelaria (don't blink) is the left-hand turnoff for the ranger station, where you register to enter the park. About one kilometer (0.6 mi) up the track is the comfortable **Hacienda El Releche** (tel. 3/301-4067 or 98/465-1922, http://haciendareleche.com, $25 pp), which has a great fireplace for drying wet clothes and can provide mules and a guide for the trek to the lakes, which can be reached after 6-7 hours of moderate uphill hiking. Meals and packed lunches are available ($6-8). El Releche also has a refuge by the lakes, **Capac Urcu** ($15 pp). It's $10 to hire the kitchen, per group. It's free to camp near the lakes or $15 near the refuge, including use of the facilities.

December-March is optimum for this hike, as there is wetter, foggier weather from April onward. The IGM *Cerros Negros* and *Laguna Pintada* 1:25,000 maps cover the area, or the route can be plotted on Maps.me.

Ecuador Eco Adventure (tel. 99/831-1282, www.ecuadorecoadventures.com) in Riobamba can provide rubber boots, advice, and directions for those wishing to hike independently. They also offer two-day, ($225 pp) and three-day ($325 pp) treks to the lakes (minimum 2 people). The climb to the summit of El Altar is thought by many to be Ecuador's finest, and most technical, climb. This takes four days and costs $525 (minimum 2 people).

Volcán Sangay

With a picture-perfect cone covered by occasional snow, **Sangay** (5,230 m/17,159 ft) might look magnificently serene, but in fact it's one of the world's most active volcanoes. It's been erupting continuously since the 1930s and regularly sends out columns of ash. In the not-too-distant past, these were accompanied by red-hot lava-rock bombs. Climbers risk being hit by falling rocks and breathing in sulfur gas near the summit. Not surprisingly, it's not one of the country's most popular climbs, but a few intrepid folk do attempt it.

Ecuador Eco Adventure (tel. 99/831-1282, www.ecuadorecoadventures.com) in Riobamba offers the seven-day expedition for $1,700 for one person or $1,200 per person for two. The best months to make the climb are October-February, the driest time in the area. July-August is sodden. Check the latest geological situation with the Ecuadorian Geophysical Institute (www.igepn.edu.ec).

The volcano can be admired with a lot less effort from the moors of Návac or from the heights of Punín, Cacha, Atillo, and Ozogoche.

Southern Sierra

South of Riobamba, the Andean cordillera is

older and less volcanically active, without the soaring mountains that are found farther north. Here, the landscape is mellower, characterized by green foothills tapestried with pastures, rising to crumpled rocky peaks. Deeper into the hills, it's more rugged and isolated, particularly in the vast chilly landscapes of El Cajas National Park and the wild forests of Podocarpus.

Many of the inhabitants of the southern Sierra are descendants of the Cañari people, who lived here long before the Incas arrived and are famous for their determined resistance of the invasion. In rural villages in the provinces of Azuay and Cañar, people still live as they have for centuries, milking their cows by hand and growing food in the traditional

Highlights

Look for ★ to find recommended sights, activities, dining, and lodging.

★ **Ingapirca Ruins:** The Inca sun temple is the centerpiece of this complex, but the more ancient Cañari archaeology is just as fascinating, including the collective tombstone of a priestess and 10 of her servants (page 196).

★ **Cuenca's Historical District:** This UNESCO World Heritage Site is a place to forget itineraries and meander the cobblestone streets and stately plazas, gazing up at church spires and geranium-covered wrought-iron balconies (page 200).

★ **El Cajas National Park:** Hike through pristine wildflower-strewn *páramo* and rugged mountains dotted with crystalline lakes and streams less than an hour from Cuenca (page 217).

★ **Podocarpus National Park:** Declared a UNESCO Biosphere Reserve for its great endemism of flora and fauna, the "Botanic Garden of America" is home to spectacled bears, *páramo* wolves, jaguars, and almost 4,000 species of plants (page 234).

★ **Vilcabamba:** Nestled in a valley surrounded by spectacular scenery, this small picturesque town is an idyllic spot to spend a few days, with excellent hiking, biking, horseback riding, spas, and wellness facilities (page 236).

Southern Sierra

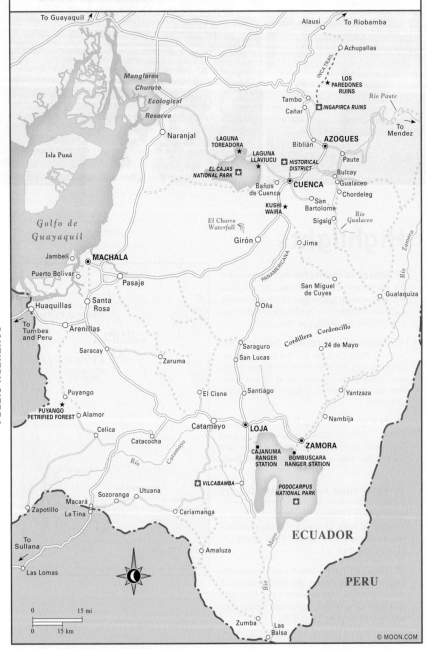

To Guayaquil

Alausi
To Riobamba

Achupallas

INCA TRAIL

LOS PAREDONES RUINS

Tambo
Cañar

Río Paute

INGAPIRCA RUINS

To Mendez

Manglares Churute Ecological Reserve

Naranjal

LAGUNA TOREADORA

LAGUNA LLAVIUCU

Biblián

AZOGUES

Isla Puná

EL CAJAS NATIONAL PARK

HISTORICAL DISTRICT

Paute
Bulcay
Gualaceo
Chordeleg

Baños de Cuenca

CUENCA

San Bartolome

Golfo de Guayaquil

El Chorro Waterfall

KUSHI WAIRA

Sígsig

Río Gualaceo

Río Zamora

Jambelí
Puerto Bolivar

MACHALA

Girón

Jima

San Miguel de Cuyes

Gualaquiza

Pasaje

Santa Rosa

Oña

PANAMERICANA

Huaquillas

To Tumbes and Peru

Arenillas

Saracay

Zaruma

Saraguro

San Lucas

Santiago

Cordillera Cordoncillo

24 de Mayo

Yantzaza

Puyango

El Cisne

PUYANGO PETRIFIED FOREST

Alamor

Celica

Catacocha

Catamayo

LOJA

ZAMORA

CAJANUMA RANGER STATION

BOMBUSCARA RANGER STATION

Nambija

Río Catamayo

VILCABAMBA

PODOCARPUS NATIONAL PARK

Zapotillo
Macará
La Tina

Sozoranga

Utuana

Cariamanga

ECUADOR

To Sullana

Amaluza

Las Lomas

Río Mayo

PERU

0   15 mi

0   15 km

Zumba
Las Balsa

© MOON.COM

way, which never stopped being organic. Some of these communities, such as Kushi Waira and Jima, have opened their doors to visitors, keen to share their way of life and keep their ancestral customs alive. The small villages near the indigenous town of Saraguro also receive tourists, sharing their gastronomy, handicrafts, music, and ancient medicines.

Traditional crafts are also still practiced throughout the region, with an astonishing level of skill, from the hand-made guitars at San Bartolomé and the beaded necklaces of Saraguro to the woven shawls of Gualaceo and the fine filigree jewelry of Chordeleg. The region's most famous export is the "Panama" hat, or *sombrero de paja toquilla*, made in villages near Cuenca.

Cuenca itself is Ecuador's third largest city and arguably its most beautiful. The colonial center rivals Quito's and is much more tranquil to explore, with a church for every week of the year and rows of pastel-colored houses with intricately carved wooden windows and doors. The historical center also has a wealth of excellent museums, restaurants, and hotels. The southern Sierra's other main city, Loja, is also worth a visit, for its wide streets leading to elegant plazas.

Just south of Loja, the countryside around Vilcabamba is a joy to explore, offering some of the best self-guided hikes in the country. This small, charming town is also the country's principal health and wellness destination, with excellent spa and yoga facilities, a bewildering range of therapies, and an abundance of organic food.

PLANNING YOUR TIME

It's worth devoting at least two days to Cuenca's historical center and museums.

After that, the city makes an excellent base from which to explore many of the region's attractions as day trips, including El Cajas National Park; Ingapirca; the artisanal towns of Gualaceo, Chordeleg, and San Bartolomé; and the El Chorro waterfall. The Cañari community tourism projects at Kushi Waira and Jima take a day each.

Those wishing to immerse themselves in traditional Andean culture could arrange a homestay for a couple of nights in Jima near Cuenca; or one of the rural communities near Saraguro, three hours south of Cuenca on the way to Loja.

Loja is an attractive city that merits an overnight stay. Just south of there, a very enjoyable few days can be spent in Vilcabamba.

Podocarpus National Park can be visited as a day trip from Loja, Zamora, or Vilcabamba. Serious hikers can hire a guide and make the two-day trek to the Lagunas del Compadre. Likewise, El Cajas National Park has a two-day trek on the Inca road to a series of lakes. Another adventurous option is the three-day Inca Trek, which starts in Achupallas near Alausí and follows the Inca road through the *páramo*, ending at the Ingapirca ruins.

The southern Sierra is often warm during the day and chilly at night, especially in Cuenca. While there is some variation between places, it's generally rainier between February and May. The weather can change quickly, so wear layers and always have a sweater with you. There are a couple of places to watch your valuables in Cuenca and Loja, but this is one of the safest areas in Ecuador. Water can be drunk straight from the faucet in much of the region.

Previous: Cuenca's Catedral Nueva; the organ in Cuenca's Old Cathedral; bougainvillea flowers in Vilcabamba.

Ingapirca

★ INGAPIRCA RUINS

Ingapirca, which means "Inca wall" in Kichwa, is Ecuador's most important set of pre-Columbian ruins, located 80 kilometers (50 mi) north of Cuenca. The sight of the Inca sun temple standing on a hill with panoramic views over the surrounding countryside is highly impressive, and the site has a fascinating history.

History

The Cañari lived here long before the Incas arrived and are famous for their determined resistance of the invasion, successfully defending their territory against the army of Inca ruler Túpac Yupanqui. It wasn't until Yupanqui's son, Huayna Capac, continued his father's campaign that the Incan empire finally conquered Cañari territory, through a combination of wars and marriages. Interestingly, following their victory, the invaders had enough respect for the Cañari to build a community together, constructing their own Temple of the Sun to complement the existing Temple of the Moon. As well as a ceremonial site, Ingapirca is thought to have had astronomical, political, and administrative functions. A few high status individuals and families resided there, visited occasionally by Huayna Capac's son, Atahualpa.

At 3,200 meters (10,500 ft) elevation, Ingapirca's position overlooking the surrounding valley was of key strategic importance, but its growth was short-lived. The complex is thought to have been destroyed shortly before the Spanish conquest, in a war between Atahualpa and his brother Huáscar in 1532. The Spanish later ransacked the site and much of the stonework was used to build churches and haciendas in Cuenca and beyond. The site lay abandoned until the Ecuadorian government began a restoration process in the mid-20th century, opening the site to the public in 1966.

The Site

Much of the site is little more than stone foundations, and it takes imagination and a guided tour to bring it to life. The **Pilaloma** complex on the south side marks the original Cañari

The three-day Inca Trek starts at Achupallas and ends at Ingapirca.

settlement. The most interesting feature is the collective tomb of a Cañari priestess and 10 of her servants, who were buried alive with her upon her death, along with thousands of spondylus shells. The tomb lies under a large stone that is thought to be linked to various astronomical calculations and was possibly used as a sacrificial altar.

Farther into the complex, there is an expansive open space where large numbers of devotees gathered for ceremonies. Just beyond this, a fragment of **Inca road** remains, part of a network that once connected religious and administrative centers across Ecuador, Peru, Colombia, Bolivia, Argentina, and Chile. Other features include ceremonial baths, agricultural terraces, and grain storage areas.

The highlight of the complex is the elliptical **Temple of the Sun,** the only one of its kind in the Incan empire, built on top of an ancient Cañari ceremonial rock. As well as a site for rituals, is thought that the structure was used to determine the agricultural and religious calendars. The most important event was Inti Raymi, the Festival of the Sun, which is still celebrated at Ingapirca every June. The mind-boggling stonework that is the hallmark of Inca construction can be fully appreciated here, with volcanic rocks hand-carved so precisely that mortar was unnecessary. The view is equally as impressive.

Next to the temple is the **House of the Chosen,** where the most beautiful girls from the neighboring villages lived as Virgins of the Sun. Removed from their families as children, they were taught how to dance, embroider, weave, and cook under the supervision of matrons called Mama Cunas. Their duties included entertaining visiting Incan dignitaries, preparing ceremonial food, maintaining a sacred fire, and weaving garments for the emperor and for rituals. They would go on to marry high-ranking men such as Incas, distinguished soldiers, and priests.

Also near the temple is a large stone with 28 holes of varying sizes, thought to have been a lunar calendar. It is believed that the holes were filled with water, which told the

date by reflecting the moon's light differently throughout the month. A 20-minute walk from the temple is a cliff in which appears a giant human face known as the **Cara del Inca,** probably a natural phenomenon.

Near the entrance is a small museum that houses a collection of Cañari and Inca ceramics, sculptures, tools, traditional dress, and a skeleton found at the site. There are several handicrafts shops and cafés selling traditional fare.

Visiting Ingapirca

Entrance to the **Complejo Arqueológico de Ingapirca** (tel. 7/221-7107, http://patrimoniocultural.gob.ec/complejo-arqueologico-ingapirca, Facebook @complejoingapircaoficial, 8:30am-5pm Mon.-Tues. and 8:30am-5:30pm Wed.-Sun., $2) includes an obligatory tour. Signs in Spanish, English, and Kichwa explain the basics of the site, but few of the guides speak much English. If you don't speak Spanish and would like to get the most out of your experience, consider going with an organized tour from Cuenca. Ingapirca is one of the best places in the country to join in the **Inti Raymi** celebrations, where Andean peoples give thanks to the Pachamama (Mother Earth) for the harvest. More than a hundred indigenous groups from Ecuador and other Andean countries gather at Ingapirca for traditional dancing, music, gastronomy, and crafts fairs. The festivities last for three days between June 17 and 23. Check the Facebook page for the exact dates.

Most tour companies in Cuenca offer organized excursions with English-speaking guides ($50 pp). Also available is a one-day hike on the Inca road through the *páramo*, ending at Ingapirca ($90 pp). See the *Cuenca* section for recommended agencies.

A more adventurous way to arrive is the three-day **Inca Trek,** which starts in Achupallas near Alausí and follows the ancient Inca road through the pristine Ecuadorian *páramo* in Sangay National Park. The hike passes beautiful lagoons and the ruins of stone buildings where Incan messengers took refuge. With a maximum elevation of 4,200 meters (13,780 ft), this is one of the highest points of the Inca road. **Community Hostel** (tel. 98/563-7714, www.communityalausi. com) in Alausí can organize the Inca Trek for $250 per person, including mules, tents, meals, and rubber boots. Unlike many agencies, they hire local guides from Achupallas. Keep in mind that you'll be hiking at over 3,000 meters (9,800 ft) elevation the whole way, and that the weather can change quickly. Bring lots of warm clothes and keep your waterproof jacket handy.

Transportes Cañar (tel. 7/284-3940) has direct buses from the *terminal terrestre* in Cuenca to **Ingapirca** (9am and 12:20pm Mon.-Fri., 9am Sat.-Sun., 2.5 hours, $3.50).

If you miss the direct bus, there are regular buses to **Cañar** (2 hours, $2) and **Tambo** (2 hours, $2.50), where you can change for Ingapirca (30 minutes, $0.50). Similarly, if you're traveling from the north along the Panamericana, get out at **Cañar** or **Tambo,** both of which have connections to Quito.

In a restored 200-year-old estate just 300 meters (980 ft) from the ruins, **Posada Ingapirca** (tel. 7/283-1120, http://posadaingapirca.com, $80 s, $113 d, breakfast included) has comfortable, rustic guest rooms, each with a chimney or heater. The restaurant ($10) is open to nonguests and has a fireplace. There are no vegetarian main courses, but most of the appetizers are meat-free, including quinoa soup.

Cuenca and Vicinity

The capital of Azuay province, Cuenca is Ecuador's third largest city and arguably its most beautiful. With only 400,000 inhabitants, it's much smaller than Quito and Guayaquil, retaining a far more intimate atmosphere. Declared a UNESCO World Heritage Site in 1996 due to the abundance of 16th- and 17th-century Spanish architecture, this is a place to forget itineraries and meander the cobblestone streets and stately plazas, gazing up at church spires and peeking into elegant courtyards. Overlooking the narrow sidewalks, rows of colonial houses have intricately carved wooden windows and doors, opening on to wrought-iron balconies hung with geraniums. Some buildings have been immaculately restored, while others are resplendent in their faded glory.

Cuenca's official name is Santa Ana de los Cuatro Ríos de Cuenca, for the four rivers that run through the city: the Tarqui, Machángara, Yanuncay, and Tomebamba. The last, with its grassy banks and fast-flowing water, is one of Cuenca's most prominent and attractive features, dividing the historical center to the north from the modern district to the south.

Cuenca is a devoutly Catholic city, both architecturally and culturally, but it's not without its bohemian streak. There is a large student population and, as in Quito, there are more alternatively dressed people here than in other Ecuadorian cities. There is also some truly wonderful street art, thanks in part to a municipal ordinance that saw dozens of artists commissioned by the council to create murals all over the city center.

Cuenca is a popular destination for foreign visitors and U.S. retirees, with an excellent range of restaurants and accommodations. Many museums, attractions, and restaurants are closed on Sundays, which also makes it the most peaceful day to roam the streets. Central Cuenca is safe to walk around, although keep your valuables out of sight near the Mercado 9 de Octubre; on the street Convención del 45; and in the area around the Barrial Blanco and the *terminal terrestre.* It's best to avoid these areas completely at night. If you're arriving at or departing the *terminal terrestre* after dark, take a taxi. At an elevation of 2,530 meters (8,300 ft), the weather can change rapidly from strong sun

Cuenca Center

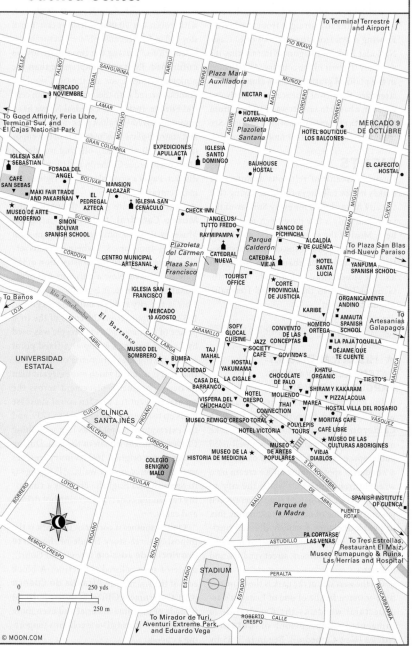

© MOON.COM

to chilly rain. Nights are cold, so bring warm clothes.

Unlike most places in Ecuador, the city water is drinkable straight from the faucet. Flowing down from the *páramos* of El Cajas National Park and Laguna Kimsacocha, it's arguably the best in the country. As reflected in the political graffiti that sits alongside the street art, the city of Cuenca is currently engaged in a battle to save its water sources from the ravages of transnational gold mining. See the *Background* chapter for more information.

SIGHTS

Cuenca's wealth of religious architecture makes it easy to believe the local saying that the city has a church for every Sunday of the year, and only a few have been mentioned here. Most of the sites of interest within the historical center are in the compact area between the river Tomebamba to the south and the streets Gran Colombia to the north, General Torres to the west, and Hermano Miguel to the east.

TOP EXPERIENCE

★ Historical District
CATEDRAL NUEVA AND PARQUE CALDERÓN

Palm and pine trees interspersed with well-maintained flowerbeds fill **Parque Calderón**, Cuenca's central square. Like most of Ecuador's *plazas*, this is a well-used public space. At the heart of the old city, it's a wonderful spot to enjoy an ice cream on a wrought-iron bench and watch the city go past, alongside felt-hatted elderly gentlemen passing the time of day. The fascinating mix of people includes formally dressed businesspeople, indigenous campesinos in traditional dress, shoe shiners, street vendors, and tourists.

On the west side of the park is the immense twin-towered facade of one of Ecuador's architectural wonders—the Catedral de la Inmaculada Concepción, or **Catedral Nueva** (New Cathedral). Begun in 1885 by an ambitious local bishop who decided the old cathedral wasn't big enough, it was originally planned as South America's largest church, with room for 10,000 worshippers. Work stopped in 1908 because of "architectural miscalculations," leaving the two square towers unfinished. Even more impressive than the pink travertine facade are the twin sky-blue domes, covered with tiles imported from central Europe. Inside, the Catedral Nueva has a sumptuous gold-leaf altar, pink marble pillars, and stained-glass windows. One of the cupolas can be climbed ($2), offering wonderful views over Parque Calderón and the historical district. Pay at a small kiosk to the right of the main entrance.

On the opposite side of the park is the **Museo Catedral Vieja** (Old Cathedral Museum, 9am-5:15pm Mon.-Fri., 10am-4pm Sat., 8am-4pm Sun., $2), where religious services were held until the construction of the Catedral Nueva. Now a museum and occasional music venue, it is well worth a visit. This is the city's oldest building, begun in 1557 with stones from the ruins of the Inca palace of Pumapungo. The steeple was used by La Condamine's group as a fixed point whilst taking measurements of the earth. Inside, it is cool and much more elegant than its newer, brasher replacement across the square. A beautiful wooden spiral staircase leads up to an organ dating back to 1739, and the extravagant pulpit looks like something Cinderella might ride in to the ball. During renovations, original 16th-century frescoes were discovered on the walls. All signage is in Spanish and English. There is a charming café in the courtyard serving hot drinks and cakes.

On the southeast corner of the park is the imposing three-story facade of the **Corte Provincial de Justicia** (Provincial Court), made of rose-colored travertine. A block east of the square, the **Alcaldía de Cuenca** (City Government Office, Bolívar *y* Borrero) is made of the same material and even more impressive, featuring Doric columns supporting a cupola.

PLAZOLETA DEL CARMEN AND PLAZA SAN FRANCISCO

West of Parque Calderón, next to the cathedral, flower vendors fill the tiny Plazoleta del Carmen, also called the **Plaza de las Flores,** with colors and scents. The white church flanking the square (with Santuario Mariano written on the side) is the **Iglesia El Carmen de la Asunción,** founded in 1682, part of the **Monasterio del Carmen.** The resident nuns, the *madres carmelitas,* sell a health tonic, *agua de pitima,* from a hatch in the side of the convent. Made from flowers, especially carnations, and sweetened with honey, the pink drink is said to be good for the nervous system and sells like hotcakes with the locals. Passion fruit and blackberry sacramental wine is also available.

One block to the south is the **Plaza San Francisco,** overlooked by the peach-and-white church of the same name, reconstructed in the early 20th century. The recently renovated square, which has sadly lost some of its original character, has a number of kiosks selling handicrafts and textiles such as alpaca ponchos and blankets.

PLAZA SAN SEBASTIÁN AND MUSEO DE ARTE MODERNO

At the western edge of the colonial center, the 17th-century **Iglesia San Sebastián** occupies the north side of the park of the same name. Facing it is the **Museo de Arte Moderno** (Sucre 15-27 *y* Coronel Talbot, tel. 7/413-4900, ext. 1960, Facebook @mmamcuenca, 9am-5:30pm Mon.-Fri., 9am-1pm Sat.-Sun., free), which was originally a *casa de temperancia* (house of temperance). In the late 19th century, the city experienced an economic boom, due to exports of wool weavings and *sombreros de paja toquilla* ("Panama" hats), which also brought an upswing in alcohol consumption. In response, a local bishop opened a treatment center for alcoholics in 1876, with cells off a central courtyard for those most affected. After passing through various incarnations as a men's jail, a nursing home, and a home for poor single mothers, the stately old structure was inaugurated as a museum in 1981, housing the donated collection of Cuencano painter Luis Crespo Ordóñez. Since 2015, the museum has been adding to this collection, displaying the pieces in the former cells.

MUSEO AND CONVENTO DE LAS CONCEPTAS

Cuenca's richest religious art collection is found in the museum of the **Convento de las Conceptas** (Hermano Miguel 6-33 *y* Jaramillo, tel. 7/283-0625, Facebook @museodelasconceptasecuador, 9am-6:30pm Mon.-Fri., 10am-5pm Sat.-Sun., $3.50), which occupies the block bounded by Córdova, Jaramillo, Borrero, and Hermano Miguel; the entrance is on Miguel. Twenty-two rooms of sculpture and painting are housed in the former infirmary, including many representations of Jesus, the Virgin Mary, angels, cherubs, and saints.

PLAZA SAN BLAS

With the **Iglesia San Blas** on one side and the twin white towers of the **Casa Provincial** on the other, **Plaza San Blas** is an attractive square with a central fountain. Several interesting discoveries were made during the extensive 2017-2018 restoration of the church, which once defined the eastern city limit. As well as murals on the walls beneath layers of paint, a cornerstone was unearthed dated 1557, indicating that construction began the same year as the Old Cathedral, the oldest European structure in the city. Perhaps the most mysterious discovery was a three-level mausoleum, the identity of whose occupants remains unknown.

Along Calle Larga and Río Tomebamba

A stroll along **Calle Larga,** running parallel to the Río Tomebamba, takes visitors past a series of museums. Two sets of stone steps adorned with street art link the *calle* with the riverside path, Paseo 3 de Noviembre. This section of the Tomebamba, known as

El Barranco, has grassy slopes just asking to be lazed upon and some beautiful buildings overlooking the fast-flowing water, including restaurants and cafés. An extremely enjoyable day can be spent meandering between Calle Larga and 3 Noviembre, with the occasional hop across the river to see the attractions on the south side. El Barranco used to be dangerous at night, but it's been revamped in recent years. Now decently lit and safe to wander, it is the heart of the city's nightlife.

MUSEO DEL SOMBRERO

At the west end of the Calle Larga is the **Museo del Sombrero** (Calle Larga 10-41 *y* Padre Aguirre, tel. 98/236-2998, Facebook @ museodelsombrerocuenca, 8:30am-6:30pm Mon.-Fri., 9:30am-5pm Sat., 9:30am-1:30pm Sun., free), where the process of making "Panama hats," or *sombreros de paja toquilla,* is displayed, step-by-step. This is also a hat finishing factory, where the *sombreros* arrive already woven with a multitude of *toquilla* strands still hanging down from the brim. It's possible to watch them being trimmed, pressed, and decorated with bands. The shop carries a wide range of styles and colors, categorized according to quality. A standard hat costs $28-35 and one labeled *fino* is $50-300. A handful of *superfinos,* which take 2-3 months to make, are kept in a locked cabinet, costing $600-900 and up. There is a café on-site.

MUSEO REMIGIO CRESPO TORAL

Two blocks farther down is the restored home of a 19th-century intellectual, **Museo Remigio Crespo Toral** (Larga 7-27 *y* Borrero, tel. 7/413-4900, ext. 1970, Facebook @casamuseoremigiocrespotoral, 10am-5pm Tues.-Fri., 10am-2pm Sat.-Sun., free). Crespo Toral was a renowned writer, newspaper founder, politician, and academic. The museum includes collections of religious sculptures, paintings, and archaeological relics, but the main attraction is the house itself, built a century ago in neoclassical style and full of original furniture. Entry is via either Calle Larga or the riverside path, Paseo 3 de Noviembre. There is a café on the riverside terrace.

MUSEO DE LA HISTORIA DE LA MEDICINA

Cross the river on to 12 de Abril to find the macabre **Museo de la Historia de la Medicina** (tel. 7/283-5859, 8am-1:30pm and 2pm-5pm Mon.-Fri., free). Housed in what was Cuenca's first hospital, built in 1876, the museum has a bizarre collection of medical history, from ledger books to an iron lung. Most unsettling are the saws and harnesses used for amputations and two mummified children aged 5 years and 8 months. With piped war-time music playing throughout the central courtyard, it's a fairly chilling experience.

PARQUE DE LA MADRE

Also on the south side of the river is **Parque de la Madre** (12 de Abril *y* Malo), which has an excellent children's playground, outdoor exercise equipment, and a running track. A planetarium offers free hour-long presentations daily.

MUSEO DE ARTES POPULARES

Cross back to the north side of the river for the **Museo de Artes Populares** (Hermano Miguel 3-23 *y* Paseo 3 de Noviembre, tel. 7/282-9451, 8:30am-5pm Mon.-Fri., free), which showcases crafts and popular arts from all over Latin America. The museum and café are housed in a beautiful converted private mansion built in 1950, accessed via 3 de Noviembre.

MUSEO DE LAS CULTURAS ABORIGINES

One of the most impressive museums along Calle Larga is the extraordinary private collection of local historian and university professor Dr. Juan Cordero, at the **Museo de las**

1: Iglesia San Blas; **2:** Panama hat display at the Museo del Sombrero; **3:** door of the Catedral Nueva; **4:** Parque Calderón

Culturas Aborigines (Larga 5-24 y Cueva, tel. 7/283-9181, Facebook @museoculturasaborigenes, 9am-6pm Mon.-Fri., 9am-2pm Sat., $4). The museum is a homage to Ecuadorian indigenous peoples, creators of the 5,000 ancient treasures on display, spanning every culture from 13,000 BC up to the Spanish conquest. Highlights include some of the oldest pottery in the Americas; the iconic Venus figures made by the Valdivia culture around 3500 BC; a Manteño stone chair; beautifully painted Inca ceremonial drinking vessels; and a skull with gold-inlaid teeth. Guidebooks are provided in English, Spanish, and French. The museum also has a handicrafts shop and a café.

MUSEO PUMAPUNGO

At the end of Calle Larga is the city's top museum, **Museo Pumapungo** (Larga y Huayna Capac, tel. 7/283-1521, 8am-5pm Mon.-Fri., 10am-4pm Sat.-Sun., free), which has beautifully laid out collections of archaeological pieces, coins, and 19th-century religious art. A whole floor is dedicated to an excellent ethnographic exhibition on Ecuador's indigenous cultures, with dioramas, re-created dwellings, examples of traditional dress, and descriptions of the various nationalities' world views. Most of the signage for the museum is in Spanish but, luckily, the most fascinating section of all, on Shuar shamanism, has translations in English. There are explanations of coming-of-age rituals; the role of the shaman; the difference between black magicians and healers; and displays of five *tsantsas* (shrunken heads). Sadly, taking photos is forbidden throughout the museum.

Visitors also have access to the **Pumapungo ruins,** one of the only remaining fragments of Tumebamba, the Incan city that preceded Cuenca. Tumebamba is thought to have been the birthplace of the Inca emperor Huayna Capac, under whose rule the Inca empire reached its greatest extent and power. He later chose to build the empire's northern capital here, modeling it on Cuzco. Most of the city was destroyed shortly before the Spanish conquest, in a war between Huayna Capac's sons, Atahualpa and Huáscar, in 1532. Nowadays, the ruins are little more than row upon row of walls and foundations, but it's still an interesting site, with a hillside setting overlooking the river. Below the ruins are ethno-botanical gardens and a bird rescue center, accessed via a door at the back of the museum. Keep going past the rather unpromising quadrangle area to reach the stepped walls and gardens.

Mirador de Turi

For spectacular views over the city and the peaks of El Cajas in the distance, head 4 kilometers (2.5 mi) south of the center along Avenida Solano up to the **Mirador de Turi.** Look closely and you can pick out the blue domes of Cuenca's new cathedral. Buses leave from 12 de Abril and Solano ($0.30), or a taxi costs about $3. Climb the stairs farther up to **Reina del Cisne,** which sells a wide range of artisanal wares.

Behind the mirador, the **Aventuri Extreme Park** (tel. 98/797-4278, 10am-7pm daily, $1) has a variety of activities, including canopy zip lines ($5), a tree house, a Tarzan swing, and a rope bridge. The highlight is the swing ($3) or *columpio*, which makes your stomach drop as you fly out over the city spread out below.

Outside the City

Located 7 kilometers (4.3 mi) to the east of the city center, the **Amaru Bioparque** (Autopista Cuenca-Azogues km 10.5, opposite the Hospital del Río, tel. 7/421-3982, www.zoobioparqueamaru.com, 9am-5pm Mon.-Fri., 10am-5pm Sat.-Sun., $6) is a sanctuary for animals that have been rescued from traffickers or were illegally kept as pets. The enclosures are ranged along a steep two-hour hiking trail, so wear comfortable shoes and bring plenty of water. Species include spectacled bears, pumas, monkeys, and jaguars. Come on weekends to see talks on the various animals. The center is involved in environmental and conservation efforts.

ENTERTAINMENT AND EVENTS

Nightlife is not nearly as raucous in Cuenca as in Quito or Guayaquil. During the week many places close early, and it's very quiet after dark. On Thursday, Friday, and Saturday evenings, though, the bars and discos along Calle Larga and El Barranco get busy, especially on Fridays. It's safe to wander and browse this area to see which spot takes your fancy. Cuenca is a fickle city when it comes to nightlife, and many places only last a year or so while they are in fashion. The venues listed here are longstanding favorites, popular with locals and visitors alike. You may be required to present ID to enter some venues, regardless of your age.

Nightlife

A great spot for pre-club drinks is **Vieja Diablos** (Calle Larga *y* Hermano Miguel, 6pm-midnight Mon.-Thurs., 6pm-2am Fri.-Sat.), which is a café and bakery as well as a bar. The *canelazo* (spiced hot fruit punch with aguardiente) is excellent and cheap ($1 per glass or $6 per bottle), and mojitos are two for $4. It's one of few bars open on Mondays and there is occasional live music. The bar at **La Cigale** (Honorato Vásquez 7-80 *y* Luis Cordero, tel. 7/283-5308, www.hostallacigale.com) has a happy hour (4pm-8pm Mon.-Sat.) and live music on Tuesdays.

On the riverside at El Barranco, **Zoociedad** (Paseo 3 de Noviembre *y* Benigno Malo, tel. 99/183-1026, Facebook @zoociedad.cafe, 9pm-2am Thurs.-Sat.) is a Cuencano institution. The $2.50 entry includes a *canelazo* or a beer—the only two drinks on the menu. Inside is a dance floor, outside is a terrace with tables. Music is eclectic but avoids *reggaetón*. There are free salsa classes on Thursdays and occasional live music. Next door, **Bumba** (tel. 99/550-3529, Facebook @bumbafruitsandbeer, 4pm-3am Tues.-Fri., noon-3am Sat.) has offers on drinks and decent bar food, including a veggie burger. There are regular live music events and DJs. **Vispera del Chuchaqui** (Calle Larga 7-119 *y* Luis Cordero, tel. 99/582-9980, Facebook @ VisperadelChuchaqui, 4pm-midnight Tues.-Thurs., 4pm-2am Fri.-Sat.) is another popular spot, with occasional live music and a fairly smart dress code.

For salsa dancing, head to the small *salsateca* **La Mesa** (Gran Colombia 3-55 *y* Ordóñez, tel. 99/286-6648, Facebook @ lamesasalsayson, 9pm-midnight Wed., 10pm-3pm Sat.). For live jazz, the place to be is the candlelit **Jazz Society Café** (Luis Cordero 5-101 *y* Juan Jaramillo, tel. 93/934-2714, Facebook @JazzSocietyCafe, Wed.-Sat. 6:30pm-10pm, $10 cover), upstairs in La Viña Italian Restaurant.

Recently opened and popular at the time of writing is swanky club **Pa Cortarse Las Venas** (Milenium Plaza, Facebook @ PaCortaLasVenas, open late Thurs.-Sat., $15 entry), which has a smart dress code.

Festivals

Cuenca is the best place in the country to participate in the January 6 **Santos Inocentes** festivities, which date back to the 5th century and commemorate the children who were massacred by Herod. Like many Ecuadorian festivals, it is a mixture of Catholic and pagan traditions. People flock to the streets in costumes and masks, and a parade remembers the main events and characters from the previous year. To demonstrate the innocence of the people, practical jokes are played.

Carnival is celebrated in much the same way as other places in Ecuador, with water fights, drinking, and general revelry, but Cuenca has a unique way of kicking off the festivities. On **Jueves de Compadres y Comadres,** leaf-wrapped dolls of bread or sugar are given to friends to strengthen bonds of solidarity and as an invitation to celebrate together over Carnival.

On **Good Friday,** thousands of people participate in a procession starting in San Blas park at 7:30pm and continuing through the city center, honoring the Passion of Christ. The Spanish **Founding of Cuenca** is marked with cultural and artistic programs on April 12. Cuenca is famous for its **Corpus Christi** celebrations, which take place in May or June and include fireworks and music in Parque Calderón. To represent the body of Christ, traditional sweets are sold in stalls next to the cathedral. The Independence of Cuenca is commemorated November 1-4 with cultural, folkloric, civic, and military events.

On December 24, Cuenca hosts the best Christmas parade in the country, known as the **Pase del Niño,** or Passage of the Child. During the festival, introduced by the Spanish almost 500 years ago, likenesses of the infant Jesus are carried through towns and villages. Organizers of the Cuenca parade claim it is the largest in Latin America, and while this claim is unproven, it is certainly one of the most important manifestations of popular religiosity in Ecuador, attended by thousands of people from all over the country. The parade features floats and cars festooned with flowers, fruits, vegetables, beer cans, liquor bottles, roasted pigs, and chickens. There are children in costumes, indigenous groups in traditional dress, bands, dancers, street performers, and stilt-walkers. John the Baptist, the wise men, and Mary and Joseph all make an appearance. At the heart of the celebration is a model of Jesus known as the Niño Viajero (Traveling Child). Made in 1823, the sculpture was taken by its owner to various holy sites around the world and blessed by the pope in 1961. For most of the year, the Niño Viajero is kept in the convent of the nuns of Carmen de la Asunción. The parade starts at 10am on Avenida Ordóñez Lasso and runs along Simón Bolívar, ending around 3pm.

Like the rest of Ecuador, Cuenca celebrates the **New Year** by burning firecracker-filled effigies. On the preceding nights, men dress as widows of the outgoing year and ask the public for funeral contributions (aka a beer fund). Cuenca follows the Sierran tradition of reading the "will" of the dying year, filled with jokes and criticisms of friends, neighbors, and the government.

RECREATION AND TOURS

All recommended tour agencies offer the most popular day trips, each costing $50-55 per person, including hiking in El Cajas National Park; a tour of Ingapirca; a visit to the artisanal towns of Gualaceo, Chordeleg, and San Bartolomé; and a trip to Girón and the El Chorro waterfall. All tours include transport, a bilingual guide, and lunch (vegetarians catered for by prior request). These are group tours and usually leave with a minimum of two people. Cuenca is easy to explore independently, but half-day city tours are available for $25. All agencies also offer private tailor-made local and nationwide tours upon request.

In addition to the standard tours, **Polylepis Tours** (Hermano Miguel 4-35 y Calle Larga, tel. 7/283-0248 or 9/851-16721, https://polylepistours.com, 9am-1pm and 2:30pm-7pm Mon.-Fri.) offers bird-watching in El Cajas National Park and other areas; a Wild Cajas hiking trip for those looking to get off the beaten track in the national park; and a visit to an indigenous Cañari community. Their full-day tour to the indigenous town of Saraguro ($120 pp) includes an artisanal factory making *liquor de agave* (a local tequilaesque drink); a workshop where the famous black-and-white Saraguro hats are made; a ritual with medicinal plants at a waterfall; and a traditional lunch. All tours are bilingual in Spanish and English. French and Italian can be arranged with prior notice. Polylepis includes extra elements to their tours, such as churches and markets or visits to local families.

Shiram y Kakaram (until recently Arutam Ecotours, Honorato Vásquez y Hermano Miguel, tel. 98/321-2728 or 99/769-7610, http://shiramykakaram.com) specializes in two- to four-day Amazon trips to Shuar communities in the province of Morona-Santiago, a region visited by few tourists. Accommodations are in tents or cabañas. Also available is a one-night jungle trip to participate in a Shuar ayahuasca ceremony in a traditional hut. Unlike many ceremonies that are offered to tourists, these are intimate experiences with just your group, plus possibly a few local people. The tour includes transport, a tobacco ritual, an ayahuasca ceremony, a dawn bathe in a river or waterfall, and breakfast. The friendly owner of the agency, Xavi, can also arrange volunteering in a Shuar community, either teaching English or helping with traditional agriculture. He sells organic Amazonian products and jewelry in the agency office to support the community. Other tours include paragliding, canyoneering, one- to two-day horseback rides, and the Inca Trek to Ingapirca (one or three days). For all these tours, the agency receives rave reviews.

Expediciones Apullacta (Gran Colombia 11-02 y General Torres, tel. 7/283-7815, www.apullacta.com) offers one- or two-day tours to Saraguro; a one-day hike on the Inca trail to Ingapirca; horseback riding in Tarqui; canyoneering at Río Amarillo; rock climbing at Cojitambo; and a canopy adventure, as well as the usual trips.

The community tourism network for the southern Sierra region, **Pakariñan Ecuador** (Mariscal Sucre 14-96 y Coronel Guillermo Tálbot, tel. 7/282-0529 or 98/795-9379, Facebook @pakarinanec) is upstairs from the fair trade store **MAKI** (www.fairtrade. ec), which is part of the same organization. Pakariñan offers tours to two community tourism projects: one at Ñamarin (see the section on *Saraguro* for more information) and another to the Cañari village of Sidsid near Ingapirca, where local guides take visitors hiking to the beautiful Laguna Culebrillas. At Sidsid, it is also possible to stay with a local family, participate in traditional organic agriculture, and learn Kichwa. Pakariñan can provide information on visiting the artisanal communities that create the products in the MAKI store, including *sombreros de paja toquilla, macana* shawls, jewelry, ponchos, and Andean clothing. Also part of the network is a project at Chobshi near Sígsig, which offers visits to caves and an archaeological site dating back 8,000 years; and one at Carmen Dejadan, 90 minutes from Cuenca, where a women-led project offers traditional weaving, ancestral medicine, agro-ecology, and traditional cuisine. The projects at Kushi Waira and Jima, plus APECAEL near Vilcabamba, featured elsewhere in this chapter, are also part of Pakariñan.

Vanservice (Hermano Miguel y Presidente Cordova, tel. 7/281-6409, www. vanservice.com.ec) offers sightseeing bus tours of the city ($8), leaving half-hourly from Parque Calderón, plus a bus trip to El Cajas National Park and a combined trip to Ingapirca, Gualaceo, and Chordeleg.

SHOPPING

The most famous product made locally is the "Panama" hat, or *sombrero de paja toquilla*. Even though these hats originate from Montecristi in Manabí province, Cuenca is Ecuador's main production and export center. Prices range from $15 to a couple of thousand dollars, depending on the fineness of the weave. **Homero Ortega Padre e Hijos** (Dávalos 3-86, tel. 7/280-9000 or 98/499-7227, www.homeroortega.com, 8am-12:30pm and 2:30pm-5pm Mon.-Fri., 8:30am-12:30pm Sat., by appointment only 9am-11am Sun.) exports sombreros around the world from a factory and shop behind the *terminal terrestre*. There is a small museum with free guided tours in English about the history and process of making the hats. Homero Ortega also has a shop in the city center (Hermano Miguel 6-84 y Presidente Córdova, 9am-1pm and 2:30pm-6:30pm Mon.-Fri.). On the same street is **La Paja Toquilla** (Juan Jaramillo 5-100 y Hermano Miguel, tel. 7/282-7863, www.pajatoquilla.com). Another good option is **Museo del Sombrero** (Calle Larga 10-41 y Padre Aguirre, tel. 98/236-2998, Facebook @museodelsombrerocuenca, 8:30am-6:30pm Mon.-Fri., 9:30am-5pm Sat., 9:30am-1:30pm Sun., free), where the Paredes Roldan family has been making hats since 1942.

Located near the modern art museum, **MAKI** (Mariscal Sucre 14-96 y Coronel Guillermo Tálbot, tel. 7/282-0529 or

98/795-9379, 10am-7pm Mon.-Fri., 10am-5pm Sat.-Sun., www.fairtrade.ec) is a fair trade store offering a high-quality selection of southern Ecuador's most emblematic handicrafts, including *sombreros de paja toquilla*, *macana* shawls, jewelry, ponchos, and Andean clothing. The shop is managed by the four communities that supply the products.

On the west side of the Plaza San Francisco, the **Centro Municipal Artesanal** or **CEMUART** (General Torres 7-33, tel. 7/284-5854, 9am-6:30pm Mon.-Fri., 9am-5pm Sat., 9am-1pm Sun.) has 84 little shops within a characterful arcade, where you can watch some of the artists at work. It's an interesting and pleasant place to browse for jewelry, leather bags, vases, dolls, painted wooden boxes, hats, embroidery, traditional sweets, and lots of other crafts.

Galapagos Artesanias (Presidente Cordova 6-37 *y* Hermano Miguel, tel. 99/119-4527, Facebook @galapagosartesanias, 9am-7pm Mon.-Sat., 10am-1pm Sun.) has a good range of high-quality handicrafts and souvenirs and can send items anywhere in the world.

Famed ceramicist **Eduardo Vega** has a workshop and gallery (Vía a Turi 201, tel. 7/415-1853, www.ceramicavega.com, 8am-5:30pm Mon.-Fri., 9:30am-1:30pm Sat.-Sun.) in the gardens of his house 60 meters (200 ft) below the Mirador de Turi.

For jewelry, it's best to go to Chordeleg, but there are several *joyerías* (jewelry shops) in Cuenca on Colombia between Aguirre and Cordero.

For organic, natural, and fair trade products, including food, health, toiletry, and household items, head to **Khatu Organic** (Hermano Miguel 5-41 *y* Honorato Vásquez, tel. 97/908-1666, www.khatuorganic.com) or **Nectar** (Benigno Malo 12-27 *y* Gaspar Sangurima, tel. 7/283-7567, https://nectarcuenca.com).

1: jewelry from Saraguro in the MAKI fair trade store; **2:** a Cuenca mural by Marco Medina **3:** colonial architecture; **4:** clay pots that are used in traditional cooking

Markets

The three main centrally located markets are the **Mercado 10 Agosto,** the **Mercado 9 Octubre,** and the **Mercado 3 Noviembre.** All are primarily **food markets,** open daily, great for fresh produce and sampling local cuisine (10 Agosto is especially recommended for its food court). Beware of pickpockets near the Mercado 9 Octubre and avoid it at night. The biggest market is 3.5 kilometers (2.2 mi) to the west of the center, the **Feria Libre,** where products arrive to be distributed to the other markets. It's open daily, but the biggest days are Saturday and Wednesday. On Wednesdays, the parking lot is closed to make space for a clothes market. Tuesdays and Fridays are "energy cleaning" days at most markets, especially 10 Agosto, where women who work with medicinal plants give brief healing sessions. Ask for the *limpiezas energéticas* and you'll be pointed in the right direction.

There are a couple of agro-ecological markets on Saturday mornings, opening around 7am. Arrive before 9am if possible. The biggest is **Biocentro Agroecológico** (Calle Rodrigo de Triana *y* La Rábida), located behind the El Tiempo newspaper office, two blocks south of the intersection between Avenida Loja and Don Bosco. There is also a smaller market on Wednesdays. More central is the Saturday morning market on **Parque del Vergel.**

There is a very photogenic **flower and plant market** in the Plazoleta del Carmen, better known as the **Plaza de los Flores,** just off Plaza Calderón to the west, next to the cathedral. A block southwest of there, the **Plaza San Francisco** has kiosks selling handicrafts and textiles such as alpaca ponchos and blankets.

There is a **handicrafts market** on the Plazoleta Santana, commonly known as the **Plazoleta Los Hippies** (Benigno Malo *y* Mariscal Lamar), that specializes in jewelry and small decorative items made from *tagua,* marble, stone, and wood. An **artisans market** on the **Plaza Rotary** (Vargas

Machuca y Gaspar Sangurima) sells woven baskets, wooden furniture and kitchen utensils, earthenware pots, and home decor items.

FOOD

Cuenca has a great selection of restaurants, the best in Ecuador outside Quito, with many excellent local and international options and plenty of choices for vegetarians.

Cafés and Sweets

★ **Moritas Café** (Hermano Miguel y Calle Larga, tel. 99/290-6777, 8am-1pm Mon.-Sat., 8am-noon Sun., $2-5) is the best spot in town for breakfasts, from fluffy omelets, pancakes, waffles, and fruit salads to local specialties such as *mote pillo*. The coffee is great and the service fast and friendly. The local owner's son, Mateo, works at the café and takes visitors hiking in El Cajas National Park. **Taita** (Calle Larga *entre* Ordoñez y Vega, tel. 98/418-6707, 8am-8pm Mon.-Sat.) is a stylish bakery and café that uses local, organic ingredients from small-scale producers. The menu includes breakfasts, sandwiches, and salads. Breads and pastries are made from traditional flours, including quinoa, corn, and barley. No processed sugar is used, only *panela de miel* (unrefined whole cane sugar syrup) from the Amazon. **Organicamente Andino** (Hermano Miguel 7 48 y Mariscal Sucre, tel. 7/282-2424, 9am-7pm Mon.-Fri., 9am-1pm Sat.) serves organic local snacks such as empanadas and *quimbolitos*, plus juices, sandwiches, and salads. On Parque San Sebastián, **San Sebas** (San Sebastián y Mariscal Sucre, tel. 7/284-3496, www.sansebascuenca.com, 8:30am-3pm Wed.-Sun., $4.50-8) is an attractive breakfast and lunch café offering bagels, pancakes, quesadillas, sandwiches, and burgers, with lots of veggie options.

Buy an ice cream at **Angelus/Tutto Fredo** (Benigno Malo y Simón Bolívar, tel. 7/282-0300, 8am-10:30pm daily), to the right of the Catedral Nueva, and enjoy it on a bench in Parque Calderón. To really indulge your sweet tooth, head to confectioner **Déjame Que Te Cuente** (Hermano Miguel y Córdova,

Facebook @DéjameQueTeCuente), which offers a range of international chocolates and pastries, including Belgian truffles, German marzipans, and Argentinian *alfajores*, made from organic, fair trade Ecuadorian cacao.

Local

The **Mercado 10 Agosto** is known for its good quality food court, which serves national and Sierran dishes at low prices. It's especially famous for its *hornado* (pork roasted in a wood-fired oven). A popular locals' spot for a good set lunch is **Karibe** (Córdova y Hermano Miguel, tel. 99/787-8966), where $2.50 will get you soup, a main course, dessert, and juice. There are also lunch places in the block around Honorato Vásquez and Borrero, most charging $2.50-3. For Ecuadorian breakfasts, lunches, and coastal specialties such as *bolón, encocados,* ceviche, and rice with seafood, head to hidden gem **Chocolate de Palo** (Honorato Vásquez 6-64 *entre* Presidente Borrero y Hermano Miguel, tel. 99/116-6481, 8am-8pm Mon.-Sat., 8am-3pm Sun.).

Many traditional Cuencan dishes have corn as the main ingredient, such as *mote pata* (corn soup with pork, sausage, bacon, and squash seeds); tamales (corn flour dough filled with pork, egg, and raisins, wrapped in leaves and steamed); *quimbolitos* (a sweet version of a tamale); *humitas* (ground corn with egg, butter, and cheese, wrapped in a corn husk and steamed); *mote pillo* (hominy cooked and scrambled with egg, onion, and cheese); and beverages such as *morocho* (a hot beverage of cooked corn, sugar, and cinnamon) and *rosero* (a cold beverage of corn, sugar, and fruit). Another Cuencan specialty is trout from Cajas.

Humitas, tamales, and *quimbolitos* are available all over Cuenca. The traditional place to go is **Las Herrerías,** a historic street full of blacksmiths and little cafés, a few minutes' walk from the Museo Pumapungo along

---

1: Mansion Alcazar; **2:** fruit vendor on a street in Cuenca; **3:** *mote pillo*; **4:** outdoor café in the historical district

Huayna-Capac. For Cuencan specialties such as *mote sucio* (hominy with pork), *habas con queso* (fava beans with cheese), *llapingachos* (fried potato patties), *carne asada* (grilled dried meat served with *mote pillo* and fava beans), head to the San Joaquín neighborhood, which is a $2.50 taxi ride from the city center. Tell the driver *"a la comida en San Joaquín."*

Open since 1952, the family-run ★ **Tres Estrellas** (Calle Larga 1-174 *y* Miguel Ángel Estrella, tel. 9/845-8015 or 7/282-2340, www.tresestrellas.com.ec, 12:30pm-3:30pm and 6:30pm-10pm Mon.-Sat., $3-11) is one of the city center's best spots for Cuencan cuisine, including *cuy* (guinea pig, $25, which must be ordered an hour in advance), *mote pillo, mote sucio, habas con queso,* and *locro de papa* (potato soup). Make sure to ask for a *canelazo* aperitif. Just down the street, **Restaurante El Maiz** (tel. 7/284-0224, Facebook @restaurante.maiz, noon-9pm Mon.-Fri., noon-4pm and 7pm-9pm Sat., $6-11) serves specialties from Cuenca and all over Ecuador. Both restaurants have veggie options.

In the city center, a good place for international and local dishes, including trout, is **Raymipampa** (Benigno Malo 859, tel. 7/283-4159, 8:30am-11pm Mon.-Fri., 9:30am-10am Sat.-Sun., $6-10), under the colonnaded arches of the New Cathedral on the west side of Parque Calderón. Open since 1933, it gets very busy with visitors and locals alike. There are plenty of veggie options.

Locally owned **Tiesto's** (Juan Jaramillo 4-89 *y* Mariano Cueva, tel. 7/283-5310, www.tiestoscaferestaurant.com, 12:30pm-3pm and 6pm-10pm Tues.-Sat.) is a gastronomic experience of Ecuadorian cuisine, with steak the house specialty. The tasting menu costs $76 for two people.

International

Recommended international restaurants in Cuenca include **Thai Connection** (Honorato Vásquez *y* Hermano Miguel, tel. 99/224-4332, noon-9pm Tues.-Sat., $7-11); ★ **Marea** (Hermano Miguel 4-79, tel. 7/282-7827,

Facebook @mareacuenca, dinner Mon.-Wed., lunch and dinner Thurs.-Sun., $7-12), which has great Argentinian-style pizza, plus wonderful chocolate brownie and apple desserts, served hot with ice cream; **Pizzalacqua** (Honorato Vásquez 5-66 *entre* Mariano Cueva *y* Hermano Miguel, tel. 99/987-1684, Facebook @PizzalacquaCuenca, 11am-10pm Mon.-Sat., 11am-6pm Sun., $4-7), a small, friendly place serving pizza, pasta, and lasagna; **El Pedregal Azteca** (Estévez de Toral 8-60 *y* Simón Bolívar, tel. 7/282-3652, www.pedregalazteca.com, noon-3pm and 6:30pm-10:30pm Tues.-Sat., 12:30pm-3:30pm Sun., $8.50-12) for Mexican food; **Taj Mahal** (Calle Larga *y* Benigno Malo, tel. 99/296-9080, $3.50-9) for Indian; and **Moliendo** (Honorato Vásquez 6-24 *y* Hermano Miguel tel. 7/410-2817, 9am-9pm Mon.-Sat., $2.50-8) for great-value Colombian specialties, including *arepas.*

Vegetarian

Cuenca has the best range of vegetarian restaurants outside Quito. Hare Krishna restaurant **Govinda's** (Juan Jaramillo *y* Borrero, tel. 7/282-2036 or 99/833-3518, Facebook @Govinda's Vegetariano, noon-4pm Mon.-Sat.) has decent set lunches for $3.50. Another good lunch option is **Good Affinity** (Capulies 1-89 *y* Gran Colombia, tel. 7/283-2469, Facebook @Good Affinity, 9:30am-3:30pm Mon.-Sat.), worth the trip into New Town, where lunch costs $3. For a bewildering range of cheap veggie meals and juices, head to **Nuevo Paraiso** (Calle Bolívar 2-52 *y* Manuel Vega, tel. 2/838-666, www.paraisovegetariano.com, open daily until 10pm), which has outside seating on Plaza San Blas and is one of the only veggie places open on Sundays. Set lunches and most dishes are around $2.50. Check the website for the other four locations around the city. Ambience and service are basic but functional.

Sofy Glocal Cuisine (Benigno Malo 5-112 *y* Juan Jaramillo, tel. 96/955-4901, Facebook @SofysCuisineCuenca, $9) is a charming brunch and dinner restaurant that serves fresh, healthy veggie and non-veggie meals, including Thai curry, ravioli, and *shakshuka* (eggs poached in a sauce of tomatoes, chili peppers, and onions). Brand-new in 2018, **Killa Pampa** (Malvinas *y* Unidad Nacional, tel. 97/908-1666, Facebook @killapampa, 9am-2pm and 5pm-8pm Mon. and Wed.-Thurs., 9am-2pm and 5pm-9pm Fri.-Sat., 9am-2pm Sun.) is a stylish, elegant restaurant with tables and decor made from recycled materials. The imaginative menu includes veggie and vegan dishes made from ethically sourced ingredients. ★ **Café Libre** (Calle Larga 5-14 *y* Mariano Cueva, tel. 99/487-2297, Facebook @CafeLibreCuenca, $4.75-10) is a gastronomic experience, serving exquisite vegan food. Don't come if you're in a hurry, and do bring warm clothes, as it's in a courtyard.

ACCOMMODATIONS
Under $10

Check Inn (General Torres 8-82 *y* Simón Bolívar, tel. 7/283-1711, $7 pp dorm $9 pp s/d, including breakfast) is great value, just two blocks from Parque Calderón. All bathrooms are shared, but each room has a basin. Some rooms have windows overlooking the city. Amenities include a shared kitchen and a rooftop terrace on the 5th floor with wonderful views. If you're a light sleeper, bring earplugs, as it's on a busy crossroads and the walls are thin. The hot water is good, but the Wi-Fi is poor.

Also two blocks from Parque Calderón is ★ **Bauhouse Hostel** (Benigno Malo 10-31, Gran Colombia, tel. 7/283-2931, Facebook @bauhousehostel $7.50 pp dorm, $8.50 with breakfast), the best dorm option in town, with spacious, airy eight-bed rooms with lockers for backpacks, a shared kitchen, and a TV room. The Wi-Fi is great, the breakfast is good, the beds are comfortable, the water is hot, and there is free tea and coffee. Staff are friendly and helpful.

$10-25

Yakumama (Luis Cordero 5-66 *y* Honorato Vásquez, tel. 7/283-4353, http://en.hostalyakumama.com, $6.50-10 dorm, $20-28 s/d) is a popular budget option. Breakfast is additional at $2, $3, or $3.50. There is a popular bar with free salsa classes on Wednesdays.

Across the road from the Museo Pumapungo, **AlterNative** (Huayna Capac *y* Casique Duma, tel. 7/408-4101, http://alternativehostal.com, $8-10 dorm, $14 s, $24 d, including breakfast) has clean rooms arranged around a light-filled central atrium. Amenities include a terrace, common room, laundry facilities, and bicycle rentals. The café serves craft beer, good coffee, sandwiches, and snacks. Staff are helpful and speak English.

In a colonial building declared part of the city's cultural patrimony, ★ **Hostal Villa del Rosario** (Honorato Vásquez 5-25 *y* Mariano Cueva, tel. 7/282-8585 or 99/225-3778, $10-15 pp) is owned by a friendly Ecuadorian couple. Rooms with shared and private bathrooms are arranged around a beautiful courtyard garden, and there is a shared kitchen. It's quiet at night. Just down the road is **Hostal La Cigale** (Vásquez *y* Cordero, tel. 7/283-5308, www.hostallacigale.com, dorm $7-10 pp, $20 s, $27 d, including breakfast), which also has a restaurant and bar. La Cigale uses local organic produce, sells organic fair trade products, collects and reuses rainwater in the toilets, and uses kitchen waste in an organic garden. The bar has a happy hour and occasional live music.

El Cafecito (Mariano Cueva *y* Mariscal, tel. 7/283-2337, www.elcafecitohostel.wixsite.com/elcafecito, dorm $11 pp, $22 s, $34 d) has large, comfortable rooms and a rooftop terrace. The friendly and helpful owner organizes group dinners, great for meeting fellow travelers. It's on Plaza Mercado 9 Octubre, so take care with your valuables when arriving and leaving.

Most of the hotels along the river are quite pricey, but **Casa del Barranco** (Larga 8-41 *y* Cordero, tel. 7/283-9763, www.casadelbarranco.com, $20-35 s, $30-50 d, including breakfast) bucks the trend. This historic house has a café overlooking the river, where breakfast is served.

$50-100

The elegant **Posada del Angel** (Bolívar 14-11 y Estévez de Toral, tel. 7/284-0695, www.hostalposadadelangel.com, $52 s, $74 d, including breakfast) has charming guest rooms around a central courtyard and friendly service. Family-owned **Hotel Campanario** (Padre Aguirre 11-84 y Gaspar Sangurima, tel. 7/282-3816, www.hotelcampanario.com.ec, $55 s, $79 d, including breakfast) has warmly decorated, comfortable rooms and friendly service.

★ **Hotel Boutique Los Balcones** (Borrero 12-08 y Sangurima, tel. 7/284-2103, www.hotellosbalconescuenca.com, $75-82 s, $90-99 d, including breakfast) has friendly staff, a great breakfast, excellent showers, a restaurant, a rooftop terrace, and a massage service.

Overlooking the Río Tomebamba, ★ **Hotel Victoria** (Larga 6-93 y Borrero, tel. 7/282-7401, http://hotelvictoriaecuador.com, $70 s, $95 d, including breakfast) is in a renovated building full of character. Most of the elegantly furnished guest rooms have views of the river, and some have private terraces. There is a gourmet restaurant, El Jardín, and a charming little café serves baked goods and ice cream.

$100-200

A pair of renovated colonial mansions have been converted into two of the best hotels in the city. The **Hotel Santa Lucía** (Borrero 8-44 y Sucre, tel. 7/282-8000, www.santaluciahotel.com, $122 s, $164 d, including breakfast) was built by Azuay's first provincial governor in 1859 and won a city-wide award for the best restoration of a historical building. The ★ **Mansion Alcazar** (Bolívar 12-55 y Tarqui, www.mansionalcazar.com, tel. 7/282-3889, $145 s, $250 d, including breakfast and afternoon tea) is one of the most stylish hotels in Ecuador, with a 19th-century ambience glittering with crystal chandeliers. There are 19 luxurious guest rooms, a gourmet restaurant, a bar, a spa, and extensive gardens.

INFORMATION AND SERVICES

Visitor Information

There's a well-staffed **Itur office** (tel. 7/282-1035, 8am-8pm Mon.-Fri., 9am-4pm Sat., 8:30am-1:30pm Sun.) on Parque Calderón. The municipality has a good website, much of it in English, at http://cuenca.com.ec/en and is on Facebook @VisitCuencaEc.

Money

Banco Pichincha has a branch and ATM half a block west of Parque Calderón, on Bolívar.

Language Schools

Spanish schools can arrange accommodations with host families or in hostels/hotels/apartments. Additional activities are usually available, such as cooking, salsa classes, and trips to attractions in the local area. Most schools also offer volunteering opportunities.

The excellent **Yanapuma Spanish School** (Hermano Miguel 8-59 y Bolívar, tel. 7/283-1504, www.yanapumaspanish.org) is the only professional school using the Communicative Language Teaching methodology, which moves away from traditional grammar-based classes. Instead, students learn through interaction with the teacher and (if in a group class) other students. Prices start at $6/hour for group classes and $9/hour for private, individually tailored classes. Study & Travel programs combine classes with exploration of Ecuador with a teacher. Volunteer programs are available whilst studying in Cuenca and Quito, where there is a sister school, or nationwide after study ends. Volunteer opportunities include an animal rescue center in the Amazon and conservation work in the Galápagos. Profits go toward the Yanapuma Foundation, a nonprofit organization that promotes sustainable development in indigenous and marginalized communities. The one-off $25 registration fee goes into a scholarship fund for disadvantaged children.

Fundación Amauta (Miguel y Córdova, tel. 7/284-6206, http://amauta.edu.ec) is a Spanish school that supports education for low-income children through scholarships, study materials, and other financial aid. **Simon Bolivar Spanish School** (Mariscal Sucre 14-21, *entre* Estévez de Toral *y* Coronel Talbot, tel. 7/283-2052, www.bolivar2.com) receives consistently good reviews. **Spanish Institute Cuenca** (Calle Larga 2-92 *y* Tomás Ordóñez, tel. 7/282-4736, https://spanishinstitutecuenca.com) combines Spanish lessons with photography classes.

Health Care

In an emergency, head to the public hospital, **Vicente Corral Moscoso** (Av. Los Arupos *y* Av. 12 de Abril, tel. 7/409-6000, http://hvcm.gob.ec).

GETTING THERE AND AROUND
Buses

Cuenca's *terminal terrestre* is two blocks northeast of the traffic circle at España and Huayna Capac, a 10-minute drive from the city center. At the time of writing, a Google search for "itinerario terminal terrestre Cuenca pdf" brought up the full timetable for all interprovincial departures. Several companies run buses to **Guayaquil** (every 30-60 minutes 24 hours, 4 hours, $8); **Quito** (at least hourly 3:20am-midnight, 10 hours, $12); and **Loja** via **Saraguro** (every 60-90 minutes 5am-midnight, 4.5 hours, $7.50).

Amazonas (tel. 3/274-0242) has departures to **Baños** (8:45am, 4pm, and 10pm, 7 hours, $10), which leave Baños for Cuenca at the same times. If you miss the direct bus to/from Baños, go via Ambato (7-8 hours, $10), from where there are frequent departures to Baños (1 hour). Alausí (tel. 98/612-2045) has departures to **Alausí** (5am and 2:45pm, 4 hours, $6); Ciudad de Piñas (tel. 7/284-3940) has departures to **Zaruma** (6:20am and 12:30pm, 6 hours, $8.75), as does Tac (tel. 7/284-7434) at 4:15pm; Patria (tel. 7/283-2729) has departures to **Riobamba** (5:30pm and 7:30pm, 6 hours, $8); Macas (tel. 7/286-9983) has a nightly departure to **Puyo** (8.5 hours, $15.50); and Pullman Sucre (tel. 7/282-2329)

has five departures daily to **Huaquillas** (5 hours, $7). Less touristy departures include Macas, Shushufindi, Lago Agrio, Gualaquiza, Machala, Atacames, and Tulcán.

Transportes Cañar (tel. 7/284-3940) has direct buses to **Ingapirca** (9am and 12:20pm Mon.-Fri., 9am Sat.-Sun., 2.5 hours, $3.50). If you miss the direct bus, there are regular buses to **Cañar** (2 hours, $2), and **Tambo** (2 hours, $2.50), where you can change for Ingapirca. For **El Cajas National Park** (45 minutes, $2), take a Guayaquil bus and ask the driver to let you off at the entrance.

Panamericana (José Joaquín de Olmedo, www.panamericana.ec) has an office a kilometer southwest of the bus station and sends luxury buses to Quito (10 hours, $12) daily at 10pm.

For Gualaceo, Chordeleg, and Sígsig, buses run every 20 minutes from the main *terminal terrestre*. Buses to other small towns and villages around Cuenca leave from Terminal Sur, close to the Feria Libre outdoor market on Avenida de las Américas.

For buses within the city, the $0.30 fare is payable only with the **movilízate** card, which costs $1.75 and is purchased from the ETAPA office (Gran Colombia *y* Tarqui). The card can be recharged at shops all over the city; just look for the logo in the window. Several people can use the same card; just swipe it several times upon entering the bus. For more information and a full list of recharge locations, see www.sircuenca.com. Alternatively, ask a friendly local to swipe their card for you and give them $0.30.

At the time of writing, an overground metro system, **Tranvía** (www.tranviacuenca.com), was in the process of being built, due to run 20 kilometers (12.4 mi) between the Fabián Alarcón bridge in the northeast of the city to the Control Sur in the southwest, with 27 stops en route, including the airport, bus terminal, and city center.

Taxis and Car Rental

The minimum taxi fare in Cuenca is $1.50, which will get you to most places within the center. All yellow taxis are required to use taxi-meters. The bus station and airport are each a $1.50-2 ride from the city center. Reputable, pre-bookable companies include **Ejecutivo** (tel. 7/280-9605) and **Andino** (tel. 7/282-3893). For car rental, try **Localiza** (www.localiza.com) at the airport (tel. 7/408 4632) or bus terminal (tel. 7/408-4631).

Air

The Mariscal Lamar airport (www.aeropuertocuenca.ec/en, tel. 7/286-7120) is 2 kilometers (1.2 mi) northeast of the town center on Avenida España. It's a 10-minute walk east from the *terminal terrestre* or a short hop by taxi or local bus. **TAME** (www.tame.com.ec) has offices in town (Florencia Astudillo 2-22, *frente a* Milenium Plaza, tel. 7/410-3199) and at the airport (tel. 7/286-6400) and flies to Quito 2-3 times daily. **LATAM** (Bolívar 9-18 *y* Benigno Malo, tel. 1800/000-527, www.latam.com) also operates three daily flights to Quito.

BAÑOS

Don't confuse this small town 8 kilometers (5 mi) southwest of Cuenca with Baños in Tungurahua province, though both places are named for the mineral rich thermal waters that flow nearby. The water that supplies **Baños de Cuenca** emerges at 75°C (167°F) from a geologic fault 400 meters (1,300 ft) wide and 10 meters (33 ft) high, known as "La Loma de los Hervideros" (Hill of the Boilers). The water is then cooled and used to create thermal baths believed to have therapeutic benefits.

In total there are seven thermal baths here, all locally owned, ranged along Avenida Ricardo Durán just downhill from the church. Most have a general open air pool at around 36-42°C (97-108°F); indoor "contrast pools" of very hot and very cold water; steam baths; and therapeutic mud. Entrance is $5-8. Be aware that the baths get busy with locals after 6pm and on weekends. Some baths also have accommodations, where the price includes entrance to the baths. Recommended are

Hostería Durán (tel. 7/289-2301 or 99/234-0985, www.hosteriaduran.com), which also has a restaurant and accommodations ($84 s, $126 d, including breakfast); and **Hostería Rodas** (tel. 7/289-2161 or 99/806-5500, www.hosteriarodas.com), which has more economical rooms ($44 s, $61 d, including breakfast). With the same owner as Hostería Durán, **Novaqua** (tel. 7/289-2354, www.no-vaqua.com.ec) does not allow children, so head there if you're looking for some peace. Massages are available. The accommodations at **Agapantos** (tel. 7/289-2015, Facebook @ HosteriaAgapantosEC, $30 s, $50 d, including breakfast) are great value, in small two-story houses with kitchens and space for four people ($25 pp).

In a class of its own is the swanky **Piedra de Agua** (tel. 7/289-2496, https://piedradeagua.com.ec, 6am-10pm Mon.-Sat., 6am-9pm Sun.), where the $35 entrance fee includes a circuit of the spa facilities, comprising steam baths, mud pools, underground hot and cold contrast baths, and outdoor pools. There are often 2-for-1 deals; check the website for details. Various packages of massages and other treatments are available.

The church in Baños is a grandiose baby blue construction, worth a look. Next to the church is a tourist information office and some stands selling street food. Specialty cuisine in Baños consists of *timbulos* (a sweet wrapped corn snack) and *cuchichaquis* (a savory wrapped corn snack). These very local items are only sold on weekends, usually served with coffee. The rest of the week, *empanadas de viento* (wind empanadas) are available. These are puffier than regular empanadas and, though they are available in a few places in Ecuador, they are thought to be especially good in Baños.

Five kilometers (3 mi) northeast of Baños, the rural village of **Uchuloma** (tel. 7/289-3566, ext. 108, comunauchuloma@yahoo.es) has created a community tourism project that offers hikes and horseback rides in the forest on ancestral paths, to visit waterfalls and for bird-watching. Uchuloma also has a mirador overlooking Cuenca, a restaurant serving traditional food, and guest cabañas.

To get to Baños, take a taxi from Cuenca ($5) or catch a local bus (line 100 from outside the Feria Libre, or line 12 from 12 Abril y Solano).

★ EL CAJAS NATIONAL PARK

Less than an hour northwest of Cuenca, the rugged landscapes of the **Parque Nacional Cajas** (tel. 7/237-0126, http://areasprotegidas. ambiente.gob.ec) are pristine. The 28,000 hectares (69,200 acres) of the park, ranging 3,160-4,450 meters (10,370-14,600 ft) in altitude, are reminiscent of the Scottish highlands, with rocky green mountains interspersed with crystalline lakes and streams. Most of the vast landscapes are covered in wildflower-strewn *páramo*, with some of the only remaining polylepis trees in the country. In stark contrast to the city, the only sounds are running water, the calls of birds, and the wind.

The *páramo* here acts as a giant sponge, forming 786 bodies of water within the park, 165 of them over a hectare (2.5 acres) in size. Here are born two of the rivers that cross Cuenca and provide its drinking water, the Tomebamba and the Yanuncay. Due to the large number of lagoons, the presence of migratory birds, and the importance of the water sources, Cajas has been recognized as a Wetland of International Importance. Despite this, it is currently threatened by megamining (see the *Background* chapter for more information).

Visitors stand a good chance of seeing wild horses and the llamas that were reintroduced to the park in the late 1990s. Other mammals in the park include rabbits, mountain wolves, deer, and pumas. Among the 157 bird species are condors, parrots, Andean toucans, tanagers, and hummingbirds.

El Cajas was used by the Cañaris, who inhabited the area before the Incan invasion, as a passage between the Sierra and the coast. Later, the Incas built a road here, the remains of which can be visited on a guided hike.

Visiting the Park

The main route to El Cajas from Cuenca is along the main road to Guayaquil, which climbs to 4,000 meters (13,000 ft) before dropping down dramatically to sea level in just 1.5 hours. Buses to Guayaquil leave from the *terminal terrestre* every half hour. Ask the driver before boarding to let you off at the national park. Buses to Cajas also leave from outside the Feria Libre. To return to Cuenca, flag down a bus on the main road outside the park entrance (they pass every half hour) or stick out a thumb.

Though there are many paths crossing the park, ranging from three hours to two days in duration, only two are recommended to undertake independently: the trails around Laguna Llaviucu and Laguna Toreadora. The other trails are not well marked, there is no cell phone signal in the park, and the weather can change in minutes, reducing visibility to near zero. It is very easy to get lost, and, with nighttime temperatures below freezing, deaths from exposure have occurred.

Just 18 kilometers (11 mi) from Cuenca is the entrance to **Laguna Llaviucu,** where a well-marked 1.5-hour trail takes visitors around the lake. This is a more scenic walk than the more popular Laguna Toreadora trail, with good bird-watching. Ask the bus driver to let you out at Llaviucu and register to enter the park at the office. Be aware that the office and lake are 2.8 kilometers (1.7 mi) from the highway, from where it's a three-hour round-trip walk.

The main entrance to the park is 34 kilometers (21 mi) from Cuenca at the **Laguna Toreadora** visitors center, where there is a well-marked, two-hour trail around the lake and a restaurant serving delicious *locro de papa* (potato soup), trout, and a set lunch. You can stay overnight at the refuge (tel. 7/237-0126), but there is capacity for only six people, so advance booking is advisable. Camping is also possible. Both the Llaviucu and Toreadora visitors centers are open until 4pm, so make sure to arrive in time to complete the walks.

For other hikes within the park, it's necessary to go with a guide. Wherever you go, stick to the paths. The *páramo* is covered with fragile, slow-growing vegetation that takes a long time to regenerate. Although it heats up considerably when the sun comes out, it's generally pretty cold. Even if the sun is blazing when you set out, it can be hailing within minutes. Bring plenty of layers, rain gear, and waterproof hiking boots (waterproof boots are not needed for the trails around Laguna Llaviucu and Laguna Toreadora). It's especially wet from mid-March through April. Be aware that it is tiring to walk at high elevation, so bring high-energy snacks and plenty of water. If you're traveling up from the coast, it's a good idea to spend a day or two acclimatizing in Cuenca before hiking in El Cajas.

Mateo Coellar (tel. 99/290-6777, coellar94@gmail.com) is a friendly local and a member of a local mountaineering club who walks every week in El Cajas. He takes tourists on a stunning three- to four-hour hike that starts at **Tres Cruces**, the highest part of the highway a few kilometers past the Laguna Toreadora visitors center. From there, the trail descends past a series of lakes before ending on the highway near **Laguna Luspa**. He can also take visitors to climb the peak at **Paragüillas,** the location of the highest meteorological radar in the world at 4,450 meters (14,600 ft), from where it's possible to see Chimborazo on a clear day. It's a fairly steep one-hour ascent and the same time to descend. Mateo, who speaks a little English, charges $25 per person with discounts for groups. This includes transport on the bus. Reserve a day before. Meet Mateo at the terminal or his mother's café, Moritas, which is an excellent place for a pre-hike breakfast.

All agencies in Cuenca offer daily group tours to the national park for $50-55 per person, including transport, bilingual guide, and lunch. The tours usually last 8am-4pm. The route varies depending on the weather, but all include Laguna Lluviacu. Other hikes can be booked as private tours, including a technical 2.2-kilometer (1.4 mi) climb to the summit of Cerro San Luis (4,264 m/13,990 ft) and a two-day, 18-kilometer (11-mi) trek on the Inca road to a series of lakes. See *Recreation and Tours* in the *Cuenca* section for recommended agencies.

Polylepis Tours (Hermano Miguel 4-35 *y* Calle Larga, tel. 7/283-0248 or 9/851-16721, 9am-1pm and 2:30pm-7pm Mon.-Fri., https://polylepistours.com) offers bird-watching tours in the national park, plus a Wild Cajas tour for those looking for a challenging eight-hour hike off the beaten track.

The **Club de Andinismo Sangay** (Mariscal Sucre 3-12 *y* Tomás Ordóñez, tel. 7/282-9958, www.clubsangay.com) is a local mountaineering club that offers occasional group hikes in El Cajas National Park ($20).

EAST OF CUENCA

The hills above Cuenca to the east contain several villages renowned for their crafts: **Gualaceo** for woven textiles; **Chordeleg** for jewelry; **Sígsig** for "Panama" hats, or *sombreros de paja toquilla*; and **San Bartolomé** for hand-made guitars. It's quite easy to visit all four in a day on the bus if you leave early, though many artisanal workshops aren't really set up for walk-in tourism. Alternatively, Cuenca tour operators offer guided trips ($50-55 pp), to Gualaceo, Chordeleg, and San Bartolomé, including pre-arranged visits to the workshops.

Gualaceo

On the banks of the Río Gualaceo, 34 kilometers (21 mi) from Cuenca, the small town of **Gualaceo** used to host the area's largest indigenous market in the central square every Sunday, selling fresh produce, household goods, handicrafts, clothes and textiles. Sadly, the market has been moved from the central square and is now housed in a building outside the town center—a trend which unfortunately is happening all over the country.

1: Laguna Toreadora and polylepis trees at El Cajas National Park; **2:** traditional ikat textiles from Gualaceo

1

2

The new **Mercado Santiago** is fairly soulless, not offering much different from the undercover markets in Cuenca. Known as the "garden of Azuay" for the surrounding rolling green hills, Gualaceo does have a fairly impressive church and an attractive central park. The local food specialties, available in the central Mercado 25 Junio, are *hornado* (roasted pork) and tortillas made from corn or wheat flour. These are served with *morocho* (a hot, sweet beverage of cooked corn, sugar, and cinnamon) or *rosero* (a cold beverage of corn, sugar, and fruit).

Gualaceo is famous for its **ikat** weaving. A technique originating in Asia, ikat has been practiced in Ecuador by the Cañari people since pre-Columbian times. Historically, the technique was used to make the *macana*, a fringed shawl that forms part of the traditional dress of the *chola cuencana*, the indigenous woman from Azuay. The shawl itself is woven on a waistloom, after which the fringes are added manually using macramé. Ikat was declared part of the Intangible Heritage of Ecuador in 2015. Today's artisans create both traditional and innovative shawls and other items such as ponchos and shoes. No two items are the same.

Ikat textiles are made by artisans in the small villages of Bullcay, Buzhún, and San Pedro de los Olivos, located on the road to Gualaceo from Cuenca. Within these communities, 18 workshops have opened their doors to tourists. The best prepared to receive visitors is the **Casa Museo de la Makana** (Sector San Pedro de los Olivos, km 10 1/2 Vía Gualaceo, tel. 98/777-8220, Facebook @CasaMuseoDeLaMakana, tejidosikat@ hotmail.com), where José Jiménez and his wife Ana Maria Ulloa give demonstrations in spinning, dying, weaving, and macramé. Considering the time and effort that goes into making the textiles, the prices are very reasonable (a shawl costs $45). To visit the workshop independently, take a bus from Cuenca and ask to be let off at San Pedro de los Olivos. To see other ikat workshops, go with a guided tour from Cuenca.

GETTING THERE

Buses run every 20 minutes between Gualaceo and Cuenca's *terminal terrestre* (1 hour, $0.80). From Gualaceo, buses leave frequently for Chordeleg and Sígsig.

Chordeleg

Just 5 kilometers (3 mi) south of Gualaceo, a pleasant two-hour walk if you're feeling energetic, this attractive, well-kept town has specialized in gold and silver craftsmanship since pre-Columbian times. Offering a huge range of jewelry items, today's artisans are especially skilled with filigree. The metals come from small-scale artisanal mines, rather than the mega-mining projects that wreak so much environmental and social damage. On the main square and dotted around town are scores of *joyerías* (jewelry shops), some of which will make custom pieces. Other shops sell handicrafts and clothing, including *sombreros de paja toquilla*. A small **Museo Comunidad** (23 de Enero, 8am-5pm Tues.-Sun., free) on the main plaza has displays on the history and techniques of making jewelry and other local crafts such as ceramics, hat weaving, and textiles.

GETTING THERE

Chordeleg is 75 minutes from Cuenca ($1) or 15 minutes from Gualaceo ($0.40).

Sígsig

Some 26 kilometers (16 mi) south of Chordeleg, **Sígsig** is known for its "Panama" hat factories, where *sombreros de paja toquilla* are woven. While many are sold wholesale to buyers from Cuenca, it is possible to buy finished hats of all grades direct from the artisans in Sígsig. The most well-known factory is just outside town, **ATMA** (Asociación de Toquilleras María Auxiliadora, tel. 7/226-6014 or 98/687-8553, 8am-5pm Mon.-Fri.). It's signposted from the town center, or take a taxi ($1). Be aware that the factories are closed on weekends and occasionally midweek. Sadly, hat making is not a profitable enterprise, and many weavers need to supplement their income with agricultural or other activities, hence the irregular opening hours. To be sure that the factory will be open, call ahead or arrange a tour in Cuenca.

Sígsig is surrounded by impressive scenery, good for hiking, with some archaeological sites. A community tourism project offers tours to the caves and archaeological site at Chobshi, 10 kilometers (6.2 mi) from Sígsig. Contact **Pakariñan,** the community tourism network for the southern Sierra region (Mariscal Sucre 14-96 *y* Coronel Guillermo Tálbot, Cuenca, tel. 7/282-0529 or 98/795-9379, https:// turismocomunitario.ec) for information. Other nearby natural attractions include the Inca ruins at Shabalula, the mountain of Fasayñan, the hills of Huallil, the lakes of Ayllon, the shore of the Río Santa Bárbara, and the lake at San Sebastián. At the time of writing, there was no tourist infrastructure to explore these sights, but local taxi drivers can provide transport.

GETTING THERE

Sígsig is 45 minutes from Chordeleg ($0.60). Buses between Sígsig and Cuenca run every 20 minutes (2 hours, $1.75), via Gualaceo. Buses from Sígsig to Cuenca via San Bartolomé leave approximately every 90 minutes. Be aware that if you get out at San Bartolomé you will have a long wait for the next bus to Cuenca. It may be quicker to come back to Sígsig and then head back to Cuenca via Gualaceo. Sígsig is not included on most organized tours of artisanal towns. Polylepis Tours (https://polylepistours. com) in Cuenca can organize a private tour, which includes the hat factory and the caves at Chobshi.

San Bartolomé

The hillside village of **San Bartolomé,** 30 kilometers (19 mi) from Cuenca, is famous for its handmade guitars, which have been crafted here for generations. It's also known for its traditional adobe houses.

GETTING THERE

San Bartolomé is 20 minutes from Sígsig and an hour from Cuenca. Buses between Sígsig and Cuenca via San Bartolomé run every approximately every 90 minutes ($1).

SOUTH TO LOJA
Girón and El Chorro

Just 45 kilometers (28 mi) southwest of Cuenca, the small town of Girón is the access point for the **waterfalls** at El Chorro, which can be visited as an easy half-day trip from the city. It's a scenic journey, as rolling green cow pastures turn into craggy peaks and dramatic rock formations near Girón. The town has a pretty central square with a museum, **Museo Casa de los Tratados** (tel. 7/227-5061, 8am-6pm daily, $1.25), which commemorates a treaty signed in 1829 between Gran Colombia and Peru shortly before the emergence of the Ecuadorian nation.

About 5 kilometers (3 mi) out of town, the waterfalls at **El Chorro** are the main attraction. Flag down a *camioneta* in Girón and arrange a pickup time with the driver ($5 each way), or follow the sign from the highway and make your way on foot, though be aware that it's uphill all the way. At the entrance to the waterfall are three restaurants specializing in trout. Activities include horseback riding and fishing. Pay the entrance fee at a small kiosk (8am-6:30pm daily, $2), from where a path leads up through the trees to a long waterfall tumbling down a cliff surrounded by lush vegetation. It's less than a 10-minute walk to reach a wooden bridge at the base of the falls, where visitors are misted with spray. On the other side, a narrow muddy path descends to a series of pools. Another waterfall can be reached via a strenuous two-hour hike. To find the trail, head back to the entrance, follow the road back toward Girón and turn off at the sign for the second waterfall. It's best to do the longer hike in the morning, when the weather is more likely to be clear; not just for the views, but to avoid getting lost if the clouds descend.

GETTING THERE

To get to Girón, take a bus heading to Machala and ask the driver to let you off (1 hour, $1). Alternatively, most tour agencies in Cuenca offer trips to the waterfalls.

Jima

About 20 kilometers (12.4 mi) southeast of Cuenca, this remote village offers some great day hikes and the opportunity to experience life with a traditional Cañari community. Many people here wear traditional dress, practice small-scale organic agriculture, and live by raising cattle, which are milked by hand. Jima is an easy journey from Cuenca, with some wonderful scenery en route, so it can be visited as a day trip or for an overnight stay. It's also the starting point for an adventurous three- to four-day trek to Gualaquiza in the Amazon.

A **community tourism** project, **Turismo Vivencial & Comunitario Jima** (Facebook @Turismo Vivencial y Comunitario Jima EATCJ) offers guided hikes to two nearby hills, Huinara and Zhimazhuma, with excellent views of the surrounding countryside. A tour of the village includes a visit to a workshop where *sombreros de paja toquilla* are finished by hand in the traditional way, with an iron filled with red hot coals. There is the option to get involved with **daily activities,** such as harvesting corn, feeding the guinea pigs, and making bread in a wood-fired oven. **Traditional cuisine,** such as trout or guinea pig with potatoes, can be sampled at the two restaurants in town, or in the homes of local families. **Homestays** can be arranged, or accommodations are available at **Hotel Jima** (Benigno Torres, tel. 7/241-8003, $10 pp). Those who stay overnight have the chance to hike to the Laguna de Zhurugüiña the following day.

Local guides are available for the three- to four-day trek to Gualaquiza, which passes through San Miguel de Cuyes, Amazonas, Ganazhuma, and La Florida, with some Incan ruins en route. Accommodations are with local families. The trek is nearly all downhill, but be aware that you'll be carrying your own pack.

Contact **Nancy Uyaguari** (tel. 7/241-8278 or 99/409-5949, caritas2011@gmail.com), who speaks English, for more information and to make reservations for day trips, overnight stays, and the trek. A week's notice is recommended, though not always necessary.

Jima's biggest annual event is the **Festival de la Chicha de Jora,** held on the first Saturday in October, which includes a contest to judge the best *chicha* (a nonalcoholic drink made from corn), along with dancing and music.

GETTING THERE

Buses with **Transportes Jima** leave Cuenca (8:30am, 11am, 1pm, and 3pm, 80 minutes, $2) from opposite the Feria Libre on Avenida de las Américas. If you get up early, Jima can be combined with the El Chorro waterfall as a day trip from Cuenca. You'll need to be on the bus to Girón at 7am or 7:30am. After visiting the waterfall, take a bus to the Redondel de Cumbe, from where buses to Jima leave (9am, 11:30am, 1:30pm, and 3:30pm). Be on the 11:30am in time for lunch in Jima. Buses back to Cuenca from Jima leave every couple of hours, including at 3:30pm and 5:30pm.

Kushi Waira

Just half an hour south of Cuenca in Tarqui, **Kushi Waira** is a rural Cañari community offering activity days, with the aim of keeping their ancestral traditions alive. After being picked up by car from Cuenca, visitors are given a welcome drink and a brief talk about the Cañari way of life and world view, followed by an organic breakfast made from locally grown ingredients.

The highlight of the day is a short, easy walk along an ancient path of medicinal plants, known as the *jumbi ñan*. It's cool and peaceful, with a soft carpet of moss underfoot.

1: the El Chorro waterfall; **2:** Energy cleansing rituals are performed at Kushi Waira. **3:** typical Southern Sierra landscape near Jima

Alfonso Saquipay, the project leader and guide, claims that just walking on the path is healing, and if that sounds crazy, ask him how old he is: You will be surprised! The *jumbi ñan* leads to the top of the area's highest hill, Jatun Urku (2,919 m/9,577 ft), where Alfonso performs rituals to clean visitors' energy, using a wind instrument to call the spirits, along with smoke smudging, medicinal plants, prayers, and incantations. Also at the top of the hill is a section of the Inca road. After an organic lunch, served communally on a long strip of fabric in an Andean style known as *pampamesa*, there are demonstrations of traditional Cañari music, dancing, wool spinning, and corn grinding using a stone. The tour lasts 8am-4pm and costs $40 per person, including transport from Cuenca. Some of the income goes toward providing free activity days for groups of schoolchildren.

For more information, see www.kushiwaira.com. To make a reservation contact **Alfonso Saquipay** (tel. 7/244-0411 or 99/747-6337, Spanish only); 24-hour notice is required.

San Lucas

Situated between Loja and Saraguro, it's worth making a quick stop at the tiny Kichwa village of **San Lucas** to see a picturesque example of a traditional rural community. A restaurant by the entrance to the village, **Inka Pungo,** open weekend lunchtimes only, serves barbecued guinea pig (*cuy asado*). San Lucas is just off the Panamericana, an hour north of Loja and half an hour south of Saraguro, and can be easily reached on any bus between the two towns. Ask the driver to let you off at the entrance to San Lucas, from where the village center is a few minutes' walk.

Saraguro

The **indigenous Saraguros,** whose name means "land of corn" in Kichwa, are a unique indigenous culture in Ecuador. It is thought that their ancestors were relocated here from Lake Titicaca on the border of southern Peru and Bolivia in the 16th century as part of the Inca *mitma* system of forced resettlement. Saraguros believe that they are descended from members of Inca leader Huayna Capac's closest circle, who were sent here to start a new colony that would adhere faithfully to their leader's beliefs. These days, over 30,000 Saraguros live in the town and surrounding villages. They usually wear black, the color worn by the Incas on special occasions. The traditional black and white hat, which is made of wool and resin, is hard and weighs 0.9 kilogram (2 lb). Many people now favor felt hats, which are lighter and more comfortable.

As well as weaving with sheep's wool, the Saraguros are known for making exquisite beaded necklaces. Part of the traditional dress for women, these hang down several inches and cover the collarbones. Building on the original pattern of simple stripes, over the years artisans have created a variety of innovative and beautiful designs. Beaded earrings are also available; the hummingbirds are particularly stunning. Saraguro's most famous food product is *queso amasado*, a type of soft cheese. These products can be bought in a number of stores around the main plaza and throughout the town, which is busiest during Sunday mornings when people from the surrounding villages come to trade and socialize.

COMMUNITY TOURISM NETWORK

Five of the rural villages that make up the canton of Saraguro have formed a **community tourism** network, Saraguro Rikuy, which has a tour operator, **Sara Urku** (tel. 7/220-0331 or 98/694-1852, Facebook @SaraurkuTurismoSaraguro, www.turismosaraguro.com), with an office one block southwest of the main plaza in the town center. The main focus of the network is to share with visitors the traditional Saraguro way of life, including customs, food, agriculture, ancestral medicine, music, and dance. With the same fundamental aim, each of the participating communities offers something different. Some provide accommodations with local families; others are visited as day trips.

The community of **Ñamarin** offers

homestays; workshops in spinning, weaving, and making beaded collars; visits to the Baños del Inca waterfall; **cultural nights** with music and dance; **horseback riding;** and participation in organic **agriculture.** Ñamarin is the only community with an English speaker. At **Gera,** it's possible to visit an archaeological site and traditional adobe houses; participate in making *guajango,* an agave drink; and possibly see condors (most likely in May). **Las Lagunas** offers homestays, Andean music, energy cleansing rituals, weaving, and gastronomy. At **Oñapaka,** it's possible to visit the Virgen de Agua Santa waterfall, sample traditional gastronomy, watch presentations of traditional music and dance, and participate in energy-cleansing rituals. **Ilincho** (Facebook @IntiWasiSaraguro) offers homestays, traditional gastronomy, dance and music presentations, and **energy-cleansing rituals.** Ilincho has its own center for Andean spirituality.

To arrange visits and **homestays** to these communities, contact Sara Urku with at least 24-hour notice. Sara Urku can also organize hikes in the surrounding mountains and cloud forest, and a three-day Sierra-to-Amazon trip that ends in Nangaritza. The journey is undertaken partly on foot and partly by car, with homestays en route.

FOOD

On the main square, **Mama Cuchara** (Parque Central, 7:15am-5pm Mon.-Fri., 7:15am-3pm Sat., $2-3) serves up traditional meals such as *mote pillo.* Profits go to a local women's association. Also on the main square is **Tupay** (tel. 96/971-4663, Facebook @Tupay Restaurante, 8am-10pm Sun.-Fri., $2.50-10), which uses organic ingredients and serves local dishes, with vegetarian options. To the northwest of the center on Parque de las Culturas, **La**

Muguna (tel. 99/593-9582, Facebook @ Saraguro La Muguna Restaurante, 10am-9pm daily, $2-10) is another good option, serving local fare in a bright, airy space with a terrace. On the central square, **Shamuico** (shamuicorestaurant@gmail.com, Facebook @Shamuico Espai Gastronomic, Wed.-Sun. 10am-10pm, $3-7) is in a class of its own, offering a gastronomic experience that receives rave reviews.

ACCOMMODATIONS

The surrounding communities provide the most authentic Saraguro experience, but it's also possible to stay in town. The best option, **Hostal Achik Wasi** (Barrio La Luz, Calle Intiñán, tel. 7/220-0058 or 99/349-8518, Facebook @Hostal Achik Wasi, $23 s, $40 d, breakfast included), part of the community tourism network, is located on a hill southwest of the center with great views. In the center, try clean, modern **Samana Wasi** (10 de Marzo *y* Panamericana, tel. 7/220-0315 or 99/115-4721, Facebook @HotelSamanaWasi, $15) or family-run **Hostal Saraguro** (Calle Loja *y* Luis Fernando Bravo, tel. 7/220-0286 or 98/632-1248, $12 s, $30 d), one block from the church.

GETTING THERE

Buses to Loja (1.5 hours, $2.10) and Cuenca (3 hours, $5) pass every half hour and stop in front of the bus companies' offices on Calle Azuay.

In Cuenca, **Polylepis Tours** (tel. 7/283-0248 or 9/851-16721, https://polylepistours. com) offers a full-day tour to Saraguro ($120 pp), including visits to artisans making *liquor de agave* (a local tequila-esque drink) and the famous black and white Saraguro hats; a ritual with medicinal plants at a waterfall; and a traditional lunch.

Loja and Vicinity

The capital of the province of the same name, **Loja** is used by visitors mainly as a gateway for accessing Vilcabamba, Podocarpus National Park, the southern Amazon, and the Peruvian border, but it's worth devoting a day to exploring this pleasant, attractive city. At 2,100 meters (6,890 ft) elevation, Loja is warmer than other Sierran towns. Its clean, wide streets make it easy to stroll between the many elegant plazas, stopping every now and then to enjoy a cup of the famous coffee, considered among the best in the country. At sunset, the surrounding mountains are tinted pink, and after dark the churches are beautifully illuminated.

Loja is home to one of the country's best universities, Universidad Técnica Particular de Loja, and a leading music conservatory. With an abundance of music classes and aficionados, it's known as the Musical Capital of Ecuador. Loja is also a leader in environmental practices. In 2001, the city won Best Community Involvement in the International Awards for Livable Communities. It has a highly organized recycling program, the first wind farm in continental Ecuador, and a fleet of electric taxis.

Loja is generally a safe city, but it's best to avoid the area around the El Panecillo and the Parque Infantile to the south of town, even during the day. Avoid the mirador at El Pedestal at night. It is possible to drink water from the faucet in Loja. Be aware that the weather is highly changeable, so come prepared for sun and rain.

SIGHTS
City Center

The Río Zamora and the Río Malacatus bracket the city center, intersecting just north of it. The streets between the two rivers are arranged in blocks, making it easy to navigate the plazas, churches, museums, and colonial architecture. A good place to start is north of the center at the **Puerta de la Ciudad** (City Gate), a replica castle that is particularly beautiful when lit up at night. It holds a small art gallery, a well-laid out local handicrafts store, and a café. Four blocks south is the **Iglesia San Francisco.**

One block farther south is the **Parque Central,** with a statue of Loja's great educator, Bernardo Valdivieso, in the center. On the east side is the city's white and gold **cathedral,** which hosts the famous Virgen del Cisne icon from late August to the beginning of November. On the north side is the municipal building, **tourist information center,** and an excellent shop, **Somos Loja**, selling local handicrafts and food products. On the south end is the **Museo de Cultura Lojana** (tel. 7/257-3004, 8am-noon and 3pm-5pm Mon.-Fri., free), which has small exhibits of pre-Columbian ceramics, modern art, and historic black-and-white photography. Half a block east of the square, the **Museo de Arte Religioso** (10 de Agosto *entre* Valdivieso *y* Olmedo, tel. 7/261-5701, 9am-5pm Mon.-Sat., $1), in the Monastery of the Madres Conceptas, has a small collection of religious art.

A block south, the **Teatro Bolívar** (Rocafuerte *entre* Valdivieso *y* Olmedo) is impressive, especially when it's lit up at night, and there are regular musical events. Next to the theater, the **Museo de la Música** (Valdivieso *entre* Riofrio *y* Rocafuerte, tel. 7/256-0033, Facebook @Centro Cultural Municipal Bernardo Valdivieso, 8am-noon and 2pm-5pm Mon.-Fri.) is housed around an attractive courtyard. Exhibitions document the city's proud musical heritage from the 19th century to 1920, including instruments and original scores. Signage is all in Spanish. The Facebook page is a great source of information on local music events.

Another two blocks south is **Parque de la Independencia** (also known as Plaza San

Loja

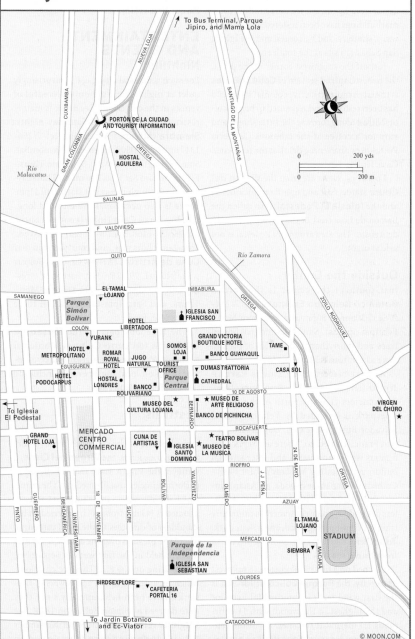

To Bus Terminal, Parque
Jipiro, and Mama Lola

NUEVA LOJA

CUXIBAMBA

GRAN COLOMBIA

Río
Malacatus

SANTIAGO DE LA MONTAÑAS

PORTÓN DE LA CIUDAD
AND TOURIST INFORMATION

ORTEGA

HOSTAL
AGUILERA

SALINAS

J F VALDIVIESO

QUITO

Río Zamora

ORTEGA

ZOILO RODRÍGUEZ

200 yds

200 m

SAMANIEGO

EL TAMAL
LOJANO

IMBABURA

Parque
Simón
Bolívar

IGLESIA SAN
FRANCISCO

COLÓN

HOTEL
LIBERTADOR

YURANK

GRAND VICTORIA
BOUTIQUE HOTEL

SOMOS
LOJA

TAME

HOTEL
METROPOLITANO

ROMAR
ROYAL
HOTEL

BANCO GUAYAQUIL

EGUIGUREN

JUGO
NATURAL

TOURIST
OFFICE

DUMAS TRATTORIA

CASA SOL

HOTEL
PODOCARPUS

HOSTAL
LONDRES

Parque
Central

CATHEDRAL

BANCO
BOLIVARIANO

10 DE AGOSTO

VIRGEN
DEL CHURO

To Iglesia
El Pedestal

MUSEO DEL
CULTURA LOJANA

MUSEO DE
ARTE RELIGIOSO

BANCO DE PICHINCHA

BERNARDO

GRAND
HOTEL LOJA

MERCADO
CENTRO
COMMERCIAL

CUNA DE
ARTISTAS

ROCAFUERTE

TEATRO BOLÍVAR

IGLESIA
SANTO
DOMINGO

MUSEO DE
LA MÚSICA

24 DE MAYO

ORTEGA

RIOFRÍO

GUERRERO

PINTO

IBEROAMÉRICA

UNIVERSITARIA

18 DE NOVIEMBRE

SUCRE

BOLÍVAR

VALDIVIEZO

OLMEDO

J J PEÑA

AZUAY

EL TAMAL
LOJANO

STADIUM

MERCADILLO

SIEMBRA

MACARA

Parque de la
Independencia

IGLESIA SAN
SEBASTIÁN

LOURDES

BIRDSEXPLORE

CAFETERÍA
PORTAL 16

To Jardín Botánico
and Ec-Viator

CATACOCHA

© MOON.COM

Sebastián). It was here that Lojanos gathered on November 18, 1820, to declare independence from Spain. All the surrounding colonial buildings have been restored with painted walls, shutters, and balconies, and the Iglesia San Sebastián sits at the south end.

Just off the southwest corner of the plaza, the pedestrianized section of **Calle Lourdes** is the city's most attractive colonial street and has been restored and repainted in bright colors. Stroll along, browse the little shops, and stop for a coffee at the fabulous Cafeteria Portal 16 or an evening drink at the renowned Casa Tinku.

Loja's best views are from the **Virgen del Churo** statue, east and uphill on Rocafuerte, and the **Iglesia El Pedestal,** also called the Balcón de Loja west of the city center on 10 de Agosto. The area around El Pedestal is not safe at night.

Outside the Center

Just south of the center is the **Jardín Botánico Reinaldo Espinosa** (tel. 7/264-2764, 7:30am-12:30pm and 3pm-6pm Mon.-Fri., 1pm-6pm Sat.-Sun., $1), which has bonsai trees and more than 200 species of orchid. Take a taxi from central Loja ($2).

A great place to take kids is **Parque Jipiro** (tel. 98/249-7853, 8am-6pm, free), 3 kilometers (1.9 mi) north of the center. The park is bounded by Velasco Ibarra, Salvador Bustamante Celi, Daniel Armijos, and Francisco Lecaro. There are replicas of famous world landmarks and international buildings, including Moscow's Saint Basil's Cathedral, a Japanese pagoda, an Asian temple, and a mosque. There are walking trails, lots of children's play equipment, a miniature train, a pedal-boating pond, and a skate park. To get here, take a taxi ($1.90) or a bus north from Universitaria.

Perched on a hill 13 kilometers (8 mi) west of the city, the **Parque Eolico Villonaco** is the first wind farm in continental Ecuador and the highest in the world, with 11 enormous 1.5 megawatt turbines. A visitors center offers guided tours. **Free Walks Loja** (tel.

98/674-5994, Facebook @FreewalksLojaec) offers a combined tour of the wind farm and Parque Jipiro ($15).

ENTERTAINMENT AND EVENTS
Nightlife

For such a musical city, Loja is surprisingly quiet at night. There are only a handful of venues in the center, and live music is mainly restricted to Friday and Saturday nights. **Siembra** (Macará y Mercadillo, tel. 7/256-1347 or 99/305-0809, Facebook @SiembraBar, 5pm-midnight Tues.-Wed., 5pm-2am Thurs.-Fri., 6pm-2am Sat.) has live music Thursday-Saturday, though it may not start until 11pm. There is also occasional live music at long-standing venue **Casa Tinku** (Lourdes y Sucre, tel. 96/959-6168, 5pm-midnight Tues.-Wed., 5pm-2am Thurs.-Sat.) and courtyard café/bar **Cuna de Artistas** (Artists Cradle) (Bolívar y Riofrio, tel. 99/428-0390, Facebook @restaurantecunadeartistas, 4pm-11:45pm Mon.-Thurs. and Sat., 4pm-1am Fri.). All three venues offer food.

The Facebook page of the **Museo de la Música** (@Centro Cultural Municipal Bernardo Valdivieso) is a great source of information on local music events, including those at **Teatro Bolívar.**

Festivals

The biggest event in Loja's calendar is the arrival of one of the country's most important religious icons, the **Virgen del Cisne,** a statue of the Virgin Mary that is believed to perform miracles, usually medical. The statue, which usually resides in a church in Cisne, 70 kilometers (43 mi) from Loja, is carried on the shoulders of devotees to the city's cathedral, where she presides over the annual festivities that are held in the first week of September, culminating on the 8th. These celebrations, which include live music and towers of fireworks, have been held annually since they were decreed by Simón Bolívar in 1824. The Virgin is returned to Cisne on November 1. Loja's **Independence** is celebrated on

November 18, coinciding with a national performing arts festival, **Festival de Loja** (www.festivaldeloja.com). On December 8, the **Feast of San Sebastián** coincides with the celebration commemorating the **Foundation of Loja,** with the festivities taking place in Plaza San Sebastián.

RECREATION AND TOURS

Free Walks Loja (tel. 98/674-5994, Facebook @FreewalksLojaec) offers bilingual walking tours of the city in exchange for tips. The two-hour tour leaves from the Parque Central at 9:15am and 3:15pm Monday-Saturday. Look for the guide's red T-shirt and umbrella. They also offer a tour of the wind farm and Jipiro Park ($15); a coffee tasting tour; and private tailor-made tours in southern Ecuador.

BirdsExplore (Lourdes 14-80 *y* Sucre, tel. 7/258-2434, www.exploraves.com) offers local and national bird-watching tours led by local expert Pablo Andrade, including to Podocarpus, Cajas, and Nangaritza.

Ec-Viator (Av. Pío Jaramillo Alvarado *entre* Chile *y* Cuba, tel. 7/258-0884, Facebook @ecviator, http://ec-viator.com, 9am-1pm and 3pm-7pm Mon.-Fri., 9am-1:30pm Sat.) offers one-day tours to Podocarpus National Park ($40) and the petrified forest at Puyango ($65 pp). Those looking for an adventure can hike to the Lagunas del Compadre in Podocarpus (2 days, 1 night, $100 pp/4 people, $115 pp/2 people), but be aware that a good level of physical fitness is required. If you have your own tent, the price is $15 lower. Groups of 1-4 people should give 3-4 days' notice for the two-day trek. Groups of five or more require three weeks' notice so that permits can be obtained.

SHOPPING

On the Plaza Central to the right of the tourism office, **Somos Loja** (tel. 99/228-3277, Facebook @somosloja, 10:30am-6pm Mon.-Fri., 10:30am-1pm Sat.) is a beautifully laid out shop selling a wide variety of local artisanal items, including handicrafts, food, and natural products, many of them organic.

The **Mercado Centro Comercial** (10 de Agosto *y* 18 de Noviembre) is one of the biggest indoor markets in Ecuador, with everything from clothing and electronics to fruit and meat.

FOOD

Loja is famous for its tamales (ground corn filled with pork, chicken, or cheese and wrapped in *achira* leaves), which are usually served for breakfast or with afternoon coffee; and *repe,* a creamy soup made from green bananas. Another soup, *arvejas con guineo,* is similar but has peas. Well-known meat specialties are *cecina* (thinly sliced sun-dried pork served with yucca) and *cuy con papas* (guinea pig with potatoes). The typical dessert is *miel con quesillo* (honey with soft unsalted cheese). As well as its excellent coffee, Loja is the birthplace of *horchata,* a pink infusion of various medicinal herbs, usually drunk hot, sometimes with aloe. *Bocadillos,* squares of raw sugar syrup and peanut that look like fudge, also originated in Loja and are available in shops all over the city and the Sierra.

The upstairs food court in the **Mercado Centro Comercial** (10 de Agosto *y* 18 de Noviembre) is a good place for cheap Ecuadorian dishes, including some local specialties, accompanied by freshly brewed *horchata.*

There are a number of recommended places to sample *lojana* specialty cuisine. Family-owned **El Tamal Lojano** (18 de Noviembre, tel. 7/258-2977, Facebook @tamallojano, 8am-noon and 3pm-8pm daily, $1.35-3.50), with another branch on 24 de Mayo and Mercadillo, is a bright, modern café offering the famous tamales, along with *bolón,* empanadas, and *mote pillo.* East of the center, **Casa Sol** (24 de Mayo *y* Eguiguren, tel. 7/258-8597, Facebook @CasaSolCafeRestaurante, breakfast, lunch, and dinner daily, $6-10) is a charming riverside café on a colonial terrace. Set lunch is $4. **Mama Lola** (Av. Salvador Bustamante Celi *y* Santa Rosa, tel. 7/261-4381, http://mamalolarest.com, noon-11pm Mon.-Thurs., noon-midnight Fri.-Sat., noon-4pm

Sun., $3-18) is where local families come for special occasions. Mama Lola specializes in *cuy* and *cecina*, so there isn't much on the menu for vegetarians.

On the pedestrianized section of Calle Lourdes, ★ **Cafeteria Portal 16** (tel. 96/948-4160, 9am-9pm daily, $1-4.50) has funky decor and wonderfully friendly service, offering a mix of local specialties (*humitas,* tamales, *quimbolitos*) and international dishes (pasta, sandwiches, wraps), plus beer and wine. Just off Parque Central, ★ **El Jugo Natural** (Eguiguren *y* Bolívar, tel. 7/257-5256, 7am-8pm Mon.-Fri., 7am-6pm Sat., 7am-2pm Sun., $2.50-5) offers an extensive vegetarian menu and drinks made with various nut and seed milks, plus sandwiches and ice cream. Just off the other side of the park, **Dumas Trattoria** (Eguiguren *y* Valdivieso, tel. 7/256-1494, Facebook @dumastrattoria, $7-13.50) is known for its great pizza ($5.50-7.50) and set lunches, which are excellent value at $4. On the south side of Parque Bolívar, **Yurank** (8am-9pm daily, $2-4.50) offers excellent, economical fruit salads with various toppings and a wide range of juices.

Most international restaurants are found on **24 de Mayo,** including Italian, Middle Eastern, Belgian, German, Mexican, and Chilean. It's a good place to browse and see what takes your fancy.

ACCOMMODATIONS
Under $10
Hostal Londres (Sucre 07-51, tel. 7/256-1936, $6 pp) is a dependable, friendly place with small, basic guest rooms and shared baths. Not easy to find, it's next to the Hotel Villonaco.

$10-25
Owned by a local family since 1969, ★ **Hotel Metropolitano** (18 de Noviembre 06-31, tel. 7/257-0007, $15 pp) is an excellent option, with comfortable beds, hot showers, and friendly service. It's centrally located but quiet at night. Near the Puerta de la Ciudad, **Hostal Aguilera** (Sucre 108 *y* Emiliano Ortega, tel. 7/258-2892, Facebook @HostalAguileraInternacional, $25 s, $55 d, including breakfast) is another decent option, though not as good value.

$25-50
Just west of the center near the river, **Hotel Podocarpus** (Eguiguren 16-50 *entre* 18 de Noviembre *y* Av. Universitaria, tel. 7/258-4912, www.hotelpodocarpus.com.ec, $34 s, $55 d) has clean, modern rooms. On the other side of the river, **Grand Hotel Loja** (Rocafuerte *y* Manuel Agustín Aguirre, tel. 7/257-5200, www.grandhotelloja.com, $37 s, $61 d, including breakfast) has a restaurant and a spa with Jacuzzi, sauna, steam room, and massage service.

$50-100
A block east of Parque Central, the glamorous ★ **Romar Royal** (José Antonio Eguiguren *y* 18 de Noviembre, tel. 7/258-2888, http://romarroyalhotel.com, $80 s, $90 d, including breakfast) has stylish, soundproofed guest rooms, helpful staff, and a good breakfast. Near the cathedral, **Grand Victoria Boutique Hotel** (Bernardo 6-50 *y* Eguiguren, tel. 7/258-3500, www.grandvictoriabh.com, $90 s, $115 d, buffet breakfast included) has a restaurant, an indoor swimming pool, a fitness center, and spa. Comfortable, elegant guest rooms have bathtubs and flat-screen TVs. Some rooms have interior views, so request a street view if this is important. Breakfast is mediocre for a luxury hotel.

A block north of Parque Central, **Hotel Libertador** (Colón 14-30 *y* Bolívar, tel. 7/257-8278, www.hotellibertador.com.ec, $54 s, $70 d) is a bit dated but has comfortable rooms, friendly service, an indoor pool, and a restaurant. The hotel uses solar panels to heat water and invests in a number of local cultural, sports, and medical causes.

SOUTHERN SIERRA LOJA AND VICINITY

1: Calle Lourdes; **2:** Puerta de la Ciudad

So, Where's the Coffee and Chocolate?

Ecuadorian coffee is among the best in the world, but order a cup in most restaurants and you'll be provided with a mug of boiling water and a jar of Nescafé. Likewise, the country's cacao is arguably the best on the planet, but head to a store and you'll find the shelves dominated by Nestlé chocolate bars. Sadly, the national coffee and chocolate industries are largely geared toward the export market, and it can be quite a challenge to find local versions of these products . . . unless you know where to look.

Though coffee is grown and processed all over the country, the best Arabica-growing regions are found in the Sierra, including the areas around **Loja, Zaruma,** and **Intag.** Organic coffee grower associations in Intag and Vilcabamba offer tours of their farms and processing plants. On the central coast, **Jipijapa** is known for its good quality beans. Not surprisingly, restaurants in and near these places are more likely to serve real coffee. A bit more hunting is required along much of the coast and in the Amazon region, though cafés serving good quality local brews are springing up in most tourist towns.

The country's biggest chocolate success story is **Pacari** (www.pacarichocolate.com), a family-owned bean-to-bar company that has won several gold medals in the World Chocolate Awards. Their organic, fair trade products are sold nationally and internationally. Besides Pacari, there are plenty of other examples of excellent local chocolate to be found in Ecuador, with associations of cacao growers and bean-to-bar companies all over the country creating delicious, high-quality treats. The best places to find these, as well as Ecuadorian ground coffee, are the independent fair trade stores, present in most tourist towns that have been included in this book. Failing that, the large supermarkets (Mi Comisariato and Supermaxi) also stock artisanal coffee and chocolate. Not only do these make excellent souvenirs to take home, but, when grown responsibly and traded fairly, these gourmet products provide a sustainable source of income for hundreds of Ecuadorian families.

INFORMATION AND SERVICES

The main **tourist information center** is on the Parque Central (tel. 7/257-0407, ext. 202, 8am-6pm Mon.-Fri., 8am-4pm Sat.). Maps and basic information are also available at the **Puerta de la Ciudad** (tel. 7/258-7122, 8am-10pm daily).

Banco Pichincha has an ATM on the southeast corner of Parque Central; **Banco Bolívariano** has one on the east side.

GETTING THERE AND AROUND

The bus terminal is a 10-minute taxi/bus ride or a 20-minute walk north of the city center on Cuxibamba. Local buses run north on Universitaria and back down Iberoamérica and Aguirre every few minutes.

There are more or less hourly departures to **Cuenca** round the clock (4 hours, $6) with Viajeros Internacional and San Luis. Buses leave for **Vilcabamba** every 15 minutes 6am-8:45pm (75 minutes, $1.30) with Vilcabambaturis and TurSur. Buses to **Zamora** (1.5 hours, $3) leave more or less hourly 2am-11:15pm with Nambija and Union Yanzatza. There are half hourly buses to **Saraguro** with Transsaraguro and 16 Agosto.

Various companies offer overnight departures to **Quito,** leaving between 7pm and 10:15pm ($14-20, 11-12 hours). Buses leave for Guayaquil at 5:30am with Cariamanga; 9:45pm, 10:45pm, and 1:30am with Nambija; and 10pm with Loja Internacional (8 hours, $9). Less touristy Ecuadorian destinations include Santo Domingo, Machala, and Gualaquiza.

If you're heading to Ecuador's southern neighbor, see the section on *Crossing into Peru.*

The Catamayo City Aiport is 34 kilometers (21 mi) west of Loja. **TAME** (24 de Mayo y Ortega, tel. 7/257-0248, www.tame.com.ec)

operates twice-daily flights to/from Quito and three flights weekly to/from Guayaquil. To get to the airport, there are buses every half hour from the *terminal terrestre* to Catamayo (40 minutes, $1), and from there, take a taxi ($1). A taxi direct from Loja to the airport costs $20.

The minimum taxi fare in Loja is $1.25 during the day and $1.40 at night. Vilcabamba is $20 in a private taxi.

EAST OF LOJA
Zamora

Located 65 kilometers (40 mi) east of Loja, **Zamora** is the capital of Zamora-Chinchipe province. The 1,000-meter (3,280-ft) descent from Loja's craggy Andean peaks to Zamora's steamy jungle-covered hills is dramatic, and you'll be discarding your sweater pretty quickly when you arrive. Though the journey is spectacular, there is little reason to stop in Zamora, except as a jumping-off point for Podocarpus National Park and the southern Amazon.

Though founded by the Spanish in 1550, there is little sign of colonial history in today's fairly characterless concrete sprawl. This is the heartland of the mining industry, with several transnational corporations extracting gold, silver, and copper from the surrounding area. The town's two nicknames—Mining Capital of Ecuador and City of Birds and Waterfalls—represent opposing visions of the region's future: one seeking to exploit natural resources for short-term gain and the other hoping to preserve these resources for generations to come. One thing is for sure; if the mining continues at its current rate, the days are numbered for the area's birds and waterfalls.

SIGHTS AND RECREATION

If you do end up here with some hours to spend, the new riverside *malecón* makes for a pleasant stroll, as do the **main plaza** and **cathedral.** Just outside the bus station is **El Reloj Gigante** (Giant Clock). Certainly the largest clock in the country and claiming ambitiously to be the largest in the world, it is set on 150 square meters (1,615 sq ft) of grassy slope. The minute hand alone is nearly 15 meters (49 ft) long.

One block northeast of the cathedral, with the main entrance at the top of Jorge Mosquera, the **Tzanka Ecological Refuge** (tel. 7/260-5692, 8am-6pm daily, $2) rehabilitates rainforest animals that have been rescued from traffickers. Those that cannot be released into the wild become life-long residents. At the time of writing, there were parrots, turtles, snakes, monkeys, and a caiman, along with an orchid garden and a small museum.

A couple of waterfalls are easily accessed from the city. **La Cascada La Rosita**, located in **Tunantza**, is less than 10 minutes northeast of the center by taxi, then a five-minute walk. Another few minutes' drive northeast in **Timbara** is the **Cascada del Aventurero,** along with several restaurants serving local cuisine. Both waterfalls are en route to Yantzaza and are accessible by bus or taxi. The **Velo de Novia** waterfall is on the road from Loja, about 15 minutes before Zamora.

Podocarpus National Park is a $4 taxi ride from Zamora. Arrange a pickup time with the driver. The park entrance is a 15-minute walk from the road. From there, there are a number of short, well-marked trails, the shortest and most scenic of which is to the Cascada Poderosa waterfall, around a 15-minute walk. Los Higuerones and El Campesino trails are longer and have fewer people. Be aware that some of the paths are steep and slippery. Wear shoes with good grip and bring rain gear, food, and water.

For tours, contact Fernando Ortega at **BioAventura** (tel. 99/906-3955, Facebook @ Bioaventuraexpeditionscom, ferbioaventura@ hotmail.com). His one-day tour of Podocarpus National Park includes the Cascada Poderosa, a visit to a Shuar center, and the grove of giant podocarpus trees ($41 pp/4 people). He also offers a one-day tour to Alto Nangaritza in the Cordillera del Cóndor, including a motorized canoe journey, a jungle hike, a visit to a waterfall, and a natural rock labyrinth, Laberinto de Mil Ilusiones (Labyrinth of a Thousand Illusions, $85 pp/4 people). A two-day Alto Nangaritza tour includes a visit to the Cueva de los Tayos. Featured in the bestselling book *The Gold of the Gods* in 1972, this mysterious cave was claimed to be the location of a vast collection of gold artifacts from an ancient civilization. BioAventura is based in the Tzanka Ecological Refuge.

FOOD

Eating options are limited in Zamora, especially for vegetarians. Fresh produce is available at the market by the bus station, where there is a food court selling Ecuadorian dishes at low prices. For set lunches, try **La Choza** (Sevilla de Oro, tel. 7/260-7246, 7am-7pm Mon.-Sat., $3). For fast food (burgers, sandwiches, hot dogs, ice cream), **King Ice** (Diego de Vaca y Tamayo, tel. 7/260-5378, 8am-11pm daily, $3-5) is just off the main square and is open on Sundays.

For healthy organic food, head to ★ **Semillas** (Pio Jaramillo y Jorge Mosquera tel. 7/260-5684, Facebook @caferestaurantezamoraec, 7:30am-4:30pm Mon.-Fri.), where a set lunch is $3. A small range of organic, local artisanal products are for sale.

Local cuisine here is definitely Amazonian, rather than Sierran, with specialties including *ancas de rana* (frog legs), tilapia, and *caldo de corroncho* (soup made from the guaraguara fish). In the town center, a good place to sample these is **Los Moros** on the *malecón,* but the two best places are a 20-minute drive outside Zamora on the road to Yantzaza: **Hostería El Arenal** (km 12 1/2 Vía Cumbaratza, tel. 7/231-8271, Facebook @hosteriaelarenal) and, 2 kilometers (1.2 mi) later, **Hostería Castillo Real** (tel. 7/231-8188, Facebook @hosterialcastillo). Both also offer accommodations and have swimming pools.

ACCOMMODATIONS

Accommodation options are similarly limited, though there are a couple of decent options, both with great views from the fourth-floor terrace. **Hotel Betania** (Francisco de Orellana y Diego de Vaca, tel. 7/260-7030, $15 pp) has comfortable rooms and friendly service. Located between the main park and the *malecón,* **Wampushkar** (Diego de Vaca y Pasaje Vicente Aldean, tel. 7/260-7800, Facebook @wampushkarhotel, $23 s, $34 d, including breakfast Mon.-Fri.) has clean, modern, stylish rooms.

About 3 kilometers (1.9 mi) east of town in far more natural surroundings, **Copalinga** (tel. 9/347-7013, Facebook @Copalinga Ecolodge Zamora Ecuador) is a birding lodge and private reserve that was recently bought by bird conservation NGO Jocotoco Foundation. Comfortable cabins either have shared bathrooms ($35 s, $56 d) or private bathrooms and balconies ($47 pp). The food is good and the service is friendly. From the dining room, hummingbirds, tanagers, tinamous, and motmots can be spotted at the feeders. Information in English about the reserve and its birds can be found on the Jocotoco website (www.jocotoco.org). A taxi from Zamora costs $3.

INFORMATION AND SERVICES

There's a **tourist office** (Plaza Central, tel. 7/260-6599, 8am-5:30pm Mon.-Fri.) on the third floor of the municipal building on the main plaza. See www.gobernacionzamora.gob.ec and Facebook @Turismo Zamora Chinchipe for more information.

The **bus terminal** (Amazonas) is a few blocks east of the plaza, across from the **market.** Buses run more or less hourly to Loja (1.5 hours, $3). There are several daily departures to Gualaquiza (5 hours, $5) and a couple of overnight departures to Quito.

★ PODOCARPUS NATIONAL PARK

Ecuador's southernmost national park, named for Ecuador's only endemic conifer, is known as the Botanical Garden of Latin America for its 4,000 plant species. Sadly, many of the podocarpus trees have been cut down for their high-quality wood, but some remain, growing up to 30 meters (100 ft) tall. A UNESCO Biosphere Reserve, the park is home to spectacled bears, mountain tapirs, ocelots, pumas, and over 600 bird species.

The park's 146,280 hectares (361,465 acres) range 960-3,800 meters (3,150-12,470 ft) above sea level, encompassing a wide variety of habitats, from *páramo* to tropical rainforest. Although poaching, illegal colonizing, and especially mining have taken their toll, large sections of the park remain untouched.

Podocarpus National Park (http://areasprotegidas.ambiente.gob.ec) has two main zones. The *zona alta*, the high Andes section, is colder and accessed via the **Cajanuma ranger station** on the road between Loja and Vilcabamba. The warmer, less visited *zona baja* (low zone) is accessed via the **Bombuscara ranger station,** 6 kilometers (3.7 mi) south of the city of Zamora.

For most of the park, October-December is the driest period overall, while February-April sees the most rain. Temperatures vary from 12°C (54°F) average in the high Andes to 18°C (64°F) in the rainforest. Be aware that some of the paths are steep and slippery. Wear shoes with good grip and bring warm clothes, rain gear, food, and water.

Visiting the Low Zone

Because it's located 14 kilometers (8.7 mi) south of Loja and 23 kilometers (14 mi) north of Vilcabamba, it's possible to reach the turnoff to the Cajanuma ranger station by bus, but be aware that the park entrance is an 8-kilometer (5-mi) uphill walk (albeit quite beautiful) from the highway. Alternatively, take a taxi from Loja ($10) or Vilcabamba ($20) and arrange a pickup time with the driver, or go with an organized tour. At the park entrance is a visitors center, a refuge (tel. 7/257-1534, $3), and several well-marked **self-guided trails** ranging 1-5 hours. The shortest is the 400-meter (1,300-ft) Oso de Anteojos trail through the cloud forest; the longest is the Sendero al Mirador, which reaches a lookout point at 3,050 meters (10,000 ft) elevation. This is also the access point for the two-day

trek to the 136 lakes known as the Lagunas del Compadre, which can only be completed with a guide.

In Loja, **Ec-Viator** (Av. Pío Jaramillo Alvarado *entre* Chile *y* Cuba, tel. 7/258-0884, Facebook @ecviator, http://ec-viator.com, 9am-1pm and 3pm-7pm Mon.-Fri., 9am-1:30pm Sat.) offers a one-day tour in the national park ($40) and the two-day trek to the Lagunas del Compadre ($100 pp/4 people, $115 pp/2 people). Be aware that a good level of physical fitness is required for the Lagunas del Compadre. If you have your own tent, the price is $15 lower. Groups of 1-4 people should give 3-4 days' notice for the two-day trek. Groups of five or more require three weeks' notice so that permits can be obtained. **BirdsExplore** (Lourdes 14-80 *y* Sucre, tel. 7/258-2434, www.exploraves.com) offers **bird-watching tours** led by local expert Pablo Andrade.

In Vilcabamba, **La Tasca Tours** (tel. 98/556-1188, Facebook La Tasca Tours—Vilcabamba/Ecuador, latascatours@yahoo.com) offers one-day ($40-50 pp) and two-day ($120 pp) horseback riding tours to a private reserve in Podocarpus and a three-day circular bike tour through Podocarpus that passes Quinara, Yananga, and Valladolid, ending up in Malacatos ($86.50 pp/day). **Vilca Adventure** (Luis Fernando de la Vega 06-40 *entre* Jose David Toledo *y* La Paz, tel. 7/264-0088 or 95/947-8749), offers various Podocarpus tours including hikes ($8-10 pp); a full-day walking and biking tour via Loja ($30 pp) or Zamora ($60 pp); camping trips ($30 pp including tent, barbecue, and transport); and biking tours ($10-25 pp). **Chino's Bikes** (Calle Sucre 03-01 *y* Diego Vaca de Vega, tel. 98/187-6347 or 98/592-7081 for English, chinobike@gmail.com, 8am-6pm daily) offers a half-day downhill biking tour ($35 pp).

If you're traveling by *camioneta* from Vilcabamba, to add an additional adventure and avoid the $20 return fare, hire bikes in Vilcabamba, put them in the back of the *camioneta* to the park entrance, and leave them locked there while hiking in the park. Once back at the entrance, ride back on the riverside path to Malacatos, 10 kilometers (6.2 mi) north of Vilcabamba. From here, a *camioneta* back to Vilcabamba costs $5.

Visiting the High Zone

The **Bombuscara ranger station** is a $4 taxi ride from Zamora, then a 15-minute walk from the road. Arrange a pickup time with the driver. At the entrance is a visitors center, a refuge (tel. 7/258-5927, $3), and a number of short, well-marked trails, the shortest and most scenic of which is to the Cascada Poderosa waterfall, a 500-meter (1,640-ft) walk through the jungle. The 1-kilometer (0.6-mi) Mirador trail leads to a viewpoint overlooking Zamora. Los Higuerones trail is a 2-kilometer (1.2-mi) circuit through an orchid garden to the Río Bombuscaro, a great spot for bird-watching.

To go with a tour from Zamora, contact Fernando Ortega at **BioAventura** (tel. 99/906-3955, Facebook @ Bioaventuraexpeditionscom, ferbioaventura@ hotmail.com), who offers a one-day tour that includes the Cascada Poderosa, a visit to a Shuar center, and a grove of giant podocarpus trees ($41 pp/4 people).

Adjoining Reserves

The **Fundación Ecológica Arco Iris** (tel. 7/256-1830 or 99/665-0896, www.arcoiris. org.ec) administers the **Reserva Arcoiris** adjoining the national park, which is the easiest access point for the gigantic podocarpus trees, some of which are hundreds of years old and up to 30 meters (100 ft) in height. There is also excellent **bird-watching.** Trails are 3-4 hours in length and require a guide ($25 for up to 3 people). Basic accommodations are available ($17 pp, $7 with own sleeping bag, $4 camping), with kitchen facilities and a hot water shower. A generator provides electricity 5pm-9pm. Reserve two days ahead by email: arcoiris.conservation@ gmail.com. Reserva Arcoiris is 30 minutes from Loja, 50 minutes from Zamora.

Bird conservation organization **Fundación Jocotoco** (tel. 2/250-5212 or 99/244-0038, www.jocotoco.org) took its name from the call of a new species of antpitta that was discovered on the park boundaries in 1998—its call sounds like a cross between an owl's hoot and a dog's bark. International funding has allowed the foundation to purchase tracts of land adjacent to the park, creating the reserves of Tapichalaca (where it's possible to see the Jocotoco antpitta), Utuana, and Copalinga. Both Tapichalaca and Copalinga have lodges.

TOP EXPERIENCE

★ VILCABAMBA

At 1,500 meters (4,920 ft) elevation, this small picturesque town is nestled in a valley surrounded by undulating Andean foothills. With spectacular scenery, a spring-like climate, and a slow pace of life, it's an idyllic spot to spend a few days. Active visitors can hike, bike, and horseback ride in the nearby mountains, forests, and rivers, including Podocarpus National Park. Those preferring to take it easy can simply sit with a cup of excellent local coffee and **watch the light change over the valley,** dramatically illuminating lush green slopes and crumpled peaks, particularly at **sunrise** or **sunset.**

Vilcabamba has historically been famous for the long lives of its population, some of whom claimed to be over 120 years old. While it is true that some old rascals were exaggerating their age (upon investigation, scientists did not find anyone over the age of 96), there was no denying the vigorous health of many elderly residents. However, as modern life has encroached, life expectancy in the so-called Valley of Longevity now differs little from other parts of the country. These days, visitors are more likely to encounter U.S. retirees and hippies than local nonagenarians, most of whom have long since passed on.

In an effort to find a new identity, in recent years Vilcabamba has successfully reinvented itself as a health and wellness destination. In

Vilcabamba

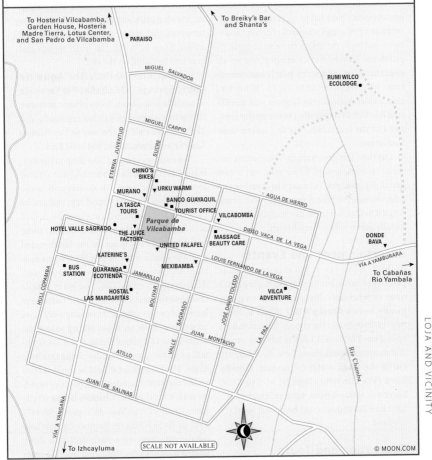

To Hosteria Vilcabamba,
Garden House, Hosteria
Madre Tierra, Lotus Center,
and San Pedro de Vilcabamba

PARAISO

To Breiky's Bar
and Shanta's

MIGUEL SALVADOR

RUMI WILCO
ECOLODGE

MIGUEL CARPIO

ETERNA JUVENTUD

SUCRE

CHINO'S
BIKES

URKU WARMI

MURANO

AGUA DE HIERRO

BANCO GUAYAQUIL

LA TASCA
TOURS

TOURIST OFFICE

VILCABOMBA

HOTEL VALLE SAGRADO

THE JUICE
FACTORY

Parque de
Vilcabamba

DIEGO VACA DE LA VEGA

MASSAGE
BEAUTY CARE

DONDE
BAVA

VÍA AYAMBURARA

UNITED FALAFEL

KATERINE'S

LOUIS FERNANDO DE LA VEGA

To Cabañas
Rio Yambala

BUS
STATION

GUARANGA
ECOTIENDA

JAMARILLO

MEXIBAMBA

HULL COPAMBA

HOSTAL
LAS MARGARITAS

BOLIVAR

SAGRADO

VALLE

JOSÉ DAVID TOLEDO

VILCA
ADVENTURE

Rio Chamba

JUAN MONTALVO

LA PAZ

ATILLO

JUAN DE SALINAS

VÍA A YANGANA

To Izhcayluma

SCALE NOT AVAILABLE

© MOON.COM

addition to excellent yoga and spa facilities, a wide range of therapies and treatments are available, including acupuncture, reiki, and hypnotherapy. There is an abundance of healthy, organic food and a bewildering range of natural and health products. And, though lifestyle has changed, one of the key reasons for the legendary longevity still remains: the mineral-rich, crystal-clear water that flows from Podocarpus National Park, which can be drunk straight from the faucet.

In contrast to its reputation, Vilcabamba is known for its *chamicos,* artisanal cigarettes made from local tobacco, often hand rolled by elderly residents. Another regional product is *panela* (unrefined whole cane sugar), though most of the artisanal producers have ceased operations after the government reclassified them as "factories" and introduced stringent regulations. Sadly, most *panela* production is now industrial. Tours are available to the remaining *trapiches,* where the sugarcane juice is extracted and boiled. The traditional local cuisine is similar to that of nearby Loja, though it can be hard to find in the increasingly internationalized Vilcabamba.

While the high numbers of foreign visitors and residents have led to increased local employment and a high standard of accommodations and food, the influx has also brought its problems. Luxury homes are popping up all over the valley, and many hotels and restaurants have been bought by expats. Many foreign residents speak only English, and there is a visible lack of integration between the gringos and the locals, who are fast losing their traditions.

Daytime temperatures in Vilcabamba average 18-20°C (64-68°F) all year, but it can get chilly at night. February to April is the rainy season, but it's not constantly wet. From August to October is the dry season, when the usually green valley turns brown.

Entertainment and Events

Nightlife is low-key in Vilcabamba, which is part of its charm, but there are a couple of bars open on weekends. Just past the town gates, locally owned **Breiky's Bar** (Calle Bolívar, tel. 99/730-2920, Facebook @BreikysBar, 8pm-2am Thurs.-Sat.) often has live music and dancing, especially on Saturdays. Slightly out of the town center to the east, **Donde Bava** (Vía Yamburara Bajo, tel. 96/740-8867, Facebook @dondebava, 6pm-midnight Fri.-Sat.) has live music, craft beer, and vegetarian food.

Recreation and Tours

An enjoyable few hours can be spent wandering the streets of Vilcabamba, taking in the main square, town gates, shops, and restaurants. Other activities include hiking, biking, horseback riding, yoga, and spa treatments.

Several hikes around town can be undertaken without a guide. If you're traveling alone, consider finding a hiking buddy in case you get lost or have an accident, and always notify your hostel of your planned route. At the time of writing, the map given out by the tourist office was fairly poor, though a project is underway to create new municipal maps. Fortunately, an excellent website, www.vilcahike.com, offers free maps of 66 hikes and three downhill mountain bike trails, each with a difficulty rating and detailed description, that can be printed or entered into smartphone GPS. All the trails mentioned here can be found on the site.

Popular hikes include the **Agua de Hierro Springs** and **Cabañas Río Yambala** (Charlie's Cabañas), from where you can climb to viewpoints, swimming holes, and El Palto waterfall on the way to Las Palmas Reserve and Podocarpus National Park.

The most spectacular hike is up to the dramatic **Cerro Mandango** rock formation that looms above the town. The shorter walk to the first peak is a 1.5-hour round-trip and can be completed by anyone with a reasonable degree of fitness, whereas the four-hour circular route to the second peak is not for the fainthearted or anyone with a fear of heights. The narrow ridge trail has extremely exposed spots, with deep drops on either side, and many people complete this section on all fours. There have been robberies on the Mandango trail, as recently as 2018, so avoid taking valuables. There is no cell phone signal and it is easy to fall, so do not consider undertaking this hike alone. The longer hike should be avoided altogether on windy, wet days. For peace of mind, go with a local guide. **Chino's Bikes** (Calle Sucre 03-01 y Diego Vaca de Vega, tel. 98/187-6347 or 98/592-7081 for English, chinobike@gmail.com, 8am-6pm daily) offers a daily guided hike to Cerro Mandango, leaving from their office a block north of the main square at 9am. The round-trip walk takes three hours and costs $25 per person (minimum 2 people, includes water and fruit). Reserve a day ahead.

The folks at **Hostería Izhcayluma** (tel. 99/915-3419, www.izhcayluma.com), 2 kilometers (1.2 mi) south of town, have created their own set of color-coded **trails** for guests, rated according to duration and difficulty. It's also a good place to meet up with fellow hikers for shared walks.

More **hikes** can be found at the east edge of town at the **Rumi Wilco Nature Reserve** (www.rumiwilco.com), an idyllic spot on the riverside with 40 hectares (99 acres) of protected forest and 12 self-guided trails, several of which are elevated and overlook the valley. A contribution of $2 allows up to three separate visits (bring change). Accommodations are also available. The reserve and ecolodge are run by Argentinian Orlando Falco, who lives on-site with his family, speaks perfect English, and is a fountain of knowledge about local ecology. Rumi Wilco is at the end of Agua de Hierro road, over the Chamba river footbridge, a 15-minute walk from the town center.

There is a very enjoyable 3-kilometer (1.9-mi) **riverside walk** from the El Chaupi bridge to the bridge at the Yamburara Park. To find the trail, head north out of town on the main road, past the town gates. Just past the Hostería Vilcabamba on the left, there is a bridge. To the right of the bridge, start following the path that runs alongside the Río Chamba, heading back toward town. When you get to Yamburara Park, you can join the main road back into town. This walk can be combined with visiting the Rumi Wilco Nature Reserve, which flanks the Río Chamba.

The Río Chamba riverside path is the last section of the **Sendero Ecológico,** a new walking trail that runs 40 kilometers (25 mi) from Loja to Vilcabamba. Beginning in Loja's Parque Lineal, the path is well maintained, well-marked, and fairly flat, connecting village to village, where you can stop and refuel. It sticks fairly close to the main road, so if you decide you're not going to make it the entire way, jump on a bus for the remainder of the journey.

To explore **Podocarpus National Park** independently, take a *camioneta* taxi to the Cajanuma entrance of the park ($20), which is 23 kilometers (14 mi) from Vilcabamba on the road to Loja. It's also possible to go by bus and ask to be dropped off, but be aware that the park entrance is an 8-kilometer (5-mi) walk (albeit quite beautiful) from the highway. From the entrance, there are several

well-marked trails ranging 1-5 hours. To add another adventure and avoid the $20 return taxi journey, hire bikes in Vilcabamba, put them in the back of a *camioneta* to the park entrance, and leave them locked there while hiking in the park. Once back at the entrance, ride back on the riverside path (part of the Sendero Ecológico) to Malacatos, 10 kilometers (6.2 mi) north of Vilcabamba. From here, a *camioneta* to Vilcabamba costs $5.

On the main square, **La Tasca Tours** (tel. 98/556-1188, Facebook La Tasca Tours—Vilcabamba/Ecuador, latascatours@yahoo.com) is a long-established agency run by friendly local René León. He offers one-day ($40-50 pp) and two-day ($120 pp) horseback riding tours to a private reserve in Podocarpus National Park; a half-day horseback riding tour to El Palto waterfall ($30-40 pp); a one-day combined tour that includes traditional coffee and *panela* factories and Podocarpus ($50 pp); the Mandango hike ($12 pp); and a three-day circular bike tour through Podocarpus that passes Quinara, Yananga, and Valladolid, ending up in Malacatos ($87 pp/day). In December/January he also offers a bike tour to see the flowering of the guayacan trees. English- and German-speaking tours can be provided by René's son and daughter, who work with him as guides.

Three blocks east of the square, another locally owned agency is **Vilca Adventure** (Luis Fernando de la Vega 06-40 *entre* Jose David Toledo *y* La Paz, tel. 7/264-0088 or 95/947-8749), run by Danny Toledo. He offers various local hikes in Podocarpus, to Mandango, to nearby waterfalls, and for bird-watching ($8-10 pp); tubing in the Bombuscaro, Vilcabamba, and Quinara rivers ($15 pp); a tour to the Polando archaeological ruins ($50 pp, minimum 2 people); a full-day walking and biking tour in Podocarpus, via Loja ($30 pp) or Zamora ($60 pp); camping trips to Podocarpus, Mandango, Yambala, and Quinara ($30 pp including tent, barbecue, and transport); local biking tours to Podocarpus and various viewpoints ($10-25 pp); and visits to artisanal workshops making café, honey, *panela, chamicos* (cigarettes), and liquor ($15 pp). Also available is a two-day, one-night Amazon tour to Alto Nangaritza in the Cordillera del Cóndor, which includes the Labyrinth of a Thousand Illusions (a natural rock maze), a river journey by paddle canoe, an overnight stay in a Shuar community with a bonfire and purification with coca leaves, and a jungle walk to a waterfall for bathing ($100 pp, minimum 4 people).

A block north of the square, **Chino's Bikes** (Calle Sucre 03-01 *y* Diego Vaca de Vega, tel. 98/187-6347 or 98/592-7081 for English, chinobike@gmail.com, 8am-6pm daily) offers motorbike rental, bike rental ($3/hour or $15/day), tours, and repairs. Three bike tours are available: a two-hour Vilcabamba city tour ($12 pp); a half-day tour to a Quinara agricultural community, an artisanal *panela* (sugar) factory, and a swimming spot at a local river ($25 pp); and a half-day downhill biking tour in Podocarpus ($35 pp). A daily guided hike to Cerro Mandango leaves at 9am, takes three hours, and costs $25 per person. All tours should be booked a day ahead.

Shopping

There are handicrafts and clothing stores around the central square. Half a block south of the square, **Guaranga Ecotienda** (tel. 98/196-0172, Facebook @guarangaecotienda, 8am-9am Mon.-Sat., 8am-5pm Sun.) offers a good range of agro-ecological, organic products from local artisans and farmers, including coffee, chocolate, bread, eggs, fresh produce, cleaning products, and health products. The **Juice Factory** on the main square has a natural and health products store in the back.

There is an organic produce market outside the bus terminal every Saturday morning. For a traditional market experience, head to Malacatos on a Sunday morning, where trading starts at 4am and ends around midday. Regular buses leave for Malacatos from the terminal, or take a taxi for $5.

Spas and Wellness

The best spa and yoga facilities are at **Hostería Izhcayluma** (tel. 99/915-3419, www.izhcayluma.com) located on a hillside 2 kilometeres (1.2 mi) south of Town. Available to guests and nonguests, the beautiful yoga studio is open on three sides, overlooking the valley. There are two classes daily in a variety of styles from hatha to air yoga. Most classes cost $5, with air yoga $7. The daily 7:30am "wake-up" class is free for hotel guests. The spa is excellent and very reasonably priced, with a 75-minute full body massage costing $22.

For spa treatments in the town center, try Karina at **Massage Beauty Care** (Diego Vaca de Vega *y* Valle Sagrado, tel. 98/122-3456), a block east of the square, who offers massage ($25 for 1 hour or $15 for 30 minutes), facials, exfoliations, and beauty treatments.

Another great option for yoga and wellness is **Lotus Center** (Calle Eterna Joventud, tel. 98/150-8358, www.lotuscenterec.com, 8am-4pm Mon.-Fri., 10am-1pm Sat.), 4.5 kilometers (2.8 mi) north of Vilcabamba in San Pedro, which is run by a physiotherapist. Various treatments are available, including physical therapy, craniosacral therapy, and Neuro Emotional Technique. Accommodations are available.

Many tourists come to Vilcabamba seeking **San Pedro ceremonies.** Like the jungle vine ayahuasca, the San Pedro cactus is a medicinal plant that is native to Ecuador. It grows in the Sierra and has been used for thousands of years by Andean shamans in spiritual and healing traditions. Both medicines are legal if prepared by a licensed *curandero,* but not for recreational use. Unlike with ayahuasca, the people who are currently administering San Pedro are not descendants of indigenous shamans but mestizos or westerners. Moreover, there is a high level of irresponsible and dangerous use of San Pedro in the Vilcabamba area. For an authentic

---

1: view from the restaurant at Hosteria Izhcayluma
2: sightseeing on horseback in Vilcabamba

experience, it's recommended to travel into the Amazon for an ayahuasca ceremony with practitioners who come from generations of healers. If you're set on a San Pedro experience, Felicia is an Austrian healer who has been working in Vilcabamba for many years and is responsible in her care of patients. See www.sacredmedicinejourney.com for more information.

Community Tourism Tours

Just across the bridge to the north of town is the small village of **San Pedro de Vilcabamba,** referred to by its residents as the *pueblo olvidado* (forgotten town) because almost none of Vilcabamba's thousands of visitors stop here. This is not due to any lack of attractions, however. San Pedro is a picturesque village with a beautiful crystal-clear river and a protected forest on its doorstep. While the residents still maintain a traditional way of life, they have created an impressive, forward-looking community tourism project, APECAEL. After starting as an association of organic coffee producers, the organization has since branched out to offer a range of tours and experiences to visitors, with the aim of improving quality of life for the community. As well as providing sustainable sources of income, APECAEL organizes workshops for local people on topics such as gender equality, self-esteem, money management, and leadership.

APECAEL (tel. 98/401-2719, www.apecael.blogspot.com, Facebook @apecael, apecael@hotmail.com) tailors its tours to suit the interests of visitors. The coffee tour includes a visit to one of the 66 organic farms in the association, where the coffee is grown in the shade of fruit trees. It's also possible to visit the facilities where the beans are sorted, skinned, fermented, washed, dried, toasted, ground, and packaged. Between April and July, visitors can participate in the process. The tour ends in the impressive coffee laboratory. Until recently, APECAEL exported all its coffee to Europe and the United States, but then made the decision to make it available to Ecuadorians at affordable prices. Initially only on sale in the Guaranga Ecotienda in Vilcabamba, it's now being requested by stores nationwide. Another excellent tour is to the **Sol del Venado** craft beer factory (tel. 98/224-5678, www.soldevenado.com), which has a barbecue on weekends (noon-6:30pm). Other activities include bathing in the river, where there is a natural swimming hole, and guided walks and birdwatching in the protected forest. A local chef can prepare a four-course traditional meal of tamales, *humitas* (ground corn with egg, butter, and cheese, wrapped in a corn husk and steamed), *repe* (creamy soup made from green bananas), *cecina* (thinly sliced sundried pork served with yucca), and *miel con quesillo* (honey with soft unsalted cheese), which would be hard to find in Vilcabamba. Vegetarians can be accommodated. There is also the option to eat at a riverside trout restaurant, **Truchas del Salado** (tel. 95/998-1316). Homestays with local families can be arranged and volunteers are accepted. APECAEL can be contacted in English or Spanish and provides tours in both languages.

Food

On weekends, there is tasty, cheap, local food at the market outside the bus station. A couple of good restaurants in town serve Ecuadorian cuisine with some Lojan specialties, both owned by local families. Half a block south of the main square on Sucre, ★ **Katerine's** (tel. 7/264-0055 or 99/796-2415, 8:30am-6pm daily) offers set lunches ($3.50) and à la carte items, including *cecina*. A block east of the square, **Vilcabomba** (Diego Vaca de Vega *y* Valle Sagrado, $3) offers similar fare. Also locally owned, but much less traditional, is the ever-popular **Shanta's** (tel. 8/562-7802, 1pm-9pm Wed.-Sun., $6-10), where the decor has a cowboy theme and the house special is pizza (gluten free and veggie options available). The trout and pasta dishes are also good. The signature drink is pickled snake moonshine; try it if you dare! To get there, head north out of town on Eterna Juventud and turn right after less than 1 kilometer (0.6 mi) at Hostería Paraíso, then take the third left.

For excellent international dishes with an unrivaled view, head up to ★ **Hostería Izhcayluma** (tel. 7/264-0095, www.izhcayluma.com, 7am-10am, noon-5pm, and 5:30pm-9pm daily, $5-7), where the open-sided, panoramic restaurant is perched on a hillside 2 kilometers (1.2 mi) south of town. The menu includes German specialties, and most meat dishes have an alternative with delicious homemade tempeh. Some ingredients come from the on-site organic gardens, most from local small-scale producers.

Other recommended international options include **United Falafel** (Facebook @ Unitedfalafel, 11am-8am Wed.-Sun., $6.50-8.50) on the main square, where falafels are served alongside wraps, sandwiches, and cakes; **Mexibamba** (tel. 98/669-9013, 10am-9pm, $6-11), which offers good Mexican food a block east of the square on Vaca de Vega; and **Murano** (tel. 98/592-7081, Facebook @ muranovilcabamba, 11:30am-8:30pm Tues.-Sun., $4-10), a Mediterranean restaurant just north of the square on Sucre. Most places in town offer veggie options, but for a purely veggie menu, head to **Urku Warmi** (tel. 98/633-2642, noon-8pm daily, $6), across the road from Murano, where the friendly Chilean owner serves organic quiches, veggie burgers, salads, pastas, and pizzas.

Accommodations

IN TOWN

At the family-run **Hotel Valle Sagrado** (Av. Eterna Juventud, tel. 7/272-1424, $7-10 pp), a block west of the square, guest rooms are basic but decent, some with shared bathrooms and some private. Two blocks south of the square, the homey **Hostal Las Margaritas** (Sucre *y* Jaramillo, tel. 7/272-1815, $15 pp, including breakfast) is great value, with comfortable guest rooms and a swimming pool.

OUTSIDE TOWN

Vilcabamba's best lodgings are found outside town, although within walking distance. Less than 1 kilometer north of town, great value can be found at Lojan-owned **Paraíso** (Av. Eterna Juventud, tel. 7/264-0266 or 98/844-8057, Facebook @HosteriaParaiso $25-30 s, $45-50 d, breakfast included), which has tropical gardens, a swimming pool, sauna, steam bath, Jacuzzi (all available to nonguests for $5), and a massage room inside a bio-energetic pyramid. Local cuisine is available in the restaurant, which uses organic ingredients where possible. Environmental policies include composting and reusing rainwater to irrigate the gardens. Slightly farther out of town, another Lojan-owned hotel, **Hostería Vilcabamba** (tel. 7/264-0271 or 98/192-2905, www.hosteriadevilcabamba.com, $43 s, $60 d), has guest bungalows set amid extensive leafy gardens. It offers a bar, restaurant, sizable pool, sauna, and steam bath. The nearby **Garden House** (tel. 96/821- 8767, Facebook @gardenhousevilcabamba, $15 s, $20 d) is a good budget option, with attractive grounds and a friendly owner. Each room has a balcony with a mountain view. Breakfast is available for $2.50.

By far the best place to stay is ★ **Hostería Izhcayluma** (tel. 99/915-3419, www.izhcayluma.com, dorm $9.50 pp, $20-39 s, $26-49 d), perched on a hill 2 kilometers (1.2 mi) south of town with unrivaled views of the valley, especially from the panoramic restaurant and open-sided yoga studio. When the German owners first bought the property, it was barren land that had been decimated by cattle grazing. Now, after extensive reforestation, the grounds are home to deer and a wide variety of birds. The ornamental gardens are truly a work of art. Accommodations are in dorms, guest rooms, and cabins with private balconies. Long-term rentals are also available ($120-500/week), some with a kitchen. A buffet breakfast ($3.90) includes homemade yogurt, bread, and granola, plus home-grown coffee. The excellent restaurant (7am-10am, noon-5pm, and 5:30pm-9pm daily) serves international dishes, with lots of veggie options made with tempeh. The spa is outstanding and reasonably priced (a 75-minute full-body massage is $22). The yoga studio offers two daily classes, with the morning class free for guests. The owners have mapped out several hiking trails and are the best source of up-to-date information about Vilcabamba and traveling onward to Peru or the rest of Ecuador, even going as far as sending volunteers to check out new travel routes and report back. Izhcayluma employs 31 local people and supports local businesses wherever possible (drivers, tour agencies, etc.). From Vilcabamba, it's a $1.50 taxi ride. There is a direct shuttle service between the hotel and the historical district in Cuenca. English, German, and Spanish are spoken.

U.S.-owned **Hostería Madre Tierra** (Amala Bajo, tel. 7/273-0362 or 99/523-0973, www.madretierra.com.ec, $22-86 s, $44-100 d, breakfast included) has immaculate guest rooms with private balconies. The spa offers a wide range of treatments ($12-37) and is available to nonguests with advance reservations, as is the restaurant, which serves healthy natural food (8:30am-8pm daily). A taxi from town costs $1.25.

For a truly natural experience on the edge of town, head to **Rumi Wilco Ecolodge** (www.rumiwilco.com, $10-23 pp, camping $5 pp), run by Argentine scientists Alicia and Orlando Falco, who worked for many years as guides in the Galápagos and the Amazon. Just a 15-minute walk from the town center, you'll find yourself in a thickly forested 40-hectare (99-acre) nature reserve offering complete seclusion. There is a choice of five adobe and four wooden cabins on the edge of the Río Chamba, with options ranging from small dorms to a mini-apartment with a kitchen. Each private cabin has a riverside balcony and fire pit. There are cooking facilities, hammocks, and Wi-Fi. Guest have access to a network of 12 self-guided trails, several of which are elevated and overlook the valley. Orlando speaks perfect English and is helpful and friendly. A third of the income from the ecolodge goes toward reforestation, trail maintenance, scientific research, and other activities on the reserve. Rumi Wilco is at the end of Agua de Hierro road, over the Chamba River footbridge. It's $2 by *camioneta*.

To get even farther away from it all, head to **Cabañas Río Yambala** (tel. 9/106-2762, www.vilcabamba-hotel.com), also known as Charlie's Cabañas. Deep in the countryside 5 kilometers (3 mi) east of town are four cabins in a beautiful riverside setting, geared toward weekly (from $150 s, $175 d) or monthly rental (from $350 s, $400 d). Kitchen facilities are available, but there are no restaurants nearby, so bring your own food. Run by American owner Charlie, who's been in Vilcabamba for 30 years, this is a favorite retreat for budget travelers seeking splendid isolation to the accompaniment of rushing water. Charlie has set up a marked trail system and can arrange hikes and horseback rides to a cloud forest refuge in the foothills of Podocarpus National Park. Cabañas Río Yambala is a one-hour uphill slog from town on foot, or take a taxi for $3. Be aware that the taxi will drop you a steep few minutes' walk from the cabins.

Information and Services

There is a **tourist office** (tel. 7/264-0090, 8am-6pm daily) on the main square.

Banco Guayaquil has an ATM on the corner of the square. Banco de Loja also has an ATM on the square; it works for international cards.

Getting There and Around

Two bus companies go between Loja and Vilcabamba every 15 minutes (75 minutes, $1.50): **TurSur** and the slightly faster **Vilcabamba Turis**. A private taxi costs $20. To travel to Cuenca, take a bus to Loja and change. Alternatively, **Hostería Izhcayluma** (tel. 99/915-3419, www.izhcayluma.com), 2 kilometers (1.2 mi) south of town, offers a daily direct minibus service to Cuenca at 8am, which terminates outside Hostal La Cigale in the historical district (4.5 hours, $15). Coming from Cuenca to Vilcabamba, it leaves at 1:30pm. To reserve a seat, email izhcayluma@yahoo.de. There is a direct bus from Vilcabamba to Quito with **Loja Internacional** at 7pm.

Crossing into Peru

The most common way to enter Peru is via the coastal town of **Huaquillas** in Machala (see the *Guayaquil and the Southern Coast* chapter for details), but it's more scenic to cross in the highlands south of Vilcabamba, where there are two main crossing points: **Zumba/ La Balsa** and **Macará.** Going via Zumba is more convenient for reaching the ruins of Chachapoyas or the Peruvian Amazon, or if you're heading to Iquitos by boat. Macará is better for the Peruvian coast or Lima. Both crossings are safe. Whichever route you take, check that your passport has been stamped upon arrival in Peru. It is fairly common for border officials to forget, and there are no computerized records here, meaning that without a stamp you will be officially in the country illegally.

MACARÁ/PIURA

With buses going directly from Loja in Ecuador to **Piura** in Peru, there is no reason to stop in the Ecuadorian border town of **Macará,** except to complete the exit/entrance formalities while the bus waits. **Co-op Loja** (tel. 7/257-1861 or 7/272-9014) has departures from Loja at 7am and 11pm (8 hours, $14). If you're traveling from Vilcabamba, you can buy a ticket in the office across from the bus station, but you must catch the bus from Loja. **Union Cariamanga** (tel. 7/260-5613, Facebook @UnionCariamanga) also has a bus from Loja to Piura at midnight. Don't worry if the bus appears to drive off while you are completing the formalities; it will wait on the other side of the bridge. Just walk over when you have received your stamp.

ZUMBA/LA BALSA/JAÉN

Historically, it was customary to spend a night in **Zumba,** 90 minutes north of the border, in order to cross at **La Balsa** the following day. These days, however, there is a direct bus from Loja to **Jaén** in Peru, which waits while passengers complete the necessary formalities in La Balsa. Be aware that the officials here may be somewhat less than official; there have been reports of passengers having to wait while Ecuadorian and Peruvian guards finish their game of football before they can cross the border.

Nambija Internacional (tel. 7/231-5177 or 7/303-9179, Facebook @coopnambija1987) has a departure to Jaén from Loja at 7am (10.5 hours, $21). The buses pass in front of the Vilcabamba bus terminal on the main road an hour after departure.

Some travelers prefer to take the old route, with an overnight stop in **Zumba,** for the experience. The 90-minute journey from Zumba to the border town of **La Balsa** is undertaken by *ranchero* (an open-sided, usually brightly painted truck fitted with wooden benches), which is a fun experience through beautiful scenery.

From Loja, **Nambija Internacional** has a departure for Zumba at 12:50pm (6 hours, $7.50); **Union Yantzaza** (tel. 98/336-2363 @ CooperativaDeTransporteUnionYantzaza) has departures at 2am and 9:45pm. **Loja Internacional** has a bus to Zumba from Vilcabamba at 8pm. Once in Zumba, take a taxi to the town center ($1), where a recommended hostel is **San Luis** (12 de Febrero *y* Brasil, tel. 99/086-2138 or 7/230-8017, $8-12 pp). In the morning, the *ranchero* to La Balsa leaves the terminal at 8am (1.5 hours, $2.25). Once on the Peruvian side, change money on the left-hand side after crossing the bridge, then take a white shared taxi or *colectivo* to **San Ignacio** (1 hour, 17 soles). If the money changer is shut, tell the taxi driver you can pay in San Ignacio, where it is also possible to change money. Ask to be dropped off where the vans to **Jaén** leave. From San Ignacio to Jaén is three hours.

The Oriente and the Amazon Basin

East of the Andes, the Amazon rainforest covers nearly half the country's geographical area, with large tracts of virgin jungle still remaining, some of it considered so sacred by indigenous peoples that even they do not tread there. These mystical forests are home to nature's most intricate and impressive orchestration of life, where one hectare can contain as many tree species as all of North America. In a single river journey, a visitor might spot pink river dolphins swimming alongside the canoe, gigantic iridescent blue morpho butterflies flitting overhead, monkeys peering down from the branches, and macaws screeching in the treetops.

Nighttime canoe rides are just as wonderful. Gliding silently across a lagoon under the Milky Way, the lily leaves illuminated by millions of

Highlights

Look for ★ to find recommended sights, activities, dining, and lodging.

★ **Cascada San Rafael:** The viewing point for Ecuador's highest waterfall is reached via a beautiful trail through a forest where wooden bridges cross rushing streams. Agoutis, monkeys, and the Guianan cock-of-the-rock are frequently spotted (page 257).

★ **Indigenous Communities:** Lago Agrio provides easy access to indigenous Kofán and Siekopai communities with grassroots tourism projects that help to preserve the rainforest and ancestral traditions (page 262).

★ **Laguna Limoncocha:** One of the top 10 birding spots in the country is this serene lake with lush jungle overhanging the water's edge. As the light fades, thousands of fireflies illuminate the lily leaves, lighting up the surface like a miniature city (page 269).

★ **Yasuní National Park:** Community-owned lodges allow the most biodiverse spot on the planet to be explored on foot, by dugout canoe, and from observation towers at canopy level (page 271).

★ **Sarayaku:** In a remote part of Pastaza province, this small Kichwa community stands at the front lines of the battle to defend the Amazon rainforest and indigenous peoples, living up to an ancient prophecy (page 286).

COLOMBIA

Cascada San Rafael ★

🔲 Indigenous Communities

Coca ○

Laguna 🔲 Limoncocha

Yasuní 🔲 National Park

ECUADOR

🔲

Sarayaku

PERU

○ Macas

0 — 50 mi
0 — 50 km

© MOON.COM

The Oriente

COLOMBIA

Pasto

Túquerres

Laguna
La Cocha

El Chical

Ipiales
Tulcán

Cotacachi-
Cayapas
Ecological
Reserve

Río

Río
Guamués

Kofán-
Bermejo
Ecological
Reserve

San

Picudo

Río

Apuela

Lago
Cuicocha

Chota

Ibarra

Cayambe-Coca
Ecological
Reserve

Lago Agrio
(Nueva Loja)

INDIGENOUS
COMMUNITIES

Miguel

Tigre
Playa

Puerto El Carmen

Otavalo

Equator

SHAYARI ★

Río Coca

DURENO

Lagunas de
Cuyabeno

Putumayo

Quito

Volcán Reventador ▲

CASCADA
SAN RAFAEL

Río Quijos

Sumaco-Napo
Galeras
National Park

La Joya de
los Sachas

Shushufindi

Tarapoa

SIEKOYA
REMOLINO ★

Río

Río
Lagartococha

Papallacta

LAGUNA
LIMONCOCHA ★

Aguarico

ZÁBALO ★

Pañacocha
Protected Forest

Cuyabeno
Wildlife
Reserve

Volcán
Antisana ▲

Baeza

Volcán
Sumaco

Río
Payamino

Coca (Puerto
Francisco De
Orellana)

Pañacocha

Río Napo

Lago
Imuya

LAGARTOCOCHA ★

Antisana
Ecological
Reserve

Cosanga

WILDSUMACO
LODGE

Loreto

LAS CAVERNAS
DE JUMANDY ★

Archidona

Río

Yasuní
National Park

TENA

SINCHI
WARMI ★

Nuevo
Rocafuerte

Puerto Napo

Misahualli

Bataburo
(Tiguiño)

Huaorani
Reserve

SEE "LOWER
RÍO NAPO" MAP

Ambato

SACHA RUNA
LODGE

Río
Tiguiño

Río

Baños

Puyo

Río

Curaray

Cononaco

Riobamba

SARAYAKU

ECUADOR

Macas

Río Paute

Río Upano

Sucúa

Pastaza

KAPAWI
ECOLODGE

Méndez

Morona

Río Zamora

Santiago

CUEVA DE
LOS TAYOS

Río Santiago

PERU

Gualaquiza

0   30 mi

0   30 km

© MOON.COM

fireflies, accompanied by the orchestra of insects and frogs, is a truly magical experience. Other jungle highlights include climbing an observation tower for a canopy-level view and visiting a parrot clay lick, where hundreds of birds flock daily in a multicolored spectacle of wings.

The Amazon region, or Oriente, is home to several indigenous nationalities: the Kofán, Siekopai, Siona, Kichwa, Waorani, Shuar, Achuar, Zápara, and Shiwiar, each with their own language and customs. Incredibly, two uncontacted tribes, the Tagaeri and Taromenane, live in Yasuní National Park. Many communities still live by hunting, gathering, fishing, and small-scale agriculture, maintaining a deep connection with the living forest. This is a land of ancestral traditions, myths, and legends, where powerful shamans practice ancient arts and, it is rumored, can shape-shift into jaguars.

These wild landscapes and indigenous peoples lay undisturbed for centuries until 1542, when a certain Spaniard, Francisco de Orellana, embarked on his ambitious, ill-fated journey in search of the gold of Eldorado. Despite founding towns such as Tena and Macas, however, the Spanish didn't settle far into the Amazon due to fierce indigenous resistance. When the 16th-century hunt for gold was replaced by the 20th-century quest for petroleum, missionaries worked together with oil companies to convert and pacify the so-called "Aucas" (savages), paving the way for drilling on a massive scale. As a result, enormous environmental damage has been done and vast tracts of land continue to be concessioned to oil companies.

The most typical Amazonian dish is *maito* (fish, grubs, or chicken grilled in a wrapped leaf). The fish might be farmed tilapia or *bagre*, a type of freshwater catfish. The grubs, known as *mayones,* are *chonta* palm worms. Farther south, the signature dish is *ayampaco* (chopped meat, chicken, or fish with palm hearts and onion, grilled in a wrapped *bijao* leaf). Throughout the region, popular accompaniments are yucca (cassava), *platano* (plantain), and *palmitos* (palm hearts). The typical drink is *guayusa*, a type of tea that indigenous people traditionally drink at dawn while analyzing their dreams. It can be served hot or cold.

Planning Your Time

Where you visit depends on your available time and budget. There is no escaping the fact that most jungle lodges are expensive, offering packages of minimum 3-4 days to make the travel worthwhile. However, Ecuador's rainforest is among the most accessible on the continent, and there are affordable options if you know where to look.

To stay in the middle of primary rainforest, the community-owned lodges in **Yasuní National Park** are your best bet, accessible via the town of Coca. The lodges get busy, so make your reservation as far in advance as possible. More economical and available last minute are tours from Coca, where Yasuní National Park can be visited in 1-3 days, often combined with the nearby **Limoncocha Biological Reserve.** Limoncocha can also be visited independently, and a Kichwa community tourism project provides economical accommodations.

Farther north, **Lago Agrio** offers access to **grassroots indigenous tourism initiatives** where the proceeds directly support the people's struggle to preserve their territory and culture. The Kofán and Siekopai nationalities have some of the best shamans in the country and provide an affordable way to experience the rainforest while sharing community life.

Lago Agrio and Coca, both oil towns, can be reached from Quito by a long bus ride (over 8 hours) or a half-hour flight. The bus has the advantage of the excellent stops en route, including the hot springs at **Papallacta** and the

---

Previous: Canoe is the main form of transportation in much of the Amazon; San Rafael waterfall; the indigenous Siekopai are known for their powerful shamans and knowledge of medicinal plants.

charming village of **Baeza,** where four forested reserves in the proximity make it an excellent base for hiking, rafting, kayaking, and bird-watching. Those venturing to Lago Agrio can easily stop off at **Cascada San Rafael,** Ecuador's highest waterfall.

Only four hours from Quito, **Tena** is a gateway to visiting Kichwa communities. The experiences tend to be cultural, rather than immersions in nature, though there are some beautiful waterfalls nearby. Tena is also Ecuador's white-water rafting center, with plenty of Class III and Class IV rapids close to town. There are more foreign visitors here than in other Amazon towns, and the tourism amenities are of a higher standard and wider range. **Puyo,** southwest of Tena, has some wonderful botanical gardens on the city outskirts. It's a popular destination with tourists from Baños who come for one- to two-day tours to nearby waterfalls and indigenous communities—a kind of "rainforest-lite" experience for those seeking a brief introduction to the region. The airport at **Shell,** near Puyo, offers access to the remote Kichwa community of Sarayaku and the even more remote Kapawi Lodge in Achuar territory. Even farther south, Macas is a good place to organize tours to Shuar communities.

Community Tourism

Wherever you decide to go, remember that indigenous peoples in the Amazon are under extreme pressure to exploit their land, not just from the oil industry, but from gold-mining companies and agricultural corporations wanting to plant African palm and malanga. Due to their geographical isolation, it is especially challenging for Amazonian communities to find alternative economic sources of income. Community-based ecotourism is often the only way for them to conserve their ancestral territories and ancient cultures. Perhaps of all the regions of Ecuador, this is where tourist dollars have the potential to make the greatest difference. It is a tragedy, therefore, that in so many parts of the Amazon, outside companies with large amounts of money to invest have monopolized the tourism industry. While local people are often employed as canoe drivers or guides, and visits are organized to their communities, they see only a fraction of the income generated in their ancestral territories.

Fortunately, there are several excellent tourism initiatives, managed by indigenous communities or families, where the income goes directly to local people, allowing them to preserve their territories and way of life. Those looking to support rainforest conservation efforts are encouraged to consider visiting one of these projects.

To visit a grassroots indigenous project, make the reservation as much in advance as possible. Remember that phone signal and/or Internet is not always reliable in the Amazon, so be patient when waiting for a response. Try not to have fixed ideas about what an indigenous community "should" be. While many still live in traditional dwellings and survive by hunting, gathering, fishing, and small-scale agriculture, the majority have adapted to western life to some degree or other. Most only wear traditional dress on special occasions, preferring jeans and T-shirts. Guns have increasingly replaced blowpipes and spears as hunting weapons, and some communities now prefer to raise chickens as a way to conserve the remaining wildlife. Try to leave preconceived notions at home, take people as they are, and be prepared for adventure.

What to Pack

Pack well for a rainforest trip, as shopping opportunities are few in the Oriente (though essentials such as rubber boots, plastic ponchos, and flashlights can be found in the region's major towns). Annual rainfall averages 300 centimeters (118 in), so bring wet-weather gear. Rubber boots are provided by most jungle lodges, but not by some of the smaller projects, so check in advance, especially if you need a large size. People with feet over U.S. men's size 10 (women's size 12) or European size 43 should definitely bring rubber boots from home, as large size footwear is hard to find in Ecuador. A rain poncho is more useful than a jacket, as it will also keep your daypack dry.

Daily highs average 30°C (86°F), so expect to sweat a lot, and bring plenty of lightweight long pants (not jeans) and long-sleeved tops, for reducing insect bites. Leggings work well for women. The sun can be strong, so pack a hat, sunglasses, and sunblock. Insect repellent is also essential. Bring lemon eucalyptus or citronella oil from home if you're looking to avoid the chemicals in DEET-based products. A flashlight is necessary for night walks and nighttime bathroom trips (when there is often no electricity). Binoculars help with spotting birds and wildlife from a canoe. There is a low risk of malaria in the Amazon basin; bite avoidance is advised, rather than anti-malarial medication. A yellow fever vaccination is recommended (these last for life, so if you've ever had one, you're protected).

Quito to Baeza

Leaving Quito and heading east, the air grows cold and thin as the road reaches 4,100 meters (13,450 ft) elevation before dropping down to 3,225 meters (10,580 ft) at **Papallacta,** the location of Ecuador's best thermal baths, 70 kilometers (43 mi) from the capital. If the weather is clear, there are magnificent views of Volcán Antisana to the south. Continuing east from Papallacta it's all downhill, with the vegetation quickly becoming more tropical near the charming village of Baeza, 110 kilometers (68 mi) from Quito, where the road forks, heading north to the San Rafael waterfall and Lago Agrio or south to Tena and Coca.

PAPALLACTA

Set in an Andean valley at a chilly 3,225 meters (10,580 ft) elevation, Papallacta is best known for its thermal baths, but it also offers great hiking opportunities. It gets cold overnight so pack warm clothes. There is no ATM in the village, so bring enough cash with you.

Hot Springs

Papallacta is within the Chacana volcanic complex that has been consistently active for more than 3 million years. The water that feeds the thermal baths is rainwater that has filtered through the caldera, absorbing heat and minerals. The baths attract crowds of Quiteños on weekends but are relatively quiet during the week.

The biggest, most upscale and popular baths are the **Termas Papallacta** (tel. 6/289-5060 or 9/275-3079, www.termaspapallacta.com), located 2.7 kilometers (1.7 mi) north of the village center ($2 by taxi). The main section (6am-9pm daily, $9 pp) has nine hot pools of varying temperatures and four that are fed by cold-water springs. Towels and lockers are available for rent ($1). The spa (9am-8pm Sun.-Thurs., 9am-9pm Fri.-Sat., $23 pp, including towel, locker, and bathing cap) offers a variety of thermal pools with water jets, a polar pool, a steam room, plus massages and other treatments. The complex includes a couple of pricey café-restaurants and a medical center. The on-site hotel ($158-200 s/d) has rooms with under-floor heating, some with Jacuzzis and/or fireplaces. The complex has been awarded the Rainforest Alliance's Smart Voyager certification of sustainable tourism, is involved with climate change research, and is planning its own organic gardens and hydroelectric plant for energy self-sufficiency. It provides financial support to local social causes and emergency medical assistance to local residents. See the *Hiking and Biking* section for details of hiking trails in a 200-hectare (500-acre) protected area owned by the company.

There are several other thermal baths. Six kilometers (3.7 mi) before Papallacta is **Jamanco** (tel. 6/289-5102, http://terjamanco.

com, $4), with hot and cold pools, a Jacuzzi, steam room, accommodations, and restaurant. Nearby, **Termas El Pantanal** (tel. 99/067-5762, Facebook @ElPntnl) overlooks a creek and is quiet even on weekends. It offers accommodations, a restaurant, and a hiking trail. Jamanco has another location just before Termas Papallacta.

Hiking and Biking

Around 15 kilometers (9.3 mi) before Papallacta, the road from Quito passes the **lake district** on the northern (left) side. This gorgeous stretch of country, filling the southern tip of the Cayambe-Coca Ecological Reserve, offers excellent hiking among glacial lakes and crumbling hills, where it's possible to see wolves and deer. It's easy to get lost in this area, and tourists frequently have to be rescued by helicopter, so do not attempt to hike without a guide. A statue of the Virgin on the south side of the road marks the start of a couple of popular four- to six-hour hikes: the **Sendero del Agua y la Vida** and **Sendero del Oso**. It may be possible to find a guide at the park's guardpost, up the dirt road opposite the Virgin, heading toward the antenna-topped hill to the north. To be sure, hire someone in advance. A recommended local guide who speaks some English is **Mario Pillajo** (tel. 99/130-6388, pillajomario@yahoo.com), who charges $50 for each hike, per group of up to 12 people. Alternatively, ask the local Ministry of the Environment (tel. 6/288-7154 or 6/288-8562) or the tourist office in Baeza (tel. 6/232-0355 or 99/478-8648) to put you in touch with a guide.

To get to the lake district, take any bus from Quito heading toward Tena or Lago Agrio and ask the driver to drop you at the Virgin de Papallacta.

Mario Pillajo offers other tours in the area, including a four- to six-hour hike in the Antisana Ecological Reserve ($50 per group of up to 12, plus $5 entry); a four- to six-hour hike to Laguna de Sucus in Cayambe-Coca National Park, with the possibility of seeing condors ($50/group plus $45 transport); a two- to three-hour hike to Laguna Loreto in Cayambe-Coca National Park ($40/group plus $10 transport); observation of Andean bears ($80/day per group plus $100/day for transport, 4-5 days recommended); bird-watching around Papallacta, Pinto, and Antisana, with the possibility of seeing condors ($80/day per group plus $100/day for transport); and bird-watching on the trails at Guango Lodge (2-3 hours, $40 per group plus $5 entry).

Termas Papallacta owns a protected area of approximately 200 hectares (500 acres), called Canyon Ranch, at the entrance of Cayambe-Coca National Park. Access is via an information and research center, the **Exploratorio,** located inside the complex, just to the right of the main baths. Five walking trails have been developed, some to waterfalls, others with views of Antisana and Cayambe. The one-hour hike ($2) can be completed independently, but the longer hikes, ranging 3-8 hours ($8-15 pp), require a guide. It's advisable to make an advance reservation for these by contacting Termas Papallacta. Be aware that some routes may not be possible after heavy rain, and that the eight-hour hikes require an 8am start. Camping is available for $6.

Food and Accommodations

Local cuisine in Papallacta consists of *trucha* (trout), *caldo de gallina* (chicken soup), corn, potatoes, and beans. The local drink is freshly squeezed *jugo de caña* (sugarcane juice). Numerous restaurants in the village center and on the road up to the Termas Papallacta offer these dishes.

Papallacta has a few accommodations ranging from budget to luxury, most with restaurants attached. All are ranged along the road that leads up to Termas Papallacta from the highway. **La Choza de Don Wilson** (tel. 6/232-0627 or 99/517-2905, http://hosteriachozapapallacta.com, $20 pp, including breakfast) has an enclosed hot pool, good views over the valley, and a popular restaurant

---

1: a parrot at a lodge in Baeza; 2: Termas Papallacta; 3: the lake district near Papallacta

serving a set menu ($7.50). Massages are available ($45/hour). The friendly **Hotel Coturpa** (tel. 6/289-5040, $22 s, $38 d, breakfast included) has rooms with thermal sheets, electric heating, TV, and private bathrooms with natural thermal water. **Hostería Pampa Llacta** (tel. 6/289-5014, www.pampallactatermales.com, $35-40 s, $85-115 d, breakfast included weekdays) has comfortable guest rooms with Jacuzzis and fireplaces. Rates include entrance to their own thermal baths. **Termas Papallacta** (tel. 6/289-5060 or 9/275-3079, www.termaspapallacta.com, $158-200 s/d) has rooms with under-floor heating, some with Jacuzzis and/or fireplaces.

The rates at **Termas El Pantanal** (tel. 99/067-5762, Facebook @ElPntal, $25 pp), 6 kilometers (3.7 mi) before Papallacta, include breakfast, plus entrance to their own thermal baths and Jacuzzi. Ten kilometers (6.2 mi) outside Papallacta to the west, on the way to Baeza, **Guango Lodge** (tel. 2/289-1880, www.guangolodge.com, $83 s, $117 d, $142 s, $237 d full board) is great for bird-watching, with 12 kilometers (7.5 mi) of hiking trails. The unique sword-billed hummingbird is a regular visitor to the feeders in the garden. A day visit costs $5.

Getting There and Around

To get to Papallacta, take any bus from Quito's Quitumbe station heading to Tena, Lago Agrio, or Coca and ask the driver to let you off (2-3 hours, $3). To continue into the Oriente from Papallacta, simply wait on the main highway in town and flag down a bus. To get to the baths from town, take a taxi ($2) or walk for 20 minutes.

ANTISANA ECOLOGICAL RESERVE

Since 1993, the **Antisana Ecological Reserve** ($5) has protected a large chunk of the Ecuadorian Andes spanning the provinces of Pichincha and Napo, with the snow-covered **Volcán Antisana** (5,704 m/18,714 ft) at its heart. Rising from cloud forest at 1,400 meters (4,600 ft), the reserve has an elevation range of more than 4,500 meters (nearly 15,000 ft), much of it *páramo*. One of the best places in the country to see condors, it's home to over 400 bird species, spectacled bears, pumas, wolves, and mountain tapir.

There is an entrance to the reserve at **Tambo,** 5 kilometers (3 mi) before Papallacta. If you have your own transport, the reserve can also be accessed via the village of Pintag, 30 kilometers (19 mi) southeast of Quito. From there, follow the road another 35 kilometers (22 mi) south to the park entrance at La Mica. Three self-guided trails of 1-3 kilometers (0.6-1.9 mi) in length explore the area near La Mica Lagoon, which is dammed to provide a quarter of Quito's drinking water. Between Pintag and La Mica, consider stopping for lunch at bird-watching lodge **Tambo Cóndor** (tel. 2/238-4601, http://www.tambocondor.com), which has an excellent restaurant (vegetarian options available).

Tours and Guides

Local guide **Mario Pillajo** (tel. 99/130-6388, pillajomario@yahoo.com), who speaks some English, offers a four- to six-hour hike in the Antisana Reserve, starting in Tambo ($50 per group of up to 12, plus $5 entry). He also offers bird-watching tours in Antisana and Papallacta, with the possibility of seeing condors ($80/day per group plus $100/day for transport). Tambo is the starting point for the 50-kilometer (31-mi) three-to five-day **Ruta del Cóndor,** or Condor Trek, from Antisana to Cotopaxi. Local guide **Victor Quinchimbla** (tel. 98/835-6566, quinchimblavictor@yahoo.es) can guide those with their own camping equipment and food ($60/day per group). **Ecuador Eco Adventure** (tel. 99/831-1282, www.ecuadorecoadventure.com) offers the trek from $550 per person including all equipment and food. The tourist office in Baeza can provide further guide recommendations.

Climbing Volcán Antisana

Rising above the *páramo* and its herds of wild horses, Ecuador's fourth-highest peak (5,704 m/18,714 ft) is one of the least climbed. Its reputation for being difficult and dangerous is due in part to the presence of active glaciers and lack of a refuge. At the summit, four peaks surround an ice-filled crater that last erupted in 1802. **Victor Quinchimbla** (tel. 98/835-6566, quinchimblavictor@yahoo.es) is a recommended local guide for the climb, leading three-day expeditions that start in Tambo.

For more information on the Antisana Ecological Reserve or for further guide recommendations, contact Juan Carlos Claudio at the tourist office in Baeza (tel. 6/232-0355 or 99/478-8648) or the Baeza Ministry of the Environment (tel. 6/288-7154 or 6/288-8562).

BAEZA

A stop at this charming mountain village is a great way to break up the long bus journey from Quito to the Oriente. Just 40 kilometers (25 mi) east of chilly Papallacta, Baeza's climate is dramatically different, verging on the tropical. A few streets of colonial houses remain in this mission settlement founded in the 16th century, sloping up steeply toward the church. Coming from Quito, the old part of town comes first, then the newer part about 1 kilometer (0.6 mi) farther on.

Baeza is attractive and well kept, with gardens full of flowers and lots of birdsong. At the foot of Volcán Antisana and surrounded by cloud-forested hills, its location close to four reserves (Antisana, Cayambe-Coca, Napo-Galeras, and Sumaco-Galeras) makes it a great base for hikers. There is excellent rafting, kayaking, and bird-watching nearby. As well as the Guianan cock-of-the-rock and plate-billed mountain toucan, the area is home to the spectacled bear and a huge variety of orchids. Despite this massive potential, the local tourism industry is not well developed, and it is mostly outside tour agencies who benefit from Baeza's wealth of attractions. Happily, this is slowly changing, with the local tourist office working with entrepreneurs and young people to expand the range of activities on offer. See http://aventura.quijos.gob.ec for more information (in Spanish).

Recreation

A couple of great hiking trails take full advantage of Baeza's dramatic scenery. To follow the **Camino de la Antena** (Antenna Trail), head up through the old part of town to the right of the church. You'll pass a cemetery on your way to a fork in the trail just across the Río Machángara. The right-hand fork continues for around 40 minutes until it reaches a waterfall, and the left fork climbs up for a couple of hours to a set of antennas overlooking the area. Whichever path you pick, the birding is bound to be great. The **Granary Trail** connects the old and new villages, beginning next to Hostería Kopal. It runs south for 15 minutes past a small waterfall and through the forested hillside to the south end of the new village. It tends to be a little muddy, so good boots are advisable. If you can't find the trailheads, the friendly family that owns Bar Restaurant Gina can point you in the right direction.

At the eastern edge of town, 300 meters (980 ft) from the main road and clearly signposted, **La Granja** ($2.50) is a small center for rescued animals and a botanical garden sitting on 4 hectares (10 acres) of regenerated land.

Between October and January, there is excellent **rafting and kayaking** on the Río Quijos and other rivers in the area. The only local tour agency is family-run **Baeza Tours** (tel. 99/897-7822, baezatours@gmail.com, Facebook @BaezaToursEcuador), inside Hostal Bambús on the main road that runs through the new part of the village. They offer rafting on the Río Quijos (Class III and IV), Río Jondachi-Hollín (Class IV), and Río Jatunyacu (Class III) for $65-75 per person per day. Class III-V kayaking is also available on the Ríos Quijos, Oyacachi, Cosanga, Jondachi, Hollín, and Jatunyacu. Kayaking courses for beginners range from two days/one night ($180 pp) to four days/three nights ($360 pp), including accommodations. Baeza Tours also offer **bird-watching** and **hiking** tours, including to nearby waterfalls, plus jungle trips. Rafting and kayaking companies in Tena also offer tours in the Baeza area. Recommended are **Caveman Adventures** (www.cavemanecuador.com) and **Torrent Duck** (Facebook @TorrentDuck).

There are 39 **rock climbing** routes on the Peña Pivico, a 75-meter (245-ft) natural rock wall at Cuyuja. At the time of writing, a group of local young people are being trained as climbing instructors. Inquire at the tourist office for information.

Twenty minutes south of Baeza is **Cosanga,** the world record holder in the Christmas Bird Count, with a total of 600 species recorded in one day. Leo, the owner of **Wasi Panka Tours** (tel. 98/182-1785, Facebook @WasiPanka.Tours) is president of the Cosanga Birdwatchers' Club and an excellent bird guide.

Arrangements to climb **Volcán Sumaco** can be made at the **Centro de Comunicación Ambiental** (Ramírez Dávilos and Rey Felipe II, tel. 6/288-7154 or 6/288-6258) in the old town. See the section on Sumaco Napo-Galeras National Park and Volcán Sumaco for more information.

Food and Accommodations

For restaurants, try **Bar Restaurant Gina** (tel. 6/232-0471, http://restaurantgina.wixsite.com/restaurantgina, Facebook @bar.restaurant.gina, 7am-9pm daily, $5-10) in the old town or **El Viejo** (tel. 6/232-0146, 7am-9pm Mon.-Fri., 7am-7pm Sat.-Sun., $6-9) in the new town. Both specialize in trout and have vegetarian rice and noodle dishes.

It's best to stay in the colonial part of the village, which is more scenic and close to the starting points for the day hikes and the tourist office. It's an attractive 1-kilometer (0.6-mi) walk from the center, either on the road or via the Granary Trail. The best place to stay is ★ **Bar Restaurant Gina** (tel. 6/232-0471, http://restaurantgina.wixsite.com/restaurantgina, Facebook @bar.restaurant.gina, $10 pp), which also has one of the best restaurants in town. The hostel is an incredible value, with clean, comfortable rooms and private bathrooms. A

second-floor balcony has great mountain views. The kind and friendly family who own it are a great source of tourist information and are generous with a spice-infused local tequila! If you're in the area on New Year's Eve, this is the place to be! They also have a house available to rent. Across the road is Dutch-owned **Hostería Kopal** (tel. 6/232-0408, www.kopalecuador.com, $34 s, $49 d), which has hand-built wooden cabins and a restaurant serving excellent pizza and burritos.

Just outside town to the west, **El Nido del Cóndor** (tel. 6/306-1671 or 98/236-3050, Facebook @ El Nido del Cóndor-Turismo Ecológico, $10-15 pp) sits on 7 hectares (17 acres) of former pastureland that have been reclaimed and reforested by the owner, who also operates an orchid rescue program. So far 2,500 plants have been retrieved from fallen or felled trees. The grounds include an animal sculpture garden and trails to two small waterfalls. The cock-of-the-rock makes a daily appearance. Three meals can be provided, with veggie options available.

In the new town, try family-run **Hostal Bambús** (tel. 6/232-0003 or 99/285-7488, hostalbambus@gmail.com, $14 pp) on the main road through the village. Rooms have private bathrooms with hot water and TV. Amenities include a heated pool, Jacuzzi, and steam room. The same family also owns Baeza Tours, the only tour agency in the village.

Information and Services

The very helpful **tourist office** (8am-5pm Mon.-Fri., tel. 6/232-0355 or 99/478-8648) is in the old town in a wooden building just up the hill from Bar Restaurant Gina. Keep going past the misleading kiosk labeled "Tourist Information"; the office is just behind it.

For information on hiking in Sumaco and climbing the volcano, including hiring a guide, stop by the **Centro de Comunicación Ambiental** (Ramírez Dávilos y Rey Felipe II, tel. 6/232-0605), a block from the tourist office.

Getting There

The road from Quito splits just west of town at "La Y" (pronounced "la YAY"). The left fork follows the oil pipeline and the Río Quijos northeast to Lago Agrio, then south to Coca. The right fork heads through the middle of Baeza to Tena (see the *South to Tena and Vicinity* section for more information).

Leaving Baeza, head to La Y for buses to Lago Agrio or Coca. For Tena, flag down a bus going through the town center. Buses to Quito (3 hours, $4) and Papallacta (1 hour $1.50) can be flagged down in either location.

★ CASCADA SAN RAFAEL

If you take the long bus ride from Quito to Lago Agrio, it's definitely worth making a stop at the highest waterfall in Ecuador, which drops 145 meters (475 ft) into the Río Quijos. It is 66 kilometers (41 mi) from Baeza (1.5 hours, $3 by bus). Ask the driver to let you off at the Cascada San Rafael. From the highway, follow the road downhill for a few minutes to the guard post, where you need to present ID.

It's a beautiful 20- to 30-minute walk through the forest to a viewing point across from the falls. The trail is wide and easy, with three wooden bridges across rushing streams. Keep your eyes peeled for agoutis, monkeys, and the Guianan cock-of-the-rock, all of which are frequently seen.

If you're traveling by bus and have luggage, the guard will happily look after it while you complete the walk, but it's a hot uphill slog to get back to the highway. Consider paying a tip to leave your bags at the **Hostería Reventador** (km 159, Vía Quito-Lago Agrio, tel. 6/302-0110, www.hosteriaelreventador. com, $39 s, $50-60 d), which is past the entrance to the falls, on the other side of the bridge marking the border with Succumbíos province. With views of Volcán Reventador and next to a boulder-strewn stream tumbling down the hillside, it's a good spot for an overnight stay. Rooms have cable TV and there is a restaurant. It's advisable to book in advance—not because it get busy, but because it's so quiet that there may not be anyone around if you show up unannounced.

Edison Hugo (tel. 99/716-9790, edisonhugocevallos@yahoo.com) leads two-hour hikes in the cloud forest near the falls, great for bird-watching ($5 pp for groups of 1-5, $3 pp for larger groups).

VOLCÁN REVENTADOR

The "exploder" is one of the most active volcanoes in Ecuador, and it justified its name by erupting suddenly in 2002, shooting 200 million tons of ash and rock 17 kilometers (11 mi) into the sky. The ash cloud covered three provinces, forcing the closure of Quito airport. **Reventador** continued to rumble into 2004, and in July 2008 it began another cycle of activity that is still ongoing. Geologists estimate that it was one of Ecuador's highest peaks before regular eruptions since 1541 cut it down to its present size of 3,562 meters (11,686 ft).

Since the first ascent by a scientific expedition in 1931, Reventador hasn't been climbed often because of its muddy approach and constant volcanic activity. The climb is further complicated by the fact that eruptions have changed the terrain significantly. The trek to the top crosses everything from jungle to lava-covered wasteland. Not surprisingly, to make the ascent, hiring a guide is essential.

Edison Hugo (tel. 99/716-9790, edisonhugocevallos@yahoo.com) leads climbs to the summit ($50/day/group of up to 5 people, $60/group/day for 5-10 people). He is available only four days every two weeks, so book in advance. It takes five hours to ascend (carrying your own pack) and four hours to descend, with an overnight on the side of the volcano (bring your own camping gear). Food can be provided upon request, or bring your own. Rain is likely, so wear waterproof clothing and rubber boots. Check on current volcanic activity beforehand at the Instituto Geofísico website (www.igepn.edu.ec).

LAGO AGRIO

The capital of Sucumbíos province, Lago Agrio (pop. 57,000) was carved from pristine rainforest as a field headquarters for Texaco after the discovery of oil in 1964. So many settlers came from the southern Sierra region that the burgeoning town was officially named Nueva Loja (New Loja), but everyone calls it Lago Agrio, meaning Sour Lake, the location of Texaco's original headquarters in Texas. Even before you arrive, the pipeline that runs alongside the road from Quito is a stark reminder of the city's raison d'être, and with transport companies named Oro Negro and Cooperative Petrolera, there is no escaping the fact that this is an oil town. Now a jungle of the concrete variety, it's a challenge to find any remaining scrap of nature in the hot, noisy streets. Even the cakes in the bakery windows look violently synthetic. While the city itself has few attractions, Lago Agrio is a gateway for the northernmost Amazon region, including the Cuyabeno Wildlife Reserve and several tourism projects managed by the area's original residents, the indigenous Kofán and Siekopai.

Lago Agrio's proximity to the Colombian border, just 25 kilometers (15.5 mi) to the north, has historically made it an unstable place and a haven for drug traffickers, guerrillas, and paramilitaries. In an infamous incident in 2008, the Colombian army crossed 2 kilometers (1.2 mi) into Ecuadorian territory just north of the city to bomb a FARC guerrilla camp, killing leader Raúl Reyes and several Ecuadorians. It is not advised to cross the border here; head to Tulcán instead.

The good news is that Lago Agrio is much safer than it used to be. At the time of writing, the U.K. foreign office still advised against traveling here, after some tourists were robbed and kidnapped in Cuyabeno in 2012, but the general consensus in Ecuador is that this recommendation is out of date. This author, a lone female traveler, felt safe whilst researching for this book. Having said that,

1: Volcán Reventador; 2: San Rafael waterfall

check www.gov.uk/foreign-travel-advice for security updates before planning your trip, stay in a town center hotel, and avoid going out after 8 or 9pm.

Recreation

The **Parque Central** (12 Febrero) is a pleasant square, with palm trees and fountains. The **Parque Turístico** (9am-5pm daily, free), bounded by Avenidas Amazonas, Petroleras, and Galapagos, has an expanse of regenerated tropical forest with walking trails. *Malocas* (huts) built by Shuar, Kofán, Siona, Siekopai, Kichwa, and Afro Ecuadorian communities have traditional products for sale. **Parque La Perla**, 3.5 kilometers (2.2 mi) northwest of the city, protects the forest around the Lago Agrio lake, where there are walking trails, a cycle path, and boat trips. Resident species include agoutis, monkeys, armadillos, turtles, frogs, capybaras, otters, caimans, piranhas, and manta rays.

To see for yourself the infamous contamination caused by Texaco, go on a **Toxi Tour,** which includes some of the former drilling sites where there are still open pits full of oil in the forest floor. Donald Moncayo (tel. 99/397-7808, donaldmoncayo@gmail.com) has been leading these tours since 2003 in an effort to spread awareness of the situation and prevent it from happening elsewhere. Donald offers his services for free, but the transport costs $80/day. A one-day tour is available, or longer tours can be arranged to multiple sites and to meet some of the affected people. Reserve as much in advance as possible. An English translator can be arranged.

As an uplifting follow-up to the Toxi Tour, a network of Amazonian permaculturists, La Red Amazónica de Permacultores, has created the Ruta Amazónica de la Esperanza (**Amazon Route of Hope**), consisting of eight family-owned projects on land that has been reclaimed and reforested after being degraded by oil exploitation and agriculture. The projects were created to show that permaculture and ecotourism are viable economic alternatives. All were born from the Clínica

Green vs. Black: Environmental Disaster in the Amazon

Before oil companies discovered oil in the province of Sucumbíos in the 1960s, the northern Amazon region was largely pristine rainforest, where indigenous Siekopai, Siona, and A'i Kofán peoples lived in harmony with the forest, as they had for thousands of years. As companies drilled for oil between 1964 and 1990, they cut costs by deliberately dumping more than 18 billion gallons of toxic wastewater, spilled roughly 17 million gallons of crude oil, and left hazardous waste in hundreds of open pits in the forest floor.

The result was, and continues to be, one of the worst environmental disasters in global history. Local indigenous people and farmers suffer from hugely increased rates of cancer, miscarriage, and birth defects. Crops fail and it's not possible to drink from, bathe in, or fish in the contaminated rivers. Some parents have lost multiple children to leukemia. A woefully inadequate $40 million clean-up campaign was largely cosmetic, and the majority of oil waste continues to poison the rainforest ecosystem. People are still dying from contamination.

In 1993, a legal case was filed in New York on behalf of 30,000 indigenous people to demand compensation to pay for an adequate clean-up operation, but the trial was moved to Ecuador's courts at the oil company's request. In 2011, the company was found guilty and ordered to pay $9.5 billion, a ruling that was later ratified by an Ecuadorian appeals court and upheld by its highest civil court. The company refused to pay, instead hiring 2,000 lawyers across 60 firms to launch a U.S. trial, accusing the plaintiffs' attorney of corruption and fraud. The affected indigenous communities were not permitted to participate in the proceedings and the judge refused to allow any testimony or evidence about the contamination and its effects. In March 2014, a judge found that the 2011 Ecuadorian verdict was obtained through unlawful means. It later emerged that the company's key witness was paid close to $2 million by the oil giant and admitted to lying under oath.

Despite being upheld by Ecuador's Constitutional Court in a unanimous 8-0 decision in July 2018, the 2011 verdict was annulled in September 2018 by an international trade tribunal made up of business lawyers. The panel ruled that Ecuador violated a trade treaty by allowing its court system to issue the $9.5 billion judgment against the oil company and ordered Ecuador to pay reparations. The oil company has asked for the full amount of the judgment against it, which it has never paid. The plaintiffs' lawyers have rejected the annulment, arguing that it is not legal for a trade tribunal to circumvent Ecuador's judiciary. While the wrangling continues, it doesn't look like the compensation will arrive any time soon.

Meanwhile, as drilling continues around Lago Agrio, other parts of Ecuador's Amazon are also being exploited or are under threat. Sadly, there is no way to extract oil without inflicting serious damage: Areas are deforested to create air strips and roads, explosions are detonated during the exploration phase, waste products contaminate rivers and lakes, and spills are inevitable. Drilling is currently ramping up significantly in Yasuní National Park, a UNESCO World Biosphere Reserve that is home to the country's last two uncontacted tribes. The Ecuadorian government is also in the process of selling 3 million hectares (7.4 million acres) of largely virgin rainforest in the southern Amazon region to oil companies in an auction known as the XI Oil Round, or Ronda Sur.

For more information and updates on the this case, see www.texacotoxico.net. Alianza Ceibo (www.alianzaceibo.org) is a Lago Agrio-based alliance of A'i Kofán, Siekopai, Siona, and Waorani people who work together to defend their territories and cultures. Amazon Frontlines (www.amazonfrontlines.org) works closely with the Ceibo Alliance and is an excellent source of information in English. To find out about the socio-environmental work that is being undertaken to heal the northern Amazon, contact the Clínica Ambiental (www.clinicambiental.org).

Ambiental, a socio-environmental project that is working to heal the northern Amazon and its people from the damage wrought by oil companies. Tours of all the projects on the route can be arranged by prior reservation. Three are in or near Lago Agrio, the most developed of which is **Amisacho** (tel. 6/286-2883 or 96/810-6800, http://amisacho. com), set on 9 hectares (22 acres) of reforested land just east of the city center. It includes a laboratory where research is undertaken on bioremediation (the science of cleaning contamination with oil-munching mushrooms). Edible mushrooms, essential oils, and other natural products are available. For information about visiting the other Lago Agrio locations on the tour, Paroto Isla and Rica Ama, or those farther afield, contact Amisacho or **Los Yapas Holistic Center** (tel. 99/284-6834, http://losyapas.org) in Puyo, which is also part of the network.

Food and Accommodations

Lago Agrio is not known for its high quality accommodations or gastronomy. For local cuisine, try **Kucha Caiman** (Guayaquil y 9 de Octubre, tel. 99/427-2803, Facebook @ Café Restaurante Kucha Caiman, 8am-4pm Sun.-Fri. and 6pm-9pm Tues.-Fri., $6-7.50), which specializes in *maito* (fish, chicken, or grubs cooked in leaves). **Folkafé** (20 Junio y Quito, tel. 98/128-9835, Facebook @folkafeoficial, 5pm-11pm Tues.-Sat., 6pm-10pm Sun., $5-8) has good Tex Mex and *micheladas* (a beer cocktail). **Restaurant D'Mario** (Av. Quito, tel. 6/283-0456, 7am-10pm daily, set lunch $3.60, entrées $6-10), in the Hotel D'Mario, does a decent pizza and has outdoor seating. There are several Chinese restaurants, including **Chifa Shang Hai** (Orellana just off Quito, 9:30am-10pm daily). The one vegetarian restaurant, **El Eden** (Calle Cofanes y Progreso, tel. 6/283-1857 or 99/101-5534), is a few blocks north of the center and offers breakfasts and set lunches ($3). **Panadería y Pastelería Manabita** (12 de Febrero y Jorge Anasco) has a self-service fruit salad bar.

There is an organic market every Saturday morning run by the **Federación de Mujeres** (Women's Federation) on Francisco Orellana y 9 de Octubre. Go early because it's all sold out before 10am.

In the center, **Hotel Heliconias** (Quito y Orellana, tel. 6/283-1562 or 98/453-1774, $20 s, $30 d) has acceptable rooms with private bathrooms, hot water, cable TV, and air-conditioning or fan. A longstanding favorite for tour groups is **Hotel D'Mario** (Quito y Pasaje Gonzonamá, tel. 6/283-0172, www. hoteldmario.com, $20-40 s, $40-60 d, including breakfast), which has a pool, Jacuzzi, and restaurant. Rooms have private bathrooms (some with hot water), cable TV, and air-conditioning. The best option, family-run **Hostal Platinum Class** (Calle César Villasis y Union, Barrio Amazonas, tel. 6/236-6797, hostal_platinumclass@hotmail.com, $30 s/d), is outside the center, but the owners are happy to provide transport.

For something more upmarket, try **Hotel Araza** (Av. Quito y Vicente Narvaez, tel. 6/283-1248, http://araza-hotel.com, $49 s, $61 d Mon.-Fri., $39 s, $51 d Sat.-Sun., including breakfast) or **Gran Hotel de Lago** (Av. Quito km 1.5 y 20 de Junio, tel. 6/283-0048, www.granhoteldelago.com, $94 s, $121 d), both of which have a pool, Jacuzzi, gym, bar, and restaurant.

To find some peace and greenery, there are a couple of rooms with shared kitchen and bathroom available at **Amisacho** (tel. 6/286-2883 or 96/810-6800, http://amisacho. com, $20 s, $25 d), a permaculture project set on 9 hectares (22 acres) of reforested land. It's $2 by taxi from the city center but feels like a world away. To find Amisacho, head east out of the city on the Panamericana. After 2 kilometers (1.2 mi), there is a junction where the Panamericana turns to the right. Turn left here, toward the airport. After a couple of hundred meters, take the turning on the right, just after Motel Trebol. Amisacho is at the end of that road, after another couple of hundred meters.

Information and Services

There are several banks in the center. **Banco Guayaquil** and **Banco Pichincha** are across the road from each other on 12 de Febrero just off Quito. The hospital, **Marco Vinicio Iza** (hmvi.gob.ec), is just east of the Parque Recreativo. The **police station** is at Avenida Quito and 12 de Febrero.

Getting There and Around

The *terminal terrestre* is 2 kilometers (1.2 mi) north of the center. There are hourly departures to Quito (5am-12:15am, 8 hours, $8) and several overnight buses to Guayaquil (14 hours, $18). There are also evening/overnight buses to Ambato, Tulcán, Santo Domingo, Esmeraldas, Manta, Tena, Puyo, Baeza, Riobamba, Latacunga, and Baños, There are fewer daytime departures. **Coop Jumandy** goes to Puyo via Baeza and Tena at 10:20am. **Transportes Baños** goes to Guayaquil at 11:45am and to Baños via Latacunga and Ambato at 2:30pm.

For buses to Coca (2 hours, $3.75), take a taxi to the *parada de buses para Coca* in the town center, from where there are frequent departures.

Transportes Putumayo runs buses and *rancheros* from outside Mercado Popular (Av. Amazonas *y* 12 de Febrero) to many Amazonian communities.

TAME (9 de Octubre *y* Orellana, tel. 6/283-0113, http://tame.com.ec) flies to/from Quito (twice daily Mon.-Fri., once daily Sat.-Sun.). Local buses run to the airport, or you can take a taxi ($2).

Taxis around town cost $1.50-2.

★ INDIGENOUS COMMUNITIES

As the security situation has improved, the number of visitors in Lago Agrio has increased. Sadly, however, most lodges in the Cuyabeno Wildlife Reserve are owned by companies from Quito; while local indigenous people are often employed as canoe drivers or guides and visits are organized to their communities, they see only a fraction of the

Speaking Kofán

- *kasete*—good morning
- *kuse kuse*—good evening
- *minga'ki*—How are you?
- *jeu*—yes
- *mein*—no
- *chigatsu afepaenja*—thank you
- *chigaikhu*—good-bye
- *na'en*—river
- *tsa'khu*—water

income generated in their ancestral territories. This is a tragedy considering the pressure that indigenous peoples are under to exploit their land, not just from the oil industry, but from gold mining companies or agricultural corporations wanting to clear the rainforest for monocrop plantations of African palm and malanga. Tourism initiatives, managed by indigenous communities or families, provide an alternative, sustainable source of income that goes directly to local people, allowing them to preserve their territories and way of life. Those looking to directly support rainforest conservation efforts are encouraged to consider visiting one of the following projects, rather than a lodge in Cuyabeno Wildlife Reserve. Not only will the costs be considerably lower, but the experience will be much more authentic. If you're looking for a luxury lodge experience where income goes directly to local communities, there are a number of options in Yasuní National Park.

A'i Kofán

The A'i Kofán people are known for their skilled ayahuasca shamans and for building the fiberglass canoes used by indigenous nationalities all over the Amazon. The canoe project was started as a way to conserve the Amazon's remaining big trees, which are felled to make the traditional wooden canoes. At the time of writing, the Kofán community of Sinangoe near Lago Agrio had just won a historic lawsuit against the government that nullifies over 50 gold mining concessions along the Aguarico River that threatened to wreak massive environmental destruction.

Avie is one of three Kofán communities within the 55,000-hectare (136,000-acre) Kofán-Bermejo Ecological Reserve. Visitors are invited to join the ayahuasca ceremonies ($45 pp) that the shaman holds with his family on Saturday nights, which require at least an overnight stay. Longer-term guests are able to share the community's daily life and visit a number of waterfalls in the area. **Accommodations** ($10 pp) and **meals** ($3) are provided by local families. The tourism project is led by Alex Lucitante, a young Kofán activist who works for rainforest defense organization Alianza Ceibo during the week in Lago Agrio and returns to his community every weekend. For more information or to make a reservation, contact him (tel. 99/946-9780, Facebook @Asentamiento Ancestral Kofan Avie). The community can also be reached (tel. 6/301-9202). To get to Avie, take a Putumayo *ranchero* destined for Santa Rosa / Barranca Bermeja from outside the Mercado Popular and ask the driver to let you out at Puerto Vega, where you cross the river. Alternatively, Alex can accompany visitors from Lago Agrio to the community.

To organize visits to other Kofán communities, contact Fidel Aguinda, vice president of **NOAIKE** (Nationalidad Originaria A'E Kofán Ecuador) (tel. 99/414-5444, canoesdefibra@hotmail.com), preferably eight days in advance. The closest community to Lago Agrio is Dureno, just 40 minutes by bus, and the most remote is Zábalo, six hours by canoe from Dureno, within the Cuyabeno reserve. If visiting Zábalo, request to stay with the community tourism project Yaikumu, and not the Cofan Survival Fund, a private initiative with links to the Summer Institute of Linguistics, a missionary organization that paved the way for Texaco to enter indigenous territories in the 1960s.

Siekopai

According to the Siekopai (which means multicolored people) the moon god (Nanëpaina) came down from the sky and found their people living underground and liberated them to live on the earth. Also known as the Secoya, they are renowned for their excellent hot sauce, made from jungle peppers. Within the **Siekoya Remolino** community, which protects 17,000 hectares (42,000 acres) of rainforest, four families have created a tourism project, Campamento Kwakwiyo. Accommodations are with families or in a covered camping area. Ayahuasca ceremonies are available with very well-respected shamans. The bird-watching is excellent and the community includes an expert bird guide. A three-night/four-day package ($200) includes a night walk; face painting; a canoe trip; a jungle hike; harvesting yucca and preparing yucca flatbread; a handicrafts demonstration; an energy cleaning with the shaman; and the chance to try *yoko*, the local coffee equivalent, made from a jungle vine. Visits of fewer or more nights are possible. One of the project's key figures is **Jimmy Piaguaje** (tel. 96/701-5578, Camping.kwa@gmail.com), a young Siekopai who also leads an environmental education project with the youth in his community and a project to preserve ancestral knowledge of medicinal plants through videos and social media. Jimmy can accompany visitors from Lago Agrio to the community, or to travel independently take a ranchero with Putumayo from outside the Mercado Popular to Puerto Los Angeles (2.5 hours), from where the community is 15 minutes by motorized canoe.

Jimmy can also arrange trips to **Lagarto Cocha,** a black lagoon environment like Cuyabeno, but bigger and more remote. Located in the far eastern part of the Amazon region, eight hours by canoe from Siekoya Remolino, it's an important spiritual center for the Siekopai. Jimmy organizes camping trips, with transport by motorized canoe, or visitors can stay at a shamanic lodge, Puerto Estrella, which is just on the Peruvian side of the border, where ayahuasca ceremonies are available.

For an organized healing retreat in the Siekoya Remolino community with an English-speaking guide, contact **José Zambrano** (tel. 99/192-7938, pantherawasi@gmail.com). A 10- to 13-day package costs around $1,600 and includes basic accommodations; two ayahuasca ceremonies; yoga; meditation; ancestral pottery lessons; an activity with the community; and an excursion such as Papallacta, the San Rafael waterfall, white-water rafting, or the Cueva de los Tayos.

Kichwa

Shayari (meaning "rise up") is a Kichwa community (tel. 6/301-9238, www.shayari.ec, Facebook @CTC Shayari) of 12 families that relocated from Pastaza province in the 1980s. Located on the edge of the Napo-Galeras Biosphere Reserve, the community protects 500 hectares (1,235 acres) of rainforest, 290 of which (715 acres) have been declared a community reserve. Unlike many of their neighbors, the people of Shayari refused to allow an oil company to conduct seismic testing in their territory. Fortunately, oil was not found in the area and the company has now left. Accommodations are in three attractive, rustic cabins with private bathrooms or in a dorm. Activities include hikes to a waterfall, to a lake, and to see gigantic trees; dugout canoe rides on the lake; and demonstrations of handicrafts and dancing. The community includes some excellent chefs, who can cook up tasty local gastronomy and will happily cater to vegetarians with advance notice. Packages include one day ($30), two days/one night ($96 pp), and three days/two nights ($155 pp). Reservations should be made 7-15 days ahead.

To get to Shayari, take a Transportes Putumayo *ranchero* from outside the Mercado

Popular (Av. Amazonas *y* 12 de Febrero) to Los Angeles (2.5 hours). The *rancheros*, which depart at 10am and 2pm, pass Cascales and then cross the Aguarico River on a boat, which is an experience in itself. Ask to be let off at Shayari. For the return journey, *rancheros* leave Shayari at 6am and 12:30pm.

CUYABENO WILDLIFE RESERVE

Most of the eastern half of Sucumbíos province falls within the beautiful **Cuyabeno Wildlife Reserve** ($20), which is characterized by vast expanses of flooded rainforest. The countless tributaries and lagoons of the Cuyabeno, Aguarico, and Lagartococha rivers are home to manatees, anacondas, pink freshwater dolphins, caimans, and giant otters.

Sadly, all the lodges within Cuyabeno are owned by companies from Quito. If you're looking to support local people in the northern Amazon region, visit one of the grassroots tourism projects in the previous section. If you're looking for a luxurious lodge experience that is community-run, head to Yasuní.

If you decide to visit Cuyabeno, the following lodges are consistently well reviewed and have comprehensive websites and offices in Quito. All offer four- and five-day packages; some also offer three and seven days. **Cuyabeno Lodge** (tel. 99/980-6153, www.cuyabenolodge.com, 4 days $260-380, 5 days $325-550) is on the Cuyabeno Lagoon. Other popular options include **Tapir Lodge** (tel. 96/936-1777, www.tapirlodge.com, 4 days $650, 5 days $787, 7 days $1,062), **Caiman Lodge** (tel. 6/282-8079, www.caimanlodge.com, 3 days $250, 4 days $290, 5 days $340), **Nicky Lodge** (tel. 2/254-6590, www.nickylodge.com, 4 days $330, 5 days $370, 4-day paddleboard program $620), and **Guacamayo Ecolodge** (tel. 2/290-4765, www.guacamayoecolodge.com, 3 days $250, 4 days $310, 5 days $350).

1: *maito;* **2:** paste made from the achiote fruit; **3:** The indigenous Siekopai decorate their bodies with fruit paste.

The Ayahuasca Experience

Ayahuasca is an ancient indigenous medicine and a central component of the spiritual traditions of most Amazonian cultures. Also known as *yagé* or *natem*, it's a potent hallucinogenic tea usually made with two plants: the ayahuasca vine and the leaves of the chacruna shrub. The Kofán believe that the vine grew from a hair that God plucked from his head when he left the earth, planting it in the Amazon and telling the people they could find guidance there when needed. Similarly, the Siekopai drink the brew to find God. Many nationalities report that their knowledge of medicinal plants was revealed to their ancestors in ayahuasca visions.

As part of the cultural heritage of indigenous peoples, ayahuasca is legal in Ecuador when administered by a legitimate shaman and has been known to alleviate a wide variety of physical illnesses, depression, addictions, and trauma. One of the most common effects is an increased feeling of connection with nature. Other drinkers report that it helped them find their purpose in life, gave them profound personal insights, made them kinder, unleashed creative inspiration, and expanded their consciousness and spiritual connection.

Ayahuasca is brewed using the ayahuasca vine and chacruna leaves.

For these reasons, an increasing number of visitors to Ecuador are looking to explore ancient plant medicines. Sadly, this has created a dangerous situation where people with little or no experience have claimed to be shamans or healers for economic gain. A young woman from the United States died during an ayahuasca ceremony in Ecuador in 2014, and others have been robbed or sexually assaulted while under the influence of the medicine.

If you are looking to participate in an ayahuasca ceremony, it is important that you choose a shaman carefully. Legitimate shamans often come from generations of healers and are prepared from childhood. The apprenticeship takes years and many sacrifices, usually involving long periods of celibacy and a very limited diet. Within Amazonian indigenous cultures, the shaman plays a key role, encompassing community doctor, moral authority, and spiritual guide, acting as the connection between the human world, the jungle, and its spirits.

Ayahuasca is not a recreational drug. Often the experience is extremely challenging, both physically and emotionally. Detoxification commonly occurs via vomiting and diarrhea. The psychedelic visions can be beautiful or terrifying, though many people experience few or no visionary effects when they first drink the medicine. The effects vary significantly from one person to another and in the same person from one ceremony to another.

Follow a cleansing diet prior to an ayahuasca ceremony. Cut out alcohol, meat, processed foods, sugar, salt, dairy, eggs, caffeine, and fermented products such as soy sauce, onion, chili, garlic, and other spices 2-3 days before the ceremony. Cutting out red meat is the most important part. Stick as closely to vegetables, fruits, and whole grains as possible. Sexual activity should be avoided during this time. Don't eat after noon on the day of the ceremony. If you are taking any kind of medication, especially antidepressants, check with the shaman before booking the ceremony about any possible contraindications. There are no English speakers in most indigenous communities, so bring a translator if needed. It is important that you are able to communicate with the shaman during a ceremony.

The Avie Kofán and the Siekoya Remolino communities near Lago Agrio both have highly recommended *ayahuasqueros.* Other communities with strong shamanic traditions are the Tsáchila near Santo Domingo and the Kichwa community of Sarayaku near Puyo. The Shiram y Kakaram tour agency in Cuenca can arrange ceremonies with the Shuar in the southern Amazon.

COCA

Officially named Puerto Francisco de Orellana, Coca is the capital of Orellana province. Like Lago Agrio, it was created by and for the oil industry, experiencing rapid growth during the boom years. While the city itself has few attractions, it is the main gateway for the rainforest along the Napo River, including Yasuní National Park.

Keep your wits about you in Coca. Avoid the central park area at night. The eastern part of the *malecón* between the dock and the bridge should be avoided after 7pm. Female travelers might choose to avoid this area even during the day, as there are a lot of men hanging around and it can feel quite hostile.

Sights

While even the ugliest of Ecuadorian towns usually boasts an attractive central square, this is not the case with Coca. Instead, head to the renovated *malecón*, which makes for a pleasant stroll. Cabins sell traditional jewelry, clothes, and handicrafts made by Shuar, Kichwa, and Huaorani women. At the time of writing, the **Feria de las Nacionalidades** was being built just next to the dock, which will offer traditional food, natural medicines, and handicrafts by the region's indigenous peoples. Also on the *malecón* is the city's most interesting attraction, the **Museo Arqueológico Centro Cultural Orellana** or MACCO (9 de Octubre y Eugenio Espejo, tel. 6/230-0277, http://macco.ec, 10am-6pm Tues.-Sun., $2.50), a modern and beautifully laid out museum with displays on the Amazon's ancient cultures and a riverside café.

Recreation and Tours

The best nightlife options are also on or near the *malecón*. One block inland from the MACCO, **Saya** (6 de Diciembre y Espejo, tel. 96/021-0529, Facebook @SayaHousecoca, 4pm-11pm Mon.-Wed. and Sun., 4pm-2am Thurs.-Sat., ID required) offers craft beer and burgers. **Pappa Dan's** (Facebook @ ElPappaDans, 5pm-midnight Mon.-Wed.,

5pm-3am Thurs.-Sat.) is a block west of the dock.

To stay at the rainforest lodges that are accessed via Coca (see the *Lower Río Napo* section for details), book directly with the lodge well in advance. Various agencies in Coca offer tours that are available last minute, are more economical than the lodges, and include overnight stays in various locations, often camping. The most ecologically minded agency is **Sumak Allpa** (Amazonas y Chimborazo, tel. 9/737-1286, www.sumakallpatours.wixsite.com/tours), half a block from the dock. The Kichwa owner, Hector Vargas, speaks fluent English. A one-day trip to Yasuní ($100 pp) includes a parrot clay lick, a visit to the Kichwa community of Añangu, and a jungle hike to admire the view from a 45-meter (150-ft) canopy tower. Two- to three-day tours ($200-300 pp) combine Limoncocha and Yasuní. A three-day tour to the Shiripuno River ($300 pp) includes a hike with Waorani guides. On the four-day tour to Cocaya ($400 pp), near the border with Peru, it's possible to see pink and gray river dolphins. Hector also offers a Toxic Tour to Shushufindi for those who would like to see Texaco's infamous contamination. Accommodations are in community tourism centers, and all tours include a visit to Sumak Allpa Island (http://sumakallpa.org), the agency's primate rehabilitation center, where monkeys roam free before being released into the wild. The center also works in the areas of biodiversity management, environmental education, and the preservation of indigenous peoples. Volunteers are welcomed.

Luis Duarte at **La Casa de Maito** (tel. 96/071-5264, cocaselva@hotmail.com) also leads tours, including camping trips in Yasuní, and can put tourists in contact with trusted local guides throughout the region. He speaks a little English.

Pablo Hualinga (tel. 99/189-4557, hualingapablo@yahoo.com) is a local bird guide who has worked at the best lodges and is now independent. Popular birding tours include Laguna Limoncocha, Yasuní for the parrot clay licks, and the Napo Wildlife Center tower for the possibility of seeing harpy eagles. He charges $80/day per group, plus canoe rental ($25/day Limoncocha, $70/day Yasuní).

Food

Restaurants in Coca are relatively expensive (a noodle dish in one of the many Chinese restaurants might cost around $6). For cheap street food, mostly barbecued meat and fish, head to Quito and Moreno.

The best spot for local cuisine is family-owned ★ **La Casa de Maito** (Espejo, tel. 6/288-2285 or 96/071-5264, 6am-10pm Wed.-Mon., 6am-6pm Tues., $6), which not only serves a variety of *maito* (fish, chicken, or grubs barbecued in a leaf) but can make excellent vegetarian food (ask the owner, Luis, for the *llapingachos de yucca* and the *plato de vegetales con salsa*).

The **restaurant** in **Hotel El Auca** (Rocafuerte *y* Moreno, tel. 6/288-0127, www. hotelelaucacoca.com, 6:15am-2pm and 6pm-10pm daily, $8-11) has a large and varied menu that specializes in tilapia (farmed fish) and includes vegetarian options (spaghetti and quinoa).

Coca has a basic **veggie restaurant** (no name, Quito *y* Bolívar, 6:30am-4pm daily), which serves set breakfasts and lunches ($2.75), though lunch may run out before closing time. **Boulevar de las Frutas** (Quito *y* Montalvo, tel. 98/893-0438, Facebook @ Boulevar de las Frutas, 7am-10pm daily) has decent coffee, breakfasts, and a fruit salad bar.

Accommodations

By far the best budget option is ★ **Hotel Lojanita** (Napo *y* Cuenca, tel. 6/230-0936 or 99/784-4435, $12-17 s, $18-26 d), which is clean, modern, and friendly. The 36 rooms over three floors have hot water, fiberoptic Wi-Fi, cable TV, and either air-conditioning or fan. There is parking and free drinking water. **Hotel Rio Napo** (Bolívar *entre* Quito *y* Napo, tel. 97/974-5448, Facebook @ ViveBienOrellana, $22 s/d) has friendly staff and well equipped, clean rooms with hot water and air-conditioning.

Hotel El Auca (Rocafuerte *y* Moreno, tel. 6/288-0127, www.hotelelaucacoca.com, $44-52 s, $67-82 d, including breakfast) has an inner courtyard filled with hammocks and flowers, a decent restaurant, gym, Jacuzzi, sauna, massage service, and beauty salon.

Information and Services

The **tourist information office** (tel. 6/288-0532, www.orellanaturistica.gob.ec, www. elcocavivelo.com in English) is on the *malecón* next to the dock. The **Hospital Francisco de Orellana** (Av. Alejandro Labaka, tel. 6/286-1831) is at the north end of the city, with the **police station** next to it.

Getting There and Around

Local buses leave from Coca's *terminal viejo* (old terminal), and interprovincial buses leave from the *terminal nuevo* (new terminal). From the latter, there are hourly departures to Tena until 6pm and then at 10pm and 11pm (4 hours, $9). Several companies operate overnight buses to Quito leaving between 7:30pm and 11:30pm (9 hours, $12.50). Loja International has a departure to Loja via Santo Domingo and Machala at 6:30pm. Putumayo has a departure to Guayaquil (13 hours) via Santo Domingo at 4:10pm. Flota Pelileo has departures to Guayaquil via Tena, Puyo, Baños, Riobamba, and Ambato at 6am and 7:30pm.

TAME (Calle Quito 29-11 *y* Enrique Castillo, tel. 6/288-1078, www.tame.com. ec) operates flights to/from Quito (3 daily Mon.-Fri., 1 daily Sat.-Sun.). **Avianca** (tel. 2/397-8000, www.avianca.com) operates a flight to/from Quito (1 daily Mon.-Fri.). Be aware that although sometimes bargains can be found, flights to Coca are more expensive than most other domestic destinations, up to $280 return.

Boats operated by various companies, locally known as *turnos*, leave the docks on Chimborazo at 7:30am heading down the Río Napo as far as Nuevo Rocafuerte on the Peruvian border (10 hours, $18.75), stopping at various locations en route.

There is only one daily departure between all the companies (except Saturday, when there is an additional departure at 8am), and they can get full, so buy your ticket one day ahead if possible. Arrive at the dock at least half an hour before departure. Coming back, boats leave Nuevo Rocafuerte at 5am or 5:30am. The 60-seat boats are covered and have toilets but no other facilities. Limited snacks are available at the dock, and the boat stops only once for lunch (rice with either fish or chicken), so bring your own food and water for the journey, plus something to read.

Lower Río Napo

Río Napo is Ecuador's largest river, born in the foothills of Cotopaxi, flowing 1,000 kilometers (620 mi) through the lowland wilderness into Peru and Brazil, where it joins the Amazon. East of Coca, the Lower Río Napo forms the northern border of Yasuní National Park, where some of Ecuador's best jungle lodges are found. Coca is the main access point for all the destinations in this section.

YARINA LODGE

Set on 470 hectares (1,160 acres) of primary rainforest, **Yarina Lodge** (tel. 2/250-4037 or 99/972-1916, www.yarinalodge.com) is the closest lodge to Coca, just one hour downriver. Activities include caiman spotting; night walks; a visit to a local Kichwa community; and bird-watching from the 40-meter (130-ft) observation tower. The lodge has an office in Quito. Available packages are three days/two nights ($370 pp), four days/three nights ($460 pp), and five days/four nights ($550 pp).

★ LAGUNA LIMONCOCHA

The **Limoncocha Biological Reserve** was created in 1985 to protect 28,000 hectares (69,200 acres) of rainforest surrounding Lake Limoncocha and a 5-kilometer (3.1-mi) stretch of the Río Napo. One of the top 10 birding spots in the country, with 470 recorded species, it comes second only to Mindo in the Christmas Bird Count. Even for non-birders, this is a magical place, with

Laguna Limoncocha is one of the best bird-watching spots in the country.

Lower Río Napo

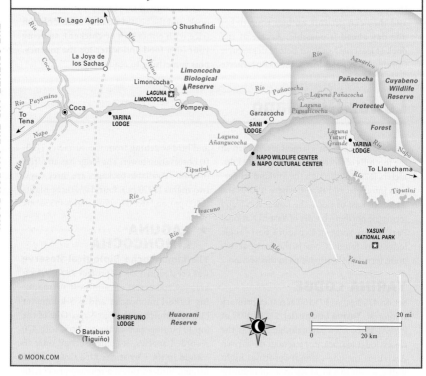

lush jungle overhanging the water's edge. During the day, the lake mirrors the blue sky and clouds and, later on, the colors of sunset. As the light fades, the frogs start to sing and thousands of insect larva illuminate the lily leaves, lighting up the surface of the lake like a miniature city. A boat trip on Lake Limoncocha is an unforgettable experience and an easy way to spot macaws, parrots, kingfishers, and various waterfowl. The trees around the lake are home to red howler and capuchin monkeys, while caimans, anacondas, and rays hunt in the water.

Despite its status as a Ramsar site (a wetland of international importance), oil companies have been drilling in Limoncocha for decades, though the damage is not visible to the casual visitor.

The entrance to the reserve, where visitors must register to enter, is a couple of minutes' walk from the Kichwa village of Limoncocha. A couple of trails are available—Laguna (2 hours) and Caiman (1 hour)—for which guides must be hired ($25). The highlight is a boat tour of the lake, for which it is necessary to hire a motorized canoe and driver ($20/day 1 person, $25/day 2-8 people), plus a local guide ($25 per day). Tours can be simply recreational or focused on bird-watching or caiman spotting. Guides can be booked in advance by calling the reserve (tel. 6/233-8062), or just turn up between 8am and 5pm.

It's also possible to hire guides for hikes, bird-watching, and canoe tours of the lake via a local community tourism project. **Cabañas Rayukindi** (tel. 98/882-4938 or 98/993-0909, Facebook @ctclimoncocha) also provides lodging ($12 pp) and meals ($5). Vegetarians can be accommodated with advance notice. Accommodations are basic with shared bathrooms and beautiful views of the lake. As well as tours, guests can participate in cultivating yucca, processing coffee, dawn *guayusa* ceremonies, and other Kichwa traditions including dances, cuisine, and handicrafts. A visit to a neighboring Siekopai community can be arranged. Advance reservations for accommodations are recommended (and required for meals and activities). In the village of Limoncocha, there are a few small stores, restaurants, and a hotel, **Hotel Limoncocha** (tel. 99/133-1507, $15 pp).

Pablo Hualinga (tel. 99/189-4557, hualingapablo@yahoo.com) is a local bird guide who has worked at the best lodges and is now independent. He leads birding tours of Limoncocha and charges $80 a day per group.

To get to Limoncocha from Coca, take any bus heading to Lago Agrio and ask to be let out at Sacha (1 hour, $1.25). In Sacha, head for Avenida Alejandro Labaka, get on a bus to Pompeya with Coop Alejandro Labaka, and ask to be let out at Limoncocha. Alternatively, take a boat, or *turno,* from Coca to Pompeya (2 hours, $4), then travel the last 15 minutes by taxi. The community tourism project will collect guests from Pompeya by reservation. From Tena, there are buses to Limoncocha (6 hours, $12) at 3:30am, 10am, and 1pm. From Limoncocha to Tena, there are departures at 6:30am, 11:30am, and 6:30pm.

If you pass through Pompeya on a Saturday, it's worth visiting the indigenous market.

TOP EXPERIENCE

★ YASUNÍ NATIONAL PARK

Yasuní National Park was discovered by scientists to be the most biodiverse spot on the planet and probably unmatched by any other park in the world for total numbers of plant and animal species. As continental Ecuador's largest protected area, it occupies over a million hectares (2.5 million acres) between the Río Napo on its northern border and the Río Curaray to the south. A UNESCO World Biosphere Reserve, just one hectare of its rainforest has as many as 655 tree species, more than all of the United States and Canada combined, some of them reaching 50 meters (165 ft) in height. Of the 610 bird species, the star attractions are the harpy eagle and agami heron. The 204 mammal species include jaguars, pumas, giant otters, and tapirs. Frequently spotted by visitors are pink river dolphins, caimans, macaws, iridescent blue morpho butterflies, freshwater turtles, and monkeys.

Yasuní forms part of the ancestral territory of the Waorani people, known for being fierce warriors and skilled hunters, adept with long hardwood spears and blowguns. Even among indigenous peoples, the Waorani (which simply means "humans" in their language) are famous for their deep connection with the rainforest. The park is also home to Kichwa communities and the country's two last known groups living in voluntary isolation, the Tagaeri and Taromenane. These nomadic tribes have no contact with the outside world, and very little is known about their way of life.

Tragically, over 30 percent of Ecuador's remaining oil reserves lie beneath the soil of the national park, and drilling is well underway. However, large sections of the park remain unscathed, offering some of the country's best opportunities to experience pristine rainforest.

Whether you stay at a lodge or organize a tour in Coca, activities include jungle hikes; climbing the observation towers that allow a canopy view of the forest; spotting wildlife from a paddle canoe; and visiting a parrot clay lick, where hundreds of birds flock daily to absorb minerals that counteract the toxic berries they eat.

Between August to October there is less rain, and therefore fewer mosquitoes. April and May are the wettest months.

The Great Yasuní Swindle

Yasuní National Park hit the international headlines in 2007 when the Ecuadorian government launched the much-hyped Yasuní ITT Initiative, hailed by some as one of the world's most innovative conservation proposals. The Initiative offered to refrain from exploiting the Ishpingo-Tambococha-Tiputini (ITT) oil field in exchange for 50 percent of the value of the reserves, or $3.6 billion, from the international community.

Other blocks within the park have been exploited for decades, but drilling in the remote ITT block is especially controversial, as it encroaches on the territories of the country's last two uncontacted tribes, the Tagaeri and Taromenane. According to Ecuador's own constitution, oil exploitation in this area is considered ethnocide.

President Rafael Correa cancelled the Yasuní ITT Initiative in 2013, blaming foreign nations for their lack of support and declaring that drilling would go ahead. Outraged Ecuadorians hit the streets en masse. To calm the situation, the government (as decreed in the constitution) promised to hold a public referendum if 5 percent of the voting population, or 600,000 people, signed a petition in favor of leaving the oil underground. Led by a newly formed civil society collective, YASunidos, a massive national effort resulted in 756,623 signatures being collected and delivered to the National Electoral Commission (CNE) on April 12, 2014, where they were due to be counted and verified in the presence of YASunidos representatives.

However, any hope of a transparent validation process was shattered on April 17, when the signatures were seized by the military and anti-riot police, who violently repressed YASunidos members with tear gas and stun guns as they tried to protect the boxes. After being seized, the signatures were moved to a military enclosure and counted behind closed doors. After rejecting 60 percent of the signatures for spurious reasons such as being "outside the box," in the "wrong ink color," or for stains on the page, on May 6, 2014, the CNE declared that insufficient signatures had been collected to call for a national referendum.

Leaked documents published in the *Guardian* showed that the government was in negotiations with a Chinese oil company to drill in Yasuní's ITT field even while seeking donations from the international community to protect it. Indeed, the infrastructure was already being built.

Oil extraction in the ITT block began in 2016, operated by state company Petroamazonas. Before drilling began, the government promised that "ecological trails" would provide access to the drilling platforms, rather than roads, and that cutting-edge technology would be used. Access to the area is tightly controlled (even the Yasuní park guards are not allowed to enter), but activists who entered in secret took photographs showing a road big enough for two or three bulldozers to pass comfortably. Park guards have reported seeing negligent practices and contamination. Those who were found gathering evidence were followed and threatened by oil company security and soldiers.

In February 2018, in a referendum containing seven questions, 67.5 percent of Ecuadorians voted in favor of reducing the oil extraction area in the ITT field from 1,030 hectares (2,545 acres) to 300 hectares (740 acres), but leaked documents show that the president is in fact considering expanding the drilling area. The new Minister of the Environment, a former oil company executive, is expected to approve the expansion plan.

In October 2018, a study by the Escuela Politécnica Nacional and the Andina Simón Bolívar University was released, showing that Correa's government committed fraud against YASunidos and the 756,623 members of the public who signed the petition in 2014. Meanwhile, drilling continues in one of the planet's most biodiverse and fragile ecosystems. Perhaps the most tragic aspect of the story is that the ITT field contains only a week's global supply of oil. For more information, contact YASunidos: https://sitio.yasunidos.org/en.

RECREATION
River Boat Trips, Canoe Tours, and Camping

For a completely different rainforest adventure, consider a camping expedition on the Río Napo and its tributaries, with transport by canoe. Fausto Andi is an excellent jungle guide who has worked at some of the best lodges and has now set up his own tour company, **Amazon Camping Expeditions** (http://amazoncampingexpeditions.com, faustoandi76@gmail.com). He offers trips ranging from two days to two weeks in length, with the maximum experience being a 1,000-kilometer (620-mi) canoe trip from Coca to Iquitos in Peru. He speaks Spanish, English, and Kichwa. All expeditions are tailor made, so email him for a quote.

Another excellent camping option is **Guinto Tour** (tel. 96/061-8624 or 98/919-5903, guintour373@gmail.com, Facebook @ touryasuniguintour), which works with the Waorani community of BamenBameno to offer six-day/five-night camping tours ($720 pp), with nights spent in various locations in Yasuní National Park and transport via canoe.

For a more upmarket experience, consider a tour on a cruise boat with comfortable air-conditioned cabins. The *Manatee* (Gaspar de Villarroel y 6 de Diciembre, Quito, tel. 2/336-0887, www.manateeamazonexplorer.com) offers trips down the Río Napo, stopping at sights of interest en route, of four days/three nights ($1,966) and five days/four nights ($2,456).

ACCOMMODATIONS

All the lodges in this section offer tours in English, can cater to vegetarians with advance notice, and have offices in Quito. Prices do not include flights from Quito to Coca (up to $285 round-trip). The bus journey from Quito to Coca takes eight hours and costs $12. Most lodges have a hefty single-person supplement and offer discounts for children. Tours often leave on specific days of the week. Book well in advance.

Napo Wildlife Center and Napo Cultural Center

The **Napo Wildlife Center** (tel. 2/600-5893 or 99/275-0088, www.napowildlifecenter.com) on the shores of Lake Añangu is an ecolodge owned and managed by the local Kichwa community, who reinvest all profits into projects such as renewable energy, education, and health care. After a two-hour motor canoe ride down the Napo from Coca, guests switch over to dugout canoes and are paddled two more hours upstream to the lake. There is a range of comfortable cabins and suites, including some with a Jacuzzi and panoramic glass floor, and a five-story observation tower. Activities include climbing the 36-meter (118-ft) canopy observation tower, visiting the Kichwa Añangu community, hiking on forest trails, enjoying two of the most easily accessible clay licks in the country, and gliding around the lake in a paddle canoe. Packages range from four days/three nights ($2,112 pp s, $1,332 pp d) to eight days/seven nights ($3,872 pp s, $2,507 pp d). Book well in advance.

Owned and operated by the women of the same Kichwa community, the **Napo Cultural Center** (tel. 2/254-7758 or 99/357-5272, www.napoculturalcenter.com) has cabins with private balconies and hammocks. Activities include hiking, kayaking, climbing the canopy tower, a dawn *guayusa* tea ceremony, a visit to a Kichwa cultural center, a sunset ride in an ancestral catamaran accompanied by magical stories and legends, paddle canoe rides, night walks, and visiting the parrot clay licks. Packages range from three days/two nights ($744 pp s, $603 pp d) to five days/four nights ($1,038 pp s, $861 pp d), with additional nights available ($130 pp s, $170 pp d).

The Añangu community members have stopped hunting and fishing on their 200-square-kilometer (77-sq-mi) territory, allowing wildlife to thrive. Solar panels generate electricity for the lodges, and organic kitchen waste provides biogas for cooking. The restaurants serve local organic produce.

Sani Lodge

On the banks of a beautiful lagoon, **Sani Lodge** (tel. 2/452-1762 or 99/434-1728, www.sanilodge.com) is owned and managed by the Kichwa community of Sani Isla, who reinvest the proceeds into education and health care. Set on 42,000 hectares (103,800 acres) of pristine rainforest, it's one of the best lodges for spotting the harpy eagle. Over 550 bird species have been identified from the 37-meter (121-ft) observation tower, which is built around a giant kapok tree. The daily paddle canoe rides are a wonderful way to spot wildlife. Birding, adventure, and cultural tours are available. As part of the family-focused tour, the guide tells children Amazonian stories and legends in the evenings. On the north side of the Río Napo, and therefore not strictly within Yasuní National Park, Sani is three hours downstream from Coca and then 30 minutes by smaller canoe along a tributary. Packages range from three days/two nights ($834 pp s, $1,001 pp d) to eight days/seven nights ($2,665 pp s, $2,221 pp d). A camping option is available at a site in the jungle with packages ranging from four days/three nights ($540 pp) to six days/five nights ($740 pp).

Eden Amazon Lodge

Just outside the park on 25,000 hectares (61,800 acres) of rainforest, **Eden** (tel. 98/286-9346 English/German or 98/409-4548 Spanish, cachi_tours@yahoo.es, www.edenamazonecuador.com) is an ecolodge owned by a community of 400 Kichwa people who use the income to fund health and education services. Cabins all have porches overlooking the Yuturi Lagoon. Activities include hiking, climbing the observation tower, and dugout canoe rides for wildlife spotting. Eden is accessed by a 3.5-hour canoe journey from Coca, followed by a 30-minute hike and a 15-minute dugout canoe ride across the lake. Packages include three nights/four days ($690

pp); four nights/five days ($880 pp); and seven nights/eight days ($1,470 pp).

Shiripuno Lodge

A joint project with the local Waorani people, **Shiripuno** (tel. 2/227-1094 or 99/593-1479, www.shiripunolodge.com, Facebook @shiripuno.lodge, shiripuno2004@yahoo.com) is one of the best lodges for spotting **wildlife** due to its remoteness. Unlike the other lodges in this section, it's not located along the Río Napo but the Río Shiripuno. Visitors are driven 2.5 hours from Coca and then taken by canoe four hours downstream. Packages of three nights/four days ($460 pp); four nights/five days ($575 pp), and seven nights/eight days ($920 pp) are available. Private tours are also offered and can be tailor made to suit specific interests, such as birding, herping (amphibians and reptiles), and photography. Costs for a private tour for two people are: three nights/four days ($828 pp); four nights/five days ($1,035 pp); and seven nights/eight days ($1,656 pp). The single-person supplement is $40 per day. For a real adventure, try one of the kayaking tours, which camp in various locations in the park.

Llanchama

Llanchama is not a lodge, but a Kichwa community in a remote part of the park, eight hours from Coca along the Río Napo, then two hours along the Río Tiputini. Of the five communities in the Tiputini parish, Llanchama is the only one that has refused to allow oil companies to drill in their territory, instead developing a community-based ecotourism project. Every visit directly supports their efforts to protect their 27,000 hectares (66,700 acres) of rainforest. Located next to the ITT oil block, this is the heartland of the Yasuní controversy.

Activities include hiking, night walks, canoe rides, and bird-watching. Ayahuasca ceremonies are available. One hike is to the Laguna Encantada (Enchanted Lake), which was, local people believe, until recently occupied by a powerful spirit or anaconda that

1: parrots at Yasuní National Park; **2:** traditional Huaorani house near Shiripuno Lodge; **3:** jungle flower; **4:** A visit to Llanchama includes a hike to Laguna Encantada.

Uncontacted Tribes: The Tagaeri and the Taromenane

Incredibly, in the digital age there are still two tribes in Ecuador who have never had contact with the outside world, the Taromenane and Tagaeri, who live a nomadic lifestyle in Yasuní National Park. It is estimated that there are 150-300 Taromenane and perhaps only 20-30 surviving Tagaeri, although these numbers are uncertain. Little is known about them, but it is said that the Taromenane cook by night to avoid detection from smoke, and that their warriors are as fast as jaguars.

The two tribes were once part of the Waorani people, whose ancestral territory covers what is now Yasuní National Park. Their name means simply "humans," and their culture values personal autonomy, sharing, and egalitarianism. Known for their skills with long hardwood spears and blowguns, the Waorani became world famous in 1956 for spearing to death five North American evangelical missionaries from the Summer Institute of Linguistics (SIL) and Wycliffe Bible Translators (WBT) who were trying to make contact with them.

Ten years later, Texaco discovered oil in Waorani territory and the pacification of the "Aucas" (a derogatory term meaning "savages") became a national priority. The Ecuadorian government, Texaco, and SIL/WBT missionaries worked together to sever the Waorani's connection with their ancestral lands in areas where the oil company wanted to operate. Using aircraft supplied by Texaco, SIL/WBT searched for Waorani homes, dropping gifts and calling out through radio transmitters. More than 200 Waorani were persuaded to leave their homes and taken to live in a distant Christian settlement, where they were told that their culture was sinful. As well as the pressure to become "civilized," the Waorani suffered the arrival of new illnesses, such as polio, against which they had no immunity. One missionary reported that "the oil people . . . are more than willing to do what they can for our operation, since we have almost cleared their whole concession of Aucas."

Rather than submit to evangelization, the Tagaeri and Taromenane groups resisted contact with outsiders by retreating farther into the forest, where they continue to live in voluntary isolation, fiercely protecting their territory from outsiders with deadly use of their massive wooden spears. Although there are records of several fatal attacks on intruders since the first arrival of oil companies in the area, the situation has worsened in recent years in response to the increased pressure on their territory caused by the expansion of illegal logging, the oil industry, and the agricultural frontier.

In a rare chance encounter between a Taromenane tribesperson and a Waorani, the former reportedly expressed anger at the noise, deforestation, and oil platforms throughout their territory, claiming that the Waorani had not done enough to prevent this incursion on their ancestral homeland. These pressures have provoked conflicts between Waorani and the uncontacted peoples, encounters that have turned into violent confrontations and even massacres. The most recent involved the spearing to death of 18 uncontacted people in October 2018.

In 1999, a presidential decree created the Tagaeri Taromenane "Intangible" Zone within Yasuní National Park, purportedly designating the area permanently off-limits for any extractive operations. But with oil drilling well underway in the ITT block of the national park, which includes part of the Intangible Zone, the situation looks bleak for Ecuador's uncontacted peoples.

whipped up a terrible storm if anyone tried to approach. The oil companies' seismic explorations dislodged the spirit and the beautiful lake is now accessible. Accommodations are in basic but comfortable wooden cabins. Food is local (fish, rice, plantain, yucca, *chicha*). Vegetarians can be accommodated with advance notice. Camping trips are also possible (bring your own tent or, for the truly adventurous, learn to make beds from leaves and hang a mosquito net from a tree).

The project is led by Yasuní Park guardian Holmer Machoa, who has an encyclopedic knowledge of the park and the fight to protect it against oil exploitation. He is one of the few people authorized to take visitors to see the rare agami heron, which is only present from March to July.

A four-night/five-day package costs $240 and includes accommodations, food, and activities. The return boat trip from Coca to Tiputini is an additional $35. Holmer can be contacted by phone or email (tel. 97/997-5544, holmerclaudio@hotmail.com). He may be without signal for up to three weeks at a time, so be patient, or leave a message with Denis Machoa (tel. 96/101-4448) or Lisardo Grefa (tel. 6/306-3833), who can reach him via radio.

South to Tena and Vicinity

BAEZA TO TENA
Cosanga

Eighteen kilometers (11 mi) south of Baeza, **Cosanga** is the world record holder in the Christmas Bird Count, with a total of 600 species recorded in one day. Leo, the owner of **Wasi Panka Tours** (tel. 98/182-1785, Facebook @WasiPanka.Tours) is president of the Cosanga Birdwatchers' Club and an excellent bird guide.

Protecting nearly 2,000 hectares (5,000 acres) of cloud forest, **Cabañas San Isidro** (tel. 2/289-1880 or 99/358-1250, www.cabanasanisidro.com, $95 s, $141 d, including breakfast) provides a wildlife corridor linking the Antisana Reserve and Sumaco Napo-Galeras National Park. Ten cabins have sitting areas, coffeemakers, and private porches with hummingbird feeders. Ten kilometers (6.2 mi) of trails lead off to archaeological sites, streams, and waterfalls. Activities include bird-watching and cooking classes. An Ecuadorian taster menu is available at the restaurant, which uses organic home-grown vegetables and sources other ingredients from local providers. Amenities include a heated pool and fireplace. The owners have opened a biology station nearby. Discounts are available for student groups. San Isidro is 3 kilometers (1.9 mi) from Cosanga. Follow the sign from the main road.

Sumaco Napo-Galeras National Park and Volcán Sumaco

Jutting from the rainforest east of Baeza, **Volcán Sumaco** is part of an ancient mountain range, isolated by ravines and deep canyons. The volcano is the star attraction of **Sumaco Napo-Galeras National Park,** a UNESCO Biosphere Reserve that protects more than 200,000 hectares (500,000 acres) of lowland and high-elevation rainforest, where the tributaries of the Ríos Napo and Coca begin. These cloud forests are unique because of their geographical isolation, and lush from the humidity rising from the Amazon below. An astonishing diversity of orchids, birds, and amphibians are found here, along with jaguars, pumas, and sloths.

The few people who venture into the park are usually intent on scaling **Volcán Sumaco** (3,732 m/12,244 ft), about which little is known due to its difficult access. Evidence suggests that there may have been volcanic activity in 1895 and 1933, but this is unconfirmed. Sumaco is not a technical climb, but it's a three- to five-day expedition, depending on fitness level and conditions. Those who dare will be rewarded with wonderful views of the Andes and Amazon. September to December is the driest time of year for the ascent.

The volcano is accessed via the community of **Pacto Sumaco,** where the local guides are the only people authorized to take visitors to the summit. The cost of $60 per person per day includes a guide, accommodations (in cabañas and refuges), and food. You can carry your own pack or pay extra for a porter. Make arrangements directly with the community tourism project in Pacto Sumaco (tel. 6/301-8324), via the Centro de Comunicación Ambiental (Ramírez Dávilos y Rey Felipe II, tel. 6/288-7154 or 6/288-6258) in Baeza's old town, or with the

Ministry of the Environment in Tena (tel. 6/287-7991). To get to Pacto Sumaco, take the Baeza-Tena road and turn off after about 50 kilometers (31 mi) onto the road heading toward Coca. After another 50 kilometers (31 mi) you'll reach the community of Wawa Sumaco, from where a dirt road leads to Pacto Sumaco.

Every mid-November Kichwa shamans from Archidonia climb the volcano, which they consider sacred, to perform rituals at the top, asking Sumaco for its energy and blessings. Tourists are welcome to join the three-to four-day expedition, known as **Jumandy Causay,** which is reclaiming an ancient tradition. Contact the Centro de Comunicación Ambiental in Baeza for more information (tel. 6/288-7154 or 6/288-6258).

Wildsumaco Lodge

Nearly 7 kilometers (4.3 mi) from Wawa Sumaco, the Swedish- and American-run **Wildsumaco Lodge** (tel. 6/301-8343, www.wildsumaco.com, info@wildsumaco. com, $140-170 pp full board, $30 day visit) offers superb bird-watching with over 500 recorded species, a spotters' deck at canopy level, and extensive forest trails. There are 10 comfortable double cabins and a dining area with a fireplace. On clear days, there are wonderful views of snow-covered Antisana, El Altar, and Tungurahua. Most of the income from Wildsumaco goes toward the lodge's own nonprofit, the Río Pucuno Foundation, which is dedicated to buying and preserving foothill rainforest (a type of forest at an elevation of 900-1,500 m/2,950-4,900 ft, lying between lowland jungle and higher elevation cloud forest). The foundation also assists local people to develop their own sustainable ecotourism projects as an alternative to felling trees; has trained several people to become local bird guides; and has recently opened a scientific research station, the Wildsumaco Biological Station. All reservations should be made via email (info@ wildsumaco.com). The lodge does not accept walk-in guests.

Archidona and the Jumandy Caves

Ten kilometers (6.2 mi) north of Tena, the small town of **Archidona** sits quietly away from the tourist crowds. Founded in 1560, the town has a rather curious striped brown-and-white church and a pleasant square, but it's best known for the caves, located 4 kilometers (2.5 mi) north of town on the Baeza-Tena road.

Las Cavernas de Jumandy (tel. 99/516-2771, Facebook @comunidadkrjumandi.kawsay, 8am-4:30pm daily except 2pm-4:30pm Wed., $15 per group of up to 5, then $3 pp) are the largest caves in the region, named after a Kichwa chief who reportedly hid here before leading an uprising against the Spanish in 1578. The caverns have also been used by shamans as ceremonial sites. It's necessary to enter with a guide (a head torch is provided), and the one-hour tour includes an underground lake, a small waterfall, stalactites and stalagmites, and a fossilized shell that is 80 million years old. Be prepared to get wet. Children under 10 are not permitted, nor is photography (except with Go Pros). The caves are set in a tourist complex (8am-5pm Wed.-Sun., $2) that includes pools, water slides, play areas, a restaurant, and a bar. When the complex is open, it's necessary to pay the $2 entrance to access the caves.

Just east of Archidona town center, **Wiñak** (Vía Sinchi Sacha, tel. 6/288-9028 or 99/577-0371, www.winak.org) is an organic chocolate company owned by an association of 257 Kichwa farmers from 57 communities, with 66 percent participation from women. In addition to cacao, Wiñak grows *guayusa* and plantain using the traditional small-scale *chakra* agroforestry system, which preserves biodiversity. Tours explain the process of making artisanal chocolate and *guayusa* tea, and include an optional visit to a *chakra.*

For excellent organic Amazonian cuisine, try **Bijao** (Transversal 16 *y* Calle 14, tel. 6/287-7167 or 99/834-4273, https://archidona. wixsite.com/bijao, 11am-5pm Wed.-Sun.) in the center of Archidona, named for the type of leaf in which much of the food is cooked. Set lunches ($5) consist of a range of local specialties, such as *maito* (chicken or fish cooked in a leaf), *caldo de gallina* (chicken soup), or tamales, accompanied by a salad, a portion of yucca or plantain, a dessert, and a glass of *guayusa*. On the central square, **Hotel Yurak** (tel. 98/348-1368, Facebook @Hotel Yurak, $25 pp including breakfast, $55 pp full board) is an excellent place to stay, with a pool, sauna, and steam room.

Archidona is on the main road from Baeza to Tena. If you're coming from Tena, buses to Archidona leave regularly from Bolívar and Amazonas with Cooperativa Expreso Napo.

TENA

The capital of Napo province, Tena (pop. 27,000, elevation 500m/1,640 ft) has an attractive location at the confluence of the Ríos Tena and Pano. Founded in the 16th century as a missionary and trading outpost, its official slogan is "the land of *guayusa* and cinnamon" (*guayusa* being a type of Amazonian tea), but Tena is more famous as Ecuador's rafting and kayaking capital. There are more foreign visitors here than in other Amazon towns, and the tourism amenities are of a higher standard and wider range, with plenty of good hotels, restaurants, and tour operators. Tena is also the gateway to several Kichwa communities, but the experiences tend to be cultural, rather than immersions in nature. There are some beautiful waterfalls nearby, and tour agencies can take visitors farther afield, into Yasuní and Limoncocha.

Sights

The **Parque Central** is a good spot to sit and watch the city go by. In the center is a statue of Jumandy, the Kichwa chief who courageously led an uprising against the Spanish colonizers in 1578. The *malecón* is the most pleasant place for a stroll. From the *malecón*, take the footbridge partway across the river to the **Parque Amazónico La Isla** (8:30am-5pm daily, $1 pp), where trails wander through 24 forested hectares (59 acres) past enclosures with native animals, including a tapir and several monkeys. There is a canopy view from the mirador and a garden of medicinal plants.

Recreation and Tours

Llaki Panka Adventours (César Augusto Rueda *y* Mariana Montesdeoca, tel. 99/256-1913, www.llaki-panka.de.rs, Facebook @llakipanka.ecuador) is owned by Juan Tapuy, a Kichwa guide who worked for various agencies for 15 years before setting up his own venture, one of very few locally owned agencies in Tena. Juan leads tailor-made tours in and around Tena, Ahuano, Llanganates National Park, Limoncocha, and Yasuní National Park. Jungle trips can be for wildlife spotting, visiting indigenous communities (including his village of Shandia), or shamanism. Adventure tours include rafting, kayaking, caving, canyoneering, tubing, and visiting waterfalls. A cacao and coffee tour is also popular. Most tours cost $40-100 per person per day all inclusive. A one-day rafting tour costs $80 per person for two people. Juan is setting up a project in Shandia on the banks of the Jatunyacu River, where volunteers can teach English at the local school and/or get involved with organic agriculture using a mix of traditional Kichwa methods and permaculture. Volunteers pay $7/night including three meals, non-volunteers pay $15. Accommodations are basic, with solar panels and a dry toilet. If Juan is out with a group when you stop by the office, send him a message on WhatsApp.

Another environmentally conscious Kichwa-owned agency is **Akangau Jungle Expedition** (12 Febrero *y* Augusto Rueda, tel. 98/617-5641, www.akangau.com, Facebook @akangau), which offers a range of community-based ecotours in the Tena area and the Amazon ranging from one day to multiple days.

Tena has developed into Ecuador's water-sports capital, and there is excellent **white-water rafting** and **kayaking** nearby, especially February to April. Half-day (around $40 pp), full-day ($65-80 pp),

Tena

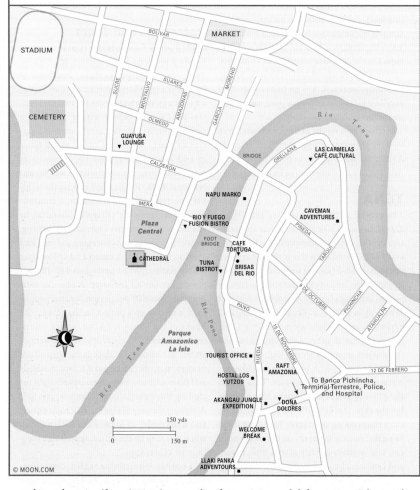

and two-day trips (from $170 pp) are available. The most famous stretches of river are along the Jondachi and Jatunyacu (both Class III), and the wilder Misahuallí and Hollín (Class IV). For more detailed information about white-water sports in this area, see the *Rafting and Kayaking* section of the *Essentials* chapter. A highly recommended operator in Tena is **Torrent Duck** (www.torrent-duck. com), which is actively involved in conservation efforts to protect the Jatunyacu River

from mining and deforestation. Other good options are **Caveman Adventures** (www. cavemanecuador.com) and Kichwa-owned **Raft Amazonia** (www.raftamazonia.com).

Shopping

On the *malecón,* **Napu Marko** (tel. 99/597-4573, Facebook @NapuMarka) is a beautifully laid out store owned by an association of local artisans and entrepreneurs. On the shelves are fair trade and organic handicrafts, coffee, cacao, *guayusa* tea, honey, liqueurs, soap, and natural toiletry products.

Food

As in much of the Amazon region, the local specialty is *maito* (fish, grubs, or chicken grilled in a wrapped leaf). The best place to try it is ★ **Doña Dolores** (15 Noviembre *y* 12 Febrero, $3.50-4.50), across from the Welcome Break hostel. The *almuerzo* places at the bus station are popular with locals, serving set lunches washed down with cold *guayusa* tea.

Right on the *malecón,* ★ **Café Tortuga** (Orellana, tel. 9/288-7340, 7am-7:30pm Mon.-Sat., 7am-1:30pm Sun., $5-6) has a wide-ranging menu including several veggie options. It's especially popular for breakfast. There is an excellent range of tourist information on the bookshelves. Despite its name, the neighboring ★ **Tuna Bistrot** (tel. 6/231-2087, 8am-9pm Tues.-Sun., $3-6) is a lovely vegetarian restaurant serving breakfasts, set lunches ($4), burritos, and burgers.

A good spot for veggies and non-veggies alike is **Guayusa Lounge** (Olmedo *y* Sucre, tel. 6/231-2561, Facebook @guayusalounge, 5pm-11pm Tues.-Thurs., 5pm-1am Fri.-Sat., $3-6), which serves pizzas, sandwiches, healthy curries, cocktails, and craft beers. There are regular salsa classes and DJs on weekends.

On the central square, U.S.-owned **Río y Fuego Fusion Bistro** (tel. 98/408-9689, Facebook @rioyfuegofusionbistro, 5pm-10pm daily, $3-12) serves Asian American fusion and is especially known for its pad thai.

Las Carmelas Café Cultural (Av. Francisco de Orellana *y* 15 de Noviembre, tel. 98/092-1969, Facebook @LasCarmelasCafeCultural, 4:30pm-11:45pm daily, $2.50-7) is an Italian café and cultural center, with weekly music, documentary nights, and a critical thinking discussion group.

Accommodations

Perched on a hill overlooking Tena, German-owned **Hostal Tena Ñaui** (Sector Las Antenas, tel. 6/231-0188 or 98/129-4330, www.hostaltena.com, $7-12 pp) is a $1.50 taxi ride from the town center, but it's worth it for the spectacular views. Breakfast is $3 extra. Rooms are large, bright, and clean, some with private bathrooms, and the service is friendly.

A more centrally located budget option is friendly, locally owned **A Welcome Break** (Augusto Rueda *y* 12 de Febrero, tel. 6/288-6301, http://awelcomebreak.wix.com/english, $8 pp dorm, $10-12.50 pp room). Guests can use the kitchen, and there's a good restaurant attached. Directly on the *malecón* is **Hostal Brisas del Río** (tel. 6/288-6444 or 6/288-6208, $9-15 pp), another friendly, locally owned place. Clean, comfortable guest rooms have a choice of shared or private baths.

Perhaps the most attractive lodging in Tena can be found at the locally owned ★ **Hostal Los Yutzos** (Augusto Rueda *y* Av. 12 de Febrero, tel. 6/288-6717, http://www.hotellosyutzos.com, $26-50 s, $45-60 d, breakfast included). Overlooking the Río Pano and Parque La Isla, guest rooms are set among leafy gardens and have either fans or air-conditioning.

Owned by an Ecuadorian/German couple, ★ **Hostal Pakay** (Av. Antisana/Perimetral *y* Manuel M. Rosales, Barrio 30 de Diciembre, tel. 6/284-7449 or 99/090-6633, http://en.ecuadorpakaytours.com, $14 dorm, $24-28 s, $32-36 d, including breakfast) is on the southeastern outskirts of the city and feels like a jungle lodge. Environmental practices include permaculture, ecological building methods, dry toilets, and biological wastewater treatment. Lunch and dinner are available ($4.50-7.50) with vegetarian options. The owners operate well-reviewed tours.

Information and Services

The staff at Tena's **tourist office** (Augusto Rueda, tel. 6/288-6452, www.tenaturismo.gob.ec, 8:15am-5pm Mon.-Fri.), on the riverside near Hostal Los Yutzos, are friendly and helpful.

There is a Banco Pichincha on 15 de Noviembre, a couple of blocks north of the *terminal terrestre*. There is a **police station** (tel. 6/288-6101) at the *terminal*. The **hospital** (15 Noviembre *y* Eloy Alfaro, tel. 6/373-1980) is a few blocks south.

Getting There and Around

The *terminal terrestre* sits about 1 kilometer south of the town center on 15 de Noviembre. Taxis to the terminal and to most destinations around town cost $1. There are more or less hourly, round-the-clock departures from/to Quito (5 hours, $6), which go via Baeza and Papallacta. There are also frequent buses from/to Baños (4 hours, $5.25), Riobamba ($7.50), and Coca (4.5 hours, $7). There are a few daily departures to Puyo (6:30am, 10:30am, 11am, 11:30am, and 9pm, 2.5 hours, $3.15) and Lago Agrio (7am, 6:30pm, and 8:45pm, 7 hours, $8) and overnight buses to Guayaquil (7:30pm and 10pm, 8 hours, $10). To get to Misahuallí (45 minutes, $0.65) head to the Jumandy Terminal a block west of the main terminal, from where there are frequent departures. Other local buses to indigenous communities (including Shandia), leave from the Centinela Terminal, a block east of the main terminal.

Misahuallí

Twenty-five kilometers (15.5 mi) southeast of Tena, the charming village of Misahuallí is the oldest port in the Amazon. Though it sees a lot less activity since the construction of the Tena-Coca road, it's still a popular spot to organize jungle tours. It also has a sandy beach that gets busy with locals on weekends. There are several tour agencies on the central square, and canoe guides wait at the dock to ferry passengers to various destinations along the Río Napo, ranging from the Kichwa community of Muyuna five minutes downstream to several days in Yasuní. Day trips include visits to various indigenous communities, waterfalls, and millennial trees. A recommended guide and good point of contact for information is **Juan Luna** (tel. 99/253-2486), a Kichwa guide from the Muyuna community.

A couple of kilometers south of the village, **Sinchi Warmi** (tel. 6/306-3009 or 96/950-2486, Facebook @SinchiWarmis, sinchiwarmis@gmail.com, $20.50 pp or $75 with 3 meals) is a community tourism project owned and run by an association of Kichwa women, who hand-built the attractive wooden cabins that are set around a small lake. Aptly, *sinchi warmi* means "strong women." The excellent restaurant serves a mix of local specialties and international dishes, with vegetarian options. Activities include a farm-to-bar chocolate tour, a dawn *guayusa* ceremony followed by a jungle walk, and a handicrafts workshop. It's $1.50 by taxi from Misahuallí.

Buses to Misahuallí from the Terminal Jumandy take 45 minutes and cost $0.65. A taxi from Tena costs $10.

Sacha Runa Lodge

Located midway between Tena and Puyo in the Arosemena Tola Canton, **Sacha Runa Lodge** (tel. 9/954-31895, www.jungleecuador. com, $8 camping, $60 s/d, including breakfast) is a private 36-hectare (89-acre) rainforest reserve located on an island in the Anzu River. Access is via cable car. Activities include night and day walks, star gazing, shamanism, swimming, a chocolate tour, a local gastronomic tour, a handicrafts workshop, and canoe rides. Rooms have private bathrooms with hot water. Amenities include a restaurant, hammock area, and Jacuzzi. The lodge works to conserve endemic flora and fauna and has a water treatment plant.

PUYO AND VICINITY

The city center of Puyo (pop. 37,000), the capital of Pastaza province, is a concrete sprawl, but look toward the edges of town and you'll find botanical gardens and wildlife sanctuaries. The surrounding waterfalls and indigenous communities provide some of the most easily accesible rainforest experiences in the country and are frequently visited on tours from nearby Baños. *Puyo* means "cloudy" in Kichwa, and wet weather is the norm, although the torrential downpours are usually brief. At 950 meters (3,100 ft) above sea level, it's cooler here than in the northern rainforest towns.

Sights

There's very little to see in the center of Puyo, but it's worth stopping by the **Museo Etnoarqueológico** (Atahualpa *y* 9 de Octubre, tel. 3/288-5605, Facebook @Museo. EtnoArqueologico.Puyo, 8am-4pm daily, free), which has an exhibition of traditional dwellings belonging to five of the province's nationalities.

On the northeast edge of town, the **Parque Etnobotánico Omaere** (tel. 98/525-0864, https://omaere.wordpress.com/english, 9am-5pm Tues.-Sun., $3 pp, minimum group price $5) is a small botanical reserve that was founded in 1993 by a Shuar woman and two French women, who bought the 15-hectare (37-acre) plot and filled it with the plants most important to Amazonian peoples. There are also traditional Shuar and Waorani houses. A guided tour (included) takes 1-2 hours. To get there, cross the footbridge over the river from the *malecón,* pass the El Jardín hostel, and continue for another 200 meters (655 ft).

A couple of kilometers farther north is the **YanaCocha Rescue Centre** (Vía Tena km 3, tel. 3/288-0000 or 98/765-4321, www. yanacocharescue.org, $3), a center for wild animals that have been confiscated from traffickers or were illegally kept as pets. At the time of writing, there were 200 animals of 43 species. Wherever possible, the animals are released back into the wild; others will be lifelong residents at the center.

Another 4 kilometers (2.5 mi) north, **Los Yapas Holistic Center** (Vía Tena km 7, tel. 99/284-6834, http://losyapas.org) is a shining example of ecotourism: a project that works to heal both the natural environment and humans. Formerly a degraded pasture, the 25-hectare (62-acre) site has been lovingly restored using permaculture techniques and now houses a botanical garden, an ecolodge, and a healing center. Tours ($4-6) of the botanical garden include an orchidarium,

bromelarium, medicinal plants garden, and reforestation area. Essential oils such as lemongrass, wild garlic, and cinnamon are for sale. Accommodations are available in beautiful wooden rooms. The healing center offers one- to- five-day holistic packages of physical and spiritual practices such as yoga, tai chi, meditation, mindfulness, and massage. The restaurant serves vegan and vegetarian food, mostly organic. The center accepts volunteers. If you're arriving by bus, ask to be let out at Fatima, from where the center is signposted. It's $5 by taxi from Puyo.

Around 3 kilometers (2 mi) south of Puyo is another botanical garden, **El Jardín Botánico Las Orquídeas** (tel. 3/253-0305, http://jardinbotanicolasorquideas.com/en, 8:30am-4pm Mon.-Sat., 8:30am-noon Sun., $5), the life's work of Omar Tello, who bought a degraded 7-hectare (17-acre) plot in 1980 and has restored it with 300 orchid species and endangered rainforest plants. A guided tour (included) takes 2-3 hours. To get there, catch bus 2 from outside the Cooperative Bank San Francisco (Atahualpa *y* 27 de Febrero, $0.25, 20 minutes) and ask to be let off at Las Orquídeas. Buses run every 15 minutes. A taxi costs $3.

Another popular day trip is to **Fundación Hola Vida** (tel. 3/303-0791, 8am-5pm daily, $1.50), with trails through 225 hectares (555 acres) of secondary rainforest and a beautiful waterfall, 27 kilometers (17 mi) south of Puyo just off the Vía Macas. The waterfall is a 20-minute walk from the entrance to the reserve and can be visited independently or with a guide ($5 per group of up to 3 people). Guides wait by the entrance to accompany visitors to the waterfall, and no reservation is required. A full-day tour (9am-6pm) is also available, for which it's necessary to book by telephone at least one day ahead. The tour includes the waterfall ($1.50 pp); a visit to a Kichwa community ($1 pp); lunch ($5 pp); a visit to a truly spectacular viewpoint, the Mirador Indichuris, with an extreme swing over the jungle ($3); a paddle canoe ride ($15 per group of up to 4); and a tour of a cacao farm ($2, including a piece of chocolate and some yucca bread). The guide for the full-day tour charges $20-25 per group of up to four people ($40 for an English-speaking guide). To get there, take any bus going to Macas from Puyo and ask to be let off at Hola Vida ($1.50), or take a taxi ($10). If you do the full-day tour, you may miss the last bus back to Puyo and have to go back by taxi. Tour agencies in Baños and Puyo offer the full-day tour with private transport for around $40 per person.

Recreation and Tours

Most travelers book rainforest tours from Baños, but Puyo has plenty of reputable operators. One of the most popular local tours combines the Hola Vida waterfall with a visit to the Mirador Indichuris, where an extreme swing flies over the jungle far below.

Run by the Sarayaku community, **Papangu Tours** (Orellana *entre* Cumanda *y* Manzano, tel. 3/288-7684 or 99/550-4983, www.papangutours.com.ec) offers the usual tours to Hola Vida, Cueva de los Tayos, Misahuallí, Yasuní, and Cuyabeno, but their most popular trip is to the Sarayaku community itself, which is a five-hour canoe journey or a 25-minute flight from Shell. Trips can be tailored to the group's interests, and English-speaking guides can be hired with advance notice. A four-day/three-night package to Sarayaku costs $107 per person per day, including accommodations and meals, for a minimum group size of four. Transport (arrival by canoe and return journey by small plane) costs an additional $180 per person.

Diego Escobar, a local environmentalist, runs **Madre Selva** (tel. 98/447-2374, www.madreselvaecuador.com), a consistently well-reviewed agency offering one- to five-day tours in and around Puyo and farther afield to Misahuallí, Yasuní, and Cuyabeno. A popular two-day local tour ($119) includes the Hola Vida waterfall, a jungle hike, a canoe ride on the Pastaza River, and a visit to an indigenous community. All tours and prices are listed on the website. **Selva Vida** (Ceslao

Marín *y* Atahualpa, tel. 99/135-3487, www.selvavidatravel.com) offers a similar range of tours.

Shopping

Waorani Hecho a Mano (Atahualpa *y* Villamil, tel. 3/288-8908), owned by an association of over 250 Waorani women, sells handmade ethnic art and handicrafts. On Sundays, head to the **Mercado de los Plátanos** (Av. Alberto Zambrano *y* Orellana, 7am-noon Sun.) to see the exotic fruits and the *chonta* palm grubs, sold live, that are popular to eat. The small section on natural medicines is the most interesting.

Food

For the best of traditional rainforest fare, try **Uchumanka** (Av. Tarqui, tel. 98/778-2645, Facebook @uchumankapuyo, 10am-4pm Sat.-Sun., $3.75-7) for specialties such as *maito* and *caldo de gallina*. It's south of the center and only open on weekends. Just north of the center, **Yuki's** (20 de Julio, tel. 96/279-6858, Facebook @yukispuyo, 7:30am-11:30pm daily, $2-6) is a popular fast food restaurant serving Amazonian fare.

In the center, ★ **Escobar Café** (Ceslao Marín *y* Atahualpa, tel. 3/288-3008, Facebook @escobar.cafe.donamadeo, 10am-midnight Mon.-Sat., noon-9pm Sun., $5-10) has a funky bamboo structure and walls adorned with photos and stories of indigenous women. Organic local products are used to make specialties such as passion fruit chicken with fried yucca. The menu features other Amazonian ingredients such as *papa china* (a starchy root vegetable) and *guayusa* tea. Breakfasts, sandwiches, salads, and desserts are also available. From the building materials to the ingredients to the decor, the Escobar is a celebration of the rainforests of the Pastaza province. The café actively supports indigenous women from various nationalities who are united

---

1: The cabins at Sinchi Warmi were hand-built by Kichwa women. 2: The Pastaza River separates the provinces of Pastaza and Morona-Santiago.

in their efforts to protect the Amazon from extractivism.

Just north of the center, ★ **Zuvar** (20 de Julio, *entre* Bolívar *y* 4 de Enero, tel. 99/886-3960, Facebook @restaurantzuvar, 7am-8pm Mon.-Thurs., 7am-3pm Fri. and Sun., $3-4) is an excellent vegetarian restaurant that serves a set lunch ($3.25) and à la carte items including pasta, tacos, burgers, and salads. Even farther north, near the *malecón*, **O'Sole Mio** (Pichincha *y* Guaranda, tel. 3/289-3310, Facebook @osolemiopizzeria59, 6pm-10pm Tues.-Sun., $5-8) is a wonderful Italian place, where the owner/chef is from Naples.

Good food can also be found in the hotel restaurants, such as **Hostería Turingia** (Ceslao Marín *y* Javier Vargas, tel. 3/288-5180, www.hosteriaturingia.com, $8-10), **El Pigual** (Tungurahua, tel. 3/289-2408, http://hosteriaelpigual.com), and **El Jardín** (Obrero, tel. 99/140-9096, noon-4pm and 6pm-10pm Mon.-Sat., $12-18, $13-22). All offer a mix of local and international cuisine.

Accommodations

In the center, **Hostería Turingia** (Ceslao Marín *y* Javier Vargas, tel. 3/288-5180, www.hosteriaturingia.com, $35 s, $55 d, including breakfast) features alpine-style cabins in gardens filled with flowers and birdsong. It has a restaurant, a bar, and a pool.

Most of the best options are just north of the town center. **Hostal El Colibrí** (Av. Manabí *y* Bolívar, tel. 98/753-0146, www.hostalelcolibripuyo.com, $20 s, $35 d, breakfast included) is one of the city's best budget options, as is **Las Palmas** (20 de Julio *y* 4 de Enero, tel. 3/288-4832, www.hostallaspalmaspuyo.com, $20-30 s, $30-45 d, breakfast included), an attractive, yellow colonial-style building with a friendly local owner. The neighboring **Posada Real** (4 de Enero *y* 27 de Febrero, tel. 3/288-5887, Facebook @posadareal, $33.60 s, $56 d pp, breakfast included) is a beautiful mustard-color colonial house with plush guest rooms.

North of town on Calle Loja, **El Pigual** (Tungurahua, tel. 3/289-2408, http://

hosteriaelpigual.com, $49 s, $91 d, breakfast and dinner included) is set in a 33-hectare (82-acre) park with trails through bamboo groves and secondary forest. Amenities include a pool, a sauna, a steam bath, and a volleyball court. Over the bridge, just before Omaere park, ★ **El Jardín** (Obrero, tel. 99/140-9096, $45 s, $77 d, breakfast included) has comfortable modern guest rooms in a wooden building overlooking charming gardens. The restaurant is one of the city's best, and there's a Jacuzzi and massage service.

Information and Services

Banco Internacional (Orellana *y* Villamil) and **Banco Pichincha** (Teniente Hugo Ortiz *y* 9 de Octubre) have ATMs in the city center. The **tourist office** (Orellana *y* 9 de Octubre, tel. 3/288-5122, ext. 250, 8am-4pm Mon.-Fri.) is next to the market. There's a **police station** (9 Octubre *y* Sucre, tel. 3/288-5102) off the main square. The **hospital** (9 de Octubre *y* Bolívar Feicán, tel. 3/288-5431, hospitalpuyo@hgp.gob.ec) is south of the center.

Getting There and Around

The main **bus terminal** is south of the town center and can be reached by buses marked "Terminal" running down 9 de Octubre, or by taxi. There are regular departures to Baños (1.5 hours, $2), Tena (2.5 hours, $3), Ambato (3 hours, $3), Riobamba (4 hours, $4), Macas (4 hours, $5), and Quito (5 hours, $5). There are also daily departures to Coca (4:30am, 5:30am, 9am, 10am, 3:30pm, and 10:45pm), Lago Agrio (4am, 4:30am, and 12:15pm), Cuenca (8:40am, 8:40pm, and 10pm), Guayaquil (6:15am, 9pm, and 11pm, 8 hours, $9), and Gualaquiza (2:20pm via Zamora and 11:30pm).

★ SARAYAKU

Sarayaku is a Kichwa community of 1,200 people who live on the banks of the Bobonazo River in a remote part of Pastaza province. Their territory covers 135,000 hectares (333,600 acres), 95 percent of which is primary rainforest. Although they live as many

Sarayaku: The Last Beacon of Resistance?

The Kichwa people of Sarayaku call themselves the People of the Zenith, after an ancient prophecy of their ancestors predicting that they would be a pillar of territorial, cultural, and spiritual defense after other communities had surrendered—a beacon of light as strong as the sun at noon. Living up to the prophecy, for decades they have stood at the frontline of the battle to defend the Amazon rainforest and the human rights of indigenous peoples.

The Sarayaku are best known for winning a historic case against the Ecuadorian state at the Inter-American Court of Human Rights (IACHR), which ruled that the government violated their rights when it granted an Argentinian oil company permission to prospect in their territory in 1996, without consulting or even notifying the community. In fact, the Sarayaku people only learned that their land had been opened for oil exploration when the helicopters arrived, followed by men with guns. For several months, the oil company carried out detonations, felled trees, dug more than 400 wells, buried more than 1.4 tons of high-grade explosives, and shattered the peace with helicopters. In 2003, the Sarayaku took their

The Sarayaku make backpacks from leaves to carry harvested yucca.

case to the Inter-American Court of Human Rights, and in 2012, after a decade-long legal battle, the judges ruled in their favor. The story is told in a documentary, *Children of the Jaguar,* made by the Sarayaku, which won Best Documentary at the National Geographic Film Festival.

Beyond their legal victory against the Ecuadorian state, this is a community that has created their own impressive democratic model, launched a professional football team, and sailed a canoe down the Seine at the Paris climate change summit.

Sarayaku is once again threatened by oil exploitation, with the Ecuadorian government planning to auction 3 million hectares (7.4 million acres) of largely virgin rainforest in the XI Oil Round, or Ronda Sur. Three of the oil blocks cover nearly all the Sarayaku territory, the borders of which are being planted with flowering trees to symbolize the community's peaceful resistance and defense of their territory.

To combat this latest threat, in July 2018 the Sarayaku launched a bold and visionary new proposal, the Kawsak Sacha Declaration. Based on existing law, the declaration describes the rainforest as a living entity with consciousness, and thus subject to legal rights. The concept for the proposal came from the *kawsak sacha*, or living forest, itself and was transmitted to the community via their shamans (*yachaks* in the Kichwa language), who act as intermediaries between the rainforest and those who protect it. After presenting the proposal in Paris at the global climate change conference and to the president of France, François Hollande, the Sarayaku have set their sights on the United Nations.

Beyond legally protecting their own 135,000 hectares (333,600 acres) of pristine rainforest, the community hopes the proposal can be used to defend indigenous territories worldwide. It also seeks to promote the indigenous world view that, rather than seeing nature as an inert space to exploit for resources, sees it as a living entity, to be respected and coexisted with. The Sarayaku believe that a shift toward this perspective could be the key to mitigating the unfolding global environmental crisis. And, with indigenous peoples acting as stewards of 95 percent of the planet's most threatened biodiverse regions and key players in the fight against climate change, the declaration could have a global impact.

For more information, see http://sarayaku.org and https://kawsaksacha.org/en.

indigenous people do, by hunting, gathering, fishing, and small-scale agriculture, this is a community like no other. For decades they have stood at the forefront of the struggle to defend the Amazon from oil companies and other threats. With its own autonomous government, Sarayaku is a sovereign territory. Highly organized, they have created their own advanced democratic model and are adept at using the tools made available by the western world, while maintaining their own strong cultural identity. Much of life in Sarayaku centers around *chicha,* a slightly alcoholic drink made from yucca, which symbolizes unity and fertility. Chewed by the women as part of the preparation process, it is fermented by bacteria in their saliva.

While activities such as canoe rides and jungle hikes are available, the main point of a visit to Sarayaku is to experience community life. There is the chance to participate in *mingas* (communal agriculture, building, or maintenance projects), traditional small-scale agriculture, and celebrations. There is also the opportunity for a consultation with a shaman (*yachak* in Kichwa) and the possibility of participating in ayahuasca ceremonies.

A visit to Sarayaku is especially recommended for those with an interest in rainforest conservation, creative resistance strategies, indigenous rights, or alternative models for living. Sarayaku is accessed from Puyo via a 90-minute taxi journey followed by five hours in a canoe, or 25 minutes by plane from the airport at Shell. The advantage of arriving by river is a stop at the *piedra de gallo,* a semi-submerged rock in the Bobonazo River where ancient shamans held ayahuasca ceremonies to decide on the names of the nearby communities according to their visions. Sarayaku, for example, means "River of Corn."

Run by the Sarayaku community, **Papangu Tours** (Orellana *entre* Cumanda *y* Manzano, tel. 3/288-7684 or 99/550-4983, www.papangutours.com.ec) in Puyo organizes trips to Sarayaku. A four-day/three-night package costs $107 per person per day, including accommodations and meals, for a minimum group size of four. Transport (arrival by canoe and return journey by small plane) costs an additional $180 per person. English-speaking guides can be hired with advance notice. Accommodations are in a beautiful *maloca,* a large hut made using traditional methods and materials, which is partitioned into bedrooms. Bathrooms are shared.

Southern Oriente

MACAS AND VICINITY

South of Puyo is the road less traveled, and Morona-Santiago is one of Ecuador's remotest provinces. Its capital, Macas (pop. 23,000), is a pleasant town with a beautiful setting and, at over 1,000 meters (3,280 ft) elevation, a mild climate. If you're coming from Cuenca or Riobamba, either road provides a spectacular descent from the Andes to the Oriente through Sangay National Park.

Sights

The modern **cathedral** on the main square boasts stained-glass windows worthy of a much larger church. Two blocks west is La Casa de Cultura (Soasti *y* 10 de Agosto), which contains the **Museo Arqueológico Municipal** (Mon.-Fri., free). The exhibition on Shuar culture includes blowpipes, funeral urns, and headdresses made of animal heads.

For beautiful views of the mountains to the west and rainforest to the east, head five blocks north along Don Bosco to the lookout at the **Parque Recreacional,** where there is also a nice café. Volcán Sangay, 40 kilometers (25 mi) to the northwest, can be seen on clear days. For an even more spectacular vista, walk to the **Mirador del Quilamo,** where there is

Headhunters: the Myths of the Shuar

The Shuar people are most famous for their tradition of making shrunken heads, or *tsantsas*. Shuar warriors believed that making a *tsantsa* was a way to capture the life force, or *arutam*, of the vanquished person, allowing the victor to become a great and powerful man, or *kakaram*.

Undertaken with great ceremony, the process of making a shrunken head was considered sacred. After decapitating his victim, the warrior would thread a vine through the mouth and esophagus before carrying the head slung over his shoulder to the ceremonial site, usually located on the banks of a stream. Here, he would meet with the master of ceremonies, the *wea*. After the skull was removed and discarded, the head was heated in almost-boiling water for 15 minutes, reducing it to around a third of its original size. The neck and eyes were then sewn shut, and the lips pinned together with sticks and secured with a vine. When the head was dry, it was filled with hot sand to cure it, a process that took 3-4 days. The final step was to add some hot stones to the inside of the head to shape the face.

Although the practice was banned in the 1930s, rumors abound throughout the Amazon region that criminal gangs do still dispatch the occasional unfortunate victim, whose shrunken head will fetch a high price on the U.S. black market. Women living alone with especially long and beautiful hair are considered especially at risk, and some even cut their hair short as a preventative measure.

It is thought that many so-called *"tsantsas"* in museums across the world are fakes, made from the heads of sloths and other animals. Telling the difference between a convincing fake and a real human shrunken head can be difficult, but the key is in the ears. Even the most skilled forgers struggled to replicate the complexity of a human ear in miniature.

Five real human *tsantsas* can be seen in the Museo Municipal in Guayaquil, three of which were missionaries who paid the price for attempting to convert Shuar people to Christianity. The other two victims were fellow Shuar, probably killed in conflicts over territory or women. The Museo Pumapungo in Cuenca has a fascinating and extensive section on Shuar shamanism, including a few *tsantsas*. In Quito, the Museo Abya-Yala is the only place in the city with a display of real shrunken human heads.

For more information about Shuar beliefs and customs, see the *Background* chapter.

a Virgin statue on top of the hill to the west of town. It's about an hour on foot, or $10 by taxi with a wait.

Recreation

Macas is a good starting point to explore the southern Oriente and to arrange stays in Shuar communities. Rafting and tubing are available, as are tours to Sangay National Park. Another popular trip is to various *cuevas de los tayos* (oilbird caves), the nesting places of strange nocturnal birds that use echolocation to find fruit by night. There are relatively few visitors in Macas, so solo travelers may end up paying extra for tours if there are no other groups to join up with.

Tsuirim (Don Bosco *y* Sucre, tel. 7/270-1681 or 99/737-2538, https://tsuirim.com) offers visits to Shuar communities (1 day $50

pp, 4 days/3 nights $240 pp), with activities such as waterfall visits, jungle hikes, cultural presentations, tobacco rituals, canoe rides, and handicrafts workshops. The most remote tour is to the community of Miazal (4 days/3 nights, $450), which is 30 minutes by plane or 12 hours by car and canoe, where there are thermal baths in primary rainforest. One- to five-day tours of Sangay National Park are available. One-day tours include rafting on the Río Upano ($30 pp) and a nearby oilbird cave ($75). A four-day/three-night tour ($450) to the oilbird cave at Coangos includes overnight stays with a Shuar community and camping underground. After traveling by canoe, visitors are lowered 75 meters (245 ft) on a cable into the caves, where ancient petroglyphs can be seen. Another agency is **Travesia Jungle** (24 de Mayo *y* Cuenca, tel. 7/252-6070 or

96/290-9718, www.travesiajungle.com), which offers a similar range of tours.

For dancing and live music, head to **La Candelaria** (Vía al Puyo, tel. 98/436-4319, Facebook @LaCandelariaMacas, 3:30pm-midnight Tues.-Thurs., 3:30pm-3am Fri.-Sat.).

Food

The specialty dish in Morona-Santiago is *ayampaco* (chopped meat, chicken, or fish with palm hearts and onion, grilled in a wrapped *bijao* leaf). The **Central Market** (10 de Agosto *y* Amazonas) is a good place to try these and other local dishes. One of the best restaurants serving local food is ★ **Mama Michi** (24 Mayo y Tarqui, tel. 9/3905-1840, 6am-2pm Mon.-Fri., $0.50-8), where specialties include *ayampaco,* barbecued meats, and *tamales de yucca.*

In the Parque Recreacional on Don Bosco is **La Semilla** (tel. 99/702-0055, https://semilladelparque.wordpress.com, 9am-8pm Sun.-Fri., 2pm-8pm Sat.), which serves a set lunch during the week for $2.75. On Sundays, there is a special lunch of local specialties such as *ayampacos* with lentil stew, rice, salad, a dessert, and a drink ($4). Snacks, coffee, juices, and craft beer are also available. Next to the park, **El Mirador** (La Randimpa *y* Riobamba, tel. 98/515-6283, $5) is very popular with locals, serving dishes such as burgers, wings, ribs, and breaded shrimp.

Chifa Pagoda China (Amazonas *y* Comín, tel. 7/270-0280, 11am-10:30pm daily, $4-6) is a decent Chinese restaurant. For Italian, try **Fiorentina** (Cuenca *y* Soasti, tel. 99/461- 6578, Facebook @fiorentinamacas). For Spanish, head to **Don Ramon Macabeo** (24 de Mayo *y* Cuenca, tel. 7/270-1334, Facebook @donramonmacabeo).

For a bohemian atmosphere and late-night drinks, head to ★ **Café Bar La Maravilla** (Soasti *y* Sucre, tel. 7/252-5533, Facebook @ LaMaravilla2017, 11am-midnight Mon.-Thurs., noon-2am Fri.-Sat., noon-10pm Sun., $3-6). The menu includes local and international dishes, including *tamales de yucca,* ribs, pastas, and salads. There's a cocktail menu and live music on weekends.

Accommodations

La Guayusa Hostal (Calle Riobamba *entre* 9 de Oct. *y* Don Bosco, tel. 7/270-4631 or 99/214-7280, http://josefc182.wixsite.com/hotellaguayusa, $16.50 s, $28 d, including breakfast) has rooms with cable TV, a garden, and parking. One of the best options in town is ★ **Hostal Casa Blanca** (Soasti *y* Sucre, tel. 7/270-0195, $20 s, $25 d, breakfast included), with clean, comfortable guest rooms and a small outdoor pool. **Hotel Angeles** (24 de Mayo *y* Gabino Rivadeneira, tel. 7/270-0337, Facebook @angeleshotelmacasms, $21 s, $34 d, including breakfast) has helpful service, cable TV, and parking. A couple of kilometers southeast of the center by the Río Upano, **Casa Upano Guesthouse & Bird Sanctuary** (Av. La Ciudad, Barrio La Barranca, tel. 7/252-5041, $50 s, $80 d, including breakfast) has balconies overlooking a garden full of birds. Service is friendly and the breakfast is good.

Speaking Achuar

- *wiña jai*—good morning/afternoon/evening
- *ja ai*—yes
- *atsa*—no
- *yaitiam*—What is your name?
- *wiyait jai...*—My name is...
- *wetai*—let's go
- *yumi*—water
- *yurumak*—food
- *maketai*—thank you
- *wea jai*—good-bye
- *arum*—see you later

Information and Services

The tourist office (Bolívar y Soasti, tel. 7/270-1480, ext. 2730) is in a small wooden cabin just west of the central park. **Banco Pichincha** (10 de Agosto y Soasti) has an ATM. There is a small **police station** in the bus terminal.

Getting There

The bus terminal is in the center of town. There are regular daytime departures to Puyo (3 hours, $4). There are daytime and overnight departures to Riobamba (5 hours, $8), Gualaquiza (5 hours, $6), Cuenca (7 hours, $10), Quito (8 hours, $12), and Guayaquil (10 hours, $12). A couple of overnight buses leave for Loja (10 hours, $12).

KAPAWI ECOLODGE

Set in pristine primary rainforest, **Kapawi Ecolodge** (tel. 98/058-9333, www.kapawi.com) is 160 kilometers (99 mi) from the closest city and a 10-day hike from the nearest road. It combines a deep cultural and natural experience in the Ecuadorian rainforest with the highest principles of community-based ecotourism, directly supporting the sustainable development of Achuar indigenous communities.

With a territory of 600,000 hectares (1.5 million acres) in the southeastern Amazon region, the Achuar have a population of approximately 7,000 individuals across 85 communities, living primarily through hunting, gathering, fishing, and small-scale subsistence farming. Once seminomadic, most Achuar now live in small villages, a result of contact with Christian missionaries in the 1960s. Their geographic isolation makes it difficult to pursue environmentally and culturally responsible economic activities, and the Kapawi Ecolodge was born to meet this need. A private indigenous partnership was created in 1993, and the lodge started operations in 1996. Since then, it has won several international ecotourism awards.

The lodge itself was built entirely with native materials and methods—incredibly, not a single metal nail was used in the construction—and energy is generated 100 percent from solar panels. Activities include visits to Achuar communities, wildlife spotting from a canoe, river kayaking with the chance to see dolphins, hiking on trails ranging from 30 minutes to 8 hours, and night walks.

Packages of three nights/four days ($1,060), four nights/five days ($1,290), and seven nights/eight days ($1,850) are available. Rates include accommodations, all meals, guides, and activities, but do not include chartered flights ($290 round-trip from Shell, near Puyo) and a fee to enter Achuar territory ($35).

North and Central Coasts and Lowlands

Ecuador's most northerly coastal province, Esmeraldas, lives up to its nickname, the "Green Province." Lush and tropical, with expanses of untamed mangroves and jungle-lined beaches dotted with palm trees, this is the heartland of the Afro-Ecuadorians, descended from escaped slaves who were shipwrecked in the 16th century. Here, the traditional musical instrument is the marimba, a West-African wooden xylophone played to a hypnotic beat, and much of the cuisine is coconut-based.

In contrast, the coast of the Manabí province is fairly arid, with the country's last remnants of tropical dry forest. Inland, as the altitude increases, the mesquite, cacti, and palo santo trees are replaced by cloud forests. Though rarely recognized as indigenous, some of the people

Highlights

Look for ★ to find recommended sights, activities, dining, and lodging.

★ **Chigüilpe:** This indigenous Tsáchila community near Santo Domingo holds ancestral healing ceremonies in a candlelit underground chamber and has a tree especially for hugging (page 296).

★ **Playa de Oro:** Here, a community-run ecotourism project protects 10,000 hectares (24,700 acres) of primary rainforest and is a release site for small wildcats rescued from traffickers (page 301).

★ **Playa Escondida:** Wake up to the sound of gentle waves lapping a pristine cove full of tide pools at this secluded ecolodge with 100 hectares (247 acres) of semitropical forest (page 302).

★ **Mompiche:** This crescent bay ending in a jungle-covered point has great surf during the day, bioluminescent plankton at night, and several deserted tropical beaches within easy walking distance (page 302).

★ **Machalilla National Park:** Protected coastal forest, archaeological relics, unrivaled whale-watching, the beautiful beach of Los Frailes, and the birdlife of Isla de la Plata are all reasons to visit (page 322).

PACIFIC OCEAN

Playa Escondida ★
Esmeraldas
Playa de Oro ★
★ Mompiche
Santo Domingo de los Colorados
Chigüilpe ★
Portoviejo
★ Machalilla National Park

0   50 mi
0   50 km

© MOON.COM

North and Central Coasts and Lowlands

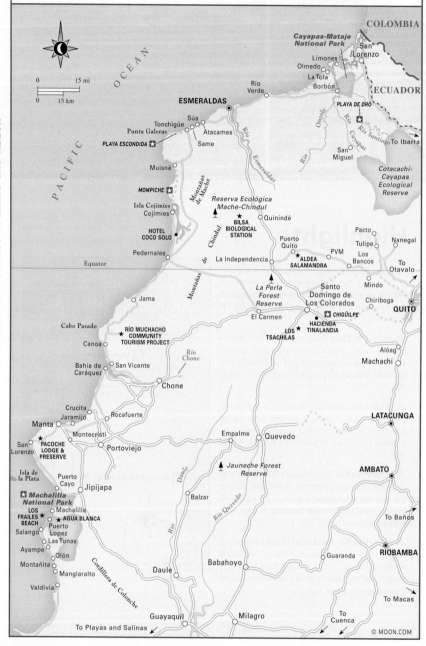

COLOMBIA

Cayapas-Mataje
National Park

San
Lorenzo

Limones

Olmedo

La Tola

ECUADOR

Borbón

PLAYA DE ORO

Río
Verde

To Ibarra

ESMERALDAS

Súa

San
Miguel

Tonchigüe

Atacames

Punta Galeras

Same

Cotacachi-
Cayapas
Ecological
Reserve

PLAYA ESCONDIDA

Muisné

MOMPICHE

Montañas de Mache

Reserva Ecológica
Mache-Chindul

Isla Cojimíes

Cojimíes

BILSA
BIOLOGICAL
STATION

Quinindé

Pacto

HOTEL
COCO SOLO

Puerto
Quito

Tulipe

Nanegal

PVM

Los
Bancos

Pedernales

Equator

La Independencia

ALDEA
SALAMANDRA

To
Otavalo

Jama

La Perla
Forest
Reserve

Santo
Domingo de
Los Colorados

Mindo

Chiriboga

QUITO

Cabo Pasado

RÍO MUCHACHO
COMMUNITY
TOURISM PROJECT

El Carmen

HACIENDA
TINALANDIA

CHIGÜILPE

Canoa

LOS
TSACHILAS

Alóag

Bahía de
Caráquez

San Vicente

Río
Chone

Machachi

Chone

Crucita

Jaramijó

Rocafuerte

LATACUNGA

Manta

Empalme

Quevedo

Montecristi

San
Lorenzo

PACOCHE
LODGE &
PRESERVE

Portoviejo

AMBATO

Isla de
la Plata

Puerto
Cayo

Jipijapa

Jauneche Forest
Reserve

Machalilla
National Park

Machalilla

Balzar

LOS
FRAILES
BEACH

AGUA BLANCA

Salango

Puerto
Lopez

To Baños

Las Tunas

Ayampe

Olón

Guaranda

RIOBAMBA

Montañita

Manglaralto

Babahoyo

Valdivia

Daule

Cordillera de Colonche

Milagro

To Macas

Guayaquil

To Cuenca

To Playas and Salinas

© MOON.COM

on this part of the coast are direct descendants of the Pueblo Manta Huancavilca, with 5,000 years of history and culture.

Those looking for beautiful beaches will find paradise in Mompiche, Playa Escondida, and Los Frailes. History and culture fans will love the archaeological site at Agua Blanca; the indigenous Tsáchila community near Santo Domingo; and Montecristi, where the "Panama" hat has been made since pre-Columbian times. Wildlife and nature lovers should head to Puerto López for unrivaled whale-watching between June and October, and the seabirds on Isla de la Plata year-round. Puerto López is also the access point for some wonderful hikes in the jungly interior, which can also be explored at Pacoche and San Sebastián. Surfers will get their fix in Ayampe, Las Tunas, San Lorenzo, Puerto Cayo, and Mompiche. Santa Marianita is the country's best kitesurfing spot, and Crucita is the place to be for paragliding.

PLANNING YOUR TIME

There are two high seasons on the central and northern coast: Christmas to Easter, when the weather is hotter with some heavy rains; and June-September, when it's cooler but still sunnier than the Montañita area, which is often gray during this period. This second high season coincides with both the vacation period for schools in the mountains and the peak period for whale-watching.

In this region, it is recommended to plan where you want to go and make specific stops, rather than aimlessly exploring. While the region has some true gems, other destinations are best avoided, either for simple lack of attractions or safety issues, or both.

A good strategy would be to traverse the region north to south, or vice versa, along the **Ruta del Spondylus,** with occasional hops inland. A whistle-stop tour of the coastal highlights might take in Playa Escondida,

Mompiche, San Lorenzo (in Manabí, not the town of the same name in Esmeraldas province), Machalilla National Park, Las Tunas, and/or Ayampe. It's worth traveling inland to hike in one of the cloud forests found at Pacoche or inland from Puerto López (e.g., San Sebastián, Río Blanco, and El Pital) and to visit the indigenous Tsáchila community. This itinerary could be completed in 7-10 days. Those wishing to visit the remote ecotourism project at Playa de Oro would need to allow a few extra days.

Some towns and cities are useful transport hubs, but lacking in visitor attractions, such as Jipijapa, Portoviejo, Pedernales, Chamanga, and Esmeraldas. Others, notably Santo Domingo and Manta, are jumping-off points for more interesting destinations nearby. South of the city of Esmeraldas, the towns of Atacames, Súa, and Same are popular with Quiteños escaping the city for the weekend, but sadly these former fishing villages have become concrete jungles with little authentically Ecuadorian about them.

Lone female travelers may find the central and northern coast more challenging than the south. From Manta and up, there is noticeably more unwelcome attention from men in the streets. While this rarely turns into anything more sinister, women, especially traveling alone for the first time, might consider giving certain destinations a miss, such as Atacames and Canoa. Robberies are also fairly common in these towns.

Sadly, the northern part of Esmeraldas province is one of Ecuador's most dangerous regions. The Colombian border zone has long been a hotbed for drug traffickers and FARC splinter groups. In 2018, there were a series of car bomb attacks and kidnaps. Travelers are advised to completely avoid the area north of the city of Esmeraldas.

Due to the wet climate, yellow fever is present (though rare) in Esmeraldas, and health professionals recommend vaccination.

Previous: fishing boats on a beach in Mompiche; the ceibo tree is part of indigenous Tsáchila ceremonies to get rid of bad energy; a chamber for ancestral healing ceremonies.

Quito to the Coast

West of Quito, the landscape changes dramatically, dropping from the Andes through cloud forests to agricultural plains, where huge banana and cacao plantations provide employment to many and riches to few. From an ecological point of view, the costs of Ecuador's agricultural boom have been high, with more than 95 percent of the lowland forests cleared in the 20th century to make way for farmland.

SANTO DOMINGO AND VICINITY

Ecuador's fourth-largest city, Santo Domingo (pop. 300,000), is far from being its fourth most appealing. Hot, noisy, and polluted, it's a useful transportation hub, but there is little of interest in the city itself. However, less than 20 minutes to the south is an indigenous village of Tsáchila people with a community tourism project offering a fascinating insight into their rich culture and ancient medicines. It was the Tsáchila that gave the town its full name, Santo Domingo de Los Colorados ("Santo Domingo of the Colored Ones") because of their use of red achiote hair paste.

★ Chigüilpe

Of the seven Tsáchila communities near Santo Domingo, Chigüilpe is the most organized for tourism. The **Centro Turístico Mushily** (Vía a Quevedo km 7, Comuna Chigüilpe, tel. 98/020-4868 or 99/387-5463, Facebook @Centro Turístico Mushily, 8am-6pm daily, $5) offers excellent guided tours of the village. The undisputed highlight is a visit to the ceremonial site, the domain of the *poné*, which is underground and entered via a tunnel. The Tsáchila believe that the earthen walls allow for greater connection with nature, and it's certainly true that the candlelit chamber possesses a remarkable energy, incredibly strong and, at the same time, deeply peaceful. The walls seem to have absorbed the healing power

of the countless ceremonies that have taken place, so that just sitting there for a few minutes can be a moving experience. While in the chamber, the guide demonstrates the instruments used during ceremonies, including the *palo de lluvia* (rain stick), a hollow branch filled with seeds, which sounds like falling rain.

Another highlight of the tour is the ceibo, a deciduous tree whose upper trunk is covered with spikes. The Tsáchila believe that this species is capable of absorbing bad energy, and that the tree is free of spikes on its lower trunk to allow for hugging. When it is saturated with bad energy absorbed from the tree huggers, the ceibo heals itself by shedding its leaves. The tour also includes a demonstration of marimba, a musical style that the Tsáchila share with Afro-Ecuadorian cultures. No reservation is required for the tour, which takes around an hour and a half. English-speaking tours can be arranged with prior notice.

There is lodging for 15 guests in traditional **cabins** ($10 pp). *Maito*, a traditional dish of fish wrapped in a leaf and cooked over a fire, is available with yucca ($5). Vegetarians can be catered with prior notice.

The Tsáchila also offer traditional **healing rituals** with the *poné*. A session costs $40 and includes a medicinal steam bath; a bath with flowers, orchids, and floral essences; a massage; an energy cleaning session with musical instruments; and a medicinal drink. Be clear about what you want when you book, otherwise you may end up with the "invigorating" treatment; i.e., a cold-water dousing at dawn with wild garlic water, like this author! Healing sessions should be booked at least one day in advance.

Ayahuasca ceremonies are held every Friday, Saturday, and Sunday at 7pm ($25, including breakfast). Participants should arrive at 4pm and expect to stay until the following afternoon at 4pm. Accommodations are either

Los Tsáchilas: The "Colored Ones" of Santo Domingo

In 1660, the indigenous Tsáchila people were living in San Miguel de los Bancos near Quito when they were struck with a deadly epidemic of smallpox and yellow fever. During a three-day ayahuasca ceremony, their shamans (known as *ponés*) received visions of their people recovering from the disease by painting themselves with black and red body paint. When they went searching for the paint substance in the forest, one of the Tsáchilas stepped on an achiote fruit and discovered the red paste inside. As per the vision, the people covered their skin with the substance and were indeed healed. To make sure all traces of the diseases were gone, the men cut their long hair and, in tribute to the medicine that had saved their lives, started to color it with achiote paste and style it in the shape of the red fruit. To the Tsáchilas, achiote represents life. They discovered the black body paint in another fruit, the *mali*, which they apply to their arms in stripes to honor the people who lost their lives in the smallpox outbreak and to protect against bad energy.

The Tsáchila rid themselves of bad energy by hugging the ceibo tree.

Following the epidemic, seven families moved from San Miguel de los Bancos to their current location, and the closest city was later named after them, Santo Domingo de Los Colorados (Santo Domingo of the Colored Ones). There are now seven Tsáchila communities living in the area and, in many ways, the people still maintain their ancestral traditions. Education is bilingual, in Spanish and their ancestral language, Tsafiki. The men wear a *mushily*, a cotton doughnut perched on top of their red hair, to symbolize the knowledge of the *poné*, and a black and white skirt in honor of the highly venomous echis snake. Women wear rainbow-colored skirts.

A variety of ancient medicinal techniques are still practiced by the Tsáchila *ponés*. The *poné* will make a diagnosis by passing a candle over the patient's body and watching the flame. Medicinal plants are then prescribed and gathered from the forest. Half the leaves are boiled to make an infusion, which the patient drinks. The rest of the leaves are placed in a hole in the ground along with fire-heated rocks, which are splashed with water to create a medicinal steam bath. The patient sits over the hole, covered in a blanket, to absorb the vapor. The *poné* also channels the energy of the rocks, trees, rivers, and waterfalls to heal patients. Ayahuasca ceremonies are held regularly, during which sacred songs are sung to cleanse a patient's energy, accompanied by traditional instruments (for more information on the ancient indigenous medicine ayahuasca, see the *Oriente and the Amazon Basin* chapter of this book).

In other ways, the Tsáchila lifestyle has changed in modern times. As Catholicism was adopted, the women started to wear sequined tops, instead of being naked from the waist up. Renowned for their weaving skills, the Tsáchila historically traded cotton textiles and garments, but the introduction of the modern clothing industry forced them to seek alternative sources of income. Though they still wear traditional woven skirts, most of the cotton bushes have been cleared to make way for yucca, plantain, sugarcane, pineapple, and citrus fruits. Agriculture is now their principal economic activity.

As the city has encroached, the rivers have become so polluted that it is no longer possible for the Tsáchila to drink, bathe, fish, or wash clothes in the water. This is especially tragic for a people whose primary food is fish, and who now have to walk for hours or travel by motorbike to fish in clean water. A people who find sacred energy in the rivers and waterfalls now have to use tanks of city water for bathing and drinking.

Despite these changes, a visit to the Tsáchila community is a fascinating and magical experience. Indeed, every visit helps the people keep their remaining traditions alive.

in the guest cabins or camping (bring your own tent). Ceremonies should be booked at least one day in advance. On the day of the ceremony, participants should eat no solid food, only vegetable soup, to prepare the body for the ayahuasca medicine.

To get to the Centro Turístico Mushily, take an Ejecutrans bus from outside the Santo Domingo bus terminal that goes to Vía a Quevedo ($0.30). Ask to be let out after 7 kilometers (4.3 mi) at Comuna Chigüilpe, from where a *mototaxi* can take you into the community ($1). A taxi from Santo Domingo costs $8-10. Arrange a pickup time with the driver.

Food and Accommodations

For those passing through Santo Domingo, there is a food court in the bus terminal offering basic local fare at economic prices. For a bit more variety, try the row of eateries across the road from the terminal, where there are a number of Chinese restaurants. **Restaurant Chef Sheratun** ($4-5) has a small selection of vegetarian pasta and rice dishes. If an overnight stay is necessary, **Santander Don Garcia** (Av. Esmeraldas *y* Av. de los Colonos, Redondel Sueno del Bolívar, tel. 99/834-9284 or 2/379-1059, $10 s/d) is a kilometer north of the terminal, tucked a block off the main road. It's great value, offering friendly service and clean rooms with private bathrooms, hot water, and TV. Most taxi drivers don't know it, but keep an eye out for the sign on the main road, or tell the driver "*ingresando por la ferretería Don Cabrera una cuadra margen derecho.*"

In the Santo Domingo city center, there are plenty of basic restaurants along 29 de Mayo serving set lunches and dinners. For something a bit better, head to **La Tonga** inside **Gran Hotel Santo Domingo** (Calle Río Toachi *y* Galápagos, tel. 2/276-7948, https://grandhotelsantodomingo.com, 7am-10:30pm daily, $8-18), which has vegetarian, international, and local specialties. The hotel also has a spa and offers decent accommodations ($80 s, $115 d, including breakfast). **Eco Spa** (Vía a Quito km 5.5, tel. 2/377-0438, Facebook @ eco.spa.5, $50 s/d) is 12 kilometers (7.5 mi) east of the city center ($5 taxi), but it's worth it for the excellent massages (1 hour for $20) and friendly service. There is a pool and it gets busy with local families on weekends, so go midweek for a peaceful experience.

Getting There and Around

Santo Domingo's **bus terminal** is 2 kilometers (1.2 mi) north of the center. To get to the center, buses run to and from the bus terminal regularly ($0.30), passing north on Tsáchilas and returning down 29 de Mayo. A taxi costs $1.50.

From Santo Domingo, there are buses every 15 minutes to Quito (3 hours, $4) and Esmeraldas (3.5 hours, $4); every half hour to Guayaquil (6 hours, $9); and more or less hourly to Ambato (4 hours, $5), Riobamba (4 hours, $6), and Manta (7 hours, $10). There are also a couple of buses daily to Machala (9 hours, $12) and Baños (5 hours, $8). Transportes Kennedy has several direct buses per day to Mindo (4 hours, $4), more convenient than going via Quito.

North Coast

Esmeraldas, the northernmost coastal province bordering with Colombia, was named by the Spanish after they arrived to find the local indigenous people bedecked in emeralds. These days, few jewels are found here, but the Green Province lives up to its name with expanses of untamed jungle and mangrove forest. Unlike Manabí, which is fairly dry, Esmeraldas is lush and tropical. Roads only arrived in the last few decades, and, cut off from the rest of the country, the region still retains its cultural identity. This is the heartland of the Afro-Ecuadorians, where the traditional musical instrument is the marimba, a wooden xylophone played to a hypnotic beat that just begs to be danced to. Much of the cuisine is coconut-based, such as *encocado* (fish or seafood in coconut sauce) and *cocadas* (sweet balls of coconut with *panela*, or raw sugar).

Sadly, the northern part of Esmeraldas province is one of Ecuador's most dangerous regions. The Colombian border zone has long been a hotbed drug traffickers and FARC splinter groups (often one and the same) and was the setting for two car bomb attacks against military targets in early 2018, leaving four soldiers dead and 39 people wounded. Travelers are advised to completely avoid the area north of the city of Esmeraldas. The situation in the province can change quickly and travelers are advised to monitor the U.K. Foreign Office website for the latest developments.

South of the city of Esmeraldas, the towns of **Atacames, Súa,** and **Same** are popular with Quiteños escaping the city for the weekend but unfortunately have become concrete jungles. Atacames is a loud, brash, fairly dangerous party town, whereas Súa and Same are lined with high-rise condos and hotels. It's not until you reach **Playa Escondida,** 65 kilometers (40 mi) south of Esmeraldas, that things start to get interesting. This secluded ecolodge protects 100 hectares (247 acres) of semitropical forest that borders a pristine private cove where sea turtles lay their eggs. At low tide, an extensive rocky reef is revealed, full of tide pools that provide warm sanctuary for octopus, shrimp, urchins, sea cucumbers, and lobsters. Sixty kilometers (37 mi) south of Playa Escondida is the small fishing village of **Mompiche,** which, unlike its northern neighbors, has preserved its rustic charm, with most hostels made from bamboo. Here, the perfect curve of the beach ends in a jungle-covered point, providing one of the best surf breaks in the country. The ocean, turquoise during the day, glows with bioluminescent plankton at night, and there are several secluded tropical beaches within easy walking distance. Another of the province's gems is the remote community of **Playa de Oro,** around 50 kilometers (31 mi) inland in 10,000 hectares (24,700 acres) of primary rainforest.

Due to the wet climate, yellow fever is present (though rare) in Esmeraldas, and health professionals recommend vaccination.

ESMERALDAS AND VICINITY

Esmeraldas started out as a fishing town before a short-lived rubber boom led to its expansion into a major port city. The oil boom in the late 1970s led to the opening of the country's largest oil refinery, the terminus for the 503-kilometer (313-mi) Trans-Ecuadorian Pipeline. These developments brought riches to few, and poverty levels and crime rates remain high. While it's safe enough to explore the city center during the day, there is little reason to make a stop here. The bus terminal south of town offers good nationwide connections, meaning that bypassing the city is easy. The airport has flights to Quito and Cali, Colombia.

If you do need to spend a day or night here, head to **Las Palmas,** the city's main beach,

Shipwrecked: the Origin of the Afro-Ecuadorians

How the Afro-Ecuadorians came to Esmeraldas is a fascinating story. Soon after the conquest, the Spanish began bringing slaves to South America. In 1553, a ship en route from Panama to Peru ran aground off the Ecuadorian coast at Portete near Mompiche. The 23 slaves on board rebelled and escaped into the forests. Despite clashes with local indigenous people, the region became a safe haven for escaped slaves due to its remote location, and the population grew rapidly. By the end of the 16th century, the community had declared themselves to be a republic of *zambos* (curly-haired people), and they lived autonomously for most of the colonial era, intermarrying with the local indigenous population. In the 19th century, the communities were finally permitted by the government to buy the land they had inhabited for so long.

Nowadays, Afro-Ecuadorians number over one million and make up approximately 8 percent of the population of Ecuador. The majority still live in Esmeraldas province, with other sizable populations in the Chota valley of Imbabura as well as in Quito and Guayaquil. While Afro-Ecuadorians fare better than indigenous people on nearly every socio-economic indicator, they still face massive inequality in terms of economic income and opportunity. Sadly, racism remains deeply ingrained in Ecuador, making it difficult for Afro-Ecuadorians to integrate with the larger society. This isolation is one reason for the maintenance of a strong association with their African heritage. This connection to their roots finds voice in the marimba, a wooden instrument resembling the xylophone that originated in West Africa, seen as an expression of freedom by many Afro-Ecuadorians. To this day, every year in May, Afro-Ecuadorians from around the province walk to Portete to commemorate the shipwreck that led to the founding of their current communities.

just north of the city center. It's been cleaned up and revamped in recent years, with an attractive *malecón,* a row of bars and restaurants, and a skate park. There are few tourists here, but plenty of local people enjoy the beach, and it's a popular spot for a few drinks on weekends. It's well-lit and safe. A taxi from the city center costs $1.50.

Food and Accommodations

In Las Palmas, there are plenty of restaurants along the new *malecón,* most offering seafood. A block inland, **Kafka Artisanal House** (Plaza Marimba, Barbizote *y* C Padiila, Facebook @kafkaartisanalhouse, 6pm-11pm Tues.-Sun., 6pm-11:40pm Fri.-Sat., $3-7) is owned by a friendly local woman. The menu includes sandwiches, crepes, salads, and empanadas, with vegetarian options. There is a good selection of teas, coffees, and juices.

Hotel Palm Beach (Av. del Pacífico *al final de la avenida,* Esmeraldas, tel. 98/066-0468 or 6/201-2447, www.palmbeachecuador. com, $45 s, $50 d, including breakfast), right on the *malecón,* has a restaurant and clean, modern rooms with cable TV.

Getting There and Around

There are several buses per hour from/to Atacames (45 minutes, $0.80). Direct buses from/to Mompiche are less frequent, with one bus every 2-3 hours (2.5 hours, $3). There are buses from/to Quito more or less hourly between 6:25am and 12:55am (6 hours, $10). There are regular buses throughout the day from/to Santo Domingo (3 hours, $4.50), Guayaquil (9 hours, $11), and Manta (10 hours, $12). Transportes Esmeraldas (http:// www.transesmeraldas.com) has overnight departures from/to Salinas (12 hours, $20), Cuenca (12 hours, $20), and Huaquillas (15 hours, $24). See the website for current schedules. Panamericana runs luxury buses from Esmeraldas to Quito and Guayaquil at 11pm.

The **Colonel Carlos Concha Torres Airport,** the airline **TAME** (tel. 1700/500-800, www.tame.com.ec) has a daily flight to/from Quito, with connecting flights to Guayaquil. There are also flights to/from Cali in Colombia. The airport is 15 kilometers (9.3 mi) northeast of the city. A taxi from the town center costs ($8).

★ PLAYA DE ORO

Playa de Oro is located 50 kilometers (31 mi) inland on 10,000 hectares (24,700 acres) of primary rainforest adjacent to the northern Sierra's Cotacachi-Cayapas Ecological Reserve. There is no "golden beach" at here; it was named for the abundance of gold found here soon after the Spanish conquest. Outside the Oriente, this is probably the farthest you can get from modern civilization in Ecuador, and a visit to this tight-knit community is an ideal way to combine a rainforest experience with the chance to support a unique ecotourism project. Playa de Oro is one of the few protected areas of the Chocó rainforest that used to stretch uninterrupted all the way to Panama, one of 34 biodiversity hot spots on the planet. It's also a release site for small wildcats rescued from illegal animal traffickers, in particular the small and beautiful margay.

The ancestors of the 50 families who live here were brought as slaves by the Spanish to pan for gold in the 16th century. One day, according to local legend, they decided to build a wooden cannon, blasted their master into oblivion, and lived for years as an autonomous community. The British went on to plunder most of the gold in the 19th and early 20th centuries. In 1992 the U.S. charity Earthways provided funding to build a lodge and reached an agreement with the villagers to establish an ecotourism project in return for designation of the territory as a reserve for wildcats, giving birth to **Playa de Oro Reserva de Tigrillos.** The community has successfully protected the rainforest from mining and timbering companies, and every visit directly supports these efforts. All tour fees go to support the **ecotourism** project, providing a sustainable source of income for the residents, who run every aspect of the project.

Guides take visitors hiking on several excellent **trails,** ranging 1-4 hours, into the forest past a succession of waterfalls. **Birdwatchers** can spot up to 330 species, and with luck, larger animals can also be seen, such as deer, sloths, anteaters, and monkeys. The six species of wildcats—jaguars, pumas, ocelots, margays, oncillas, and jaguarundis—are elusive, but their tracks are often seen, and you can sometimes hear the grunting of ocelots close to the lodge at night. To go farther into the rainforest, you can rent a boat with a guide. It's refreshing to take a dip in the river at the end of a long hike.

In the village of Playa de Oro, there are plenty of activities to get involved in with the locals—from fishing to gold panning (there are small deposits remaining). There are also wooden carvings and drums for sale, which help to supplement the local income.

The **lodge** ($75 pp per night) includes all meals, guides, and activities, except additional boat trips. There is also a $10 reserve entrance fee. There is no electricity, hot water, phones, or Internet—a small price to pay for a few days of complete isolation—but there are toilets and cold showers in the lodge. Visits are by prior reservation only, ideally two weeks in advance. Reservations are handled by Maquipucuna Reserve & Bear Lodge (tel. 99/421-8033, www.maquipucuna.org) near Mindo, partners of Playa de Oro and allies in their efforts to protect Ecuador's pristine ecosystems from mining.

The Maquipucuna Reserve coordinates all transport for visitors to Playa de Oro, which is accessed via canoe from Selva Alegre in Esmeraldas province. The return canoe trip from Selva Alegre costs $200 per group of up to 12. To get to Selva Alegre, Maquipucuna provides private transfers from Quito or Ibarra. From Quito, the journey takes six hours, and the round-trip transfer costs $530 for 1-2 people, $550 for 3-6 people, or $600 for 7-9 people. By flying from Quito to Esmeraldas, the journey can be cut down to four hours, but the flight is an additional cost. From Ibarra, the round-trip transfer costs $310 for 1-2 people, $390 for 3-6 people, or $450 for 7-9 people.

SOUTH OF ESMERALDAS
★ Playa Escondida

Playa Escondida (Vía Tonchigue-Punta Galera km 10, tel. 99/650-6812 or 6/302-7496, www.playaescondida.com.ec, $25 pp, camping $7 pp) is a truly special place. Since 1991, this secluded ecological getaway has been protecting 100 hectares (247 acres) of semi-tropical forest from hunters, logging, cattle, shrimp farming, and commercial tourism. Fourteen kilometers (8.7 mi) from the closest village, Playa Escondida lives up to its name (Hidden Beach), and the tranquility is wonderful. Rustic wooden guest rooms in the forest have spectacular views overlooking a pristine private cove, and at night the only sounds are gentle waves and the insect chorus. When the tide recedes, an extensive rocky reef is revealed, full of tide pools that provide warm sanctuary for octopus, shrimp, urchins, sea cucumbers, and lobsters. With its sheltered beach, rock pools, and calm waters, this is a wonderful place to bring children. Inland, the grounds include a bamboo grove, a river, and an estuary, great for birding. The area's biodiversity led to the creation of the Marine Reserve Galera-Cabo San Francisco, which spans the coastline from Mompiche to Atacames and includes Playa Escondida.

The **guest rooms** have comfortable beds with mosquito nets, and each room has a private (cold water) shower, basin, and unlimited drinking water. The composting toilets are shared. The **restaurant** serves a range of seafood, meat, and vegetarian dishes, with some of the ingredients coming from the on-site permaculture gardens. Water comes from the lodge's own well. Volunteers are accepted.

Playa Escondida is halfway between Tonchigüe and Punta Galera. To get there, take a bus from Esmeraldas or Atacames bound for Punta Galera or Estero de Platano and ask to be let off at Playa Escondida (45 minutes from Atacames, 90 minutes from Esmeraldas). These buses run approximately every hour. Alternatively, take a bus from Atacames, Esmeraldas, or Mompiche to Tonchigüe and then a taxi, local bus, or *camioneta*. A taxi from Atacames to Playa Escondida costs around $20.

★ Mompiche

The small fishing village of Mompiche is set on a crescent-shaped white sand beach that ends in a jungle-covered headland, where trees and vines overhang turquoise waters. Fishing boats cluster at the southern end of the beach, where fishers bring in the daily catch. Unlike the concrete jungles further north, Mompiche has retained its rustic charm, with most hostels built from wood and bamboo, topped with traditional woven *cade* roofs. Fortunately, the locals are determined to keep it that way. Many hostels are right on the oceanfront, with delicious sea breezes. The village might be small, but it has plenty of character and a laid-back atmosphere. With one of the best left-hand breaks in the country, Mompiche fills up with surfers during the season (December to April). By day, there is great snorkeling; by night, bioluminescent plankton. A number of secluded beaches are within easy walking distance. Guided hikes are available in the tropical jungle just inland, and a couple of hostels offer kayaking tours to the island of Portete. Mompiche itself is safe, but it's not advisable for women to walk alone on the beach at night. Note that there is no ATM in Mompiche; the closest are in Atacames and Pedernales.

RECREATION

For experienced **surfers,** Mompiche offers one of the longest left-hand point breaks in South America, while beginners can practice on the beach break. Local surfer **Morongo Garcia,** owner of the Punto de Encuentro hostel (tel. 97/927-5514) at the southern end of the *malecón,* offers classes for $25, including use of the board for two hours afterwards. He also rents boards. Be aware that out of season

1: Playa Negra; **2:** kayaking between the island of Portete and Mompiche; **3:** Playa de Oro is a release site for margays.

(May to November) there may not be waves, even for beginners.

Other ways to enjoy the ocean include **snorkeling** by day and **bioluminescent plankton** at night, best seen after 10pm. To see the plankton, cross the river at the southern end of the beach and continue walking approximately 200 meters (655 ft) past the protruding rocks. Walk into the water up to chest height and move around to see the glow. A couple of territorial dogs en route have bitten a few people at high tide when there is less beach, so walk close to the ocean and take a stick. As with any beach in Ecuador, it's not advisable to walk alone at night. Hidden House hostel organizes nightly visits to see the plankton.

Just past the fishing boats to the south of town is a shelter for stray dogs and cats, run by a local woman. **Rescate Animal Mompiche** (tel. 99/139-8467, Facebook @rescateanimalmompiche) offers horse-riding tours for $20, with income going toward the shelter. Donations of food are gratefully received, and volunteers are welcome.

The coast to the south of Mompiche offers some spectacular walks, possible on the beach in low tide or inland at high tide. At the very end of the beach, a path leads up into the jungle onto the headland. It's only a few minutes' walk to the tip of the headland, with beautiful views of the coves farther south. En route, the path passes through a very picturesque **cemetery** with views looking back at Mompiche. Keep following the coast south, either on the beach or the road, to reach the tiny secluded cove of **La Meseta,** 1.5 kilometers (0.9 mi) from Mompiche. Half a kilometer farther along the coast is **Playa Negra,** a stunning beach with soft black titanium sand. Local people recently won a battle to save the beach from industrial titanium extraction, and, happily, it is now protected.

Four kilometers (2.5 mi) south of Mompiche is a small dock where boats wait to ferry passengers across a narrow strip of water to the island of **Portete** ($1). The long, almost-deserted, coconut-fringed beach is where the ancestors of the province's Afro-Ecuadorian population escaped a 1553 shipwreck. The island is also the location of the luxury Royal Decameron hotel. Near the dock on Portete, locals sell beer and seafood. Their humble bamboo cabins used to be on the other side of the island until they were forced to move by Decameron, due to concerns that the presence of the cabins might ruin the view for the hotel guests. With the gigantic resort on one side of Portete and luxury lots for sale on the other, locals can only traverse the island via a narrow path lined with barbed wire. The same boats that ferry visitors to Portete also go to the nearby **Isla Jupiter,** which has even fewer people.

An alternative way to visit Portete is on a **kayak tour** with **Casa Banana** (tel. 99/823-6133, Facebook @casabanana.mompiche), an environmentally minded hostel on the *malecón* of Mompiche. They have their own kayaks and hire local guides.

The rainforest inland of Mompiche can be explored on a tour with local guide **Ramon Cotera** (WhatsApp 99/739-6244), who owns and protects 15 hectares (37 acres) of tropical forest. On his land are four freshwater springs, a small waterfall, a lake, and an organic cacao and fruit farm. Visitors might glimpse howler monkeys, wild boars, and a wide variety of birds. The tour is around 3.5 hours, made shorter or longer upon request. Activities include hiking, bathing in the waterfall, and making face-masks from therapeutic mud. The cost per person is $20 for 1-2 people or $15 for 3 or more, including transport from Mompiche (15 minutes by truck) and fruit from the farm. Tours are in Spanish only and should be booked via WhatsApp two days in advance. Ramon can also be contacted via Casa Banana (tel. 99/823-6133, Facebook @casabanana.mompiche) on the *malecón*. Wear mosquito repellent, especially between January and May. Ramon hopes to offer camping in the future. His love and gratitude for nature are a joy to witness.

FOOD

Mompiche has some good seafood shacks offering ceviche, *encocado* (fish or seafood in coconut sauce), and fried fish. One of the most well established is **La Langosta** (tel. 9/8165-4068, Facebook @RestaurantLangosta, 7am-7pm daily, $5-10), one block south of the center on the main street. At the crossroads of the main street and the *malecón*, **El Económico** ($3-10) is owned by local fishers who serve their own fresh catch, as is **Atardacer de Mompiche** ($5-10), a block inland.

On the main street, ★ **La Chillangua** (tel. 98/148-6131, Facebook @La Chillangua Restaurant, 7am-8pm daily) is a family business owned by a friendly local woman. The menu includes a variety of breakfasts and a set lunch with a vegetarian option ($3.50). Specialties are *encocado* and *cazuela de mariscos* (seafood stew). Another good option for vegetarians is the nightly veggie dinner at **Hidden House** hostel (Av. Fosforera, tel. 97/928-0589, www.hiddenhousehostel.com, $4, sign up before 6pm, non-guests welcome).

Argentine-owned ★ **La Chocolata** (tel. 6/244-8077, Facebook @lachocolata-mompiche, 9:30am-2:30pm and 6pm-10:30pm Wed.-Mon., $1-7) offers healthy freshly made breakfasts, crepes, desserts, salads, homemade pasta, and sandwiches with lots of veggie options, including a veggie burger. The smoothie bowl breakfast is absolutely wonderful. Wine and craft beer are available.

Premadham Permacultura (tel. 95/876-6250, Facebook @PremadhamPermacultura, $5-9), right on the beach just past the fishing boats, is an organic vegetarian restaurant offering sandwiches, pizzas, salads, ravioli, lasagna, and desserts. It's the only restaurant in the province with a certificate of conscious consumption (see www.consumoconsiente.info). Among other requirements, it does not use any meat or egg derivatives, GMOs, industrial products, white sugar, or disposable plastic. On sale are a variety of organic, fair trade products, such as honey, powdered *guayusa* tea, and coffee from the Amazon.

ACCOMMODATIONS

Most hostels are rustic, with guest rooms made from bamboo and wood with woven *cade* roofs. Many don't have hot water, so check in advance if this is important to you. There are mosquitoes, so make sure your bed has a fan and/or a mosquito net. Most places don't include breakfast.

At the southern end of the *malecón*, ★ **Punto de Encuentro** (tel. 97/927-5514, Facebook @Punto de Encuentro Morongo Garcia, $35-40 s/d) is one of very few locally owned hostels, built and run by friendly surfer Morongo Garcia. The second-floor common area has a wonderful sea breeze, with seats and hammocks offering incredible views of the headland and the hive of activity around the fishing boats. There is free water, tea, and coffee in the communal kitchen. Downstairs is a pizza restaurant. Guest rooms have shared or private bathrooms. There are two houses for rent, each sleeping 8-9 people ($110/night for the house). Morongo also manages ★ **La Jungla** (tel. 97/927-5514, www.lajunglabungalows.com, $20 s, $30 d), just inland from Punto de Encuentro. Cabins for 1-4 people are set in peaceful tropical gardens with private, outdoor showers filled with plants.

Just behind La Jungla is another locally owned place, **Casa Coral** (tel. 99/911-1806, Facebook @casacoralmompiche, $15 pp). There are four light, airy rooms with shared or private bathrooms and a communal kitchen. The local owner and his Canadian wife have a farm and provide free fruit to guests. They also offer horseback riding tours.

Opened in 2018, English/Ecuadorian-owned ★ **Hidden House** (Av. Fosforera, tel. 97/928-0589, www.hiddenhousehostel.com, $7 dorm, $10-15 pp, including breakfast) is a sister hostel to Hidden House Montañita. Rooms have private or shared bathrooms with hot water and fans. There is a nightly vegetarian dinner ($4). Like its sister hotel, it's great value, friendly, and an excellent spot to meet fellow travelers. There is a bar and there are nightly group walks to see the bioluminescent plankton. Other local tours are also available.

★ **Premadham Permacultura** (tel. 95/876-6250, Facebook @ PremadhamPermacultura, $12 pp) is an idyllic spot right on the beach just past the fishing boats. Two cabañas have mosquito nets, fans, and incense! The shared shower has hot water, and there is a shared compost toilet. The owners are in the process of restoring the mangrove forest that backs onto the property. There are permaculture gardens and a vegetarian restaurant on-site. Camping is available for $5 per tent (bring your own tent). Permaculture and bioconstruction workshops are available.

In the middle of the *malecón*, **Casa Banana** (tel. 99/823-6133, Facebook @casabanana.mompiche, $25 s, $30 d) is owned by an environmentally minded Brazilian and managed by local guide Ramon Cotera, who offers jungle tours. Large bamboo cabins have oceanfront balconies and there is a shared kitchen. The hostel sells natural soap, handmade paper, and organic cacao. Visits to an organic farm and kayaking tours to the island of Portete are available. The owner has established Fundación Aullador (Howler Monkey Foundation), which aims to conserve the remaining local Chocó rainforest by linking sustainable economic activities (e.g., organic cacao production) with conservation, and another foundation that provides subsidized sterilization programs for local dogs and cats.

Half a block inland from the north end of the *malecón*, **La Caleta** (tel. 98/015-6165, Facebook @La Caleta Mompiche, $20 s, $25 d, including breakfast) is Portuguese owned, but run by a friendly local. Two guest cabins share a bathroom. The restaurant (6pm-10pm) serves homemade ravioli and desserts. The small organic garden grows herbs, fruit, and vegetables.

One block in from the *malecón*, **La Facha** (tel. 99/804-4604 or 6/244-8024, www. lafachahostel.com, $15 dorm, $20-35 s, $30-40 d, including breakfast) has decent guest rooms with shared or private bathrooms and hot water. The friendly Argentinian owner, a surfer and chef, is in the process of implementing solar panels and biodegradable cleaning products. The restaurant serves a good variety of local and international dishes, including veggie options. Organic coffee from the province of Carchi is on sale. Surf classes and boat tours are available.

GETTING THERE

There are a few direct buses daily from Esmeraldas (3 hours, $4), with the last departure at 4pm. Unlike the other buses, which drop passengers on the main road 7 kilometers (4.3 mi) from Mompiche, these direct buses go into Mompiche itself. Alternatively, take a bus headed to Muisne and change at El Salto, and then take a taxi for the last 45 minutes, or take any bus heading south and ask to be dropped off at the entrance to Mompiche. From there, unofficial taxis wait (or will soon appear) to ferry passengers into the village ($1). From Canoa, take a bus to Pedernales (2 hours, $3.50), another to Chamanga (1 hour, $2), and then a bus heading north to Esmeraldas, and ask to be dropped off at the entrance to Mompiche (40 minutes, $1). From Montañita, take a bus to Puerto López (75 minutes), then to Portoviejo (2 hours), then to Pedernales (5 hours), then to Chamanga (1 hour), and finally to Mompiche (40 minutes).

If arriving after 6pm, it is safer to get dropped off in the neighboring town of Tres Vías rather than at the entrance to Mompiche, as there is little transport to the village after this hour. Taxis and tuk-tuks are easy to hire in Tres Vías, just 1 kilometers (0.6 mi) and 5 minutes away.

Central Coast

Ecuador's largest coastal province, Manabí, borders Esmeraldas less than an hour south of Mompiche. Those traveling by bus will probably pass through the transport hubs of Chamanga and Pedernales en route to more interesting destinations farther south.

A couple of hours from the border near **Canoa,** it's possible to stay with families at **Río Muchacho,** a small agricultural community offering walks and horseback rides to bathe in a waterfall, and maybe see howler monkeys.

Another two hours south, the port city of **Manta** is the jumping off point for **Santa Marianita,** a mecca for kitesurfers, and **Montecristi,** the birthplace of the Panama hat. Also within easy reach of Manta is the **Pacoche Marine & Coastal Wildlife Reserve,** which protects the beautiful beach at **San Lorenzo,** and the semi-dry tropical forest at **Pacoche.**

Puerto López, two hours farther south again, is the country's principal whale-watching destination between June and October. It's also the best base from which to explore **Machalilla National Park,** including **Isla de la Plata,** home to many Galápagos species; the pristine beach of **Los Frailes;** and the ancestral community of **Agua Blanca.**

The southernmost villages in Manabí, **Ayampe** and **Las Tunas,** both have good waves for surfing and offer a more peaceful alternative to Montañita, their rowdier neighbor on the southern coast. Las Tunas is an ecologically minded community that has been recognized by the United Nations for its conservation work, including efforts to protect the world's second smallest hummingbird, the critically endangered *estrellita Esmeraldeña,* or Esmeraldas woodstar.

CANOA

Canoa is the kind of destination that puts a travel writer in a dilemma. While it has consistent waves for surfing and a long stretch of beach overlooked by cliffs and caves to the north, there is no escaping the fact that this is a town with serious social challenges. In the 2016 earthquake, 118 people lost their lives, an enormous number for such a small town, and 50-60 percent of the buildings were leveled, leading to a traumatized population and a decimated tourist industry. While the buildings are being reconstructed and visitors are starting to come back, the holes in people's lives will take longer to heal. Sadly, robberies and drug use have increased since the earthquake, and assaults on female travelers are not unheard of. Having said that, tourism is the town's best hope of getting back on track and, rather than advising travelers to simply avoid Canoa, instead this book aims to inform visitors about the potential risks and guide them toward those people and projects that are working to build a hopeful future for the town.

The center of town, *malecón,* and beach are reasonably safe during the day. Visitors should completely avoid the inland area surrounding the Calle de Alegria, which runs between the Hotel Mediterraneo on the main road and Posada Olmito on the *malecón.* This is the domain of local drug addicts, and robberies are common. At sunset, it is advisable to stick to the northern part of the *malecón* and beach, as robberies have been reported farther south. A good guideline is to stay north of the big Canoa sign. It is not advisable to go to the beach at night. Canoa is much less safe than Ecuador's other famous surf/party town, Montañita. If you're a lone female traveler looking for a safe place to party, you might be better off heading there.

Entertainment and Events

All the bars mentioned are on the *malecón.* There are three spots for late night dancing—**Barquito, Ventarron,** and **Flavio**

The 2016 Earthquake

On Saturday April 16, 2016, at 6:58pm, an earthquake of 7.8 magnitude struck Ecuador. It was the country's largest recorded earthquake since 1979, and tremors were felt as far as Colombia and Peru. The epicenter was the town of Pedernales in the province of Manabí. At least 676 people were killed and 16,600 people injured, with 75 percent of the casualties in Manta, Pedernales, and Portoviejo. Around 7,000 buildings were destroyed, including all of Manta's central commercial shopping district, Tarqui. Widespread damage was caused across Manabí province, where structures hundreds of kilometers from the epicenter collapsed. Following the earthquake, more than 26,000 people were living in shelters. Hundreds of strong aftershocks caused widespread panic in the following days and weeks.

While the disaster prompted a huge outpouring of donations from the Ecuadorian public, recovery has been marred by widespread corruption and large-scale theft by state entities and NGOs. While shining new malls and high-rises have sprung up in Manta, there are still families living in tents outside Canoa, and many in the town still lack basic services such as running water.

Bamboo houses were built for some of the earthquake victims by NGOs; however, most of the organizations that flooded into the area in the days and weeks following the disaster have now left, leaving the remaining displaced people to fend for themselves. People who fled into the countryside immediately after the earthquake have formed small communities, many of them still living in makeshift tents. Counseling and mental health care is nonexistent for these traumatized and grieving people, many of whom lost family members as well as their homes.

One group that is still doing excellent work in the area is the **Bomberos Unidos Sin Fronteras** (BUSF, United Firefighters Without Borders, https://busf.org). Since the earthquake they have been using donations and volunteers to build houses for those most in need. One recipient of a new home was a young woman whose 6-year-old son was killed in her arms by a falling beam when her house collapsed. She was sleeping under a tarpaulin, but now she and her husband are living in a simple bamboo cabin and expecting a baby. The firefighters also built a home for an elderly woman with four deaf-mute sons who had been widowed just before the disaster. At the time of writing, they had just built 10 homes for a group of displaced people outside Canoa. To make a donation or volunteer for BUSF, contact Jesus Luch Ferrer, General Director (jesus@busf.org).

Light—all open until midnight Monday-Thursday and until 2am Friday-Saturday. **Beach Boys** (6pm-2am Mon.-Sat.) sometimes has live music. **Suki Bar** caters to a slightly older crowd

Recreation

Canoa has 18 kilometers (11 mi) of beach with consistently good waves for surfers of all levels. With no rocks or rip tides, it's a great spot for beginners. The peak surf season is from December to April, though there are rideable waves year-round. The best place for surf classes or board rental is **Happy Happy Kiki Surf** (tel. 98/418-1341, Facebook @kikisurf-school), located in the bamboo structure on the beach in front of the Canoa sign. Owned by friendly local surfer Kiki, the school is open

daily and offers classes ($25 including use of the board all day) and board rental ($3/hour or $10-15 all day). Kiki, who was taught to surf by his grandmother at the age of two on a homemade wooden board, serves as Canoa's semi-official lifeguard and has saved a number of lives. He also mentors local youngsters, encouraging them to get involved in surfing rather than less healthy extracurricular activities.

One block in from the northern end of the *malecón*, **VerdeTur** (tel. 98/471-0814, http://verdetur.com) is owned by a friendly young local, Oscar Ortiz. A variety of day tours are available, including a community-operated boat trip through the mangroves of Isla Corazón ($25 pp/2 people or $20 pp/3 people); kayaking tours to three islands, including Isla

Corazón ($40); paragliding ($45); horseback riding ($20); hiking in the tropical dry forest at Cerro Seco ($25 pp/2 people or $20 pp/3 people); and a tour of a cacao farm, fruit farm, and artisanal beer company in Río Canoa ($25 pp). Oscar also runs cultural nights around a bonfire, where visitors learn about the traditional way for coastal men to woo women, with verses.

Shopping

Angel Montaño is an artisan with a stall on the *malecón* opposite the Costa Azul restaurant. He makes jewelry and souvenirs, including models of traditional fishing boats, from local materials, including carved wood, *tagua* nut, and bone.

Food

There are numerous seafood shacks on the *malecón*. Owned by a friendly local, **Charly Bar** (tel. 99/879-0493, Facebook @Charly Bar, 8am-7pm Thurs.-Sun.) is one of the best. Charly also offers breakfasts, crepes, and sandwiches, with vegetarian options. At the north end of the *malecón*, **Hotel Bambú** (tel. 5/258-8017 or 9/926-3365, http://hotelbambuecuador.com, 7:30am-10pm daily) has a wide-ranging menu, including vegetarian options, and good service. A vegetarian dinner is available most nights at **Coco Loco** (tel. 95/910-4821, www.hostelcocoloco.com), a hostel on the *malecón*, for guests and nonguests alike ($3.50-4.50).

Accommodations

Canadian-owned ★ **Coco Loco** (tel. 95/910-4821, www.hostelcocoloco.com, $10 dorm, $12-16 s, $22-26 d) is an attractive, well-kept place with friendly staff. Rooms are airy and clean with private or shared bathrooms. Amenities include a bar, fire pit, communal kitchen, and balcony with hammocks overlooking the ocean. Dorm rooms have decent beds and individual lockers big enough for backpacks. The hostel employs local people and is known for treating them fairly.

There is a full breakfast menu and a vegetarian dinner is available most nights for guests and nonguests ($3.50-4.50). **Hotel Canoa's Wonderland** (tel. 5/258-8163, www.hotelcanoaswonderland.com.ec, $35 s, $65 d, including breakfast) has clean, modern, comfortable guest rooms with hot water, balcony, and air-conditioning. Rooms have big windows and flank the central path, so the second floor offers greater privacy. There is a pool, children's play area, and restaurant. The area inland from Coco Loco and Wonderland is not safe, even during the day, so make sure to come and go via the *malecón* and take care at night. Consider arriving by taxi after dark.

The last hotel at the north end of the *malecón* (quieter and safer than the southern end) is Dutch-owned **Hotel Bambú** (tel. 5/258-8017 or 9/926-3365, www.hotelbambuecuador.com, $10 dorm, $10 glamping, $20 s, $40 d), which offers a range of accommodations in attractive gardens with colorful common areas. The glamping is great value, with a comfortable bed, bedside table, and safe inside each spacious tent. There is a decent restaurant and bar, open 7:30am-10pm daily. Yoga classes are available. The hotel offers free cocktails in exchange for cleaning up the beach. However, it appears that part of the hostel was built on a supposedly protected mangrove forest.

Ten minutes south of Canoa on the Ruta del Spondylus, ★ **Casa Ucrania** (tel. 99/581-3480, http://lacasaucraniana.com, $50 s/d), is a good option for those wanting to stay outside Canoa. Owned by a friendly Ukrainian family, the hotel is set in tropical gardens right on the beach in a peaceful location. Guest rooms are clean and comfortable. The open-air restaurant serves a mix of Ukrainian and local cuisine. The owner made great efforts to support the people displaced from their homes following the 2016 earthquake.

Information and Services

There is no ATM in Canoa. The closest is in the shopping mall in Bahía de Caráquez.

Getting There

Buses between San Vicente (30 minutes, $0.65) and Pedernales (2 hours, $3.50) pass through Canoa every half hour. There are also buses every half hour to Bahía de Caráquez (30 minutes, $0.65), over the bridge on the other side of the bay.

Reina del Camino (https://reinadelcamino.ec) operates a direct overnight service between Quito's Quitumbe terminal and Canoa (8 hours, $11), leaving Quito at 11pm and arriving in Canoa at 7:45am. From Canoa, it leaves at 9:45pm and arrives in Quito at 5am. There are buses every couple of hours between Quito and Bahía de Caráquez, and Quito and San Vicente (both $8 hours, $9). There are more or less hourly buses between Guayaquil and San Vicente, and Guayaquil and Bahía de Caráquez (both 6 hours, $8). Then just hop on the local bus to Canoa (30 mins, $0.65), or take a taxi (20 minutes, $6)

RÍO MUCHACHO

Fourteen kilometers (8.7 mi) northeast of Canoa, 80 families live by the idyllic Muchacho River in simple cabins with gardens full of flowers. To supplement the humble income they earn from growing maize, plantain, cacao, peanuts, and beans, they have created a **community tourism project.** Walks and **horseback rides** ($10) are available in the nearby forest, where it's possible to see and photograph howler monkeys and bathe in a waterfall.

Guests are given the opportunity to share in the daily life of the community, with activities such as fishing for river shrimp and making chocolate, cheese, butter, and *pan de yucca* (manioc bread). It's possible to visit for a day trip or to stay in spacious tents erected inside bamboo **shelters** ($10 pp). **Meals** are available for $3, with vegetarian options available by prior request. Reservations should be made at least a week in advance with **René Herrera Benavides** (tel. 5/302-0415 or 99/151-3906), who can also arrange transport from Canoa ($5 each way per group of up to four).

There is a well-known organic farm in the area, but it's not recommended to visit, as there is much speculation over its treatment of employees and use of donated items following the 2016 earthquake. Those looking to make ethical travel choices that benefit local people are encouraged to visit the Río Muchacho community tourism project.

Take a walk or horseback ride into the forest with a community tourism project.

MANTA AND VICINITY

A major port since pre-Inca times, **Manta** was officially established by the Spanish in 1565 as a supply point between Panama and Peru. Today, it's second only to Guayaquil in the volume of imports and exports and has become the center of the Ecuadorian tuna industry. The arrival of a U.S. military base in 1999 brought an economic boom, and the city developed quickly, with a string of high-rise hotels and shopping malls. The military base was closed by President Rafael Correa in 2009.

Manta is a useful transport hub, with an airport and regular bus services to most major cities around the country, but that's one of the few reasons for tourists to visit Manabí's biggest city. The seafood is good, though it's not the most picturesque place to enjoy it. Those seeking to extend their tourist visas might consider visiting the Ministerio de Relaciones Exteriores just inland from Playa Murcielago, which is a quieter alternative to the offices in Quito and Guayaquil.

Manta was hit hard by the 2016 earthquake but has recovered well. The neighborhood of Tarqui was completely flattened and won't be rebuilt in its previous location due to the high water table. The barrios of Jocay and Cuba have taken Tarqui's place as Manta's most dangerous and should be avoided, even during the daytime. The city center is safe enough, though there is some prostitution along the Murcielago *malecón*. Female travelers may find themselves subjected to unwelcome catcalls and comments from groups of men near the port.

The good news is that Manta is the jumping-off point for some much more appealing destinations, all easily accessed in 30-40 minutes, including the beaches of Santa Marianita and San Lorenzo; the protected semi-dry tropical forest at Pacoche; and Montecristi, birthplace of the famously misnamed woven hat.

Recreation

Manta's main beach, **Playa Murcielago** (Bat Beach), is a fairly unappealing stretch of sand encroached by the city. The *malecón* is lined with seafood restaurants and there are shaded deck chairs for rent. Across from the Oro Verde Hotel (*malecón y* Calle 23) is the workshop of surfboard shaper René Burgos (reneburgos_surf@hotmail.com), who makes great quality custom boards for economical prices ($350-400).

On the other side of the port to the east is **Playa Tarqui.** As the location of the fish market, it's not very clean or scenic, but it's interesting to watch hand-built wooden boats being assembled on the beach just east of the market.

The **Museo Centro Cultural** (*malecón*, tel. 5/262-6998, 9am-5pm Tues.-Fri., 10am-5pm Sat.-Sun.) has exhibits on modern art and the Manteño culture that existed along the coast from AD 800 to 1500.

Entertainment and Events

For nightlife, head to **Avenida Flavio Reyes,** where there are plenty of bars and discos. The current "in" place to be is **Piedra Larga,** 10 kilometers (6.2 mi) west of the city, where there are restaurants, cafés, and bars.

Food

A kilometer in from the *malecón*, the **Mercado Central** (8am-7pm daily) is a good place for local dishes at low prices ($2-3), e.g., *caldo de pato* and *caldo de gallo* (duck soup and chicken soup). **Rincon Criollo** (Av. Flavio Reyes *y* Calle 20, tel. 05/262-3183, noon-6pm daily, $6-10) is another great option for local fare, and not just seafood. The menu includes steak, chicken, and some vegetarian soups.

For fresh seafood, head to **Playita Mia,** part of Tarqui Beach, where the fishers bring in their catch every morning at 6am. Of the string of restaurants there, one of the best is **Acuario** (tel. 99/134-3022, Facebook @ MantaAcuario, 8:30am-9:30pm daily, $4-15). Another good seafood place is **Cevichería Juventud Italiana** (Av. 24 *y* Calle 9, Facebook @Cevicheria Juventud Italiana, 8:15am-2:30pm Wed.-Sun., $4-6), named after a local football club, which serves great

Manta

PACIFIC OCEAN

HOSPITAL ■

AVENIDA CIRCUNVALACIÓN

To
Hostal El Náufrago

CALLE 18

CALLE 16

CALLE 16A

AVENIDA 35

FINISTERRE ▲

AVENIDA CIRCUNVALACIÓN

CALLE 26

FLAVIO REYES

HOSTAL
CASA LATINA ●

Cementerio
General

AVENIDA 12 A (M4)

M3

M2

CALLE M1

AVENIDA 35

CALLE 17

GOVINDA'S ▼

CALLE 18

AVENIDA 28

CALLE 17

AVENIDA
FLAVIO REYES

AVENIDA FLAVIO REYES

CALLE 22

HOSTAL
MANAKIN ●

RINCÓN
CRIOLLO ▼

Mal del
Pacífico

ORO
VERDE ●

POLICE ■

Malecón
Escénico

Playa Murciélago

AVENIDA 25

AVENIDA 24

AVENIDA 23

AVENIDA 22

CALLE 20

CALLE 19

HOTEL
BALANDRA ●

AVENIDA CIRCUNVALACIÓN

★ MUSEO
CENTRO CULTURAL

TOURIST OFFICE ■

CALLE 12

HOTEL
PACÍFICO ●

CALLE 12

CALLE 11

CALLE 10

CALLE 9

CALLE 8

CEVICHERÍA
JUVENTUD ITALIANA ▼

AVENIDA 18

AVENIDA 17

AVENIDA 16

CALLE 17

CALLE 15

AVENIDA 13

CALLE 14

CALLE 13

★ MERCADO
CENTRAL

CALLE 11

AVENIDA MALECÓN

CALLE 9

BANCO
PICHINCHA ATM ●

TO
TARQUI, PLAYITA MÍA,
BUS TERMINAL, AIRPORT,
AND HOSTAL EL CASTILLO (ARROW)

Bahía
Manta

Bahía
Manta

0   250 yds
0   250 m

© MOON.COM

ceviche and *encebollado* (a fish soup made with cassava root, tomatoes, onions, and cilantro).

For something upmarket, try **Finisterre** (Calle 27 *y* Av. 35, tel. 5/262-1884, www.finisterre-manta.com, noon-4pm and 6:30pm-midnight Mon.-Fri, 6:30pm-12:30pm Sat., $9-24), which has a wide-ranging menu, including vegetarian options.

For vegetarian lunches, head to ★ **Govinda's** (Calle 17 *entre* Av. 27 *y* Av. 28, *diagonal a* Parque Santa Monica, tel. 98/117-2017, Facebook @govindasmanta, noon-3pm Mon.-Fri., noon-2pm Sat., $3.50) The daily set menu includes a soup, main course with side salad and brown rice, and a juice or tea.

Accommodations

There aren't many decent budget options in Manta. One of the few places with dorms is **Hostal El Castillo** (Vía Puerto Aeropuerto, Barrio La Florita, tel. 98/336-5950, Facebook @Hostal El Castillo Manta, $8 dorm, $30 s/d) near the airport. **Hotel Pacífico Central** (Av. 22 *y* Calle 12, tel. 99/952-0844, $15 s, $27 d) is 3 kilometers (1.9 mi) inland from the beach. **El Naufrago** (Av. Circunvalación, behind the Rodríguez Zambrano Hospital, tel. 99/500-0437, Facebook @El Naufrago Hostal, $25 s, $35 d) is consistently well-reviewed, though there is no hot water. Centrally located ★ **Hostal Casa Latina** (Calle 26 *y* Av. Flavio Reyes, tel. 5/262 9846 or 99/682-7180, www.hostalcasalatina.amawebs.com, $27 s, $44 d) has clean, airy rooms with hot water, private bathrooms, air-conditioning, and cable TV. It gets busy, so book in advance.

The following places are all near Playa Murcielago. ★ **Hostal Manakin** (Calle 20 *y* Av. 12, tel. 5/262-0413, Facebook @ Hostal Manakin, $40 s, $68 d, including breakfast) has 10 comfortable, sound-proofed guest rooms, retaining an intimate atmosphere missing in many other hotels in Manta. Book ahead, as it gets busy. For even more comfort, the next step up is the **Hotel Balandra** (Av. 7 *y* Calle 20, tel. 5/262-0545, www.balandrahotel.com, $120-180 s/d, including breakfast), which has cabins set in tropical gardens and rooms with sea views. Amenities include a good restaurant, gym, sauna, and pool. The swankiest place in town is the high-rise **Oro Verde** (*malecón y* Calle 23, tel. 5/262-9200, www.oroverdemanta.com, $159 s, $170 d), which has all the amenities you might expect from a luxury hotel.

Information and Services

There is a **tourist information office** on the Playa Murcielago *malecón,* and **Banco Pichincha** has an ATM a couple of blocks inland (Av. 2 *entre* Calles 11 *y* 12). There are **police stations** on Playa Murcielago (Calle 1, tel. 5/262-3076) and Playa Tarqui (Villa Puerto Aeropuerto *y* Calle 105, tel. 5/238-0755). The public hospital, **Rodríguez Zambrano** (Calle 12 *y* Av. 38, tel. 5/261-1849, www.hrz.gob.ec) is a couple kilometers inland.

Getting There and Around

The bus terminal is northeast of the city center, near the airport. Provincial buses leave every few minutes to Montecristi (6am-7:45pm, $0.50-1), Jipijapa (6am-7:45pm, $1.65), and Portoviejo (6am-9pm, $3.25). There are also departures to Bahía (11 departures daily 6am-6pm, 3 hours, $3) and Canoa (Coop Turístico Manabí, noon, $4.50).

The Co-op Manglaralto bus goes to Santa Elena every half hour 4am-6pm, stopping in Montecristi ($0.75), San Lorenzo ($1.25), Los Frailes and Machalilla ($3.50), Puerto López (2 hours, $3.75), Ayampe ($4.50), Montañita ($5.50), Olón ($5.80), Manglaralto ($5.90), and Santa Elena ($7.50).

Interprovincial buses run to Guayaquil (at least hourly between 2am and 8:30pm, 4 hours, $6), Esmeraldas (15 departures daily 3am-8pm, 9 hours, $11.50), Santo Domingo (more or less hourly 1:30am-10:45pm, $7.50), and Quito (at least hourly 3:30am-10pm, 8 hours, $11). Flota Imbabura has a 10pm bus stopping in Otavalo ($14), Ibarra ($14), and Tulcán ($17). Carlos Alberto Aray has buses to El Coca ($21) via Papallacta ($15) at 9:30am and 12:30pm. Reina del Camino has a nightly departure to Huaquillas (10:20pm, $13).

To avoid the bus station, **Panamericana** (Calle 12 *y* Av. 4, tel. 5/262-5898, www.panamericana.ec) runs a comfortable bus to Quito at 9:45pm, leaving from a couple of blocks inland from Playa Tarqui.

The **Eloy Alfaro Airport** is 5 kilometers (3 mi) northeast of the city center. **TAME** (www.tame.com.ec) has an office on the *malecón* near Plaza Cívica (Calle 13 *y* 14, tel. 5/261-0008) and operates daily flights to/from Quito. **Avianca** (www.avianca.com) also flies daily to/from Quito.

Santa Marianita

Just 25 minutes from Manta, **Santa Marianita** is being increasingly developed, but it's still a world away from the city's urbanized landscape. This long, curved bay is Ecuador's kitesurfing mecca, and there isn't much else to do, but it's still a hands down better beach experience than Murcielago or Tarqui.

KITESURFING

Kitesurfers flock here for the thermals created when the Humboldt Current meets Manta's hot, dry climate. Most days between May and December there is a stable cross onshore wind of 15-22 knots, making this the ideal spot for riders of all ability levels. One of the best kitesurfing schools is **Ocean Freaks** (tel. 99/924-0658, www.oceanfreaks.com), at the far north end of the *malecón*. With a restaurant and bar, it's a good spot to meet fellow kitesurfers. A private eight-hour course over 2-3 days costs $350 for beginner, intermediate, or advanced level. A one-day, three-hour course costs $150. By the hour, instruction costs $50/hour and equipment rental $25/hour. Also recommended is **Ecuador Kitesurf** (tel. 99/572-9775, www.ecuadorkitesurf.com), where a private two-hour class costs $65, an eight-hour course costs $280, a 12-hour course $380, and a 20-hour course $600.

FOOD AND ACCOMMODATIONS

There is a cluster of locally owned **seafood cabañas** in the middle of the *malecón*, open until around 6pm.

Budget accommodation options are limited. **Ocean Freaks** (tel. 99/924-0658, www.oceanfreaks.com), a local family business, has three simple guest rooms ($12 pp). Their restaurant and bar **Gnomo Lounge** serves mostly seafood but does have a veggie bowl. Another great budget option is ★ **Punta La**

Ocean Freaks kitesurfing school

Barca (tel. 95/983-9180, www.puntalabarca. com, $12 dorm, $15-20 s, $27 d, including breakfast), on a hill just south of the main beach. Owned by a friendly Ecuadorian/ Belgian family, guest rooms are rustic and cozy, and the balcony has wonderful views. With discounts for long-term stays, fast Internet, and a co-working space, it's an ideal option for digital nomads. Camping is available for $5.

On the *malecón*, **Don Willy** (tel. 99/114-3179, $45-60 s/d, including breakfast) is a family-run seafood restaurant and hostel. Surprisingly attractive guest rooms are inside a revamped shipping container. Group rooms are available for $15 per person, not including breakfast. ★ **Casa Blanca** (tel. 99/135-4729, $50 s, $70 d, including breakfast) has light, airy rooms with balconies overlooking the ocean. The owner is friendly and there is a pool. Dinner is available for $12-14.

Santa Marianita is 25 minutes southwest from Manta. Taxis cost $8-10. Shared *camionetas* leave from outside the central market when they are full and cost $1. Once in Santa Marianita, there are no taxis and few buses, so move around on foot or in the shared *camionetas* that ply the main road.

San Lorenzo

San Lorenzo, 40 minutes southwest of Manta, is much less developed than Santa Marianita and more picturesque, with an oft-deserted beach ending in dramatic rock formations to the north. The waves are impressive, and it's a popular spot for advanced surfers. A nesting site for turtles, the beach is part of the 13,445-hectare (33,225-acre) **Pacoche Marine & Coastal Wildlife Reserve.**

There are a couple of locally owned seafood restaurants on the beach: **Delfín Azul** and **Delicias del Mar.** The latter can make a decent omelet with *patacones* (fried plantain) for vegetarians. Canadian-owned **The Lookout** (tel. 5/255-8015 or 98/122-3499, www.thelookouthostel.com, $10-20 s, $40-50 d, including breakfast) has decent guest rooms (the cheaper ones with bunk beds) and a pool. Owned by an Ecuadorian/Norwegian couple, **El Faro Escandinavio** (tel. 99/112-2336, www.elfaroescandinavio.com, $122 s, $145 d, including breakfast) has bungalows in tropical gardens, a pool, and a small lighthouse with an observation platform. Lunch and dinner are available on request.

Shared *camionetas* to San Lorenzo wait outside Manta's central market and leave when they are full (40 minutes, $1).

Pacoche

As well as protecting the stretch of coastline that includes San Lorenzo, the **Pacoche Marine & Coastal Wildlife Reserve** also encompasses one of the last remaining pockets of semi-dry tropical forest on the coast. An oasis of lush greenery in the arid Manta region, this *garua* (drizzle) forest has its own misty microclimate. It is home to the critically endangered Ecuadorian Capuchin monkey, howler monkeys, kinkajous, agoutis, jaguarundis, and ocelots, as well as over 250 species of birds. Among the native tree species is the *tagua* palm, source of the vegetable ivory used for carving souvenirs.

The ★ **Pacoche Lodge & Reserve** (Vía Manta-Puerto Cayo, Carretera E 15 km 582, tel. 99/810-3178 or 5/605-1951, www. pacochelodge.org) occupies 10 hectares (25 acres) within the larger reserve and can be visited as a day trip ($5) or an overnight stay. Three trails range 30-90 minutes and can be explored independently or with a guide. English-speaking tours are available by prior reservation. The reserve's three families of howler monkeys, often heard and sometimes seen, are recovering from a mysterious incident in 2016, when 50 individuals died from unknown causes.

The **lodge** ($67 s, $100 d, including breakfast) has attractive cabins inside the forest. A variety of birds, and sometimes monkeys, can be seen from the balconies. With 360-degree views of the forest, the restaurant serves meat, seafood, and vegetarian options. The lodge is the base for **Greenearth Ecuador** (www.

greenearthecuador.org), a nonprofit that undertakes environmental education programs with local communities and has a project to reduce plastic waste in Manabí.

Pacoche is 30 minutes from Manta, on the way to San Lorenzo. Shared *camionetas* to San Lorenzo leave from outside Manta's central market when they are full and cost $1. Ask to be let out at Pachoche. Alternatively, take a Co-op Manglaralto bus heading to Puerto López from the station in Manta and ask to be let out at Pacoche.

Crucita

Like many small coastal towns that were once fishing villages, **Crucita** is increasingly developed, but it's worth a visit if you're looking to learn or practice paragliding. Lessons are available at **Hostal Voladores** (Nueva Loja *y* Principal, tel. 5/234-0200, Facebook @ ParapenteCrucita, $15 pp), which has a pool. A 12-minute tandem paraglide costs $35. Crucita is 45 minutes north of Manta. Buses leave from the terminal.

Rocafuerte

The small town of **Rocafuerte** is known for its traditional sweets, including *alfajores* (shortbread cookies with a *dulce de leche* filling), *cocadas* (balls of coconut with sugar or *panela*), fruit and vegetable jellies, and meringues. Also available is *rompope*, a sweet, alcoholic eggnog-like drink. All the sweets are vegetarian, but not all are vegan. Most cost $0.05. Of the many confectioners, one of the best is **Los Almendros** (Av. Sucre Vía Chone, tel. 5/264-5508 or 99/971-9839, Facebook @ LosAlmendrosDulceria). Rocafuerte is 45 minutes north of Manta. Buses leave from the terminal.

Montecristi

Montecristi was the birthplace of Ecuador's liberal president and revolutionary hero, Eloy Alfaro. After serving twice as president (1899-1901 and 1906-1911), Alfaro was assassinated by an angry mob in Quito in 1912 and his body burned in El Arbolito Park. During his time in office, he oversaw the construction of the Guayaquil-Quito railroad and a range of progressive legislation, including separating church from state; introducing a state education system; and allowing women to work.

Montecristi's profile was raised considerably in 2008 when President Rafael Correa chose to base the temporary National Assembly here to draft a new constitution. The assembly building, high above the town, houses two museums. The **Centro Cívico Ciudad Alfaro** (tel. 5/231-1210, www.ciudadalfaro.gob.ec, 8:30am-5pm daily, free) documents the life of Eloy Alfaro and includes a mausoleum housing his ashes, overlooked by the sculpted faces of dozens of fellow revolutionaries. Next door is an impressive museum with displays on traditional handicrafts from the province of Manabí, with signage in English, and some handicrafts shops. To get to the museums, take a taxi ($1.50) from the town center. To get back into town, arrange a pickup time with the driver or ask the museum staff to call a taxi for you.

SHOPPING

From **Montecristi's** central park, which has an attractive white church, the main street, 9 de Julio, heads northeast and is lined with shops selling *sombreros de paja toquilla* and other woven goods.

One of the best places to buy a hat is the workshop of **Freddy Pachay** (Calle Quito *y* Av. Manta, tel. 99/759-1155, www.torranzo.com), who presses up to 50 hats per day, giving them their final touch before they're ready for sale. Unlike most hat pressers, who have transitioned to electric machines, Freddy still works with a manual machine from 1880, passed down from his father and grandfather, who started the family business. The workshop is open to visitors, who can choose their hat and watch it being pressed. The hats cost anywhere from $40 to $2,000. Freddy's workshop is north of the central park. To get there, find the hardware store Zambrano on the main road that runs through Montecristi, and from there turn onto Calle Quito.

The Panama Misnomer: Montecristi Hats

weaving *paja toquilla* in Montecristi

It's thanks to U.S. president Theodore Roosevelt that Panama was given credit for the iconic hat, which in fact originated in the small Ecuadorian town of Montecristi just outside Manta.

Known locally as a *sombrero de paja toquilla*, these lightweight woven hats have been made in Ecuador since pre-Columbian times. In the early 19th century, Spanish entrepreneurs recognized the quality of the hats and began exporting them via Panama. After independence, the trade continued to grow rapidly. When construction of the Panama Canal began in 1904, exiled Ecuadorian president Eloy Alfaro, whose father had exported the hats for many years, noticed the discomfort of thousands of workers toiling in the hot sun, and he ordered 220,000 hats to be sent from Ecuador. U.S. president Theodore Roosevelt heard about the popularity of the hat and was photographed wearing one while visiting the canal construction in 1906. The photo of the president was published worldwide with the caption "The president and his Panama hat," and the misnomer was born.

The traditional weaving of *paja toquilla was* declared an Intangible Cultural Heritage of Humanity by UNESCO in 2012. It's a process that provides a livelihood for hundreds of families. First, the *toquilla* palms are harvested for their shoots, which are beaten on the ground, the leaves removed, and then tied into bundles, boiled, dried in the sun, and bleached. The resulting "straw" is then woven into hats, which are pressed to set their shape. Crafters from Montecristi introduced the weaving technique to other parts of Ecuador, most notably Cuenca. However, the Montecristi hats are considered the finest because the weavers adopt a painful bent over position that results in a tighter weave. In contrast, hat makers near Cuenca work seated at tables.

There are three classes of hat, graded according to the number of fibers per inch. A *subfino* hat might sell for $15-20, whereas a *superfino* might fetch as much as $2,000. Considering that the most basic hat might take a week to weave, it's not surprising that there are fewer hatmakers than there used to be.

As well as hats, Montecristi's craftspeople are also known for weaving wicker furniture from the bejuco vine that winds its way up trees in the jungles of Esmeraldas. One of the best wicker workshops is **Taller Artesanal Creativo** (tel. 99/477-0920), a block from the main square, where the friendly owner, Nicolas, is happy to explain the whole process, from harvesting to weaving. A medium-sized chair takes three days to weave, costs $160, and will last for 30 years.

FOOD

The best place to eat is ★ **Trattoria de Gabriel** (Ciudadela Eloy Alfaro, tel. 99/325-7790, http://trattoriadagabriele.com, noon-3pm and 7pm-10:30pm Sun.-Tues., $10-18), a charming restaurant perched on the hill above town, owned by a friendly young local woman who inherited it from her Italian father. All dishes are freshly prepared to order, and the chefs are happy to accommodate dietary and special requests. The tiramisu is wonderful, as are the views! Nearby, a good place to stay is **Balcones de Cerro** (San Andres Callejón 6, tel. 5/231-0135, www.balconesdelcerrohotel.com, $67 s, $85 d, including breakfast).

GETTING THERE

Montecristi is between Portoviejo (30 minutes, $0.75) and Manta (20 minutes, $1.10). Buses run regularly from the terminals in both towns, or flag one down on the main road.

Portoviejo

Portoviejo (pop. 228,000) is the capital of Manabí province, and after Manta it is the largest city in the province. It's also officially the hottest city in Ecuador. Statistics aside, there is little of appeal in this dusty, busy commercial center. Portoviejo is an important transportation hub with a large bus terminal, so you may have to pass through. If you are stuck, **Hotel Ceibo Dorado** (Espejo y Pedro Gual, tel. 5/265-7080, www.hotelceibodorado.com.ec, $45 s, $65 d, including breakfast) and **Hotel-Boutique Casa Lolita** (Calle Nueva y Av. Universitaria, tel. 5/263-6333, Facebook @ hotelcasalolita, $62 s, $90 d, including breakfast) are both centrally located good options.

Buses run every 15 minutes to Jipijapa (45 minutes, $1.50, change here for Puerto López) and Guayaquil (4 hours, $6) and at least hourly to Manta (50 minutes, $2). There are frequent departures to Quito (8 hours, $11) until 2:45pm and then no more until the overnight departures start at 8:20pm.

PUERTO LÓPEZ

The horseshoe bay of **Puerto López** is full of fishing boats and surrounded by green forested hills. The town has had a facelift in recent years, with an attractive new *malecón* lined with cabañas offering seafood, fruit salads, and cocktails. All boat trips now leave from a pier, which is open for visitors to stroll along. There isn't much to see in Puerto López itself, but it's the best base from which to explore **Machalilla National Park.** Between June and October, it's the country's principal whale-watching destination.

Recreation and Tours

Over the last 20 years, tourism has transformed Puerto López. Whale-watching and Machalilla National Park have allowed many residents to move away from the fishing industry and concentrate on these more sustainable sources of income. While the whale-watching tours are regulated by the Pacific Whale Foundation to minimize impact on the animals, and tour guides do provide information on the threats faced by marinelife, drinks onboard the boats are still served in single-use plastic cups from disposable plastic bottles. Tour operators are more likely to switch to a more sustainable alternative (such as Facebook @empaqueverdeec) if enough visitors request it, so consider speaking up if it's a change you'd like to see implemented.

While whales can often be seen from Ecuador's beaches, it's worth taking a boat trip for awe-inspiring close-up views. As well as **whale-watching** ($25 pp), most operators

Migration of the Giants

In an epic 7,000-kilometer (4,350-mi) migration from Antarctica, humpback whales or *ballenas jorobadas* come to breed in the warm waters of Ecuador between June and October. The shallow waters near Puerto López are also a humpback nursery, where mothers can protect their offspring from predators. Female humpbacks can reach up to 16 meters (52 ft) in length, weighing in at 36,000 kilograms (80,000 lb)—equivalent to 500 people or six elephants. The males are smaller at a mere 13-14 meters (43-46 ft). During the breeding season, a female is accompanied by a principal male escort, who tries to maintain his position at her side while rival males attempt to displace him using high speed, breaching, growls, and crashes.

The unique scars and deformations on humpbacks' tails, or flukes, allow them to be individually identified. International conservation organization The Pacific Whale Foundation has a record of 6,000 whale flukes. If you send them a photo of a new, unregistered tail, the whale will be named after you. Send your photos to research@pacificwhale.org or WhatsApp 99/546-4860.

in town offer tours to Machalilla National Park, including boat trips to **Isla de la Plata** ($40-45 pp, with whale-watching en route in season) and mainland visits to the beautiful beach of **Los Frailes** and the community-run archaeological site at **Agua Blanca** ($40 pp for both). Another popular boat trip is to **Isla Salango** for bird-watching and snorkeling ($25 pp). Several dive shops offer day dives and courses. Bike tours, kayaking, and bird-watching are also available. Most tours are available in English, but check at the time of booking. Whatever your destination, avoid the touts in the street and stick to the recommended agencies. It's best to book a couple of days in advance if possible, but if you turn up on the day, go around 8am, as most tours leave at around 9am.

Machalilla Tours (*malecón y* Eloy Alfaro, tel. 5/230-0234 or 99/492-5960, http://machalillatours.org) is a reputable and long-standing agency with another office in Montañita. They specialize in the national park but offer a wide variety of tours, including community-led hikes, horseback rides, and camping in the tropical rainforest near Río Blanco, home to toucans and howler monkeys. They also have a dive shop. A consistently well-reviewed agency is **Aventuras la Plata** (tel. 5/230-0105 or 99/731-9691, http://www.aventuraslaplata.com), which offers all the popular boat trips. **Naturis** (General

Córdova *y* Juan Montalvo, tel. 5/230-0218 or 98/495-1841, https://naturis.com.ec) offers all the usual tours, plus community-managed horseback rides and hikes in the tropical forest near El Pital and the tropical dry forest near El Rocio. **Exploramar Diving** (*malecón*, tel. 99/950-0910, www.exploradiving.com) offers diving trips and PADI (Professional Association of Diving Instructors) certification. Exploramar helped found, and provides ongoing financial and practical support to, the Fundación Megafauna Marina del Ecuador, an NGO that studies and protects the country's whale sharks and giant manta rays.

There are a few things to do and see in Puerto López itself. At the far north end of the beach is a sea turtle rescue center, **Centro de Rehabilitación de Fauna Marina del Parque Nacional Machalilla** (Facebook @ Centroderehabilitacionmarina).

Toward the north of the *malecón*, **Tentáculo** (tel. 98/336-0849, Facebook @ Tentaculoclasesycultura) is an environmentally and community-minded cultural center run by a friendly local/Californian team. There are classes and workshops in Spanish, salsa, surfing, ceviche preparation, and making souvenirs. Natural facials are available and there is a selection of local, environmentally friendly products for sale. To give something back, join the weekly beach cleanups, held every Sunday. Spanish classes and a weekly language exchange night are available at **Clara Luna** (tel. 99/062-5479, www.claraluna. ec, $10/hour, $190 for 20 hours/week, $145 for 15 hours/week), with proceeds supporting community education projects, including after-school programs, tutoring, English classes, and reading initiatives. Volunteering is available for those wishing to get involved with these activities.

Entertainment and Events

The town hosts a festival dedicated to the arrival of the humpback whales, the **Festival de los Ballenas Jorobadas**, in mid-June, featuring street parties and parades.

Nightlife is very quiet in Puerto López, and bars open and close sporadically during high season. **Wett** (Alejo Lascano y Juan Montalvo, tel. 98/437-3635, https://discotecawett. business.site, Facebook @wettbarpuertolopez, 7pm-midnight Mon.-Thurs., 9pm-2am Fri.-Sat.) is a club located a block in from the malecón.

Shopping

On the malecón, **El Artesan** (tel. 99/353-2108, www.elartesan.com.ec) specializes in palo santo products, including soap, shampoo, massage oil, essential oil, and incense. The owner, Dante Bolcato, only uses wood from fallen branches or dead trees, and some of the proceeds from the shop go toward reforestation of the tropical dry forest. If the owner is there, he is happy to give a free tour that demonstrates the process of harvesting the wood, extracting the oil, and making the products. Advance reservations for the tour can be made by phone.

Food

One of the local specialties is bolón, a butter-fried ball of plantain stuffed with cheese and/or ham, traditionally a breakfast dish served with fried eggs and coffee. Bolones are available in cafés all over town and in the mercado, a few blocks inland on García Moreno. The mercado is also a good place for fresh produce and decent, cheap almuerzos.

The beach cabañas along the malecón offer tasty fruit salads right on the sand. Just across the road are plenty of good seafood restaurants. **Carmita's** (malecón, tel. 99/372-9294, $6-12) is probably the best of these, with the specialty being fish in seafood sauce. Chicken, pasta, and rice dishes are also available. A block inland is **Patacón Pisa'o** (General Córdoba, tel. 99/377-1915, $7-9), which serves Colombian specialties such as arepas, including vegetarian options, and good coffee. At the far northern end of the malecón, ★ **Café Madame** (tel. 98/436-7851, http://cafemadame.com, Facebook @ CafeMadameorg, 9am-8pm Tues.-Fri., 9am-11:30pm Sat., 9am-7pm Sun., $5-7) offers sandwiches, omelets, crepes, and desserts. The drinks menu includes juices, smoothies, local craft beer, good coffee, and cocktails. The ingredients are mostly local and organic, with coffee from Jipijapa and vegetables from Agua Blanca or the café's own small organic garden. The decor is rustic chic.

Accommodations

Book ahead on weekends during the whale-watching season as the best accommodations fill up fast. The north end of the beach is quieter than the south but farther from the amenities.

A good budget option is **Sol Inn** (Juan Montalvo y Eloy Alfaro, tel. 5/230-0234, http://hostalsolinn.machalillatours.org, Facebook @hostal.sol.inn.puerto.lopez, $8 dorm, $12 pp s/d), a block in from the middle of the malecón, with a shared kitchen and attractive gardens and common areas.

In a peaceful location at the north of the malecón, **Cabanas Playa Sur** (tel. 5/230-0335, Facebook @CabanasPlayaSur $20 s, $30 d) has rustic cabins with private bathrooms, hot water, fan, and Wi-Fi.

With balconies overlooking the ocean, **Hostal Los Islotes** (malecón y General Córdoba, tel. 98/066-7047, Facebook @ losisloteshostel, $10 dorm $25-30 s/d) is a friendly, colorful place with comfortable beds. Cheaper rooms have an interior view.

The bar and restaurant is open from 6pm and offers veggie food.

Half a block from the *malecón*, **Hotel Ancora** (Eloy Alfaro *y* Juan Montalvo, tel. 5/230-0319, www.hotelancoraec.com, $34 pp, including breakfast) is a stylish, immaculate, newly built hotel owned by an Ecuadorian/Spanish couple. Comfortable, individually decorated guest rooms feature original local art on the walls, air-conditioning, and TV. Amenities include a pool, Jacuzzi, massage service, and a restaurant serving Spanish/Ecuadorian dishes and good coffee. The hotel is LGBTQ friendly.

A couple of places in Puerto López have sound environmental policies. Owned by a friendly Ecuadorian couple, ★ **Tuzco Lodge** (Calle General Córdoba *y* Juan León Mera, tel. 5/230-0120 or 98/428-7362, www.tuzcolodge.com, $30 pp, including breakfast) has attractive guest rooms set around a central plant-filled courtyard. There is original local art on the walls and decor made from recycled materials. Lunch and dinner are available upon request, and there is a shared kitchen. A swimming pool is set in extensive organic gardens with ornamentals, maize, watermelon, mandarins, passion fruit, and medicinal plants. The gardens are watered using a gray water system and collected rainwater, and a closed system filters, cleans, and reuses the water in the pool. Every Sunday the owners run an environmental club for local children, with workshops on organic gardening and making crafts from recycled materials.

At the very north end of the *malecón*, ★ **Hostería Mandála** (tel. 5/230-0181 or 99/951-3940, www.hosteriamandala.info, $55-115 s, $65-115 d, including breakfast) has a range of cabins set in dense tropical gardens, providing a feeling of privacy and immersion in nature. The cabins are spacious and comfortable, with balconies and hammocks. Each painstakingly and individually decorated, some have intricate wooden floor mosaics in druid and Chinese patterns. Unusually for Ecuador, there are accessible facilities. There is no air-conditioning, TV, or pool. Instead, there are fans, a music room, books, board games, and beach toys. Massages are available. The Swiss and Italian owners speak English and are a great source of tourist information. The gardens are home to 120 iguanas and the northern ghost bat, which is white in color and can be seen roosting during the day. Next to Mandála is a 15.7-meter (52-ft) skeleton of a whale that was washed up on the beach—the biggest male found on the coast to date. In front of the hotel on the beach are cabins strung with hammocks for guests to use. The hotel uses gray water to irrigate the gardens, biodegradable cleaning products, and a vermicomposting system. Employees are local, as are all goods and services. The hotel supports the community by providing plants and trees for reforestation projects as well as donating to local day care centers and the sea turtle rescue center.

Information and Services

There is a helpful tourist office on the pier. The **Banco Pichincha** has an ATM on the *malecón*.

Getting There and Around

Co-op Manglaralto buses run every 20 minutes or so along the Ruta del Spondylus south to Montañita (50 minutes, $1.50) and Salinas (3 hours, $3), and north to Jipijapa (1.5 hours, $1.50) and Manta (2 hours, $2.50). These stop on the main road next to the market, a five-minute walk to the waterfront, or you can take a *triciclo* taxi ($0.50).

From the bus terminal just outside town, there are buses to Quito (10 hours, $12) at 5:30am, 9:10am, 7pm, and 8pm with Coop Reina del Camino (tel. 5/230-0140) and Coop Carlos Alberto Aray (tel. 5/230-0178). Coop Jipijapa runs 12 buses daily to Guayaquil (3.5 hours, $5) between 4am and 5pm.

★ MACHALILLA NATIONAL PARK

Established in 1979, **Machalilla National Park** (tel. 5/230-0170, http://areasprotegidas. ambiente.gob.ec) preserves what's left of the tropical dry forest that once stretched all the way to Panama. Only about 1 percent of the original forest remains in Ecuador, and Machalilla contains most of it—about 40,000 hectares (100,000 acres); the other 20,000 hectares (50,000 acres) of the park is ocean. On the mainland, the principal attractions are the beautiful beach at Los Frailes and the archaeological site and sulfur lake at Agua Blanca. Off the coast, the islands of Salango and La Plata make great day trips for **bird-watching** and **snorkeling.** The biggest wildlife draw is the singing, somersaulting population of **humpback whales** that visit June-September.

Isla de la Plata

Isla de la Plata, 37 kilometers (23 mi) northwest of Puerto López, is often referred to as the "poor man's Galápagos" for the number of species that it shares with the famous archipelago. It's well worth a visit, especially between June and September, when tours include whale-watching.

Archaeological investigations reveal that Isla de la Plata was an important ceremonial site from 3500 BC. The island's name (Silver Island) arose from a legend that Francis Drake, the English sea captain (or pirate, depending on your point of view) buried treasure here after an assault on a Spanish galleon at the end of the 16th century. The island was a refuge and resting place for pirates throughout the 17th and 18th centuries.

With the pirates long gone, these days it is **birds** that use the island as a resting (and nesting) place, including blue-footed, red-footed, and masked boobies; magnificent frigate birds; and waved albatross. There is a small colony of sea lions, but it's rare to see them. Due to currents that bring in nutrients and plankton, the ocean just off Isla de la Plata is home to **marine animals** such as hammerhead sharks, giant manta rays, and sea turtles. Though fishing is banned within the park, it does still happen, and sadly these species are often accidentally caught up in nets. Between June and September, the shallow waters provide a safe nursery for humpback whales.

Boats to Isla de la Plata leave from Puerto López around 9am and land at Drake Bay after approximately 90 minutes. In season, the whale-watching en route is spectacular. Once on land, visitors are given the choice of three trails of differing difficulty and length, the longest taking around three hours. Much of the island is closed to protect the waved albatross, which is sensitive to the presence of humans. Coinciding with the migration of the whales is the nesting season of the boobies and frigate birds. The boobies, who begin courtship in June and are nesting by July, lay their eggs on the ground, often right in the middle of the footpath. It's a sobering fact that the incubation period for chicks on the path is three days longer than those on open ground, due to the stress caused by human traffic. While the popularity of the park provides employment for local people and allows for its continued protection, it does feel like an invasion to walk so close to birds protecting eggs or chicks. Visitors should take care to minimize stress by walking quietly past the nests and not getting too close. Outside nesting season, the seabirds use the island as a resting place. After hiking on the island, visitors return to the boat for lunch and snorkeling among tropical fish in the bay, before arriving back in Puerto López around 5pm.

Bear in mind that the boat journey can be rough, so skip breakfast and take seasickness medicine if you are prone. It can be very hot and dry on the Island, especially between December and May, and there is very little shade on the walk, so bring sunscreen, a hat,

1: Machalilla National Park offers spectacular whale-watching between June and September. **2:** Isla de la Plata is a nesting and resting site for blue-footed boobies.

and plenty of water. For recommended tour operators, see the *Puerto López* section.

Agua Blanca and San Sebastián

One of the most well-established community tourism projects in the region is found at **Agua Blanca,** an ancestral village of around 300 people, some of whom are descendants of the Manteño culture (AD 800-1500). Here were found the remnants of U-shaped stone chairs, thought to have been used by shamans during ancient ceremonies, as well as funeral urns and other ceramics. Aside from being an important archaeological site, Agua Blanca is an easy access point for the tropical dry forest, and there is a natural sulfur lake of therapeutic water and healing mud.

Guides from the community are available daily to take visitors on a tour ($5, no reservation required) that includes the archaeological museum and a two-hour forest walk that takes in the Manteño ruins. The forest is filled with towering *ceibo, barbasco,* and fragrant palo santo trees. There are views up to San Sebastián from lookout points, and the tour ends with a refreshing but pungent dip in a natural sulfur pool, where the mud is thought to have healing properties for the skin.

Farther inland, the landscape rises to 800 meters (2,625 ft), where dry forest becomes cloud forest in **San Sebastián.** The forest, which is home to orchids and bromeliads, as well as howler monkeys, anteaters, and *tigrillos,* can be explored with a guide on foot or on horseback.

GETTING THERE

To get to Agua Blanca, take a bus north from Puerto López (5 km/3.1 mi) and then walk the dusty 5-kilometer (3.1-mi) trail up a dirt track, or, better, hire a *mototaxi* ($5 one-way, $10 round-trip). Alternatively, go with an agency from Puerto López. Machalilla Tours and Naturis offer tours to Agua Blanca and San Sebastián.

Playa Los Frailes

With pristine waters, a perfect crescent-shaped beach of soft golden sand, and a backdrop of forested hills, **Los Frailes** (8am-4pm, free) is rightly regarded as one of Ecuador's most beautiful beaches. It is a special place, and if you come early enough, you may have it to yourself. Swimming and sunbathing can be combined with a short walk to a lookout point at the north end. For a longer hike, it's possible to approach Los Frailes via a 3-kilometer (1.9-mi) cliff-top footpath through dry tropical forest, passing the beaches of Playa Prieta, Playa Negra, and La Tortuguita en route.

If you're planning on walking, bring plenty of water and set off early to arrive before it gets too hot. There is no shade on the beach, but parasols can be rented for $4 a day in the car park. Drinks and ice cream are available for purchase, but not much else, so bring snacks/food with you. Los Frailes is rarely crowded, but for even fewer people come midweek.

Los Frailes is 10 kilometers (6.2 mi) north of Puerto López. There are guided tours, often in combination with Agua Blanca, but it's easy to visit on your own. A taxi from Puerto López costs $7 one-way, or $15 round-trip (arrange a pickup time with the driver). Alternatively, take a bus ($0.50, 10-15 minutes) heading to Manta, check with the driver that it will pass the Parque Nacional Machalilla, and ask to be let off. At the entrance, present ID and register to enter the park. From there, take a tuk-tuk ($2-3) to the beach or walk for an hour on the well-marked cliff-top path that starts a few hundred meters from the entrance.

SALANGO

Salango is a fishing village 6 kilometers (3.7 mi) south of Puerto López on the edge of Machalilla National Park, with **Isla Salango** just off the coast. The **Mirador de Salango,** perched on a cliff just to the south of the village, has truly wonderful views of Isla Salango and the coast stretching out below. It's best to go by taxi, as it's a hot, steep, dusty climb on foot.

The inhabitants of Salango are direct descendants of the Pueblo Manta Huancavilca, with 5,000 years of history and culture. They have established a community-based ecotourism operation (tel. 5/257-4304, www.salango.com.ec, Facebook @turismo.comunitario) that includes accommodations, a restaurant, an archaeological museum, a viewpoint, and boat trips to Isla Salango.

The heart of the operation is the **Museum Arqueológico,** which displays 245 relics dating back to 4,500 years before the conquest. Guided walks are available in the tropical dry forest at **Río Chico,** 20 minutes from Salango. The community has also established a native plant nursery for reforestation. Whale-watching trips are available in season.

The highlight is a boat trip to **Isla Salango,** home to blue-footed boobies, frigate birds, and pelicans, and thought to have been the most important ceremonial center for six pre-Columbian cultures (Valdivia, Machalilla, Chorrera-Engoroy, Bahia, Guangala, and Manteña). Just off the island is a marine shelf 3 meters (10 ft) deep, perfect for snorkeling among tropical fish and corals. To directly support the community, organize boat trips to Isla Salango directly with them, rather than an agency in Puerto López. If you'd prefer to go with an agency, consider choosing one that works with the Salango tour operators, rather than taking tourists in its own boat. Boat trips cost $30-35.

The Salango community also offers accommodations in **beachfront cabins** ($15 pp) with hot water and fans, next to the museum. A **restaurant** offers local cuisine, specializing in seafood. Packages of accommodations, food, and activities ranging from six hours to two days are detailed on the website.

To get to Salango, flag down any bus going in the right direction on the Ruta del Spondylus and ask the driver to let you off.

LAS TUNAS AND AYAMPE

Located between Montañita and Puerto López, the southernmost villages in the province of Manabí are **Las Tunas** and **Ayampe,** which share a long beach with good waves for surfers of all levels. A defining feature of this stretch of coast is a striking rock formation, Los Ahorcados, that rises out of the ocean to form a backdrop for sensational sunsets. Nightlife is pretty much nonexistent, and Ayampe in particular has become increasingly popular with visitors looking for a quieter alternative to the more lively beach town Montañita. While both are small and peaceful, Ayampe can feel somewhat like a gringo bubble, whereas Las Tunas provides a more integrated experience with the local community.

Between Ayampe and Las Tunas is the beautiful **Río Ayampe** estuary, part of the Ayampe River Reserve, created by Fundación Jocotoco (www.jocotoco.org) to protect the world's second smallest hummingbird, the *estrellita Esmeraldeña* or Esmeraldas woodstar. Only slightly bigger than the world's smallest bird, Cuba's bee hummingbird, the *estrellita Esmeraldeña* was thought to be extinct due to the destruction of its dry forest habitat, but it was rediscovered in Ayampe in 1990. Critically endangered, this tiny creature is found only in the Ayampe/Las Tunas area.

The Ayampe River Reserve is also the release site for an even rarer bird, the green guacamayo, a type of macaw that disappeared from Machalilla National Park 50 years ago due to deforestation and trafficking. There are estimated to be only 30 individuals remaining in the country. Fundación Jocotoco is undertaking a breeding and reintroduction program in the reserve and at the time of writing eight birds had been released, with another six on the way. For more information, see Facebook @proyectoguacamayosayampe.

A couple of excellent local **bird-watching** guides offer tours of the reserve. **Byron Delgado** is president of the Las Tunas Ecological Club and owner of the Wipeout restaurant (tel. 98/474-7014, Facebook @wipeoutcabana). He speaks a little English. Tours ($40 pp/1 person, $30pp/2 people, $25 pp/3 people, including a bird list and a

drink) start at 6am and last 3-6 hours, depending on the visitor's enthusiasm, and include a visit to the estuary to see migratory birds. **Sandra Plua** (tel. 99/886-1819, http://guiaspnm2008.wixsite.com) leads birding tours of the Ayampe River Reserve and another local birding hot spot, Río Chico (7am-12:30pm daily, $40-45 pp). She is a licensed Machalilla National Park guide and speaks fluent English.

Las Tunas

Having adopted it as their emblem, the ancestral community of Las Tunas is heavily involved with efforts to protect the *estrellita Esmeraldeña*. Working with Fundación Jocotoco, local people have been restoring its habitat by planting 10,000 native trees, especially the *pechiche*, which provides not only food for the hummingbird but fruit for making jam. On the first Sunday in April the **Festival del Pechiche** raises awareness about conserving the dry forest and its species, and includes the sale of *pechiche* jams and crafts made from recycled materials. Throughout the year, environmental education activities are carried out with children and adults, as well as waste collection and recycling initiatives.

Las Tunas owns and protects a 4,000-hectare (9,900-acre) **community reserve,** which includes the **Ayampe River Reserve.** As well as the Esmeraldas woodstar and green guacamayo, the reserve is a nesting site for green and olive ridley sea turtles. In recognition for its conservation efforts, the community of Last Tunas was a finalist in the United Nations' Equator Prize 2017, an initiative that recognizes outstanding community efforts to reduce poverty through the conservation and sustainable use of biodiversity.

FOOD

Las Tunas has a couple of excellent restaurants on the beach serving traditional cuisine, both owned by friendly local families. Guests can choose to eat in the restaurants or out on the beach under bamboo shelters strung with hammocks. ★ **Jinmy's** (tel. 5/234-7033, Facebook @Restaurante De Jinmy, 8am-8pm daily, $5-14) offers mainly fish and seafood dishes, with the specialty *robalo con camaron al maní* (sea bass with shrimp in peanut sauce). Omelets, pasta, and rice dishes are available for vegetarians. Next to Jinmy's, ★ **Wipeout** (tel. 98/474-7014, Facebook @wipeoutcabana, $5.50-12) is owned by Byron Delgado, president of the Las Tunas Ecological Club and a bird-watching guide. The wide-ranging menu includes breakfasts, seafood, meat and chicken dishes, and an imaginative vegetarian selection. Specialties include seafood with passion fruit, cooked in bamboo, and *cazuela*, seafood cooked with plantain and peanut. Guest rooms are available ($20 pp, including breakfast), or Byron can arrange homestays with local families ($20 pp including all meals). He can also organize tours, including horse riding on the beach or in the forest.

For great pizza, try **Pizza de Guillo** (tel. 99/326-8602, Facebook @PizzaDeGuillo), another locally owned restaurant located inland just north of the main *malecón*. Deliveries are available and can be ordered via WhatsApp, along with beers and wine—great for those recovering from the day's surf.

ACOMMODATIONS

Nearby, **Casa Esperanto** (tel. 99/970-4569, http://takeme2ecuador.com) offers surf and yoga packages, with the option of combining a stay in Las Tunas with the sister Hostal Esperanto in Montañita. Contact the owner, Jorge Moran, who speaks fluent English, for details. Casa Esperanto sleeps eight people and can be rented as a holiday home. Built by local people using local materials, Casa Esperanto has an enormous wooden balcony with hammocks and a gray water system to irrigate the garden.

Cabañas Mirada del Mar (tel. 5/234-7011 or 99/921-7400, http://cabanasmiradaalmar.wixsite.com/hostel, $12.50 pp) is a local

---

1: Playa Los Frailes; **2:** kayaking around Isla Salango

family-owned hostel on the *malecón*. Rooms have private bathrooms, hot water, and fans. There is a shared kitchen and a rooftop terrace with hammocks.

Ayampe

There are only a few streets in Ayampe, so it's easy to navigate. A good place to start is the southernmost entrance into the town from the Ruta del Spondylus. Where this street hits the village's main crossroads, signposts have helpfully been erected, pointing the way to many of the village's hostels and restaurants. Before the crossroads on the left is an unofficial and helpful tourist information office.

Also on the southernmost entrance from the highway are two of the best places to eat, both locally owned. **Los Corales** (tel. 5/257-5045, Facebook @restobarloscorales01, 8:30am-4pm daily, $4-20) specializes in seafood, with some meat, chicken, and vegetarian options. Breakfasts and a set lunch ($5) are also available. Next door, ★ **El Paso** (tel. 5/257-5013 or 98/916-7035, www.elpasoayampe.com, 9am-8pm daily, $4-13) has an extensive menu, including seafood and fish, an excellent vegetarian selection, plus breakfasts, sandwiches, fruit salads, and omelets. Specialties include *bolón*, fish in peanut sauce, and ceviche with peanut sauce. Both restaurants stay open late in high season. El Paso has basic rooms for rent ($15 s, $25 d).

Just over the bridge to the north of town by the side of the highway, the **Cabaña del Corviche** is a longstanding favorite with locals, offering one coastal specialty: *Corviches* are deep-fried balls of mashed green plantain and peanut, stuffed with fish.

Canadian-owned ★ **Otra Ola** (tel. 5/257-5017 or 98/884-3278, www.otraola.com) is a Spanish, surf, and yoga school with a café. The menu offers organic food, good coffee, *guayusa* tea, and *kombucha*. It has a peaceful vibe and sound environmental practices, with compost toilets and a policy of using as little plastic as possible.

On the Ruta del Spondylus is a Hare Krishna temple and hostel, **La Cabaña de Jagannatha** (tel. 9/682-3678, Facebook @ yogapeeth, govindasvegetariano@hotmail.com, $10 dorm, $5 camping). There are single-sex dorms, shared bathrooms, and a camping area in an open-sided wooden rooftop terrace (tents can be provided). The shared kitchen is for meat-free use only. Yoga and meditation classes are offered for donations. The temple protects 42 hectares (104 acres) of land, and the Hare Krishnas are planning a reforestation program, as well as trails and a viewing point. Volunteers are accepted to work in the gardens and grounds. Full-time volunteers stay for free; part-time volunteers pay $3 per day.

Cabañas De La Iguana (tel. 5/257-5165 or 93/967-9436, Facebook @laiguanacabanas, $11 dorm, $18 s, $30 d) has cabins set in extensive gardens. There is hot water, a shared kitchen, and free drinking water. Camping is available ($8) and breakfast can be provided upon request ($5). ★ **Spondylus Lodge** (tel. 93/918-2247, http://sponduluslodge.com, $15 dorm, $25-35 pp suite/room) is entered via a flowering tunnel of vegetation, and the rest of the hostel is just as attractive, with extensive gardens and a range of clean, stylish rooms and cabins, all with hot water and balcony. There is an outdoor Jacuzzi and a shared kitchen with free tea, coffee, and drinking water. Yoga classes are available. It's worth the uphill walk to get to **Finca Punta** (tel. 99/189-0982, http://fincapuntaayampe.com, $30 pp), which has wonderful views from its position overlooking the beach. The rooms are looking a bit tired, but the cabins are newer and great value, with balconies. There is a pool and a restaurant ($6-15) with several vegetarian options.

To get to Las Tunas and Ayampe from anywhere on the Ruta del Spondylus, flag down any bus going in the right direction and ask the driver to let you out at Las Tunas/Ayampe. Buses pass along the highway every 10-15 minutes.

Guayaquil and the Southern Coast

Ecuador's largest city has finally begun to stand up as a tourist destination and bury its bad reputation. Previously considered dirty and dangerous, Guayaquil (pop. 2.7 million) has undergone a major redevelopment in recent years. If you're arriving from the mountains, there's quite a contrast between Quito's cool, colonial charms and Guayaquil's hot, humid vivacity. Although it can hardly rival the capital in terms of beauty, it's worth spending a day exploring the city's highlights, especially the renovated waterfront of the River Guayas, the Malecón 2000, which leads to the bohemian district of Las Peñas; and the Parque Histórico, with a wildlife sanctuary, cacao farm, and restored colonial buildings.

To the west of Guayaquil, beaches are the main reason to visit the

Highlights

Look for ★ to find recommended sights, activities, dining, and lodging.

★ **Montañita:** Popular with Ecuadorian and foreign visitors alike, Montañita offers world-class surf, legendary nightlife, plenty of activities, and a free-spirited vibe (page 334).

★ **Olón:** Montañita's northern neighbor has blossomed into a flourishing destination in its own right, with more of a family atmosphere, gentler waves, and seafood shacks right on the beach (page 342).

★ **Dos Mangas and the Cordillera de Chongón:** The coast's lush green interior can be explored on a bike ride to this sleepy village or a trip to the nearby tropical forest, with pools, waterfalls, and howler monkeys (page 344).

★ **Ayangue:** This picturesque fishing village has one of Santa Elena's few sheltered bays, with calm turquoise seas for swimming, snorkeling, and scuba diving (page 346).

★ **Bosque Petrificado de Puyango:** Fossilized aquatic creatures are found among the giant trunks of stone trees in the largest petrified forest in South America (page 370).

★ **Zaruma:** it's a joy to wander the steep, winding streets of this charming mountain town, with its panoramic views, traditional wooden architecture, and well-founded claim to produce Ecuador's best coffee (page 371).

© MOON.COM

★ **Cerro de Arcos:** Inside the seemingly impenetrable rock formation towering above the *páramo* is an enchanted labyrinth of caves, gnarled moss-covered trees, and natural rock sculptures (page 375).

province of **Santa Elena**. As many national as international tourists flock here to enjoy the laid-back lifestyle, great surf, and sensational sunsets. While **Montañita** is the province's star attraction, the nearby beaches all have their own character and charm, notably **Olón, Manglaralto,** and **Ayangue**. As well as riding waves, there are plenty of other activities available along the coast, including yoga, salsa lessons, Spanish classes, cycling, horseback riding, snorkeling, scuba diving, and paragliding, though many visitors are happy to simply watch the world go by from a hammock. Inland is a lush green interior, which can be explored with a bike ride to **Dos Mangas** or a trip to the protected tropical forest of the **Cordillera de Chongón**.

South of Guayaquil, the province of El Oro is rarely visited by tourists, except as a stopover en route to Peru. This is not through any lack of attractions—quite the contrary, the region is astonishingly diverse—but simply because so few people know of its hidden treasures. Even the most popular destinations, the charming mountain town of **Zaruma** and the petrified forest at **Puyango**, receive relatively few foreign visitors. Other highlights include the dramatic labyrinthine rock formations rising from the *páramo* at **Cerro de Arcos** and the lush green birders' paradise of **Buenaventura.** These are truly roads less traveled, and they are quite spectacular.

PLANNING YOUR TIME

Guayaquil is worth a day for sightseeing, with an overnight stay for the restaurants and nightlife. There's no escaping the fact that the city is hot and humid (28-32°C/82-90°F year-round). January-April is the hottest, wettest period, with an average of 12-15 days of rain and high humidity levels. It is drier June-December, with overcast, slightly cooler days.

The highlights of the **Santa Elena** province can be seen in a whistle-stop tour of 4-5 days, but be aware that the area has become a semipermanent, or even permanent, home for many visitors who originally planned to do just that! **Montañita** and **Olón** can be explored in a couple of days, though most people choose to stay longer to relax or take surf lessons or Spanish classes. Both make good home bases from which to make day trips to **Dos Mangas**, the **Cordillera de Chongón,** and **Ayangue** (though the last certainly merits an overnight stay).

Santa Elena province is easy to navigate, as most of the attractions are located along the **Ruta del Spondylus**, the main coastal highway, which is well served by buses and taxis.

The peak high season on the coast runs from New Year to Easter, when the days are hot (around 30°C/86°F), the waves most consistent, and overnight rains keep the vegetation lush. Ecuadorians (especially Guayaquileños) flock to Santa Elena's long beaches during high season weekends and national holidays, so be prepared for crowds in Montañita and Olón at these times. Be aware that hotel rates may double at New Year's, Carnival, and Easter. The prices quoted in this chapter are for high season (excluding national holidays) and include tax. Between Easter and June, the weather and waves are still good but there are fewer visitors. All along the coast, whales can be seen from the shore between June and September, or with a whale-watching trip. In July, the cloudy days start to appear and gradually increase until gray skies are the norm from August to November, with the occasional sunny interval. Some people prefer low season, when the beaches are almost deserted, temperatures are in the low 20s C (68-75°F), and there are still rideable waves most days. Significant discounts are available at many hotels during this time. Whatever the time of year, be sure to bring sunblock, good sunglasses, and a hat, as the sun can be vicious, even on a cloudy day.

Allow perhaps 10 days to see the highlights

GUAYAQUIL

Previous: a surfer at sunset; Ayangue's sheltered bay; a colorful colonial building in Zaruma.

Guayaquil and the Southern Coast

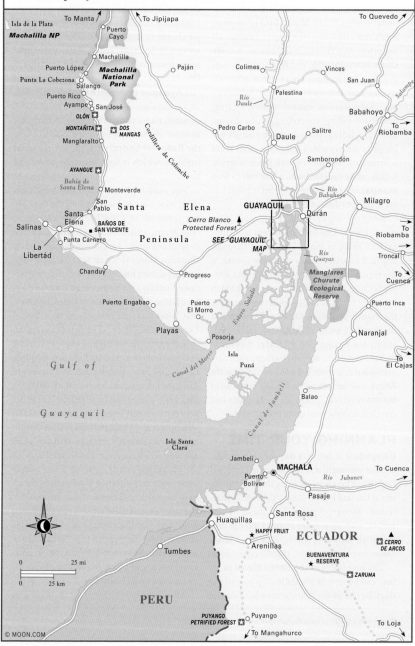

To Manta
To Jipijapa
To Quevedo

Isla de la Plata
Machalilla NP

Puerto Cayo

Machalilla

Paján
Colimes
Vinces

Puerto López
San Juan

Punta La Cabezona
Machalilla National Park

Salango
Río Daule
Palestina

Puerto Rico
Babahoyo

Ayampe
San José
To Riobamba

OLÓN
Pedro Carbo
Salitre

MONTAÑITA
DOS MANGAS
Daule

Manglaralto
Samborondón

AYANGUE
Río Babahoyo

Bahía de Santa Elena
Monteverde
GUAYAQUIL
Milagro

San Pablo
Santa
Elena
Durán

Santa Elena
Cerro Blanco Protected Forest
To Riobamba

Salinas
BAÑOS DE SAN VICENTE
SEE "GUAYAQUIL" MAP

Punta Carnero
Peninsula
Río Guayas
Troncal

La Libertad
Chanduy
Progreso
To Cuenca

Manglares Churute Ecological Reserve
Puerto Inca

Puerto Engabao
Puerto El Morro
Naranjal

Playas
Posorja
To El Cajas

Gulf of
Isla Puná

Canal del Morro

Guayaquil
Estero Salado
Balao

Isla Santa Clara
Canal de Jambelí

Jambelí
MACHALA
To Cuenca

Puerto Bolívar
Río Jubones

Pasaje

Santa Rosa

Huaquillas
★ HAPPY FRUIT
ECUADOR
★ **CERRO DE ARCOS**

Tumbes
Arenillas
BUENAVENTURA RESERVE

0 25 mi
0 25 km
ZARUMA

PERU

PUYANGO PETRIFIED FOREST
Puyango
To Loja

To Mangahurco

© MOON.COM

of **El Oro** province. **Puerto Jelí** makes a good home base, where it's worth spending half a day on a boat trip of the mangroves. Another half day could be spent at the **Happy Fruit** agro-ecological farm, where the owners can help you plan the rest of your time in the province. From Puerto Jelí, the petrified forest at **Puyango** and the island of **Santa Clara** make excellent day trips (the latter especially worthwhile during whale-watching season). The **Buenaventura** reserve makes a good day-trip en route to Zaruma, though birders should allow 2-3 days. You'll probably want to spend 2-3 days in **Zaruma** and two days at **Cerro de Arcos.**

As the only province with both *páramo* and mangroves, El Oro contains so many ecosystems at different altitudes that it's not possible to generalize about the climate. Indeed, with countless micro-climates, there is no bad time to visit El Oro.

El Oro is generally well served by buses, especially Machala, Santa Rosa, and Zaruma. Buses will drop you off a few kilometers from the more remote locations (e.g., Puyango, Cerro de Arcos, and Buenaventura), which must then be accessed by car or on foot. Options include going with a tour operator, by taxi, with your own vehicle, by arranging collection with someone from the destination you are visiting, or by walking the final distance. However you choose to travel, you'll find the local people friendly and happy to help visitors.

Santa Elena Province

Each of Santa Elena's many beaches offers something different. With a world-class point break, legendary nightlife, and lots of accommodation options, **Montañita** is most popular with backpackers, artisans, surfers, and party-goers. As a tourist hub, there are plenty of activities on offer, including surf, yoga, salsa, and Spanish classes—though if you're offended by the wafting scent of marijuana, you may be happier in **Olón.** Montañita's neighbor to the north has blossomed into a flourishing destination its own right, with more of a family atmosphere, some great restaurants, and gentler waves for beginner surfers. Montañita and Olón make good jumping-off points for exploring the rest of Santa Elena, or for trips to the neighboring province of Manabí, for whale-watching or to visit Machalilla National Park.

To the south of Montañita, the peaceful village of **Manglaralto** has a long stretch of quiet beach and a beautiful stand of mangroves. It's definitely worth taking a day to visit the lush green interior just inland, either with a bike ride to the sleepy village of **Dos Mangas,** where the inhabitants still practice traditional agriculture and handicrafts, or a trip to the protected tropical forest of the **Cordillera de Chongón**, where jungle pools and waterfalls can be explored on foot or horseback. A little farther south, the picturesque fishing village of **Ayangue** is one of the province's few sheltered bays, with calm turquoise seas for swimming, snorkeling, and scuba diving.

While the Sierra and Amazon are well known for their indigenous peoples, fewer people know that the coast is also inhabited by ancestral communities, descendants of ancient, pre-Columbian civilizations that lived in the area as early as 3500 BC. These communities are found throughout the province of Santa Elena, including the villages of **Valdivia, Barcelona,** and **Sitio Nuevo.**

MONTAÑITA AND VICINITY

★ Montañita

In the 1970s, the discovery of a world-class point break began to attract surfers to the small farming village of **Montañita,** which at the time was little more than a cluster of rustic houses. As the surfers kept coming, a few low-key hostels and restaurants started springing up to accommodate them.

These days, Montañita is a thriving tourism hub and Ecuador's premier surf destination, home to some of the best surfers on the continent. The right-hand break at **The Point** (La Punta), a 10-minute walk north along the beach from the town center, is for advanced surfers only, but Montañita's long beach break provides year-round rideable waves for all levels.

In high season, Montañita also hosts the country's most vibrant nightlife. As many national as international tourists flock here, and visitors will find themselves sharing a dance floor with backpackers, locals, surfers, Ecuadorian holidaymakers, and Guayaquileños escaping the city for the weekend. Midweek is much quieter.

Even if you're not into surfing or partying, this small town has plenty to offer, from yoga and Spanish classes to bike rentals. Montañita also has several good restaurants. However you choose to spend your time in this small coastal town, the infectious energy of the place is undeniable.

For those seeking a quieter alternative to the town center, the Point has a peaceful rustic charm and is only a 10-minute walk from the action, with decent midrange hotels and a couple of good bars and restaurants.

It's not advisable to walk along the beach alone at night, especially for women. Assaults are infrequent but do occur, especially around holiday periods. Drink spiking is fairly common, so don't leave your beverage unattended. Don't accept flyers from anyone on the street, as they may be dusted with scopolamine, a substance that leaves victims in a docile state, vulnerable to robbery or assault.

ENTERTAINMENT AND EVENTS

Clubs in Montañita stay open later than anywhere else in Ecuador, some until 4am or 5am. Most play a mix of *reggaetón*, pop, electronic, and salsa; any visitor with even a rudimentary knowledge of the latter will not be short of partners on the dance floor. Montañita is more LGBTQ friendly than most places in Ecuador.

At the epicenter of the action is **Cocktail Alley** (open nightly except Sunday), a whole street of cocktail stands that play competing ear-splitting music until the early hours. A bewildering array of drinks are available, and bartenders are happy to add an extra shot to any drink that doesn't put enough hairs on your chest. Of the many stalls, particularly recommended are **Cocteles d'Gloria** and **Charlie's**. A quieter spot for a cocktail is **Surfiesta** (10 de Agosto, Facebook @surfiest, 7pm-2am Mon.-Thurs., 2pm-4am Fri.-Sat.), owned by a friendly local surfer who offers two cocktails and a shisha pipe for $10.

Right on Cocktail Alley is longstanding favorite **Caña Grill** (tel. 99/306-4642, Facebook @CanaGrill, 9pm-4am Wed.-Mon. Jan.-Mar., 9pm-4am Wed., Fri., and Sat. Apr.-Dec.), Montañita's most legendary, albeit low-key, nightclub. The house band is excellent and plays covers at 11pm, followed by a DJ. Flip-flops are discarded in the corners of the sand dance floor for unencumbered dancing. No one minds if a few toes are stepped on due to the uneven surface. **Nativa Bambu** (tel. 4/206-0095, Facebook @Nativa.Bambu, 9pm-4am Fri. and Sat.), the big bamboo structure on the *malecón,* is more upscale than Caña Grill, with prices to match. There is often live music. **Abad Lounge** (tel. 99/386-4688, Facebook @abadlounge, 7pm-4am Mon.-Sat.), on Cocktail Alley, is the best spot for giving your salsa skills a whirl.

El Otro Lado (tel. 98/924-6785, Facebook @ElOtroLadoMontanita, 10am-midnight

Montañita

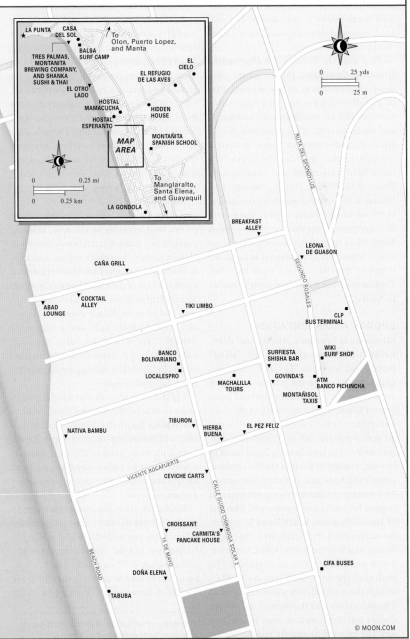

LA PUNTA
CASA DEL SOL
To Olon, Puerto Lopez, and Manta
BALSA SURF CAMP
TRES PALMAS, MONTAÑITA BREWING COMPANY, AND SHANKA SUSHI & THAI
EL CIELO
EL REFUGIO DE LAS AVES
EL OTRO LADO
HOSTAL MAMACUCHA
HIDDEN HOUSE
HOSTAL ESPERANTO
MAP AREA
MONTAÑITA SPANISH SCHOOL
0   0.25 mi
0   0.25 km
To Manglaralto, Santa Elena, and Guayaquil
LA GONDOLA

0   25 yds
0   25 m

RUTA DEL SPONDYLUS

BREAKFAST ALLEY
LEONA DE GUASON
CAÑA GRILL
SEGUNDO ROSALES
COCKTAIL ALLEY
ABAD LOUNGE
TIKI LIMBO
CLP BUS TERMINAL
WIKI SURF SHOP
BANCO BOLIVARIANO
SURFIESTA SHISHA BAR
LOCALESPRO
GOVINDA'S
ATM BANCO PICHINCHA
MACHALILLA TOURS
MONTAÑISOL TAXIS
TIBURON
NATIVA BAMBU
HIERBA BUENA
EL PEZ FELIZ
VICENTE ROCAFUERTE
CEVICHE CARTS
CALLE GUIDO CHIRIBOGA SOLAR 2
CROISSANT
CARMITA'S PANCAKE HOUSE
15 DE MAYO
CIFA BUSES
BEACH ROAD
DOÑA ELENA
TABUBA

© MOON.COM

Wed., Thurs., and Sun., 10am-3am Fri.-Sat.) is the only gay bar in the area, and it's situated on the beach near the Point, a few minutes' walk north from the town center. The staff are friendly and there are lots of colorful hammocks and sun loungers.

Also near the Point is the **Montañita Brewing Company** (MBC, noon-10pm daily, closes Monday in low season). Part of a small complex called Tres Palmas that also includes an excellent sushi restaurant and rooms to rent, MBC is the first oceanfront microbrewery in Latin America. Friendly, English-speaking staff serve craft beers, hard fruit ciders, and imaginatively flavored *kombucha*. During the day, Tres Palmas is the spot for watching the surfers at the world-class break right in front; later on it's without doubt the best place to watch Montañita's spectacular sunsets. Most visitors to Montañita don't make it as far as the Point, so the vibe is much more peaceful. There is often live music from 6pm Thursday to Sunday.

SPORTS AND RECREATION

Montañita is Ecuador's premier surf destination, with local surfers Dominic "Mimi" Barona and Jonathan "El Gato" Chila frequent champions on the pro circuit. Waves at the Point, the world-class right-hand point break 1 kilometer (0.6 mi) north of the town center, can reach 3 meters (10 ft) and it can get pretty crowded. Advanced surfers surf either the Point or the adjoining beach break to the left, directly in front of the Tres Palmas complex/Montañita Brewing Company. This break provides both rights and lefts and is good for tricks and maneuvers. The rest of Montañita's long beach break is suitable for surfers of all levels, although the neighboring beach to the north, Olón, has fewer people and gentler waves for beginners. The peak surf season is from January to May, though there are rideable waves year-round. The water is warmer during high season but doesn't warrant a wetsuit even in low season. The waves in Montañita and the nearby breaks work best two hours before and two hours after high tide. Check www.magicseaweed.com for the tide schedule.

Surfboard rental and **surf classes** are readily available, but quality varies. Take care to choose a qualified instructor who speaks English if your Spanish isn't good. In Montañita town center, the best option for classes and board hire is **LocalesPro** (tel. 98/528-0392, Facebook @LocalesPro) on the main street, run by national champion longboarder Isidro Villao ($25 for a 2-hour lesson). For surf supplies, head to **Wiki Company** (Calle 15 de Mayo, tel. 97/889-6736, www.wiki-company.com, 10am-9pm daily), which sells boards, wax, leashes, and clothing.

Sumpa Trip (tel. 98/034-2989, http://sumpatrip.com) is one of very few locally owned tour agencies in the area, offering paragliding, salsa classes, whale-watching (June-October), horseback riding, and trips to Machalilla National Park and the protected tropical forest of the Cordillera de Chongón. Sumpa Trip only works with trusted operators, and all tours include door-to-door service from friendly, safe, and professional drivers. Sumpa Trip can also organize Galápagos cruises. There are several tour operators in Montañita offering similar experiences, but quality varies.

For last minute whale-watching trips and tours to Machalilla National Park, head to **Machalilla Tours** (tel. 93/984-5839, http://machalillatours.org, 8:20am-10pm daily), just off the main street in the town center. If you turn up at 8:20 when the office opens and there is availability, they can organize same-day tours.

Machalilla Tours also rents bikes for $15 per day. One of the area's most pleasant bike rides is to the peaceful village of Dos Mangas, 7 kilometers (4.3 mi) inland from the neighboring village of Manglaralto. Another brief excursion by bike or on foot is the cliff above the Point between Montañita and Olón,

---

1: hostels and restaurants in Montañita; 2: sunset view from Montañita Brewing Company

which provides spectacular views of endless sandy bays stretching out to the north. The **Santuario de la Virgen Rosa Mística** church clings precariously to the cliff edge. To get there, take the left fork at the surfer statue by the Point and follow the road to the top of the hill.

Parasailing is available on the beach in Montañita ($25). There are several **dive shops** in Montañita, but there isn't much to see at the local dive sites. It's better to head to Puerto López and dive there or at Isla de la Plata.

Perched on the hill across the highway from the town center, the **Montañita Spanish School** (tel. 4/206-0116 www.montanitaspanishschool.com) is an excellent language school offering individual or group lessons ($170 and $240 for 20 hours per week, respectively). Students can combine Spanish lessons with learning to surf, cook, dance salsa, practice yoga, or volunteer. An imaginative four-week package allows students to design and make their own surfboard with a local shaper. The school can provide accommodations in its own cabañas or with a local family.

The best place for **yoga** is **Casa del Sol** (tel. 9/248-8581, http://yogamontanita.com) at the Point, which offers 1-2 classes daily in various styles ($8 per class, 5 classes $35, 10 classes $65). Private classes are also available ($30 on-site, $45 off-site). Seven-day yoga and surf retreats are scheduled monthly ($690-895). A month-long, 200-hour yoga teacher training course is available, usually in March and November (around $2,000).

Massages are available in tents on the beach ($30 for an hour). For more privacy, try **Balsa Surf Camp's spa** at the Point (tel. 98/971-4685, http://balsasurfcamp.com), where treatments range from $30 for 40 minutes to $40-50 for 90 minutes, or contact **Colleen Geis** (tel. 93/982-6410, cgeis63@gmail.com), an excellent massage therapist who does home appointments ($35 for 60 minutes).

SHOPPING

The streets of Montañita are lined with artisans selling **hand-made jewelry.** Many will make custom pieces on request. Quality varies and haggling is advised. Several boutiques sell hand-made clothes.

Montañita is a good place to pick up souvenirs made from *tagua* nut. Also known as vegetable ivory, *tagua* comes from the seed of a palm tree that grows on the coast and is used to make jewelry, pipes, tiny sculptures, and home decor items.

Pre-Incan style ceramic **figurines and masks** are another popular souvenir, sold by mobile vendors who walk the streets and beach. These pottery replicas are based on artifacts made by ancient indigenous peoples such as the Valdivians, who lived in the provinces of Guayas and Santa Elena as early as 3500 BC, one of the oldest settled cultures recorded in the Americas.

FOOD

Montañita has a wide range of good, cheap street food. Alongside the international options (rotisserie chicken, burgers, burritos, and pizzas) are classic Ecuadorian snacks such as empanadas (pastry turnovers filled with cheese or meat), *choclo* (grilled corn on the cob with chimichurri and parmesan), and *carne en palito* (barbecued meat skewers).

The street food most popular with international visitors is ceviche, a dish made from fresh raw fish, shellfish, or shrimp marinated in lime juice, spiced with chili, and served with tomato sauce and toasted corn kernels ($6). There are **ceviche carts** (Vicente Rocafuerte *y* Guido Chiriboga, 7am-7pm daily) with seating in the town center, while others ply their trade on the beach. **El Pez Feliz** (Vicente Rocafuerte, 8am-1pm daily, $2.50) is a stall serving *encebollado,* a traditional fish soup served with yucca, plantain fries, and bread. Local people swear it's the only hangover medicine you'll ever need.

At the east end of Cocktail Alley, away from the ocean, is **Breakfast Alley** (8am-10pm daily, $2-3.50), a row of stalls selling fruit salads, crepes, juices, smoothies, and omelets.

The town center has several good cafés and restaurants offering more diverse fare than other destinations in Ecuador. Establishments tend to open and close so fast that it's hard to keep up, but the following are longstanding favorites.

One of the best options for an Ecuadorian set lunch, or *almuerzo*, is **Doña Elena** (tel. 99/070-7416, 8am-5pm Mon.-Fri., 8am-11pm Sat.-Sun.), near the church, where $3.50 will buy a soup, a main course (typically rice, fish or chicken, salad, and plantain chips), and a juice. Open since 1974, Doña Elena is the town's oldest restaurant and famous for its shrimp empanadas with cheese ($5). Across the road is **Croissant** (6:30am-10pm daily), the best bakery in town, owned by friendly locals. Try the pastries stuffed with mushrooms, or the legendary chocolate croissants.

Locally owned **Hierba Buena** (Vicente Rocafuerte *y* Guido Chiriboga, 9am-10pm daily, entrées $3-8) is another good option for Ecuadorian food, and its central location on the corner of Montañita's two main streets makes it a good spot for people watching. A popular dish is grilled fish with peanut sauce, rice, and plantain chips. There are plenty of vegetarian options. Juices and beer are available. Wine drinkers can bring their own from a nearby store and ask for glasses.

For vegetarian and vegan food, try ★ **Govinda's** (10 de Agosto, noon-9pm daily $3-9), which offers a good set lunch ($3.75) and some excellent soya burgers. Another recommended option for veggies and vegans is **Carmita's Pancake House** (Guido Chiriboga *entre* Rocafuerte *y* San Isidro, tel. 4/206-0030, Facebook @Carmita's pancake house, 8am-5pm Sun.-Fri., 8am-10pm. Sat., $3-$7), half a block from the park and owned by a friendly local woman. The menu includes meat-free set lunches, sandwiches, burgers, ceviches, salads, and, of course, pancakes.

Tucked away on the first floor of the main street, locally owned ★ **Tiburón** (Calle Principal, tel. 99/384-3579, Facebook @ TiburonRestaurante, noon-10pm daily, $5-10) is a real gem, serving excellent seafood, typical Ecuadorian dishes, and Asian fusion, including several vegetarian options. Specialty dishes are Thai curry served in a pineapple and giant baked empanadas with savory or sweet fillings. Everything is made from scratch and the chef is open to special requests. If there is no wine in stock, the owner doesn't mind if you bring your own from a nearby store.

For the best range of international cuisine, including Asian, Italian, and Mexican as well as vegetarian and vegan options, head to ★ **Tiki Limbo** (Chiriboga, tel. 99/954-0607, www.tikilimbo.com/en, $6-9). The Polynesian decor is stylish and the outdoor seats provide one of the best spots in town for people watching.

Ecuador might not be the first place you'd expect to find good sushi, but ★ **Shankha Sushi 'n' Thai** (Facebook @ ShankhaSushiNThai, $8-11), located at the Point, is excellent. Also on the menu are Thai curries and yummy desserts (the aptly named killer lime pie is to die for), with plenty of vegetarian options. Drink-wise, if the cocktail menu isn't your thing, the attached Montañita Brewing Company serves craft beers, ciders, and *kombucha*. The restaurant and bar, collectively known as Tres Palmas, provide the best place in Montañita to watch the sun go down and admire the skills of the surfers at the world-class break right in front. There is often live music at sunset Thursday to Sunday.

For excellent pizza, try locally owned **La Leona del Guason** (Ruta del Spondylus, tel. 98/541-9893, Facebook @LaLeonadelGuason, $7 pp), which has a restaurant on the highway and also offers delivery.

ACCOMMODATIONS

Montañita has a huge number of hostels and hotels for such a small town. In peak season the popular places fill up fast, so advance bookings are advisable, especially for weekends. Definitely book ahead if you're planning on visiting around New Year's, Easter, or Carnival, and be aware that rates may double during these holidays. Significant discounts are available in low season (June-November, especially August-October).

Where you stay depends on how much sleep you want to get. The town center is packed with hostels, but the music and revelry is very noisy throughout the night, particularly on weekends. The rapidly developing inland neighborhood of Tigrillo, just north of the town center by the bridge, is farther from the ocean, but also farther from the noise, offering several budget options, including camping. For a peaceful night's sleep only 10 minutes' walk from the action, consider staying at the Point, where there are several midrange options. Don't walk to the Point along the beach at night; take a taxi for $1.50.

Just over the bridge from Montañita town center, alongside the river, is one of the town's best budget options. Slightly tucked away, ★ **Hostal Mamacucha** (tel. 99/374-9395, $6 dorm, $8 s/d) is quieter than the town center hostels. The attractive common area has a pool table, and it's a great place to meet fellow travelers. What really sets the hostel apart is the friendly local owner, Colorado, who goes out of his way to make sure his guests enjoy their stay. He's also a wealth of knowledge about Ecuador and can organize tours.

Farther down the same street is **Hostal Esperanto** (tel. 99/970-4569, www.esperantohostel.com, $16 pp), which is very clean with friendly, helpful staff. The pentagonal building has a rooftop bar with lots of hammocks. The two dorms sleep four people, and the four private rooms sleep 3-5 people in bunk beds. The hostel has a system that reuses gray water to irrigate the gardens.

In Tigrillo, at the end of the first street on the right, **Hidden House** (tel. 97/928-0589, www.hiddenhousehostel.com, $8-10 dorm, $25-30 s/d) is a large English/Ecuadorian-owned hostel with inviting common areas in attractive gardens. The vibe is friendly and laid-back. Bedrooms are wooden cabins with fans and mosquito nets, most with shared bathrooms. Two double rooms with private bathrooms have a small private patio. There are nightly activities (movie night, barbecue, beer pong, etc.), a communal kitchen, and a bar. A restaurant should be built by the time this guide is published. Hidden House accepts volunteers.

Farther down the Tigrillo road on the right is **Refugio de las Aves** (tel. 4/459-3414 or 4/206-0137, Facebook @refugiodelasaves, $15-20 pp, including breakfast), one of the first hostels in the neighborhood. The gardens feature native trees and plants (banana, lemon, orange, bamboo), and the hostel was built using natural local materials and traditional methods. Owned by Ecuadorians who converted their family home, the hostel has six rustic but charming cabañas sleeping 2-10 people. Most are self-contained with their own kitchen and living space. A gray-water system irrigates the garden.

Even farther down the Tigrillo road, down the fourth street on the right, is friendly, Canadian-owned **El Cielo** (Facebook @elcielomontanita, $10 dorm, $28 s/d), which has two private double rooms, a four-person dorm, and an apartment-style seven-person dorm for group bookings ($40 per night). There is a communal kitchen. Breakfast is available upon request ($3).

Two hundred meters (655 ft) south of the town center, in front of a quiet stretch of beach, is family-run ★ **La Gondola** (tel. 99/183-1488 or 98/512-5249, http://lagondolaecuador.com, $30 s, $50 d, breakfast included). Bamboo bungalows with air-conditioning and hammocks are set in peaceful gardens, with a charming wooden shack restaurant opening onto the sand.

On the *malecón*, **Tabuba** (tel. 4/206-0145, http://tabubamalecon.com, $50 s/d, $60 Fri.-Sat., breakfast included) has friendly service and wonderful ocean views, especially from the bedrooms on the upper floors and the rooftop terrace. Rooms have air-conditioning and television.

Located at the Point, ★ **Balsa Surf Camp** (tel. 98/971-4685, http://balsasurf-camp.com, $25-45 pp, breakfast included) is perhaps the best place to stay in Montañita. Built by a local surfboard shaper, Rasty, and his wife, Julie, using bamboo and wood, the rooms are set amid tropical gardens filled with art. One of the rooms is a refurbished VW van! The vibe is friendly and the staff are welcoming and helpful. As well as a restaurant, spa, and plenty of hammocks, there is free daily yoga and surf classes are available ($25 for 90 minutes). Julie and Rasty organize beach clean-ups and recycled art workshops with a group of local kids. Workshops are also held on meditation, alternative medicines, and healing methods. They also founded a group that established a permaculture project in the area affected by the 2016 earthquake. Attached to the hotel is a gallery of Rasty's unique balsawood surf boards, made from sustainably harvested wood. Some are decorated with encrusted stones or indigenous art.

Next to Balsa is Canadian-owned **Casa del Sol** (tel. 9/248-8581, http://casadelsolmon-tanita.com, $15 dorm, $25-30 pp private room, breakfast included). The common area has big sofas with colorful cushions, and the walls are covered with murals. The friendly bar is a gathering spot for guests and nonguests alike, making Casa del Sol a great place for meeting people. There is an excellent on-site yoga studio with daily classes ($8) as well as a Spanish school. Surf board rental, surf classes, and yoga-and-surf retreats are available.

Also at the Point, right in front of the surf break and part of the ★ **Tres Palmas** complex, are three rooms to rent, with air-conditioning, hot water, Wi-Fi, and parking (WhatsApp 99/352-8422, geofflynch1610@ hotmail.com, $30 s, $50 d). Surfboards, fishing poles, and snorkel gear are available to rent ($5/hour or $20 day). Tres Palmas also has a sushi restaurant and craft brewery.

INFORMATION AND SERVICES

There is no tourist office, but **Machalilla Tours** (tel. 93/984-5839, http:// machalillatours.org, 8:20am-10pm daily), just off the main street in the town center, can help you out by providing information about the area.

Montañita is the only town in the area with ATMs, and there are several in the town center. Most reliable for international cards are Banco Pichincha and Banco Bolivariano. There are several Internet cafés.

There is a pharmacy to the right of the church. In case of serious illness or injury, take a taxi to the hospital in the neighboring village of Manglaralto (24 de Mayo y 10 de Agosto, tel. 4/290-1192, 24 hours daily).

GETTING THERE AND AROUND

The bus company Cooperativa Libertad Peninsular (CLP, http://libertadpeninsu-lar.com) has a direct bus service between Montañita/Olón and the Guayaquil bus station *terminal terrestre*. In Guayaquil, the ticket office is on the third floor of the bus station. The journey takes three hours and costs $6.25. Buses leave hourly 5am-4pm, then at 4:30pm, 5pm, 5:30pm, 6:30pm, and 7:30pm. In Montañita, the CLP office is on the Ruta del Spondylus, just south of the town center. It's advisable to buy tickets the day before, especially in high season. Buses leave for Guayaquil daily at 4:45am, 5:45am, 7am, 10am, 1pm, 2pm, 5pm, and 6:30pm, with additional 8am and 9am departures Friday-Sunday.

If the CLP bus is full, it's possible to travel to/from Guayaquil indirectly via the new bus terminal in Ballenita, near the provincial capital, Santa Elena. In the Guayaquil bus station, head for windows 86 to 88 and buy a ticket for a CLP, CICA, or Liberpresa bus to Ballenita ($3.75, 2 hours). Once in Ballenita, buy a ticket for a CITUP or TransManglaralto bus to Montañita ($1.75, 1-1.5 hours). The last bus from Guayaquil to Ballenita leaves at 9pm, from Ballenita to Montañita at 8pm. If you miss the last bus to Montañita, a taxi from the Ballenita bus station costs $25. A taxi between Guayaquil and Montañita costs around $90.

To travel indirectly from Montañita to Guayaquil, flag down any southbound CITUP (blue) or TransManglaralto (green) bus on the Ruta del Spondylus. Buses pass roughly every 20 minutes 5am-9pm, and Ballenita is the last stop. From Ballenita, there are buses to Guayaquil (every 20 minutes with CLP, CICA, or Liberpresa), Quito (overnight only, with Transportes Esmeraldas, www.transportesesmeraldas.com), and Baños (overnight only, with Cooperativa de Transportes Baños, www.cooperativabanos.com.ec).

Going north from Montañita, the CITUP buses travel as far as La Entrada, just north of Olón. The TransManglaralto buses travel via Puerto López (1 hour) to Manta (3 hours).

The most direct way to travel to Quito from Montañita is with **Wanderbus** (www.wanderbusecuador.com), which has departures from Montañita town center at 6:30am on Thursday, Saturday, and Monday, arriving in central Quito at 7pm ($25). The bus goes via Puerto López, and there is the option to spend the night there and continue to Quito the following day. Tickets can be bought online or in person at the Go Montañita tour agency (Segundo Rosales *y* Vicente Rocafuerte, tel. 98/667-9985, Facebook @ GoMontanita). Wanderbus also has a route from Cuenca to Montañita at 6:30am on Wednesday, Friday, and Sunday, with a stop in Cajas National Park, arriving at 6:30pm in Montañita ($59). These routes include guided tours.

CIFA (www.cifainternational.com) operates a bus service between Montañita and Piura in Peru, with stops in Guayaquil, Machala, Huaquillas, Tumbes, and Mancora. The bus departs daily at 8pm from the CIFA office a block from the park in Montañita.

Getting around Montañita is easy; everything is within walking distance. It's not advisable to walk along the beach alone at night, especially for women. Assaults are infrequent but do occur, especially around holiday periods.

There are two taxi companies in the area: Montanisol (http://montanisol.com, tel. 96/891-1333 or 98/279-5312), based in Montañita town center, and Manglaralto Express (tel. 9/826-7367, 96/863-5659, or 99/843-1588), based in Manglaralto. Both offer safe and reliable service. A taxi from Montañita to the Point or Manglaralto costs $1.50; to Olón $2.

★ Olón

The village of **Olón**, to the north of Montañita on the other side of the Point, has a fine beach and slightly calmer seas for beginner surfers. In recent years Olón has blossomed into a flourishing tourist destination in its own right, with plenty of good accommodation options, some excellent restaurants, and lots of seafood shacks and cocktail stands on the beach. There are some bars in Olón but no nightclubs, resulting in a different vibe from Montañita; it's fairly buzzing with life in high season, particularly around the central park, but has a more family friendly atmosphere than its rowdier neighbor to the south.

The **Olón Surf School** (Escuela de Surf Olón, tel. 99/735-6565, Facebook @ EscuelaDeSurfOlon) on the beach offers safe, good quality surf classes in English or Spanish with experienced instructors ($20 for 2 hours).

Outdoor Ecuador (Calle Othmar Stahelli, *frente a* Pacho's house, tel. 99/962-4398 or 95/940-0161, www.outdoorecuador. com) is a small, friendly Spanish school with alfresco classrooms. Also available, to students and non-students alike, are activities including mountain biking, jungle tours, island tours and treks, snorkeling, parasailing, custom surf trips, and volunteer programs. Spanish classes are available for all levels and cost $8/hour for group classes and $10/hour for individual classes. An intensive course of 15 hours per week costs $105 (group class) or $140 (individual).

FOOD

Next to Outdoor Ecuador is Olón's best café, ★ **Café de la Negra** (tel. 9/8260-6062, Facebook @OutdoorEcuador, 8am-5pm daily Dec.-May only, $2.50-6), run by a welcoming English-speaking local, Karen Teran. The café serves great coffee, imaginative salads and sandwiches, and yummy breakfasts and desserts, all freshly made to order. The vegetarian sandwich with homemade hummus, guacamole, cheddar cheese, vegetables, and sundried tomatoes is delicious, as are the chocolate frappuccinos!

There are street food vendors by the park, which is a lively spot in the evenings. Also right by the park is **Rasimar** (tel. 96/754-2009, Facebook @kathitaandrade21, 8am-5pm and 7pm-11pm daily, $3-15), which serves dishes such as *pescado encocado* (fish in coconut sauce). The friendly local owner studied culinary arts in Spain and is happy to accommodate special requests, including vegetarian and vegan. At the south end of the beach, ★ **Spondylus** (tel. 99/046-7975, http://spondylusrestaurant.com, 8am-11am and 5pm-10pm Wed.-Sun., $8-10) has a wide-ranging menu including pasta, Asian food, burgers, grilled meat/fish, and vegetarian options. Home delivery is available.

ACCOMMODATIONS

One of the best places to stay is ★ **Hostería Isramar** (Calle Santa Lucia *y malecón*, tel. 99/463-9191 or 4/278-8096, www.isramarhosteria.com, $50-70 s/d), next to the beach. Owned by a friendly local couple, the rooms are spotless and there are attractive common areas and a garden with tropical plants and hummingbird feeders. The café serves breakfasts, pizza, good coffee, and juices.

There are few budget places to stay in Olón, but **La Jungla** (13 de Diciembre *y* Alberto Pote, *junto a la* Casa Comunal, tel. 98/680-6782, http://lajunglahostal.wixsite.com/olon, $10-17 s, $16-20 d) is a friendly, decent option, located four blocks in from the ocean. The owner is a trained chef and offers breakfast ($4) and dinner on request, as well as Ecuadorian cooking courses. Bring earplugs if you're a light sleeper, as it's in the middle of the village.

San José and La Entrada

North of Olón is the quiet village of **San José**, where the long beach is often almost empty. There are a couple of hostels and restaurants, including **Cuna Luna** (tel. 99/128-5389 or 99/961-0927, www.cunaluna.com, $80 s/d, breakfast included), right on the beach. This tranquil retreat was conceived as a project to revitalize the village, offering work, training, and development to the local inhabitants. Most of the breezy thatched rooms and cabins have sea views, balconies, and hammocks. Construction is from local materials and uses bioclimatic design principles. The beachfront restaurant serves seafood dishes.

Just north of San José, the houses in the village of **La Entrada** have been painted with beautiful murals. Right on the Ruta del Spondylus is the area's most famous bakery, **Benito's** (tel. 9/6918-4985, Facebook @losdulcesdebenitooficial, 9am-8pm daily), which serves up tasty treats such as tiramisu, pistachio cheesecake, and passion fruit pie.

Manglaralto

The word almost universally used to describe Manglaralto, Montañita's neighbor to the south, is *tranquilo*. This small village is a great option for those wishing to stay somewhere quiet with easy access to Montañita, which is a 30-minute walk along the beach or a five-minute taxi ride away ($1.50). The village is named for its beautiful mangrove forest (literally translating as "tall mangrove"), one of the few remaining on this part of the coast. The long stretch of beach is quiet even in high season, and the visitors are mostly local. The surf break is fast and breaks close to the shore, so it isn't suitable for beginners.

Nightlife in Manglaralto is practically nonexistent, but in high season (December-May) there is a charming, rustic bar open on the *malecón*. **Ocaso** (tel. 97/986-0373, Facebook @Ocaso bar, noon-8pm Tues.-Thurs., noon-midnight Fri.-Sat.), owned by two local surfers, offers friendly service, great cocktails, and spectacular views of the long stretch of beach to the Point in Montañita.

It's a wonderful place to check out the sunset. **Playa de James,** on the *malecón* next to the river, caters to an older, expat crowd.

FOOD

There are few restaurants in Manglaralto, and most close before sunset. For economical local cuisine, head for the row of rustic cabañas on the beach next to the mangroves. At the end of the row, ★ **Punta Manglar** (tel. 98/953-8132, 8am-6pm, $3-6) has by far the best food and service. The family-owned café offers typical coastal dishes such as ceviche and grilled fish with rice and plantain chips, but the specialty is *bolón*. This butter-fried ball of mashed plantain, stuffed with cheese or ham, comes with coffee and/or juice and an optional side of fried eggs. Traditionally eaten for breakfast, *bolones* are delicious but heavy; you may not need lunch! Vegetarian options include a burrito.

Another excellent option is **Pizza Di' Alegria** (6pm-10pm Thurs.-Sun.), a wooden cabin in the middle of the village that opens on weekend evenings to offer delicious pizzas and gluten-free tacos (veggie and vegan options available). The friendly local owner started his business with a mobile pizza oven on a tricycle before establishing a more permanent establishment. Popular with locals, it's a welcoming hive of activity.

On Sunday mornings there is small organic market next to the church, where farmers sell fruit, vegetables, and local specialties such as raw cacao, coffee, tamales, and corn crackers.

ACCOMMODATIONS

There are a few good accommodation options. At the southern end near the hospital, ★ **Tagua Lodge** (Calle 10 de Agosto *y* Flavio Alfaro, tel. 4/290-1274 or 99/942-6819, www.tagualodge.com, $6-15 pp) is a friendly place with an attractive plant-filled common area and outdoor kitchen. Clean, simple rooms have private baths, hot water, and fast Wi-Fi. The owner, Luis Chavez, speaks fluent English and often stocks the kitchen with plantain, avocados, and yucca from his nearby

organic farm. Camping is available ($4), with tents and mattresses provided under individual shelters. Discounts are available for long-term stays ($180-300 monthly for a private room).

A block from the beach on the main street, **Manglaralto Sunset Hostel** (El Oro *y* Constitución, tel. 99/440-9687, www.manglaraltosunset.hostel.com, $25 pp, breakfast included) has clean, simple rooms, each with private bathroom, hammock, hot water, air-conditioning, and Wi-Fi. The local owners, Jorge and Adele, are extremely friendly and helpful. Jorge speaks excellent English.

Outside the village to the north, **Kamala Hostel** (tel. 99/813-2693, www.kamalahostel.com, dorm $7-11 pp, $30 s/d) is right on the beach next to the mangroves. Rustic cabins are set around a swimming pool, and there's a bar, a restaurant, and a dive school. Kamala is a party hostel and it's a great place to meet fellow travelers.

★ Dos Mangas and the Cordillera de Chongón

Just a few kilometers inland, the village of **Dos Mangas** feels like a different world. The slow-paced life in this small community, which depends on agriculture and traditional crafts, continues much as it has for decades. Here you can see horses carting in bamboo from the nearby forest; cowboys driving their herds; *toquilla* palm leaves (used to make Panama hats) being dried and woven; and *tagua* (vegetable ivory) being sculpted into tiny works of art. Both sides of the Vía Dos Mangas, the road running through the village, are lined with little stores selling traditional crafts and souvenirs.

The most enjoyable way to get to Dos Mangas is by renting a bicycle in Montañita, to fully appreciate the lush greenery of the countryside; it's a world away from the beach. A couple of places en route sell **iced coconuts** (*coco helado*) to drink from, and a woman in the village sells homemade **ice cream** for $0.25 (try the peanut flavor—*helado de maní*).

Another option is to take a *colectivo* (an adapted flatbed truck used as a shared taxi) from the junction where the Ruta del Spondylus meets the Vía Dos Mangas ($0.50) just north of Manglaralto. Traveling by *colectivo* is a great way to meet local people, but the five-passenger minimum rule means there may be a wait before departure. Those short on time can get a taxi from Manglaralto ($3, 10 minutes) or Montañita ($4, 15 minutes).

Located 4 kilometers (2.5 mi) down the Dos Mangas Road, **Bromelia Retreat & Healing Center** (http://bromelialodge.com) is an oasis of tranquility. Set amid beautiful gardens next to a forested river, the center offers various healing services, including reiki, massage, and Advance Tachyon Technology. Classes in chi kung, yoga, reiki training, meditation, and Japanese jujitsu are available for groups, private classes, or retreat packages. Bed-and-breakfast and long-term stays are sometimes available; contact the center for more information.

Just before the Bromelia Center, the **Santa Maria de Fiat** is an organic farm and store, selling a wide variety of organic products, including cow milk, soya milk, eggs, cheese, ham, jam, natural yogurt, and homemade cookies.

Dos Mangas is the starting point for hikes or horse rides into the protected tropical dry forest of the **Cordillera de Chongón**, where two alternative routes lead to waterfalls or natural pools. Howler monkeys are often heard and sometimes seen. The entrance to the reserve is a via an information center a couple of hundred meters past the village, and it's necessary to hire a guide ($20, up to 8 people per guide). Be aware that the paths can be very muddy after heavy rain and it may be a good idea to rent rubber boots ($0.50). Guided horseback rides are also available ($40 for a group of up to 4). Make your own way to the information center via Dos Mangas, or book a tour with **Sumpa Trip** (tel. 98/034-2989, http://sumpatrip.com).

Valdivia and Vicinity

The village of Valdivia, 20 minutes south of Manglaralto on the Ruta del Spondylus, is famous for being the home of one of the oldest settled cultures recorded in the Americas. Pre-Columbian ceramics made by the Valdivians, who lived in the area between 3500 and 1800 BC, are found in museums all over Ecuador. Considering this, the **Museo Valdivia** (tel. 99/360-3187, Facebook @museovaldiviaoficial, 9am-6pm daily, $2) is a small and humble affair, probably because the best artifacts are in the city museums, but the village is still inhabited by the descendants of the ancient culture, who make replica figurines and masks that are good souvenirs.

A few minutes north of Valdivia is a grassroots animal rehabilitation center, the Valdivia Marine Rescue Center, better known as the **Acuario Valdivia** (tel. 98/298-3994, Facebook @acuariovaldiviaecuador, 10am-12:30pm and 1:30pm-4pm Wed.-Sun. free), where visitors can see rescued sea lions, turtles, penguins, blue-footed boobies, and pelicans. Animals that cannot be returned to the wild will be life-long residents. If you find an injured creature on any of the local beaches, this is the place to contact, or bring it if you can (animals are accepted even when the center is closed).

Just inland from Valdivia is the ancestral community of **Barcelona,** where the people have been making *sombreros de paja toquilla*, or Panama hats, for over 100 years. Here you can see the *toquilla* palm plants being grown, cooked, dried, and woven into the famous headwear.

Midway between Manglaralto and Valdivia, near the village of Libertador Bolívar, is **Playa de Bruja** (Witch's Beach), where it's possible to go **paragliding/parapenting** (http://opeturmo.com or Facebook @ParapentePlayaBrujaEcuador, $30 for 15-20 minutes, including transport to/from Montañita by prior reservation, or just turn up 11am-6pm daily).

★ Ayangue

Sheltered bays are hard to locate on the Ruta del Spondylus, but the petite fishing village of **Ayangue** is a notable exception. Here the sea is calm, turquoise, and so warm in peak season it's like taking a bath. The horseshoe-shaped, white-sand beach fills up with local families on weekends and is reasonably quiet midweek. Activities include **snorkeling, paddle boarding,** and **whale-watching** (June-September). There is also a PADI dive shop, **Ray Aguila** (Brisas del Mar, opposite Cabañas Sumpa, tel. 4/291-6162, www.ray-aguila.com, 8am-4pm Tues.-Sun.).

The seafood **restaurants** on the beach are all part of a local women's association, offering the same fare at the same prices ($4-8). There's not much here for vegetarians, but most places can make up a plate of rice, salad, plantains, and *menestra* (lentil stew). After the restaurants close at around 7pm, local women set up barbecues in the streets.

Great places to stay include the family-owned, environmentally conscious **Muyoyo Lodge** (tel. 99/158-8610, www.muyuyolodge.com, $35 s, $60 d) at the west end of the beach. As well as eight rooms, there are three self-contained cabins for families and groups ($25 pp) made from 100 percent local materials, including bamboo and wood. There are free water refills and the lodge recycles plastic and glass. Owned by a friendly Italian/Peruvian couple, another delightful option is **Nautilus Casa de Mare** (tel. 4/459-1180 or 98/286-8450, www.nautilusea.com, $55-65 s, $85-95 d), right on the beach just southeast of the park. The front windows and terrace have stunning ocean views, and the back overlooks a picturesque lake. Cuisine from both Italy and Peru is available by reservation.

Ayangue is 3 kilometers (1.9 mi) off the Ruta del Spondylus. There are taxis waiting by the highway to take visitors to the village ($1.50).

SALINAS AND VICINITY

The beach resort of Salinas is packed with Guayaquileños during high-season weekends, but, apart from a community of retired U.S. expats, foreign visitors tend to give it a miss. This may be because Salinas has the feel of a wannabe Miami Beach; there's very little authentically Ecuadorian about the concrete *malecón* lined with high-rise apartments. On the plus side, there are good restaurants and the ocean is calm for swimming. The neighboring bay to the west, Chipipe, has a long, slightly quieter beach.

Entertainment

During high-season weekends, Salinas is a real party town for wealthy young Guayaquileños. Be aware that robberies on the beach have been reported at night.

The bar at **Chesco's** (*malecón junto al Banco Guayaquil*, tel. 4/277-0875, Facebook @chescoshostel) has wonderful ocean views, a good cocktail menu, and happy hour 7-9pm. For late-night entertainment, **Balu Beach** (Av. Naciones Unidas *y* Calle 50, tel. 99/127-2127, Facebook @BaluBeachClubSalinas, 8:30pm-3am Thurs., 8:30pm-4am Fri.-Sat.); **Samoa Beach** (Hotel Chipipe, Calle 12 *entre* Av. 4 *y* 5, tel. 99/473-0329, 8:30pm-4am Fri.-Sat.); and **Eleven Beach Club** (Calle 34, Chipipe, tel. 97/870-8979) are all popular with wealthy Ecuadorians and foreign visitors, while **Rockabar** (Calle 25 *entre* Av. General Enríquez *y* Av. Malecón Salinas, tel. 98/941-0939, Facebook @RockabarSalinasDisco, 9pm-3am Thurs., 9pm-4am Fri.-Sat.) attracts a more local, eclectic crowd.

Recreation and Tours

Most visitors spend their time sunbathing and swimming. Salinas also has plenty of water sports, from pedal boats to waterskiing, all of which can be arranged on the beach. At the west end of the *malecón*, **Hotel Casablanca**

1: Hostería Ecológica El Faro; **2:** Cordillera de Chongón; **3:** Olón's long sandy beach

(tel. 99/760-6121, Facebook @hotelcasablancasuites) rents bicycles for $3/hour.

Escuela Paradise Surf (General Enríquez Gallo, tel. 98/855-8124, http://sergbzn.wixsite.com/surfparadise, 6am-6pm Mon.-Fri., 6am-7pm Sat.-Sun.) is a friendly, family-run surf school that offers classes at all the local breaks, depending on ability level. The head instructor, Victor Bazán, is a national champion surfer and president of the Salinas Lifeguard Association. A 90-minute surf class costs $20, including transport and all equipment. ID is required for board rental ($20-25 per day). Stand-up paddleboard rental is available for $20 with a free class. Victor also offers tours of the local area (3 hours, $25 pp for 5 people).

To take a tour and see the shorebirds that gather at lagoons about 5 kilometers (3 mi) southwest of town, look for Ben Haase at the **Oystercatcher Bar** (General Enríquez Gallo *entre* Calle 47 *y* Calle 50, tel. 4/277-8329), who offers a morning trip ($40) for up to 10 people in English or Spanish. Ben also offers whale-watching trips in a 50-foot sailing boat between June and October.

Within the grounds of the Ecuadorian Air Force (FAE, 6am-7pm daily), **La Chocolatera** is the most westerly point of continental South America. It's a pretty barren spot, but its location at the intersection of oceanic cross currents creates some impressive crashing surf. More interesting is the nearby **Lobería**, home to a colony of male sea lions that come to recuperate after losing fights with more dominant males in their native Peru. There is a 2.5-kilometer (1.6-mi) trail between the two spots, both of which have decent breaks for advanced surfers. It's a long walk from the FAE checkpoint by Chipipe beach, so hire a bicycle in Salinas or find a taxi by the checkpoint to drive you to both spots and wait ($4).

Food

One of the highlights of Salinas is the food. The wealthy locals that frequent the resort expect good-quality restaurants, and there are several of them, mainly along the western half of the *malecón*. Prices are slightly higher than elsewhere, but there are plenty of places to eat for $5-8.

The **Mercado Central,** just off 22 de Diciembre, across from the Parque Sindicato de Sales (7:30am-4pm daily), is fairly small, but clean and well organized, with a good selection of fruit, vegetables, fish, and seafood. It's also a great place to sample local cuisine at low prices.

Jhimy's Food (Av. Jaime Roldós Aguilera *y* Calle 37, tel. 99/077-3789, 8am-9pm Tues.-Sun.) is the best budget option in town, serving set lunches, ceviches, *bolones,* and Peruvian dishes starting at $2.50.

Chesco's (*malecón junto al* Banco Guayaquil, tel. 4/277-0875, Facebook @chescoshostel, $2.50-11) serves breakfasts, *arepas* (griddled corn cakes with various fillings), and burgers, including vegetarian options. A couple of blocks west of Chesco's, **Luv'n'Oven** (tel. 9/995-78101, Facebook @luvnoven.ec, open for breakfast, lunch, and dinner daily) is one of the best restaurants in town, serving seafood and Italian dishes. A few blocks inland from the *malecón*, **Cevichería El Velero** (Leonardo Aviles/Av. 6 *y* Eduardo Espiazu/Calle 18, tel. 4/277-1379, 8am-7:30pm daily, $7-9) is an excellent spot for ceviche.

For something a bit different, try ★ **Big Ralph's** (tel. 4/312-7120, www.bigralphhostal.com, 6pm-9pm Wed.-Thurs., 6pm-10pm Fri.-Sun., $11-18), a friendly place owned by a British chef and his Ecuadorian wife. Located at the far eastern end of the *malecón*, just after the road turns the corner and heads inland, the restaurant serves British cuisine, including fish and chips and braised beef, plus Thai curry (with a vegetarian option) and gnocchi (also vegetarian).

With seafood everywhere, Salinas isn't an easy place for vegetarians. Apart from Chesco's and Big Ralph's, **Lui e Lei** (*malecón y* Calle 29, tel. 99/957-8101, 8am-10pm daily, $5-10) has a garbanzo bean salad, a cooked vegetable salad, and a quinoa salad.

Accommodations

In the heart of the action, ★ **Chesco's**

(*malecón junto al* Banco Guayaquil, tel. 4/277-0875, www.chescos.com, $10 dorm, $30-40 s/d) is the best budget option in town. Rooms are simple and clean with air-conditioning. Attractive, airy common areas have colorful, quirky decor, and the bar has postcard-worthy ocean views. Breakfast is not included, but it's available at the café downstairs. Located just after the east end of the *malecón* turns a corner and heads inland, family-owned **Big Ralph's** (tel. 4/312-7120, www.bigralphhostal.com/hostal, $27 s, $36 d) is another excellent budget-friendly option. Clean, simple rooms have air-conditioning and private bathrooms. A small courtyard garden holds a fountain. Service is friendly and bilingual. Breakfast is available for $8.

At the west end of the *malecón*, ★ **Hotel Casablanca** (tel. 99/760-6121, Facebook @@ hotelcasablancasuites, $50-60 s/d) is the best midrange option. The 26 spotless rooms are individually decorated with original art on the walls, each featuring a TV, fridge, safe, and air-conditioning. There is a lovely patio area by the pool, and a rooftop terrace offers a Jacuzzi overlooking the ocean—a great spot for sipping cocktails from the downstairs bar. A buffet breakfast is served in the on-site restaurant ($7), which also offers lunch and dinner. Free tea and coffee are available in reception. The service is friendly and professional. Located a block inland from the *malecón,* **Palmira Inn** (Av. Gnrl. Enríquez Gallo *y* Luis Alberto Flores, tel. 4/277-2678, http://palmirainn.com, $55 s, $75 d) is another good midrange option, with equally good service. The rooms are modern and spotless, and there is an on-site café.

Located on the oceanfront a few minutes' drive from the town center, ★ **Hostería Ecológica El Faro** (Cdla. La Milina, Manzana G, *entrando por la* UTE, tel. 4/293-0680, http://hosteriaecologicaelfaro.com, $112 s/d) is an oasis of nature and tranquility in the concrete desert of Salinas. When the owner, Gabriel Faidutti, bought an empty plot here 25 years ago, he planted trees that are now fully grown, providing the feeling and wonderful aroma of being in a forest. He built the whole place from scratch as a home to raise his daughter, who now runs the hotel with him. The income from the hotel goes toward feeding and caring for a number of animals, including parrots, a peacock, tortoises, and a monkey, all of which were rescued from traffickers or illegally kept as pets. The buildings have a nautical theme, with a replica lighthouse and a beautiful deck overlooking the ocean, complete with a ship's wheel. Everything has been put together with style and attention to detail. Original artwork adorns the walls. The rooms are immaculate and thoughtfully equipped, the shower is a joy, and the Wi-Fi works everywhere. Breakfast is included and guests are welcome to use the kitchen to prepare other meals. Gabriel is a kind, thoughtful host and loves to take his guests out on excursions. It's a $0.30 bus ride or $2 taxi to the central *malecón.*

Information and Services

There are several ATMs along the *malecón.* For incoming boaters, the **Capitanía del Puerto** is on the *malecón* at Calle 30.

Getting There and Around

To get to Salinas, take a taxi ($4) or bus from the new bus terminal in Ballenita, 13 kilometers (8 mi) to the west. The terminal (www.terminaltsantaelena.com) has frequent buses to/from Guayaquil (2 hours, $3.75), Montañita (75 minutes, $1.75), Puerto López (2.5 hours, $3), and Manta (4.5 hours, $7.50). Cooperativa Baños (www.cooperativabanos.com.ec) has overnight buses to Quito (several departures 7:30pm-9:30pm, 9-11 hours, $18) and to Baños (8pm and 9pm, 9 hours, $25).

Museo Los Amantes de Sumpa

Just outside the provincial capital of Santa Elena is the small **Museo Los Amantes de Sumpa** (Vía Libertad-Salinas, tel. 4/294-1020, 8:30am-4:30pm Tues.-Fri., 9am-5pm Sat.-Sun., free), with various exhibits on the history, culture, and customs of the inhabitants of the Santa Elena Peninsula. It also tells the story of an archaeological dig in the 1970s that unearthed 200 skeletons, including the well-preserved bones of a man and woman in an 8,000-year-old embrace, known as the "Lovers of Sumpa"; the museum is named after them. Free guided tours are available. All information is in Spanish. Buses heading east from La Libertad or west of Santa Elena can drop you off nearby, or take a taxi.

Guayaquil and Vicinity

While Quito is Ecuador's capital and cultural center, Guayaquil (pronounced WHY-a-keel), is the country's economic hub and largest city, with a population of 2.7 million. Previously notorious for being dangerous and dirty, Guayaquil used to have little to offer visitors but has undergone a major transformation in recent years, winning a United Nations award for redevelopment. It's much cleaner and safer than it used to be, with policed pedestrianized zones. While it's still undeniably hot, polluted, and noisy, it's worth devoting a day to exploring the highlights of this vibrant, steamy city.

Guayaquil's tourism centerpiece is the **Malecón 2000**, a 3-kilometer (1.9-mi) promenade along the Guayas River featuring botanical gardens, sculptures, museums, and cafés. The *malecón* leads to the colorful artistic district of **Las Peñas**, where cobbled streets are lined with colonial balconies and inviting cafés, and a set of 444 stairs leads to a lighthouse with impressive views of the city. In the **Parque Bolívar**, urban iguanas laze in the trees and on the lawns. Cross the impressive Puente de la Unidad Nacional to the swanky neighborhood of **Entre Ríos** to visit the **Parque Histórico**, one of the city's best attractions, with a wildlife sanctuary, cacao farm, and restored colonial buildings.

For restaurants and nightlife, **Las Peñas** and the neighborhood of **Urdesa** are the places to be. There are good quality hotels to suit every budget in Urdesa and the downtown area.

You don't have to travel far outside the city to connect with nature, with the **Manglares Churute** mangrove reserve an hour southeast of the city, and the **Cerro Blanco** tropical forest an hour to the west. The Gulf of Guayaquil, where the Guayas River empties into the Pacific, offers opportunities to experience a side of the city rarely seen by visitors, including community tourism projects in the mangrove reserve at **Cerrito de los Morreños,** to see dolphins near **Isla de Puná,** and to an Afro-Ecuadorian community on the **Isla Trinitaria.**

With a new airport and bus terminal, Guayaquil is an efficient transport hub for international and domestic destinations. Within the city, the Metrovía trolleybus system, modeled on Quito's, makes exploring quick and economical.

SAFETY CONSIDERATIONS

Poverty levels are high in Guayaquil and crime is a serious issue, though the Malecón 2000 and Las Peñas have a high security presence and are considered safe, even after dark. Avoid aimless wandering at any time of day—go directly from place to place, and stay on the main streets in the center. Stay alert and keep valuables out of sight. Muggings are fairly common, as are "express kidnappings," where rogue taxi drivers briefly abduct passengers, relieve them of their possessions, and force them to take cash out of an ATM. The surest way to avoid this is to ask your hotel or restaurant to call a radio (prebooked) taxi, or call one yourself (for telephone numbers, see the *Getting There and Around* section). For detailed information on the safe use of taxis in Ecuador's cities, see the *Getting Around* section of the *Essentials* chapter.

One Day in Guayaquil

Start the day the Ecuadorian way with a *bolón*, a butter-fried ball of mashed plantain stuffed with cheese or ham. **El Café de Tere,** with various locations across the city, is a good option for *bolón* and other traditional breakfasts.

Take a short hop out of the city center by bus or taxi to the **Parque Histórico** and spend the morning learning about local wildlife, rural traditions, and colonial history.

For lunch, make your way to the neighborhood of **Urdesa** to browse the many excellent eateries on the Avenida Victor Emilio Estrada.

In the afternoon, head to the **Parque Bolívar** for close up encounters with urban iguanas, then walk to the **Museo Municipal** and its gruesome yet fascinating display of shrunken heads. Continuing on foot, pass the impressive facades of the government buildings at the **Plaza de la Administración** to reach the **Malecón 2000.** Spend the rest of the afternoon strolling the impressive riverfront promenade, with its botanical gardens and museums.

Arrive at **Las Peñas,** at the north end of the *malecón,* in the early evening and climb the 444 steps to catch the sunset over the city. Find an inviting spot for dinner among the cobbled streets of Las Peñas before catching some live music at **Diva Nicotina,** at the foot of the steps, or mingling with the arty crowd in the city's most iconic bar, **La Paleta.**

SIGHTS

Most of Guayaquil's tourist attractions are concentrated about 5 kilometers (3 mi) south of the bus station and airport in the downtown center, which spreads out westward from the Malecón 2000. Traffic in the city is terrible, especially during the week, but most attractions are within walking distance. The municipal tourism site (www.guayaquiles-midestino.com) has themed walks and other things to do.

Malecón 2000

In the late 1990s, an ambitious project was launched to completely overhaul the rundown waterfront of the Guayas, resulting in the **Malecón 2000** (7am-midnight daily, tel. 4/252-4530, www.malecon2000.com), the pride of Guayaquil and symbol of its redevelopment. This 3-kilometer (1.9-mi) promenade is the biggest attraction in the city, with historical monuments, modern sculptures, museums, botanical gardens, fountains, bridges, children's play areas, shopping outlets, and restaurants. The cool breezes off the river and the watchful eye of security guards make a stroll along the Malecón 2000 a relaxing and pleasant experience. Along the boardwalk are public bathrooms, drinking fountains,

stations for charging cell phones, and free Wi-Fi spots.

A focal point is **La Rotonda,** where the *malecón* meets the Boulevard 9 de Octubre. This semicircular statue is the *malecón*'s most important historical monument, depicting a famous meeting of South America's two most prominent liberators, José de San Martín and Simón Bolívar (see the *History* section of the *Background* chapter for more information).

South of La Rotonda, past the **Moorish Clock Tower,** is the *Henry Morgan* (tel. 99/108-5820, Facebook @elbarcomorgan, departs 4pm, 6pm, and 7:30pm daily, plus 12:30pm and 2pm Sat.-Sun., $7), a replica of the famous Welsh pirate's 17th-century ship that takes passengers on one-hour river trips. There are late-night departures Thursday-Saturday with a free bar ($20).

North of La Rotonda is a large children's playground and the **botanical gardens**, a highlight of the *malecón*, with plenty of quiet benches amid the trees and plants. North of the botanical gardens is Guayaquil's answer to the London Eye, **La Perla** (10am-10pm Sun.-Thurs., $3.50, 10am-midnight Fri.-Sat., $5).

Across from La Perla is the **Museo Guayaquil en La Historia** (tel. 4/256-3078, 8am-4:30pm Mon.-Fri., 10am-6:30pm

Guayaquil Center

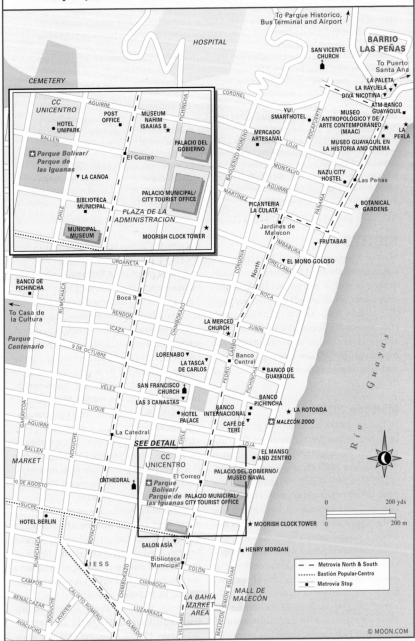

HOSPITAL

CEMETERY

To Parque Historico,
Bus Terminal and Airport →

BARRIO
LAS PEÑAS

SAN VICENTE
CHURCH

To Puerto
Santa Ana

LA PALETA
LA RAYUELA
DIVA NICOTINA
ATM·BANCO
GUAYAQUIL

LA
PERLA

CORONEL

CC
UNICENTRO

AGUIRRE

PICHINCHA

POST
OFFICE

MUSEUM
NAHIM
ISAAIAS B

HOTEL
UNIPARK

BALLEN

PALACIO DEL
GOBIERNO

★ Parque Bolívar/
Parque de
las Iguanas

El Correo

▼ LA CANOA

BIBLIOTECA
MUNICIPAL

CHILE

MUNICIPAL
MUSEUM

PALACIO MUNICIPAL/
CITY TOURIST OFFICE

PLAZA DE LA
ADMINISTRACION

MOORISH CLOCK TOWER ★

YUI
SMARTHOTEL

MERCADO
ARTESANAL

BAQUERIZO MORENO

ROCAFUERTE

MUSEO
ANTROPOLÓGICO Y DE
ARTE CONTEMPORÁNEO
(MAAC)

MUSEO GUAYAQUIL EN
LA HISTORIA AND CINEMA

LOJA

MONTALVO

AGUIRRE

MARTINEZ

PICANTERIA
LA CULATA

Jardines de
Malecon

NAZU CITY
HOSTEL

PANAMA

Las Peñas

★ BOTANICAL
GARDENS

IMBABURA

▼ FRUTABAR

North

ORELLANA

▼ EL MONO GOLOSO

CORDOVA

ROCA

GUAYAQUIL
GUAYAQUIL AND VICINITY

URDANETA

BANCO DE
PICHINCHA

RUMICHACA

Boca 9

CHIMBORAZO

RENDON

← To Casa de
la Cultura

ICAZA

Parque
Centenario

9 DE OCTUBRE

VELEZ

GARAYCOA

LUQUE

AGUIRRE

NOGUCHI

LA MERCED
CHURCH ★

JUNIN

LORENABO ▼

LA TASCA
DE CARLOS

CARBO

PEDRO

Banco
Central

PICHINCHA

■ BANCO DE
GUAYAQUIL

SAN FRANCISCO
CHURCH

LAS 3 CANASTAS

BANCO
PICHINCHA

● HOTEL
PALACE

BANCO
INTERNACIONAL

La Catedral

CHILE

CAFÉ DE
TERÉ

★ LA ROTONDA

✚ MALECÓN 2000

LOJA

BALLEN

MARKET

10 DE AGOSTO

CATHEDRAL

SEE DETAIL

CC
UNICENTRO

El Correo

★ Parque
Bolívar/
Parque de
las Iguanas

PALACIO MUNICIPAL/
CITY TOURIST OFFICE

PALACIO DEL
GOBIERNO/
MUSEO NAVAL

▼ EL MANSO
AND ZENTRO

Río Guayas

SUCRE

HOTEL BERLIN

RUMICHACA

BOYACA

IESS

CAMPOS

BENALCAZAR

NOGUCHI

LAVAYEN

CHIMBORAZO

CALIXTO ROMERO

SALON ASÍA

Biblioteca
Municipal

COLON

CHIRIBOGA

OLMEDO

LUZARRAGA

LA BAHÍA
MARKET
AREA

VILLAMIL

MALECON SIMON BOLIVAR

★ MOORISH CLOCK TOWER

■ HENRY MORGAN

MALL DE
MALECÓN

AYACUCHO

0   200 yds
0   200 m

— — Metrovia North & South
· · · · · Bastión Popular-Centro
■ Metrovia Stop

© MOON.COM

Sat.-Sun., $3), which tells the history of the city from prehistoric times to the present in 14 beautifully crafted miniature scenes with narration in Spanish or English. Above the museum is a **cinema** (www.malecon2000.com). The north end of Malecón 2000 culminates in the Banco Central's impressive **Museo Antropológico y de Arte Contemporáneo** (MAAC, tel. 4/230-9400, 8:30am-4:30pm Tues.-Fri., 10am-4pm Sun., free), which has exhibitions on ancient history and modern art, and a huge collection of pre-Columbian ceramics. Enter via the downstairs entrance if the upstairs entrance is locked.

Las Peñas

The north end of Malecón 2000 connects with the colorful artistic district of **Las Peñas,** the oldest neighborhood in Guayaquil, with cobbled streets and colonial architecture. Like the waterfront, this area used to be run-down and dangerous but has been completely regenerated in recent years, with freshly painted balconies and security guards. The main draw is the climb up 444 steps past cafés and art galleries. It's a hot walk, so come in the early evening and stay for a drink in the many inviting bars. At the top you'll find a small chapel and a lighthouse, which can be climbed for fabulous views over the city, Guayas estuary, and Santay Island to the east.

As well as climbing the hill, you can also walk around to the right from the bottom of the steps along the cobbled street called **Numa Pompilio Llona,** named after the Guayaquileño who wrote Ecuador's rousing national anthem. There are several art galleries and the city's most interesting bar, **La Paleta.**

Puerto Santa Ana

There are four museums in the Astillero building at the northern end of Numa Pompilio Llona, where the old district meets the ultramodern offices and apartments of **Puerto Santa Ana.** On the ground floor, the **Museo Barcelona S.C.** (tel. 4/228-1385, http://museobarcelonasc.com) and

Museo Club Sport Emel (tel. 4/207-5054, Facebook @museo.emelec.3) are dedicated to Guayaquil's two major soccer teams (both open 10am-6pm Wed.-Sun., free). The second floor houses the **Museo de la Música Popular Guayaquileña Julio Jaramillo** (tel. 4/207-5004, 10am-5pm Wed.-Sat., 10am-3pm Sun., www.museomunicipaldel-amusicapopular.com, free) named after one of Ecuador's most famous singers. The museum tells the history of the city's music scene, focusing on the melancholic *pasillo*, considered the national music style. Next door is a museum dedicated to the history of brewing, **Museo de la Cerveza** (tel. 4/207-5004, 10am-5pm Wed.-Sat., 10am-3pm Sun., free).

Parque Centenario

From La Rotonda on the Malecón 2000, follow the Boulevard 9 de Octubre to the **Parque Centenario,** central Guayaquil's largest square. The trees are a welcome oasis and in the center stands the Monument to the Heroes of Independence. On the west side of the square is the **Casa de la Cultura** (Facebook @CCENucleoGuayas, tel. 4/230-0500, 9am-1pm and 2pm-5:30pm Mon.-Fri., free), which has a pre-Columbian art museum on the 6th floor. Two rooms house exhibitions of artifacts made from gold and precious metals, ancient ceramic figures, and shamanic objects. Signage is in Spanish. The rest of the building hosts regular cultural events, including art exhibitions, music and dance performances, and film festivals.

Plaza de la Administración and Vicinity

A couple of blocks south of La Rotonda are the grand buildings of the local government, the most impressive of which is the Renaissance-style **Palacio Municipal,** whose Corinthian columns support an arched interior passage covered by a glass ceiling. One block inland from the *malecón* is a pleasant pedestrianized zone around the **Plaza de la Administración,** with statues, fountains, and a monument to Mariscal Sucre.

Parque de las Iguanas

The white, neo-Gothic **cathedral**, rebuilt in 1936 after it was destroyed by fire, dominates the west side of Parque Bolívar, also known as Parque Seminario or **Parque de las Iguanas**. The centerpiece of the park is an imposing monument of South American liberator Simón Bolívar on horseback, but even Bolívar can't compete with the sight of dozens of urban iguanas lazing around in the trees and on the lawns. There's also a fish pond filled with turtles.

Museo Municipal

One block southeast of the Parque de las Iguanas is the **Museo Municipal** (Sucre y Chile, tel. 4/259-4800 ext. 7402/7308, www. museoarteyciudad.com, 9am-5:30pm Tues.-Sat., free), one of the oldest museums in Ecuador. Downstairs are exhibitions on natural history and the history of the city. Upstairs is a room of portraits of Ecuadorian presidents, nicknamed "the room of thieves," and another with medals and coins. Also upstairs is the museum's most interesting, and gruesome, exhibit: a display of five shrunken heads, three of which were unfortunate missionaries who paid the price for attempting to convert Shuar people to Christianity. The other two heads were fellow Shuar, killed in conflicts over territory or women. Alongside the display is a step-by-step explanation, with diagrams, of how the heads were made. All signage is in Spanish, but free English tours are available. Identification is required to enter the museum (one ID per group is sufficient). The museums hosts regular temporary exhibitions and music events.

Parque Histórico

Across the bridge in the wealthy district of Entre Ríos, the 8-hectare (20-acre) **Parque Histórico** (tel. 4/283-2958, www.parquehistorico.gob.ec, 9am-4:30pm Wed.-Sun., free) is definitely worth the trip out of town. The park is divided into three zones. The wildlife zone was created out of the natural mangroves of the Río Daule and houses over 50 species of wild animals, all of which were rescued from traffickers or illegally kept as pets. This zone is explored via raised wooden walkways through various ecosystems, with animals including ocelots, monkeys, a tapir, and a harpy eagle. The traditions zone depicts rural life, including a cacao farm and a large ethnobotanical orchard growing ancestral medicinal plants, fruits, and vegetables. An on-site store sells the produce of the farm, and there are displays on domestic permaculture and organic farming techniques. In the urban architecture zone, some of Guayaquil's lost colonial buildings have been reproduced, and the upmarket **Casa Julián** is a beautiful spot to have an afternoon tea and gaze over the river. There are buses to Entre Ríos from the terminal, or get a taxi from downtown ($5).

ENTERTAINMENT AND EVENTS
Nightlife

Guayaquil's nightlife rivals Quito's, and the locals, of course, will tell you that it beats the capital hands down. As in Quito, bars are usually empty before 9pm, and the night gets going toward midnight on weekends. It can be a bit expensive, with cover charges ranging $5-20 in the upmarket joints.

The breezy, bohemian atmosphere of Las Peñas makes it the most pleasant area to visit at night, with countless bars, cafés, and restaurants. It's also far safer than alternative nightspots in the city, under the watchful eye of security guards. At the bottom of the steps, one of the best bars to catch live music is **Diva Nicotina** (tel. 4/504-8763, Facebook @DivaNicotinaBar, 7pm-midnight Tues.-Thurs., 7pm-2am Fri.-Sat.). Many of the city's best musicians play here—everything from Latin rock to jazz and Cuban habanera. Some music nights are free; others have a $10 cover. Farther up the steps, there are plenty

---

1: macaws at the Parque Histórico; **2:** iguanas in Parque Bolívar; **3:** shrunken heads, or *tsantsas*, in the Museo Municipal; **4:** the Malecón 2000

of endearing little bars serving beer, cocktails, and tapas, some with great views over the river.

Instead of climbing the Las Peñas stairs, follow the cobbled street Numa Pompilio Llona round to the right to find **La Rayuela** (tel. 98/339-7261, @RayuelaEc, 6pm-3am Tues.-Sat.), a restaurant and bar with frequent live music nights.

Farther down Numa Pompilio Llona is one of Guayaquil's most iconic bars, ★ **La Paleta** (tel. 4/232-0930, 8:30pm-2am Tues.-Sat., $15 minimum). The city's creative crowd comes here to enjoy the eclectic, colorful decor, low ceilings, cozy nooks and crannies, and wide-ranging menu of cocktails and tapas. Epitomizing the arty atmosphere of the district, this is one place you shouldn't miss.

As an alternative to the city center, the northern district of **Urdesa** ($3 by taxi from downtown) has thriving nightlife, with countless restaurants and bars lining the main street, Victor Emilio Estrada. **El Manantial** (Estrada *y* Las Monjas, tel. 4/288-4288, Facebook @elmanantialbar, 2pm-midnight Mon.-Wed., 2pm-3am Thurs.-Sat.) is a Guayaquil institution. It's an informal bar-restaurant where you can fill up on Ecuadorian staples accompanied by pitchers of beer. Afterward, head farther down the street to another long-standing favorite, **Chappus** (Estrada *y* Las Monjas, tel. 4/288-1181, Facebook @chappusbeeroficial, 7pm-3am Tues.-Sat.), a rustic wooden bar open since 1984. Either have a quiet drink upstairs or shake it on the dance floor downstairs later on. The nearby **Frutabar** (tel. 4/600-0828, www.frutabar.com, 11am-midnight Mon.-Sat., 11am-11:30pm Sun.) serves good cocktails and sangria in a colorful space with surfboards and tropical murals on the walls. For something a bit different, try the **Pop-Up Teatro-Cafe** (Circunvalación Sur #405 *entre* Ebanos *y* Diagonal, Urdesa, tel. 99/123-4500, @PopUpTeatroCafe, from 8pm Wed.-Sun., $5), a bohemian café, bar, and performance venue showing several short theater productions each night (Spanish only).

The municipal calendar of events can be found at www.guayaquilesmidestino.com.

Festivals

The biggest parties in Guayaquil take place at **New Year's,** when the city is filled with fireworks and burning effigies representing the old year. The heart of the action is the Malecón 2000, where there is a huge street party with live bands. From mid-December to mid-January, up to 40 giant papier-mâché sculptures of characters such as Darth Vader, Jack Sparrow, and Godzilla are located around the downtown area to form the **Ruta de los Monigotes Gigantes** (Route of the Gigantic Dolls). Following pleas from the firefighters, these effigies are no longer burned. **Carnaval** is celebrated in February or March, with parades, concerts, and raging water fights, but many residents head for the beach and much of the city has a deserted air. There are more concerts and parades to celebrate the **Foundation of Guayaquil** on July 25 and the **Independence of Guayaquil** on October 9. For more information, see www.guayaquilesmidestino.com or Facebook @ TurismoGuayaquil.

RECREATION AND TOURS

El Manso (*malecón y* Aguirre, tel. 4/252-6644, http://manso.ec) offers two bicycle tours of the city ($20 pp): a daytime tour of the historic downtown area and an evening brewery tour. El Manso also offers several ecotours showing aspects of the city rarely experienced by visitors. All are managed and operated by local communities or organizations, with all economic benefits going directly to them. Tours include a full-day trip to a cooperatively run agro-ecological cacao farm; full-day and overnight trips to a community ecotourism project in Cerrito de los Morreños, with boat trips through mangroves in the Gulf of Guayaquil and lodging provided by local families; and a three-hour excursion to an Afro Ecuadorian community on the Isla Trinitaria, including a boat trip through the mangroves, visits to local grassroots organizations, a marimba dance class, and an Afro Ecuadorian meal. For more information and prices, see the website.

Tangara Guest House & Tours (Sáenz y O'Leary, Ciudadela Bolivariana, Bloque F, Casa 1, tel. 4/228-4445 or 4/228-2828, www. tangara-ecuador.com) offers day tours of Guayaquil and trips to Quito, Cuenca, the Galápagos, and the coast for bird-watching. Most interesting are the tours to various indigenous community tourism projects in the Amazon, Andes, and coast.

SHOPPING

Shopping in Guayaquil covers the whole budget spectrum from bustling open-air markets to pristine air-conditioned malls offering luxury goods at U.S. prices. The high street stores of downtown are somewhere between the two extremes.

La Bahía, opposite Malecón 2000 north of Olmedo, is the city's black market. You can find everything here—shoes, clothing, electronics, and, unfortunately, most of the city's stolen cell phones. It's all semi-legal with a faint air of danger, so take care and don't go with much money or valuables.

For souvenirs and handicrafts, head to the artisan market a few blocks inland from the north end of the *malecón*. The **Mercado Artesanal** (Loja *entre* Moreno y Córdova, www.mercadoartesanalguayaquil.com, 9am-7pm Mon.-Sat., 10am-4pm Sun.) has over 250 stores offering indigenous clothing, Panama hats, bags, leather goods, handicrafts, paintings, and ornaments. Quality varies but there are some treasures to be found. Visitors are generally left to browse in peace, making it a pleasant experience. Be sure to haggle! For Panama hat specialists, head to **Ecua-Andino** (Ciudadela Albatros Mz. 28 solar 4, tel. 4/228-2500, www.ecua-andino.com, 8am-5pm Mon.-Fri.).

Las Peñas is a charming spot to browse the dozens of alluring little stores selling artisanal wares, paintings, and sculptures.

Remember that if you want your tourist dollars to benefit Ecuadorians, it's much better to shop at locally owned businesses, but if you're looking for big supermarkets, international chain stores, and movie theaters, you'll find them in Guayaquil's many *centros comerciales* (malls). Major malls include: **Policentro** (www.policentro.com. ec), **San Marino** (www.sanmarino.com. ec), **Mall del Sol** (www.malldelsol.com. ec), **Mall del Sur** (www.malldelsur.com. ec), and **City Mall** (www.citymall.com. ec). The city's most economically priced mall is inside the bus terminal, the **Centro Commercial Terminal Terrestre** (http:// ttg.ec/centro-comercial-terminal).

FOOD

The **Mercado Central** (Av. 6 de Marzo y 10 de Agosto), a few blocks inland from the iguana park, and the smaller, better organized **Mercado Este** (Carlos Gómez Rendón y Chimborazo), just south of the Malecón 2000, are good places to pick up fresh produce.

For local organic produce, head to **La Molienda** (Dátiles 416 y la Sexta, Urdesa, tel. 98/517-1743, Facebook @organicfoodmarket, 10am-7pm Wed.-Fri., 9am-3pm Sat.), which also sells natural health and beauty products. Another option is the **Feria Bona Terra** organic market (www.fundacioninterris.org) that takes place every other Saturday morning at the Balandra Cruz del Sur school in the neighborhood of Los Ceibos, where small-scale farmers and artisans sell fresh fruit, vegetables, dairy products, jams, cotton clothes, cookies, seeds, and vegan food.

For restaurants, Las Peñas is the most pleasant place to browse, while the Urdesa neighborhood's main avenue, Victor Emilio Estrada, is lined with good eateries.

Asian

Chinese restaurants (*chifas*) abound in Ecuador, but most are poor quality. Sucre and Chile is Guayaquil's *chifa* corner, with plenty of restaurants offering passable entrées for $3-6. Of these, **Salon Asia** (tel. 4/232-8088, http://salonasia.ec, 11am-9pm daily, $3-6) was the city's first Chinese restaurant, established in 1940. Salon Asia also has restaurants in Urdesa and downtown. Located in the Las Terrazas mall in upscale Samborondón, **Hong Kong Deli** (tel. 4/283-7221, Facebook @HKDeli, 12:30pm-10pm Tues.-Thurs. and Sun., 12:30pm-10:30pm Fri.-Sat., $8-15) is generally considered the city's best Chinese. Try the dim sum ($4-6).

Noe Sushi has three locations in Guayaquil, all in malls (Mall del Sol, San Marino, and Bocca, www.noesushibar.com, $7-20). Just as good is **Isao** (Bálsamos 102 *y* Estrada, Urdesa, tel. 4/288-9936, Facebook @isaosushiec, noon-11pm Tues.-Sat., noon-10pm Sun., $8-12).

Bakeries and Cafés

A block from the *malecón* is one of the city's best bakeries, **El Mono Goloso** (Luzarraga *y* Panama, tel. 99/802-1567, Facebook @elmonogoloso, 8am-6:30pm Mon.-Fri., 11am-5pm Sat., $0.50-3). Another good downtown bakery is the **Galleta Pecosa** (10 de Agosto *y* Boyacá, tel. 4/251-8636, Facebook @PasteleriaGalletaPecosa, 9am-8:30pm Mon.-Sat., 9am-6:30pm Sun., $1-3). In Urdesa, ★ **Camellias Tea** (Victor Emilio Estrada *y* Ficus, tel. 4/503-4031, 11am-8:30pm Mon.-Thurs., 11am-10pm Fri.-Sat.) is a stylish teahouse and café offering a wide range of drinks, healthy, organic food with plenty of vegetarian options, and yummy desserts. For a slice of beach chic, head to **Frutabar** (www.frutabar.com, 11am-midnight, Mon.-Sat. 11am-11:30pm Sun., $7-12) at its downtown location (*malecón y* Martínez, tel. 4/230-0743) or in Urdesa (Estrada *y* Las Monjas, tel. 4/600-0828). A huge selection of *batidos* (fruit shakes), sandwiches, and imaginative burgers are served in a colorful space with surfboards and tropical murals on the walls.

Ecuadorian

The center is full of cheap places offering $2-3 *almuerzos* (set lunches), but quality is variable. To eat with the locals, head for the food courts at **Mercado Central** (Av. 6 de Marzo *y* 10 de Agosto) or the **Mercado Este** (Carlos Gómez Rendón *y* Chimborazo).

A good option for Ecuadorian breakfasts is **El Café de Tere** (www.elcafedetere.com, 6:30am-2pm daily, $2-7), which has a few locations around the city, including downtown (*malecón y* Pichincha) and near the airport (Av. Hno Miguel *y* R. Nazur, tel. 4/262-7348). The specialty is *bolón*, a butter-fried ball of mashed plantain stuffed with cheese or ham. Also downtown, **El Jardín** (Chimborazo *y* Venezuela, tel. 4/244-3048, Facebook @restaurant.eljardin, 8am-3:30pm daily, $3.50-7) offers a range of national dishes and has won awards for the city's best *caldo de bolas*, a traditional coastal soup consisting of plantain dumplings stuffed with meat and vegetables served in a beef broth with corn and yucca. In Urdesa, **Lo Nuestro** (Estrada *y* Igueras, tel. 4/228-9330, noon-11pm daily, Facebook @RestauranteLoNuestroEc, $10-15) offers a wide range of traditional dishes with an old-school ambience to match. Open since 1974, **La Canoa** (within the Hotel Continental, Chile *y* Av. 10 de Agosto, tel. 4/232-9270, 24 hours daily, $5-20) offers pricey but good Ecuadorian dishes such as goat or chicken stew. The soup of the day is a steal at $1.22.

Seafood

Lo Nuestro (Estrada *y* Igueras, tel. 4/228-9330, noon-11pm daily, Facebook @RestauranteLoNuestroEc, $10-15) offers lots of good seafood dishes. Near the *malecón*, **Picanteria La Culata** (General Cordova *y* Mendiburu, tel. 99/230-8348, 6am-midnight Mon.-Thurs., 6am-2am Fri.-Sat., $5-10) is a no-frills place offering ceviche, *encocado* (shrimp or fish cooked in a rich, spiced coconut sauce), and seafood rice. For a gourmet experience, try **El Caracol Azul** (9 de Octubre *y* Los Ríos, tel. 4/228-0461, http://elcaracolazul.ec, noon-11pm daily, $20-25), established over 40 years ago and considered the city's best seafood restaurant. If you want to eat like a true Guayaquileño, head to a *casa del cangrejo* (crab house). In Urdesa, the **Red Crab** (Estrada *y* Laureles, tel. 4/288-7632, www.redcrab.com.ec, 11:30am-4pm and 6pm-11pm Mon.-Thurs., 11:30am-midnight Fri.-Sat., 11:30am-10:30pm Sun., $15-20) serves crab, shrimp, and lobster cooked every way imaginable.

Steak Houses

The huge **La Parillada del Ñato** (Estrada 1219 y Laureles, Urdesa, tel. 4/238-7098, www.parrilladelnato.com, noon-11:30am daily, $5-12) is famous for its mammoth portions and is always packed. There are platters of barbecue for meat eaters, and soups, pastas, and pizzas for vegetarians. There are five other branches across Guayaquil.

Vegetarian

All the vegetarian restaurants listed offer *almuerzos* (set lunches) consisting of a soup, a main course, and a juice/soft drink. For more vegetarian restaurants in Guayaquil, see www.happycow.net.

Right on the *malecón,* inside the Manso Boutique, is ★ **Zentro** (Malecón y Aguirre, tel. 98/794-9376, Facebook @zentroeco, 7:30am-11am daily, noon-10pm Mon.-Fri., 6pm-10pm Sat.-Sun.), an agro-ecological restaurant that serves breakfast and dinner, as well as set lunches. There are regular cultural and musical events in the evenings.

A few blocks inland from La Rotonda on the *malecón* is vegan restaurant **Lorenabo** (Francisco Paula de Icaza y Cordova, tel. 99/383-7990, noon-5pm Mon.-Fri., *almuerzo* $3), which also has an à la carte menu featuring mainly brown rice, noodle, and spaghetti dishes with soy meat ($4).

It's a little bit out of the way, but **Emilia Restaurante Vegetariano** (Av. Quito 2809 y Calle 21, 11:30am-3:30pm Mon.-Sat., *almuerzo* $2.50) is a no-frills gem, and one of the few veggie places open on Saturday (there are even fewer on Sunday). Tasty and nutritious food is efficiently served by friendly people.

In Urdesa, **Amaranto** (Estrada *entre* Higueras y Ilanes, tel. 4/512-4307, noon-5pm Sun.-Wed., noon-9:30pm Thurs.-Sat., Facebook @amaranto1light, *almuerzo* $6) is

a more stylish, upmarket option. Unlike the others, it is open every day.

Other International

For cheap, tasty pizzas cooked in a clay oven, try **El Hornero** (Estrada 906, Urdesa, tel. 4/460-4788, 11am-11pm Mon.-Sat., 11am-10pm Sun., $5-15). For pizzas with a difference, try **Pizza Alta** (Av. Las Monjas, Urdesa, http://pizzaalta.com, tel. 4/601-4579, 1pm-10:30pm Tues.-Thurs., 1pm-11pm Fri.-Sat., 5:30pm-9:30pm Sun., $5), where all the pizzas are 5 centimeters (2 in) thick with fillings inside and topped with sauce, like pies. One of the best Italian restaurants in town is **Riviera** (Estrada 707 y Ficus, tel. 4/460-2628, http://rivieraecuador.com, 12:30pm-11pm Mon.-Sat., 12:30pm-5pm Sun., $13-23). All three restaurants offer home delivery.

For Spanish tapas and paella, head to **La Tasca de Carlos** (Gral. Cordova 1002, tel. 4/283-6680, 8am-6pm Mon.-Fri., $10-15).

ACCOMMODATIONS

For security reasons, many hostels and hotels in Guayaquil don't loudly advertise their presence and can be quite hard to find. Many have discreet signs next to closed doors and a bell to ring.

$10-25

Downtown has several fairly decent budget options. Three blocks from the iguana park, **Hotel Berlin** (Rumichaca y Sucre, tel. 4/252-4648, Facebook @hotelberlingye, $12-15 s/d) is excellent value for its rock bottom prices. Rooms are basic but have private bathrooms and air-conditioning. Amenities include a café, a communal kitchen, and a washer/dryer that guests can use for free. Staff are helpful and friendly. The downside is the traffic noise, so bring earplugs. A block from the Parque Centenario, **Hotel Sander** (Luque 1107 *entre* Quito y Pedro Moncayo, tel. 4/232-0030, http://www.hotelsander.com.ec, $16-18 s, $20-24 d) is also good value. Rooms are basic but clean, most with air-conditioning. Breakfast isn't included but there is a restaurant attached. **Hotel Jeshua** (Padre Vicente Solano y José Mascote, tel. 4/239-6253, www.hoteljeshua.com/en-gb, $24 s, $47 d) is owned by a friendly local family. Rooms come with both air-conditioning and fan. Prices include breakfast. Laundry and airport transfers are available. **Hotel Simmonds** next door is owned by the same family with rooms at the same price.

Dreamkapture Inn (Juan Sixto Bernal, Manzana 2, Villa 21, tel. 4/227-3335, www.dreamkapture.com, dorm $9-10.50, $17-19 s, $24-26 d, breakfast included) is a decent budget option near the airport. Most rooms have fans, some have air-conditioning. Staff speak English. It has a communal kitchen and a women-only dorm, in addition to the coed dorms. Airport pickup by the hostel costs $10; a taxi can be reserved for the return journey for $5. Urdesa's best budget option is ★ **Nucapacha** (Bálsamos Sur 308, tel. 4/261-0553, www.nucapacha.com, $11.50 dorm, $23-28 s, $29-35 d, breakfast included). The hostel is clean, modern, and friendly, with a tourist information desk, outdoor patio, bar, and pool, but no hot water or air-conditioning (rooms have fans). A free English-speaking tour of the city leaves daily at 10:30am.

$25-50

Ten minutes' walk from the airport, **DC Suites** (www.dcsuitesgye.com, $27 s, $31-36 d) is owned by a friendly local family who converted their home into the hostel, which is newly remodeled with plans for a solar water heater. Rooms are clean and modern with air-conditioning. Rates include free transfers to and from the airport, except midnight-6am, when they cost $5. Breakfast is available for $4.

Located right on the *malecón,* **Nazu City Hostel** (*malecón* y Montalvo, http://nazu-cityhostel.com, $15 dorm, $41 s, $49 d) is a delightful place. The walls and doors are covered with original work by visiting artists, and the furniture is made from recycled materials. There is a communal kitchen and exercise room. The hostel is pet friendly. Staff are friendly and speak English. Prices include

breakfast. Farther south on the *malecón,* ★ **El Manso** (*malecón* 1406 y Aguirre, tel. 4/252-6644, www.manso.ec, $15 dorm, $38-55 s, $48-63 d) is the city's most ecological option, aimed at travelers seeking to "expand their consciousness through contact with culture and nature." Each room is uniquely decorated and has air-conditioning. The hostel offers bicycle rental, has an on-site restaurant using agro-ecological and organic products, and organizes urban ecotourism experiences. Pets pay the same as human guests. See the website for their environmental policy.

Tucked away between Urdesa and downtown, **Tangara Guest House** (Sáenz y O'Leary, Ciudadela Bolivariana, Bloque F, Casa 1, tel. 4/228-4445 or 4/228-2828, www.tangara-ecuador.com, $35 s, $56 d, breakfast included) is a haven of peace, with paintings of birds, murals of vines, and lots of plants. Rooms have TV and air-conditioning. The people are friendly and speak English. There is a laundry service and free water, tea, and coffee. Two blocks from the Malecón del Salado, ★ **Hostal Villa 64** (Hurtado 808 *entre* Tulcán y Carchi, tel. 4/219-1034, www.hostalvilla64.com, $35 s, $55 d, breakfast included) has 10 immaculate and stylish rooms, each inspired by a different region of Ecuador, all with private bathrooms and air-conditioning. The owners are friendly and speak English.

$50-100

Conveniently located near Las Peñas, **Yu! Smarthotel** (Vicente Rocafuerte 250 y Manuel de J. Calle, tel. 4/259-7850, www.yuhotels.com, $59 s/d) is clean, modern, and very purple! Staff are friendly, professional, and speak English. Prices include a continental breakfast.

Between the airport and downtown, ★ **Hostal Macaw** (Cdla. Guayaquil Av. Victor Hugo Sicouret, tel. 4/229-6799, www.hostalmacaw.com, $60 s/d, breakfast included) is a family-run, environmentally friendly place. The ambience is warm and welcoming. The wood for the doors, fittings, and furniture comes from an invasive tree species in the Galápagos, and the fruit for breakfast is sourced from local organic farmers. The hotel uses no unnecessary chemical products; the rooms are scented with wood soaked in essential oils. The owner has an urban garden and tends the plants in a local park. The family speaks English, French, Italian, and some German.

Near the iguana park are two good options, both with English-speaking staff, great service, an included buffet breakfast, and similar facilities (restaurants, gym, deli): the newly remodeled **Unipark Hotel** (Clemente Ballen *entre* Chile *y* Chimborazo, tel. 4/232-7100, www.uniparkhotel.com, $85 s/d) and **Hotel Palace** (Chile 214 *y* Luque, tel. 4/232-1080, www.hotelpalaceguayaquil.com.ec, $85 s/d).

Family-run **Nazu House** (Av. Carlos J. Arosemena km 3.5, Ciudadela La Cogra, tel. 4/462-2523, http://nazuhouse.com, $85 s/d) is tucked away just west of Urdesa. It's hard to find, but its hilltop location offers a different lodging experience to the rest of Guayaquil. With friendly service, lush gardens, a pool, and great views of the city, it's worth seeking out. It's pet friendly. In Urdesa, **El Escalon** (Diagonal 419 *y* Circunvalación Sur, tel. 4/238-8239, www.escalonhotel.com, $67 s, $117 d, including breakfast) has friendly staff and an attractive garden that backs onto the river. The interior is colorful, with original art on the walls and furniture made from recycled materials.

Over $200

Over the bridge inside the Parque Histórico is the opulent **Hotel del Parque** (Av. Río Esmeraldas, Samborondón, tel. 4/500-0111, www.hoteldelparquehistorico.com, $400 s/d, including buffet breakfast and afternoon tea), a luxuriously renovated 19th-century property with a waterfront restaurant and a spa inside the bell tower of the original restored chapel.

INFORMATION AND SERVICES

Money

The most reliable ATMs for international cards are **Banco Guayaquil** (www.bancoguayaquil.com), which has nearly 300 ATMs across the city; **Banco Internacional** (www.bancointernacional.com.ec); and **Banco Pichincha** (www.pichincha.com). See their websites for up-to-date maps and lists of locations. **Western Union** has several branches across the city. See their website for locations and opening hours (www.westernunion.com).

Communications

The **post office** (Correos del Ecuador, www.correosdelecuador.gob.ec) has its main office a couple of blocks from the *malecón* at Aguirre and Pedro Carbo (8am-6pm Mon.-Fri., 9am-2pm Sat.). See the website for locations of the other eight branches. **Internet cafés** with **telephone cabins** are everywhere.

Health

If you are seriously ill or injured, the not-for-profit **Hospital Luis Vernaza** (Loja 700 *y* Escobedo, tel. 4/256-0300, www.hospitalvernaza.med.ec) near Las Peñas offers free emergency care. For private health care, head to the **Clínica Kennedy** (Av. del Periodista *y* Callejón, tel. 4/228-9666, www.hospikennedy.med.ec), renowned for its specialists and emergency services. There are also branches in Alborada and on Vía Samborondón. Ambulances are slow, so it's best to take a taxi to the hospital.

Foreign Embassies and Consulates

Several nations have consulates in Guayaquil, including: **Australia** (SBC Office Centre Building, Office 1-14, 1st Fl., km 1.5 Vía Samborondón, tel. 4/601-7529, 9am-1pm and 2pm-4:30pm Mon.-Fri.), **Canada** (Francisco de Orellana No. 234, Blue Towers Building, 6th Fl., office 604, tel. 4/263-1109, ext. 101, 9am-1pm Mon.-Fri.), **United Kingdom** (General Córdova 623 *y* Padre Solano, tel. 4/256-0400, ext. 318 or 336, 9:30am-12:30pm Mon.-Thurs.), and the **United States** (Calle

Santa Ana *y* Av. José Rodríguez Bonin, San Eduardo Sector, tel. 4/371-7000, 8am-5pm Mon.-Fri.). For details of other consulates, see www.embassypages.com/ecuador.

Other Services

The **Tourist Office** (tel. 4/252-4100, www.guayaquilesmidestino.com/en, 9am-5pm Mon.-Fri.), opposite the Palacio Municipal, stocks general information about the city and area. The website, in English, has plenty of suggestions for activities in the city. For maps, stop by the **Instituto Geográfico Militar** (IGM, Av. Guillermo Pareja #402, Cdla. La Garzota, tel. 4/224-3909, www.igm.cl). Maps can be requested in person at the office or online (see *Servicios* on the website).

For visa-related queries, head for the **Ministerio de Relaciones Exteriores y Movilidad Humana** (Edif. Gobierno del Litoral, Av. Francisco de Orellana *y* Justino Cornejo, tel. 4/206-8492). Take a Spanish speaker with you and be prepared to wait.

GETTING THERE AND AROUND
Air

Five kilometers (3 mi) north of the city center, Guayaquil's award-winning **José Joaquín de Olmedo International Airport** (Las Américas, tel. 4/216-9000, www.tagsa.aero) is Ecuador's only international airport besides Quito's.

The following airlines serve Guayaquil direct to/from domestic destinations: **TAME** (1700/500-800, www.tame.com.ec) flies to/from Galápagos (Baltra) and Quito. **Avianca** (tel. 1800/003-434, www.avianca.com) and **LATAM** (tel. 1800/000-527, www.latam.com) fly to/from Galápagos (Baltra and San Cristóbal) and Quito. Flights to other national destinations go via Quito.

The following airlines serve Guayaquil to/from international destinations: **AirEuropa** (tel. 1800/000-648, www.aireuropa.com, to/from Madrid), **American Airlines** (tel. 1800/010-357, www.aa.com, to/from Miami), **Avianca** (tel. 1800/003-434, www.avianca.

com, to/from San Salvador, Bogota, Cali, and Lima), **Avior Airline** (tel. 4/268-9150, www.aviorair.com, to/from Barcelona in Venezuela), **Condor** (www.condor.com, to/from Munich, Frankfurt, and Dusseldorf), **Copa Airline** (tel. 4/230-3211, www.copaair.com, to/from Panama), **KL** (tel. 4/216-9070, www.klm.com.ec, to/from Amsterdam), **LATAM** (tel. 1800/000-527, www.latam.com, to/from Lima, Santiago de Chile, and New York), **Spirit Airlines** (www.spirit.com, to/from Fort Lauderdale), and **TAME** (tel. 1700/500-800, www.tame.com.ec, to/from Bogota, Cali, Lima, Fort Lauderdale, and New York).

A taxi from the airport to the center of Guayaquil takes about 10-15 minutes and costs around $5. Make sure that you take a taxi with a Cooperativa de Taxis Aeropuerto logo on the side. Most hotels and hostels can arrange airport pickups, starting from $10 (some charge $20 at night). Check when making reservations for details.

International Buses

See the *Essentials* chapter for information on international buses to/from Guayaquil.

National and Local Buses

Guayaquil's new bus terminal is just north of the airport. It's clean, safe, efficient, and doubles as a shopping mall. All buses depart from the 2nd and 3rd floors. There are departures for just about every city in the country. Frequent buses depart for Santa Elena/Ballenita ($3.75, 2 hours), Montañita ($6, 3 hours), Machala (4 hours, $5), Manta (5 hours, $7), Cuenca (5 hours, $7), Riobamba (5 hours, $7), Ambato (6 hours, $8), Baños (7 hours, $10), and Quito (9 hours, $12). There are several daily and overnight departures to Huaquillas (5 hours, $7) and Loja (9 hours, $12). There are overnight departures to Puyo (7 hours, $10) and Coca (15 hours, $23).

Confusing routes, heavy traffic, and overcrowding mean that local buses ($0.30) are not really worth it. The Metrovía service is cleaner and faster.

Metrovía

The three main Metrovía lines include stops at the bus station, the airport, Las Peñas, and the cathedral (the most convenient stop for the downtown sights). For maps of the routes, see www.metrovia-gye.com.ec and click on *Mapa de Rutas*. From the main bus terminal, be aware that you'll need to cross six lanes of traffic to reach the Metrovía terminal. Pickpockets are a problem on the Metrovía, so don't carry valuables, and be vigilant. The flat rate is $0.30.

Taxis

Taxi drivers in Guayaquil are notorious for driving badly and overcharging foreigners. Few of them use meters, so negotiate the price in advance. It's worth asking at your hotel for the approximate price and then telling the driver, rather than waiting for them to give you an inflated price. As a rough guide, short journeys around downtown should be about $3, and trips from downtown to the airport, bus station, Urdesa, and other northern districts $4-5.

Guayaquil is the worst place in the country for "express kidnappings," where rogue taxi drivers briefly abduct passengers, relieve them of their valuables, and force them to take cash out of an ATM. Victims are usually released unharmed, but these incidents are terrifying and can turn violent. The surest way to avoid this is to ask your hotel or restaurant to call a radio (prebooked) taxi, or call one yourself. Reliable firms include **FastLine** (tel. 4/282-3333, www.fastline.com.ec), **Solservice** (tel. 4/287-1195 or 4/287-2837), and **Wayose** (tel. 4/212-0234 or 4/212-2569). If you choose to flag a taxi down in the street, there are several measures that you can take to minimize the risk. For more information, see the *Getting Around* section of the *Essentials* chapter.

Car Rental

Renting a car in Guayaquil is expensive, starting at around $50 per day before insurance, tax, or gasoline. It's not recommended, as the standard of driving is atrocious, and the excess charges are alarmingly high. If you really must, major companies at the airport include: **Avis** (tel. 4/216-9092, www.avis.com.ec), **Budget** (tel. 4/216-9026, www.budget-ec.com), **Hertz** (tel. 4/216-9035, www.hertz.com), and **Thrifty** (tel. 4/216-9088, www.thrifty.com.ec). More information about car rental is included in the *Essentials* chapter.

Train

Tren Crucero (tel. 2/265-0421, http://trenecuador.com/en) offers various scenic day-trip train rides departing from Durán, a suburb to the east of the city. Round-trip excursions range $30-112. One route goes to Alausí, the departure point for the Devil's Nose train ride. For more information, schedules, and prices, see the website.

NEAR GUAYAQUIL
Cerro Blanco Protected Forest

If Guayaquil leaves you craving fresh air and green spaces, this is the nearest place to get it. **Cerro Blanco** (tel. 98/622-5077, http://bosquecerroblanco.org, 8am-4pm daily, $4 pp, camping $4 pp) protects 6,000 hectares (14,800 acres) of tropical dry forest in the Chongón-Colonche hills. A tenth of this area has been reforested with native trees grown in the on-site nursery, which produces 100,000 saplings annually from collected seeds—a project that won a prize in the Latinoamerica Verde (Green Latin America) 2016 competition. There is also a sanctuary for animals rescued from traffickers or illegally kept as pets. The reserve accepts volunteers.

Cerro Blanco's biggest draw is the birdlife, with over 250 species including the endangered great green macaw, the symbol of the reserve. Known as the "*papagayo*" of Guayaquil," the macaw is endemic to the area, and only 50 remain in the wild. Lucky visitors might spot howler monkeys, whose low roar can often be heard. Jaguars are also present, although these are only seen on camera traps.

Only the shortest trails can be hiked independently, one of which goes to a butterfly garden. The longer trails require a guide (1-5 hours, $30-40 per group for English-speaking tours). Spanish-speaking tours are half price. Reservations are needed during the week with advance payment via bank deposit (easily made at a Banco Pacífico ATM). No reservations are needed on weekends. Some level of fitness is required, as the hikes are steep in places.

Cerro Blanco is about an hour west from the bus terminal in Guayaquil. Take a Villamil bus from the terminal ($1.50) and ask the driver to drop you off. It's a short walk from the highway to the information center.

Playas and Vicinity

As the closest beach resort to Guayaquil (1.5 hours), **General Villamil,** better known as Playas, is flooded with city dwellers at high-season weekends, but midweek the hotels and long beach have a deserted air. Fans of seafood will find it in abundance, though it's not the most scenic setting and the beach has a lot of litter. The beaches farther north are much more attractive with more to offer visitors.

RECREATION AND ENTERTAINMENT

Most people come to Playas to lie on the beach, drink a few beers, and fill up on seafood.

There are surf breaks for various ability levels, but no board rental, so bring your own. Playas is a fairly popular surf destination in peak low season, when sun and swell can be elusive in the Montañita area. On these days, both can often be found in Playas, making it an occasional day trip for wave-starved surfers and sun worshippers.

Nightlife is limited and only happens on high-season weekends. It's been reported that both **Blue Hawaii** (Av. Jaime Roldos y Gral Villamil) and **Joy Vip** (Av. Pedro Menendez Gilbert y 24 de Septiembre, tel. 98/092-0203, Facebook @JoyVipDiscotec, Thurs.-Sat. 8pm-3am) are decent, security-conscious clubs. Joy Vip has a formal dress code (no shorts or sandals). Blue Hawaii is most popular with foreign visitors.

FOOD

There are seafood shacks all along the ocean-front and they all serve pretty much the same fare: fish and shrimp fried, grilled, steamed, or breaded, as well as hot soups and cold ceviche. For a slightly more wide-ranging ocean-front menu, try **La Cabaña Típica** (*malecón,* tel. 4/276-0464, lunch and dinner daily, $4-10). Widely considered the best restaurant in town, **Juan Ostra** (Av. Zenon Macias, tel. 99/140-7215, Facebook @JuanOstras) is 2 kilometers (1.2 mi) inland and serves, not surprisingly, seafood.

Playas is not an easy place for vegetarians, but **Coffee D'Galo**, next to the square across from Banco Pichincha, offers fruit salads, sandwiches, *bolones* (fried plantain balls with cheese), and juices. Just down from Banco Pichincha on Avenida Jaime Roldós is **Dulces de Benito,** selling delicious cheesecakes, desserts, and pies.

The best place to try Playas' famous empanadas (fried pastry turnovers with various fillings) is **Empanadas Chilenas de Playas** (Roldós, in front of Parque Infantil, tel. 98/256-3293, 3pm-11pm Mon.-Fri., 10am-11pm Sat.-Sun., $1.30), at the east end of the *malecón.*

Fresh produce is available at the central market, **Mercado Municipal Pedro Pascual** (Av. 15 Agosto). At the time of writing, the **Centro Ecológico Turístico de Playas** (tel. 99/455-0692, Facebook @cepvillamil), just outside town to the west, was re-establishing its organic gardens with a view to selling fresh produce (and accepts volunteers).

ACCOMMODATIONS

Accommodations in Playas are underwhelming and quite pricey for the standard. Discounts are often available mid-week, even in peak high season.

An acceptable budget option is **Hotel Marianela** (Av. Jaime Roldos y Av. Paquisha, tel. 4/276-1507 $15 s, $19 d), where rooms are basic with private bathrooms and fans. Next to Banco Pichincha, **Hostal Descanso Quijote** (tel. 4/236-9677, descansoquijote@

yahoo.com, $28-40 s, $33-45 d) has rooms with air-conditioning, friendly service, a rooftop terrace, and an attractive common area and kitchen. Owned by a friendly, helpful local family, ★ **Hotel D'Laverdy** (Av. Jaime Roldos y Calle 3 de Noviembre, tel. 4/276-2501, www.hoteldlaverdy.com, $28-45 s, $33-56 d) is one of the best options in town. Some rooms have ocean views and balconies, and some have air-conditioning. Prices remain the same year-round, even during public holidays. There is a good restaurant that can cater to vegetarians.

Twelve kilometers (7.5 mi) east of the town center on the main coastal road, ★ **El Jardín de Playas** (km 10.5 Vía Playas/Posorja, tel. 4/276-6071, www.eljardinde-playas.com.ec, $35-45 pp) is a hidden gem. Self-contained cabins and suites are set in bougainvillea-filled gardens with lots of birds. It's a family-run place, with trees named after the owner's nieces and nephews. It has an outdoor pool, a children's play area, free drinking water, and lots of hammocks. A good restaurant (8am-8pm) caters admirably for vegetarians. Environmentally friendly, LGBTQ friendly, and pet friendly, El Jardín has a gray water system, organizes beach clean-ups, and provides space for community workshops on tourism, dental health, organic food cultivation, and commercial jam-making. The hotel also organized anti-parasite treatment for 300 local children. The owner, Maria Gabriela, is a wonderful host with a permit as a naturalist guide on the Galápagos Islands, where she leads small, tailor-made group tours that support small, eco-friendly businesses.

INFORMATION AND SERVICES
There are a few Internet cafés with telephone cabins in the center of town. The Banco Pichincha ATM is on the main plaza; the Banco Guayaquil ATM is near the central market.

GETTING THERE AND AROUND
Frequent buses to Guayaquil (1.5 hours, $2) leave with Transportes Posorja (near the church and the main plaza) or the faster Transportes Villamil (Guayaquil and Paquisha). The easiest way to travel between Playas and Santa Elena or Salinas is to take a Guayaquil-bound bus and transfer at Progreso. In Playas, *mototaxis* charge $0.50 for short journeys within the town.

Posorja, Isla de Puná, and Puerto El Morro
To support a real grassroots community ecotourism project, head to **Posorja**. This fishing town 20 kilometers (12.4 mi) southeast of Playas is the gateway for reaching the **Isla de Puná,** a large island inhabited by the direct descendants of the Punaes Indians, who fought bravely against the Spanish conquistadores.

The current islanders, who eke a meager living raising animals and growing coconuts, have started offering boat trips in the **Canal de Morro**, taking visitors to see rocky islands full of seabirds, including blue-footed boobies and frigate birds, and a group of dolphins that reliably come to feed on fish from the mangroves. Call or WhatsApp Francisco Parrales (tel. 99/710-3462) 2-3 days in advance to book a tour ($25 pp for 2-10 people, Spanish only) that includes the boat trip, a tour of the Isla de Puná and its mangroves, a traditional lunch, and a visit to an artisan who makes jewelry and handicrafts from local materials. Francisco, who leads the fledgling ecotourism project, hopes that it will provide much-needed income for his community. Sadly, they face some fairly overwhelming environmental threats, including a constant battle against litter from the Guayas River and a planned deepwater port that endangers the mangroves. His optimism in the face of this adversity is deeply affecting.

Boat trips to see the same dolphins and bird species (1.5 hours, $5) also leave from **Puerto El Morro,** a village to the east of Playas. A longer route (3 hours, $8) includes a walk on the **Isla de los Pájaros**. Boat trips need a minimum of six passengers, so solo travelers and small groups are recommended to visit on weekends, when there is more chance of joining another group. Two community tourism projects operate from the *malecón* in Puerto Morro: **Ecoclub Los Delfines de Puerto el Morro** (tel. 4/252-9496, www.puertoelmorro.blogspot.com) and **Fragatas y Delfines** (tel. 98/272-8928, http://ctcpuertodelmorro.wixsite.com/fragatasydelfines).

Buses to Posorja and Puerto Morro leave from Playas town center and take 30 and 15 minutes respectively.

Puerto Engabao

The small fishing village of Puerto Engabao is home to one of the most consistent waves in Ecuador and is an increasingly popular destination for surfers, who come to ride the right-hand point break or the beach breaks to the left of the point.

The few hostels and cafés are in the vicinity of the lighthouse. The **Cabaña de Miguelito** (tel. 96/782-9243) is the best spot to eat. Located one block from the bamboo church, ★ **Hostal Suyuña** (tel. 99/001-7953, Facebook @hostalsuyuna, $8 dorm, $20-25 s/d) is run by a friendly local couple. It's a charming and colorful place, with furniture made from recycled materials. The nearby **Hostal Puerto Engabao Surf Shelter** (tel. 98/012-3734, Facebook @hostalpuertoengabao) is another friendly option, run by local surfers. Rooms have mosquito nets and fans. Board rental and surf lessons are available. Both hostels have a communal kitchen/barbecue and hammocks.

Puerto Engabao can be reached via a fairly bone-shaking 30-minute bus ride from Playas; don't get off at Engabao, but stay on the bus for another 3 kilometers (1.2 mi) to reach Puerto Engabao.

Manglares Churute Ecological Reserve

Located 40 kilometers (25 mi) south of Guayaquil, **Manglares Churute** (tel. 93/919-6806, 8am-5pm daily, free), protects 50,000 hectares (124,000 acres) of land, much of it mangrove forest, from the ravages of shrimp farming. The reserve also includes fresh-water lakes and hilly forest. As well as over 300 bird species, the reserve is one of the few places in the region with larger, endangered animals such as jaguars and other wild cats, howler monkeys, porcupines, crocodiles, and caimans. It is also home to ancestral communities who live within the reserve and sustainably fish for crab.

A couple of 1.5- to 2-hour **hikes** are signposted and can be completed independently. Lucky visitors might spot howler monkeys and sloths. A decent level of fitness is required, as the hikes are hilly. Also be aware that the mosquitoes are savage, so wear plenty of repellent as well as a long-sleeved T-shirt and pants.

For a more informed experience, contact the reserve a day in advance to book a **guide,** some of whom speak English ($20-30 per group). Bird-watching guides are also available. There is a campsite at the reserve ($4 pp), and a couple of seafood restaurants are across the highway from the entrance.

The road between Guayaquil and Machala passes the entrance to the reserve at kilometer 49, and it's a short walk to the information center. In the Guayaquil bus station, buy a ticket to Manglares Churute from the Cooperativa de Transportes SAN (Facebook @cooperativasan, $1.50) and ask the driver to let you off there.

Boats to explore the mangroves ($30) can be hired in the mornings and on weekends. To reach the pier, get off the bus at La Flora, 5 kilometers (3 mi) before the main entrance to the reserve. From there, take a mototaxi to the *muelle* (pier).

Machala and Vicinity

Ecuador's fifth biggest city and the capital of El Oro Province, Machala (pop. 240,000) proclaims itself to be the "banana capital of the world." More than 1 million tons of the fruit is exported every year through nearby Puerto Bolívar, and if you live in North America, chances are one has ended up in your fruit bowl. In addition to bananas, income from cacao, coffee, shrimp, and, more recently, banking and commerce, has helped Machala become a fairly wealthy city with decent hotels, good infrastructure, and great food.

While it lacks visitor attractions, Machala makes a good jumping-off point for other destinations. Many visitors are just passing through on their way to Peru, but both Machala and Santa Rosa, 30 kilometers (19 mi) to the south, are good bases from which to explore the rest of El Oro, which is incredibly biodiverse. The only province with both *páramo* and mangroves, it also has expanses of tropical forest. Highlights include South America's largest fossilized forest in Puyango; the dramatic labyrinthine rock formations rising from the *páramo* at Cerro de Arcos; the lush green birders' paradise of Buenaventura; and the charming mountain town of Zaruma. Boat trips are available to explore tangled mangrove forests and to the island of Santa Clara, which has a community of sea lions and more birds per square kilometer than anywhere else in the country. Despite this wealth of attractions, El Oro receives very few international visitors. As the province's natural resources are increasingly threatened by mining, shrimp farming, and deforestation, the fledgling tourism industry provides the best alternative, sustainable source of income for its inhabitants. Those who do venture here will find the people warm, welcoming, and eager to strike up conversation.

SIGHTS

Machala's main artery, 25 de Junio, runs along the northeast side of the **Parque Central** and the city's **cathedral.** This is the heart of the city and the most attractive part, with wide, well-lit streets that are safe even at night. One block southwest is **La Casa de Cultura** (Bolívar *entre* 9 de Mayo *y* Juan Montalvo, tel. 7/293-0711, 9am-noon and 1:30pm-5pm Mon.-Fri., free), which houses a small museum on the third floor. Exhibits include pieces of the Puyango petrified forest and various ancient shamanic artifacts. If you speak Spanish, it's worth a visit for the interesting guided tour; if you don't, give it a miss, as there is no signage and the displays will make little sense. The **Parque Central, Parque Diego Minuche** (*entre* Rocafuerte *y* 25 de Junio), and **Parque Colón** (Buenavista *y* Olmedo), which has a replica galleon, are all pleasant places to find a bench, enjoy the free public Wi-Fi, and watch the city go by.

ENTERTAINMENT AND EVENTS

Machala's biggest event is the **World Banana Fair** (Feria Mundial del Banano, Facebook @ feriabananoec) in the third week of September, featuring the election of the World Banana Queen and a best banana competition for small producers across the continent. A series of concerts and parades culminate in the **Fiestas de Machala** on June 25, celebrating the creation of the *cantón* of Machala.

For nightlife, head to **Soneros** (Facebook @ Soneros Música en vivo, 8pm-2am Fri.-Sat.) for live salsa music; to **Sinatras** (Santa Rosa *entre* Pichincha *y* Arizaga) for three dance floors playing music for different generations; and to **Fizz LoungeBar** (Manuel Serrano *entre* Buenavista *y* Colón, Facebook @ FizzLoungeBar, 4pm-midnight Mon.-Thurs., 4pm-2am Fri.-Sat., ID required) for current music. Fizz is located in the Zona Rosa, which is not safe at night, so take a taxi there and don't wander. Three kilometers (1.9 mi) southeast of the town center, **Jacú Café & Music** (Av. Marcel Laniado y Circunvalación Norte, see Facebook @JacuCafe for opening hours) is another good option for live music, with some nightclubs in the nearby streets.

FOOD

For fresh produce, head to one of the city's markets. The cleanest and best organized are the **Mercado Municipal Bueños Aires** (Carrera 7ma Oeste y Av. Central 9 de Octubre, 6am-6pm daily) and the **Mercado Sur** (Juan Montalvo y Bolívar, 6am-6pm daily). Both have food courts serving local fare at low prices.

★ **Marthina** (Santa Rosa y Sucre, tel. 7/500-3432 or 99/851-6849, Facebook @ marthinacoffee.wine.restaurant, 7:30am-3pm Mon.-Fri., $1-4) serves set breakfasts and lunches, plus local specialties including *bolones*, *tigrillo* (mashed plantains with cheese and egg), and *tortillas de verde* (plantain patties stuffed with cheese). The friendly local owner is on a mission to encourage Machaleños to read more. There is a reading room at the back of the café, with books to borrow and exchange, complete with a tree of books on the wall.

Right in the heart of the action, **El Monito** (Ayacucho y 25 de Junio, tel. 7/292-3542, Facebook @elmonitomachala) is a popular spot with the locals, offering the usual breakfast dishes, plus burgers, pastries, and cakes. With two locations near the central park, **Chesco Pizzeria** (Pichincha y Ayacucho, tel. 7/293-0114, and Guayas y Sucre, tel. 7/293-6418, www.chescopizzeria.com, 11am-11pm daily, $4-10 pp) has good pizzas.

The best seafood is found in the string of *cevicherías* along the docks of **Puerto Bolívar,** west of town, though it's a fairly industrial setting. It's five minutes by cab ($3) or 10 minutes by bus ($0.30) from the center. Bus numbers 1 and 13 leave from the corner of Sucre and Guayas. For more central seafood,

try **Heike Marisquería** (Carrera 6ta Oeste y Av. Arízaga, tel. 7/292-4602, Facebook @ Heikemarisqueria, $9-15).

Machala is a surprisingly good for vegetarians. **Maranatha** (Sucre y Santa Rosa, tel. 98/991-2143, Facebook @LightMaranatha, 7:30am-8pm Mon.-Sat., 9am-3pm Sun., $3-5) is an entirely vegetarian restaurant, offering a wide range of à la carte dishes and set breakfasts, lunches, and dinners. Portions are large and the food is tasty. **El Paraiso De La Vida** (Ayacucho *entre* 25 de Junio y Rocafuerte, tel. 98/977-8035, Facebook @elparaisodelavida) offers vegetarian set lunches with a salad bar until 3pm ($4).

Fruit fans will be in heaven in Machala, with several places offering ridiculously large, delicious fruit salads at economical prices, including **Siloe Light** (Sucre y Ayacucho, tel. 96/959-6683, 7:30am-7:30pm Mon.-Sat., $2-5) and **La Casa de Jim** (Ayacucho y 25 de Junio, tel. 2/600-2328, 9am-11pm daily).

ACCOMMODATIONS

Hostal Madrid (Av. 25 de Junio y Guayas, tel. 7/292-2995, $18 s, $30 d) has the best location, just off the main square. It's surprisingly quiet at night, with helpful staff, comfortable beds, good Wi-Fi, and air-conditioning. There's no hot water, but Machala is so warm that you may not need it. **Hostal Saloah** (Colón y Rocafuerte, tel. 7/293-4344, $20 s, $30 d) has hot water, friendlier service, and nicer rooms but is a few blocks farther from the square. Rooms have air-conditioning, Wi-Fi, and television.

Two blocks from the central square, the **Gran Hotel Montecarlo** (Guayas y Olmedo, tel. 7/293-1901, www.hotelgranmontecarlo. com, $35 s, $50 d, breakfast included) is an excellent option. Guest rooms are light and airy with air-conditioning, cable TV, and room service. There is an on-site restaurant and laundry. A few blocks southeast, the **Grand Hotel Americano** (Tarqui y 25 de Junio, tel. 7/296-6400, http://hotelesmachala.com, $46 s, $59 d, breakfast included), has immaculate guest rooms decorated in warm colors, each with cable TV and air-conditioning. There is an on-site restaurant and parking.

The best luxury option is the **Hotel Oro Verde** (General Telmo Sandoval *y* Av. Edgar Cordova, tel. 7/298-0074, www.oroverdem-achala.com, $145 s/d, breakfast included), set in tropical gardens in the Unioro suburb 10 minutes east of town. Amenities include a pool, gym, sauna, tennis and squash courts, restaurant, and piano bar.

INFORMATION AND SERVICES

There's a **Banco Pichincha** (Rocafuerte *y* Guayas) and half a dozen other banks/ATMs near the Parque Central. Machala's **post office** is at Bolívar 733 at Montalvo. For **laundry**, head to Boyaca and Santa Rosa.

For immigration matters, the **Ministerio de Relaciones Exteriores y Movilidad Humana** (Rocafuerte *y* Guayas, tel. 7/292-0050, 8:15am-4:15pm Mon.-Fri.) is on the east corner of the central park.

The **city tourist office** (tel. 7/293-2106, 8am-1pm and 2:30pm-5:30pm Mon.-Fri.) is on the southeast corner of the main plaza. Staff are helpful and speak basic English.

For English-speaking half-day and full-day tours of the city and the province, contact **Trip&Life** (Arizaga *y* Bolívar, tel. 7/293-5350, Facebook @triplifecu). Packages include a Puyango tour; a full-day bird-watching tour that takes in the reserves at Buenaventura, Humedal La Tembladera, and Arenillas, plus the mangroves at Puerto Jelí; a half-day kayaking trip at Humedal La Tembladera; a full-day tour of Zaruma and the Buenaventura reserve; and a half-day tour of Machala. Prices range $40-80 per person for two people, with prices dropping to $20-50 per person for larger groups.

GETTING THERE AND AROUND

Machala's new **bus terminal** (www.termi-nalterrestremachala.gob.ec), opened in 2018, is 5 kilometers (3 mi) east of the city center on Avenida Ferroviária. There are frequent departures to Huaquillas (75 minutes, $2) and Guayaquil (4 hours, $5), and hourly departures to Zaruma (2 hours, $3.75), Cuenca (3 hours, $7), and Loja (6 hours, $8). There are departures every couple of hours to Quito (10 hours, $14).

There are several taxi companies near Guayas and Pichincha, including **Coop de Turismo OroGuayas** (tel. 7/293-4382), which runs an efficient hourly service to Guayaquil ($10 pp).

Machala's closest airport is in Santa Rosa, 30 kilometers (19 mi) to the south, with daily flights to/from Quito.

NEAR MACHALA
Isla Jambelí

Isla Jambelí is much touted as a tourist attraction in Machala, and perhaps at one time it merited a visit, but these days it serves as an example of the disastrous results of unchecked mass tourism and shrimp farming. Apart from its value as a cautionary tale, it's not recommended as a destination.

Santa Rosa and Vicinity

Thirty kilometers (19 mi) south of Machala, Santa Rosa is an excellent base from which to explore the province's considerable attractions, and a good place to spend the night en route to/from Peru.

The best place to stay is ★ **Hostal Gualingo** (tel. 7/216-1038, Facebook @turismopuertojely, $20 s, $25 d), a few minutes' drive from the town center in Puerto Jelí, where the *malecón* is lined with great seafood restaurants and local fishers offer tours of the mangroves. The hostel is owned by an Ecuadorian couple, Magaly and Edwin, who are simply wonderful hosts, going to incredible lengths to make sure that their guests enjoy their stay. They can organize tours within the province and also make delicious artisanal ice cream. Puerto Jelí is a $0.30 bus journey or $2.50 taxi ride from the Santa Rosa bus station.

Twenty minutes south of Santa Rosa is ★ **Happy Fruit** (tel. 96/959-6356, www.

fincahappyfruit.com/en, Facebook @finca-happyfruit), an idyllic agro-ecological farm serving garden-to-table gourmet vegetarian meals. The owners, Tanya and Jorge, are a friendly bilingual Ecuadorian couple who offer tours of the farm, where they grow nearly 100 different fruits and other organic products. Options include a three-hour tour with a juice and snack ($10), a tour with lunch (11am-4pm, $25), and a tour with breakfast and lunch (9am-4pm, $30). All tours must be booked at least a day in advance and include as much fruit as you can eat! At the time of writing, guest rooms were being built. Camping is also available. To get to Happy Fruit, take a bus from Santa Rosa to Arenillas and then a taxi ($1.50).

Tanya and Jorge also own **AllSur** (tel. 95/983-6717, Facebook @allsurecuador), a tour operator specializing in ecotourism and bird-watching trips in El Oro. Having spent five months exploring the province to create the municipal tourist map, they are experts on the region. Tours are available in English and range 1-4 days. Destinations include Zaruma, Cerro de Arcos, Humedal La Tembladera, Buenaventura, and Puyango. Jorge is a naturalist guide with a permit to take visitors to Isla Santa Clara, an island with more birds per square kilometer than anywhere else in Ecuador.

The airport in Santa Rosa operates one flight daily to/from Quito with TAME (www.tame.ec). Transportes CIFA and Cooperativa El Oro run buses every few minutes between Santa Rosa and Machala (30 minutes, $0.60). From Santa Rosa, there are buses to Guayaquil (every 30 minutes), Loja, Cuenca, and Peru.

Mangahurco

The flowering of the guayacan trees in Mangahurco takes place once a year, usually in early January. Two days after the first heavy rains, hundreds of these trees burst into brilliant yellow bloom, creating a natural spectacle that lasts for only eight days. As the petals start to fall, the forest floor is carpeted in yellow, adding to the visual impact.

AllSur (tel. 95/983-6717, Facebook @allsurecuador) offers three-day/two-night tours to see the guayacans in bloom ($120 per day, including transport from Santa Rosa, accommodations, and all food). Thousands of people descend on the tiny village of Mangahurco to see the phenomenon, so finding accommodations independently can be almost impossible. Many villagers will allow a tent to be erected in their garden for $10/night, offering visitors the local specialty cuisine, *chivo al hueco*, or goat-in-a-hole. To get there, head to Zapotillo by bus and change there for Mangahurco. Keep an eye on the Facebook page @mangahurco for updates on when the trees start to flower.

★ Bosque Petrificado de Puyango

Hidden far off the beaten track near the Peruvian border, the **Bosque Petrificado de Puyango** (Facebook @Fosilizados, bosquepuyango@hotmail.com, 8am-5pm daily, $1 pp) is the largest petrified forest in South America, extending over 2,658 hectares (6,568 acres). Experts believe that about 100 million years ago, volcanic eruptions covered the forest in ash. Subsequent floods caused the minerals from the ash to seep into the trees, hardening them into underwater rocks. As the land was later reclaimed from the sea, the forest rose again into what we see today; this is evidenced by the presence of fossilized aquatic creatures such as ammonites, sea turtles, and fish.

The gigantic stone trunks, some 15 meters (49 ft) long and 2 meters (6.5 ft) in diameter, are surrounded by tropical dry forest, which is lush and green January-May and leafless the rest of the year. The forest is home to 130 species of birds and several living trees that match their stone counterparts in size.

The forest has 3 kilometers (1.2 mi) of trails, suitable for all fitness levels. It's possible to enter only with a guided tour (included in the entrance fee, though tips are appreciated). An English-speaking guide can be hired by prior reservation. Despite being a protected forest, Puyango is threatened by deforestation carried out by local people felling trees for sale. Tourism is the best alternative source of income for these communities.

FOOD AND ACCOMMODATIONS

The only accommodation options are **Casa Posado** (inquire with the staff at the petrified forest), a six-bed dormitory in the village of Puyango, or camping (bring your own tent). The closest food is **La Olla de Barro**, on the main road about 15 kilometers (9.3 mi) north of Puyango, a charming roadside café that uses traditional cooking methods, including a wood-fired earth oven and ceramic pots over a fire. Specialties are cheese empanadas and local coffee.

GETTING THERE

Getting to Puyango is a bit of a challenge, but it's a beautiful journey, through lush forested hills. There are buses from Huaquillas (1 hour, $2.50) with CIFA Internacional (5am) and Cariamanga Internacional (11:30am). Transportes Loja and CIFA both make the trip three times daily from Machala (2.5 hours, $3); get on a bus destined for Alamor and ask the driver to let you off. If you miss the direct bus from Machala, take a bus to Arenillas and then a pickup truck to Puyango (45 minutes, $5). All buses will drop you off on the highway, by the turnoff to the forest. A taxi driver, Galo Torres (tel. 7/309-6151), lives at the turnoff, in the yellow house opposite the military checkpoint. For $5 he will take you to the entrance of the forest, via an interpretive center where you pay the entrance fee and pick up a guide. Alternatively, for $3 he will drop you off at the interpretive center and you can walk an hour to the entrance.

If you have the budget, it's easier to hire a driver or go with a tour operator. In Machala, **Doris Tour** (Guayas y Pichincha, tel. 7/293-3208 or 7/293-6809) will make the round-trip journey in a 10-seater vehicle for $100 (transport only). **Trip&Life** (Av. Arizaga y Bolívar, tel. 7/293-5350, Facebook @triplifecu) offers a six-hour tour, including transportation and

English-speaking guide, for $45 per person for two people, $35 per person for 3-5 people, and $25 for 6-9 people.

★ Zaruma

Zaruma's dramatic location, clinging improbably to a steep hillside, offers panoramic views over the surrounding lush green peaks and valleys. It's a pleasure to wander the winding streets of this charming town, taking in the traditional wooden architecture and stopping to enjoy a cup of its famous coffee. The climate is warm during the day and pleasantly cool at night, when a light fog starts to roll in and is romantically illuminated by old-fashioned streetlights.

The dark side of this picturesque town is hidden beneath the ground. Ever since the arrival of the Incas in the 15th century, the mountain underneath Zaruma has been heavily mined for gold and other metals; indeed, it has been likened to a gruyère cheese, riddled with thousands of kilometers of labyrinthine tunnels. The majority of Zarumeño men work in the mines or the processing plants in neighboring Portovelo, employed by national and foreign companies, or operating independently as artisanal miners. It's low-tech, dangerous work and there are regular fatalities. The mining industry also causes environmental problems, including air pollution, water contamination, deforestation, and subsidence. Some mining operations were closed after a school disappeared into a hole in 2016, creating mass unemployment. As one life-long resident of the town commented, if the city doesn't start to leave mining behind, its days are numbered.

These issues are not apparent to the casual visitor, and Zaruma is still a very attractive town with much to offer in terms of natural beauty, architecture, history, and cuisine. By making the most of these considerable renewable resources and fulfilling its potential as a tourist destination, Zaruma has a chance to free itself from mining. In that sense, every visit helps to steer the town toward a sustainable future.

SIGHTS

The heart of the town is the attractive **Plaza de Independencia,** overlooked by the main church, **Santuario de la Virgen del Carmen.** Just off the north side of the square is the **Museo Municipal** (9am-4pm Wed.-Sun., free), which has a small archaeological collection of pottery and tools. Next to the museum is a tourist office (tel. 7/297-3533, Facebook @Turismo.Zaruma.Oficial, 8am-5:30pm Mon.-Fri., 8am-4pm Sat.), with helpful staff who can provide maps and information on the sights in and around town.

The main attraction in the town itself is the disused gold mine, **Mina Turística El Sexmo** (tel. 7/297-2227, Facebook @ElSexmo, 8am-noon and 1pm-4pm daily, free), where visitors can explore a 500-meter-long (1,640-ft-long) tunnel. The tunnel has a peaceful atmosphere, which some attribute to the presence of a large quantity of quartz rock. For this reason, some people come to the mine to practice meditation, yoga, and reiki. This particular tunnel is wider than most, with electric lights. It's sobering to reflect that most miners working for companies in Zaruma spend their days in much smaller tunnels, lit only by torchlight, and artisanal miners work in tunnels so small that it's only possible to crawl inside.

A basic tour of the mine is available, but to really get the most out of your visit, hire the services of **Tito Castillo** (tel. 7/297-2761 or 9/309-4707) of Oro Adventure, who has a small office on the main square. For $25 per group he will provide a two-hour tour in Spanish of the mine and Zaruma town center. A life-long resident of the town, he is full of knowledge and amusing stories. For $70, he will provide a group of up to four people with a full-day tour of the local area, including the Buenaventura reserve ($15 entry fee not included), Portovelo, Zaruma, and Piñas.

Dulces de Doña Clema (tel. 7/214-4071, 8am-5:30pm Mon.-Sat., 8am-noon Sun.), 3.5 kilometers (2.2 mi) north of the town center, is run by a local family who have been making sweets and pastries for three generations, still using the 14 secret recipes of Clemencia Maria Natividad Aguilar, aka Doña Clema, who died in 1913 aged 115. Most of the ingredients, including sugarcane, milk, coffee, and cacao, come from the family farm. The products are sold nationwide. A taxi from Machala costs $2.50.

Seven kilometers (4.3 mi) from Portovelo is the **Cascada Arco Iris,** a 17-meter (56-ft) waterfall that gets its name from the presence of rainbows in the surrounding clouds of water vapor. It's a beautiful spot to bathe, but check on conditions locally before setting out: After heavy rains, the road to the falls can be blocked by mudslides, and there may be sediment and branches in the water. It's a $12-15 taxi journey from Zaruma (each way).

FOOD

A cup of local coffee is the perfect accompaniment to the town's specialty breakfast dishes, which are served throughout the day: *tigrillo* (mashed plantains with cheese and egg); *bolón* (a ball of plantain with cheese, peanuts, or ham, best served with fried eggs); and *humitas* (a whole ear of mashed corn steamed in its leaves, served with cheese). Countless establishments offer these dishes; a couple of the best options are **Café Uno** (Sucre *y* Eugenio Espejo, tel. 7/297-2440, $3-4) and **Cafeteria Central**, on the central square. Also on the central square is an artisanal ice cream café, **Mix Heladeria.**

The best restaurant in town is Café Zarumeño, better known as ★ **200 Millas** (Honorato Márquez, tel. 7/297-2600, 7am-10:30pm daily, $4-10), down the hill from the center. Owned by a friendly local woman, it has a wider ranging menu than most places, with chicken, seafood, and salads, though the specialty is still *tigrillo*.

1: garden to table gastronomy at the Happy Fruit agro-ecological farm; **2:** Bosque Petrificado de Puyango; **3:** Zaruma is famous for its wooden architecture. **4:** Machala's Parque Central and cathedral

ACCOMMODATIONS

Zaruma has limited hotel options, but they are mostly of a decent standard, locally owned and very good value. None include breakfast. The most upmarket is **Hotel Roland** (Alonso de Mercadillo, tel. 7/297-2703, rolandhotel@hotmail.com, $20-30 s, $40-45 d), a friendly family-run place with a swimming pool, parking, and great views of the valley. The only drawback is that you have to walk up a steep hill on the busy main road to reach the town center.

In the center, the best-located hotel is **Romeria Hostal** (Plaza Independencia, tel. 7/297-3618, $13.50 s, $22 d), with a view of the main square from the balcony; the café below is also popular. Going down the hill on Calle Sucre are a number of options: **Cerro de Oro** (tel. 7/297-2505, www.cerrodeoro.galeon.com, $12 pp); **Aguila Dorada** (tel. 7/297-2230 or 7/297-2775, Facebook @aguiladoradahotel, $12 pp), which has parking; and ★ **Hotel Zaruma Colonial** (tel. 7/297-2742, Facebook @HotelZarumaColonial, $15 pp), the cleanest and most modern, with wonderful views from the top floors and great service. Family-run **Hotel Blacio** (tel. 7/297-2045, $10 pp) is a little farther down, on the corner of Sucre and El Sexmo.

INFORMATION AND SERVICES

There is a Banco Pichincha ATM just down the hill from the town center on Avenida Alonso de Mercadillo.

GETTING THERE AND AROUND

Despite its remote location, Zaruma is well connected to major cities in Ecuador. There are two bus companies in town, Cooperativa Piñas Interprovincial (tel. 7/297-2955) and Cooperativa de Transportes TAC (tel. 7/297-2156, Facebook @asociadostac), both of which have offices on 8 de Diciembre at the bottom of the hill (take a taxi if you have luggage, $1.50).

TAC has buses to Cuenca (12:30am, 2:30am), Guayaquil (12:15am, 2am, 3:30am, 9:15am, and 2:15pm, 5 hours, $8.25), Huaquillas (4:30am and 7:20am, 2 hours, $3.75), Loja (3am and 6am daily, and 5pm Fri., 3pm Sun., 4 hours, $6); Machala via Piñas (daily every hour 3am-6pm, then at 9:30pm Sat. and 7pm Sun., 2 hours, $3.75), Machala direct (6:45am, 12:45pm, and 5:45pm, 2 hours, $3.75), and Quito (4am, 5:30pm, and 6:30pm, 13 hours, $15.20).

Cooperativa Piñas Interprovincial has buses to Ambato (8:30pm), Cuenca (1:15am, 4:45am), Guayaquil (1am, 3am, 12:45pm), Quito via Santo Domingo (6:45pm), and Quito via Ambato (7:15pm).

Getting around town is easy, and you can walk to most places. Yellow taxis and white pickup trucks will also take you around ($1.50 for journeys in town).

Reserva Buenaventura

Less than an hour from Zaruma and 90 minutes from Santa Rosa, the lush, verdant greenery of the Buenaventura Reserve ($15) feels like a different world. Owned by the **Jocotoco Foundation** (www.jocotoco.org), this 2,000-hectare (5,000-acre) reserve protects one of the largest tracts of cloud forest in the region, where only 5-10 percent of the original forest remains. It was established to protect a newly discovered endemic bird species, the El Oro parakeet, which is only found in the province's high altitude spots. With the help of a nest box project, the endangered parakeet has recovered from the brink of extinction and there are now nearly 450 individuals on the reserve. Over 330 other bird species have also been recorded, of which 12 are globally threatened and 34 are regional endemics. The bizarre long-wattled umbrella bird is found here, as are hummingbirds, monkeys, sloths, and pumas.

The reserve has a **hummingbird garden** and three **trails,** which can be explored independently, with a tour operator guide, or with a guide from the reserve ($30/day per group). The reserve's guides don't speak English, except to name the birds. Guided tours must be booked in advance, by phone (1 day in advance, tel. 2/250-5841) or email (3-4 days in advance, info@jocotoco.org). If you wish to hike independently, make your way to the visitors center first, to pay the entrance fee and be briefed by a guide.

The income from the on-site **lodge** ($150 pp, including 3 meals and guided hikes) goes toward the foundation's conservation efforts. Rooms are simple but comfortable, with beautiful views from the balconies. Vegetarians can be accommodated with advance notice. Camping is also available ($8, bring your own tent). Those coming for a day trip can make advance reservations for meals.

The entrance to the reserve is 9 kilometers (5.6 mi) from the town of Piñas, which is easily reached by bus from Zaruma (30 minutes, $1.20), Santa Rosa (1 hour, $2.40), and Machala (2 hours, $2.65), with hourly departures from each. From Piñas, it's $12 by taxi or pickup truck to the reserve. Alternatively, ask the bus driver to let you off at the sign for the Jocotoco Foundation and Selva Alegre and walk 5 kilometers (3 mi) to the reserve, or make arrangements with the foundation for a guide to pick you up.

★ Cerro de Arcos

High in the remote *páramo*, dramatic rock formations tower above the grasses and wildflowers. From the outside, **Cerro de Arcos** looks like an impenetrable rock fortress, but inside is a labyrinth of caves, stone arches, and natural rock sculptures. Gnarled trees cling to nooks and crannies, hung with beards of moss and lichen. In the center is a circular flat area that summons images of ancient rituals and magic (indeed, there is a nearby lake where current-day shamans come to perform ceremonies). It's a fascinating and mysterious place, made all the more so by the profound silence of the *páramo*, punctuated only by the occasional call of a bird or drip of water. Sitting here quietly for a few minutes really brings it home how rarely we experience true silence.

It's easy to get lost on the *páramo*, where clouds can suddenly descend, reducing visibility to almost zero. Go with a guide from the nearby Refugio Cerro de Arcos (tel. 7/302-9074, $25 per group of up to 15 people). The rock formations are a 40-minute walk from the refuge, and exploring the labyrinth inside can take 3-4 hours. It's 3,680 meters (12,075 ft) above sea level; remember that walking at altitude can be exhausting. Bring water, snacks, sunblock, and walking shoes.

Aside from Cerro de Arcos, other hikes are possible from the refuge, and horseback riding

Cerro de Arcos

is also available ($20/day). Climbing routes up to 15 meters (49 ft) high have been created in the rock formations behind the refuge. The best time to visit is August, when the *páramo* is carpeted with flowers and there is the best chance of spotting condors. Lucky visitors might also see a rare and endemic hummingbird that was discovered at Cerro de Arcos in 2017, the critically endangered *estrella garganta azul* or blue-throated hillstar.

Built by the Mato Grosso Foundation, income from **Refugio Cerro de Arcos** (tel. 7/302-9074, 98/034-9678, or 98/070-1679, frankterry.blu@gmail.com, $20 pp, including breakfast) supports the foundation's work with local communities, including the provision of medical assistance and the construction of houses. The foundation also provides local people with clean water and vocational training in wood carving, furniture making, and mosaics. The refuge, which took volunteers three years to build, was constructed around a giant rock that occupies pride of place inside the lodge, with orchids still flowering on its craggy sides. The next project is to install photovoltaic panels for renewable energy. The refuge is rustic but comfortable enough, with hobbit-sized bedrooms and shared bathrooms. All stays at the refuge must be reserved a minimum of three days in advance. Lunch and dinner are available for $7-10. Vegetarians are accommodated by prior request. Note that no English is spoken by the staff or guides. There is no Internet, and it is cold at night, so bring warm clothes.

To reach the refuge, take the 6:30am Trans Guanazan bus (2.5 hours, $3) that leaves from the outside the *coliseo* in Zaruma and ask the driver to let you off 500 meters (1,640 ft) after the village of Sabadel, where there is a sign for Cerro de Arcos. It's a bone-shaking journey that will take you past some truly remote rural communities and beautiful scenery. By prior reservation, someone from Cerro de Arcos will meet you at the sign in a four-wheel-drive and drive you to the refuge ($5), or you can make the hour's hike on foot. Coming from Cuenca, take a bus headed

for Loja and get off in Saraguro (3 hours), then take a Cooperativa Trans Suroriente or Transportes Manú bus to Manu (every hour, 2.5 hours). In Manu, take the 2:30pm Trans Guanazan bus headed for Zaruma and get off at the Cerro de Arcos sign just before Sabadel (1 hour).

Crossing into Peru: Huaquillas

In previous years, travelers had to walk across a bridge in the not-too-pleasant town of Huaquillas to make the border crossing between Ecuador and Peru, running a gauntlet of black market money changers and other shady characters. Fortunately, the construction of new immigration offices has made the process much safer and more convenient, with Ecuadorian and Peruvian border officials sitting side by side in the same building.

The new offices are 15 minutes south of Huaquillas. To get there, take a bus to Huaquillas and then a taxi ($5) to the joint Ecuador-Peru migration office. Once there, join the queue to leave Ecuador at the "Salida del Ecuador" desk, then queue up again to enter Peru at the "Ingreso al Peru" desk. On your way out, a green-and-yellow sign shows the fixed-rate taxi fares to a dozen different destinations in Peru in dollars and soles (e.g., $10 or S/33 to Tumbes, and $50 or S/165 to Mancora. The drivers accept both currencies. Entering Ecuador from Peru, the process is the same in reverse.

International buses between Ecuador and Peru will wait outside the immigration offices while passengers complete the formalities.

Coming from Peru, it's best to get rid of Peruvian money before crossing into Ecuador, to avoid the dodgy money changers—or use what you have left for your onward taxi journey within Ecuador. Once in Ecuador, you can take out dollars at one of the ATMs in Huaquillas (Banco Pichincha near the main plaza), Santa Rosa (at the bus terminal and town center), or Machala.

Huaquillas is not a town you want to hang around for long, and luckily there is sufficient transportation to shuttle you south to

Peru or north to more pleasant destinations in Ecuador. If you do get stuck in Huaquillas for the night, head to the **Vallejo Hotel** (Av. La República y 9 de Octubre, tel. 98/755-2090, Facebook @VallejoHotel, $16 s, $26 d, breakfast included), which is modern, clean, and friendly. There's an attached café and a pizza place across the road. On the central square, another decent option is **La Habana** (tel. 7/299-5077, www.lahabanahotel.com.ec, $28 s, $43 d), which has a good restaurant.

Huaquillas does not have a central *terminal terrestre*; each bus company operates from its own office. **Panamericana** (Teniente Cordovez y 10 de Agosto, www.panamericana.ec) runs eight daily direct buses from/to Quito 6am-9:30pm (11 hours, $15), plus one departure from Huaquillas to Tulcán via Ibarra and Otavalo (4pm), and one to Ambato (8pm). **Transportes Occidentales** (R Gómez, www.transportesoccidentales.com.ec) has nine daily departures from/to Quito 5:20am-8:45pm, and one departure from Huaquillas to Esmeraldas at 7pm. **Transportes Esmeraldas** (11 de Noviembre y 1 de Mayo, www.transesmeraldas.com) departs for Quito at 6pm, 7pm, and 9pm, and to Esmeraldas at 3:45pm and 7:30pm. **CIFA** (Santa Rosa y Machala, www.cifainternacional.com) has frequent buses from/to Machala (75 minutes, $2) and Guayaquil (4.5 hours, $6).

CIFA also operates several buses per day between Guayaquil and Tumbes in Peru, and between Guayaquil and Piura in Peru. Both services go via Machala and Huaquillas. There is also one direct daily bus between Montañita and Mancora in Peru, stopping in Guayaquil, Machala, Huaquillas, and Tumbes en route. It departs Montañita at 8pm, stops in Huaquillas at 4:30am, and arrives in Mancora at 7am. Coming from Peru, it leaves Mancora at 8:30pm, stops in Huaquillas at 11pm, and arrives in Montañita at 7am. These international buses wait while you complete the immigration formalities.

chapter contributed by Lisa Cho,
author of *Moon Galápagos Islands*

The Galápagos Islands

The Galápagos archipelago is one place on earth that lives up to and surpasses expectations. There are insufficient superlatives. It is unquestionably the best place on earth for wildlife-watching because the wildlife watches you as much as you watch it. The lack of natural predators has left the animals fearless. The only timid species are the fish, the food supply for so many. Every other creature on the islands is either unconcerned by the presence of visitors or is intent on communicating.

The Galápagos are also heaven for bird-watchers. Here you don't need to get up at dawn and wait with binoculars for a glimpse of birdlife in the trees. Instead, the birds proudly display themselves—the male frigates inflate their red chests to the size of a basketball, the albatross

Highlights

Look for ★ to find recommended sights, activities, dining, and lodging.

★ **Tortoise Reserves:** No Galápagos trip would be complete without seeing **giant tortoises** in their natural habitat—this site is by far the easiest place to spot them (page 398).

★ **Seymour Norte:** This island is the best place to see the impressive mating display of the red-chested **frigate bird** year-round. It's also home to a large population of land iguanas and **blue-footed boobies** (page 402).

★ **Isla Lobos:** Here you'll find excellent **snorkeling** among a colony of playful sea lions and colorful fish (page 412).

★ **Kicker Rock (León Dormido):** Dramatic cliffs shaped like a sleeping lion make this one of the most famous landmarks in the Galápagos. Visitors enjoy exceptional **snorkeling** with sharks, turtles, and fish (page 412).

★ **Sierra Negra and Volcán Chico:** The **best hike** in the Galápagos is a trip along the rim of this enormous active caldera (second largest in the world), followed by walking on the moonlike landscape of Volcán Chico (page 426).

★ **Devil's Crown:** An eroded **volcanic crater** forms the jagged shape of a crown in the sea off the coast of Floreana. Snorkelers swim in the middle with a variety of marinelife (page 436).

★ **Bartolomé Island:** This jagged rock jutting out of the sea is the most frequently

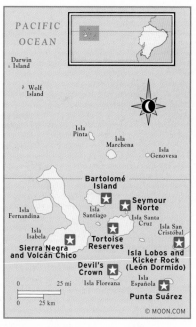

photographed sight in the Galápagos (page 437).

★ **Punta Suárez on Española:** Punta Suárez is most famous as the only site to see the rare **waved albatross,** which nest here from April to November (page 439).

The Galápagos Islands

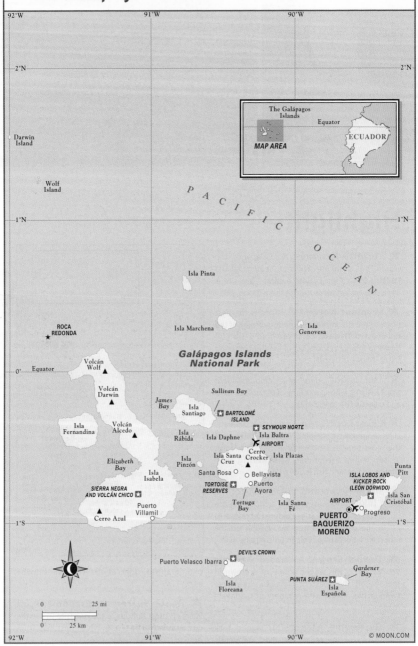

© MOON.COM

entertain with their circular clacking dance, and pelicans dive-bomb the ocean in search of lunch.

A visit to these islands changes you, as it changed Charles Darwin, who was inspired to form his monumental theory of evolution after visiting in 1835. The Galápagos' isolation and inhospitable volcanic terrain have been their greatest assets, saving them from colonization and degradation. With the South American coast 970 kilometers (603 mi) to the east and nothing but blue Pacific Ocean all the way to French Polynesia, over 5,000 kilometers (3,100 mi) to the west, the Galápagos were hidden away for centuries.

Today, the Galápagos are a glimpse of what life was like before humans—and a reminder that when we seek out perfection, we throw a wrench in nature's works. Evidence of human activity on the Galápagos is everywhere—the number of endemic species hunted or driven to near extinction by introduced species is alarming. The archipelago was on the UNESCO List of World Heritage in Danger from 2007 until 2010. Its removal was criticized by scientists and conservationists, but welcomed by the travel industry. The islands continue to struggle with illegal fishing, water pollution, fossil fuels, invasive species, and growth in tourism and local population.

The effort of conservationists to restore the ecological balance is inspiring. Tread lightly and you will return home filled with a sense of wonder and a clearer view of nature's fragile beauty.

Visiting the Islands

PLANNING YOUR TIME
When to Go

The Galápagos are a year-round destination. **December-April** is the rainy, hot season and includes the **busiest tourist period** around Christmas and early January. The weather is sunny and interspersed with periods of rain. The seas are at their calmest and warmest, but mosquitoes and the sun are the most intense. **June-October** is the cool, dry season, with fewer mosquitoes and more comfortable temperatures. However, the landscapes are more barren and the sea is considerably rougher. **June-August** is **another high season,** with many travelers coming for summer vacations. The **low seasons** in **May** and **September** are the best times to secure last-minute availability. Cut-price **deals** can be found year-round if you look hard enough and are flexible.

Entry

To enter the Galápagos, you must obtain the mandatory **$20 transit control card** from your departure airport (either Quito or Guayaquil). This helps to regulate the exact number of visitors. Upon arrival there is a mandatory **$100 national park entrance fee,** payable in cash. This fee helps to preserve the islands' fragile ecosystem. If you have a student or cultural visa, you pay $25, while Ecuadorians pay just $6.

Booking a Tour

The farther you are from the Galápagos, the more you pay. Cruises, land tours, and diving tours can all be arranged in your home country or through a travel agency in Ecuador. Keep in mind that when booking a tour from abroad, a **deposit** of at least $200 per person, via wire transfer or Western Union (no credit cards by Internet or phone),

Land Tour or Cruise...or Both?

The first decision you need to make is whether to take a cruise or a land tour. Or do you? While most travelers do either one or the other, it is also reasonably common to do both. Some travelers like a couple days to relax in the islands before flying home, and others choose to spend those days scuba diving—an activity not allowed aboard cruises with the exception of a few live-aboard diving boats. If you must decide, however, the tradeoffs are below.

ADVANTAGES OF LAND-BASED TOURS

- **Avoiding seasickness** is one of the top reasons people choose land tours. However, although you do get to sleep in a comfortable hotel room on dry land, you also spend significant time in transit on small boats that are prone to rocking. You can avoid interisland speedboat ferries by buying interisland flights instead, but some of the best day-trip sites are a 45-minute to 2-hour boat ride from port. Though you will likely be less seasick on a land tour compared to a small tourist- or tourist-superior-class yacht, you will likely be more seasick compared to being on a 50- to 100-passenger cruise ship.

- **Saving money** is another reason people choose land tours, particularly if you choose to travel independently. Your overall trip cost can be much lower, and your hotel room will likely still be nicer and more spacious than your cruise cabin.

- **You're not stuck on a boat** on a land tour. You can take a walk after dinner, grab a drink, or have extra time for souvenir shopping in the ports. You can eat at a variety of restaurants (though the gourmet food aboard first-class and luxury cruises is usually better than the restaurants in the ports).

- **You can customize your itinerary** to your interests, including hiking, wildlife visits, snorkeling, and even camping. You can travel spontaneously and independently without a fixed itinerary, booking tours just the day before as it suits your whims.

- **You can explore sights near the ports** independently; if you're lucky, you might even find yourself completely alone in nature.

- **You can scuba dive**—an activity that is not allowed on regular cruises, only on a few specialized live-aboard dive cruises.

is usually required. Travel agencies in Quito and Guayaquil advertise tours, so if you're booking in Ecuador, shop around. Holding out for **last-minute deals** may save you 5-35 percent, but be aware that it may leave you stranded as well. Some travelers with time on their hands even fly to the Galápagos, book into a cheap hotel for a few days, and take their chances on finding a last-minute cruise, saving 50 percent in some cases; but there are no guarantees.

Transportation

Transportation to the islands is generally not included in the price of a tour. Flights depart from Quito and Guayaquil daily. There are two entrance **airports** in the Galápagos: one on **Baltra,** just north of the central island of Santa Cruz, and one on **San Cristóbal.** The airport on Isabela is only used for interisland flights, and there are no airports on Floreana. Make sure you're flying to the correct island to begin your tour. Prices are about $350 round-trip from Guayaquil and $400 from Quito.

If you are traveling to the islands without a tour reservation, **Puerto Ayora** is the best place to arrange a **budget tour.** Note that getting from Baltra to Puerto Ayora is a journey in three stages involving two bus rides and a ferry ride. There are daily ferry shuttles

- Land-based tours **support the local Galápagos economy** much more than cruises.

- **You see more of the culture** of the Galápagos when you spend time in the ports. Note, however, that the Galápagos region is not famous for its local culture, and Quito is a much better option if you really want to experience Ecuador's rich history and culture.

DISADVANTAGES OF LAND-BASED TOURS

- The Galápagos archipelago is famous for its unique wildlife and varied pristine landscapes, and **you simply don't see as much** of these on land tours. Fernandina, Española, Genovesa, Rábida, and many of the best sites on even the inhabited islands are off-limits. Some of those sites are home to animals that you won't see anywhere else. Visitors on a land tour don't see the waved albatross, flightless cormorant, or fur seal at all, and they also miss the largest colonies of other animals, such as the red-footed boobies on Genovesa. If you choose a shorter central-islands cruise, however, you can indeed see the large majority of the same sites on a land tour.

- **Significant daylight hours are spent in transit,** so you generally see fewer sites in the same number of days, and you may experience seasickness aboard the small boats used for day tours.

- Day tours often employ **Class One naturalist guides,** who have less knowledge and experience than the Class Two or Class Three guides found aboard the higher-end cruise ships.

- If you book day tours on your own, you will likely have a single guide with a mixed-language group, hence **all information is repeated:** once in English and again in Spanish. Note, however, that this is also true of some of the smaller cruise boats.

- Many land tours involve **island-hopping,** which requires you to pack and unpack your suitcase frequently to move to hotels on different islands. You travel between islands aboard an uncomfortable speedboat or a more pricey interisland flight.

- Though there are some eco-hotels with excellent environmental practices, **land tours usually have a larger environmental impact.** As land-based tourism grows, more workers and infrastructure on the islands are needed, and more goods are imported on cargo ships.

from $30 per person one-way to the other three other ports—Baquerizo Moreno on San Cristóbal, Puerto Velasco Ibarra on Floreana, and Puerto Villamil on Isabela.

CRUISES

Tour boats are organized into four classes. **Economy/tourist-class** boats are basic and appropriate for those on a limited budget; **tourist superior-class** boats are the most common, with a bit more comfort and better guides; **first class** and **luxury tours** offer gourmet food, comfortable cabins, and service that matches those in the finest hotels on the mainland, and guides are qualified scientists.

Prices vary widely, but all prices should include food, accommodations, transfers to and from your boat, trained guides, and all your shore visits.

A good guide is the most important factor in your visit. All Galápagos guides are trained and licensed by the National Park Service and qualify in one of three classes, in ascending order of quality. When booking a tour, ask about your guide's specific qualifications and what language(s) he or she speaks.

A tour of at least five days is recommended, but seven or eight days are even better, as it takes half a day each way to get to and from the islands.

Tour Operators:

- Angermeyer Cruises/Andando Tours (P.O. Box 17210088, Mariana de Jesús E7-113 at Pradera, Quito, tel. 2/323-7330, www. visitGalápagos.travel)

- Lindblad Expeditions (www.expedititons. com)

- Ecoventura (www.ecoventura.com)

- Silversea (www.silversea.com)

LAND TOURS

Land tours are now the most popular way to visit the Galápagos—especially for those who are on a budget, prefer independent travel, suffer from seasickness, or want to scuba dive. You stay in a hotel in a port town on one of the four populated islands, take day trips, and shuttle between the islands via speedboat.

Tour Operators:

- Backroads (www.backroads.com)

- GAdventures (www.gaventures.com)

- Pikaia Lodge (www.pikaialodgegalapagos. com)

- ROW Adventures (www.rowadventures. com)

TOP EXPERIENCE

DIVING

With such an astonishing array of marinelife, it's no surprise that the Galápagos rank among the world's best dive destinations. In 1998, protection of the land sites was extended to a marine zone 74 kilometers (46 mi) offshore, and there are now some 60 dive sites around the archipelago, many of them closed to nondivers.

Diving in the Galápagos is not for beginners. Local dive schools offer PADI training, but it is overpriced and far from the best place to learn. You are better off not only learning elsewhere but also getting a few dives under your belt first. Currents are strong, and visibility is often poor, ranging 10-25 meters (33-82 ft). Many dives are in unsheltered water, meaning that holding on to coral is not only permitted but essential. It is not ideal for the health of the coral, but it is certainly important for your health.

For those with sufficient experience, the diving is world-class. Schools of fish stretch out for what seems like eternity, and you're almost guaranteed close encounters with a variety of sharks—small white-tipped reef sharks, larger Galápagos sharks, hammerheads, and, off the more remote western islands, enormous whale sharks. You may see manta rays, marine iguanas, and the surprisingly fast penguins, the diving in the Red Sea or the Caribbean will pale in comparison.

The law requires that every boat in the Galápagos must be either a nondiving cruise boat or a dedicated dive boat, so divers are forced to choose between expensive live-aboard charters, or a land-based tour with day trips to dive sites. This far cheaper option is popular, but is restricted to sites within easy reach of Santa Cruz, San Cristóbal, and Isabela.

Santa Cruz has the most dive sites and the greatest number of dive agencies, with access to **Santa Fé, Gordon Rocks, Daphne Minor, Mosquera, Seymour Norte, Cousins Rock,** and excellent sites off the coast of **Floreana.** San Cristóbal has relatively fewer: **Kicker Rock,** the **Caragua wreck, Roca Este, Roca Ballena,** and **Islote 5 Fingers.** Isabela has **Isla Tortuga** and the more advanced sites **La Viuda** and **Cuatro Hermanos.**

Most of the other dive sites at Española, Isabela, and off Marchena can only be experienced on a live-aboard cruise. The most spectacular diving is around Darwin and Wolf, but requires a minimum experience of 50-100 dives. These islands are a full day's sail north of the main island group. Hundreds of hammerheads can be seen off Wolf, and gigantic whale sharks cruise slowly by between June and November. Bottlenose dolphins are common at Darwin's Arch.

The best diving is during the cold season (June-November). Temperatures drop to 15°C (59°F), so a six-millimeter wetsuit with hood, booties, and gloves becomes necessary. It's best to bring your own equipment, as renting locally is expensive and can cause problems because many itineraries go straight to the boat. Bring a mask, dive alert whistle, and sausage or scuba tuba. Boats supply tanks, air, and weights.

Because most visitors depart by plane, you must leave a day free at the end of your dive trip to avoid possible decompression problems (most dive tours spend the last day on Santa Cruz).

Dive Operators

Choosing the right dive company is essential for your own safety. Most operators in Puerto Ayora and Puerto Baquerizo Moreno are reputable, but steer clear of any operator who doesn't ask you in detail about your experience. For example, any operator willing to take novices to Gordon Rocks should be avoided. The best operators ask you to fill out a detailed questionnaire to assess experience.

Most large Galápagos tour agencies can book dive trips aboard the small number of equipped boats. A PADI Open Water certificate is essential, and some companies ask for a minimum number of dives, although this depends on the difficulty of the site. A PADI Open Water course generally costs around $450 per person for a four-day training course.

Santa Cruz and Nearby Islands

The economic, tourist, and geographic center of the Galápagos, Santa Cruz is the best base from which to explore surrounding islands on day tours and pick up last-minute deals. Many of the island's attractions can be seen independently.

Puerto Ayora is the tourism hub, with the widest selection of hotels and restaurants, and can be used as a base to explore the central islands.

On the edge of town is **Charles Darwin Research Station,** the most convenient place to view giant tortoises up close. A 45-minute walk west of Puerto Ayora is the sandy expanse of **Tortuga Bay.** The brackish waters of **Las Grietas,** fissures in the lava rocks that make for a relaxing, cool dip, are another short hike from town.

In the verdant highlands, several attractions make an interesting day trip: Two 30-meter-deep craters called **Los Gemelos** (The Twins) have abundant birdlife. East of Bellavista are the **lava tunnels** formed by the solidified outer skin of a molten lava flow, as well as the beautiful beach **Playa Garrapatero.** The biggest highland attraction is the huge **tortoise reserves,** where these giants roam in their natural habitat.

Near Santa Cruz Island are several small islands that can be visited as day-trip tours. Some of the most popular day trips leave for the iconic Pinnacle Rock on **Bartolomé,** to see land iguanas on **Santa Fé** and **Plaza Sur** islands, observe nesting frigate birds on **Seymour Norte,** and take advantage of the excellent snorkeling with sharks, turtles and sea lions at **Pinzón.** In addition, day trips leave for the populated islands Isabela, San Cristóbal, and Floreana, though staying the night is often a better idea.

Santa Cruz also has the most dive agencies. Divers frequently see schooling hammerheads at **Gordon Rocks,** and there are several other excellent options for diving day trips: **Floreana, Seymour Norte,** and **Daphne** are among the most popular.

PUERTO AYORA

If you're expecting a deserted island paradise, Puerto Ayora will be a surprise, with a permanent population of about 18,000 and thousands more temporary residents and travelers. The waterfront is filled with tourist eateries, travel agencies, gift shops, and hotels. While conservationists may wish the port away, it's hard to dislike Puerto Ayora. Set in a sheltered

Santa Cruz and Nearby Islands

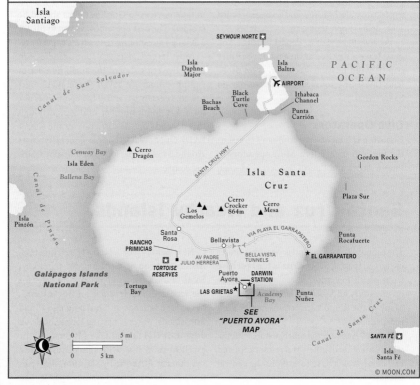

bay lined with cacti and filled with dozens of anchored yachts, the town is a pleasant place to be based for a few days. The docks are particularly attractive, with a jetty that is lit up at night. To the east near Banco del Pacífico, a small fish market attracts pelicans and sea lions looking for scraps.

If you're traveling independently, it makes a lot of sense to stay here to pick up day tours or last-minute cruises. However, note that Puerto Ayora has its drawbacks—there's too much noise and traffic, especially the countless white-truck taxis shuttling around town. Go just a block or two inland, and you'll find unattractive piles of construction debris and half-finished building projects. Day tours by boat are increasingly expensive. More serious are the problems with the water supply, and

the construction of a decent sewage treatment facility is long overdue. The water supply here is dirtier than in mainland Ecuador, so don't drink it, and use bottled water to clean your teeth.

Sights

TOP EXPERIENCE

CHARLES DARWIN RESEARCH STATION

At the Charles Darwin Research Station (Av. Charles Darwin s/n, Puerto Ayora, tel. 05/252-7013 ext. 101, darwinfoundation.org, 7:30am-5pm, free admission), the primary attraction is the **Tortoise Breeding Center Fausto Llerena.** The center opened in the 1960s as a

Puerto Ayora

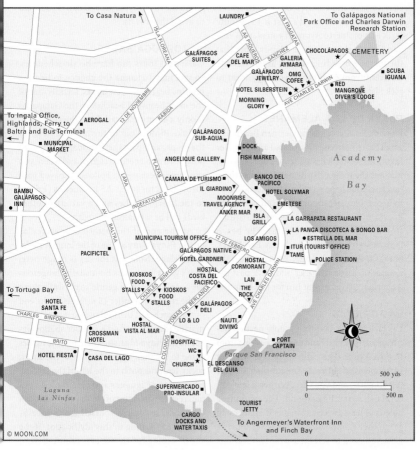

place for endangered subspecies to be hatched and cared for until they can be safely released into the wild. Adult giant tortoises of different species and land iguanas are easy to spot among the rock enclosures. Tiny giant tortoises of different subspecies are nurtured and protected in mesh-top boxes until their shells harden. One of the boxes contains baby tortoises from the island of Española. This is the station's biggest success story: After the population had fallen to only 14 individuals, conservationists have been able to breed and repopulate thousands of tortoises

to the island. The biggest failure is also on display: the meticulously preserved body of **Lonesome George,** the last surviving member of the Pinta Island species, which became extinct in 2012.

In addition to the breeding center, the research station complex houses buildings dedicated to scientific research; unfortunately, these are closed to the public. However, a small visitors center has a mixed bag of exhibits about the tortoises and other Galápagos flora and fauna. There's also a small beach just outside the station, **Playa de la Estación**

(7am-6pm daily), that is a good place to relax and spot the occasional marine iguana. It's easy to visit the Charles Darwin Research Station on your own; it's just a 15-minute walk east of Puerto Ayora. If you plan to visit San Cristóbal and Isabela Islands, note that the tortoise breeding centers aren't terribly different from each other; you may want to pick just one.

PLAYA DE LOS ALEMANES

Playa de los Alemanes, or German Beach, is a small beach conveniently located a short water taxi ride ($0.80 each way) from Puerto Ayora. It is not the most pristine beach, nor is there much wildlife to be seen, but it is the most easily accessible place to sunbathe and swim near Puerto Ayora, and makes a good sunbathing stop on the way to Las Grietas. The beach is right in front of the Finch Bay Eco Hotel, but it's open to the public. To get there, take a water taxi from the pier and walk past the Angermeyer Waterfront Inn for five minutes.

LAS GRIETAS

Las Grietas is a swimming hole nestled between red rock cliffs and easily accessible from Puerto Ayora. The calm turquoise water is surrounded on both sides by stunning 6-meter (20-ft) cliffs, and you can even see a few colorful fish swimming around. The swimming hole is at least twice as long as it appears; to get to the second half that far fewer tourists visit, you need to scramble over two sections of treacherous, slippery rocks. If you're feeling adventurous, there's a short underwater tunnel on the right side of the channel that goes under the second rocky scramble. To get your bearings, hike the short **bay trail** that veers left from the main path and has viewpoints over Las Grietas as well as Academy Bay.

To get to Las Grietas from Puerto Ayora, take a water taxi across the bay ($0.80 each way) and head inland past Finch Bay Eco Hotel; it's then an easy 15-minute walk along a well-maintained trail. There is a staircase to enter the swimming hole. Bring water shoes for climbing over the rocks. Las Grietas is

popular among locals and included as part of all the bay tours. Go early in the morning or climb the rocks to the second half if you want to avoid the crowds.

★ TORTUGA BAY

Galápagos tours can have hectic schedules, so you may welcome the chance to lie on a pristine beach for a few hours. Luckily, one of the most beautiful beaches in the Galápagos is only a 45-minute walk from Puerto Ayora.

Take Binford out of town to the west, up the steps, and past the national park guard post, where you need to sign in and where you can buy refreshments. Follow the paved path through cactus forest 2.5 kilometers (1.6 mi) to the beach. Finches and a variety of other birds can be seen along the path.

At the end of the path is a spectacular beach, **Playa Brava,** one of the longest in the archipelago. Note that the sea is rough here, so it's good for surfers but usually dangerous for swimmers. For a gentle soak, walk along to the right for another 15 minutes to the end of the beach and turn inland past a group of marine iguanas to find a smaller shallow lagoon and **Playa Mansa,** where marine turtles come to lay their eggs. Don't miss the short, rocky **iguana path** to the left of the lagoon, where marine iguanas and blue-footed boobies rest. During most of the day the water can be cloudy, so content yourself with sunbathing and swimming in this idyllic spot. If the sun is shining and the water is calm and clear, you can see tortoises, white-tipped reef sharks, and stingrays by swimming around the bay. It's a long way around the periphery, so bring fins. You can also rent kayaks ($10 pp) and ride along the mangroves lining the bay.

Note that the beach closes at 5pm, so you should set out earlier than 3pm to have enough time to enjoy it. There are no facilities, so bring water and refreshments, and be sure to take the trash back with you. Those

1: the pristine mangroves of Tortuga Bay; **2:** tour boats anchored at Puerto Ayora; **3:** Las Grietas; **4:** display at the Charles Darwin Research Station

wishing to avoid the walk to Tortuga Bay can take a boat ($10 each way), which departs from the dock at 9am or noon and returns after a couple hours.

Tours

Puerto Ayora's tour agencies line the blocks near the boardwalk, making it easy to book any tour—as well as rent bikes, purchase ferry tickets, and book last-minute cruises. However, on occasion different agencies charge different prices for the same tour and yacht, so get quotes from at least two agencies before booking.

The tours on Santa Cruz Island, such as the bay tour and highlands tour, only take half a day, and you can usually find both morning and afternoon departures. The other tours take a full day, leaving early in the morning and returning late in the day. Full-day tours must be booked the night before at the latest, but tours sometimes fill up, making it necessary to book a couple days in advance, especially in high season. You can also book ahead of time from abroad to ensure that you get on the tours you want, though prices tend to be higher.

HIGHLANDS TOURS

The **highlands tour** ($45) goes to El Chato Tortoise Reserve, the nearby lava tunnels, and Los Gemelos collapsed craters. Alternatively, you can see many of these sights independently with a taxi driver for about $40 for a half day, divided among your group.

BAY TOURS

The half-day **bay tour** ($35) takes in several highlights near Puerto Ayora. Bay tours go to the small islet **La Lobería** and observe the small colony of sea lions. Depending on conditions, the tour includes a snorkel here or in the shallower waters of **Punta Estrada** in the bay. From there the boat coasts by the cliffs to look for blue-footed boobies and other seabirds before you disembark for a short walk to **Canal del Amor,** a lookout point where you can observe white-tipped

reef sharks resting in the shallows, and a rather generic beach, **Playa los Perros.** The tour concludes with a visit to **Las Grietas,** an excellent swimming hole near port; this site can also be visited easily on your own. Tours leave at 9am and 2pm every day and take about four hours. Tip: Request free fin rental from your tour agency when you buy the ticket. Not all agencies provide them for the half-day trips, and you will see many more fish if you're moving faster while snorkeling. The boats for the bay tour are small and generally slow because distances are short; some ($40 pp) have a glass bottom for observing marinelife.

DAY TOURS

Full-day tours from Puerto Ayora to nearby uninhabited islands are the most desirable tours and are also the most expensive.

A day trip to **Seymour Norte** ($160-250) has a walk among colonies of nesting frigate birds and a snorkel along cliffs. A day trip to **Plaza Sur** ($140-250) includes a walk on the island to see land iguanas and sea lions. A day trip to **Bartolomé** ($160-250) features climbing the hill for the famous view of Pinnacle Rock and snorkeling in the bay. Day trips to **Santa Fé** ($160-250) land on the island to see the Santa Fé land iguana, endemic only to that island, followed by snorkeling, though a cheaper artisanal fishing trip ($120) that only includes snorkeling is also possible. Each of these tours features a secondary, less famous beach as a spot to rest and relax after the main visit; these beaches tend to change between tour operators and days of the week. The range of prices depends primarily on whether you book a luxury or regular yacht; there is also some fluctuation depending on whether you are in high or low season.

These day tours operate aboard "day-tour yachts." These are a step up in comfort from the speedboats—typically with tables outside, booths inside, an area for sunbathing on the stern of the yacht, and a bathroom for changing out of wet clothes. A couple luxury-class yachts offer more even more amenities, such as hot food cooked onboard, the stability of a catamaran, and a couple cabins for taking a nap. Since tourism on Santa Cruz is more developed than on the other islands, these yachts are also more comfortable than you will find on day tours from the ports on Isabela and San Cristóbal. Always ask which yacht when booking a tour and try to get pictures if possible.

There's no consistent class ranking for day tour yachts, and it's worth double-checking since boats change frequently. Currently the most luxurious day tour yachts are the *Adriana* (tel. 99/171-6411, www.adriana-galapagos.com) and *Promesa* (Galápagos Daily Tours, Baltra at Tomás de Berlanga, tel. 5/252-7337). Standard day tour yachts include the *Española* (www.espanola-tours.com.ec), *Altamar* (tel. 5/252-6430, Galápagosaltamartours.com), and *Sea Finch* (tel. 99/980-3147, www.seafinch.com).

TOUR OPERATORS AND AGENCIES

Most of the offices are on or near the main road, Avenida Darwin. Recommended agencies for day tours include **Galápagos Voyager** (Darwin at Colón, tel. 5/252- 6833, Galápagosvoyages2008@hotmail.com), **Moonrise Travel** (Darwin, tel. 5/252-6348, www.Galápagosmoonrise.com), **We Are the Champions Tours** (Darwin, tel. 5/252-6951, www.wearethechampionstours.com), **Galapatur** (Rodríguez Lara and Genovesa, tel. 5/252-6088), and **Galápagos Deep** (Indefatigable and Matazarno, tel. 5/252-7045, www.Galápagosdeep.com).

Recreation
KAYAKING AND SUP

Kayak rentals are available in three locations in Santa Cruz—the dock (for exploring the bay), Tortuga Bay (where you can kayak among mangroves), and El Garrapatero Beach. Rentals cost $10 per person. You can rent SUP boards to go around the bay for $25 for the day at **Galadventure Tours** (tel. 5/252-4119, www.galadventure.com).

BIKING

Biking is a fun, off-the-beaten-path way of visiting the highlands.

The easiest ride is to take the bus or taxi to Bellavista (6 kilometers) or Santa Rosa (15 kilometers), then take a long **downhill ride to Puerto Ayora.** Buses for Santa Rosa ($1.50) and Bellavista ($1) leave Mercado Central; some have bike racks and others allow bikes on board in the back, so check with the driver. There is a protected bike lane that separates the frequent taxi and bus traffic. This lane ends shortly after Santa Rosa, so biking past there isn't recommended. You can, however, take a detour along **Guayabillos,** a paved road reminiscent of a country lane that passes numerous farms and houses before it loops back to the main highway. There's no bike lane, but practically no traffic either. It is not marked, but it's the only paved road on the right side of the road on your way back, between Santa Rosa and Bellavista.

If you're up for a challenge, from Santa Rosa, descend five kilometers via the bumpy dirt road to **El Chato** or **Rancho Primicias,** visit the giant tortoises, ascend back to Santa Rosa, and ride mostly downhill to Puerto Ayora. This section is only possible when it hasn't been raining recently.

Another fun option is to take the bus to Bellavista, bike to **El Garrapatero** beach (14 km/8.7 mi), and catch a taxi back. From Bellavista, it's a scenic climb (7 km/4.3 mi, 100-m/328-ft climb) along verdant highland farms to the tiny town of Cascajo, where you can buy water and ice cream. From there, it's another 7 kilometers (4.3 mi) of easy descent to the beach; it's interesting to watch the change of scenery from the green highlands to the low, arid coast. There are more challenging rides possible as well; the entire route is 21 kilometers (13 mi) each way (this is the biking portion of the Galápagos Challenge triathlon). The ascent from the beach back to Cascajo isn't recommended; it's a sweaty and unrewarding slog.

For all of the longer routes, a couple shops in town have good rental bikes, but many of them are clunkers; if you're going on unpaved roads, you should try to find one with shocks. Most bike rental places open at 8am; if you want to start a long ride earlier, get the bike the day before.

DIVING

Diving tours can be booked at specialist diving operators. Day tours are becoming more popular among divers because live-aboard cruises are expensive and are no longer allowed to mix diving with land visits. Note that although you can learn to dive on the Galápagos, it's expensive. More importantly, the strong currents and predominance of drift dives mean it is better suited to more experienced divers. Academy Bay and La Lobería are popular beginner dive sites near Puerto Ayora. There are also good sites for novices and intermediate divers at Santa Fé, Seymour Norte, and Floreana, while Gordon Rocks is definitely for more experienced divers. Most diving tours meet in Puerto Ayora, then take a 45-minute bus ride north to Ithabaca Channel (provided by the diving operator), where the boat departs for the dive site. A couple of diving tours visiting dive sites south of Puerto Ayora leave directly from Puerto Ayora.

Day tours cost from $170 to $200 per person for two dives per day, although there are sometimes last-minute discounts.

Galápagos Sub-Aqua (Darwin, Puerto Ayora, tel. 5/252-6350 or 5/252-6633, Guayaquil tel. 4/230-5514 or 4/230-5507, www.Galápagos-sub-aqua.com) is the longest-operating dive center on the islands, with 20 years of experience and a good safety record.

Scuba Iguana (Darwin, tel. 5/252-6497, www.scubaiguana.com) is one of the most highly respected operators and is run by dive master Matías Espinosa, who was featured in the *Galápagos* IMAX movie. Daily dive prices start at $200 per person and fill up well in advance. They also book live-aboard trips.

Academy Bay Diving (Darwin, tel. 5/252-4164, https://academybaydiving.com) and **Nauti Diving** (Darwin, tel. 5/252-7004, www.nautidiving.com) are also reputable.

There is a decompression chamber in the main hospital in Puerto Ayora; your dive operator will help you in the event of an emergency.

The most famous site you can visit via day tour is **Gordon Rocks,** where schools of hammerheads are frequently seen, just 45 minutes away from Ithabaca Channel. Due to the strong currents, it is only recommended for experienced divers with 30 or more dives under their belt.

Seymour Norte, Mosquera, and **Daphne** are other places within 30 minutes of Ithabaca Channel. Seymour Norte sometimes has strong currents, and it is home to many species of sharks. Daphne is a drift dive with moderate currents. Mosquera is in relatively calm waters above a sandy area with Galápagos eels.

Farther north, **Beagle Rocks, Bartolomé,** and **Cousins Rock** are off the coast of Santiago (90 minutes by boat from Ithabaca Channel). Divers at Beagle explore three large rocks and can often find manta rays and reef fishes. Bartolomé has moderate currents and a variety of reef fishes, sharks, and rays. Cousins normally does not have strong currents; it's home to seahorses, barracudas, sharks, and sea lions.

The dive sites **Champion Island, Punta Cormorant,** and **Enderby** are right off the coast of Floreana, and are home to Galápagos sharks, white-tipped reef sharks, and sea turtles. Ironically, you can only dive there via a day trip from Puerto Ayora (two hours), because there are no local diving agencies on Floreana.

Shopping

Puerto Ayora has the best souvenir shopping, with a concentration of stores along Avenida Darwin toward the Charles Darwin Research Station.

The colorful **Angelique Gallery** (Darwin and Indefatigable, tel. 5/252-6656, 9am-1pm

---

1: green sea turtle at Gordon Rocks; **2:** kayaking along El Garrapatero

and 3pm-9pm Mon.-Sat., 3pm-8pm Sun.) features the work of U.K. expat Sarah Darling. Her wild imagination captures the islands in vivid swirls of color, painted on mirrors, silk pillows, and scarves. She also makes handcrafted jewelry.

Galápagos Jewelry (Darwin and Piqueros, Darwin and Indefatigable, tel. 5/252-6044, www.Galápagosjewelry.com, 9am-12:30pm and 3pm-9pm daily) has two locations showcasing elegant creations in shining sterling silver.

At the end of the block, **Galería Aymara** (Darwin and Piqueros, tel. 5/252-6835, www.galeria-aymara.com, 8am-noon and 3pm-7pm Mon.-Sat.) hosts artwork from Latin American artists, including some from indigenous communities.

Food

Puerto Ayora has the best selection and variety; it has both the cheapest and the most expensive meals in the archipelago. The $5 *almuerzos* (lunches) are the best deals. International restaurants are along the *malecón*.

SNACKS AND COFFEE

OMG Galápagos (Darwin at Piqueros, tel. 098/916-9540, 7:30am-7:30pm Mon.-Sat., 3pm-7:30pm Sun., espresso drinks $4) single-sources coffee beans from farms in the highlands of Santa Cruz and roasts them on-site. In addition to the espresso drinks, frozen yogurt, snacks—and in the afternoon, air-conditioning.

Chocolápagos (Darwin and Marchena, tel. 096/738-9575, 10am-5pm Mon.-Sat.) makes artisanal truffles on-site. and hosts demonstrations of the chocolate-making process by reservation ($15).

ECUADORIAN AND SEAFOOD

Opposite the ferry docks, **El Descanso del Guia** (Darwin, tel. 5/252-6618, 6:30am-7:30pm daily, fixed lunch $5, entrées $8-12) is the preferred choice of guides, as its name

(Guides' Rest) suggests. Fill up on large plates of chicken, fish, and meat staples).

For fresh fish, head a couple of blocks inland to the string of ★ **Los Kioskos,** along Charles Binford east of Avenida Baltra, busy in the evening with locals and tourists wolfing down cheap, tasty specialties. Try the bright red brujo or lobster and langostino in season, cooked to your preference. Several of the stalls serve a fixed-course *almuerzo*; **Servisabroson** (Binford, tel. 5/252-7461, lunch and dinner daily, fixed-menu lunch $4, entrées $10-13) is one of the best.

INTERNATIONAL

The **Galápagos Deli** (Berlanga and Baltra, no phone, 7am-10pm Tues.-Sun., $5-10) is a cute café and pizzeria just behind the main strip with good-value pizzas, fresh salads, and homemade sandwiches. It is also one of the few cafés with free Wi-Fi.

Popular ★ **Il Giardino** (Darwin and Binford, tel. 5/252-6627, www.ilgiardino-galapagos.com.ec, 8:30am-11:30pm Tues.-Sun., entrées $7-14) serves a wide range of Italian specialties in a relaxed garden café atmosphere.

The Rock (Darwin and Naveda, tel. 5/252-7505, www.therockgalapagos.com, 8:30am-11pm Tues.-Sun., entrées $8-18) is a casual gastropub named after the first bar established here in the 1940s. It serves a hodge-podge of international food, with juices, shakes, and cocktails to wash it all down.

Known for the fantastic views of the harbor, especially at sunset, **Almar** (Red Mangrove Hotel, Darwin, tel. 98/462-7240, http://almargalapagos.com, 7am-10pm daily, entrées $15-25) serves international and seafood specialties with mostly local ingredients.

★ **Anker Mar** (Binford at Plazas, tel. 05/252-4994, 6pm-10pm Tues.-Sun., entrées $18-27) serves famed farm-to-table and haute cuisine concepts with creativity beyond the other restaurants in town. Try the tender brujo ceviche, roasted octopus, or indulge in the six-course tasting menu ($55).

MARKETS

The **Supermarket Pro-Insular** (Darwin and Malecón, 8am-9pm daily) is located by the pier. For a more local experience, head to the **Municipal Market** (Baltra and Calle No 55, 5:30am until they run out, daily), where stands sell fresh fruit, vegetables, and eggs. To buy fresh fish, lobster, and langostino, head to the **fish market** (Darwin and Indefatigable, open morning and evening daily).

Accommodations

In Puerto Ayora, you can pay anything from $20 per person to more than $200 per person. Many of the cheap and midrange places charge higher rates via online platforms like Booking.com, so it's cheaper to reserve via email or phone.

UNDER $50

Unless noted, rooms include Wi-Fi, private bathrooms, hot water, and air-conditioning.

If you don't need air-conditioning, **Los Amigos** (Charles Darwin, tel. 05/252-6265, $15 s, $30 d, no breakfast) has the cheapest rooms in town. Some have shared bathrooms as well, but they are popular for being clean and right on the main strip.

Hostal Morning Glory (Darwin at Floreana, tel. 099/680-5789, jmarcox@gmail. com, $20 s, $40 d, breakfast $5) is the cutest and also one of the cheapest budget options. Small, colorful rooms are centered around a small garden.

Vista al Mar (Baltra at Binford, tel. 05/252-4109, $30 s, $50 d, no breakfast) has just a couple of centrally located rooms with lukewarm showers and a sunny patio. The real reason to stay here is that bike rental, snorkels, and fins are all included.

The **Crossman Hostal** (Binford and Montalvo, tel. 5/252-6467, www.crossmanho-tel.com.ec, $20 dorm, $30 s, $50 d, no breakfast), located by Laguna Las Ninfas, a 10-minute walk from town. It is one of the few places in town to offer dorms and a shared kitchen.

Estrella del Mar (12 de Febrero at Charles Darwin, tel. 5/252-6427, estrellademar@an-dinanet.net, $30 s, $50 d, no breakfast) is easily the cheapest hotel on the waterfront; some of the rooms have ocean views. Simple rooms have cable TV, air-conditioning, a mini-fridge, and hot water.

$50-100

Hotels in the midrange are comfortable and include the basic amenities of Wi-Fi, hot water, and air-conditioning. You get a more spacious room and nice decor, and many include breakfast.

★ **Hostal Flightless Cormorant** (Darwin and 12 de Febrero, tel. 05/252-4343, hostalcormorant2016@outlook.com, $30 s, $60 d, breakfast $5) is right on the main drag. The comfortable rooms are a fine value and a few even have large windows. You can cook in the shared kitchen and relax on lounge chairs overlooking the bay.

Hidden in a side street by the municipal market, the six-room **Bambu Galápagos Inn** (Parque Alborada at Isla Duncan and Albatros, tel. 5/252-4085, elbambuGalapa-gos@hotmail.com, $60 d, $75 t, $75 suite, no breakfast) has attractive, rustic rooms. There is no breakfast, but there is a small shared kitchenette.

Hostal Costa del Pacifico (Berlanga at Isla Plazas, tel. 05/252-6222, costadelpacifi-cogalapagos.com, $45 s, $70-80 d, $105 t, no breakfast included) has clean, modern rooms in a central location. Though it's generic, the balconies make it stand out.

A couple blocks inland, ★ **Galápagos Native** (Berlanga and 12 de Febrero, tel. 5/252-4730, www.Galápagosnative.com.ec, $60 s, $70-90 d), has friendly service, spotless and spacious guest rooms in cheery colors, and breakfast next door at Villa Luna included. Request a room on the second floor to avoid street noise.

$100-200

These hotels have transparent pricing with minimal bargaining, so it book in advance.

At the west end of town, inland from the docks near Laguna de Las Ninfas, family-run **Casa del Lago** (Moises Brito and Juan Montalvo, tel. 5/252-4116, $115 s, $140 d) has a bohemian vibe, with bougainvillea vines climbing the walls. Colorful guest rooms are equipped with kitchens.

Worth the short walk north of town, ★ **Hotel Fiesta** (Moises Brito and Juan Montalvo, tel. 5/252-6440, www. Galápagoshotelfiesta.com, $100 s/d, $140 t, $156 q) feels like a desert paradise retreat. 28 elegant guest rooms are equipped with locally crafted furniture and mini-fridges. Regular rooms overlook the pool, while quiet cabanas are in the back. Guests can walk along the mangroves on a wooden walkway on Laguna de Las Ninfas.

For a more intimate setting and personalized service, **Galápagos Suites** (Cucuve and Floreana, tel. 5/252-6209 or 9/744-8110, www. Galápagossuites.com, $110 s, $138 d, $179 t) is a friendly, family-run place with just six modern guest rooms, each with a private balcony and a hammock. Note that despite the name, rooms do not have kitchens or separate sitting areas.

Hotel Santa Fe (tel. 5/252-6419, www. santafegalapagos.com.ec, $117 d, $159 suite) offers large, immaculate rooms. Suites have a small sitting area, a fully equipped kitchen, and a balcony overlooking the pool. It's a short walk to the main strip and the local market, making cooking convenient. The owners also run the tour agency Galápagos a la Carte, where you can create your own custom package.

OVER $200

These top-end venues are popular with tour groups. Booking them as part of your tour for the best rates.

On the main strip, elegant **Hotel Silberstein** (Darwin and Los Piqueros, tel./ fax 5/252-6277, www.hotelsilberstein.com, $240 d) is a villa with charming arches, a tropical courtyard, a swimming pool terrace, and spacious guest rooms with solar-heated water. It's part of Galextur, which can organize island hopping, cruises, and diving with the on-site Dive Center Silberstein.

★ **Red Mangrove Hotel** (Darwin, tel. 593/5252-6564, www.redmangrove.com, $350-370 d, $550 suite) lives up to its name, with 16 elegant rooms nestled within a mangrove forest overlooking the bay. Rooms have top-quality furnishings and amenities including robes flat-screen TV, and spa toiletries. Breakfast is served in the elegant waterfront Almar restaurant. Free bicycle rental is an added plus.

Across the harbor and accessible by water taxi, the **Angermeyer Waterfront Inn** (tel. 9/472-4955, www.angermeyer-waterfront-inn. com, $274-374 d, $475 suite) feels like a secluded Mediterranean villa overlooking the bay. Lava rocks and driftwood, coral give it a maritime theme. Well-appointed rooms are have great views.

The **Sol y Mar** (Darwin near Banco del Pacífico, tel. 5/252-6281, $285-300 d) has plush rooms appointed with California king-size beds and balconies with ocean views. Enjoy the sunny patio, pool, and Jacuzzi.

Beachfront ★ **Finch Bay Eco Hotel** (tel. 2/250-8810, ext. 2810, www.finchbayhotel. com, $509 s, $538 d, $752 suite) has a large pool and comfortable lounge area overlooking Playa de los Alemanes. Rooms are elegant and designed for unwinding; there are plenty of hammocks but no TV. It is the most ecologically sound hotel in the archipelago, with its own freshwater system and solar panels. It's a short walk to Las Grietas with a free water taxi service across to town.

Luxury glamping resort **Galápagos Safari Camp** (Finca Palo Santo, Salasaca, tel. 2/204-0284, www.Galápagossafaricamp.com, $548 s, $753 d) boasts stylish canvas tents with real beds and private bathrooms with hot water, an outdoor pool, and great views of the highlands. A taxi into town is approximately $10 each way, though most guests book the all-inclusive tour packages.

Information and Services

The **Cámara de Turismo** office (Darwin and 12 de Febrero, tel. 5/252-6206, www. Galápagostour.org, 9am-5pm Mon.-Fri.) and the **Ministry of Tourism** office (Binford and 12 de Febrero, tel. 5/252-6174, 9am-5pm Mon.-Fri.) both have maps, brochures, and helpful staff. The Cámara de Turismo only has maps and information about Santa Cruz; go to the Ministry of Tourism for information on all the islands. The **Galápagos National Park Office** (tel. 5/252-6189 or 5/252-6511, www.Galápagospark.org, 7am-12:30pm and 2pm-7pm Mon.-Fri.) is just before the Charles Darwin Research Station at the edge of town.

Banco del Pacífico on Darwin has an ATM. **Banco de Bolivariano** also has an ATM next to the supermarket opposite the ferry dock. Internet access is available around town, but it's slow.

The **hospital** (Baltra and Darwin, tel. 5/252-6103) has a 24-hour emergency room and is just up from the docks. The **police station** (tel. 5/252-6101) is behind the TAME airline office, down a side road off Avenida Darwin on the waterfront.

Getting There and Around
AIRPORT

The main **airport** serving Santa Cruz Island, **Aeropuerto Seymour de Baltra** (airport code: GPS, www.ecogal.aero, tel. 5/253-4004) is actually located on Baltra, a small island just north of Santa Cruz. Getting to Puerto Ayora from the airport takes a few steps. First take one of the free **airport buses** located right after the luggage claim. The airport buses come frequently, take 15 minutes, and drop you off at the dock. From the dock, take a **ferry** across the channel to Santa Cruz Island ($1); they run about every 15 minutes and take 10 minutes. Once you arrive at the dock on Santa Cruz, the easiest way to get to Puerto Ayora is by **taxi** (45 minutes, $25). Note that taxis almost always break the speed limit of 50 kilometers per hour (31 mph) and sometimes hit birds as a result.

A cheaper and more eco-friendly option for getting from the dock to Puerto Ayora is the **bus** ($2), which takes a little over an hour, though the schedule is sporadic; they leave at different times depending on when the flights land and when there are enough passengers, and they usually stop running by 10am. Going the opposite direction, buses leave Puerto Ayora for the dock 6:30am-8:30am. The bus stop in Puerto Ayora is in the *terminal terrestre* (bus station), a long walk from downtown or a $1.50 taxi. If you miss the last bus, then your only option is a taxi.

To change flights between the Galápagos and the mainland, you can head to one of the airline offices in town: **TAME** (Darwin and 12 de Febrero, tel. 5/252-6527), **AeroGal** (Rodríguez Lara and San Cristóbal, tel. 5/244-1950), and **LAN** (Darwin, www.latam.com).

INTERISLAND FERRIES

Daily services connect Santa Cruz with San Cristóbal and Isabela. Ferries connecting Floreana and Santa Cruz run three to four times a week, but the schedule is sporadic, so check with the tourist agencies in town when making your plans. All routes cost $30 per person one-way and take about two hours. Tickets can be purchased at one of the kiosks by the dock or at any of the tour agencies in town.

Speedboats leave Puerto Ayora for Isabela and San Cristóbal at 7am and 2pm, and for Floreana at 8am. The reverse trip from Isabela to Puerto Ayora departs at 6am and 3pm; from San Cristóbal to Puerto Ayora, at 7am and 2pm; and from Floreana to Puerto Ayora, at 3pm.

INTERISLAND FLIGHTS

If you're in a hurry or prone to seasickness and can spare the extra cost, take an interisland flight with **Emetebe** (Los Colonos and Darwin, top floor, tel. 5/252-6177) or **FlyGalápagos** (tel. 5/301-6579, www.flyGalápagos.net). Small eight-seat planes fly half-hour routes among San Cristóbal, Baltra, and

Isabela several times per week. Fares start at $160 one-way, $240 round-trip or for any two flights (even different routes).

AROUND PUERTO AYORA

White *camionetas* (pickup truck taxis) are available for hire around town and cost $1.50 for trips within the city limits, but the town is small so often it's easier to walk or rent a bike. You can also negotiate taxi prices to go into the highlands (usually $40 for a half day). **Water taxis** wait at the dock to shuttle passengers to boats waiting in the harbor ($0.80 pp by day, $1 pp at night) and across to the dock of Angermeyer Point to reach Playa de los Alemanes and Las Grietas.

SANTA CRUZ HIGHLANDS

It's worth venturing inland and up 600 meters to experience a different environment than the coast—misty forests and green pastures. Guided tours include Los Gemelos, the lava tunnels, and El Chato combined into a half-day tour ($40). Alternatively, you can visit many of the attractions on your own via bicycle or taxi.

TOP EXPERIENCE

★ Tortoise Reserves

The most famous draw of the highlands is the tortoise reserves on private land. Most tourism agencies describe this experience as "watching the giant tortoises graze in their natural habitat." However, it's best to think of it as watching the tortoises in a *more* natural environment compared to the enclosures at the tortoise breeding stations. The reality is that the reserves are former cattle ranches, where the native *escalesia* forests were cleared and replaced with grass. Wild giant tortoises come and go at will between these private lands and the neighboring national park land, attracted to the reserves for the muddy ponds and delectable fruit from introduced trees. The reserves are similar, so most people just visit one.

About a 30-minute drive from Puerto Ayora is **El Chato Tortoise Reserve** (no phone, 8am-5pm daily, $5). You can wander around on your own and explore lava tunnels on-site. Don't miss the muddy pools where tortoises gather to cool off. There's a slightly dubious photo opportunity where visitors can wear the heavy shell of a dead tortoise. Free coffee and tea are included with entrance, and there's a restaurant on-site that sells decent *almuerzos*.

A similar but slightly less popular private ranch where you can see giant tortoises and lava tunnels is **Rancho Primicias** (no phone, 8am-5pm daily, $5), which borders El Chato.

A third option, **Cerro Mesa** (daily, $5), is on the east side of the island at higher elevation. You can spot giant tortoises here, though there aren't as many and there aren't great walking paths as at El Chato and Rancho Primicias. On the other hand, this site tends to have fewer tourists, and the lookout tower has a spectacular 360-degree view of Santa Cruz Island. There is also a huge collapsed crater on-site, similar to Los Gemelos. Bring good hiking shoes; the trail to descend is steep.

Los Gemelos

A few kilometers up from Santa Rosa on either side of the road are 30-meter-deep craters called **Los Gemelos,** formed when caverns left empty by flowing lava collapsed on themselves. The view into the now verdant craters is impressive; Galápagos hawks, barn owls, and vermillion flycatchers flit through damp *Scalesia* forests. The trail bordering these craters is short; it doesn't take more than 15 minutes to visit.

Lava Tunnels

Lava tunnels are formed by the solidified outer skin of a molten lava flow. They are a popular stop combined with a visit to the tortoise reserve and Los Gemelos. Most people visit the popular tortoise reserves **El Chato** or **Rancho Primicias** and explore the lava

1: Los Gemelos; **2:** giant tortoise; **3:** sea lions on the beach on Santa Fé; **4:** tourists visiting Plaza Sur

tunnels on those reserves, which are included with the entrance fee. The largest lava tunnel at El Chato is extremely well-illuminated and popular with tour groups, although there are a couple small tunnels where you need a flashlight. The tunnel at Rancho Primicias is also illuminated with artificial light, and it is longer, about 600 meters (2,000 ft).

The most spectacular lava tunnels are the **Bellavista lava tunnels** ($3.50), which have a length of 2,200 meters (7,219 ft), though only a 1-kilometer section is currently open for tourists. With a longer length, far fewer tourists, a more natural rocky path, and only minimal artificial lighting, these tunnels feel more like exploring a cave. The Bellavista tunnels are an easy walk from Bellavista, which is accessible by bus from Puerto Ayora ($0.50).

Cerro Crocker and Puntudo

Hiking here is rare on tour group itineraries literally off the beaten path. Trails are often muddy, much of the area has been impacted by invasive plants, and the views are obscured by fog. However, you can walk among lush endemic greenery and perhaps get a fleeting view of the Galápagos petrel in the morning. If you're lucky and the weather is clear, you can also see the island from Cerro Crocker—the highest point on the island. The starting point is a trailhead north of the small town of **Bellavista,** north of Puerto Ayora. From the trailhead, it is about a two-kilometer walk north to **Media Luna,** or "half moon," a volcanic formation covered in native miconia trees. Continuing north past Media Luna, you will reach a fork in the road. To the right is **Cerro Crocker** at an elevation of 860 meters (2,822 ft), 5 kilometers (3 mi) north of Media Luna. To the left is **Puntudo,** another, less popular peak. Hikers have become lost trying to hike directly between Cerro Crocker and Puntudo and there is no trail; you must backtrack to the fork and then take the left branch to get to Puntudo. Having a guide is advised but not required. If you don't go with a guide, take a friend or two and make sure to download an offline

GPS map (maps.me is accurate). Fit walkers can do this hike in three hours; budget an extra couple hours if you plan to backtrack and visit Puntudo as well.

To get to the trailhead, take a taxi from Puerto Ayora ($10/ hour including waiting for you). You can also take the bus to the small town of Bellavista ($0.50) and walk three kilometers uphill along the dirt road to the trailhead. The walk to the trailhead has decent scenery, passing endemic escalesia trees, coffee farms, and the occasional cow, though it has significant elevation gain. You'll need to budget an extra two hours for the walk up and down the dirt road. A third alternative is to just ask for a taxi dropoff at the trailhead from town ($18) and then return downhill along the dirt road to Bellavista to catch the bus back to Puerto Ayora.

SANTA CRUZ ISLANDS
Eastern Santa Cruz Island
EL GARRAPATERO

El Garrapatero, 19 kilometers (12 mi) northeast of Puerto Ayora, is one of the most beautiful beaches in the archipelago. Located in a large, sheltered bay, it has calm turquoise waters. Though it's not as long as the beach at Tortuga Bay, you will often find fewer tourists due to the more remote location. The snorkeling is not great, but it is a nice place to relax, rent kayaks ($10 pp), and look for elusive flamingos at the inland lagoon. With a kayak rental, you can coast near the rocky, mangrove-lined shore by the remote stretches of beach on the opposite side of the bay. Note that you can't walk on the beach as it's a tortoise nesting area, but you can wade around in the shallows. It's also possible to swim to the stretches of beach on the opposite side of the bay with fins if you're a strong swimmer (approximately 1.6 km/1 mi round-trip), though it's not recommended because the water is cloudy and there's not much to see. The beach is easy to visit independently; taxis from town charge $40 round-trip, including waiting for you at the beach, though you can also get here by bike (see Biking). There is a bathroom at the registration office.

Northern Santa Cruz Island

Some day tours stop at Bachas Beach on their way to Seymour Norte or Bartolomé. **Black Turtle Cove** and **Cerro Dragón** are accessible only by cruise.

BACHAS BEACH

This beach is named for the remains of U.S. military barges wrecked during World War II. The remains are usually buried, though sometimes after a high tide the rusty metal parts are visible jutting out of the sand. The white-sand beach is often covered in Sally Lightfoot crabs and is also a sea turtle nesting site, while the lagoons behind the beach are home to flamingos. The site is often included on cruise ship itineraries and on day tours combined with other sites such as Seymour Norte, due to its proximity to the dock on the north side of Santa Cruz. Despite its proximity to the dock, it is not possible to visit independently.

BLACK TURTLE COVE

Just west of the canal between Santa Cruz and Baltra, this shallow mangrove lagoon extends far inland. There is no landing site, so visitors are restricted to a slow tour on a *panga* (small boat). Above water, there is abundant birdlife: herons, gulls, frigate birds, and boobies all nest in the tangled branches of red and white mangroves. Beneath the surface, golden and spotted eagle rays glide by, and green sea turtles are often seen mating September-February. You may also be lucky enough to see white-tipped reef sharks resting in the shallows. The only way to visit this site is via a cruise; it is often included at the beginning or end of cruises due to its proximity to the airport on Baltra.

CERRO DRAGÓN (DRAGON HILL)

This visitor site on the northwest side of the island has a dry or wet landing, depending on the tide. A lagoon is sometimes filled with flamingos, and a 2-kilometer (1.2-mi) trail through a dry landscape of palo santo and opuntia cacti leads to the top of Cerro Dragón, which commands good views of the neighboring volcanic tuff cones. This is a good spot to see groups of land iguanas, which gave the hill its name. The only way to visit is via cruise.

SURROUNDING ISLANDS

★ Santa Fé

This small island is midway between Santa Cruz and San Cristóbal, about two hours from each. There's a wet landing on the northeast side and trails through a forest of **opuntia cacti,** which grow up to 10 meters (33ft) high. The trail is rocky in places, and you have to cross a steep ravine, so bring good walking shoes. The highlight is the yellowish **Santa Fé iguana,** endemic to the island, and you may be lucky enough to see Galápagos hawks in the forest. It is a popular cruise site and day-tour site. Day tours landing on the island start at $160, while artisanal fishing tours (about $100) are limited to the snorkeling sites around the island, where sea turtles, manta rays, white-tipped reef sharks, and sea lions can be seen in the shallow waters. Take care, as some of the sea lion bulls can be bad-tempered.

★ Plaza Sur

Off the east coast of Santa Cruz are the two tiny Plaza Islands. You can only visit the south island, Plaza Sur, one of the smallest visitor sites in the archipelago at just two square kilometers.

The dry landing onto the docks usually includes a welcoming party of negligently stretched-out sea lions. A trail climbs through colorful landscape past a small colony of land iguanas to the far side of the island, where the cliffs teem with birdlife—red-billed tropic birds, frigates, and swallow-tailed gulls. There is less food on the Plaza Islands for the land iguanas compared to Seymour Norte, and consequently the **land iguanas** here are smaller and less brightly colored, and have evolved unique adaptations—such as attacking and eating birds to survive. The presence of both land and marine iguanas has led to a small hybrid colony, the offspring of both species mating, although sightings are rare. Like most hybrids, they are sterile. There is also a small sea lion bachelor colony, separated from the main colony, plotting their next challenge to the dominant males below. Note that swimming or snorkeling here is usually avoided due to the aggression of sea lion bulls. Like Seymour Norte, Plaza Sur is a busy visitor site, and prices start at $140 for a day tour.

★ Seymour Norte

A tiny island off the north coast of Santa Cruz, Seymour Norte is the best place to see large colonies of **blue-footed boobies** and magnificent **frigate birds.** You can decide for yourself which has the most interesting mating ritual: the boobies marching around displaying their blue feet, or the frigates inflating their red chests to the size of a basketball. Both present great photo opportunities. After you make a somewhat tricky dry landing on some rocks, you can hike the 2.5-kilometer (1.6-mi) trail that loops around the island and takes over an hour. At the end, you can appreciate the amazing sight of marine iguanas, sea lions, and red Sally Lightfoot crabs sharing the rocky beaches. Offshore there is a good swell, and sometimes you can see the sea lions bodysurfing. There is excellent snorkeling along the cliffs of the island, where you can see sharks and tropical fish. This is a popular spot for cruises, and day tour prices start at $160.

Pinzón

Pinzón, east of Santa Cruz, is one of the best snorkeling spots available via day tour from Puerto Ayora. The excellent snorkeling is the only attraction here; there is no landing site on the island. Visitors can see a huge variety of marinelife, including sea lions, colorful fish, rays, sea turtles, and white-tipped sharks, in the shallow, calm water.

Artisanal fishing day tours cost $100-140. They include an attempt to catch fish and a relaxing visit to a nearby beach. Some also include a visit to **Daphne Major.**

Daphne Major

Off the north coast of Santa Cruz, about 10 kilometers (6.2 mi) west of Seymour Norte, the two small Daphne Islands are not included on most itineraries, and access is restricted. The larger island, Daphne Major, is an important research site. This is where Peter and Rosemary Grant researched finches, documented in the Pulitzer Prize-winning book *The Beak of the Finch,* by Jonathon Weiner.

Day trips to bird-watch from the boat, snorkel, and fish off the coast of Daphne depart regularly from Puerto Ayora ($100-140). It's highly recommended to look for a tour that combines this site with the excellent snorkeling at **Pinzón.**

San Cristóbal

The most easterly island and the geologically oldest island in the Galápagos is San Cristóbal. Its port, **Puerto Baquerizo Moreno** is the capital and administrative center of the islands. It's not nearly as busy as Santa Cruz, and while Puerto Ayora has boomed in recent years, Baquerizo Moreno is a more modest tourism hub and quiet off-season. Its quiet vibe belies a troubled history, however; in the late 19th century it was the site of a large penal colony, inland at the small town of El Progreso. These days San Cristóbal is pleasant, with excellent boat trips into the national park, excursions into the highlands, and walks to nearby beaches. However, unlike on Santa Cruz, you can't really fill more than a few days here.

If you are staying on the island just a couple days, make sure to do the **360 tour,** which hits many of San Cristóbal's famous sites, including **León Dormido,** in one day.

San Cristóbal

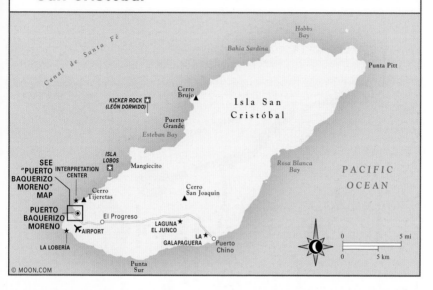

Then take a day trip to **Española,** a site that was previously accessible only by cruise, for its excellent bird-watching and to see the waved albatross. Spend your last day visiting the **Interpretation Center,** climbing to the viewpoint and snorkeling at **Cerro Tijeretas,** and seeing the huge sea lion colony at **La Lobería** in the afternoon. If you have extra time, you can fit in more snorkeling among sea lions at **Isla Lobos** or a trip to the highlands.

San Cristóbal has made significant progress in renewable energy. After an oil spill, wind turbines were installed in 2007. Over the next eight years these turbines provided 30 percent of the energy used by the town. This is part of the government's ambitious multipronged Zero Fossil Fuel on the Galápagos Islands initiative, which aims to eliminate fossil fuel usage by 2020.

PUERTO BAQUERIZO MORENO

The capital of the Galápagos Islands has a different feel from Puerto Ayora on Santa Cruz.

It's smaller, cheaper, and not completely dependent on tourism—fishing and administration are also important. The port has a waterfront walkway where sea lions lounge lazily, and the beach just west of the center is the sleeping area for an entire colony—dozens congregate here at night. The air has a fishy smell: there are few places on the boardwalk where you can avoid it. Nonetheless, Baquerizo Moreno is a popular place to visit, with many sights within easy reach independently or on day tours. Española is widely regarded as one of the top three or four sites in the archipelago, and for many years it was only accessible by cruise. It is now a fantastic though pricey day tour from Puerto Baquerizo Moreno.

Sights

A 10-minute walk northeast of the center along Alsacio Northia is the small, popular **Playa Mann,** which gets busy on the weekend. Note that the water is not particularly clean. Opposite the beach is a branch of the University of San Francisco de Quito, and

Puerto Baquerizo Moreno

@ MOON.COM

To Hospedaje Milena →

← To Airport

J. COBOS

NAVAL BASE

CASA DE LAURA

AVENIDA DE LA ARMADA

RESTAURANT LA PLAYA

HOTEL KATARMA

QUITO

GIUSEPPE'S

TAME

SUPERMARKET

HOSPITAL

J. COBOS

AVENIDA

PORT CAPTAIN'S OFFICE

CALYPSO

FISHERMAN'S STATUE

TOURIST OFFICE

IGNACIO HERNÁNDEZ

ALSACIO NORTHIA

CATHEDRAL

HOSTAL ANDRY

CHARLES

LEON DORMIDO

NATIVO

Shipwreck Bay

FLORES

MARKET

12 DE FEBRERO

LEON DORMIDO TOURS

JOSE DE VILLAMIL

DARWIN

LAVA WAVE SURF

LUCKY'S

ROSITA

SCUBA EDEN

PATAGONIA

TEODORO WOLF

TONGO REEF BAR

GALAPAGOS SUNSET

CASA BLANCA

ESPAÑOLA

CRI'S BURGER FACTORY

POLICE

CASA MABELL

HERMAN

LA ZAYAPA

GABRIEL GARCIA

MÁRQUEZ

MELVILLE

DESCANSO MARINERO

DELICIAS DEL MAR

CEVICHERIA

DIVE AND SURF CLUB

GALAPAGOS BLUE EVOLUTION

SUP GALAPAGOS

GALAPAGOS

CASA OPUNTIA

0

0

500 yds

500 m

To The Highlands, El Junco, and Progreso

PANADERIA CUENCAN

TASTE

AVENIDA ISABELA

Playa de Oro

To Interpretation Center

MUYU & GOLDEN BAY HOTEL

CASA IGUANA MARY SOL

HOTEL CASA DE NELLY

FRESCO'S AND HOSTAL GALAPAGOS

FISHERMAN'S DOCK

students are frequent visitors to the beach. There is also a small food stall that serves basic $8 *almuerzos.*

Playa Punta Carola, east past Playa Mann, is a beach area protected by a rocky outlet. Try snorkeling off the beach; you can sometimes spot sea turtles and sea lions. Go during high tide because of the rocky terrain.

Past Playa Punta Carola, the paved path curves to the right and you will see a large hill called **Cerro Tijeretas.** Cerro Tijeretas has two **viewpoints** with sweeping views of the cove below and neighboring beaches. *Tijeretas* means "scissors" in Spanish; the site is named after the scissors-like tails of the frigate birds that inhabit the hill. Keep an eye out for frigate birds soaring above or perched in the trees, particularly in the morning. There is also a good swimming and **snorkeling spot** in a protected cove just below the hill, which is best at high tide. There is a wooden platform for entry into the water, but at low tide you will still need to scramble over the rocks.

Past Cerro Tijeretas lookout point, the path descends and turns into a rocky trail. There are some difficult sections with rocky scrambles over sharp, uneven lava rock. Though the path to **Playa Baquerizo** is only 2 kilometers (1.2 mi) from this point, it frequently takes an hour to arrive from Cerro Tijeretas (Cerro Tijeretas is 30 minutes from town and 1 hour from Playa Baquerizo). Those who do make the trek out will be rewarded with the least crowded beach accessible from town. You can snorkel and swim here, too, though there's not much to see. Wear hiking shoes and be especially careful if it has rained recently, as slippery mud and sharp lava rocks are a dangerous combination.

You can easily visit all these sights on your own in less than a day. Starting in the morning, first visit the **Interpretation Center** to learn about history and environmental problems in the Galápagos. Walk to Playa Punta Carola for a refreshing dip and snorkel before continuing your trek up the hill to Cerro Tijeretas lookout. After watching the birds, start the strenuous hike out to Playa Baquerizo. You can eat lunch, relax, and cool off in the waves. Break up your hike back with a dip at the snorkeling point at Cerro Tijeretas.

TOP EXPERIENCE

INTERPRETATION CENTER
Walk farther up from Playa Mann to reach the **Interpretation Center** (tel. 5/252-0358, 8am-5pm daily, free), which has detailed informational displays about the islands' history, geology, development, and current environmental problems. It's even better than the smaller exhibition at the Charles Darwin Research Station in Puerto Ayora on Santa Cruz.

★ LA LOBERÍA
On the opposite end of town from Playa Mann is **La Lobería,** a rocky beach where there's a large colony of **sea lions** lazing around. It's a 30-minute walk along an unmarked road near the airport, with not much to see but some dry cacti, so it's better to bike or take a taxi ($4) to the trailhead, which is only a quarter mile from La Lobería. Arrange a pickup time or walk (or bike) back. This is the only place on the island where you can walk among a sea lion colony, and there are usually dozens of these mammals stretched out on the beach and rocks. Snorkeling is common, though it is best at high tide to avoid swimming in shallow rocky areas, and visitors should beware of currents on the sides of the inlet. Though the trail from La Lobería is only about 1 kilometer (0.6 mi), it is a difficult path across large, sometimes loose lava rocks. Wear good shoes.

Tours
HIGHLANDS TOUR
The half-day **highlands tour** ($40) visits La Galapaguera, Puerto Chino, El Junco, and occasionally Casa del Ceibo. You can save money by hiring a taxi to visit the same places ($10/hour).

BAY TOUR

You can take a half-day **bay tour** ($60) near Puerto Baquerizo Moreno by either kayak or SUP. Glass-bottom boats and dinghies are no longer allowed in the bay because they disturb the wildlife.

DAY TOURS

Day tours visit **León Dormido** ($100) or **Isla Lobos** ($80) in combination with a nearby beach. Day tours to visit **Punta Pitt** ($150) don't leave every day; on these tours you disembark on the island and hike to the top, unlike the artisanal fishing tour to Punta Pitt.

The most expensive and most spectacular tour that leaves from Puerto Baquerizo Moreno is to see the waved albatross on **Española** ($200).

ARTISANAL FISHING TOURS

One of the most popular tours is the **360 tour** ($140), which circumnavigates San Cristóbal and visits five sites in one day. It starts with snorkeling at the calm lagoons of Bahía Rosa Blanca, coasts by Punta Pitt to observe the birdlife on the coast (but you do not disembark), and has a rest stop at a beautiful white-sand beach, Bahia Sardinia. The tour then coasts by rock formations at Cerro Brujo to observe the scenery, and finishes with snorkeling at León Dormido. It includes a stop for fishing; if you're lucky, you may get fresh ceviche. Total navigation time is four hours, so avoid this tour if you get seasick easily.

TOUR OPERATORS AND AGENCIES

Lava Wave Surf (tel. 5/252-1815, info@lavawavesurf.com) has surfboard rentals, surf classes, yoga classes, and guided bike tours of the highlands. They can also book almost any other tour on the island.

León Dormido Tours (Villamil at Darwin, tel. 99/445-1667, http://leondormidogalapagos.com.ec) is a popular tour agency that offers almost everything, including bike rentals, diving, ferry boat tickets, and day tours.

SUP Galápagos (Malecón at Melville, tel. 93/967-8592, reservas@Galápagos.tours) is the only outfit in town that organizes stand-up paddleboarding tours of the bay.

Most tour agencies also sell dive tours, but for the best information, go directly to the dive operators.

Dive and Surf Club (Melville, tel. 8/087-7122 or 8/634-7256, www.divesurfclub.com) operates daily dive tours as well as discovery dives, PADI courses, and night dives.

Scuba Eden (Teodoro Wolf and Darwin, tel. 5/252-0666, http://scubaedengalapagos.com) operates daily snorkel and dive trips to Kicker Rock.

Galápagos Blue Evolution (Melville at Hernández, tel. 5/301-0264, http://Galápagosblueevolution.com.ec) is a dive operator that offers a full list of dive certifications, from open water to dive master.

Recreation

SURFING

San Cristóbal has a strong surfing culture, and some of the agencies in town rent boards for $20 per day. Pass the military base at the east edge of town along Armada Nacional, and you will find some of the best surfing spots, **El Cañon** and **Tongo.** Note that these are rocky areas recommended only for experienced surfers, and there is no beach for sunbathing. You will need to show identification to walk through the military base on your way to these sites. Other surfing spots include **Punta Carola,** at the west edge of town, and **Manglecito** (accessible only by boat; look for an organized surf tour if you wish to go).

BIKING

Tour agencies in town rent mountain bikes for $20 per day, or $10 for a half day. It's a fun option for visiting the highlands, and there is a protected bike lane that extends a decent way up toward the highlands. Be ready for a

1: Sally Lightfoot crabs; **2:** surfing on San Cristóbal Island; **3:** the path to Cerro Tijeretas; **4:** sea lions sleeping on La Lobería

grueling day if you go all the way to Puerto Chino in the highlands and back.

KAYAKING

Guided kayaking tours ($60) leave from the port and go either around the bay, along the coast, to the snorkeling spot at Tijeretas, or, in rare cases, take a longer kayaking trip all the way to Playa Ochoa. Unfortunately, kayaking independently is no longer allowed due to tourists getting lost.

DIVING

San Cristóbal has excellent diving, although there are fewer dive operators based here. There is a hyperbaric chamber at the Port Capitania. Prices for most trips are $140-160, although going to Punta Pitt or Española costs about $200-250. There are open water dive certification courses for people who arrive without certification, and you can even get advanced level, rescue diver, and dive master training.

Tijeretas and the Caragua wreck is a trip particularly recommended for divers who need a refresher. Tijeretas is a relatively shallow site where they can review their skills among tropical fish. Caragua Wreck is where the boat that brought Manuel J. Cobos rests. Cobos is infamous for founding the sugarcane plantation on the island, terrorizing his workers, and later being murdered by them. The boat's skeleton forms an artificial underwater reef with schools of fish. There is a buoy rope between the wreck and the surface that you can climb down for greater control.

The most famous dive site on San Cristóbal is **Kicker Rock**, where divers frequently see hammerheads, sea lions, eagle rays, and stingrays. The site is suitable for all levels.

Dive trips to **Punta Pitt** are also possible, combining a short hike to see red-footed boobies with two immersions at Cerro Pitt (home to fish, sea turtles, and beautiful coral) and Bajo Pitt (home to Galápagos sharks, hammerheads, rays, and sea turtles). The drawbacks are the two-hour boat ride each way and the hefty price tag of $200.

A dive trip to **Española** visits the famous site of the waved albatross, Punta Suárez, and does two nearby immersions in Gardner Bay.

There are a couple more sites for advanced divers. **Islote 5 Fingers,** named for the five rocks that stick out of the water, is a good place to see schools of Galápagos sharks. **Roca Este** is a coral rock reef that hosts a wide variety of fish, Galápagos sharks, and rays. **Roca Ballena** is similar to Roca Este but deeper, and it often has more sharks. The **Hitler Caves** are three large underwater caves with calm, well protected waters, bizarrely named after a local fisherman (of no relation to the Nazi party) who discovered them.

Food

Compared to Puerto Ayora, Baquerizo Moreno's restaurants lack variety. Mom-and-pop restaurants serve passable Ecuadorian and fast food. Some of the upscale seafood restaurants also serve pizza and pasta, but you won't find many other options for international food.

SNACKS

Panadería Cuencan Taste (Northia at Isabela, 5/301-0846, 2pm-9pm Mon.-Sat., rolls $0.25-0.50) is where the whole town buys their bread. There is a large variety of rolls, along with a few treats like empanadas, chocolate rolls, and cakes.

ECUADORIAN AND SEAFOOD

Many informal restaurants serve breakfast, burgers, sandwiches, and snacks.

On the *malecón* are **Patagonia** (tel. 5/252-0017, breakfast, lunch, and dinner daily, $5-10) and **Tongo Reef Bar** (tel. 5/252-1852, breakfast, lunch, and dinner daily, $5-10). The food is just passable, and overpriced for the quality, but they are the only places in town that serve breakfast early enough to eat before 7:30am day tours. For breakfast, there's American or continental breakfast as well as more local specialties such as the *bolon* (a fried plantain ball).

Farther north, **Casa Blanca Café** (Malecón and Melville, no phone, breakfast, lunch, and dinner daily, $5-12) overlooking the bay has similar typical food but in a more lively café atmosphere. The sandwiches are just adequate, but it is a popular spot for traditional snacks such as tamales or *humitas* (mashed corn filled with chicken, vegetables, or cheese) and cocktails, particularly at sunset.

One of the best cheap set meals in town is at **Lucky's** (Villamil and Hernández, no phone, 8am-9pm Mon.-Fri., 8am-2pm Sat.-Sun., $4), a hole-in-the-wall popular with locals that serves up an excellent-value two-course lunch and dinner, as well as simple breakfasts.

Cevicheria Delicias del Mar (Northia and Melville, no phone, 8:30am-3pm daily, $10-12) is where the locals go for ceviche and a beer or two. Pull up a plastic chair and choose between the basic fish ceviche or pricier mixed shrimp, oysters, and *canchalagua* (a local mollusk) ceviche. They all come with fried banana chips and popcorn.

Rosita (Villamil and Hernández, tel. 5/252-1581, noon-3pm and 5pm-10pm daily, entrées $15-20, *almuerzos* $6) is a popular restaurant among both tourists and locals. Outdoor seating, soccer jerseys, and flags of the world give it a fun, informal vibe. It has fish, shellfish, and meat dishes on the menu, prepared 10 different ways, but there is also a simpler set-meal lunch and dinner for $6.

The ★ **Descanso Marinero** (Northia and Melville, no phone, 8am-9pm daily, $15-20) has excellent food in large portions and a fun tropical atmosphere, complete with hanging lobster shells, surfboards, paper lanterns, and plenty of tropical greenery. Families sit in the larger tables in the center of the restaurant while couples prefer the rustic booths where tropical plants and straw create little hideaways. There is a wide variety of rice, chicken, shrimp, and fish dishes, but the specialties are the dishes *a la plancha*, which come on a sizzling iron skillet.

INTERNATIONAL

The best hamburger in town is at **Cri's Burger Factory** (Teodoro Wolf and Hernández, tel. 99/423-6770, 5pm-10pm daily, $7-12), a joint frequented by tourists and locals alike. The patties made with local beef are huge and grilled right out front, and the toppings are creative and heaping. The Hawaiian comes with pineapple chutney, while the Pepe has bacon, sweet corn, onion, and barbecue sauce. Pizza, hot dogs loaded with toppings, grill platters, and a couple salads round out the menu.

★ **Fresco's** (7:30am-6pm, breakfast $4, *almuerzos* $8 Mon.-Sun.) is a casual restaurant near Playa Mann with good breakfasts (avocado and egg toast), espresso drinks, and excellent international *almuerzos*. True to the restaurant's name, the food here is considerably fresher than at most places in town, and it's cooked to order. Note that they are open until 6pm but only serve espresso drinks and snacks after 3pm.

Giuseppe's (Darwin at Manuel Cobos, tel. 99/763-8540, 4:30-10:30pm daily, $10-20) has a wide range of Italian dishes, including pizza, pasta, seafood, and meat dishes.

Nativo (Malecón, no phone, 10am-10pm daily, $10-20) is a casual place for alfresco waterfront dining. There's an eclectic international menu of salads, seafood dishes, pizzas, wings, and drinks, made with mostly locally sourced ingredients. The prices are reasonable despite the location and a clientele that is almost all tourists.

Calypso (Darwin and Cobos, tel. 5/252-0154, 5:30pm-midnight daily, $10-15) is a friendly restaurant popular with tourists, with inviting decor and breezy outdoor tables right along the *malecón*. The varied menu has seafood, chicken, and burgers, but the specialty is gooey deep-dish pizza with traditional Italian toppings.

The top restaurant in Puerto Baquerizo Moreno is ★ **Muyu** (Malecón inside Golden Bay Hotel, tel. 05/252-0069, 7-10am, noon-3pm, 5-10pm daily, entrées $20-35, tasting menu $65, menu bar menu $7). The farm-and sea-to-table concept means that all their food is sourced in the Galápagos, unlike most places where ingredients are imported from mainland Ecuador. The high-quality ingredients are well presented and served in a setting with panoramic windows overlooking the ocean. If the prices blow your budget, there's a less-sophisticated set of $7 meal-size bar bites that you can order at the seaside bar.

MARKETS

If you want to cook, there are numerous little convenience stores in town that have a limited selection of fruit, vegetables, and meat. The **supermarket** is located at Quito and Flores, though it also lacks fresh produce.

The best selection of fruits and vegetables is at the **Municipal Market** (12 de Febrero and Flores, no phone, 6am-6pm Mon.-Fri, 4am-2pm Sat., 6am-noon Sun.), a farmers market on the outskirts of town, but note that during the week almost all the food for sale is imported from mainland Ecuador, meaning it is more expensive and less fresh. On Saturdays the local farms come to the market to sell local organic produce.

Fresh, locally caught seafood including lobster can be purchased at the **Muelle de Pescadores** (fishing dock) from about 7am until they run out. Lobster season (when fishers are allowed to catch and sell a limited quantity of lobster) is September 8 to January 8. The rest of the year is langostino season. (Langostino is similar to lobster in taste and texture. The main difference is that the langostino lacks big front claws.)

Accommodations

Puerto Baquerizo Moreno has plenty of options for accommodation, particularly in the budget range. It lacks a large selection of mid-range and top-end hotels, which is not necessarily a bad thing because tour groups prefer to stay in Santa Cruz, keeping San Cristóbal quieter.

UNDER $50

Baquerizo Moreno has many informal, family-run *hostales,* which are converted family residences. Many have sprawled inland to rather inconvenient locations, and, despite the inconvenience, aren't really any cheaper than the locations in town. Budget *hostales* in Baquerizo Moreno typically have only Spanish-speaking staff, spotty Wi-Fi, and no breakfast (unless noted). Rooms have private bathrooms unless noted.

One of the best budget options is ★ **Casa de Laura** (Callejón 2 and Armada, tel. 5/252-0173, www.hostalcasadelaura.com, $20 pp). At the end of a quiet cul-de-sac, it is one of the most tranquil budget options in town. The *hostal* has hammocks and an inviting lounge, but the bright, air-conditioned rooms overlooking a beautiful tropical garden edged by lava rocks are the real reason to stay here. Some rooms even have a mini-fridge.

Another family-run option is **Casa de Huéspedes Milena** (Serrano at Northia, tel. 99/013-6604, milepibu11@hotmail.com, $25 pp), which has well-maintained, spacious guest rooms a little inland, but not as far as many other similar guesthouses.

More centrally located is the family-run **Hostal León Dormido** (Jose de Villamil and Malecón, tel. 5/252-0169, $25 s, $50 d), which has decent, though unfashionable, guest rooms with air-conditioning and TVs, a cozy lounge area, and a small coffee shop downstairs.

Travelers who want to cook head to the centrally located family house **Casa Mabell** (Melville and Northia, tel. 98/125-8617, $30 s, $40 d), one of the few *hostales* with a shared kitchen. The rooms are somewhat small but are more comfortable and modern than the other budget options in town. Rooms have air-conditioning and TV, and common areas have Wi-Fi.

$50-100

There are not too many hotels in the midrange in Puerto Baquerizo Moreno.

Hostal Andry (12 de Febrero at Ignacio Hernández, tel. 5/252-1652, hostal_andry@outlook.es, $30 s, $60 d, breakfast not included) is a good value and centrally located. The rooms are simple and clean; ask for a room with a mini-fridge. There's an in-house tourist agency as well.

Hostal Galápagos (Playa de Oro, tel. 05/301-0947, www.hostal-galapagos.com, $50-60 s/d) has some of the least expensive beach-view rooms and is just next to the exclusive Golden Bay Hotel. Only the two rooms in front have views of the beach; the inland rooms are slightly cheaper. The detached, single-story rooms somewhat resemble *cabañas* (cabins) and are surrounded by cactus gardens. There are even hammocks out front, although the furnishings are on the plain and modern side. The included breakfast at **Fresco's** is excellent.

Just inland is the bright, whitewashed **Hostal Casa de Nelly** (Tijeretas and Manuel Agama, tel. 5/252-0112, saltosnelly@hotmail.com, $50 s, $70 d), a friendly *hostal* with nice terraces. The three-story building has cheerful, rustic rooms, a shared kitchen, and a couple hammocks for relaxing. Playa Mann is just a few blocks away.

La Zayapa (Darwin at Melville, tel. 99/643-9541, www.lazayapahotel.com, $60 s, $90 d) has comfortable, clean, modern rooms in a great location. The interior rooms lack views, but the exterior rooms have wide views of the bay.

Casa Blanca (Malecón and Melville, tel. 5/252-0392, www.casablancagalapagos.com, $70-120 d, $150 suite) on the waterfront is distinctive for its whitewashed Moorish architecture and bright blue cupolas. Inside, the rustic-chic guest rooms have hammocks, wide balconies with views of the harbor, and the most personality in this price range.

$100-200

Hotel Katarma (Northia and Esmeraldas, tel. 5/252-0300, $170 s, $200 d) is a boutique property with only 13 rooms and a beautiful courtyard where mosaic seahorses, fish, and a sphinx overlook a serpentine swimming pool. The rooms are plainer, without the artistic touches of the common areas, but are spacious. There is a sunny terrace and sauna. The only downside is the inland location for a hotel of this price.

Galápagos Sunset Hotel (Charles Darwin at Melville, tel. 5/252-0529, http://Galápagossunset.com.ec, $138 d, $220 ocean-view suite) is a newly built, upscale boutique lodging on prime real estate on the *malecón*. Windows have panoramic views of the scene.

Casa Opuntia (Darwin, tel. 2/604-6800 in Quito, www.opuntiaGalápagostours.com, $120-160 s, $150-185 d, $180-220 t) is one of the most well-known luxury options in San Cristóbal. The hotel has 13 elegant guest rooms, half of which overlook the harbor. The other rooms in the less-expensive extension overlook the pool, where visitors sun themselves during the day and swim up to the bar at night. The beautiful seaside restaurant is in a breezy open-air terrace with a cactus and lava-rock garden.

OVER $200

The port has a few top-end hotels, but not as many as Puerto Ayora.

For an intimate experience, try the boutique hotel ★ **Casa Iguana Mar y Sol** (Alsacio Northia, tel. 5/252-1788, http://casaiguanamarysol.com, $135-285 d). The hotel has five suites, all with huge beds, separate sitting areas, and bay views. The largest are twice the size of the smallest and have a mini-kitchenette. The hotel is modern and was built in 2009. However, leopard-print bedding, artisanal touches, and rustic artwork remind you that you are in a tropical paradise.

Golden Bay Hotel & Spa (Playa del Oro, tel. 5/252-0069, www.goldenbay.com.ec, $305-410 d, $525 suite) is leaps and bounds ahead of the competition for poshest digs on San Cristóbal, with sumptuous beds, rainfall showers, an on-site spa, and, of course, the highest prices. The all-white interiors are soothing and designed to highlight the fantastic panoramic views of Playa del Oro through the floor-to-ceiling windows. A pool, a rooftop terrace with a hot tub, and the farm- and sea-to-table restaurant Muyu round out the amenities. If you really want to splurge, get a suite with a soaking tub.

Information and Services

The **CAPTURGAL** tourist information office

(Hernández, tel. 5/252-1124, 8am-noon and 2pm-5pm Mon.-Fri.) and the **municipal tourist office** (Darwin and 12 de Febrero, tel. 5/252-0119 or 5/252-0358, 8am-noon and 2pm-5pm Mon.-Fri.) have helpful maps and information.

Wi-Fi can be found at most hotels and cafés around town, though the speed is extremely slow.

Other services in town are the **post office,** at the western end of Darwin, past the municipal building; the **police station** (Darwin and Española, tel. 5/252-0101); and the town's main hospital, **Oscar Jandl Hospital** (Northia and Quito, tel. 5/252-0118), which has basic medical care and a 24-hour emergency room.

Getting There and Around
AIRPORT

The **San Cristóbal Airport** (airport code: SCY) is at the west end of Avenida Alsacio Northia past the radio station. Take a taxi ($2) from the airport to town or walk (20 minutes).

INTERISLAND FERRIES

Traveling between islands is easy, with daily services on small launches connecting Santa Cruz with San Cristóbal and Isabela. All routes cost $30 per person one-way and take about two hours.

The ferries leave Puerto Ayora on Santa Cruz for San Cristóbal at 7am and 2pm. The reverse trip from San Cristóbal to Puerto Ayora leaves at 7am and 2pm.

Getting from San Cristóbal to Isabela in the same day is possible, though unpleasant, because it takes two ferries; take the morning ferry (7am) from San Cristóbal to Puerto Ayora, then the afternoon ferry (2pm) from Puerto Ayora to Isabela. For the reverse trip, take the morning ferry (6am) from Isabela to Puerto Ayora, then the afternoon ferry (2pm) from Puerto Ayora to San Cristóbal.

Getting from San Cristóbal to Floreana in the same day is not possible due to ferry schedules.

INTERISLAND FLIGHTS

Small eight-seat planes fly half-hour routes among San Cristóbal, Baltra, and Isabela several times per week. Fares start at $156 one-way, $240 round-trip or for any two flights (even different routes). You can book interisland flights through either **Emetebe** (tel./fax 5/252-0615, www.emetebe.com.ec) or **FlyGalápagos** (tel. 5/301-6579, www.flyGalápagos.net).

AROUND TOWN

Taxis are affordable and cost only $1 within Baquerizo Moreno. To visit sites in the highlands you can hire a taxi for about $10 per hour. **Buses** leave from the *malecón* half a dozen times daily for El Progreso in the highlands, or take a **taxi** (about $3).

OFF THE COAST
★ Isla Lobos

Isla Lobos is a tiny, rocky island 30 minutes north of Baquerizo Moreno by boat. Walking on the island is prohibited, so just jump straight in for excellent snorkeling with sea lions in the channel between the islet and the shore. Boobies and frigates can also be seen nesting here. Day trips cost $80 and combine Isla Lobos with a nearby beach for sunbathing and swimming.

Bahía Rosa Blanca

This peaceful bay is an excellent snorkeling spot. Its protected, crystalline waters turn interesting shades of turquoise depending on the sun, and visitors can snorkel among a wide variety of fish, white-tipped reef sharks, and sea turtles that take refuge here. The only way to visit this site is to take the 360 tour leaving from Puerto Baquerizo Moreno, which circumnavigates the island.

★ Kicker Rock (León Dormido)

One of the Galápagos's most famous landmarks is **Kicker Rock,** also known as León Dormido (Sleeping Lion). Some people think it looks like a foot, while others see the shape of a lion. Whichever name you prefer, this is one of the best snorkeling and dive sites. The sheer-walled volcanic tuff cone has been eroded in half with a narrow channel between. This is a prime place to spot sharks—white-tipped reef sharks are commonly seen in and around the channel, while divers can go deeper to see awesome schools of hammerheads. Sea turtles and a wide range of rays are also common. Boats are not allowed in the channel, waiting at either end while you snorkel or dive. Snorkeling day trips cost $100 and stop at one of three beaches—**Cerro Brujo, Puerto Grande,** or **Manglecito,** depending on the day of the week, for more relaxed swimming, snorkeling, and sunbathing. **Cerro Brujo** is often said to be the most beautiful, with a long stretch of white sand capped by rocky cliffs, and cruises sometimes stop here for kayaking as well.

Punta Pitt

On the northeast tip of San Cristóbal, the farthest site from the port is **Punta Pitt.** A wet landing is followed by a long and fairly strenuous hike uphill (two hours round-trip) past an olivine beach through thorny scrub and past tuff cones. The rewards are panoramic views and, more importantly, the only **red-footed booby** colony in the archipelago outside Genovesa, and the only spot where you can see all three booby species together. There are also populations of frigate birds, storm petrels, and swallow-tailed gulls.

Punta Pitt is common on cruise ship itineraries. There are day tours that visit from Baquerizo Moreno, although only a handful of agencies go here, and those that do charge a hefty premium ($150-200). There are also 360 tours, which do not disembark and hike up the hill but just coast by to observe the birds at a distance before sailing on.

SAN CRISTÓBAL HIGHLANDS

Most of these sights can be visited on a guided tour ($40 pp), or you can save money by sharing a taxi (from $10/hour). Enthusiastic bike riders can rent a bike in town (about $20/day) to get to these, but with a steep incline and 25 kilometers to the farthest point one-way, it is not a ride for the casual biker. Hiring a taxi to help somewhat is popular. One option is to be dropped off with a bike at the highest point (Laguna El Junco); you can bike downhill to La Galapaguera and Puerto Chino, and then bike back (you still have to climb the hill on the way back).

Casa del Ceibo

Avenida 12 de Febrero climbs north out of Baquerizo Moreno to **El Progreso,** a notorious former penal colony that's now a quiet farming village. There's not much to see, but for a unique experience, visit the **Casa del Ceibo** (near the main street, tel. 5/252-0248, www.lacasadelceibo.com, 9am-12:30pm and 1:30pm-5:30pm daily, $1.50), a small tree house in a huge kapok tree. The tree is a whopping eight meters wide and is claimed to be the world's widest of its kind. You can rappel up the side, relax in the hammocks, and drink the local coffee. A maximum of two people can stay overnight in the quirky tree house for $25 per person.

Laguna El Junco

From El Progreso, the road continues north to the settlement of Soledad, near an overlook at the south end of the island, and east to Cerro Verde and Los Arroyos. About 10 kilometers (6.2 mi) east of Progreso on the way to Cerro Verde, a turnoff to the right goes along a steep dirt track to the **Laguna El Junco,** one of the few freshwater lakes in the Galápagos. At 700 meters (2,300 ft) above sea level, the collapsed caldera is fed by rainwater and shelters wading birds, frigates, the Chatham mockingbird, and seven species of Darwin's finches. It's also a good place to observe typical highland tree ferns. A narrow trail with spectacular panoramic views encircles the rim, and it's a leisurely 45 minutes to go all the way around. Note that this site can get muddy in the rainy season (January-April).

Puerto Chino

The road from Cerro Verde continues across the island to **Puerto Chino,** an isolated beach on the south coast that is frequented by local surfers. Swimming and snorkeling are not recommended due to the strong waves, but there is a *mirador* (viewpoint) toward the right side of the beach where blue-footed boobies can be seen. It's possible to camp here with permission from the national park office in the port, though you will need to bring your own equipment. If you're in San Cristóbal on Sunday, instead of an expensive taxi you can take a bus that goes from the *mercado* in Puerto Baquerizo Moreno to Puerto Chino and back

($2). Buses leave the market at 8am and 9am; to get back, the bus leaves the beach at 4pm.

La Galapaguera

A few kilometers inland from Puerto Chino is **La Galapaguera** (no phone, 6am-6pm daily, free), a giant tortoise reserve where San Cristóbal tortoises reside in 12 hectares of dry forest. Mature tortoises from San Cristóbal Island are kept in captivity to breed, and baby tortoises are protected from invasive species until they are five years old. The baby tortoises are kept in raised enclosures, though the adults frequently wander across the stone walkway.

Isabela

Isabela is by far the largest island in the Galápagos and, at nearly 4,600 square kilometers (1,776 sq mi), accounts for half the archipelago's total landmass. At 100 kilometers (62 mi) long, it's four times the size of Santa Cruz, the next largest island.

One of the Galápagos's youngest islands, Isabela boasts a dramatic landscape dominated by six intermittently active volcanoes. From north to south, these are Wolf (1,646 m/5,400 ft) and Ecuador (610 m/2,000 ft), which both straddle the equator; Darwin (1,280 m/4,200 ft); Alcedo (1,097 m/3,600 ft); Sierra Negra (1,490 m/4,888 ft); and Cerro Azul (1,250 m/4,100 ft).

As the giant of the archipelago, it's only fitting that Isabela has one of the largest populations of giant tortoises, which feed on the abundant vegetation in the highlands. There are five separate subspecies here, one for each volcano (except tiny Volcán Ecuador). The slopes of Volcán Alcedo have the biggest population—more than 35 percent of all the tortoises in the archipelago.

The west coast of the island receives nutrient-rich, cool waters from both the

Humboldt and Cromwell Currents. This is why the marinelife is so abundant, with large populations of whales, dolphins, and flightless cormorants, which dive down into the cool waters in search of fish and no longer need their wings. Isabela also has the largest population of Galápagos penguins.

Isabela's only port, **Puerto Villamil,** where most of the island's population of 2,000 lives, is slowly turning into a tourism hub, but on a much smaller scale than Puerto Ayora. There are plenty of visitor sites near the port as well as excursions inland to the volcanoes, but many of the best coastal sites are on the west side of Isabela, accessible only to cruises. Most cruises stick to the central and southern islands, and fewer than 25 percent make it out to Isabela due to the distance involved. Those that do are rewarded with some spectacular visitor sites.

Notable among the several visitor sites accessible to those staying in Puerto Villamil are the **Tortoise Breeding Center** (the largest in the archipelago) and the islets of **Las Tintoreras,** which offer great snorkeling with reef sharks, the stunning archways of **Los Túneles,** and nearby snorkeling. In the highlands, one of the best hikes in the Galápagos

1: Cerro Brujo; 2: whale-watching near Kicker Rock

Isabela

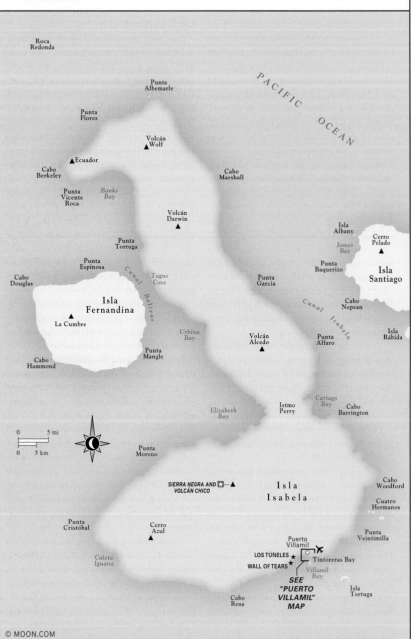

Roca
Redonda

PACIFIC OCEAN

Punta
Albemarle

Punta
Flores

▲ Volcán
Wolf

▲ Ecuador

Cabo
Berkeley

Cabo
Marshall

Punta
Vicente
Roca

*Banks
Bay*

Volcán
Darwin
▲

Isla
Albany

Cerro
Pelado
▲

*James
Bay*

Punta
Tortuga

Punta
Baquerizo

**Isla
Santiago**

Punta
Espinosa

Cabo
Douglas

Canal Bolívar

*Tagus
Cove*

Punta
García

Cabo
Nepean

**Isla
Fernandina**

Canal Isabela

Isla
Rábida

▲ La Cumbre

*Urbina
Bay*

Volcán
Alcedo
▲

Punta
Alfaro

Cabo
Hammond

Punta
Mangle

*Elizabeth
Bay*

Istmo
Perry

*Cártago
Bay*

Cabo
Barrington

0   5 mi

0   5 km

Punta
Moreno

SIERRA NEGRA AND ✪▲
VOLCÁN CHICO

**Isla
Isabela**

Cabo
Woodford

Cuatro
Hermanos

Punta
Cristóbal

Cerro
Azul
▲

Punta
Veintimilla

Puerto
Villamil ✈
LOS TÚNELES ★   ○
WALL OF TEARS ★   Tintoreras Bay

*Caleta
Iguana*

*Villamil
Bay*

***SEE
"PUERTO
VILLAMIL"
MAP***

Isla
Tortuga

Cabo
Rosa

© MOON.COM

is to **Sierra Negra,** Isabela's highest volcano, which boasts the second-largest active crater in the world. Marine sites accessible only to cruise boats include *panga* (dinghy) rides into the mangroves of **Punta Moreno** to see penguins and **Elizabeth Bay** to see flightless cormorants. **Urbina Bay** contains a fascinating raised coral reef, and **Tagus Cove** is notable for the graffiti left by generations of pirates as well as a hike to the deep-blue saline **Darwin Lake.**

PUERTO VILLAMIL

About 2,000 people live in this small port on the southeast tip of Isabela. As well as fishing and a developing tourism industry, the locals have worked on all manner of projects—from sulfur mining in nearby Sierra Negra volcano to lime production and coffee farming. The charming town is far more laid-back base than the two larger ports in the archipelago. With a small selection of hotels and restaurants as well as nearby beaches, a lagoon, and highland hikes, Puerto Villamil has plenty to keep you busy for a few days. Bring cash, because there is no ATM on the island and credit cards are rarely accepted.

Sights
PLAYA GRANDE
The town's main beach is a beautiful three-kilometer-long stretch of white sand ideal for a relaxed stroll, a swim, and watching the sunset. It starts in town, with a rickety wooden structure serving as a lookout point, and continues west, the beach becoming more and more pristine the farther you walk. Keep an eye out for blue-footed boobies, which are occasionally spotted here in huge feeding frenzies, diving in unison.

CONCHA DE PERLA
Concha de Perla is a great free place to go snorkeling on your own. Bring your own snorkel or rent one in town and simply walk toward the dock from town for about 15 minutes. No guide, tour, or taxi is needed. The sheltered cove has calm water where fish, sea

lions, and rays can be seen. The access path is a raised wooden pathway that goes through a tangle of mangroves to the dock.

Tours
HIGHLANDS TOURS
The classic must-see tour of Isabela's highlands is the hike to **Sierra Negra Volcano and Volcán Chico** ($40). Some of these tours include downhill bike riding back to town. A less popular trek available only via private tour is to the **sulfur mines** ($100 pp, minimum four people).

BAY TOURS
The half-day **Tintoreras Bay tour** includes great snorkeling around the islet, a small walk along lava fields, and a visit to a channel where white-tipped reef sharks rest. The classic way to visit is by small dinghy ($40), though kayaking ($50) and SUP tours ($50) of the bay are also possible. Note that the kayaking and SUP tours don't disembark.

ARTISANAL FISHING TOURS
The artisanal fishing tour to **Los Túneles** ($110) is widely regarded as the best tour available from Puerto Villamil. The tour to **Isla Tortuga** ($110) is less popular and does not leave every day. Both include a stop to attempt to catch fish for lunch.

TOUR OPERATORS AND AGENCIES
GalaTourEx (Gil, tel. 5/252-9324, gala-tourex2017@hotmail.com) can help organize an overnight stay at Campo Duro EcoLodge for camping ($70), as well as tours ($48) to hike Sierra Negra combined with breakfast and a nice buffet lunch at Campo Duro (most other operators serve box lunches) and the onsite giant tortoise refuge.

Rosadelco Tour (Conocarpus at Pinzón, tel. 5/252-9237 or 99/494-9693, http://rosedelco.com.ec) is a reputable operator in town. They offer all the usual suspects—tours of Los Túneles, Sierra Negra volcano, Tintoreras, and snorkeling at Isla Tortuga.

Galápagos Bike & Surf (Escalesias at

Puerto Villamil

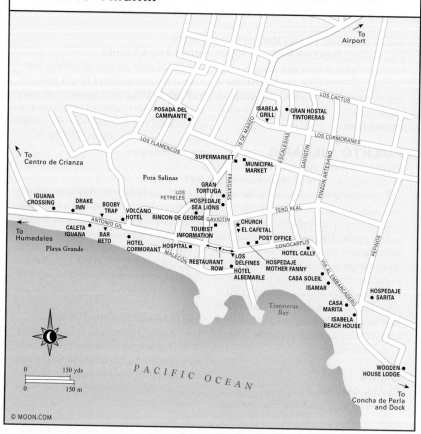

Tero Real, tel. 99/488-5473 or 5/252-9509, www.Galápagosbikeandsurf.com) has surfing classes for $45, surfboard rentals for $25 full day or $15 half-day, and bike rentals for $20 for the day. They're also the only outfit in town that goes to Tintoreras by SUP rather than dinghy (tours $50 including snorkeling). A couple times a week, they also offer tours of Sierra Negra that return by downhill biking.

Recreation
BIKING

Puerto Villamil is a fun place to ride a bike around town. You can get more easily to the

spectacular far end of Playa Grande and see Los Humedales and the Wall of Tears independently. Hard-core bikers can ascend into the lush highland areas where the locals have farms, though it's steep. A less extreme ride is to rent a good mountain bike, get a taxi to drop you off at the trailhead, El Cura, for $25 and bike down.

Ask the travel agency where you rent the bike ($15/day) to call ahead and make a reservation at one of the excellent destination farm restaurants in the highlands for a nice lunch break. Note that this largely depends on luck; they primarily cater to tour groups and may not accept reservations for just one or two people unless they are already cooking that day. Of the highland restaurants where you can stop for lunch, **Campo Duro** is also a campground with a giant tortoise reserve, **Flor de Recuerdo** next door is an intimate, family-run farm that makes chicken on lava rocks, and **Hauser's** is an upscale, romantic restaurant with a well-appointed dining room. After lunch, stop at the volcanic caves **Cuevas de Sucre.**

DIVING

Isla Tortuga is a great intermediate dive site just 30 minutes from the port. Divers can spot giant manta rays and hammerheads in relatively calm waters. There are advanced dive sites off the coast of Isabela—**Cuatro Hermanos** and **La Viuda**—but it is currently hard to find a day tour due to the popularity of Isla Tortuga and the lack of dive operators on the island.

There is currently only one dive operator on Isabela, **Isla Bella Tour** (Antonio Gil and Escalesias, tel. 5/252-9151, harrymoscoso@yahoo.com), which runs trips to Isla Tortuga most days for $150. Unlike at Puerto Ayora, however, there is no hyperbaric chamber on the island.

There is one other operator, **Natural Selection Tours** (Gil at Escalesias, tel. 96/837-6151, http://Galápagosnaturalselection.com) that does discovery dives near Tintoreras, but the company does not go to the more spectacular Isla Tortuga. They also offer PADI open water dive certification.

Nightlife

Nightlife in Isabela is low-key and limited to a handful of bars and a couple of seedy *discotecas* (dance clubs) inland.

The most popular place in town is the **Caleta Iguana Bar** (Gil, no phone, 7pm-midnight Mon.-Sat.), right at the Caleta Iguana *hostal*, with a chill bohemian vibe. The location right on the beach and the 5pm-7pm happy hour make it an excellent place to watch the sunset. Later you can test your state of sobriety by trying to walk on the slackline, or if that doesn't work, relax in the hammocks or by the beach bonfire.

A quieter place for a drink is next door at **Bar Beto** (Gil, no phone, 7pm-midnight Mon.-Sat.), a beach bar at the western edge of town. The cocktails are rather pricey, but the beer goes down well with the sea view.

Food

Restaurant options in Puerto Villamil are pretty limited. The highest concentration of restaurants is along the main road, Antonio Gil, and along the *malecón*, though most of the best options are elsewhere. Visitors should be aware that food in restaurants is more expensive than for the equivalent quality in Puerto Ayora and Puerto Baquerizo Moreno due to the higher cost of importing food to Isabela.

ECUADORIAN

The **mercado municipal** (town market, 16 de Marzo, 7am-6pm daily, though it closes for lunch noon-2pm) has a couple nondescript stalls with the cheapest eats in town; you can find a passable breakfast or lunch for $5-6, and deep-fried empanadas for $1. Dinner isn't served, though.

The south side of the main square is **restaurant row,** with several popular casual restaurants that cater primarily to tourists and have a cute rustic ambience and similar menus and prices. The most popular item on the menu is the fixed-price breakfast ($6), and lunch and dinner for $8, though you can ask for only the main plate for $6. A couple serve pizza and pasta as well. The food is just passable—heaps of rice and beans, small portions of fish or chicken, microscopic sides of vegetables, watery soup, and sugary juice. The primary draw is the fun atmosphere and the fact that it is the cheapest food in town aside from the market.

Across from the main strip of restaurants, the inviting patio of **El Cafetal** (Fragatas and Gil, tel. 5/301-6775, www.elcafetalgalapagos.com.ec, 9am-1pm and 3pm-10pm daily,

$15-25) is well touristed. The small menu has pasta dishes, sandwiches, and a selection of seafood and cocktails. The vegetable and rice sides are nothing special, but it manages to justify its high prices with the nice ambience, skillful preparation, and large portions; the huge fish steak is particularly good.

★ **Coco Surf** (Gil at 16 de Marzo, tel. 5/252-9465 or 96/986-3340, cocosurfisabela@hotmail.com, noon-2pm, 6pm-9pm Mon.-Sat, 6pm-9pm Sun., $12-25) is a casual restaurant with a focus on creative presentation and fresh ingredients primarily sourced from the islands. The *patacón pisao* is a smashed plantain topped with crispy rice, crab, chicken, or beef. The seafood fajita is also excellent; it comes heaped with fish, shrimp, octopus, and fresh veggies. The rustic patio seating is unassuming and easy to mistake for a cheap *almuerzo* (set-lunch) joint, but the quality of food here isn't much of a secret. The restaurant's popularity and small size mean you may want reservations around prime dinner time.

If you like a good dive, head inland to ★ **La Casa del Asado** (Av. Mercado Municipal at Cormoran, tel. 93/968-2481, 6:30pm-10pm daily, entrées $7-12, grill platters for two $20). It's a fun mix of outdoor patio seating, a huge sidewalk grill, tropical music, and a crowd of mostly locals. The most popular items are the big platters to share; the mixed seafood grill ($20), with fish, octopus, and shrimp plus sides for two, is highly recommended. There are also chicken and beef platters if you're sick of the seafood.

For a larger variety of meat, try the **Isabela Grill** (16 de Marzo and Los Jelies, tel. 5/252-9104, 10am-2pm and 5pm-10pm daily, $15-25), which offers everything from T-bone to filet mignon cooked over a charcoal grill, as well as chicken, pork, and seafood. Though the atmosphere is casual, it is one of the few indoor restaurants where you can hide from the mosquitoes.

INTERNATIONAL

Sun & Coffee (Gil at Petreles, tel. 5/252-9447, 7am-noon, 5pm-10pm daily, sandwiches and crepes $6-14, entrées $15-20) is a casual café-deli with fruit salads, large omelets and continental breakfasts, espresso drinks, crepes, ice cream, toasted sandwiches on homemade bread, and an assortment of seafood dishes. Grilled octopus in cacao sauce and the raw tuna *chabelas* (thin fried smashed plantain topped with fish) are some of the specialties. There's indoor seating with air-conditioning and a small patio outside.

The ★ **Booby Trap** (Gil, tel. 5/252-9500, 11am-3pm, 5pm-8:30pm Tues.-Sun., entrées $8-20, lobster $30) has it all—fresh, high-quality ingredients, large portions, great atmosphere, and reasonable prices. The menu is large, with several options for seafood and meat platters, tacos, pizzas, and burgers. For dinner, arrive at sunset time and enjoy the beach view from one of the charming wood-slab tables on the second floor. The raw tuna-avocado-octopus tartare and seared tuna tataki are particularly good.

Casa Marita Restaurant (Gil, tel. 5/252-9301, www.casamaritagalapagos.com, 7am-8:30pm daily, $15-25) boasts an elegant ambience and great views of the beach from the third floor of Casa Marita Hotel. The hotel is owned by a Peruvian/Italian couple, and many of the specialties in the restaurant—Peruvian ceviche and seafood pasta—come from their respective home countries. There are also the standard Ecuadorian seafood, meat, and chicken dishes with a good selection of sides.

The town's only gourmet restaurant overlooks the lagoons and is inside **Iguana Crossing** (Gil, tel. 5/252-9484, www.iguanacrossing.com.ec, 7am-9pm daily, $20-25). It serves local and international specialties, including standard grilled seafood as well as more imaginative dishes such as passion-fruit chicken and coconut lobster.

1: Isabela; **2:** marine iguana with blue-footed boobies

MARKETS

If you stay in a *hostal* with a kitchen, it is possible to cook for yourself, though ingredients are more limited in variety compared to Puerto Ayora. You can buy fresh fruit and vegetables at the **municipal market** (16 de Marzo, 7am-6pm daily, though it closes for lunch noon-2pm). Next door is a small **supermarket** where you can find dry goods and staples.

Accommodations

There are fewer hotels in Puerto Villamil than Puerto Ayora, but there is a range from budget to luxury. For two people, below $40, prepare to sacrifice air-conditioning, location, or maintenance. The midrange of $50-100 has lots of perfectly clean and spacious rooms that are centrally located. If you're willing to spend $200 or more, there's a good number of luxury digs with fantastic views that will happily part you from your money.

UNDER $50

The cheapest place to stay is **Posada del Caminante** (near Cormorán, tel. 5/252-9407, https://posadadelcaminante.com, $18 s, $36 d, no breakfast) is about a 15-minute walk inland. Rooms are just adequate and are fan-only, but it's a good place for cooking as there's a shared kitchen and the lodging is a short walk to the municipal market. There are two wings to the hotel: the primary location and the secondary wing across the street. The best rooms for the same cost are on the upper floor of the secondary location (Posada del Caminante II).

A slightly nicer choice for travelers wanting to cook is **Hospedaje Sarita** (Pepinos at Gil, tel. 5/301-6769, hospedaje.sarita@gmail.com, $30 d with fan, $50 suite with a/c and kitchen, no breakfast). All rooms are basic and have either an en-suite mini-kitchen or access to the shared kitchen. The suite with private kitchen and air-conditioning is a great value. Compared with Posada del Caminante, the rooms are nicer and the location is significantly closer to the beach, Concha de Perla, and the central square with restaurants and

tourist agencies, though farther from the municipal market where you'll buy your groceries.

If you don't plan to cook, then **Hospedaje Mother Fanny** (Gil at Escalesias, tel. 97/997-9678, hospedajemotherfanny@yahoo.com, $25 s, $40 d, no breakfast) has the cheapest doubles with air-conditioning; rooms are small and nondescript though well located smack dab in the center of town.

The nicest budget rooms are at ★ **Casa Sea Lions** (Fragatas and 16 de Marzo, tel. 5/252-9198, www.hotelgrantortuga.com, $30 s, $50 d, no breakfast), which is run by Hostal Gran Tortuga next door. Compared to Hostal Gran Tortuga, Casa Sea Lions has similar cheerful, bright, slightly smaller rooms on the second floor, without breakfast, as well as a great central location.

Casa Soleil (Conocarpus at Malecón, tel. 9/940-3069 or 5/252-9121, oseegers@gmx.de, $40-45 s, $50-60 d, breakfast $5) is the best budget option directly on the beach. The friendly, family-run house has only three basic rooms. Owners speak English, German, and Spanish. The room upstairs is by far the best and well worth the extra dollars. Book direct for the best price.

$50-100

Hotels in this range all have air-conditioning, hot water, and Wi-Fi, and include breakfast.

A solid midrange option inland is the **Gran Tortuga** (Fragatas and 16 de Marzo, tel. 5/252-9198, www.hotelgrantortuga.com, $45 s, $67 d, $105 t), a small *hostal* with friendly service and bright, cheerful rooms with large, firm beds. The doubles are a good value, particularly on the second floor. There is a third-floor terrace strung with hammocks.

Another reliable choice is **Rincón de George** (16 de Marzo and Gil, tel. 5/252-9214, rincondegeorge@gmail.com, $55 s, $70 d, $105 t), with comfortably furnished guest rooms with firm beds, hot water, and TV. The owner of Rincón de George is a registered tour guide. Continental breakfast is served on the fourth-floor terrace, and there's a nice kitchen for cooking.

A good option farther inland is **Gran Hostal Tintorera** (Escalesias at Cormoran, tel. 5/252-9248, http://Galápagostintorera.com, $40 s, $70 d). Compared to the previous two options, you can get a slightly larger room and an idyllic courtyard with fruit trees and hammocks. The trade-off is an additional four-block walk inland.

Hotel Cally (Gil at Piquero, tel. 5/252-9072, http://hotelcallygalapagos.com, $60 s, $90 d, $140 t) is a medium-size hotel with immaculate, if generic, rooms with large beds in a new building close to the beach and downtown. There are also noisier but equally clean rooms on the first floor for $35 per person.

The ★ **Wooden House Lodge** (Gil, tel. 5/252-9235, www.thewoodenhouse.com.ec, $45 s, $90 d) is a cute cabin-style lodge on the east side of town. Notably, it is the closest hotel to the snorkeling at Concha de Perla. Comfortable rooms with wood interiors and a quaint exterior make it cozy. The dipping pool isn't very inviting, but you'll probably go snorkeling instead, anyway. It is a 10-minute walk into town.

Tanned beach-bum types choose **Caleta Iguana** (Gil, tel. 5/252-9405, www.iguana-cove.com, $30-100 d), also known as the Casa Rosada. The *hostal* boasts its own surf camp and tour agency as well as a fantastic location on the beach. Choose among options from basic, fan-only rooms facing the road ($30, no breakfast) to ocean-view rooms with air-conditioning and breakfast for $100. Rooms are run-down for the price, but nonetheless popular for the social atmosphere and location. The on-site bar is the most popular in town, which can make the rooms noisy at night.

The beachfront **Drake Inn** (Gil, tel. 5/301-6986, www.drakeinngalapagos.com, $98-130 d, $178 two-bedroom suite) has perhaps the most character in town, with cheerful, breezy rooms and a fun nautical theme. You can peer out a port window, admire a large statue of Poseidon, or relax in the aqua-colored lounge. There are two sunny terraces; visitors can pick between soaking away their cares in the sea-view Jacuzzi or enjoying the view from the third-floor terrace, which overlooks the beach on one side and the lagoons on the other.

$100-200

Puerto Villamil is beginning to cater to luxury land-based tours, and some top-end hotels have opened.

Run by an expat from the United States, the **Isabela Beach House** (Gil at Pepino, tel. 5/252-9303, theisabelabeachhouse@gmail.com, $132 d, $160 d with ocean view, $200 t) is a beachfront house that prides itself on friendly, personalized service. The cute, simple rooms are purposely beachy, with plenty of fish and seashells to go around. Breakfast ($10 pp) is served on tables on the beach.

At the east end of town on a quiet strip of beach is the artsy **Casa Marita** (Gil, tel. 5/252-9301, www.casamaritagalapagos.com, $115-125 d, $170-220 suite), a 20-room beach house with uniquely decorated guest rooms and suites, each housing eclectic art and furniture handpicked by the Peruvian and Italian owners. Each room has a mini-fridge but no TV. You won't miss the TV, however, when you can watch the sunset from beachside lounge chairs and hammocks. The elegant upstairs restaurant has Italian, Peruvian, and Ecuadorian specialties. The cheaper extension wing across the street is more mundane and doesn't have any views.

Opened in 2017, the modern ★ **Hotel Cormorant** (Av. Antonio Gil *y* Calle Los Pinquinos, tel. 5/252-9192, $160 interior view, $180 ocean view, $250 suite) impresses with panoramic views of the ocean, polished wood, and accents of lava rock. The charming courtyard hosts blue-footed boobies and frigate birds painted across the polished concrete floors. Solar panels provide hot water, and breakfast is served across the street at the Sun & Coffee restaurant. The interior-view rooms don't have the lovely views and they're not as impressive as the ocean view rooms or suites.

OVER $200

Right downtown, the **Hotel Albemarle** (Malecón, tel. 5/252-9489, www.hotelalbemarle.com, $165 d pool view, $235 d ocean view) has 17 rooms, 12 with spectacular ocean views. The other rooms face a central courtyard, where you can bathe in the dipping pool among tropical greenery. All rooms are well-appointed with high ceilings and modern coastal decor.

The **Isamar** (Gil, tel. 593/99 555-3718, isamargalapagos.com/en/home, $148 d, $266 d with ocean view) is an upscale lodge of just eight rooms on a prime beachfront location. Rooms are large and modern, with tidy white linens, security boxes, and sofa chairs. Rooms are arranged in single-story rows; the few best ones have unobstructed views of Isabela's long, sandy beach. The deck has lounge chairs overlooking the beach.

Swanky **Iguana Crossing** (Gil, tel. 5/252-9484, www.iguanacrossing.com.ec, $288 d, $457 suite) overlooks the beach on the quiet west side of town. There are 14 elegant guest rooms, each with stylish decor, flat-screen TV, mini-fridge, and views of the ocean. The deck has a small pool and enormous lounge-chair-beds. The third-floor terrace is even more spectacular, with more couches, a Jacuzzi, and a 360-degree view of both the beach and the lagoons. The on-site restaurant serves gourmet local and international specialties.

If money is no object, glamping at the **Scalesia Lodge** (tel. 593 3/250-9504, www.scalesialodge.com, $331 s, $442 d) in Isabela's lush green highlands is a completely different camping experience, inspired more by the luxury safari camps in Africa. Due to the difficulties in getting to and from the lodge, most visitors here opt for the all-inclusive packages and island-hopping packages.

Information and Services

There is no bank or ATM on Isabela; some top-end hotels accept credit cards, but you are strongly advised to bring enough cash for the duration of your stay.

The local **iTur** tourist office (16 de Marzo and Las Fragatas, tel. 5/301-6648, 9am-5pm Mon.-Fri.) is two blocks inland. The **national park office** (Gil and Piqueros, tel. 5/252-9178, 7am-12:30pm, 2pm-7pm Mon.-Fri.) is one block from the main plaza.

Getting There and Around
AIRPORT AND INTERISLAND FLIGHTS

The **General Villamil Airport** (airport code: IBB) is just north of town, a short taxi ride away. It only serves interisland flights to San Cristóbal and Baltra; you cannot fly directly to Isabela from mainland Ecuador.

Small eight-seat planes fly half-hour routes among San Cristóbal, Baltra, and Isabela several times per week. Fares start at $160 one way, $240 round-trip or for any two flights (even different routes). Interisland flights can be booked through **Emetebe** (tel./fax 5/252-0615, www.emetebe.com.ec), or **FlyGalápagos** (tel. 5/301-6579, www.flyGalápagos.net).

INTERISLAND FERRIES

Interisland **ferries** leave for Puerto Ayora (2-2.5 hours, $30 pp one-way) daily at 6am and 3pm from the main dock. The reverse trip leaves Puerto Ayora for Isabela at 7am and 2pm. It is possible (though tiring) to take the morning ferry, arrive in Puerto Ayora, and take the afternoon ferry for San Cristóbal the same day, but there are no direct routes. Water taxis from the ferry to the dock charge $1 per person. The dock charges a $10 tax per person when you land ($5 for Ecuadorian residents).

AROUND TOWN

Buses leave only once a day at the crack of dawn for the highlands, and you need a guide to visit the volcano Sierra Negra anyway, so you're better off exploring on a guided tour.

Taxis can be picked up near the main plaza and will take you around town for $1 and to nearby visitor sites for $10 per hour.

Bicycles can be rented in town for $3 an hour and are the most popular way to explore Los Humedales.

NEAR PUERTO VILLAMIL
Los Humedales and Centro de Crianza

The most famous sight in Los Humedales (The Wetlands) is the Wall of Tears, a reminder of Isabela's history—but there are also beaches, lookout points, a tortoise breeding center, and tons of lagoons. The farthest point is six kilometers west of town, so you can visit on a guided tour with a van ($25 pp) for a half-day tour. If you have all day, you can rent a bike ($3/hour) or hike. The route to the Wall of Tears and the wetlands is easy—mostly flat along the beach, though it is a long distance, and the last section to the Wall of Tears is uphill along a hot, exposed road. To visit the Centro de Crianza requires a long walk along an exposed trail that branches off the main trail. Hence, riding a bike is a more popular way to see the wetlands than hiking. The bike ride can be sweaty on sunny days, but you can take a dip at one of the beaches to cool off. Another option is to get a taxi to drop you off at the Wall of Tears ($5) and walk or bike back to town.

Before leaving Puerto Villamil, check out **Laguna Salinas**, a lagoon at the west end of town where flamingos can sometimes be spotted. There isn't much to see otherwise, but it's right on the edge of town so it's worth a quick check.

CENTRO DE CRIANZA

Go 1.6 kilometers inland from the main road, following the signs, and you will reach the **Centro de Crianza (Tortoise Breeding Center).** Parallel to the main road, there is a hiking path that passes by several lagoons where you may be able to spot flamingos. There are some 850 tortoises separated into eight enclosures, all from Isabela Island, as well as an information center documenting the life cycle of these fascinating creatures and an excellent program to boost the populations of Isabela's five subspecies. After visiting the breeding center, you will have to backtrack to the coast to visit the rest of the sights in Los Humedales. Note that this breeding center is similar to Charles Darwin Research Station on Santa Cruz and La Galapaguera on San Cristóbal; most people need only visit one.

LAGOONS AND BEACHES

At the western edge of town is a set of lagoons with sizable populations of flamingos that flock here to mate. **Poza de los Diablos (Devil's Pool)** is actually the largest lagoon in the entire archipelago. Wooden walkways take you past the lagoons before joining a trail through a forest. The **Pozas Verdes** are smaller lagoons filled with greenish water and surrounded by cactus. Afterward, see if you can find the **Poza Escondida (Hidden Lagoon)** at the end of a short trail.

It's easy to miss the turnoff to the tiny, sandy cove known as **Playita (Small Beach),** which has a small strip of sand, rocks with marine iguanas, and a calming view of the sea.

Next, there is a forked path off the main trail. To the left you will find **Playa del Amor,** a small but beautiful beach with a large population of marine iguanas. To the right is the **Túnel del Estero**—a short walk to see a small, rocky tunnel and a view of the sea.

The **Camino de Tortuga** is a short trail lined on either side by lush, green majagua trees and leading to a calm mangrove-lined inlet where you can wade in the water to cool off.

WALL OF TEARS AND MIRADOR ORCHILLA

Bike another 30 minutes uphill from the Playa del Amor (or walk another hour), and you will reach the last two stops in Los Humedales. **Mirador Orchilla** is a wooden stairway and lookout point with an excellent panoramic view of the island. **Muro de las Lágrimas (Wall of Tears)** is just a wall, 100 meters (328 ft) long and 7 meters high, but the brutal story behind it is interesting. It was built by convicts from a penal colony in the 1940s and served no real purpose except punishment, which only adds to the tragedy of the men who suffered and died building it. There is a set of steps up to an impressive view of the wall and the surrounding landscape. If you are lucky, you might spot wild giant tortoises here that have been repatriated from the breeding center.

Tintoreras Bay

Just off the coast of the dock at Puerto Villamil is the best spot for snorkeling, a set of islets called **Las Tintoreras,** named after the reef sharks that frequent them. The islets are visited by a small *panga* (dinghy) ride, during which you can spot penguins, sea lions, and blue-footed boobies on the rocks. After disembarking on a dry landing, you take a short trail over otherworldly, rocky terrain, where whitish-green lichens top flat fields of craggy, black volcanic rocks. Along the trail, Sally Lightfoot crabs scuttle and marine iguanas nest. At the end of the trail is a channel where white-tipped sharks can be observed resting from above. The tour also includes snorkeling in clear, shallow water where rays, sea lions, and lots of fish can be observed. Day tours cost $40 per person.

Los Túneles

Take a 45-minute boat ride south of town to the amazing rock formations of **Los Túneles,** also known as Cabo Rosa and El Finado. Boats navigate mazes of rocks, where stone archways form the namesake tunnels over the ocean. The tour includes a short walk on the rocky terrain; you can see blue-footed boobies perched at the foot of endemic opuntia cactus trees while majestic sea turtles glide through the water below. After the walk, tours include excellent snorkeling in the vicinity, where there are many sea turtles resting. Day tours cost $110 per person.

Isla Tortuga

Crescent-shaped **Isla Tortuga** is about an hour boat ride away from the port and is best known as a diving site. Nonetheless, snorkeling tours also come here to attempt to spot the same Galápagos sharks, hammerheads, and manta rays that divers often spot in deep water at the cleaning station. The tradeoff is that the currents here can make for difficult snorkeling. Some tours also combine Isla Tortuga with a visit to Cuatro Hermanos, another islet farther afield. Day tours cost $110 and do not run every day.

ISABELA HIGHLANDS

TOP EXPERIENCE

★ Sierra Negra and Volcán Chico

The best excursion to take from Puerto Villamil, and perhaps the most impressive geologic sight in the entire archipelago, is the hike up to the active Sierra Negra, Isabela's oldest volcano. The last eruption was in 2005 and took geologists by surprise.

The more popular trek is to the crater of Sierra Negra and Volcán Chico. After you hike about an hour, your toils will be rewarded with fantastic views of the **Sierra Negra crater,** which is 10 kilometers (6.2 mi) in diameter. You then descend for about an hour and a half to **Volcán Chico,** a fissure of lava cones northwest of the main crater. On this side, there is less mist and rain, offering spectacular views over the north of Isabela and across to Fernandina. This trek takes five hours walking at a brisk pace with minimal breaks. Alternatively, it is possible to just go to the edge of the crater and back at a leisurely pace in two hours. Some tours include visits to nearby **Mirador de Mango,** a lookout spot with a 360-degree view of the island, and the **Cuevas de Sucre,** a nearby lava tunnel not unlike the lava tunnels on Santa Cruz. Still others combine a trip to the crater with lunch and a visit to the tortoise reserve at **Campo Duro Ecolodge.** There are also tours that combine a trip to the volcano with **downhill biking** back to town. Standard day tours cost $35 per person; lunch at Campo Duro and downhill biking cost more.

The longer and far less popular trek is to **Las Minas de Azufre** (Sulfur Mines).

It takes seven hours in total and is tougher, particularly in the rainy season, when it gets muddy. The hike culminates in a dramatic descent into the yellow hills of the sulfur mines, which spew out choking gas (hold your breath!). Because this tour is less popular, tour agencies only offer private tours. Try to find other travelers who want to go and then approach a tour agency together. The cost will depend on the number of people. For a group of four people, you would pay around $90-100 per person. Even more expensive and less popular are camping tours here.

Nautilus (Gil and Las Fragatas, tel. 5/252-9076, www.nautilustour.com) charges $40 per person for the Sierra Negra and Volcán Chico trek.

NORTHERN AND WESTERN ISABELA ISLAND

Some of Isabela's best sites are along the western side of the island. All of the following visitor sites are off-limits to land-based visitors and are **only accessible to cruise tours.**

Punta Moreno

This visitor site is often the first point on Isabela for boats approaching from the south. It is reachable via a *panga* ride along the sea cliffs and into a grove of mangroves where penguins and great blue herons are often seen. After a dry landing, a 2-kilometer (1.2-mi) hike inland along a pahoehoe lava flow lined by cacti leads to a handful of brackish ponds frequented in season by flamingos and white-cheeked pintails. There are impressive views of three of Isabela's volcanoes. Wear comfortable shoes because the lava rocks are difficult to negotiate in places, and note that it's a strenuous hike; take plenty of water and sunblock.

Elizabeth Bay

North of Punta Moreno, Elizabeth Bay has no landing site, so it can only be explored by *panga*. There are small populations of flightless cormorants and marine iguanas in the bay. The marine iguanas here are comparatively big, munching themselves to a healthy size on the abundant supplies of algae. Farther in is a set of shallow lagoons where you can see rays, turtles, and, occasionally, white-tipped sharks. The *panga* then heads out to some rocky islets called Las Marielas, where there is a small colony of nesting penguins.

Urbina Bay

This bay was created by remarkable geologic activity in 1954. A volcanic eruption lifted a chunk of seabed, including a coral reef, six meters above the water's surface. After a wet landing on the beach, you can enjoy the somewhat surreal experience of seeing coral littered with bones and the shells of marinelife. The short loop trail is easy and takes less than two hours. Land iguanas can be observed, and if you are lucky you might also spot a giant tortoise or two; the juveniles are repatriated from the breeding center and stay until they reach sexual maturity, and the females come to Urbina Bay from Volcán Alcedo to nest. Along the shoreline, flightless cormorants, blue-footed boobies, and penguins can often be seen, and there are rays and sea turtles in the bay.

Tagus Cove

Tagus Cove is the best place to see how humans have left their mark—literally—on the Galápagos. The rocks above this popular anchorage in the Bolívar Channel are covered in graffiti. It's a strange but interesting sight, with the oldest readable record from whalers dating to 1836.

The 2-kilometer (1.2-mi) hike from the cove to the interior is strenuous but worth the effort. A dry landing leads to a trail through a steep gully to a wooden staircase and then along a gravel track. At the top is an impressive view over the deep blue **Darwin Lake.** This eroded crater is 12 meters (39 ft)deep, and the waters have a high salt content, so it's largely lifeless. Scientists have concluded that seawater seeped in through the porous lava rocks beneath the surface. The small round pebbles covering the trails began as raindrops that collected airborne volcanic ash and hardened before hitting the ground. The trail leads to the lower lava slopes of Volcán Darwin, and there are spectacular views over the entire island of Isabela.

After the hike, there is a *panga* ride, and you can cool off with excellent snorkeling along the rocky northern shore. Highlights include sea turtles, Galápagos penguins, flightless cormorants, marine iguanas, and sea lions.

Punta Vicente Roca

Punta Vicente Roca is easily the best spot for snorkeling with sea turtles. The snorkeling site is in a protective cove at the base of Volcán Ecuador, where they can be spotted resting in the calm waters by the dozens, along with flightless cormorants, penguins, and fish. Snorkeling is often followed by a *panga* ride along spectacular cliffs and a cave formed out of tuff (compacted ash), and to a rocky area where fur seals make their home.

Other Sites

There are various other sites on Isabela, most of which have restricted access. Just north of Tagus Cove is **Punta Tortuga,** a beach surrounded by mangroves, and one of the few spots to see the mangrove finch. At Isabela's northern tip, **Punta Albemarle** was a U.S. radar base in World War II. There is no landing site, but there is plenty of birdlife to see from the boat, including flightless cormorants and penguins.

On the east side of Isabela, there is a landing site at **Punta García,** one of the few places on this side where flightless cormorants can be seen. This is the beginning for the trail up to **Volcán Alcedo,** famous for its 7-kilometer-wide (4.3-mi) crater and the largest population of wild giant tortoises on the islands. This particular species of giant tortoise is endemic to Volcán Alcedo and is the most "giant" of all the giant tortoises. Unfortunately the site is now closed to tourists, and only scientists can visit.

Floreana

Floreana is the smallest of the inhabited islands, with an area of just 174 square kilometers (67 sq mi) and a tiny population of only 130 people. Southern cruises stop here for the tranquil, mangrove-lined coast, the chance to mail a postcard at the quirky post barrel, and the excellent snorkeling on the nearby islets. People come on day tours to take in a bit of Floreana's mysterious history, dip their toes in black-sand beaches, and swim with sea turtles. Visitors stay on the island to get away from it all, and to experience Galápagos life at its slowest. If you do stay, come well prepared (food options are limited and there is no bank or ATM), and bring bug spray since it has the worst mosquito population of any of the ports.

Floreana's best sites include the beautiful beaches **Playa Negra** and **La Lobería;** the peaceful, mangrove-lined coast of **Mirador de la Baronesa;** and outstanding snorkeling spots at the submerged volcanic cone of **Devil's Crown,** along with **Enderby** and **Champion Island.**

PUERTO VELASCO IBARRA

The tiny port of **Puerto Velasco Ibarra** feels like a scene from the past. The people meander slowly up dirt roads, stopping to smile and greet each other as they pass. Everyone knows everyone. It is the only town in the Galápagos where tourism takes a back seat to farming and fishing. There are no banks, no markets or convenience stores, and no cell-phone coverage, and the only mail service is through the Post Office Bay barrel.

Sights

Beautiful black-sand **Playa Negra** is directly in front of Hotel Wittmer but is open to the public. Tour groups often spend a couple hours here in the afternoon after returning from the highlands, but at other times it is surprisingly peaceful, and you may even find it empty if you are lucky. Sunbathing on the shore is idyllic, and swimming and snorkeling off the beach are also good, though there is not nearly as much marinelife as at La Lobería nearby.

If you come on a day tour, you will head out for snorkeling at **La Lobería.** There is a small population of sea lions, but the primary attraction is snorkeling among the marine turtles that come here to feed. Hotel-based visitors can walk south from town along a scenic 900-meter (2,950-ft) walking path, mostly through gravel and sand. The path overlooks the ocean and crosses through black lava and dry cactus forest. This is also the most spectacular site near Puerto Velasco Ibarra to watch the sunset.

Tours

A **day tour** from Puerto Ayora to Floreana costs approximately $80 and is the most common way to visit Floreana, though it's not recommended due to the long time in transit. The boat takes about two hours each way and takes in Asilo de la Paz, the tortoise reserve, Playa Negra, and La Lobería. Tourism based on Floreana is in its nascent stages. There are no dive operators on the island; no naturalist guides live here either. If you are staying on the island, you can visit many of the sites yourself or, if you prefer, tag along with the day trip ($20) from Puerto Ayora by showing up at the dock at around 10am when the day tour arrives.

Other activities aren't included on the day tour and can only be done by staying on the island and booking through **CECFLOR** (Centro Comunitario Floreana) and its affiliated tour operator **Floreana Post Office Tours** (tel. 5/253-5055, reservas.postofficetours@gmail.com), which is the sole tour operator on the island. Plan in advance or bring friends because tours don't leave every day, and they require a minimum of four people. Though these tours

are available, at this writing prices have not yet been set by CECFLOR.

- A guided **hike to Post Office Bay and Mirador de la Baronesa** (three hours to arrive; includes snorkeling and a speedboat back to port). Note that some visitors walk on their own from the port; this is against national park rules and may result in a hefty fine.

- A tour to **kayak to Post Office Bay and Mirador de la Baronesa.** You need to be reasonably in shape to do this one; each direction is 1:30-1:45 in kayak.

- **Kayak rentals** for exploring the bay

- A kayaking trip to **La Botella** ($45 per person/2 person minimum), an excellent snorkeling spot. Kayaking along the coast is part of the fun and takes 40 minutes each way.

In the near term, bicycles are on their way to Floreana, and the following tours are scheduled to launch in the near future. Contact CECFLOR for confirmation and rates.

- **Bicycle rentals** for exploring the dirt roads of the highlands

- **Bicycle tours** through the local farms in the highlands

In the future, the larger vision of the project includes **camping tours** at the beautiful and remote **Mirador de la Baronesa** and tours to **Devil's Crown** (currently accessible only via cruise), but it's not certain whether these will obtain approval.

Food

If you come on a day tour, your lunch will be included. For independent travelers, food options are limited. All the restaurants are informal and have outdoor patio seating; there are no international or upscale establishments. Restaurant hours are unpredictable, as most do not cook or stay open if there are no customers. It is recommended that you stop by a restaurant and let them know you are coming two hours in advance. Prices are the same at

Floreana

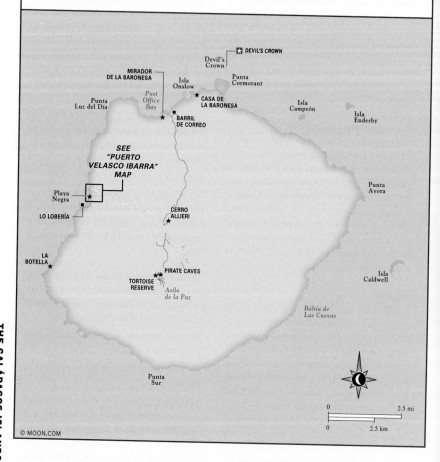

all the restaurants: $7 for breakfast, $12 for lunch, and $15 for dinner.

On the main strip, the **Canchalagua** (12 de Febrero, no phone, lunch, coffee, and dinner daily) is the town's only coffee shop and café. The specialty of the owner, Cookie, is *canchalagua* pizza and burgers—made with a local mollusk. Despite the nondescript atmosphere, visitors love the Canchalagua for the friendly service and home-cooked food.

Farther up the main road, try the **Devil's Crown Bar-Restaurant** (12 de Febrero, no phone, breakfast, lunch, and dinner daily, set menu). The atmosphere is nothing special, but the fried fish is delicious.

At the end of the main road is the **Oasis de la Baronesa** (12 de Febrero, tel. 5/253-5006, lunch and dinner daily). They serve standard fare of fish, rice, and a small salad, with a soup for a starter.

Off the main strip, **Leila's Restaurant** (Juan Salgado, tel. 5/253-5041, breakfast and lunch daily) is one of the most popular restaurants with tour groups. The food is about the same as the other restaurants on the island—fixed menus with soup and rice with fish or

Community Tourism

Floreana has been a day tour destination from Santa Cruz for years. The residents of Floreana call it "lightning tourism" because big tour groups "strike" the island for an instant and then are gone. While visitors may eat lunch at a restaurant in town, the residents see little of the profits. Floreana residents don't want the large-scale development of the other ports. The challenge has been to maintain Floreana's slow pace of life while creating economic opportunities for the locals.

To that end, Floreana has worked with the national park and several conservation organizations to develop a different model of tourism. The goal is to serve a limited number of tourists and ensure that the profits flow equitably into the community. Unlike Santa Cruz where multiple tour operators tout their services every time you walk down the street, Floreana has only one: CECFLOR (Centro Comunitario Floreana) directs the flow of group tours to hostels and restaurants and is the only company authorized to operate day tours to the beautiful Post Office Bay, Mirador de la Baronesa, and La Botella. When large tour groups arrive, people are assigned to stay in community-run guest houses and eat in community-run restaurants on a rotation schedule. A percentage of the proceeds goes back to CECFLOR for its operating costs, to support the local school and other projects to benefit the community.

There are no naturalist guides living on Floreana, so the national park has authorized CECFLOR to send tourists to protected areas with locals instead. These local guides have other jobs outside of tourism; these tours are a source of extra income. Their English may be limited and they don't have the training that naturalist guides go through, but they know the sites well and can point out animal species to you.

As an outsider, it may seem unfair that you aren't allowed to walk on your own to Post Office Bay and Mirador de la Baronesa, but Floreana residents can go alone. Keep in mind, however, that many residents of Floreana are older; they lived on the island before the national park came into existence in 1959. For years the national park only allowed visits with a naturalist guide, but since no naturalist guides live on Floreana, it effectively prevented anyone from going unless they were on cruise ships. Under the new rules, residents can finally return to their favorite childhood haunts.

chicken, but the atmosphere is pleasant, with long wooden tables, plants, and hammocks.

The restaurant inside **Hotel Wittmer** (Playa Negra, tel. 5/253-5033, erikagarciawittmer@hotmail.com) is the nicest place in town, as well as the only restaurant with views of the beach and the only indoor restaurant where you can escape the bugs at night.

Accommodations

There are only 10 options for accommodations on the island, with capacity for about 100 guests, and none is as luxurious as you will find on the other three inhabited islands. They do all come with hot water, and there's Wi-Fi throughout the town.

HOSTELS AND HOTELS

Both Black Beach House and Hotel Wittmer have the unique aspect of living history; they are run by the descendants of the Wittmer family, some of the earliest inhabitants of the Galápagos, whose lives have been well documented in several books and a film. Hotel Wittmer and Floreana Lava Lodge cater primarily to large tour groups.

★ **Black Beach House** (Playa Negra, tel. 5/252-0648 or 98/475-5473, ingridgarciawittmer@hotmail.com, $30 pp) is a two-room house built out of brick with a fantastic location right on the beach and friendly personal service. The rooms are spacious, and there's a living room with views of the beach and hammocks outside. The fully equipped kitchen is a huge benefit since eating out on Floreana is more expensive and less convenient than on any other island. If you plan to cook, the safest bet is to purchase all your food from Santa Cruz.

The beachfront **Hotel Wittmer** (Playa

Negra, tel. 5/253-5033, erikagarciawittmer@hotmail.com, $30 pp) is a *hostal* with a sense of history; the sitting room has a small exhibit on the history of Floreana and the Wittmer family. The second-floor rooms have some of the best views on the islands. The guest rooms and bungalows are simple but comfortable, with hot water and ceiling fans; some have mini-fridges as well. There are no room keys, but there is a safe-deposit box for valuables. The *hostal* is primarily occupied by organized tour groups.

The most expensive place in town is the **Floreana Lava Lodge** (road to La Lobería, tel. 5/253-5022, malourdes.soria@hotmail.com, $138 s, $153 d or t, breakfast included), a collection of 10 oceanfront pine cabins in a private area tucked away from town and overlooking the ocean. It is one of the few places in town with air-conditioning. Rooms, though compact, are fully equipped with reading lamps, hair dryers, and safe-deposit boxes; the triples have bunk beds. The lodge is mainly occupied by organized tour groups. The kayaks and stand-up paddleboards at the lodge are only for guests on all-inclusive packages.

COMMUNITY TOURISM GUESTHOUSES

In addition to the regular *hostales*, Floreana also has seven mom-and-pop guesthouses that are affiliated with the community tourism project. These houses currently offer the same price of $35 per person, though there is a surprising variation in quality and amenities. The following list is ordered roughly in order of quality, best options first. Unless noted, these guesthouses do not include breakfast or air-conditioning. Note that there are plans to continue investing in renovating the guesthouses; prices may potentially increase.

None of these guesthouses use online booking platforms; make your reservation through the direct emails provided below or through CECFLOR with a special request for the guesthouse of your choice.

Casa Santa Maria (Ignacio Hernández, tel. 5/253-5022, malourdes.soria@hotmail.com, $35 pp), run by the seasoned owners of the Floreana Lava Lodge, boasts six relatively modern rooms with mini-fridge, safe-deposit box, and hot water; it's a block inland. Ask for a room on the third floor.

Casa de Emperatriz (12 de Febrero, tel. 5/253-5014, orquideasalgado@hotmail.com, $35 pp) has three rather dingy rooms a couple blocks inland by the main road, but it is the only budget option on the island with air-conditioning. Some rooms also have mini-fridges.

Casa de Lelia (Ignacio Hernández and Oswaldo Rosero, tel. 5/253-5041, leliaflorimarc8@gmail.com, $35 pp), a block inland, has pleasant rooms with remodeled bathrooms, hammocks, and hot water; some rooms have mini-fridges.

Los Cactus (Oswaldo and La Baronesa, tel. 5/253-5011, loscactus.gps@gmail.com, $35 pp), is slightly inland near the dock. There are four basic, modern-style guest rooms; the two on the second floor have limited views of the bay. There is a kitchen that guests are sometimes allowed to use, but it's best to ask.

Casa El Pajas (Wittmer at Zavala, tel. 5/253-5002, hospedaje.elpajas@gmail.com, $35 pp) has an attractive tiki-style log cabin vibe but is located farther inland than the other options. There is also a breezy second-floor sitting area and a couple hammocks.

Cabañas Leocarpus (12 de Febrero, tel. 5/253-5054, veritoemi2006@gmail.com, $35 pp) on the main street has a similar rustic vibe. The guest rooms on the second floor have a distant view to the sea. Each has one double bed and one single bed.

Casa de Huéspedes Hildita (12 de Febrero and Juan Salgado, tel. 5/253-5079, $35 pp) has five guest rooms built around an empty gravel courtyard. Be aware, however, that while water is a precious resource on the entire island, this *hostal* has the strictest water usage policy.

Information and Services

There are few services on Floreana. Bring all the cash you need because there's no ATM or bank. Bring clean clothes because there's no launderette.

There are no supermarkets to buy food or snacks, and the one **minimarket** is frequently closed. If you are desperate for a snack, there is a small *panadería* (bakery) by the power station at the east edge of town that sells loaves of bread, rolls, and soft drinks. If you stay the night, it is highly recommended to bring snacks from Puerto Ayora. You can bring food including fruit and vegetables as long as it does not contain seeds (apples, bananas, pineapples, and pears are permitted; passion fruit is not).

You can drink the tap water if you boil it first, though many *hostales* have large dispensers of drinking water.

The **CECFLOR** office is by the main dock and is the only source of tourist information on the island. Like most businesses in Floreana, it is open from morning to late afternoon, though hours are sporadic.

There is no hospital, but there is a small **medical clinic** along the main road for minor cuts and bruises.

There are no Internet cafés or phone cabins for making international calls. If you need to use the Internet, there is a free public Wi-Fi network that reaches most of the town.

Getting There and Around
INTERISLAND FERRIES

There is no airport on Floreana, so the only way to get there is either on a cruise or a speedboat from Puerto Ayora on Santa Cruz.

Ferries don't leave every day, so ask for the ferry schedule before making your plans and booking accommodation. Ferries ($30) depart Puerto Ayora at 8am and arrive around 10am. The return trip leaves Floreana at approximately 2:30pm and arrives in Santa Cruz at 4:30pm.

Organized island-hopping tour groups occasionally charter speedboats directly between Floreana and Isabela or San Cristóbal, but there are no public ferries. If you run into such a group, you can try your luck finding the captain or guide and buying your way on

board, but don't plan on it; most like to keep their exclusive group tours exclusive.

AROUND PUERTO VELASCO IBARRA

There aren't any **taxis** in Puerto Velasco Ibarra as in the other ports, because the town is so small.

The local *chiva* ($1), a rustic open-air bus, is the only form of public transportation, and it leaves just two times a day at 6am and 3pm. It leaves port from the main road (12 de Febrero) and goes to the highlands, stopping at local farms to drop off locals and stopping at Asilo de la Paz if there are tourists. It picks people up and returns to port after an hour and a half.

FLOREANA HIGHLANDS

Away from the dry port of Velasco Ibarra, Floreana is beautifully lush and green in the highlands.

Asilo de la Paz

Head inland from port 8 kilometers (5 mi) into the boundaries of the national park and you will reach the visitor site Asilo de la Paz, a lush green area in the hills where you can explore a tortoise reserve, a freshwater spring, and even pirate caves, all in close proximity along a well-marked path. First is the **tortoise reserve,** where you can walk right among the animals on a dirt path. Unlike the tortoise reserves on the other islands, this one has no breeding center. The tortoises here used to be the pets of the islanders before the national park prohibited it and moved the animals to this reserve. Next, follow the path past the tortoise reserve and you will find a tiny **freshwater spring** through the fence, where water trickles over rocks into a reservoir. It is not much to look at, but it is a fascinating indicator of the history of Floreana, since this tiny spring used to supply the entire island. Around the corner is a stone carving of a face, reminiscent of moai on Easter Island, but don't get too excited about ancient civilizations as this was done by the Wittmer family kids. Last are the **pirate caves**. These small shelters were carved out of the hill by pirates centuries ago and were later used as the temporary home of the island's earliest inhabitants (the Wittmers) when they first arrived on the island. There aren't any remnants of the early inhabitants, but it's fun to crawl inside a cave and let your imagination run wild.

This site is often included on day tours, though visiting it independently is also possible if you can wake up in time for the 6am *chiva* to the highlands ($1, 45 minutes). The *chiva* returns to port after an hour and a half, so it is possible to catch it after your visit to get back, but it will be a rushed visit. For a more leisurely visit, take the *chiva* to Asilo de la Paz and then walk back afterward, downhill 8 kilometers (5 mi), stopping to take in Cerro Alieri on your way back. There is another *chiva* at 3pm, but it's not recommended because if you miss the *chiva*, you may be walking back as it is getting dark. It is possible to walk there and back (16 km/10 mi round-trip) if you start early. Keep in mind, though, that getting there is significantly harder because it is uphill. The path is hilly and the weather is unpredictable, so bring a jacket and good walking shoes.

Cerro Alieri

Cerro Alieri is a hill about halfway between town and Asilo de la Paz. The trailhead is well marked on the left-hand side on the main road to Asilo de la Paz. Visitors ascend a steep path and staircase for about 20 minutes and are rewarded with fantastic views of both sides of the island, from Puerto Velasco Ibarra and Post Office Bay to the green hills of the highlands. Darwin's finches can also be spotted along the trail. The walk from town to the trailhead isn't terribly interesting, but it only takes an hour each way (head inland away from port along the main road). It is also possible to eliminate the walk by taking the 6am or 3pm *chiva* ($1); ask to be dropped off at the trailhead and then picked up on the *chiva*'s way back down. A third option for visiting is to take the *chiva* to Asilo de la Paz, walk down

to Cerro Alieri (1.5 hours), and then return to town walking (one hour).

THE COAST AND SURROUNDING ISLETS

The coast and surrounding islets of Floreana have some of the best snorkeling sites. Only **La Botella, Post Office Bay, and Mirador de la Baronesa** are accessible by **day tour** from Puerto Velasco Ibarra. The rest are currently only accessible by cruise.

Diving at Punta Cormorant, Enderby, and Champion Island is possible via a day trip from Puerto Ayora on Santa Cruz Island, but ironically cannot be done as a day trip from Puerto Velasco Ibarra since there are no dive agencies there.

La Botella

Beyond La Lobería is a protected bay with great snorkeling with marine turtles, fish, and the occasional rays. Farther from town and with calmer waters, it has considerably more to see than La Lobería. The beach is a sea turtle nesting ground. Despite its proximity to port, this site is not reachable on foot as there is no trail, and the only way to arrive is by kayak tour.

Post Office Bay

Post Office Bay is one of the quirkiest sites in the Galápagos. You wouldn't imagine that a mailbox would be of much appeal, but it has an interesting history and is also a bit of lighthearted fun. Back in 1793, whalers began the practice of leaving mail in a barrel for homeward-bound ships to collect. Crews would then hand-deliver the letters to their destination in a remarkable act of camaraderie. These days the tradition has been carried on, mainly by tourists. Leave a postcard for a fellow national to collect, and take one home with you. Tradition dictates that you should deliver it in person, but paying the postage is probably preferable these days to turning

1: giant tortoise; **2:** a ground finch; **3:** the famous mailbox at Post Office Bay

up on a stranger's doorstep. The barrel has evolved into a wooden box on a pole surrounded by an assortment of junk.

A visit to the bay begins with a wet landing directly onto the brown-sand beach. Just a few meters beyond the barrel is a lava tunnel, and you often need to wade through water to reach it. There are also the rusted remains of a Norwegian fish operation dating back to the 1920s, as well as a football field used by crews who may invite you to a game. Be aware that there are sizable populations of introduced wasps, and their sting is painful, so take care. A more scenic end to the visit is a *panga* (dinghy) ride past a sea lion colony, where you can also spot sea turtles and occasionally penguins.

Mirador de la Baronesa

Mirador de la Baronesa (Baroness's Lookout) was where the baroness of Floreana Island would often sit and watch for passing ships. Nowadays, cruise ships often stop at this idyllic mangrove-lined lagoon for snorkeling, kayaking, or a *panga* ride to spot the blue-footed boobies, sea lions, and occasionally penguins sitting on the rocky shores, which are covered in black lava and endemic cacti.

Punta Cormorant

Visiting this site on the north side of Floreana starts with a wet landing onto a beach colored green by olivine minerals, which are silicates of magnesium and iron. A 720-meter (2,362-ft) trail leads up to a saltwater lagoon. Along the trail, Floreana's comparatively lush surroundings can be appreciated. The lagoon is a good spot to see flamingos and other wading birds, such as white-cheeked pintails, stilts, and gallinules. The lagoon is surrounded by gray, seemingly lifeless palo santo trees. Among the vegetation is abundant birdlife, including yellow warblers and flycatchers. Beyond is a beautiful beach, nicknamed

"Flour Beach" for its incredibly fine white sand. Stingrays and spotted eagle rays are common near the beach, and sea turtles nest here November-February. There are signs to keep out of their nesting areas, but you may be lucky enough to see the turtles swimming. Note that snorkeling and swimming are not allowed. The only drawback of this site is its perplexing name—there are no flightless cormorants here.

Diving at Punta Cormorant is possible via a day trip from Puerto Ayora on Santa Cruz Island. Day tours cost up to $200 per person for two dives per day.

★ Devil's Crown

Offshore from Post Office Bay, the jagged peaks of this submerged volcanic cone poke out of the water and supply its name, Corona del Diablo (Devil's Crown). The nooks and crannies of this marine site offer some of the best snorkeling, either outside the ring or in the shallow inner chamber, which is reached through a side opening. There is a rich variety of tropical fish—parrot fish, angelfish, and damselfish—and you can occasionally see sea lions and sharks. Note that the current can be strong on the seaward side, so pay close attention to your guide. It is currently accessible only by cruise.

Enderby and Champion Island

These two sites are popular with snorkelers and divers. Enderby is an eroded tuff cone where you can snorkel with playful sea lions, and Champion Island is a small offshore crater, a popular nesting site for boobies. Landing is not allowed, but the snorkeling and diving are great, with the chance to see many species of sharks, fish, and sea turtles. Snorkeling at these sites is currently only possible from cruise ships. Diving at these sites is available via a day trip from Puerto Ayora on Santa Cruz Island. Day tours cost up to $200 per person for two dives.

Remote Uninhabited Islands

The uninhabited islands are the most pristine, least visited, and most fascinating places in the Galápagos. With the exception of Española, Bartolomé, and Sullivan Bay, the only way to arrive is by cruise.

SANTIAGO

Stepping onto the Galápagos's fourth-largest island, **Santiago,** is like stepping back to the beginning of time. Blackened lava dominates the landscape, and small plants and cacti are the first signs of life sprouting from the ashes.

One of the most popular sites on the island is **Sullivan Bay** on the east side. An eruption in 1897 left the area covered in mesmerizing patterns of black lava, known as pahoehoe (a Hawaiian word for rope) because of its tendency to buckle when it cools. The lava's glassy, almost ceramic feel comes from its high silicate content. The walk over the 1.5-kilometer (0.9-mi) loop takes about 1.5 hours and is uneven—it's a natural trail—so bring good walking shoes.

A freshwater source made **Buccaneer Cove** a haven for pirates in the 17th and 18th centuries. A few years back, divers found evidence in the form of ceramic jars on the seabed, still intact and filled with wine and marmalade. There is no landing spot, but cruises either take *panga* boats or allow passengers to kayak along the coast to appreciate the steep cliffs and dark-red volcanic sand beach.

On the west side of Santiago, a popular visitor site is **Puerto Egas,** named after the owner of a salt mine that operated on the island in the 1960s. There is a wet landing onto the long black-lava shoreline, home to a small colony of sea lions and large populations of marine iguanas.

A 2-kilometer (1.2-mi), three-hour loop trail leads inland past the rusted remains of the salt mine and a rather makeshift soccer field built by cruise crews. Look to the

skies and you may be lucky enough to see Galápagos hawks, circling in search of prey in the form of Galápagos doves and mockingbirds. Farther down the trail are the famous fur-seal grottoes, where the ocean fills a series of pools and underwater caverns occupied by seals, sea lions, and bright-red Sally Lightfoot crabs. There are great snorkeling opportunities here.

At the north end of James Bay, five kilometers from Puerto Egas, is **Espumilla Beach,** another good spot for snorkeling and swimming. Visitors make a wet landing onto a beach where sea turtles can sometimes be spotted; they come ashore at night to lay their eggs. A short trail (2 km/1.2 mi round-trip) leads inland through the mangroves to a lagoon populated by Galápagos flamingos, herons, and other wading birds.

★ BARTOLOMÉ ISLAND

This tiny island off the southeast coast of Santiago is one of the most photographed sights in the archipelago. A wooden staircase leads 114 meters (374 ft) up to a summit with a breathtaking view—and for once, this is no exaggeration. In the foreground the mangroves are flanked on either side by twin half-moon beaches. Rising up behind is the famous 40-meter-high (131-ft) **Pinnacle Rock,** a jagged volcanic formation that has endured years of erosion as well as the U.S. Air Force using it for target practice during World War II. The blackened lava fields of Santiago in the background complete a perfect photograph.

A dry landing is followed by a 30-minute round-trip hike to take in the view. It's a steep but short climb. Afterward, you take a short boat ride to the two beaches, where there is excellent snorkeling with a small colony of sea lions as well as the occasional chance to see Galápagos penguins. Out of the water, a trail winds through the mangroves to the beach on the other side (500 m/1,640 ft each way). Swimming is not allowed on this side, but look closely and you may glimpse stingrays, white-tipped sharks, and sea turtles that come ashore at night to lay their eggs. In the mangroves, bird-watchers should keep their eyes open for Galápagos hawks, herons, and oystercatchers.

Bartolomé is included on many cruise itineraries, but as a day trip it has become more expensive and will set you back $180 per person with tour operators in Puerto Ayora. Some day trips combine Bartolomé with Sullivan Bay, whereas others visit Bachas Beach (on the north side of Santa Cruz) instead. It is also possible to dive here on a day tour from Puerto Ayora ($200).

RÁBIDA ISLAND

About 5 kilometers (3 mi) south of Santiago, this small island, also known as Jervis, is the exact geographic center of the Galápagos archipelago. There's a wet landing onto a rust-colored beach filled with dozens of sea lions stretched out; this is a great spot to walk among a colony and listen to their snorts and snoring. It's also an excellent place for snorkeling, but note that the male sea lion population is quite large (it's mainly a bachelor colony), so take care. The beach is also one of the best places to see brown pelicans nesting. Chicks have a high mortality rate, so don't be surprised to stumble across numerous corpses. Still, there are plenty of live ones filling the skies and crying to their parents, who are busy dive-bombing the ocean in search of the family lunch.

Aside from the beach, there is a 1.1-kilometer (0.7-mi) loop trail through the palo santo forest and along a brackish lagoon. On the trail, look for Galápagos hawks perched watchfully on tree branches as well as Galápagos flamingos and yellow-crowned night herons stabbing at fish and shrimp in the salt ponds.

SOMBRERO CHINO

This tiny island off the southeast tip of Santiago, just south of Bartolomé, is a volcanic cone with the rough shape of a "Chinese hat" (hence the name). Most cruise tours simply pass it to admire the shape, because landing access is restricted to boats carrying 12 people or fewer. Sombrero Chino has a small sea lion colony, marine iguanas, excellent snorkeling, and a short 700-meter (2,297-ft) trail across the island that takes half an hour and commands impressive views.

FERNANDINA

At under one million years old, **Fernandina** is the youngest volcanic island in the archipelago and also the most active. It's where flightless cormorants stretch out their vestigial wings between trips into the water, and enormous marine iguanas fight over territory on the rocks.

Fernandina has just one visitor site, **Punta Espinosa,** on the island's northeast corner across from Isabela's Tagus Cove, but it's arguably one of the best sites in the archipelago. A dry landing among the mangroves leads 250 meters (820 ft) to a sandy point partly covered by lava from recent flows, both the rippled glass-like surface of pahoehoe lava and the rough, rocky lava. Nearby is the dramatic sight of the largest colony of marine iguanas in the archipelago sunning themselves on the rocks. The high population is due to the abundance of food from the cold currents in this side of the archipelago. In the afternoon you may be able to see the largest males head-butting as they fight over territory.

Next you pass a large sea lion colony with the sound of barking bulls filling the air. This is also one of the biggest nesting sites of flightless cormorants. Watch out for males returning from fishing to bring lunch to their mate, who sits in a tangled nest of seaweed and twigs near the water's edge.

After retracing your steps, you can take a longer 750-meter (2,460-ft) trail leading over jagged lava spotted with lava cacti (bring good shoes). Brilliant vermilion flycatchers often sit in the mangrove branches. At low tide a pool offers excellent bird-watching. The tour usually ends with a *panga* ride out into the strait, where schools of dolphins are often seen. There is excellent snorkeling at several locations around Punta Espinosa, offering chances to see penguins, marine iguanas, flightless cormorants, and sea turtles.

ESPAÑOLA

The southernmost island in the Galápagos is also the oldest in the archipelago, at nearly 3.5 million years, compared with Fernandina in the northwest, which is less than one million years old. It's the only place in the world to view the waved albatross. Whether you see the enormous creatures nuzzling beaks in their mating ritual or landing at the "albatross airport," it is sure to be a highlight of your trip. The waved albatross that nest here April-November are the island's main draw. Witness these enormous birds taking off and landing, and enjoy their amusing mating dance. Española is accessible via cruise or as a pricey day tour ($200) from Puerto Baquerizo Moreno on San Cristóbal.

On the northeast side of Española, the beautiful crescent beach at **Gardner Bay** is reached by a wet landing. There are no hikes, so the main draw is the excellent snorkeling. Highlights include frolicking with playful sea lions (there's a colony here) as well as spotting stingrays or occasional white-tipped sharks. The beach is an important nesting site for marine turtles, so you might be lucky enough to see them. **Turtle Rock,** a short *panga* ride offshore, is another good snorkeling spot with a rich variety of bright tropical fish, such as moorish idols, damselfish, and parrot fish.

On the beach, you can walk among the sea lion colony, but try to give the males a wide berth. At the east end, there are marine iguanas and Sally Lightfoot crabs, and you can often see the endemic hood mockingbirds.

★ Punta Suárez

On the western tip of Española, **Punta Suárez** is one of the top visitor sites in the Galápagos. A dry landing leads to a trail toward the cliffs on the south side of the point. Unique to Española is a subspecies of **marine iguanas,** nicknamed "Christmas iguanas" that are splotched with bright red and green colors around the end of the year. Along the way there are cliffs where Nazca boobies or blue-footed boobies nest, depending on the time of year. Watch your step, as these tame birds remain utterly unconcerned by your presence and sit in the middle of the trail.

The best is yet to come. If you visit between April and November, farther along the trail is the biggest breeding site of **waved albatross** in the world; this site is even nicknamed the "albatross airport." Some 15,000 couples congregate on the island, and it's quite a sight to witness these massive birds with their 2.5-meter (8.2-ft) wingspans taking off from the cliffs. Seeing them land is also impressive but rather less elegant, as they often fall over, being unsteady on their feet after long flights. The highlight is their entertaining courtship, as the couple dance around each other in a synchronized circular walk, clacking and calling skyward. In November, there are fewer adults, but the babies can be seen waddling about with fluffy gray feathers.

This site is teeming with birdlife, and aside from the boobies and albatross, you can see Galápagos hawks, Galápagos doves, swallow-tailed gulls, oystercatchers, red-billed tropic birds, and finches. The views of the cliffs below are equally impressive, with waves crashing into rocks and water spurting high into the air through blowholes. The rocks are often covered in marine iguanas sunning themselves; these iguanas are more colorful than those found on other islands, with turquoise tinges to their backs and legs, perhaps the result of eating algae endemic to Española.

The entire trail is about 3 kilometers (1.9 mi) round-trip and takes about two hours.

GENOVESA

Genovesa is home to the largest colony of red-footed boobies in the world. They inhabit a beach and cliffs surrounding an enormous submerged crater, along with a slew of other native birds. Genovesa, also known as Tower Island or even **Booby Island**, is famed for its

abundant birdlife, notably the world's largest colony of red-footed boobies, but it takes some getting to—about eight hours by boat overnight, so stock up on seasickness tablets. The bay is actually a large submerged volcanic crater. Interestingly, there are no land reptiles on Genovesa, only a small population of marine iguanas.

After a tricky entrance into **Darwin Bay,** where you pass rocks decorated with graffiti from visiting ships, there is a wet landing onto the beach. A short trail (approximately 1.5 km/0.9 mi round-trip) leads inland to the mangroves filled with the nests of red-footed boobies and frigate birds. Masked boobies and swallow-tailed gulls also nest here, and you may spot storm petrels and short-eared owls. The end of the trail leads over rough rocks next to a series of tidal pools, where you can see yellow-crowned night herons half-asleep by day. At high tide, you may be wading through this part of the trail. Other species to watch for include mockingbirds, Galápagos doves, and Darwin's finches. The opuntia cacti you see on the trail are noticeably softer than on other islands. Scientists believe this is because the plants don't need to defend themselves against giant tortoises (there has never been a tortoise population on the island). Visitors can also snorkel off the beach or along the rocky coastline and spot a wide variety of tropical fish and the occasional shark.

Named in honor of a royal visit in the 1960s, **Prince Philip's Steps** are near the tip of Darwin Bay's eastern arm. A *panga* ride along the bottom of the cliffs provides glimpses of red-billed tropic birds landing in their crevice nests and a large population of frigate birds. If you're lucky, you may glimpse elusive fur seals. Ashore, a steep-railed stairway leads to a dramatic trail along the top of the cliffs (1.5 km/0.9 mi round-trip). Masked and red-footed boobies nest here with frigate birds lurking nearby, ready to scavenge. It's also a good area to see Galápagos doves and sharp-beaked ground finches, also known as "vampire finches" because they peck away at boobies' tails. Storm petrels are also seen in large numbers, and occasionally you may spot the Galápagos owl. The *panga* ride and hike combined take about two hours.

WOLF AND DARWIN ISLANDS

These tiny islands, about 215 kilometers (134 mi) northwest of the main island group, are hidden jewels visited only by diving tours. It takes a full night to get here, but the rewards are rich indeed—these islands rank among the best dives in the world. You might even recognize **Darwin's Arch**—a striking stone formation just east of Darwin Island—from magazine articles. The waters around Wolf and Darwin attract whale sharks June-November. Other shark species commonly seen are hammerheads, Galápagos sharks, and reef sharks. Manta rays, dolphins, and turtles abound.

MARCHENA AND PINTA ISLANDS

Midway between Wolf and Genovesa in the far north of the archipelago, these two medium-size islands are closed to visitors, although diving is possible in the waters off the coast of Marchena. It has a 343-meter-high (1,125-ft) volcano at its center that last erupted in 1991. Pinta is famous as the original home of the tortoise known as Lonesome George; and giant tortoises are currently being repopulated there.

1: a waved albatross on Española; **2:** Bartolomé Island

Background

The Landscape

The old adage "small is beautiful" applies to Ecuador. Few places in the world have such a rich variety of breathtaking landscapes packed into such a diminutive space; in fact, it's the most biodiverse country in the world per unit area. The fourth-smallest country in South America (only Uruguay, the Guyanas, and Suriname are smaller) extends over 283,561 square kilometers (109,484 sq mi) on the northwestern shoulder of the continent, with Colombia to the north, Peru to the east and south, and the Pacific Ocean to the west. The Galápagos Islands are over 1,000 kilometers (620 mi) west of the mainland. Named for the

equator that bisects it, Ecuador is roughly the size of Colorado and slightly bigger than the UK.

From the tourist's point of view, its small size is a huge asset. You can get from one end of Ecuador to the other in a day. And what a day it is—moving from Pacific beaches up through misty cloud forests and windswept *páramo* moorlands, past snowy volcanic peaks and down again to the Amazon rainforest. With coast, Sierra, Amazon, and Galápagos, it is no exaggeration to call Ecuador "four worlds in one."

GEOGRAPHY
The Coast

The coastal lowlands stretch from the cloud-forested foothills of the Andes west to the Pacific. The entire 2,237-kilometer (1,390-mi) coastline is lined with sandy beaches, most of which are exposed to strong Pacific currents—heaven for surfers but less ideal for swimmers. Only pockets remain of the mangroves that were once present along much of the coast. Running parallel to the beaches from Esmeraldas to Guayas are the low mountain ranges of Mache-Chindul and Chongón-Colonche, which protect much of the region's remaining tropical forests, including tropical dry forest, cloud forest, and tropical wet forest. Over 95 percent of these have been destroyed, and much of the lowland is now agricultural plantations, especially banana. The northern coast is wetter and greener than the south.

Two main rivers carve through the lowlands. To the north, Río Esmeraldas flows 320 kilometers (199 mi) to the Pacific. Farther south, the Río Babahoyo and Río Daule merge into Río Guayas, which flows for 60 kilometers (37 mi) into the Gulf of Guayaquil. In the gulf, Isla de Puná is the largest island in Ecuador outside the Galápagos. There are other, smaller islands along the coast, the best known being Isla de la Plata in Manabí.

Around half of the country's population lives on the coast. Guayaquil, with a population of 3 million and rising, is by far the country's biggest city. Portoviejo, Manta, Machala, and Santo Domingo all have populations of over 200,000.

The Sierra

The Andes run through the country like a spine. Though these mountains and their foothills fill only about one-quarter of Ecuador's land area, they certainly pack a punch, with 10 peaks over 5,000 meters (16,400 ft) and another dozen over 4,000 meters (13,000 ft). In the southern Sierra, the cordillera is older and less volcanically active, without the soaring mountains that are found in the north. Two parallel mountain ranges run north-south—the Cordillera Occidental (Western Range) and the wider and higher Cordillera Oriental (Eastern Range). Between them is one of the most spectacular drives on the continent: the aptly named Avenue of the Volcanoes, which runs along the Panamericana south of Quito.

The 10 main intermountain basins, called *hoyas*, are where about half of Ecuador's population lives. All the main cities in the Sierra—from north to south, Tulcán, Ibarra, Otavalo, Quito, Latacunga, Ambato, Riobamba, Cuenca, and Loja—sit at 2,000-3,000 meters (6,500-10,000 ft) above sea level. Above the tree line but below the snow line, at 3,000-5,000 meters (9,800-16,500 ft) above sea level, are the windswept Andean grasslands, or *páramos*, surrounding the icy peaks. Due to high moisture retention in the soil, the *páramos* are the birthplace of several of Ecuador's rivers and a key source of water for much of the country, including major cities such as Quito and Cuenca.

The Oriente

With only 5 percent of the population, Ecuador's slice of Amazon rainforest makes up half the country's land area. East of the

Andes, the land slopes down through cloud forest to rainforest that becomes increasingly pristine near the Colombian and Peruvian borders. The Amazon has been affected by oil exploration, especially in the north, where the damage has been devastating, and large areas continue to be opened up for drilling.

There are a few towns and cities, but only Lago Agrio has more than 50,000 people. In descending order come Puyo, Coca, Tena, and Macas. East of these towns, the rivers are the main mode of transportation. In the north, Río Coca and Río Aguarico feed into Río Napo, Ecuador's longest river at 855 kilometers (530 mi). The Río Pastaza drains Pastaza Province and lies just north of the Río Zamora, which becomes the Río Santiago in Peru.

GEOLOGY

It comes as no surprise that a country with an Avenue of Volcanoes has a violent geological heritage. The country sits right on the Pacific Rim of Fire, where two tectonic plates—the Nazca Plate and the American Plate—grind together.

About 65 of Ecuador's peaks began as **volcanoes,** and at least six have been recently active. **Cotopaxi,** one of the world's highest active volcanoes, rumbled into life in April 2015 by emitting a 10-kilometer (6.2-mi) ash plume, culminating in an eruption in August 2015. Tremors were felt in the surrounding towns, and gas and steam were released over the following weeks, along with thousands of tons of ash that covered the surrounding countryside, even reaching Quito.

By far the show-stealer in the past decade has been **Tungurahua** ("throat of fire" in Kichwa), which awoke from an 80-year sleep in 1999, forcing an evacuation of nearby tourist town Baños. Since then, the volcano has remained in an eruptive phase. The 2006 eruptions caused pyroclastic flows on the volcano's western slopes (fortunately Baños lies to the south), and ashfall reached Guayaquil, nearly 300 kilometers (185 mi) away. Further eruptions occurred in 2010,

2012, 2013, and 2014, when an ash plume reached 10 kilometers (6.2 mi) into the sky. Other recent eruptions include **Reventador,** the aptly named "Exploder," which lived up to its name in 2002, and **Guagua Pichincha,** which showered Quito in ash in 1999. **Sangay** is one of the most active volcanoes on earth, with a constant pool of lava bubbling in its crater.

More destructive than volcanoes in recent decades have been **earthquakes.** On April 16, 2016, an earthquake of 7.8 magnitude struck the province of Manabí. It was the country's largest recorded earthquake since 1979, and tremors were felt as far as Colombia and Peru. At least 676 people were killed and 16,600 were injured. In 1998 a quake of magnitude 7.1 devastated the coastal city of Bahía de Caráquez. In 1987 an earthquake in the northern Oriente killed hundreds of people and caused $1 billion in damage, including the destruction of 40 kilometers (25 mi) of oil pipeline.

On a smaller scale but also deadly are **landslides,** usually triggered by heavy rain. Avalanches of melted ice, snow, mud, and rocks can reach 80 kilometers per hour (50 mph) when careening downhill, and there are landslides every year in the Andes and the foothills. Five people were killed in the Pastaza Valley outside Baños in 2010, and 39 people were killed in a landslide near Papallacta in 2001.

CLIMATE

Ecuador's climate is so varied that it is impossible to make sweeping generalizations. Often the weather varies more with altitude than geography; sometimes you can be sweltering in one place and then freezing less than an hour's drive away. Even without moving an inch, some of the Sierran cities are well known for showing visitors "four seasons in one day." The good news is that there is no bad time to visit Ecuador. If you're coming from colder climes, never underestimate the strength of the equatorial sun; always wear sunscreen, even on a cloudy day.

The Coast

On the coast, the climate is clearly defined by two contrasting ocean currents. December-April, the Equatorial Counter Current from the north brings heat, humidity, and heavy rain. Daytime temperatures average 30-33°C (86-91°F) and the sun can be brutal. It cools down a little at night, but a fan or air-conditioning is a must. Rains can be torrential, especially overnight, and flooding is common. Despite the occasional downpours, the sun and consistent surf bring the crowds, and this is the high season on the coast. The northern coast (from Puerto López up) experiences a second high season from June to September.

After May, the Humboldt Current comes up from the south, bringing cooler weather, gray skies, and drizzle, with daytime temperatures averaging 20-25°C (68-77°F). A light sweater is often required and nights do not require a fan or air-conditioning. The ocean is colder and the waves are choppier, although surf can still be decent. May-July there are still frequent sunny days, but August-November is usually dreary. During this peak low season, sun is more frequently found to the south of Salinas and north of Manta.

Every few years, the rainy season is made far worse by the famous El Niño climate pattern, which brings abnormal quantities of rain. Flooding wreaks massive damage along the coast, and many roads become impassable.

The Sierra

The Andes climate is often described as ideally "springlike," but this is an oversimplification. You will probably need several blankets overnight and wake up to a chill in the air, but it can heat up quickly by midday. Daytime temperatures average 15-20°C (59-68°F), occasionally peaking at 25°C (77°F), with nights falling to 7-8°C (45-46°F) but sometimes dropping to 0°C (32°F).

The driest, warmest season is June-September. October and November are cooler, with showers common in the mornings. December-May is the rainy season.

Whatever the time of year, the weather can change quickly, so wear layers and always have a sweater and sun cream with you.

The Oriente

In the Amazon, it's not a question of whether it will rain, but rather how much. The wettest period is April-May, when the rivers are more easily navigated and the seasonally flooded rainforest is underwater. August-October is drier and has fewer mosquitoes. Year-round, daily highs average 30°C (86°F), with night-time lows around 20°C (68°F). Rainstorms tend to be torrential and brief.

The Galápagos

The climate in the Galápagos more or less mirrors that of the coast, with the two ocean currents pulling the strings. December-May, seas are calmer and the weather mostly sunny and hot, with rain falling mainly in the highlands of the larger islands. February and March are the warmest months. June-November, the weather is cooler, and the sea becomes rougher and colder for swimming. The temperature peaks at over 30°C (86°F) in March and cools to the low 20s C (low 70s F) in August.

ENVIRONMENTAL ISSUES
Problems

Ecuador has a reputation for being an environmental pioneer, largely due to its 2008 constitution, which was the first in the world to grant legal rights to nature. Sadly, however, the opposite is true. According to Mongabay, Ecuador has the highest deforestation rate and worst environmental record in South America. The discrepancy can partly be explained by the recent Correa government's world-class marketing department and control of the media. For example, while Ecuador was lauded in the international press for its 2015 Guinness World Record-breaking effort to plant 647,250 trees of 200 species in a single day, it was largely unreported that 3 million hectares (7.4 million acres) of largely virgin rainforest were being simultaneously auctioned to oil companies. The sale of the Amazon is just one example of Correa's extractivist policies, which wrought large-scale destruction through oil exploitation and mega-mining, and are currently being ramped up by his successor, Lenín Moreno.

Ecuador is not a safe country for environmental defenders, who are criminalized, threatened, attacked, and even assassinated for attempting to uphold the rights of nature decreed in the constitution. While the overt incitement to hatred against environmental activists ended when Moreno replaced Correa as president and some imprisoned indigenous leaders were freed, the intimidation and threats continue. In 2018, there were several attacks against members of the Collective of Amazonian Women, which works to defend the Amazon from oil and mining. Two (including Patricia Gualinga from Sarayaku) had rocks thrown through their bedroom windows at night; Margoth Escobar had her house intentionally set on fire; and others received death threats. Also in 2018, three water defenders—including the president of Ecuarunari (a confederation of indigenous peoples), Yaku Pérez Guartambel—were kidnapped by mine workers believed to have been following orders from above. An angry mob kicked, dragged, and tortured Pérez Guartambel, accusing him of leading anti-mining efforts. They planned on crucifying him and started gathering materials, until a group of journalists broke through with cameras and rescued the water protectors.

Coast

The coast has suffered the worst deforestation of all the regions of Ecuador. Once, tropical dry forests extended along the coast from Colombia to Panama and, inland, the low mountain ranges of Mache-Chindul and Chongón-Colonche were covered with cloud forest and tropical wet forest. Tragically, over 95 percent of these have been destroyed to make way for agricultural mono-crop plantations, especially banana and cacao, which provide employment to the many and riches to the few. Of the mangroves that used to line much of the coastline from north to south, nearly all have been cleared for shrimp farms and tourism.

Real estate and tourist development is another enormous threat. One example is a multimillion-dollar complex that is being built on 7,000 hectares (17,300 acres) of land adjacent to the small fishing village of Engabao, near Guayaquil. As well as 3,000 condos and town houses, the complex will include tennis courts, swimming pools, retail units, and restaurants. Other multimillion-dollar residential developments have sprung up all along the coast, many of them condos for city dwellers that are uninhabited for most of the year. Other development is touristic, such as the all-inclusive resort on the previously unspoiled island of Portete near Mompiche. Not only does the construction of these huge projects cause massive environmental damage, but their ongoing operation pollutes the ecosystem and uses precious local resources such as water. Some formerly peaceful fishing villages have been converted into concrete jungles of high-rise hotels and apartments. In a country where money supersedes the law, the few building codes that exist to protect the environment can easily be bypassed. The influx of tourists also causes problems. When people descend en masse on a place that lacks the infrastructure or resources to handle it, it causes contamination (e.g., raw sewage being released into the ocean) and water shortages. Litter is another big issue.

Other coastal ecosystems are threatened by mega infrastructure projects. The government is in a partnership to build a $1 billion deep-water port in Posorja near Guayaquil to increase global trade. At the time of writing, construction was only in its first phase and already a lifeless wall of stones has replaced

1, 2: Pits of oil have been left in the Amazon near Lago Agrio. 3: water contamination caused by mining

the supposedly protected mangroves where dolphins feed daily. The new port will also end a community tourism project that depends on the presence of the dolphins. Dredging the channel will cause further destruction. Another forthcoming mega project is a new airport for Guayaquil, which in 2024 is set to replace the still immaculate José Joaquín de Olmedo airport, opened in 2006. With a budget of $80 million, the new airport will take up 2,020 hectares (5,000 acres) of land near the Cerro Blanco Protected Forest, which shelters a 6,000-hectare (14,800-acre) fragment of tropical dry forest in the Chongón-Colonche hills, 95 percent of which has already been destroyed. Cerro Blanco is home to the endangered great green macaw, of which only 50 remain in the wild, plus jaguars and howler monkeys.

Fishing causes the death of untold quantities of marinelife. All along the coast, especially in low season, turtles and even occasionally sea lions are washed up dead on the beach, victims of fishing nets, propellers, or hooks. Even within Machalilla National Park, where fishing is banned, it does still occur, with endangered species such as hammerhead sharks and giant manta rays being accidentally caught up in the nets.

Sierra

Mega-mining projects for gold and copper pose the biggest threat to ecosystems in the Sierra. There has been gold mining in Ecuador since the arrival of the Incas, but it remained fairly small scale and national until a series of laws opened the gates for transnational mega-mining projects. Following the oil price crash, Correa increasingly turned to minerals to pay for government spending, passing a controversial water rights law in 2014 that prioritized the use of water for mining over human consumption and agriculture and creating a mining ministry in 2015. The value of Ecuador's mining industry is forecast to jump from $1.1 billion in 2017 to $7.9 billion in 2021.

Two of Correa's five strategic mega-mining projects are located in the Andean province of Azuay: Kimsacocha and Rio Blanco in El Cajas National Park. The other three projects are in the Amazon region. By definition, throughout the cordillera, wherever there are water sources, there are minerals. The Kimsacocha and Rio Blanco mines are located in the *páramo*, a fragile and threatened moorland ecosystem that provides water for the city of Cuenca and thousands of indigenous campesinos, as well as habitat for endangered animals such as the spectacled bear and Andean tapir.

Mining causes contamination and desertification. Obtaining 10 grams (0.35 oz) of gold generates between 20 and 60 tons of waste and uses 7,000 liters (1,850 gallons) of water, which is normally contaminated with cyanide, arsenic, and other heavy metals. Despite 92 percent of local people voting against the Kimsacocha mine in a referendum attended by international observers, the ombudsman's office, and human rights organizations, the project is currently in its exploration phase and already water quality has been affected. Indigenous leaders who oppose the mine have been threatened and criminalized. In 2016, the government of Azuay unanimously resolved to prohibit metal mining in the province's *páramos*, and in 2017, the Council of the County of Cuenca declared its territory and water sources free of metal mining. A month later, one of the mining companies involved announced the sale of CAD$24 million in shares in order to continue exploring in the area. The company's own feasibility study for the project predicted that the mine will produce 5.5 million tons of toxic waste over 12 years, while generating only $9 million per year.

In a rare and historic environmental victory, in June 2018 a judge ordered the closure of the Rio Blanco mine, arguing that the project was undertaken without consulting indigenous communities as required by the constitution and international law. In August 2018, the verdict was upheld and the judge ordered the immediate suspension of mining activities. It was the first time that a court ordered the closing of an active gold mine with millions of dollars of foreign investment in Ecuador. The mine continued operations in defiance of the ruling, however, and indigenous people who protested at the site were met with brutality.

Mining in the Sierra is not limited to the government's strategic projects. The Intag region in the northern Sierra, located at the confluence of two of the world's biological hot spots, has also been concessioned to mining interests. The cloud forests here are home to threatened species, including Andean bears, jaguars, pumas, ocelots, Andean tapirs, and mantled howler monkeys, and 40 percent of the bird and plant species are found nowhere else on the planet. At the time of writing, a transnational mining company was finishing its exploration for copper. Depending on the results of its investigations, a mega-mining project is planned for 2020. The initial exploration phase has already been damaging, drilling forests with perforations that release chemicals into the water. If it goes ahead, the mine would destroy thousands of hectares of primary forest, force four communities to relocate, and contaminate rivers and streams with heavy metals. In fact, 95 percent of the Intag region has been concessioned, threatening all but one of the water sources. Most of the neighboring Los Cedros Biological Reserve, which protects nearly 7,000 hectares (17,300 acres) of tropical forest and cloud forest as well as four major watersheds, has also been concessioned to mining interests.

The small town of Zaruma, near the Peruvian border in the province of El Oro, has 17 stories of gold-mining tunnels underneath it, and processing plants have contaminated the local rivers. Some tunnels were closed after a school disappeared into a hole in 2016, but many operations continue. Mining has also been announced within the nearby 2,000-hectare (5,000-acre) Buenaventura Reserve, which protects one of the largest tracts of cloud forest in the region, where only 5-10 percent of the original forest remains.

Agriculture is another major threat to Sierran ecosystems. The rolling tapestries of hills dotted with cows might look picturesque, but they were once covered with forests. The biggest threat to the pristine *páramos* of the El Ángel Ecological Reserve in the northern Sierra is clearance for potato farming and cattle grazing.

Oriente

The biggest threat facing the Amazon region is oil exploitation, which has been devastating the rainforest and its communities ever since the discovery of petroleum reserves in the 1960s. While drilling for oil between 1964 and 1990, an oil company deliberately dumped more than 68 billion liters (18 billion gallons) of toxic wastewater, spilled roughly 64 million liters (17 million gallons) of crude oil, and left hazardous waste in hundreds of open pits in the forest floor. The result was, and continues to be, one of the worst environmental disasters in global history. Meanwhile, other parts of Ecuador's Amazon are being exploited or are under threat. Drilling is currently ramping up significantly in Yasuní National Park, a UNESCO World Biosphere Reserve that is home to the country's last two uncontacted tribes. The Ecuadorian government is also in the process of selling 3 million hectares (7.4 million acres) of largely virgin rainforest in the southern Amazon region to oil companies in an auction known as the XI Oil Round, or Ronda Sur. Sadly, there is no way to extract oil without inflicting serious damage: Areas are deforested to create air strips and roads; explosions are detonated during the exploration phase; waste products contaminate rivers and lakes (for each oil barrel extracted, 9 barrels of toxic waste are produced); and spills are inevitable.

Mega-mining is an enormous threat in the Amazon, too. Three of the Correa government's five flagship gold and copper megamining projects are being developed in the southern Amazon region, in the provinces of Zamora-Chinchipe and Morona-Santiago. The Fruta del Norte, Mirador, and Panantza-San Carlos mines are set to wreak irreversible destruction, requiring the construction of new roads, generating huge amounts of contaminated waste, and using vast quantities of water. At the end of the projects' 12- to 25-year life-spans, the opencast mines will be filled with water, creating further contamination problems, especially in an area with so much rainfall. With 41,000 hectares (101,000 acres) allocated to it, the Panantza-San Carlos project will be the world's second largest copper mine. The Mirador project, less than half the size of the Panantza-San Carlos project, is estimated to generate 26,000 tons of solid rock waste per day, all contaminated by heavy metals (a total of 180 million tons over its 18-year life-span), and will use and contaminate over 1 million liters (264,000 gallons) of water per day. All this in the Cordillera del Condor, one of the most biodiverse areas on the planet and the birthplace of the Amazon headwaters. For more information, see the documentary *Paradise Under Threat: The Mirador Mine in the Condor.*

The Ecuadorian army has facilitated the mining invasion by forcibly removing Shuar communities from their ancestral lands. After the community of Nankints was violently evicted in 2016, the area was militarized to quell protest, patrolled by soldiers and police in tanks, trucks, and helicopters. In the village of Tandayme, the school and church were demolished to make way for the Mirador project. Communities that are not evicted will no longer be able to fish or farm due to contamination and will be at a greatly increased risk of cancer. Jobs promised by the mining companies rarely materialize, and indigenous leaders who oppose the mining projects are threatened and criminalized. The body of one anti-mining activist, José Tendetza, was found floating in the Río Zamora just days before he was due to travel to the climate change summit in Peru to denounce the environmental damage caused in the Mirador project. Two other Shuar men have died in mining-related circumstances: schoolteacher Bosco Wizuma in 2009 and Freddy Taish in 2013.

There is hope, however. Following the historic victory in Rio Blanco, in 2018 the Kofán community of Sinangoe near Lago Agrio won a historic lawsuit against the government that nullifies over 50 gold-mining concessions along the Río Aguarico that threatened 30,000 hectares (74,000 acres) of their territory.

In 2010, Correa's government announced the construction of eight flagship hydroelectric power stations in the Amazon and Sierra. In 2018, three are functioning and the other five are still in construction. The new projects are already following the historical pattern of Ecuador's dams, leaving enormous environmental footprints without delivering the promised energy benefits. By diverting water to produce electricity, dams dry up rivers, destroy aquatic ecosystems, and displace local people. As with oil and mining projects, affected communities are rarely consulted, and almost every hydroelectric project being developed in Ecuador faces intense opposition from locals and environmentalists.

Located on the border of Napo and Succumbíos provinces, the Coca Codo Sinclair hydroelectric facility is the largest energy project in Ecuador's history, financed and built by a foreign loan. Completed in 2016, an audit of the project found 7,648 cracks in the structure and the dam running at only half capacity. The facility is located on a bend in the Coca River that is home to the country's highest waterfall, the San Rafael Falls, and forms a natural barrier with steep canyon walls that protects a vast rainforest wilderness area, designated by UNESCO as a Biosphere Reserve. Not only was a network of access roads built in previously untouched parts of the Sumaco Biosphere Reserve, but the dam has reduced the water flow at San Rafael. International Rivers reported in 2007 that a total of 226 hydroelectric projects had been proposed in Ecuador.

The roads built for oil, mining, and hydroelectric projects are a major trigger of deforestation. Beyond the immediate forest clearance for their construction, roads allow loggers to access vast tracts of previously untouched rainforest. The ancient cultures of formerly isolated communities are irreversibly altered by easy access to urban areas. Furthermore, roads allow incursion by national and foreign tourism companies with large amounts of money to invest. Plans are currently underway, for example, for companies from Baños to use roads built by oil companies to construct new tourist lodges in Pastaza province. This kind of development doesn't just cause environmental damage, but siphons income away from local grassroots tourism initiatives, which can't compete in terms of resources. This is a situation already seen in the Cuyabeno Wildlife Reserve, where all the jungle lodges are owned by companies from Quito. While local indigenous people are often employed by the lodges, they see only a fraction of the income generated in their ancestral territories. This is a tragedy considering that community-run ecotourism projects, where income goes directly to local people, are often the only chance they have to conserve their territories and cultures.

In an attempt to make South America more functional to the needs of global goods, production, and circulation, a transport corridor is planned, due to stretch from the port of Manta in Ecuador to Manaos in Brazil. Cargo such as hydrocarbons, minerals and metals, agricultural and fishing products, wood, and biofuels would be transported via road, hydro-way, port, and airport. If it goes ahead, the ecological cost of this corridor would be very high, as it would cut through the Limoncocha Biological Reserve, Cuyabeno Wildlife Reserve, and the national parks of Llanganates, Yasuní, and Sumaco Napo-Galeras. Perhaps the most damaging aspect for the environment and indigenous communities would be the dredging of the Río Napo, which borders the northern side of Yasuní National Park, to make it a navigable hydro-way.

Vast tracts of Ecuador's Amazon have been cleared by agricultural corporations to make way for mono-crop plantations of African palm and, more recently, malanga, a type of root vegetable. Areas of rainforest are also cleared for cattle grazing and small-scale agriculture. The problem is compounded by the poor quality of the shallow soil below the rainforest. After a year or two, the nutrients are washed away and it's necessary to use large quantities of chemicals to grow crops.

Hunting has caused the near extinction of many rainforest species, though many indigenous communities have banned the killing of certain species, notably the tapir, to allow populations to recover. Raising chickens is an increasingly popular alternative.

Galápagos

Meanwhile, the Galápagos Islands are experiencing the effects of exploding tourism, luxury real estate developments, a fast-growing population, and introduced species. Organized tourism, which began with 4,500 visitors in 1970, has spiraled out of control. While studies dictate that no more than 180,000 tourists should enter the Galápagos every year, over 224,000 visited in 2015. With several planes landing and departing the islands' four airports daily, yachts and cruises transporting tourists from island to island, and thousands of visitors trekking through the landscape, the impact of irresponsible tourism is severe. Often basic services do not work and sewage is discharged into the sea. Immigration rates have also soared, putting increased pressure on the fragile ecosystems.

It is estimated that international luxury hotels and operators take 80 percent of profits from tourism in the Galápagos, a figure that is set to increase since the moratorium banning new hotel infrastructure was lifted in 2014. That same year, plans for a luxury $90 million hotel and residential complex on San Cristóbal Island were announced, including a hotel, spa, 18-hole golf course, and an urban development of "private, massive, awe-inspiring residential villas." In 2015, it was reported that at least 20 new hotel projects, some of them million-dollar investments aimed at the wealthy, were awaiting approval. Of these, 11 would be on San Cristóbal and nearby Floreana, seven on Santa Cruz, and two on Isabela, causing irrecoverable damage and destruction to natural ecosystems.

Invasive species such as goats and rats, introduced by sailors hundreds of years ago, eat native species' food and eggs. More recently, a type of parasitic fly was accidentally introduced that sucks the blood of fledgling finches, resulting in the possible extinction of the Galápagos mangrove finch. The threat can be invisible; even a seed or spore attached to clothing could launch an invasion.

Solutions

With much of the environmental damage enabled by the state, it's not surprising that the best solutions come from grassroots actions. Supporting these efforts is the best way for visitors to help conserve what is left of Ecuador's staggering biodiversity.

The most effective ways to defend threatened ecosystems tend to be community-led and multifaceted, incorporating a variety of strategies, including nonviolent resistance and direct action, legal action, habitat regeneration, and the creation of alternative, sustainable sources of income that reduce dependence on extractivism and destructive agricultural practices.

The historic 2018 suspension of the Rio Blanco mine was a result of both legal and social resistance. For a decade prior to the court decision, water defenders had been organizing peaceful protests and roadblocks to filter access to their territories. Solidarity was another key factor, with support from local media, other indigenous communities, and urban citizens in Cuenca, whose water sources are also threatened by the mine.

Since 1995, the communities of the **Intag** region have been engaged in a battle to protect the cloud forest ecosystem from mining. As well as direct actions such as roadblocks, residents have created an alternative development model, including renewable energy from small-scale hydroelectric plants and a diversified, sustainable economy based on ecotourism; small-scale fruit farming; an organic coffee growers association; artisanal natural soaps, shampoos, and creams; and handicrafts made from woven sisal. With the coffee grown in the shade of native trees, the conservation (rather than destruction) of the region's cloud forest is incentivized. A café and store in the tourist hub of **Otavalo** sells Intag's products and raises awareness of their struggle. See www.decoin.org and http://codelcoecuador. com for more information.

Sarayaku (http://sarayaku.org) is another community that has successfully employed a variety of tactics to protect their 135,000 hectares (333,600 acres) of primary rainforest territory. Like Intag residents, they are also building a sustainable, alternative economy based on ecotourism and agro-ecology. After winning a historic legal battle against the Ecuadorian state, which illegally allowed an oil company to explore for oil in their territory, they used some of the settlement to create a small airline, providing the region with an alternative to one of the biggest threats facing the rainforest: the expanding network of roads. In 2018, the Sarayaku launched a bold and visionary proposal, the Kawsak Sacha or Living Forest Declaration, which describes the rainforest as a living entity with consciousness, and thus subject to legal rights. The community hopes the proposal can be used to defend other indigenous territories as well as their own.

Other projects involve the regeneration of damaged ecosystems. One of the most inspiring examples started in 1985 when an Ecuadorian couple, Rebeca Justicia and Rodrigo Ontaneda, decided to protect and restore an area of degraded cloud forest north of Quito. After establishing the 6,500-hectare (16,100-acre) **Maquipucuna Reserve** (www. maquipucuna.org), they spent three decades reforesting it with native species, including a type of wild avocado—a favorite food for the Andean or spectacled bear, which had all but disappeared from the area. Attracted by the avocados, the bears started coming back. The reserve now provides a safe haven for at least 60 of these endangered mammals and is the best place in the world to see them in the wild. Recognizing the importance of this achievement, the government of Quito declared Maquipucuna and the surrounding area a protected bear corridor, preserving a total area of 65,000 hectares (161,000 acres). In 2018, UNESCO announced the creation of the new **Chocó Andino de Pichincha Biosphere Reserve,** with Maquipucuna at its core—a simply monumental accomplishment.

The Maquipucuna Foundation was also instrumental in protecting the neighboring 2,600-hectare (6,400-acre) reserve of **Yunguilla** (www.yunguilla.org.ec). Until the late 1990s, the 60 families that inhabit the reserve were felling their forests for charcoal production to make ends meet. When the Maquipucuna Foundation realized the extent of the threat posed by their neighbors' unsustainable land-use practices, they assisted the Yunguilla community to find alternative sources of income. Funds were raised for the purchase of a building to serve as a hostel and the headquarters of a community enterprise that produces orchids, handicrafts, and organic cheeses and jams. Rather than felling trees, the families now practice reforestation, soil conservation, and organic gardening.

Another great example of a regenerative project is the **Clínica Ambiental** (www.clinicambiental.org) in the northern Amazon region, which works to heal the ecosystem and local communities from the damage wrought by oil companies and agriculture. As part of this effort, a network of Amazon permaculturists has created the **Esperanza Tour** (Hope Tour), a series of projects designed to show that permaculture and ecotourism are viable economic alternatives, with products such as essential oils and organic jams providing income. A laboratory undertakes research on bioremediation (the science of cleaning contamination with oil-consuming mushrooms; http://amisacho.com). There is a sister project, **Los Yapas** (http://losyapas.org), in Puyo.

On the coast, the ancestral community of **Las Tunas** is involved with efforts to protect the world's second smallest hummingbird, the critically endangered *estrellita Esmeraldeña*, or Esmeraldas woodstar. Working with **Fundación Jocotoco** (www.jocotoco.org), local people have been restoring its habitat by planting 10,000 native trees, especially the *pechiche*, which provides not only food for the hummingbird but fruit for making and selling jam. In recognition of its conservation efforts Las Tunas was a finalist in the United Nations Equator Prize 2017, an initiative that recognizes outstanding community efforts to reduce poverty through the conservation and sustainable use of biodiversity.

Running through these success stories is the common thread of finding sustainable economic alternatives to destructive practices. Examples include organic coffee, cacao, jam, essential oils, and crafts made from *tagua* nut. **El Artesan** (www.elartesan.com.ec) in Puerto López is a store that specializes in palo santo products, including soap, shampoo, massage oil, essential oil, and incense. The owner only uses wood from fallen branches or dead trees, and some of the proceeds from the shop go toward reforestation of the tropical dry forest. A craftsman near Canoa is working with a local community who currently fell native trees to make furniture, teaching them instead to make intricate wooden boxes, which are more profitable and can be made with fallen branches. In **Montañita,** Balsa Surf Camp is working on replicating machines that can turn plastic waste into raw material and is planning on distributing them to people who collect trash on the beach.

ETHICAL TOURISM

While irresponsible or mass tourism can cause severe environmental impacts, **ethical tourism** is often the best solution for preserving threatened ecosystems. Ecotourism, defined as "responsible travel that conserves natural environments and sustains the well-being of local people," is a good start, but **community-based ecotourism** goes one step further. Community-based ecotourism initiatives are led by local people, with the income going directly to them, enabling them to preserve their ecosystems and culture. This is in contrast to some ecotourism projects, where local people are employed, often as cooks, cleaners, and drivers, but see only a tiny fraction of the income generated in their ancestral territories and are not involved in decision making. With community-based ecotourism, often a percentage of the proceeds goes toward improving the quality of life for the community, funding health care, education, and conservation projects. Visitors are usually invited to share aspects of daily life, providing an authentic cultural experience. A good community tourism project should be well organized; should reinforce collective identity and revitalize culture; should practice economic solidarity; and should strengthen the defense of territory. This type of tourism is especially important in indigenous communities, whose ancestral cultures, languages, and knowledge of plant medicines are in danger of disappearing. An excellent resource on community tourism is the **Federación Plurinacional de Turismo Comunitario del Ecuador** (www.feptce.com).

There are several excellent examples of community ecotourism in Ecuador. In Esmeraldas province, the residents of **Playa de Oro** worked with U.S. charity Earthways to build a tourist lodge and establish their territory as a release site and reserve for wildcats. The community has successfully protected the rainforest from mining and timbering companies ever since, and every visit directly supports these efforts.

Near Ibarra, the residents of the small Kichwa village of **San Clemente** (www.sclemente.com) have opened their homes up to guests, with the income going back into the community. One of the requirements of joining the project is that no chemicals are used in the cultivation of produce, so the whole community now eats fresh, organic food and is almost entirely self-sufficient. As well as sharing the Andean cosmovision and culture with visitors, the project also involves local indigenous youth, aiming to keep Kichwa traditions alive.

Another Kichwa village in Bolívar province, **Salinas de Guaranda,** has a number of successful community cooperatives making cheese, chocolate, nougat, dried fruit and mushrooms, jam, herbal teas, woollen yarn, and clothes. Under the brand **Salinerito** (www.salinerito.com), it has several stores throughout the country and exports internationally. Profits are reinvested back into the cooperatives and used for the development of the community, including initiatives in social support, education, permaculture, and agroecological farming.

In the Amazon region, there are community-based ecotourism projects in **Yasuní National Park,** including the Napo Wildlife Center and Napo Cultural Center, Sani Lodge, Eden Amazon Lodge, and Llanchama. In the northern Oriente are the Kofán **Avie** and Siekopai **Remolina** communities and, in the far southeast, **Kapawi Ecolodge.**

Throughout the country, private individuals and organizations, such as the nonprofit Jocotoco and Jatun Sacha Foundations, have small reserves dotted around the country, including **Wildsumaco** and **Cabañas San Isidro** in Napo province; **Pacoche Lodge** in Manabí; and **Sacha Runa Lodge** in Cotopaxi. Some use income from tourism to purchase and protect hectares of forest.

Environmental solutions are also found in urban spaces. Of note are **El Manso** hotel in Guayaquil and the restaurants **Tandana** and **Flora** in Quito, all of which are actively implementing creative ecological and social projects. Alliances between urban and rural, mestizo and indigenous causes are also important. A recent program for young leaders in Quito run by human rights organization **INREDH** (www.inredh.org) brought together activists from across the movements, including indigenous, LGBTQ, and anti-extractivist, to work together to find common solutions.

As a visitor to Ecuador, you have the potential to make an enormous impact toward the conservation of its incredible biological and cultural diversity. Think carefully about where you spend your tourist dollars. Consider supporting the projects mentioned here and featured throughout this book. Purchase goods directly from local producers or fair trade stores that stock their products (**Camari** in Quito, for example). Choose hotels and restaurants owned by local families. Look for accommodations with sound environmental policies, which may include renewable energy, recycling, conservation of water and energy, ecological building methods, waste management practices (i.e., gray water systems, composting), use of biodegradable cleaning products, support of local producers, organic gardens, and environmental education. These establishments are included in this guide wherever they were found. If you see examples of incoherence with environmental principles, speak up. For example, boat tours in Machalilla National Park provide information on the threats faced by marinelife, but then serve drinks in single-use plastic cups from disposable plastic bottles. Tour operators are more likely to switch to a more sustainable alternative (such as **EmpaqueVerde Ecuador** products, www.empaqueverde.com) if enough visitors request it. Travel with your own refillable water bottle, lunch container, and cutlery. Say no to disposable plastics and explain why. Reach out to environmental organizations (some are mentioned in the *Resources* chapter). Consider volunteering at one of the projects listed in this chapter. Learn what you can about environmental problems and solutions in Ecuador and spread the word when you get home.

Plants and Animals

Ecuador is the ninth most biodiverse country in the world. Measured per unit area, it's the most biodiverse. Covering less than 0.005 percent of the planet's surface, it boasts 10 percent of all plant species on earth (almost 20,000, more than in all of North America) and one-sixth of all birds (more than 1,600 species, compared with 844 in North America). There are also over 840 species of reptiles and amphibians, 341 species of mammal, and thousands of butterfly species. Much of this diversity is found in the Amazon region, which makes up nearly half of Ecuador's territory.

Ecuador is one of the best countries in the world for bird-watching. Of the myriad species, perhaps the **hummingbird** (*colibrí*) deserves special mention, for its presence in all of the mainland regions: coast, Sierra, and Oriente, from sea level to the snowcapped mountains. They are even spotted buzzing around in Quito and Guayaquil. Ecuador is home to over 132 hummingbird species, almost half of the world's total, including the world's second smallest, the *estrellita Esmeraldeña* (or Esmeraldas woodstar). Also of note is the sword-billed hummingbird, which totes a 10-centimeter (4-in) beak.

THE COAST

Ecuador's oceans are home to five species of marine turtle: green, olive ridley, loggerhead, leatherback, and hawksbill. All are considered either vulnerable or endangered, and the hawksbill is critically endangered. The leatherback is the largest marine turtle in the world, measuring up to three meters. Sadly, turtles are most commonly spotted washed up dead on the beach, victims of fishing boats, nets, hooks, and garbage. Occasionally, the babies are seen at various hatching sites along the coast. It is possible to snorkel and dive with marine turtles at Isla de la Plata and the Galápagos.

Abundant tropical fish, including parrot fish and clown fish, can be seen at Isla de la Plata and other sites in Machalilla National Park, where hammerhead sharks and giant manta rays also lurk. Isla de la Plata has a small colony of sea lions, but it's much easier to see them at La Lobería near Salinas. Humpback whales are present off the coast from Salinas up to Atacames June-September. The best place to watch them is around Puerto López in Machalilla National Park. Farther south in the estuaries of the Gulf of Guayaquil, dolphins come to feed in the mangroves and are spotted daily in the Canal de Morro, which separates the mainland from the island of Puná.

All along the coast, pelicans and frigate birds are the most iconic and commonly spotted marine bird species. Magnificent frigate birds can be seen inflating their red chests at several locations, including Isla Corazón near Bahía de Caráquez, Isla de la Plata, and the Canal de Morro. Blue-footed boobies can be spotted at the latter two sites. Isla de la Plata is also a resting and nesting site for waved albatross, red-footed boobies, and masked boobies. In El Oro province, the island of Santa Clara has a community of sea lions and more seabirds per square kilometer than anywhere else in the country.

Pockets of mangroves can still be found along the coast, providing habitat for crustaceans such as crab, nurseries for fish, and nesting sites for birds. The biggest area around the Gulf of Guayaquil includes the Manglares Churute Ecological Reserve, which shelters larger, endangered animals such as jaguars and other wildcats, howler monkeys, porcupines, crocodiles, and caiman, as well as over 300 bird species. Santa Rosa near Machala is another good place to visit mangroves. Bioluminescent plankton are present nightly in Mompiche in Esmeraldas.

Inland, parts of the northwestern coast fall within the Chocó bioregion, which contains some of the most biologically diverse forests on earth, where up to one-fifth of the plants are endemic—half in some areas! Part of the Chocó, Playa de Oro is a release site for six species of wildcats: jaguars, pumas, ocelots, margays, *oncillas*, and jaguarundis. Ocelots and jaguarundis are present at the Pacoche Marine & Coastal Wildlife Reserve, a pocket of semi-dry tropical forest near Manta, which is also home to the critically endangered Ecuadorian capuchin monkey, along with howler monkeys, kinkajous, and agoutis.

Running parallel to the coast from Esmeraldas to Guayas, the low mountain ranges of Mache-Chindul and Chongón-Colonche protect the remnants of the region's tropical forest. Much of this is tropical wet forest, home to the *tagua* palm, source of the vegetable ivory used for carving souvenirs. Plant species include orchids, bromeliads, and *Carludovica palmata* or *toquilla* palm, a palm-like plant whose leaves are used to weave into *sombreros de paja toquilla* ("Panama" hats) and other items. In 2010, scientists working in the protected forest of the Cerro Pata de Pájaro near Pedernales in Manabí province announced that they had discovered several new reptile and amphibian species, including a gecko so tiny that it that can sit on top of a pencil eraser; a glass frog whose beating heart can be seen through its transparent skin; and a salamander that has no lungs, but breathes through its skin. Mammal species include howler monkeys, anteaters, and *tigrillos* (northern tiger cats).

The Chongón-Colonche range also includes expanses of tropical dry forest, such as the protected forest at Cerro Blanco west of Guayaquil. Among the 250 bird species is the endangered great green macaw, of which only 50 remain in the wild. Howler monkeys and jaguars are also present, though the latter are only seen on camera traps.

In southern Manabí, Machalilla National Park shelters tropical dry forests, where plant life consists of water-stingy varieties such as the palo santo, ceiba, barbasco, balsa, and mesquite trees, along with cacti. Birds such as the vermilion flycatcher, Pacific pygmy owl, and long-tailed mockingbird live among the dry hills, which are also home to armadillos, opossums, and *oncillas* (northern tiger cats). Slightly farther south, the Ayampe River Reserve protects the world's second smallest hummingbird, the critically endangered *estrellita Esmeraldeña*, or Esmeraldas woodstar.

The area is being reforested with the native *pechiche* tree, which provides food for the tiny bird. The reserve is also the release site for an even rarer bird, the green guacamayo, a type of macaw with only 30 individuals remaining in the wild.

El Oro is Ecuador's most southerly coastal province and the only one with both *páramo* and mangroves. It also has expanses of tropical forest and South America's largest fossilized forest in Puyango, near the Peruvian border. El Oro is famous for the annual flowering of the guayacan trees in Mangahurco, where hundreds of trees burst into brilliant yellow bloom every January in an eight-day spectacle. Also in El Oro, the cloud forests of the Buenaventura Reserve protect the El Oro parakeet, which is only found in the province's high altitude spots. The bizarre long-wattled umbrella bird is another resident, as are hummingbirds, monkeys, sloths, and pumas.

THE SIERRA

In the Sierra, the valley interiors were once covered with a thorny woodland, giving way to a low evergreen forest toward the valley edges, then to the grasslands of the *páramo* at higher elevations. The foothills are now mostly covered with a rolling tapestry of agricultural fields, which, sadly, have become more quintessentially Ecuadorian than the forests they replaced.

Páramo

Situated between the tree line and the snow line at an elevation of 3,000-5,000 meters (9,800-16,500 ft), the windswept grasslands of the *páramo* rise to rocky mountains interspersed with crystalline lakes and streams. Acting as giant sponges, these moorlands give birth to a number of Ecuador's rivers and provide water for many Sierran towns and communities.

Much of the *páramo* is sprinkled with wildflowers, but at very high elevations few flowers can survive. A notable exception is the orange thistle-like *chuquiraga*, regarded as the national flower. Another iconic plant

is the *frailejón*, a spiky-headed relative of the sunflower that, despite only growing one centimeter every year, can reach several meters in height. *Frailejones* are particularly abundant in the El Ángel Ecological Reserve in the northern Sierra, which protects some of Ecuador's most pristine high elevation terrain. Other impressive *páramos* can be found near Otavalo in the northern Sierra; in the Cotopaxi, Chimborazo, and Sangay National Parks and near Quilotoa in the central Sierra; and in the Cajas and Podocarpus National Parks in the southern Sierra.

The most famous avian resident of the *páramo* is the Andean condor, the world's largest flying bird, with a wingspan of more than 3 meters (10 ft) and weighing up to 15 kilograms (33 lb). The condor is Ecuador's national bird and a symbol of Andean identity. A type of vulture, it is critically endangered, with between 50 and 100 mating pairs in the country. The best place to see condors is the Antisana Reserve, accessed via Papallacta. Cotopaxi National Park is the best place to see the carunculated caracara, the largest member of the falcon family, with its bright red face, yellow bill, and black body. Locally known as a *curiquingue*, the caracara was a sacred bird for the Inca.

The mammalian star of the show is the highly endangered Andean spectacled bear, named for white patches around its eyes. The only bear native to South America, the *oso andino* can be found in the cloud forest as well as the *páramo*. The males can reach 2 meters (6.5 ft) in length. In the Sierra, the best places to see them are the Antisana Reserve, accessed via Papallacta, and Podocarpus National Park. They are also present in the reserves of Cayambe-Coca, El Ángel, and Iliniza, as well as several locations in the cloud forest.

South America's high-elevation relatives of the camel—llamas, vicuñas, and alpacas—were hunted to extinction, but reintroduction programs using animals from Chile and Bolivia have been highly successful in the Chimborazo Fauna Reserve. Wild horses and reintroduced llamas can be seen in Cotopaxi National Park.

The *páramos* are also home to the highly endangered Andean tapir, highland wolves, Andean foxes, and the world's smallest deer, the pudu.

Cloud Forests

Cloud forests are found on both the eastern and western slopes of the Andes, between the high elevation *páramo* and the lowland rainforest. Cloud forests are cooler than rainforests, characterized by fast-moving, clear rocky rivers and beautiful views due to the mountainous terrain. Rainforests are hotter, with larger, silt-laden, slow-moving rivers and flatter terrain. Rainforests have a greater diversity of trees, but cloud forests have more epiphytes, with mosses on the trunks of trees, orchids between the mosses, ferns and bromeliads growing on branches, and algae covering the leaves.

Andean cloud forests provide some of the best bird-watching in the world. The bright-red feathers of the Andean cock-of-the-rock make it a favorite with birders, who watch their mating displays in courtship clearings called leks. Golden-headed quetzals have bright turquoise plumage and live in tree cavities next to vivid tanagers and toucans, while antpittas skulk in the shadows.

Maquipucuna, a cloud forest reserve north of Quito, is the best place in the country to see Andean bears, as they come to feed in wild avocado trees. Bears are also present in Intag, Los Cedros Biological Reserve, Podocarpus National Park, and the area around Baeza. Other cloud forest mammals include jaguars, pumas, ocelots, margays, Andean tapirs, mantled howler monkeys, agoutis, Andean coatis, three-toed sloths, and white-fronted capuchin monkeys. Crystalline streams provide habitat for a number of glass frog species and escape routes for the famous basilisk or "Jesus Christ lizard," which can walk on water.

Beautiful cloud forests can be found in the north of the country at Mindo, Los Cedros Biological Reserve, and Intag. The latter is notable for being at the confluence of two of the world's biological hot spots, the Chocó-Darien Western Ecuadorian and the Tropical Andes. Incredibly, 40 percent of Intag's bird and plant species are found nowhere else on the planet. East of Quito, Baeza is a great jumping off point for a number of forested reserves nearby. In the far south, Podocarpus National Park and Buenaventura Reserve both have beautiful cloud forest.

RAINFORESTS

Rainforests are defined by low elevation (up to 1,000 m/3,300 ft), high temperatures (25-30°C/77-86°F), and high levels of rainfall (200-300 cm/80-120 in per year). The result is a warm, humid environment as perfect for unbridled growth as any on earth. Among the oldest of all ecosystems, some rainforest plants and animals have had hundreds of millions of years to evolve into their particular niche.

Rainforests are among the least understood of the planet's ecosystems, at least by the Western world. Scientists are just beginning to understand the incredible biological diversity of the Amazon, where 3,000 different types of beetles have been found in study plots of 12 square meters (129 sq ft), and 87 species of frogs and toads were found in 1 hectare (2.5 acres). Ecuador's Yasuní National Park was recently discovered by scientists to be the most biodiverse spot on the planet and probably unmatched by any other park in the world for total numbers of plant and animal species. Just one hectare (2.5 acres) of its rainforest has as many as 655 tree species, more than all of the United States and Canada combined.

For all the richness that lies in the rainforest, the soil underneath is surprisingly thin and poor. In contrast with temperate forests and their rich, deep layers of humus, rainforests have most of their nutrients suspended in the vegetation itself—in both living and dead matter—instead of the ground. Countless bacteria, fungi, and insects are crucial in quickly breaking down dead matter and returning the nutrients to the pool of life. In fact, less than 1 percent of forest nutrients are thought to penetrate deeper than 5 centimeters (2 in) into the soil. As a result, when rainforests are cleared for agriculture, the thin topsoil washes away in a few years to reveal an impenetrable layer of clay on which little can grow.

Although deforestation and oil exploration have seriously impacted the Amazon region, there are still vast areas of primary rainforest stretching east to the Colombian and Peruvian borders.

Plants

The Oriente includes both primary and secondary forest. Primary forest is largely untouched, usually within the context of logging activities, whereas a secondary forest has been logged or disturbed in a significant way and is in the process of growing back. Often, the difference between the two is not obvious to the casual observer, especially if the secondary forest was logged a few decades ago. The easiest way to identify primary forest is the presence of massive trees, some of which can grow up to 50 meters (165 ft) tall and 5 meters (16 ft) across at the base. King of the rainforest trees is the towering ceiba (kapok). To the indigenous residents of the rainforest, the types of forest are very different. Primary forest is considered more sacred, but secondary forest is often more useful, especially if the forest was previously cleared for small-scale agriculture or human habitation. This is where edible and medicinal plants are more likely to be found, planted by previous inhabitants, as well as trees used in traditional construction methods. Some indigenous people would add the third forest category of "virgin rainforest," which is so undisturbed that even they rarely tread there.

Each large tree in the rainforest supports a veritable zoo of aerial plant life, starting with huge, woody lianas that climb host trees to reach the sun. Epiphytes, aerial plants that get all their nutrients and water from the air, include orchids and bromeliads, which resemble the tops of pineapples (they're in the same taxonomic family). Inside each bromeliad's leafy crown, a small puddle of rainwater can support hundreds of insects, amphibians, and even other epiphytes.

An incredible array of medicinal plants, long known to native people, have only recently begun to be appreciated by modern science. Many familiar substances were discovered this way—among them nicotine, caffeine, strychnine, Novocain, and quinine, the first effective medicine against malaria. Indeed, indigenous peoples often refer to the rainforest as their pharmacy.

Of these medicinal plants, of particular note is the ayahuasca vine (*Banisteriopsis caapi*), which forms a central component of the spiritual traditions of most Amazonian cultures. Together with the chacruna plant it is brewed into a powerfully hallucinogenic tea, used to cure illness and emotional maladies, to find spiritual guidance, and to communicate with the forest itself.

Birds

Aside from insects, birds are the most abundant animal life you'll see in the Oriente. You'll have the best chance of spotting them from a canoe, along the borders of clear-cut areas, at a salt lick, or from a lodge's canopy tower. Of the hundreds of different species (there are over 600 in Yasuní National Park alone), a few stand out. Hoatzins are unmistakable, with their Mohawk crest, ungainly body, and prehistoric squawk. The smell of decomposing leaves, which is used to deter predators, gives these birds the nickname "stinky turkeys." The liquid call of an oropendola is unmistakable—like a large drop of water falling into a deep well—and it's one of the most attractive sounds in the rainforest. Their long woven nests are commonly seen dangling from tree branches. Harpy eagles, South America's largest birds of prey, use their daggerlike claws to snatch monkeys out of tree branches and can be best spotted in Yasuní National Park. Also present in Yasuní from March to July is the spectacular but elusive agami heron, much coveted by birders.

Twenty species of toucans use their huge bills for reaching and opening fruit and seeds

in the canopy. Forty-five species of macaw can be seen here, including the blue-and-yellow and the chestnut-fronted. Macaws are often spotted from a canoe, squawking as they fly overhead in a small flock. It is possible to see hundreds of parrots and parakeets at clay licks, where they gather daily to absorb minerals that counteract the toxic berries they eat. The most famous lick is in Yasuní near Napo Wildlife Center.

Mammals

Large mammals do exist in the Amazon, but they are rarely seen. Even indigenous residents of the forest may have had only one or two sightings of a jaguar in their lives. This magnificent big cat is worshipped by many nationalities as one of the rainforest's most powerful spirits, often invoked in ceremonies by shamans. Indeed, it is said that the most powerful shamans can transform into jaguars. Either jet black or spotted, this highly endangered feline is the only member of the *Panthera* genus found in the Americas and the third-largest cat in the world after the tiger and lion, usually weighing 56-96 kilograms (123-212 lb). Also present in the Amazon are the puma and smaller cats such as the jaguarundi and the ocelot.

Even bigger than the jaguar, the Amazonian tapir is one of the continent's largest mammals, weighing in at 160-270 kilograms (350-600 lb). These herbivorous animals have been hunted almost to extinction, and many indigenous nationalities have banned further hunting to allow populations to recover. Also frequently hunted are peccaries, a type of wild pig.

Ten monkey species inhabit the Ecuadorian Amazon, including the pygmy marmoset, the smallest monkey in the world. The loudest is the red howler, named after the roaring call of the males, which is audible for kilometers. The long-haired spider monkey is named for its long, thin limbs and tail. Common squirrel monkeys live in large groups and are quite frequently spotted. Brown woolly monkeys are named for their thick coats. White-fronted capuchins, along with other capuchins, are thought to be among the most intelligent of monkeys.

Other Amazon mammals include the bush dog; the world's largest rodent, the capybara; two- and three-toed sloths; and 100 species of bat. Beneath the waters, pink river dolphins often feed where joining rivers produce clashing currents that confuse fish. Manatees and giant otters can also be found in the rivers.

Reptiles and Amphibians

Ecuador has around 840 species of reptiles and amphibians, of which more than 400 are frogs and toads, representing the highest frog and toad diversity per unit area of any country in the world. Most of these are found in the Amazon, where they join the insects to create a wonderful nighttime orchestra of millions of voices and wings. The notorious poison-arrow frog raises its tadpoles in cups of water trapped in bromeliads. Their neon red, blue, and green spots give warning to potential predators of some of the most potent toxins in the animal kingdom, applied by indigenous hunters to their arrow and dart tips.

Like the jaguar, the anaconda is revered by many indigenous peoples as one of the jungle's most powerful spirits, often evoked in ceremonies. A type of boa constrictor, it can grow up to 7 meters (23 ft) long and is semiaquatic. Mainly feeding on fish, rodents, and occasionally small caimans, the anaconda squeezes the life out of its prey. Seven other types of boa are present in the Amazon, including the beautiful rainbow boa. There are countless other snake species, but they are very hard to spot, unless they're sleeping curled around a riverside tree branch as you pass by in a canoe. While it's extremely rare for visitors to get bitten by snakes, they are the most dangerous of all the jungle animals for local people, who have to take great care when cutting the undergrowth. Particularly feared are the

1: a red-footed booby; 2: cactus on Plaza Sur in the Galápagos Islands; 3: gigantic trees of Ecuador's primary rainforest; 4: land iguana on Santa Cruz Island

fer-de-lance (spearhead), locally known as the "X" (pronounced "ekkis") and the coral snake, both of which can deliver potentially fatal bites. The danger lies in surprising one dozing in the foliage, so always wear rubber boots when walking in the jungle.

Flashlight beams on nighttime canoe rides might catch the glittering eyes of caimans. Growing up to 6 meters (20 ft) long, the black caiman is the largest predator in the Amazon ecosystem and has been hunted to near extinction. They do not seek out humans but may attack if approached. Fortunately, locals are usually aware of where black caimans live. They usually sleep during the day and can be spotted more easily on night canoe excursions (they don't tend to attack boats). The three smaller species (white, brown, and crowned dwarfs) are fairly harmless, feeding mostly on crustaceans and small fish. Freshwater turtles can sometimes be spotted as they doze on fallen trees by the riverside.

Fish

There are around 300 species of fish in the Oriente. The Amazon catfish is the largest freshwater fish in the world, often topping 200 kilograms (440 lb). Locally known as *bagre*, they form a key part of Amazon cuisine. Fear of piranhas shouldn't keep you out of the water completely; these small fish do have a powerful set of choppers, but they rarely attack an animal that isn't bleeding already, and some species feed solely on fruit. Stingrays, however, hide in muddy shallows and can inflict an excruciating sting with a barb on the end of their whiplike tail.

Insects

Four-tenths of a hectare (1 acre) of Ecuador's rainforest may contain as many as 70,000 species of insect. Listening to the nightly chorus of crickets, this isn't too hard to believe.

Probably the most common type of insect you will see is the leafcutter ant, columns of which will cross your path, each individual carrying a piece of leaf. When the ants get back to their nest, the leaves are chewed up, fertilized with ant feces, and set in carefully tended gardens to grow a particular type of fungus that the ants then eat. The lemon ant has developed a unique relationship with the *Duroia hirsuta* tree, which it defends by injecting formic acid into the stems of any plant which attempts to grow near the tree. The clearings created by the ants are known locally as "devil's gardens" and were once believed to be the work of an evil spirit. Live lemon ants are a popular snack for local people. Another interesting, albeit gruesome, ant-related phenomenon is that of the *Cordyceps* fungus. This parasite lives inside ants and other insects, feeding on their non-vital organs; then, when it is ready to produce spores, the fungus grows into the host's brain and releases chemicals that make the insect climb to the top of a plant and attach itself. The *Cordyceps* then kills the host by devouring its brain and sprouts a mushroom out of its head, from which it disperses spores over the surrounding area. The nastiest of the Amazon ant species is the 3-centimeter (1.2-in) conga ant, known locally as *veinte-quatros* ("twenty-fours") for the day-long pain of their potent bite, so keep your distance.

With wingspans of 20-38 centimeters (8-15 in), electric-blue morpho butterflies are one of the most eye-catching creatures in the forest, flitting through patches of light on their way down forest trails or waterways. Less picturesque, the papery nests of termites are a common sight, made of digested wood cemented together with droppings. Termites play a crucial recycling role in the rainforest by digesting dead wood with the help of microbes.

History

EARLIEST CULTURES

If you've ever noticed the similarities in features of American indigenous people and Asians, you're not imagining it—most experts agree that the Americas were first colonized by nomadic hunter-gatherers who crossed the Bering Strait from Siberia about 18,000 years ago. They gradually moved south, reaching Latin America a few thousand years later to become the continent's original inhabitants. Archaeologists have found instruments carved from stone and arrowheads made from obsidian and flint dating back 10,000 years, when it is thought that small family groups roamed the area. From then, numerous cultures thrived for thousands of years before the Inca and Spanish invasions.

The pre-Columbian civilization can be divided into four periods: Pre-Ceramic, Formative, Regional Development, and Integration. The best places to see archaeological remains from the pre-Columbian period are museums in Quito and Cuenca.

Pre-Ceramic Period

The earliest Ecuadorian culture, Las Vegas, can be traced to the Santa Elena Peninsula as long ago as 9000 BC. After starting out as hunter-gatherers, they began farming around 6000 BC. The best-known remains are the skeletons called the Lovers of Sumpa, housed in the Museo Los Amantes de Sumpa in Santa Elena. Around the same time, the area near present-day Quito was inhabited by nomadic hunters known as the Inga.

Pristine areas of Amazon rainforest are usually considered to be ancient, untamed jungles untouched by human hands. But that perception is starting to change, with evidence suggesting that ancient peoples played a key role in the ecological development of the rainforest as long as 8,000 years ago. Like other populations, they changed the land to suit their needs by burning, cutting, tilling, planting, and building. Before European-introduced diseases decimated indigenous populations around 500 years ago, many parts of the Amazon were probably as cultivated as regions in Europe. Research indicates that many rainforest tree species appear to be abundant because they were cultivated for food or building by pre-Columbian cultures, including cacao, rubber, caimito fruit, and tucuma palm.

Formative Period

Around 4500 BC, people evolved from hunting-gathering and simple farming into more permanent settlements with more developed agriculture and the use of ceramics. Emerging from the Las Vegas culture around 3500 BC, the Valdivia culture inhabited the Santa Elena Peninsula near the modern-day town of Valdivia. They produced some of America's oldest pottery and are best known for producing female ceramic figures known as the Venus of Valdivia. They were followed by the coastal Machalilla culture between the second and first millennia BC, who were experts at crafting objects from shells and practiced skull deformation as a sign of status.

Traces of cocoa dating back to around 3200 BC have been found in ancient pots in the Ecuadorian Amazon; this is the oldest proof of cocoa use ever found, predating the domestication of cocoa by the Maya in Central America by some 1,500 years. This evidence was collected at the Santa Ana La Florida archaeological site near Palanda in the southern Amazon region, where there are traces of a house and a ceremonial site belonging to the Mayo Chinchipe, the oldest known Amerindian civilization in the upper Amazon. The presence of seashells, such as spondylus and strombus, demonstrates that there were communication links between the peoples of the coast and the Oriente.

The Narrio culture appeared in the

southern Sierra around 1500 BC and made funeral offerings depicting their ancestors with shells, evidencing commerce between the coast and Sierra. Living on both the coast and in the Andes, the Chorerra (to 300 BC) produced beautiful polished and painted pottery in the form of fruit, animals, and people.

Regional Development

Between 300 BC and AD 700 several cultures flourished along the coast (Bahía, Guangala, Jambelí, Jama-Coaque, La Tolita) and in the Sierra (Tuncahuán and Panzaleo). The La Tolita people on the northern coast were remarkable craftspeople in metallurgy, using gold, copper, and platinum, this last being worked in Ecuador for the first time in the world. Felines were their principal deity and were represented in their art. Their famous gold sun-mask is the symbol of the Banco Central.

Integration Period

Coastal cultures reached their peak between AD 700 and 1460. The Manteños were the last of the pre-Columbian cultures in the coastal region and are famous for making U-shaped stone chairs, thought to have been used by shamans during ancient ceremonies. Theirs was a trading culture, and they were specialists in diving for spondylus shells.

In the Sierra, the Cara people arrived in what is now Quito in the 10th century, defeating the local Quitu tribe. The combined Quitu-Cara culture was known as the Shyris or Caranqui civilization and thrived until the Inca invasion, against which they fought valiantly. The Cañaris, descended from the Narrío culture in the southern Sierra, would also put up fierce resistance to the invaders.

THE RISE AND FALL OF THE INCAS

The Incas, or "Children of the Sun," had roots in two previous great empires: Tiwanaku (circa AD 300-1100), based around Lake Titicaca between Peru and Bolivia; and the Wari (circa AD 600-1100), who occupied the Cuzco area for about 400 years. By about AD 1250, the Incas began to expand from Cuzco. By the 14th and 15th centuries they had built an empire called Tawantinsuyu that stretched from what is now northern Chile to the southern edge of present-day Ecuador.

In 1463 the ruling Inca, Túpac Yupanqui, began the push into Ecuador from Peru. In the Sierra, Inca armies met fierce resistance, notably from the Cañaris and Quitu-Caras. It wasn't until Yupanqui's son, Huayna Capac, continued his father's campaign that the Incan Empire finally conquered these territories. Following their victory, the invaders had enough respect for the Cañari to build a community together at Ingapirca.

Once a complex with ceremonial, astronomical, political, and administrative functions, Ingapirca is Ecuador's most important Inca site. It is thought that the Temple of the Sun, which is still standing, was used as a site for rituals and determining the agricultural and religious calendars. The most important Inca event was Inti Raymi, the Festival of the Sun, which is still celebrated by indigenous communities across Ecuador every June solstice.

Ingapirca also includes a fragment of Inca road, part of a 40,000-kilometer (25,000-mi) network that once connected religious and administrative centers across Ecuador, Peru, Colombia, Bolivia, Argentina, and Chile, described by *Smithsonian Magazine* as "arguably the biggest, most complex construction project ever undertaken." Paved in parts with stone, the roads allowed teams of relay runners to make the 470-kilometer (290-mi) journey from Cuenca to Quito in two or three days, crossing suspension bridges and resting in stone shelters along the way. Messages carried over longer distances would have involved hundreds of oral exchanges, and to preserve the correct meaning of the original message, *quipu*—coded assemblies of strings and knots—were probably used to help the memory of the runners. One of the highest sections of the Inca road passes through what is now Sangay National Park, reaching an elevation of 4,200 meters (13,780 ft), and can be hiked on the three-day Inca Trek from Achupallas to Ingapirca. Another fragment of Inca road can be seen in El Cajas National Park. El Salitre, a small Inca *pucara* (fortress), can be visited on the eastern edge of Cotopaxi National Park.

Huayna Capac chose to build the empire's northern capital where Cuenca is today. Modeled on Cuzco, the city was called Tumebamba, and the ruins can be visited at Pumapungo. Most of the city was destroyed shortly before the Spanish conquest, in a war between Huayna Capac's sons, Atahualpa and Huáscar, in 1532.

That same year, the arrival of the Spanish conquistadores coincided with the Inca's weakest moment, divided as they were by war. The Spanish were able to defeat the Children of the Sun, putting an end to their 50-year reign in Ecuador. During this brief period, the Inca left a strong imprint on the culture and landscape. Agriculture was diversified and centralized, grown on terraced fields watered by complicated systems of irrigation. Though the Quechua language (which evolved into Kichwa) predates the Incas, they enforced it as the official language of the empire. The Incas are thought to have brought the ancestors of the Andean Saraguro and Salasaca people from southern Peru and Bolivia in the 16th century as part of the *mitma* system of forced resettlement. Saraguros believe that they are descended from members of Huayna Capac's closest circle, who were sent here to start a new colony that would adhere faithfully to their leader's beliefs. To this day, the majority of the 30,000 Saraguros in Ecuador wear black—the color worn by the Incas on special occasions.

THE CONQUISTADORES
The Spanish Conquest Begins
Most conquistadores (literally, "conquerors") were low-ranking Spanish noblemen heading to the New World for wealth, fame, and adventure. Of these, Francisco Pizarro went on to lead an expedition that conquered the Inca empire and claimed the lands for Spain.

Pizarro was an illiterate and illegitimate fortune-seeker who accompanied explorer Vasco Núñez de Balboa on a 1513 expedition that was credited with the European "discovery" of the Pacific Ocean. A decade later, Pizarro received permission from the Spanish crown for a voyage along the west coast of South America with fellow adventurer Diego de Almagro.

In 1526, while Pizarro was exploring what is now Panama and Colombia, his main captain, Bartolomé Ruiz, sailed down the Ecuadorian coast on a reconnaissance mission and captured a Manta merchant vessel laden with gold and jewels. This news convinced Pizarro that the region contained untold riches. Following several largely unsuccessful voyages, Pizarro returned to Spain to ask King Charles I for permission to undertake a conquest. He traveled again to the New World having been granted all the authority of a viceroy, arriving in Tumbes in northern Peru in 1532 with 180 men. After meeting with hostility from the Incas, Pizarro's party relocated to the island of Puná in the Gulf of Guayaquil. Here, he met even fiercer resistance from the indigenous inhabitants, resulting in a full battle. Despite being hopelessly outnumbered, the Spanish massacred the locals with superior fighting skills and firepower that included muskets and cavalry. Over 400 natives died, but just three Spaniards did. Pizarro sailed back to Tumbes and decided to move inland in the hope of avoiding further battles and finding the riches he craved.

Atahualpa's Fate
After defeating and capturing his half-brother Huáscar in the civil war of 1532, the Inca leader had decamped to Cajamarca in the mountains of northern Peru. As Pizarro was heading inland, he was alerted to the whereabouts of Atahualpa and a meeting was arranged. The ensuing scene would have been fascinating to witness: Two leaders meeting in the sunbaked central plaza under the eyes of dozens of Spanish soldiers and thousands of Inca warriors, with tension resonating in

the air. Atahualpa, considered a living god by his people and with an army of thousands at his disposal, made the fatal mistake of underestimating a band of less than 200 Spaniards. Upon the Inca leader's refusal to accept Christianity and Charles V as his master, Spanish soldiers fired cannons and charged their horses into the heart of the Inca garrison. Within hours, the Incas had been defeated, the Sun King had been taken captive by Pizarro, and the fate of South America's greatest empire had been sealed.

During the nine months of his imprisonment, Atahualpa learned Spanish, chess, and cards while retaining most of his authority. Thinking that Pizarro planned to depose him in favor of Huáscar, Atahualpa ordered his captive half-brother killed. When it became clear that his own life hung in the balance, Atahualpa offered to buy his freedom with the wealth of his entire kingdom. He is said to have reached high on the wall of a room 5 meters wide by 7 meters long (16 by 23 ft), offering to fill it once with gold and twice with silver. The ransom—one of the largest the world has ever known—was assembled and was on its way to the capital when Pizarro went back on his word, fearful of the Inca leader's power. Atahualpa was put on trial for polygamy, idolatry, and crimes against the crown and was sentenced to be burned at the stake. He reacted with horror at this news because he believed that such a fate would prevent his body from passing into the afterlife. He agreed to be baptized and was strangled with a garrote on July 26, 1533, in Cajamarca. The ransom, quickly hidden en route from Cuzco, has never been found.

The Conquest Is Completed

In November 1533, just four months after Atahualpa's death, Cuzco fell to Pizarro and the Inca empire was finished. The Spanish victors were welcomed as liberators by many indigenous groups, who had resented and fought against the yoke of the Incas. A few battles remained to be fought: In May 1534, Sebastián de Benalcázar (Pizarro's second in command) found himself facing 50,000 Inca warriors under the guidance of Rumiñahui, the greatest Inca general, who had deserted and burned Quito rather than surrender it to the invaders. Benalcázar, aided by Cañari soldiers, defeated "Stone Face," whose capture, torture, and execution signaled the end of organized indigenous military resistance.

By 1549, fewer than 2,000 Spanish soldiers had defeated an estimated 500,000 indigenous people. Although these numbers seem unbelievable, they can be explained by a combination of battle tactics, epidemiology, and luck. In the 16th century, Spanish soldiers were among the best in the world, almost invulnerable to attack from the ground when mounted on their war horses in full battle armor. A dozen mounted soldiers could hold off and even defeat hundreds of Inca foot soldiers. In addition, European diseases, to which the indigenous people had no immunity, killed them by the thousands.

The End of the Conquistador Era

Victory did little to dampen the Spanish conquerors' lust for power, and they quickly began fighting among themselves. In 1538, Diego de Almagro contested Pizarro's right to govern the new territory of Peru. He was defeated, tried, and sentenced to death in Lima, garroted in the same way as Atahualpa. Francisco Pizarro was stabbed to death in his palace in 1541 by the remaining members of Almagro's rebel army, led by his son.

The Spanish crown tried to restore order by imposing the New Laws of 1542, aimed at controlling the unruly conquistadores and ending the enslavement of the indigenous peoples, already a widespread practice. A new viceroy, Blasco Núñez Vela, was sent to oversee the budding colonies in 1544, but Gonzalo Pizarro (Francisco's brother) organized resistance and fought and killed Núñez in the battle of Añaquito near Quito in 1544. Pizarro, in

1: gold mask made by the La Tolita culture; 2: pre-Columbian pottery at the La Casa de Alabado

turn, was defeated by royal troops near Cuzco in 1548 and beheaded on the field of battle.

THE COLONIAL PERIOD

From 1544 to 1720, Ecuador existed as part of the Viceroyalty of Peru, one of the divisions of Spain's New World colonies. In 1563, Quito became a royal Audience of Spain, thus, permitting it to deal directly with Madrid on certain matters instead of going through the Viceroyalty in Lima. The territory of the Audience of Quito greatly exceeded that of present-day Ecuador, encompassing the north of present-day Peru, the city of Cali in the south of present-day Colombia, and much of the Amazon River Basin east of present-day Ecuador.

Farms and Slaves

As Spanish settlers replaced the conquistadores, and female immigrants evened the balance of the sexes, a new form of land tenure was born in the Sierra. The *encomienda* system gave settlers (*encomenderos)* the title to tracts of the best land, along with the right to demand tribute and labor from the indigenous people who lived there. In exchange, the *encomendero* agreed to defend the land and convert its inhabitants to Christianity. The Spanish crown strove to impose rules governing the treatment of the native Ecuadorians, but, in many cases, they were forced into virtual slavery, subjected to extreme punishment and death if they resisted. By the early 17th century, about 500 *encomenderos* controlled vast tracts of the Sierra, with around half of the population living on them. The rich volcanic earth of the Andean highlands bore bumper crops of wheat, corn, and potatoes, which thrived in the mild climate, along with cattle, horses, and sheep. Another important source of income for the Spanish in the Sierra was textile *obrajes* (workshops), where indigenous people were forced to weave from dawn to dusk, often chained to their looms in brutal conditions. The hacienda system was also introduced,

consisting of large privately owned estates, often owned by minor Spanish nobles. Local indigenous laborers were tied to the haciendas by various forms of debt peonage that continued well into the 20th century.

On the coast, the main crops were bananas, cacao, and sugarcane, though agriculture was hampered by rampant tropical diseases like malaria and yellow fever and a subsequent lack of natives to enslave. Instead, the coastal economy revolved around shipping and trade. Despite being destroyed by fire several times, Guayaquil became a thriving port city and the largest ship-building center on the west coast of South America.

In 1553, a ship en route from Panama to Peru ran aground off the Ecuadorian coast at Portete near Mompiche. The 23 African slaves on board rebelled and escaped into the forests. Despite clashes with local indigenous people, the region became a safe haven for escaped slaves and, by the end of the 16th century, the community had declared themselves to be a republic of *zambos* (curly-haired people). They lived autonomously for most of the colonial era, intermarrying with the local indigenous population and giving rise to today's population of Afro-Ecuadorians, who still mostly live in Esmeraldas province.

The Roman Catholic Church was a cornerstone of life during the colonial period for indigenous people and immigrants alike. By a majority vote, the Vatican had decided that indigenous people actually did have souls, making their conversion a worthwhile endeavor. A sweltering climate, impassable terrain, and fierce indigenous groups kept most settlers out of the Oriente except a few missionaries, many of whom were speared to death or ended up as shrunken heads.

INDEPENDENCE FROM SPAIN
First Sparks

During the colonial period, the Spanish stood at the top of the social ladder, whether they were born in Spain (known as *peninsulares*) or the New World (criollos). Mixed-blood mestizos were in the middle, keeping the urban machinery going as shopkeepers, craftspeople, and skilled laborers. This middle class, aspiring to wealth and status as they looked down on the native masses, was politically unstable and easily provoked by fiery rhetoric—a ready source of fuel for the spark of independence. Following the conquest, countless numbers of indigenous people had died of imported diseases like smallpox, measles, cholera, and syphilis, to which they had no natural immunity. Those that remained, numbering 750,000-1 million by the 16th century, made up most of colonial society and provided the forced labor.

Just as things had settled into a routine of oppression in the colonies, a series of events unfolded that would eventually shake the continent. From 1736 to 1745, the French mission to measure the shape of the earth at the equator spread ideas of rational science and personal liberty, courtesy of the Enlightenment. Revolutions in the United States (1776) and France (1789) set the stage for the wars of independence in South American countries.

In Ecuador, the physician and writer Eugenio Espejo was a liberal humanist who demanded freedom and a democratic government for the colonies. Hailed as one of the fathers of independence, Espejo was thrown in jail repeatedly and even exiled for his books and articles, before contracting dysentery in a Quito prison and dying in 1795. Across the country, uprisings among both indigenous people and mestizos protested their treatment at the hands of Spain.

The 18th century was a period of economic hardship in Spain, and thus its colonies. The wealthy were harder hit than the poor, resulting in the criollos joining the revolutionary movement. The final straw came in July 1808 when Napoléon invaded Spain, deposed King Ferdinand VII, and installed his brother Joseph Bonaparte on the throne. Monetary demands on the colonies—always a source of friction—skyrocketed as Spain sought funds to fight for the deposed Ferdinand, and the colonists decided enough was enough.

Early Uprisings

Resentful of the privileges afforded to the peninsulares, on August 10, 1809, a group of elite criollos jailed the president of the Audience of Quito and seized power, but the coup was short-lived and brutally quelled. In the decade that followed, the criollo population unsuccessfully tried several times to take control of the Audience of Quito.

The Battle for Independence

Simón Bolívar's success in Bogota inspired the faltering independence struggle in Ecuador. In 1820, a junta in Guayaquil under the leadership of poet José Joaquín Olmedo declared Ecuador's independence from its colonial master. Unlike in earlier independence attempts, Olmedo appealed for outside assistance, asking Simón Bolívar and his Argentinian counterpart, José de San Martín, for support. In response, Bolívar sent his best general, Antonio José de Sucre, at the head of an army. The combined Ecuadorian and foreign forces won a number of successive victories against the Spanish before finally being stopped in Ambato. In the nick of time, San Martín's reinforcements arrived and Sucre's army went on the offensive again, heading for Quito via an arduous climb over the Pichinchas. On the muddy slopes of the volcano, within sight of the capital, they fought the largest Spanish force in Ecuador. After three hours and 600 lives lost, Sucre's army prevailed and the Audience of Quito formally surrendered. The Battle of Pichincha was the decisive victory that forever drove the Spanish from Ecuador.

Simón Bolívar arrived in Quito three weeks later and arranged his famous meeting with José de San Martín in Guayaquil on July 26, 1822, commemorated with a monument on

El Libertador

Revered and despised, **Simón Bolívar** embodied all the contradictions of the continent he helped free from Spain. Whether as the heroic liberator of South America or the tyrannical despot chasing an impossible vision of continental unity, Bolívar is considered by many as the most important figure in Latin American history. At his death, his dream remained only half fulfilled: He had freed his beloved land, but he couldn't unify it.

Born in Caracas on July 24, 1783, to a wealthy family of planters, Simón Antonio de la Santísima Trinidad Bolívar y Palacios saw both his parents die before his 10th birthday. Relatives and friends helped raise him in the cultured circles of the New World's upper class. His early teenage years were spent in military school, where his records reveal innate martial talent. His studies continued in Europe, and his attention was soon captured by the rising star Napoléon Bonaparte, who had just crowned himself emperor of France for life. As he soaked up the rhetoric of Rousseau and Voltaire, advocating the sacred duty of a monarch to protect the common man by means of the law, Bolívar was solidifying his own ideas for South America. He came to believe that the best way to organize the struggling republics would be through a strongly centralized, even dictatorial government. At the helm would preside a lifetime ruler with limitless power who would labor for the greatest good—a "moralistic monarch."

When Bolívar returned to Venezuela in 1807, he found a population divided between loyalty to Spain and independence. When Napoléon invaded Spain in 1808, many Venezuelans felt that they no longer owed allegiance to Spain. Bolívar was an important advocate for independence during this time, and indeed, on July 5, 1811, the First Venezuelan Republic voted for full independence. The Spanish quickly regained control, however.

Bolívar, defeated, went into exile, heading to New Granada (now Colombia) to become an officer in the growing independence movement there. With 200 men, he aggressively attacked all Spanish forces in the area, and his prestige and army grew. By the beginning of 1813, he was ready to lead a sizable army into Venezuela and rode victoriously into Caracas, quickly establishing the Second Venezuelan Republic. The people named him El Libertador (The Liberator) and made him leader of the new nation.

the city's waterfront. It was decided there that Bolívar would lead the charge into Peru, the last Spanish stronghold on the continent. Bolívar and Sucre's subsequent victories at the Battle of Junín and the Battle of Ayacucho sealed South America's independence. Spain was beaten and withdrew its administrative apparatus from the Americas.

For eight years, Bolívar ruled over what was then known as Colombia, encompassing the present-day nations of Bolivia, Peru, Ecuador, Colombia, Venezuela, and Panama. His grand plan for a united South America soon succumbed to regional rivalries, and he resigned as leader April 1830. In August of that year, Ecuador withdrew from Colombia and became fully independent. A constituent assembly drew up a constitution for the State of Ecuador, thus named for its proximity to the equator. A general, Juan José Flores, was put in charge of political and military affairs.

EARLY YEARS OF THE REPUBLIC

Ecuador's childhood as a nation was marked by power struggles among *criollo* elites, in particular aristocratic conservatives from Quito and free-enterprise liberals from Guayaquil. Meanwhile, the new republic had little effect on most of the country—the poor, in other words, stayed poor.

Juan José Flores ruled ruthlessly 1830-1845, either directly as president or through puppet figures, until widespread discontent forced him to flee the country. Between 1845 and 1860, 11 governments and three constitutions came and went, as the economy stagnated and the military's influence in politics

Spain struck back, occupying Caracas in 1814, and Bolívar went into exile once again. When he returned, he found Venezuela devastated by fighting between pro-independence and royalist forces. He turned his sights to Bogota, where he planned on destroying the Spanish base of power in northern South America. After an arduous two-month crossing of the Andes, Bolívar and his army marched into Bogota in 1819, winning the battle of Boyaca en route. After that, it was only a matter of time before the remaining Spanish forces in New Granada and Venezuela were defeated. On June 24, 1821, Bolívar crushed the last major royalist force in Venezuela and declared the birth of a new republic: Colombia, which would include the lands of Venezuela, New Granada, and present-day Ecuador, with himself as president. After driving the Spanish out of present-day Ecuador and Peru, the nation of Bolivia was created and named after him. Bolívar now ruled over the present-day nations of Bolivia, Peru, Ecuador, Colombia, Venezuela, and Panama. It was his dream to unite them all, creating one unified nation, but it was not to be.

It was in peace that the newly freed nations would disappoint him, and his noble-minded revolution soon dissolved into a bloody struggle between disparate factions. In a last-ditch attempt to reconcile the warring populations, Bolívar organized a peace congress in Panama in 1826. Only four countries showed up.

Bolívar became depressed by his failure to build a united continent, and in April 1830 he resigned as leader of Colombia, declaring: "America is ungovernable; all who served the revolution have plowed the sea." He planned to go into exile but lost his final battle, with tuberculosis, at age 47 on December 17, 1830. He never answered the question of whether a South America unified under a monarch would have prospered, or if he simply would have recreated in the New World the system he fought to dispel. Shortly before he died, the fiery general seethed with bitterness at what he saw as the betrayal of his dream: "There is no good faith in America, nor among the nations of America. Treaties are scraps of paper; constitutions, printed matter; elections, battles; freedom, anarchy." Even on his deathbed, though, his thoughts were full of hope for his beloved federation: "Colombians! My last wishes are for the happiness of our native land."

grew. By 1860 the country was on the brink of chaos, split by provincial rivalries and tension over border disputes with Peru and Colombia.

Theocracy and Conservatism

In 1860 a new player rose to the top. Gabriel García Moreno so much embodied devout Sierra conservatism that some historians have dubbed his regime a theocracy. He grew up during the chaos of the preceding decades and was determined to impose religious and political order on Ecuador.

Conservatives loved him, seeing him as a great "nation-builder" who saved Ecuador from falling into chaos. Under his iron rule, the economy improved and corruption was dramatically decreased. An improved education system now accepted women and *indigenous people, and* new roads, hospitals, and railroads were built (often using forced indigenous labor). Deeply religious, García Moreno established Roman Catholicism as the official state religion, with membership a prerequisite for citizenship and voting. Free speech was tightly controlled and political opposition squashed.

Not surprisingly, García Moreno's firm stance made him many enemies among liberals, who dubbed him a ruthless tyrant. In 1875, after being elected to a third term, he was hacked to death on the steps of the presidential palace. His last words were reportedly "God doesn't die."

INTO THE 20TH CENTURY
Secularism and Liberalism

Two decades of jousting between the Liberal and Conservative Parties ended with the ascension to power of General Eloy Alfaro. Both his terms as president, 1897-1901 and 1906-1911, started with armed coups. Credited with separating church from state, Alfaro embodied the Radical Liberal Party as much as García Moreno typified conservatism. He toppled the Catholic Church from its domination by seizing church lands, instituting freedom of religion, secularizing marriage and education, and legalizing divorce. Civil rights, such freedom of speech and the rights of workers and indigenous Ecuadorians, were expanded, with native slaves being freed from haciendas. He also completed the Quito-Guayaquil railroad and rode triumphantly aboard it in 1908. However, as with García Moreno, Alfaro made many enemies and became a hated figure for conservatives. He lost power in a coup in 1911 and was exiled. Upon re-entering the country and attempting another coup, he was arrested and brought to Quito. An angry mob broke into the prison where he was held and shot him dead, dragging his body through the streets and burning it in Parque El Ejido. It was a barbaric end for the "old warrior," who is considered the hero of Ecuador's liberal revolution. There is a museum dedicated to Eloy Alfaro in Montecristi, his birthplace.

Following Eloy Alfaro's death until 1925, a number of Liberal presidents took power, including his bitter party rival General Leónidas Plaza Gutiérrez. During this second half of the Liberal rule, however, the power was really held by a plutocracy of agricultural and banking interests. According to Ecuadorian historian Oscar Efrén Reyes, the Commercial & Agricultural Bank of Guayaquil was so powerful that presidential and ministerial candidates had to seek its approval before running for office.

Crisis and War

In 1926, the Ecuadorian Socialist Party (PSE) welcomed indigenous activists to its 1926 congress. At the time, Sierran indigenous communities were engaged in land struggles with haciendas, demanding better conditions and salaries for sharecroppers (*huasipungueros*) who, in exchange for a plot of land, were required to provide labor to hacienda owners; their wives were also obliged to work as domestic servants. A number of indigenous activists considered their efforts to be part of a broader class struggle and joined forces with the nascent PSE.

That same year, Isidro Ayora was elected as president. He restructured fiscal and monetary institutions, bringing a prosperous half decade that saw the establishment of several social agencies and progressive social programs. His skillful financial management couldn't survive the 1929 Great Depression, however, putting an end to his presidency. The 1930s saw another 13 presidents come and go, including José María Velasco Ibarra, who said, "Give me a balcony, and I will become president." The first leader to appeal to both liberals and conservatives, he was elected a total of five times between 1934 and 1961, though was overthrown from four of his five terms.

The border between Ecuador and Peru, outlined only roughly by the colonial Audience of Quito, had been a bone of contention since Ecuador became a country. Boundary talks broke down into skirmishes, and in 1941 Peru took advantage of the rest of the world's focus on World War II by seizing Ecuador's southern and easternmost provinces. Fearing a coup, President Carlos Alberto Arroyo del Río kept the best troops in Quito during the border fighting, and the Ecuadorians were easily defeated. In 1942, Peru and Ecuador signed the Protocol of Peace, Friendship, and Boundaries, also known as the Río Protocol, overseen by the United States, Chile, Argentina, and Brazil. Not only did Ecuador have to sign away more than 200,000 square kilometers (75,000 sq mi) of territory to its neighbor, but it also lost the Amazon River port of Iquitos, its main river access to the Atlantic. Ecuador continued to dispute the Río Protocol, and the border between the two countries was militarized. Running through the ancestral lands of the Siekopai people, it divided communities and families.

Between and 1920s and 1940s, indigenous communities started to collaborate, regionally consolidating their struggles against agrarian capitalism and organizing several protest marches against forced hacienda labor that converged on Quito. The fledging indigenous movement was supported by the PSE, which included demands for expropriation of hacienda lands in their general platform; raised funds for local indigenous causes; publicized their struggles in the socialist press; provided logistical support for the 1931 First Congress of Peasant Organizations; and assisted indigenous organizations in presenting demands to the government. In return, socialist candidates received electoral support from indigenous organizations. In 1944, the Federación Ecuatoriana de Indios (FEI, Ecuadorian Federation of Indians) was founded, representing the first successful attempt to establish a national organization by and for indigenous peoples.

Postwar Ecuador: Instability and Military Rule

Ecuador sided with the Allies in World War II, during which the United States built a naval base in the Galápagos and tried to remove all German settlers from the archipelago. After the war, Ecuador enjoyed a decade of relative political stability and prosperity, despite a massive earthquake that completely destroyed the city of Ambato and the surrounding villages in 1949. Even old Velasco Ibarra was finally able to finish a full term—his third—in 1952. When a wave of disease ravaged Central America's banana crop, Ecuador stepped in to supply the huge U.S. demand with the help of the United Fruit Company. Exports jumped from $2 million in 1948 to $20 million in 1952, and Ecuador's position as world banana king became official.

By the late 1950s, however, the banana boom was over and political chaos returned. Velasco Ibarra, who was re-elected in 1960, began a proud Ecuadorian political tradition by renouncing the Río Protocol in his inaugural address, to the delight of the crowd.

His left-leaning policies proved ill-timed, however, coming at the height of the Cold War. A gunfight in the congressional chamber proved how bad things had become at the top. In November 1961, the military removed Velasco Ibarra from power; two years later replaced his successor with a four-man junta.

Ecuador's first experiment with outright military rule was short-lived, barely managing to pass the well-intentioned but ultimately ineffectual Agrarian Reform Law of 1964. Though land distribution was minimal, the new law did end the brutal *huasipungo* system of forced indigenous labor on haciendas. After flourishing for two decades, the Ecuadorian Federation of Indians started to decline after achieving this key aim. Instead, new indigenous organizations surfaced that focused on defending their culture, religion, medicine, and bilingual education. The first significant of these was the Shuar Federation, formed in the early 1960s, followed by the Federación Nacional de Organizaciones Campesinas (FENOC, National Federation of Peasant Organizations) and Ecuarunari (Confederation of Kichwa Peoples of Ecuador). The latter represents Sierra Kichwas, and the name is a shortened version of a phrase meaning "to awaken the Ecuadorian Indians."

After the military government succumbed to concerns over another economic slump, Velasco Ibarra was re-elected in 1968 for the fifth time with barely a third of the popular vote. For two years he enjoyed military support as he dismissed Congress and the Supreme Court, suspended the constitution, and dictated harsh and unpopular economic measures, before being once again overthrown by the military in 1972.

A few years earlier, it had been discovered that Ecuador had the third-largest petroleum reserves in Latin America. In 1972, the military government paraded the first barrel of oil through the streets of Quito, extracted from the jungle by a consortium between Texaco and the fledgling state oil company, and hailed as the answer to Ecuador's economic woes. The junta instituted a firm strategy of modernization and industrialization. While the middle class grew in numbers and power, further attempts at land reform met the stone wall of the landholding elite. Not surprisingly, the poor and indigenous suffered from the oil-boom inflation and environmental devastation without reaping the attendant benefits.

The Return to Democracy

Coups in 1975 and 1976 caused splits within the military, and they sought to return Ecuador to civilian rule. In January 1978 a national referendum voted for a new constitution, universal suffrage, and guaranteed civil rights. The following year, highly popular and charismatic left-winger Jaime Roldós Aguilera took office in a landslide election victory. During an era of military dictatorships throughout Latin America, he embodied the hope for change. He found himself at the wheel of a country unfamiliar with democracy, but with a government budget increased more than 500 percent by the oil windfall. Roldós's center-left government began programs of improving rural literacy and housing. He championed human rights, formed a friendship with the Sandinista government in Nicaragua, challenged the oil contracts negotiated with foreign companies, and turned down an invitation to Ronald Reagan's inauguration. In May 1981, shortly after presenting a draft reform of the hydrocarbons law in favor of national interests, Roldós and his wife were killed in a mysterious plane crash, which has never been properly investigated by the authorities. Left-wing Panamanian leader Omar Torrijos died in a similar incident a few months later. Both leaders had failed to toe the U.S. line, and a common view is that they were assassinated by the CIA. You can read about these theories in John Perkins's 2004 book *Confessions of an Economic Hitman*. An excellent documentary, *La Muerte de Roldós* by Manolo Sarmiento, also examines Roldós's life and tragic death.

In 1980, the Shuar Federation joined other organizations to form the Confederación de Nacionalidades Indígenas de la Amazonía Ecuatoriana (CONFENIAE, Confederation of Indigenous Nationalities of the Ecuadorian Amazon) to battle for the common interests of all Amazon communities, including the lowland Kichwa, Shuar, Achuar, Siona, Secoya, Kofán, and Waorani.

The early 1980s brought a succession of crises. Border fighting with Peru flared up and the disastrous 1982-1983 El Niño climate pattern caused enormous drought and flood damage, ruining rice and banana crops along the coast. Sudden declines in petroleum reserves left the country with a foreign debt of $7 billion by 1983, when inflation hit an all-time high of 52.5 percent.

Conservative León Febres Cordero defeated eight other candidates to win the presidency in 1984. A neoliberal, Febres Cordero favored a pro-U.S. foreign policy, free market economic policies, and strong-arm tactics that led to accusations of human rights abuses. In January 1987, Cordero was kidnapped by air force troops under orders from an imprisoned mutinous general. Only by granting them general amnesty was the president able to secure his own release after 11 hours in captivity, a move widely perceived as cowardly by Ecuadorians. That same month, an earthquake in Napo Province killed hundreds and ruptured the all-important oil pipeline, causing Ecuador to suspend interest payments on its $8.3 billion foreign debt.

In 1986, CONFENIAE joined Ecuarunari in the highlands to form the Confederación de Nacionalidades Indígenas del Ecuador (CONAIE, Confederation of Indigenous Nationalities of Ecuador) to combine all indigenous peoples into one national pan-indigenous movement. CONAIE's central and most controversial demand was to revise the constitution to recognize the plurinational character of Ecuador. Other fundamental objectives were to consolidate the indigenous peoples and nationalities of Ecuador; to defend indigenous territories; to fight for bilingual education (in their native tongues and Spanish); to combat the oppression of civil and ecclesiastical authorities; to protect the cultural identity of indigenous peoples against colonialism; and to uphold the dignity of indigenous peoples and nationalities.

In 1988, social democrat Rodrigo Borja Cevallos won the presidency and introduced reforms, including a literacy program and legislation to protect civil liberties.

In 1990, indigenous peoples led by CONAIE organized the largest ever uprising in the country's history, frustrated by stalled talks with the government over the recognition of Ecuador as a plurinational state, land reforms, and other issues. The protests blocked roads, cut off the food supply to the cities, and effectively shut down the country for a week. In 500 years of struggle, it was the first time the indigenous movement had articulated itself nationally, and it rocked Ecuador's white and mestizo power base. President Borja Cevallos agreed to meet with CONAIE to negotiate and, while the talks failed to meet the key demands, bilingual education was restored and an Indigenous Affairs Office established. Ecuador's indigenous movement had established itself as a force to be reckoned with. Over the next couple of decades, it would become one of the strongest on the continent, due to its ability to mobilize and inclusion of a diverse range of ethnic groups.

Ecuadorian voters swung back to the right in 1992, electing Christian Socialist Sixto Durán Ballén as president. Harsh austerity measures were masterminded by vice president Alberto Dahik, who fled to Costa Rica in a private plane, accused of embezzling millions of dollars in state funds. A government cover-up, which involved the seizure of Central Bank vaults that held incriminating microfilm, led to the resignation of ministers and the impeachment of one Supreme Court judge.

In 1992, two thousand Kichwa, Shuar, and Achuar peoples embarked upon a 385-kilometer (240-mi) march from the Amazon to Quito to demand legalization of land holdings. Two years later, indigenous organizations again organized a "Mobilization for Life" campaign in protest of an agricultural reform law that would allow communal land to be divided and sold, jeopardizing indigenous territories. Protests were prolonged and violent, with 15 of the 21 major transport arteries closed. In response, the law was reformed in consultation with CONAIE.

The political turmoil was compounded when tensions with Peru erupted into outright war in January 1995. During six weeks of combat near the headwaters of Río Cenepa, elite units of Shuar soldiers distinguished themselves, enabling Ecuador to claim victory.

After a decade of rejecting politics, in 1995 CONAIE made a U-turn and helped form a political movement, Pachakutik, in coalition with non-indigenous social movements. Identifying itself as part of a new Latin American left, the party opposed the government's neoliberal economic policies and favored a more inclusive and participatory political system. In both the 1996 and 1998 elections Pachakutik candidates won seats at all levels of government, from town councils to Congress.

El Loco

Desperate times led the voters to desperate choices. In 1996, the same year Jefferson Pérez became Ecuador's first-ever Olympic medalist by winning gold for speed walking, Abdalá Bucaram became president. The grandson of a Lebanese immigrant, he had carved out a successful political career as founder of the Partido Roldista Ecuatoriano (PRE), named after his brother-in-law Jaime Roldós. Bucaram had been mayor of Guayaquil and built a reputation for his eccentric style and rousing speeches. His nickname was "El Loco" (The Crazy One), and he was an energetic campaigner who often used to sing at political gatherings. He was seen as a political outsider, an image that he exploited to perfection, marketing himself as the people's hero who would lead them out of poverty.

From the start, it was clear that El Loco wasn't firing on all cylinders. His inaugural address was described as a two-hour "hysterical diatribe." One day he was raising money for charity by shaving his mustache on live TV; the next he was having lunch with Ecuadorian American Lorena Bobbitt, who infamously cut off her husband's penis in 1993. The president released an album titled *A Madman in Love* and crooned at beauty contests. More importantly, he outraged his supporters by introducing austerity measures that led to skyrocketing utility bills, and he was accused of large-scale corruption. A general protest strike paralyzed the country, with an estimated 3 million indigenous people participating, and on February 6, Congress determined that he was unfit to govern on grounds of mental incapacity. Bucaram holed up in the presidential palace for days before finally fleeing to exile in Panama, allegedly with suitcases filled with public money, a mere six months after taking power.

Vice President Rosalía Arteaga became Ecuador's first woman president for two days before the male-dominated Congress re-wrote the constitution to allow the president of the Congress, Fabián Alarcón, to be installed. He repealed the austerity measures and muddled through for another year or so until another election was called.

INTO THE 21ST CENTURY
Economic Crises and Dollarization

After the pantomime of Bucaram's brief presidency, Ecuadorians thought that things couldn't get much worse, but how wrong they were. A second El Niño hit the country in 1998, washing out roads, devastating the country's farming and fishing industries, and killing off wildlife in the Galápagos. In August, an earthquake of magnitude 7.1 hit near Bahía de Caráquez, knocking out water and electricity supplies and even more roads.

It was a good year for the indigenous movement, however, when the new 1998 constitution finally recognized Ecuador as a multicultural and multiethnic nation. After the Texaco lawsuit and several other instances of

oil drilling on indigenous territories without their permission, it also decreed that communities must give consent before any project is carried out on their land. The government almost immediately violated this last right, as successive regimes have continued to do, by selling two blocks of Achar, Kichwa, and Shuar lands to an oil company without their consent.

The new constitution came into effect on the same day as the new president, former Quito mayor and Harvard graduate Jamil Mahuad, came to power. Things began well when Mahuad finally laid to rest the longstanding border dispute with Peru. Indigenous Siekoya communities and families who had been divided by the militarized border were reunited after 50 years. However, the rising cost of El Niño, depressed oil prices, and plummeting confidence of foreign investors led to Ecuador's worst economic crisis in modern times. The country's currency, the sucre, fell dramatically, the economy shrank by more than 7 percent, and inflation rocketed to 60 percent. Mahuad pressed ahead with deeply unpopular economic austerity measures, and in a disastrous decision, froze more than $3 billion of bank deposits, preventing millions of Ecuadorians from making withdrawals. Worse news came when Ecuador became the first country to default on its Brady bonds. Filanbanco, the country's largest bank, then folded, taking $1.2 billion in public funds with it. Mahuad's last-ditch policy was to adopt the U.S. dollar as Ecuador's official currency, causing massive unrest.

Mahuad likened the situation to the sinking of the *Titanic* in a state-of-the-nation speech. Widespread protests ensured that the captain went down with the ship, including roadblocks by CONAIE and a coalition of indigenous groups. On January 21, 2000, a thousand protesters, mostly indigenous, burst through a military cordon and rushed the National Congress building. Some of the soldiers who had previously placed barbed wire around the building had stepped aside, indicating that a faction of the military had shifted allegiance. By mid-morning, the rainbow-colored flag of the indigenous movement was hanging from the roof of Congress. The protesters proceeded inaugurate their own National Peoples' Parliament, joined by a high-ranking army colonel and about 200 army officials. A short time later, a three-member junta was declared, composed of Army colonel Lucio Gutiérrez, a former Supreme Court judge, and the president of CONAIE, Antonio Vargas (marking a key moment in the indigenous movement). Later that afternoon, Mahuad was informed that the security of the presidential palace could no longer be guaranteed, forcing him to flee. The rebellion was short-lived, however, as Colonel Gutiérrez lacked the confidence of the military high command. He was replaced in the junta by General Carlos Mendoza, the armed forces chief of staff, who announced that Vice President Gustavo Noboa would assume the presidency.

Noboa pressed ahead with the dollarization plan and introduced austerity measures to obtain $2 billion in aid from the International Monetary Fund. By 2001, the economy had begun to stabilize, but by then 500,000 Ecuadorians had already emigrated to North America and Europe.

In 2002, Colonel Lucio Gutiérrez was elected president. His campaign painted him as a friend of the downtrodden, and his ascent was seen as part of a general leftward political shift in Latin America, but it didn't last long. As soon as he got into power, Gutiérrez's policies moved markedly to the right. He dropped his early opposition to the adoption of the U.S. dollar, befriended U.S. president George Bush, and introduced austerity measures to finance the country's massive debt. He then filled Supreme Court positions with political allies and announced plans to allow his old ally Abdalá Bucaram to return, prompting massive public demonstrations. After being ousted by the National Congress and losing the support of the army in April 2005, Gutiérrez was forced to flee in fear for his life, leaving by helicopter from the roof of the presidential palace in Quito. On the positive side, the country's economy grew by 7 percent in 2004, in part due to higher oil prices.

Rafael Correa and 21st-Century Socialism

Alfredo Palacio took over from Gutiérrez and managed the country until the next election in 2006, when a new figure burst on to the political scene. A young economist, Rafael Correa, appeared during a time of political vacuum, founding a new party, Alianza Pais. He exploited perfectly the anti-elite feeling of the time, raising anti-establishment banners and reviving leftist narratives based on social justice. He reached out directly to indigenous and environmental movements, wearing a poncho, speaking Kichwa, and promising to "create a country where humans could live as part of nature, not as its principal destroyer."

Correa took office in January 2007 and, true to his election campaign promise, quickly pushed through a referendum to replace Congress with a constituent assembly, tasked with drafting a new constitution. The 2008 constitution was the first in the world to grant legal rights to nature and to define water as a human right. Controversially, it also substantially consolidated executive powers to levels never experienced before in Ecuador.

Within his first months in office, Correa transferred control over the public oil corporation, PetroEcuador to the military. Vowing to end "the long dark night of neoliberalism," he closed the U.S. military base in Manta and declared the World Bank representative "persona non grata." The rhetoric against U.S. imperialism, however, gave way to a new wave of Chinese investments, as Correa negotiated a series of billion dollar loans and megaprojects in preserved areas. With record oil profits, his government enjoyed the biggest economic boom in Ecuador's history. In what Correa termed the "Citizen's Revolution," the administration oversaw the construction of highways, hospitals, schools, hydroelectric dams and other mega infrastructure projects. Access to public education and health care improved, while poverty, infant mortality and illiteracy rates fell. Correa was riding high, in 2009 becoming the first Ecuadorian president in 30 years to be re-elected, finally bringing some political stability to the country.

Cracks soon started to show, with allegations of financial irregularities in government construction projects. The much-touted new roads turned out to be among the most expensive in the world, with the price per kilometer over 15 times what it would cost in Germany. The Anti-Corruption Commission denounced the lack of accountability when the Manduriacu dam project came in US$102 million over budget, 82% higher than the contract. This overpricing became a characteristic of Citizen Revolution projects, with little transparency over the missing money. In early 2019, an audit commissioned by the UN announced that roughly half of the $5 billion the state had paid for oil-related infrastructure projects over the previous decade was lost to corruption.

In 2012, international oil companies were invited to bid for 3 million hectares of largely virgin rainforest in the southern Amazon in an auction known as the Ronda Sur. After his 2013 re-election, Correa announced plans to drill for oil in the Yasuní National Park,

a UNESCO World Biosphere Reserve. He passed a draconian decree regulating rights of association, allowing the government to control NGOs. He used this legislation to shut down the National Teachers Union and one of the country's most prominent organizations, the Pachamama Foundation, which had been active in efforts to preserve the Amazon.

While the government positioned itself in the international media as a champion of free speech by offering asylum to Julian Assange in 2012, at home it implemented the most repressive media legislation in Latin America. In 2013, Congress passed a law granting broad powers to regulate, censor and prosecute the country's news outlets. Correa branded the private media his "biggest enemy" and used his weekly public address to name and threaten journalists, activists and opponents. Several journalists received death threats, sometimes in deliveries of flowers. What set Correa-ism apart from prior authoritarian regimes was a world class marketing department that proactively defined Ecuador's brand. Public relations and marketing were the biggest ministerial expenditures, used to generate a smokescreen behind which the government could largely implement its own agenda. Nonetheless, public discontent

a 2014 indigenous march protesting mega-mining in community water sources

started to build. Protests against Correa's environmental policies, attacks on freedom of expression and labor laws were met with brutal police force.

By 2015, the oil boom was over and the country was in economic crisis. That August, Correa was faced with the most widespread and vociferous civil unrest of his time in office, sparked by a proposed package of 16 constitutional amendments. Confirming his increasingly dictatorial style, the most controversial of these allowed the indefinite re-election of the President and other government officials. These protests were inconveniently timed, coming just ahead of the Pope's state visit. The Cotopaxi volcano chose that moment to erupt and the government declared a State of Emergency, not just in the affected province but nationwide. Under cover of the decree, the military and police brutally quelled protests across the country, with multiple arrests and injuries. Homes were raided in the indigenous community of Saraguro, over 500 kilometers from the volcano. Despite the protests, and polls indicating that 82% of the people wanted the constitutional changes decided by a referendum, the amendments were pushed through by the National Assembly, where the ruling party had an absolute majority. Though a provision was adopted to prevent Correa from running in the 2017 election, many expected him to install a puppet leader for the following term and then return to power.

In line with the fall of 21st century socialism across Latin America, Correa's reign ended in authoritarianism and widespread allegations of corruption and financial mismanagement. Although his government cannot be compared to the violence of military regimes like Pinochet's, it was nonetheless a totalitarian regime that criminalized almost one thousand journalists, dissident politicians, indigenous authorities, and social activists over its decade in power. Correa's major legacy is the largest licensing of land for extractive industries in the history of Ecuador, not just for oil exploitation but also mega-mining,

much of it in indigenous territory. This has increased Ecuador's dependency on the export of raw commodities, especially oil. It also led nature defenders to redefine Correa's regime as neither right or left wing, but extractivist.

Moreno and the Return of Neoliberalism

Lenín Moreno, who served as Correa's Vice President from 2007 to 2013, was nominated to run as his successor in the 2017 election, with center-right banker Guillermo Lasso his major contender. With Moreno promising a continuation of Correa-ism, many normally left-leaning Ecuadorian civil society groups, indigenous organizations, academics, activists and NGOs united behind Lasso. After Moreno narrowly won in a contentious second round, Lasso contested the results, providing evidence of election fraud. Nevertheless, Moreno assumed office on 24 May 2017, becoming the world's only currently serving head of state to use a wheelchair, after being shot in a 1998 robbery attempt.

Once in office, Moreno unexpectedly broke with Correa-ism by pardoning several indigenous activists who had been jailed for their involvement in protests in 2015. Through a referendum, he reversed several key pieces of legislation passed by the previous administration, most notably the constitutional amendment allowing indefinite reelection, thereby blocking his predecessor from returning to power. He allowed the prosecution of Vice President Jorge Glas (a loyal Correa-ist), who was sentenced to six years in prison for pocketing $13.5 million in bribes, part of the Odebrecht scandal that engulfed the continent. Moreno, branded a traitor by Correa, was sacked from the Alianza País party, but continued as head of state.

In sharp contrast to Correa's fiery, divisive rhetoric, Moreno adopted a conciliatory style, easing pressure on the media and advocating engagement with civil society. However, Ecuador remains a dangerous place for nature defenders, with several being threatened and attacked in 2018. Crucially, Moreno is also accelerating Correa's extractivist policies. The referendum that ended indefinite re-election also included proposals to decrease oil drilling in the Yasuní National Park and to ban metal mining in protected areas. Although both received nearly 70 percent public support, it appears that the Moreno administration is doing exactly the opposite, expanding drilling in Yasuní and licensing more protected areas to mining. In 2018, he appointed a former oil executive to head the Ministry of the Environment, indicating the priority given to extractive investments.

Moreno's government marks a rupture with the "pink tide" of 21st Century Socialism that swept across Latin America. While Ecuador has not joined those countries that have elected far right leaders in the backlash, it appears that Moreno is moving the country back towards neo-liberalism. During a June 2018 visit by U.S. Vice President Mike Pence, the two leaders agreed to improve U.S.-Ecuador relations, which had been strained under Correa. They announced a joint security effort, with Ecuador buying weapons, radar, helicopters and other military equipment. According to Defense Minister Oswaldo Jarrin, co-operation will include training and intelligence sharing. In a further sign of a closer relationship with the U.S., Moreno has taken a much harsher stance towards Julian Assange than his predecessor. He has reached a financing agreement with the World Bank and has met with the IMF, as well as continuing Correa's pattern of borrowing from China.

Shortly after coming to power, Moreno was forced to admit that the public debt was over twice the $28 billion admitted by Correa at the end of his tenure, at nearly $58 billion. In 2018, a criminal investigation was opened against Correa and other officials for concealing the extent of the debt. Correa is also being investigated for ordering the 2012 kidnapping of political opponent Fernando Balda in 2012 and is currently a fugitive from justice after ignoring an injunction to appear in Quito every two weeks as a preventative measure. The judge has requested Interpol to capture the former president, who has applied for asylum in Belgium, where he has lived since the end of his presidency.

Government and Economy

POLITICS

The Republic of Ecuador is a representative democracy with compulsory suffrage for all literate persons aged 18-65, optional for all other citizens. There are three main branches of government: executive, legislative, and judicial. The executive branch is made up of the president and vice president, 28 ministers, provincial governors, and councilors. The legislative branch, the National Assembly, is responsible for passing laws and consists of 130 assemblypersons representing the country's 24 provinces. The president and assemblypersons may be re-elected once and serve a four-year term. The president must be elected by at least a 50 percent majority, frequently leading to runoff elections. The judicial branch is made up of the National Court of Justice, provincial courts, and lower courts.

Added to these are the electoral branch, which organizes, conducts, and controls elections and referendums; and the Transparency and Social Control branch, which combats corruption and promotes accountability via overseers such as the comptroller general and the ombudsman.

Twenty-four *provincias* (provinces) are ruled by governors who oversee 219 *cantones* (counties) and around 1,000 *parroquias* (parishes). There are also around 2,000 *comunas*, like mini municipalities that are governed by their own laws and regulations, with communally owned territories.

Ecuador's tumultuous political history is

characterized by instability, corruption, and inequality. Since independence from Spain in 1822, there have been nearly 90 changes of power and almost 20 constitutions. Less than a quarter of those governments came to power as a result of a democratic election, and many regimes have been toppled by the military or mass civilian protest. Without the opportunity to mature, any well-intentioned governmental institutions have been unable to address Ecuador's constantly re-emerging problems. The economy is also in constant flux due to its dependence on a few export commodities, such as oil. The vast majority of the nation's wealth sits in the hands of a very few, with a highly inequitable economic and social structure that has existed since the colonial era. Due to large-scale corruption, any periods of economic boom tend to further enrich the wealthy, while more than half of the country's population hovers at or below the poverty level.

While Correa brought a decade of relative political stability to Ecuador, he did so by concentrating all state powers. Any party or candidate that opposed his government was forced to confront all the state apparatus, making it very difficult for a credible opposition to exist. Of the 137 seats in the National Assembly, 74 are held by Alianza Pais and pro-government independents. Only two other parties hold more than 10 seats, both center-right: CREO, founded in 2012 by former presidential candidate Guillermo Lasso, holds 32 seats, and the long-standing right-wing Social Christian Party, has 15. Pachakutik, a coalition of indigenous and social movements, holds 4 seats.

ECONOMY

Ecuador is substantially dependent on its petroleum resources, which have accounted for more than half the country's export earnings and approximately 25 percent of public sector revenues in recent years. Frozen shrimp have overtaken bananas as the country's second largest export earner after petroleum. Ecuador is still the largest banana exporter in the world, exporting more than twice its closest competitors, the Philippines and Costa Rica. The cut flower industry, especially roses, has grown substantially, with the country now occupying third place in the world after the Netherlands and Colombia. Cacao is another key export.

According to government statistics, the monthly cost of basic food for a family (known as la canasta básica) stood at over $700 in 2018, while the average monthly income is $437 and the minimum wage just $386 ($11/day). Unemployment may be relatively low at 4.6 percent, but this doesn't tell the whole story. Informal craftspeople and vendors make up close to 40 percent of the workforce, and the real problems are precarious employment, underemployment, and low pay. The poverty rate fell from 49.9 percent in 2003 to 21.5 percent in 2017, with 9.4 percent of people living on less than $3.20 a day. Indigenous peoples are much more likely to experience poverty, with 63 percent impoverished.

In the two years after Ecuador began to export petroleum in 1971, government income quadrupled. However, the initial bonanza was relatively short-lived, and just five years after production began, a flood of foreign borrowing was needed to sustain economic growth. Ecuador has been able to secure large loans for its size because of its oil reserves and has accumulated a staggering foreign debt. At the same time, the benefits of oil development have not been well distributed. Ecuador's wealth is concentrated with a few people at the top of the social ladder with little trickling down to the rest. Furthermore, oil development has accentuated Ecuador's dependence on export markets and foreign investment, technology, and expertise rather than providing the answer to its economic difficulties.

After the devastating economic crisis of 1999-2000 the economy recovered well in the early 2000s, with GDP growth peaking at 7.9 percent in 2011. Rafael Correa's government, which came to power in 2006, benefited from the biggest economic boom the country has ever known, managing $400 billion in 10 years. Record oil profits and massive borrowing enabled Correa to preside over the construction of highways, hospitals, schools, and hydroelectric dams.

In 2008, Correa expelled the World Bank representative and allowed the country to default on its U.S.-backed debt, deeming it "immoral and illegitimate." A year later, he turned to China to fill the void, with an initial $1 billion loan from PetroChina to Petroecuador. After that, Chinese money began to flow for massive infrastructure projects across the country, but with stringent conditions. Along with steep interest payments (up to 10.5 percent, making the loans among the most expensive on the planet), Ecuador is usually required to use Chinese companies and technologies on the projects. Much of the financing has to be paid back with oil, meaning that Ecuador has pre-sold almost 100 percent of its exportable surplus of Amazon crude to meet repayments. This led to an unprecedented situation in 2015, where Ecuador was forced to import 30 million barrels of oil for use in its own refinery in Esmeraldas.

In December 2009, Ecuadorian debt totaled $10.199 billion, equivalent to 16.3 percent of GDP. By November 2015, that figure had risen to $32.8475 billion, representing 32.9 percent of GDP. When Correa left power in May 2017, he admitted to a $28 billion public debt. Just two months later, in July 28, 2017, his successor, Lenín Moreno, conceded that the figure was actually $57.8 billion, a difference of nearly $30 billion. In 2018, a criminal investigation was opened against Correa and other officials for concealing the extent of the debt. The same year, Correa's successor, Lenín Moreno, reached a $400 million dollar financing agreement with the World Bank and secured a new $900 million loan from China. This brings China's total lending to Ecuador in the last 10 years to over $19 billion, which doesn't include $6 billion in cash-for-oil payments.

For the first eight years of Rafael Correa's government, oil prices were high, averaging $70 a barrel but at times reaching $140. In 2014, the country experienced a severe crisis caused by falling oil prices, which were dependent on the market, and high extraction costs, which were locked into service contracts signed by the government with international corporations such as Halliburton. With the cost of extracting a barrel of oil higher than its market worth value, the industry collapsed. The 3.8 percent GDP growth rate in 2014 fell to 0.1 percent in 2015 and -0.12 percent in 2016. Following the introduction of austerity measures growth was 2.4 percent in 2017.

After the oil crash in 2014, the government's focus turned to mining; thus, the value of Ecuador's mining industry is forecast to jump from $1.1 billion in 2017 to $7.9 billion in 2021.

People and Culture

DEMOGRAPHY

Ecuador's population stands at nearly 17 million, fairly evenly spread between the coast and the Sierra, with less than 5 percent of Ecuadorians living in the Oriente. Two-thirds of the population lives in densely populated urban areas, with nearly 3 million in Guayaquil.

Ecuador's population continues to grow at over 1 percent per year, and large families are still considered normal, not least because the predominant Roman Catholic religion frowns on birth control, and abortion is illegal. Sadly, Ecuador has the highest rate of teenage pregnancy in South America; 16.9 percent of girls aged 15-19 are mothers. People still tend to marry young and have children quickly, resulting in a very young population—35 percent are under age 15—in contrast to the aging populations of North America and Europe.

However, things are beginning to change, particularly in the wealthier classes, with people marrying later and having fewer children. Life expectancy stands at a respectable 76.6 years.

The largest racial group is mestizo—people of mixed Spanish and indigenous heritage—making up 72 percent of the population. According to 2010 census, 6.8 percent of the population self-identify as indigenous, though other estimates are considerably higher. The Confederation of Indigenous Nationalities of Ecuador (CONAIE) states that indigenous peoples make up 25-30 percent of the population. Similarly, there is a gap between the official figures for Afro-Ecuadorians (5 percent) and NGO estimates (10 percent). These differences have to do with questions of classification of Afro-descendants and indigenous peoples, including the self-identification of those who have intermarried with non-black or non-indigenous people, and those who live in urban areas. Whites are estimated at 6.1 percent, mostly of colonial-era Spanish origin, known as *criollos.*

Between the 1980s and mid-2000s, a series of economic crises led 10-15 percent of the population to emigrate overseas. Today, an estimated 1.5-2 million Ecuadorians live abroad, mostly in Spain, Italy, and the United States. In the early 2000s, thousands of Colombians migrated to Ecuador. More recently, Ecuador has seen a massive influx of Venezuelan migrants escaping the humanitarian crisis there, with 2,000 entering the country every day in 2017 and 2018. Around 20 percent of these stay in Ecuador, while the others are en route to other countries.

RACISM AND REGIONALISM

Ecuador is far from being a racially equal society, and a look back at history reveals why. Many of the country's richest and most influential families can trace their power directly back to colonial times, when their Spanish ancestors took ownership of the choicest plots of land. The brutal systems of forced indigenous labor implemented by the colonizers would continue for 400 years, only being finally abolished in the 1960s. While indigenous people are often still treated as second-class citizens, and the word *indio* is used in a derogatory way, it's more common to hear overtly racist comments from older people about Afro-Ecuadorians and immigrants from Colombia and Venezuela. Happily though, things are changing and the younger generation is much more open minded. There were both anti-immigration and anti-xenophobia protests in 2018.

Regional prejudice between the mountains and the coast, particularly between Guayaquil and Quito, is just as pervasive. Traditionally, *costeños* view *serranos* as uptight, conservative, two-faced, and hypocritical, whereas *serranos* see *costeños* as brash, lazy, uncultured, and frivolous. A *serrano* who moves to the coast may never really be accepted into their new community and vice versa. Again, though, things are changing with the younger generations. It's certainly true that young people on the coast laugh at the Andean visitors, in their jeans and closed shoes, but it's more good natured than malicious.

INDIGENOUS GROUPS

Indigenous nationalities inhabited mainland Ecuador for thousands of years before the Inca invasion and are still found all over the country, which is officially recognized as a plurinational state. While each has its own culture and customs, most of these groups are struggling to defend their ancestral territory from the ravages of oil exploitation, mining, industrial agriculture, and development. Indigenous leaders who spearhead these resistance efforts are often criminalized. Another common struggle is for bilingual education. Many ancient languages are in danger of dying out, and some have already been forgotten. Some of today's coastal residents are direct descendants of the region's pre-Inca civilizations, but they have lost not just their native tongue but most of their traditions. Indeed, they are rarely recognized as "indigenous." At the other end of the spectrum are the country's last two remaining groups who have never had contact with the outside world and live a seminomadic life as hunter-gatherers in Yasuní National Park. Most of Ecuador's indigenous groups are somewhere between the two extremes, having adapted to various degrees to the western way of life while preserving some of their ancestral customs. Most indigenous communities have a church and at least one shaman, blending Catholic and animist beliefs. Many maintain a strong connection to nature and the Pachamama (Mother Earth), and an encyclopedic knowledge of medicinal plants is often passed down the generations. Ecuador's indigenous peoples are represented by the Confederation of Indigenous Nationalities of Ecuador (CONAIE, https://conaie.org), which fights for social change and land rights. CONAIE is best known for its organization of popular uprisings (*levantamientos populares*) that include marches and road blockades. See the *History* section for more information on the indigenous struggle.

The Coast

Seven communities of **Tsáchila** people live near Santo Domingo after their ancestors relocated from Quito in the 1600s following a smallpox epidemic, which they cured with paste from the achiote fruit. In tribute, the men still color their hair with achiote and style it in the shape of the red fruit. To represent the knowledge of their shamans, or *ponés,* they wear a *mushily,* a cotton doughnut perched on top of their head. The Tsáchila still maintain many of their ancestral traditions, especially the practice of ancient healing techniques, including steam baths with medicinal plants and ayahuasca ceremonies in a subterranean chamber. Education is bilingual, in Spanish and Tsafiki. The Chigüilpe community has a well-organized tourism project, the Centro Turístico Mushily.

The 3,500 members of the **Awá** nationality live in the provinces of Imbabura, Carchi, and Esmeraldas. According to their ancestors, they are descended from the Mayas of Mexico, who arrived in Ecuador 300 years ago. Their language is called Awapit. Symbolism is important to the Awá; coming face-to-face with a hummingbird means that someone close is going to die, for example. They believe that children should not be allowed to play or bathe after four o'clock in the afternoon, because it can give them bad air, and that fallen fruits eaten after three in the afternoon can cause tumors.

Almost 90 percent of Santa Elena province is the territory of 68 ethnic communities made up of direct descendants of the **Guancavilcas**, who inhabited the area prior to the Inca invasion. During the colonial period, the natives managed to recover their lands from the Spanish. In modern times, these indigenous groups have adapted to the western way of living perhaps more than any others in the country, losing their ancestral traditions, and are thus rarely recognized as "indigenous." However, their descendants can be traced through family lineages, with surnames such as Yagual, Borbor, Tomala, and Oralla.

The Sierra

The majority of Ecuador's indigenous people live in the Sierra and are of Kichwa nationality. The Sierran Kichwas are subdivided into numerous groups, including the Natabuelas, Otavalos, Karanquis, Kayampis, Kitu Karas, Pastos, and Paltas in the northern Sierra; the Panzaleos, Salasacas, Chibuleos, Puruhás, Gurangas, Kisapinchas, and Warankas in the central Sierra; and the Cañaris and Saraguros in the southern Sierra. The majority of these groups are represented by Ecuarunari, the Confederation of Kichwa Peoples of Ecuador, and between them, six dialects of Kichwa are spoken. Each group has its own traditions and style of dress, often featuring woollen shawls and ponchos, embroidered shirts and skirts, felt hats, and beaded necklaces. Hair is often long and braided. Many highland Kichwas are small-scale farmers (campesinos), growing crops such as corn, potatoes, and beans or keeping cattle for milk. Others make a living with traditional handicrafts such as weaving, embroidery, and jewelry-making.

At the heart of the Andean indigenous cosmovision is the concept of *sumak kawsay,* or good living in harmony with nature and community—a concept that was adopted in the 2009 Ecuadorian constitution but not upheld. As part of community life, people work together to complete agricultural, construction, and maintenance tasks in joint efforts known as *mingas.* A traditional Andean way of eating is the *pampamesa,* where food is eaten communally on a long strip of fabric on the ground.

It is thought that the **Saraguros** and **Salasacas** are descended from people relocated from southern Peru and Bolivia in the 16th century as part of the Inca *mitma* system of forced resettlement. Other indigenous groups were present in Ecuador long before the Incas and fought valiantly against the invasion, such as the **Cañari**. In fact, the Inca had so much respect for the Cañari that, after finally defeating them, they built a community together at Ingapirca and added a Temple of the Sun to complement the existing Temple of the Moon. Also at Ingapirca is the tomb of a Cañari priestess and 10 of her servants, who were buried alive with her upon her death.

Probably the most famous of the Andean Kichwa groups is the **Otavalos,** who, after being brutally oppressed by the Incas and Spanish, found financial success in the 20th century due to their weaving skills. Otavalo and the nearby villages are great places to participate in traditional indigenous celebrations such as Inti Raymi. Farther north, the **Pastos** are stewards of the eerily beautiful El Ángel Ecological Reserve, which protects some of the most pristine *páramo* in the country, where a ghost of a Pasto chief is said to appear at Laguna Voladero at the solstice. Not far from Ibarra, the **Karanqui** village of Zuleta is known for its embroidery, in which intricate, colorful designs are sewn onto white cloth shirts, napkins, table cloths, and wall hangings. The nearby community of San Clemente is a shining example of community tourism, offering the opportunity to discover the Karanqui way of life, their culture and traditions.

In the central Sierra, the communities around Cotopaxi and Quilotoa are **Panzaleo.** Of these, Sasquili is known for its indigenous market, whereas Tigua is famous for its paintings on sheepskin that depict Andean scenes. Nearby, farmers make a yearly pilgrimage to the top of Amina hill, which is shaped like a gorilla, to ask for blessings for their crops. Pujilí is the best place in the country to join in the Corpus Christi celebrations, which blend Catholic and Panzaleo traditions. The **Puruhás** have been living on the flanks of the Chimborazo volcano since time immemorial. Native guides take visitors to the Templo de Machay, a sacred cave at 4,560 meters (14,960 ft) altitude, where their ancestors conducted rituals asking Chimborazo for blessings, a practice still carried out today. The population of Guaranda, the capital of Bolívar province, is largely **Waranka.** The nearby town of Salinas has become a model for self-sufficiency and community development through a number of successful food cooperatives that were set up by the Warankas with the help of a Salesian monk. Near Baños, the **Salasacas** still weave in the ancestral way, using sheep wool and plant dyes, with the women spinning and the men sitting at the looms. Indeed, the women can be seen spinning as they sit outside their stalls in the craft market, or even as they walk along the street.

In the southern Sierra, Cuenca provides easy access to the **Cañari** communities of Jima and Kushi Waira, both of which have tourism projects to share their way of life. Rural Cañari villages can also be visited near Alausí, where some campesinos still live in traditional indigenous dwellings made of mud and straw on the windswept *páramo.* Between Cuenca and Loja, the **Saraguros** are known for their black and white hats and for making exquisite beaded necklaces. Five of the rural villages that make up the canton of Saraguro have formed a community tourism network, where visitors can participate in handicrafts workshops, traditional agriculture, music and dance. One of the villages, Ilincho, has a center for Andean spirituality offering energy cleansing rituals.

The Oriente

The Confederation of Indigenous Nationalities of the Ecuadorian Amazon (CONFENIAE, https://confeniae.net) represents 11 nationalities: Kichwa, Shuar, Achuar, Waorani, Sápara, Andwa, Shiwiar, A'i Kofán, Siona, Siekopai, Chachi, Épera, Andoa y Kijus, and Chicha.

The **A'i Kofán** moved down from the foothills of the Andes centuries ago to inhabit a large territory between the Río Aguarico in the northern Ecuadorian Amazon and the Guamués River in southern Colombia. Before the arrival of the Spanish, it is estimated that there were 15,000-20,000 A'i Kofán, but a brutal history of colonization, disease, forced religious conversion, and the invasion of the extractive industry reduced their numbers to approximately 2,100 people who live in a vastly decreased territory. The A'i Kofán are known for their skilled ayahuasca shamans and for building the fiberglass canoes used by indigenous nationalities all over the Amazon. The canoe project was started as a way to conserve the Amazon's remaining big trees, which are felled to make the traditional wooden boats. The Avie community, accessed via Lago Agrio, offers the best opportunity to visit the A'i Kofán.

The Secoya, or **Siekopai** (which means multicolored people) are renowned for their shamanic acumen and knowledge of medicinal plants, with uses for over 1,000 different plants. According to Siekopai legend, the moon god (Nanëpaina) came down from the sky and found their people living underground and liberated them to live on the earth. Their language is called Pai'koka. The Siekopai wear crowns and arm bands made of leaves and flowers and paint their bodies and faces with geometric designs. They once had an immense territory that stretched an estimated 2.8 million hectares (7 million acres) from Ecuador into Colombia and Peru. There are around 900 Siekopai remaining in Peru and 600 in Ecuador, where they have been corralled into a territory of 20,000 hectares (50,000 acres). After their lands were divided by the militarization of the Ecuador-Peru border in the 1940s, some communities and families did not see each other for 50 years, until the signing of the 1998 peace treaty allowed reunification. To keep their ancestral knowledge alive, the Siekopai Remolina community has created a medicinal plant garden and is documenting their shamans' knowledge in online videos with English subtitles, available at www.amazonfrontlines.org. It is possible to visit the Remolina community via Lago Agrio.

Lowland Kichwas are the largest group of Amazonian indigenous people in Ecuador, numbering 30,000-40,000 and comprising two different ethnic groups. The Napu-Kichwa live in the provinces of Napo and Sucumbíos and also in Colombia and Peru, whereas the Canelo-Kichwa (also referred to as Kichwa of Pastaza) live in the province of Pastaza. The two groups speak similar versions of Kichwa that vary greatly from that spoken in the Sierra. Amazonian Kichwas are known for producing beautiful ceramics and for putting chili in the eyes of newborn babies to teach them to be brave, or as a punishment for naughty children. Despite this painful tradition, they are known for being people of peace. A Kichwa leader told this author of a meeting he had with his counterparts from neighboring Achuar and Waorani communities, some of which still practice swift and merciless indigenous justice with spear or gun if members commit a serious crime. The Achuar and Waorani leaders were laughing at the Kichwa, calling them cowards for being slow to pick up a spear. The Kichwa leader responded by claiming that his people were real men of the jungle because, after killing a monkey to eat, they practiced the custom of slicing off and eating the creature's testicles, raw. In surprise, his neighbors stated that they too practiced this tradition and, in discovering this unexpected common ground, newfound respect was fostered between the three leaders. Kichwa communities can be visited near Lago Agrio (Shayari community), via Tena and Misahuallí (Sinchi Warmi), via Coca (Limoncocha, Yasuní), and via Puyo (Sarayaku).

The **Waorani,** who currently number around 2,000, once maintained one of the largest territories of all indigenous Amazon peoples in Ecuador, within the modern provinces of Orellana (including Yasuní National Park), Napo, and Pastaza. Their word for themselves, *wao*, simply means "humans," as opposed to *cowode*, the "non-humans," which refers to all outsiders. They live in extended families, under one roof (the *maloca*), with each group organized around an elderly person, considered the wisest. Traditionally, marriage is by arrangement of the bride's father, and men are allowed to have multiple wives. Waorani legend states that they descend from the union between a jaguar and an eagle, so they never hunt these animals. They are known for being fierce warriors and skilled hunters, adept with long hardwood spears and blowpipes. Even among indigenous peoples, the Waorani are famous for their deep connection with the rainforest. In their world view, there is no difference between the physical and the spiritual world. The jungle is considered a safe place, where they are protected from spells and attacks, while the outside world is full of threats. Animals are seen as equals and, to compensate for the offense of hunting, the darts they use are prepared in a ritual by their shamans. The Waoranis traditionally lived as nomadic hunter-gatherers, but missionary groups, working directly with oil companies, relocated many families into larger communities with the purpose of converting them to Christianity and clearing the way for oil exploitation. The Waorani are the most recently contacted of all Ecuadorian indigenous peoples, with the first "successful" interaction happening in 1958. Two years previously, they became world famous for spearing to death five Summer Institute of Linguistics missionaries. Since being contacted, the Waorani territories have been greatly reduced and theirs is the nationality with the greatest presence of oil companies within its remaining lands. Two Waorani groups, the Tagaeri and Taromenane, have continued to reject contact and live in Yasuní National Park in a state of voluntary isolation. The Waoranis can be visited at Shiripuno Lodge in Yasuní National Park.

The **Shuar,** whose territory is found in

The indigenous Sarayaku are Lowland Kichwas who live in Pastaza.

the provinces of Morona-Santiago, Zamora-Chinchipe, and Pastaza, are most famous for making shrunken heads (*tsantsas*). Central to their belief system is the concept of *arutam*, the life force that allows men to be successful warriors, husbands, and fathers, and enables women to excel as wives, mothers, and cultivators of food. *Tsantsas* were made as a way to capture the *arutam* of the vanquished, allowing the victor to become a great and powerful man, or *kakaram*. So many Shuar women were left widowed by battles (often with other Shuar) that the tradition arose of men having more than one wife. Renowned for their fierceness, the Shuar successfully defended their territory for centuries, repelling both the Incas and the Spanish. They were the first of Ecuador's indigenous nationalities to organize in defense of their land and human rights, forming the Shuar Federation in the early 1960s. In 1995, elite units of Shuar soldiers enabled Ecuador to claim victory in the Battle of the Cenepa, a border dispute with Peru. Twenty years later, the Ecuadorian army fired on some of the same Shuar warriors after violently evicting the community of Nankints to make way for a mega-mining project. The Shuar Federation's open letter on the issue, *Letter from the Shuar Arutam People to the Country & the World*, can be found online. In addition to ayahuasca, which they call *natem*, Shuar shamans use the tobacco plant and the powerfully hallucinogenic flowers of the brugmansia or angel's trumpet tree in their rituals. When they come of age, young men are given brugmansia in order to receive visions of their future. They believe in *tsentsak*, invisible darts that a shaman shoots into a patient's heart, allowing the diagnosis and healing of illness. In their cosmovision, every waterfall is sacred and has its own living spirit. Several Shuar communities can be visited from Macas.

GENDER AND SEXUALITY

Ecuadorian culture is very sexually polarized, with machismo and male dominance running through society from top to bottom. Girls are brought up to be "princesses" and to spend a lot of time on their appearance. Many women work (often casual, part-time jobs or in the family business), but they are also expected to manage the home and raise the children. Men who get involved in domestic chores are mocked with the derogatory term *mandarina*, which roughly translates as "under the thumb." Traditional indigenous cultures often have especially fixed ideas about gender, with roles very clearly defined.

While it is common to see men out playing football after work, enjoying a few drinks, or gathered around a television watching the game, it is rare to see a group of women out enjoying themselves or having time for hobbies. Most young women are expected to live with their parents until they are married. The few who attempt to live alone, with friends, housemates, or a boyfriend, may face being ostracized by their family. Even those who share an apartment with other students for the duration of their university studies are expected to move back to the family home as soon as they graduate.

It is pretty much expected for men to cheat on their wives and to visit brothels, which are legal and present in every town. Domestic violence and femicide rates are high, with a woman killed every 84 hours, usually by an intimate partner.

Abortion in Ecuador is illegal except in the case of a threat to the life or health of a pregnant woman (when this threat cannot be averted by other means) or when the pregnancy is the result of the rape of a mentally disabled woman. Not surprisingly, unsafe abortion is a leading cause of injury and death. Women can be sentenced to up to two years in prison for having an abortion, and even harsher penalties apply to medical professionals who perform them. Ecuador's former president, Rafael Correa, threatened to resign if Congress passed a law decriminalizing abortion in cases of rape, and the congressmember who proposed the motion was accused of treason and sanctioned to 30 days of silence.

See the *Women Travelers* section of the *Essentials* chapter for advice on dealing with machismo and staying safe as a foreign female visitor.

Until just over 20 years ago, homosexuality was considered a crime punishable by prison in Ecuador, but fortunately things have changed dramatically since then. In fact, the 1997 constitution included some of the world's most progressive LGBTQ-friendly legislation, including full anti-discrimination laws on grounds of sexual orientation, and the equalization of the age of consent (which now stands at 14 for everyone). Since 2008, same-sex couples can legally register their civil union and receive the same rights/benefits as straight couples (except for adoption), but the arrangement is not yet officially referred to as a marriage.

Nevertheless, Ecuador's largely conservative and macho culture tends to view gender queerness negatively, especially the older generations. Many traditional indigenous cultures have especially fixed ideas about gender identity. Anti-gay humor is common, with the word *maricón* used to derogatively describe gay or effeminate men. Many LGBTQ people are either in the closet or share their orientation very selectively.

There are some suggestions and advice for LGBTQ travelers in the *Essentials* chapter.

RELIGION

Since the first conquistador planted a cross in honor of God and the king of Spain, Roman Catholicism has been a linchpin of Latin American culture, and Ecuador is no exception. After the constitution of 1869, the official religion became Catholicism and only Catholics could obtain citizenship. In 1899, the liberal government of Eloy Alfaro made a new constitution that respected all faiths and guaranteed freedom of religious choice. The public education is supposedly secular (though sex education regarding contraception is very limited in schools even today).

According to the Ecuadorian National Institute of Statistics and Census (2010), 91.95 percent of the country's people have a religion, 7.94 percent are atheists, and 0.11 percent are agnostics. Of those with a religion, 80.44 percent are Catholics, 11.30 percent Protestants, 1.29 percent Jehovah's Witnesses, and 6.97 percent have other faiths (notably Mormonism).

After the Spanish conquest many indigenous people were pressured into converting to Catholicism for fear of what their new masters would do if they refused. The pressure to convert continued into the 20th century, with missionaries working directly with oil companies in the 1960s and 1970s to "civilize the Aucas" (a derogatory term meaning savages) and clear oil concessions of indigenous peoples. Missionaries are still present in Ecuador today, though their tactics are somewhat gentler. Though churches are found in even the most remote of Amazon communities, many of the ancient traditions have prevailed, resulting in a fusion of animist beliefs and Catholicism. Many indigenous people see no conflict between participating in a shamanic ritual that evokes the spirits of the anaconda and jaguar and then going to church the next day.

A fusion of indigenous and Catholic traditions can also be seen in many of Ecuador's celebrations. For example, in the Corpus Christi celebration in Pujilí, the priest of the rain dances through the streets accompanied by people in animal and devil masks. La Mama Negra celebration in Latacunga exhibits an even more complex racial mix, blending together Afro-Ecuadorian, indigenous, and Catholic beliefs.

While an increasing number of young people are not religious, the older generations tend to frown upon atheism, so it may be best to keep your beliefs, or lack of them, to yourself.

LANGUAGE

Spanish is Ecuador's official tongue and is spoken by the vast majority of the population. As a plurinational country, there are also 21 indigenous languages, comprising nine varieties of Quechua plus Waorani, Shuar, Kofán, Achuar-Shiwiar, Awa-Cuaiquer, Chachi, Tsafiki, Epena, Secoya, Tetete, Sápara, and Media Lengua. Many indigenous people are bilingual, though some elders speak only their native tongue. Conversely, a growing number of young people speak only Spanish, and the ancient languages are in danger of dying out. Only a handful of elderly people in the jungles of Pastaza province still speak Sápara, for example. Some indigenous nationalities, often led by young people, are starting to take measures to rescue their native tongues. For more information on languages in Ecuador, see www.ethnologue.com.

Few people speak English in Ecuador, mainly wealthy Guayaquileños and Quiteños, and some people working in tourism. You will struggle to communicate without some knowledge of Spanish, so it's a good idea to learn some basics before your trip, or take classes once you get here.

ARTS AND ENTERTAINMENT
Visual Arts

Early colonial sculptors and painters remained anonymous, remembered only for their gloomy but heartfelt images of the Virgin and Gothic-style saints. Indigenous influences began to emerge with the onset of the Renaissance and baroque styles, allowing artists like Gaspar Sangurima, Manuel Chili (aka Caspicara), and Miguel de Santiago more freedom for personal expression in their works. Works by these artists can be seen in the Museo Fray Pedro Gocial, the Museo Nacional de Arte Colonial, and the Museo de San Agustín in Quito and the Convento de las Conceptas in Cuenca.

The Quito School, encompassing the artistic output of the Audience of Quito during the colonial period (1542-1822), is famous for its mastery of polychrome carvings of the Virgin Mary, Jesus, and numerous saints. It was particularly well known for its use of realism, emphasizing the suffering of Christ and even using real human hair. Notable artists include Isabel de Santiago and María Estefanía Dávalos y Maldonado.

The 19th century and independence brought "popular" art to the fore, and the Quito School's influence faded, as it was synonymous with Spanish rule. Concerned with the secular as much as the holy, it consisted of intense colors and naturalistic images of landscapes and people. This was followed in the 20th century by the reverberations of impressionism and cubism. Powerful representations of the dignity and suffering of Ecuador's indigenous peoples dominated the work of Camilo Egas (1889-1962), Manuel Rendón (1894-1982), and Eduardo Kingman (1913-1999). Kingman painted exaggerated renditions of hands that inspired Oswaldo Guayasamín (1919-1999), probably Ecuador's most famous modern artist. Guayasamín's final magnum opus, the *Capilla del Hombre* (Chapel of Man), is dedicated to the struggles of indigenous peoples. Other works include *La Ternura*, depicting the tenderness of a mother and child's embrace, and *El Toro y el Cóndor*, symbolizing the struggle between Spanish and Andean identities. The Museo Fundación Guayasamín in Quito is located in the artist's former home and is the best place to see his work. Araceli Gilbert (1913-1993) is famous for her brightly colored geometric abstracts, one of which (*Manhattan*, painted in 1985) has been replicated as a mural on the side of the Casa de Cultura in Guayaquil.

Originally painted on ceremonial drums, Tigua paintings are now painted on sheep hide stretched over a wooden frame. Common themes include religious festivals and daily Andean life. The Cotopaxi volcano is present in the majority of the work, often painted with a human face, expressing the Kichwa world view of mountains as living beings. The paintings are sold nationwide, but the best place to see them is in Tigua at the gallery of Alfredo Toaquiza, a prominent artist whose father pioneered the use of sheepskin at the suggestion of Hungarian artist and collector Olga Fisch.

Ecuador's most famous graffiti artist is Quiteño Juan Sebastian Aguirre, better

Contemporary Ecuadorian Music

Listening to contemporary artists is a great way to immerse yourself in the culture and also learn Spanish. All the artists and songs mentioned here can be found on YouTube. With the prevalence of *cumbia*, *reggaetón*, pop, and salsa, however, you are unlikely to hear any of this music when you're out and about; a lot of Ecuador's music scene remains fairly grassroots and underground.

Ecuador has a thriving hip-hop scene. Quiteño rapper **Chango** (Facebook @medicenchango) rightly won an award for the wonderful video to "Vengo de un País" (I Come from a Country), a love song to Ecuador from his debut album *Me Dicen Chango* (They Call Me Chango). His second album, *Animal*, includes songs written from the perspective of the Andean condor and Lonesome George, the famous Galápagos tortoise. With over 6 million hits on YouTube is **Barrio 593**'s "Hip Hop Ecuador." Their name is a reference to Ecuador's international dialing code. On his album *Polemica*, **Una Voz** (Facebook @unavozqm) addressed a direct message to Rafael Correa in "Sr Presidente, Permítame Faltarle El Respeto" (Mr President, Permit Me to Disrespect You) regarding the exploitation of the Amazon. The video has English subtitles on YouTube. Also speaking out for the Amazon is **Mateo Kingman** (Facebook @mateokingmanoficial) from Macas, who fuses folklore influences with hip-hop. His debut single, "Lluvia," was released in 2016, and "Religar," the first single from his second album, was released two years later. Also from the Amazon region are rapper **Jota Al Cuadrado** (Facebook @jos3phjara) and Kichwa group **Kambak,** whose best known song, "Sikwanka," is about the toucan bearing witness to the oppression of indigenous peoples.

Andean hip-hop group **Los Nin** (Facebook @losninoficial) has been around for over a decade and is still going strong, using pan flutes and rapping alternately in Spanish and Kichwa. Check out their 2009 single "Identidad" and, from 2018, "Unan Las Manos." **La Mafia Andina** is also an Andean hip-hop group mixing Spanish and Kichwa, this time with an indigenous female singer/rapper **Taki Amaru. Curare** is another band using Andean instruments such as pan flutes, but this time to create metal music. Check out their songs "Morenita" and "Tinku." Even heavier is the band **Colapso.** A graduate of Quito's National Music Conservatory, **Lascivio Bohemia** (Facebook @lasciviobohemiaec) samples and remixes Afro-Ecuadorian sounds, coastal beats, and the native music of the Sierra, as can be heard on his 2016 album, *Afro Andes EP.* Starting to make it on the international stage is **Nicolá Cruz,** who fuses music from the Andes to the Amazon with traditional instruments and *cumbia* beats, to create an electronic sound. Check out his tune "Colibria." Another band using traditional Ecuadorian sounds is guitar-based **Guardarraya** (Facebook @guardarraya), whose song "Chuchaqui" is the repentant tale of a hangover.

Da Pawn (Facebook @dapawn) creates folksy low-fi tunes such as "Ballenas de Ruido," which has chalked up well over a million YouTube hits. Influenced by reggae and ska, **Sudayaka** (Facebook @sudakayaec) is amazing live, as are the **Swing Original Monks** (Facebook @swingoriginalmonksofficial), one of Ecuador's better known bands. Check out their song "Caminito." Like the Arctic Monkeys that inspired them, **Lolabúm** (Facebook @lolabum) were teenagers when they got together in 2014 and are still going strong, taking a noisier, darker turn. Iguana Brava is a *cumbia* band from Guayaquil.

known as Apitatán (Facebook @elapitatan), who has painted murals all over the country, Latin America, the United States, and Europe. Many of his distinctive pieces depict indigenous themes.

Music and Dance

Made famous throughout South America by Guayaquileño Julio Jaramillo in the 1950s and 1960s, *pasillo* is considered the national music style. To learn more about these melancholic acoustic guitar-based love songs, head to the Museo de la Música Popular Guayaquileña Julio Jaramillo in Guayaquil, where there is also a *pasillo* school that works with young people to keep this music tradition alive.

The haunting melodies and wistful lyrics of the Ecuadorian Andes are played by groups throughout the highlands. The music can be extremely beautiful, although there is

Public Holidays and Major Festivals

Ecuador is a country with a thriving tradition of holidays, festivals, and celebrations: some Catholic, some indigenous (or a blend of the two), others marking important historical occasions. Many Ecuadorians don't have paid vacation and the long weekends created by public holidays or *feriados* are the only chance they have to go on holiday. During these periods, accommodations should be booked in advance and may be more expensive (especially around New Year's Day and Carnival). Traveling is best avoided, as buses will be full and there are more accidents on the roads. Some cities become ghost towns (e.g., Quito), with all the residents gone to the beach; others become overrun (e.g., Cuenca, and any beach destination). If the date of a public holiday falls on a weekend or midweek, it will often be moved to the Friday or Monday. In addition to the national festivities, each city commemorates its founding date with street parties. Smaller towns and villages hold annual *fiestas patronales* in honor of their patron saint.

- **January 1: New Year's Day**—a national holiday.

- **January 6: Fiesta de los Santos Inocentes**—street party in Cuenca commemorating the children who were massacred by Herod. People flock to the streets in costumes and masks, and a parade remembers the main events and characters from the previous year.

- **February or March** (weekend closest to new moon): **Carnival**—the country's biggest party, with four days of festivities and water fights. The Monday and Tuesday are national holidays. Guaranda is the most traditional place to join in the fun. **Pawkar Raymi** (Blossoming Festival) is the Quechua equivalent of Carnival, celebrating the fertility of the earth. Festivities last for 11 days and include fireworks, parades, musical events, and rituals. Otavalo and the surrounding villages are the place to be.

- **March or April** (40 days after Ash Wednesday): Easter Week or **Semana Santa**—a long weekend with parades on Good Friday (a national holiday) remembering the passion of the Christ, notably in Quito and Cuenca.

- **May 1: Labor Day**—a national holiday with workers parades around the country.

- **May 24: Battle of Pichincha**—a national holiday to commemorate the decisive 1822 battle that resulted in independence from Spain.

- **May or June** (9th Thursday after Easter): **Corpus Christi**—honors the Eucharist, particularly celebrated by indigenous people in the central Sierra. During the festival in Pujilí, the "priest of the rain" dances through the streets in an elaborate costume to the beat of a drum, accompanied by a colorful cast of characters. Cuenca is another fun place to be, with sweet stalls lining the streets, fireworks, and parades.

- **June: Fiesta del Coraza**—celebrated at Laguna San Pablo near Otavalo between June 9 and 15, including a race on the lake between floating horses made of reeds. Key personages are the *coraza*, painted white to represent the Spanish, with his face covered in silver chains to symbolize greed; and the *pendonero*, who represents resistance to the Spanish invasion, dressed as a warrior waving a blood-red flag.

- **June 21-29: Inti Raymi** (Quechua for Sun Festival) is the Inca festival of the northern solstice and the most important Andean celebration. Every indigenous group has its own specific dates and traditions, but the main event starts on June 21 and continues for several days. There is a celebration at the Inca sites of Ingapirca on June 21·and Las Tolas de Cochasquí on June 22. In the Otavalo area, people gather to bathe in sacred rivers and waterfalls on June 22 to eliminate negative energies accumulated during the previous year, to purify themselves and kick off the festivities. The Peguche waterfall is a popular spot to participate in this cleansing ritual, which also takes place at Laguna Quilotoa.

- **August 10: Independence Day**—a national holiday commemorating the country's first (failed) uprising against the Spanish in 1809.

- **End of August: Fiesta del Yamor**—held in Otavalo from the end of August until the first week of September. This festival dates back to pre-Incan times and centers around a drink, a type of *chicha,* which is made from seven varieties of corn and represents the unity of the people.

- **September:** The biggest event in Loja's calendar is the arrival of one of the country's most important religious icons, the **Virgen del Cisne,** a statue of the Virgin Mary that is believed to perform miracles. The statue is carried 70 kilometers (43 mi) from Cisne to Loja's cathedral, where she presides over the annual festivities that are held in the first week of September, culminating on 8th.

- **September 23-24: Fiesta de La Mama Negra**—the more authentic, raucous version of Latacunga's flamboyant festival, combining not only Spanish and indigenous traditions, but also African elements, culminating in the arrival of a blackened man in women's clothing throwing milk and water.

- **October 9: Independence of Guayaquil**—a national holiday with parades and fireworks in Guayaquil.

- **November 2: Día de los Difuntos**—a national holiday, better known as Day of the Dead. Families bring food, flowers, and offerings to the graves of loved ones, or prepare tables of food for them at home and call for their spirits to come and eat. Don't miss the delicious *colada morada,* a sweet purple fruit drink.

- **November 3: Foundation of Cuenca**—a national holiday and the city's biggest celebration, which merges with the previous holiday.

- **Saturday prior to November 11: Fiesta de La Mama Negra**—the more sedate, state-sponsored version of the festival.

- **December 21: December solstice**—a festival held at the Inca site Las Tolas de Cochasquí.

- **December 24: Christmas Eve**—Cuenca hosts the biggest Christmas parade in the country, the **Pase del Niño,** where likenesses of the infant Jesus are carried through towns and villages accompanied by floats, indigenous groups in traditional dress, bands, dancers, street performers, and stilt-walkers. Most locals celebrate Christmas with a family dinner and gifts at midnight.

- **December 25: Christmas Day,** a national holiday.

- **December 28: Día de los Inocentes**—commemorating the children who were massacred by Herod. To demonstrate the innocence of the people, practical jokes are played.

- **December 31: New Year's Eve**—life-size effigies of prominent figures of the outgoing year are burned at midnight.

Ecuador's Traditional Celebrations

gorilla effigy for New Year's Eve

Ecuador is a country that takes great pride in its traditions, and visitors are welcomed into the fun with open arms. **New Year's Eve** is celebrated by burning effigies (*monigotes*), often of cartoon characters or public figures who symbolize the outgoing year (unpopular politicians being a favorite). In a wonderful blend of pyromania and personal reflection, the effigies are stuffed with lists of things that people would like to leave behind. Some people complete a symbolic act at midnight that represents their hopes for the forthcoming year; e.g., walking around the block with a suitcase to manifest travel. In Montañita, the surfers catch a midnight wave. In some Sierran towns, people read out the old year's Last Will and Testament, which is filled with jokes and criticisms of friends, neighbors, and the government.

On the nights preceding New Year's Eve, especially on the coast, men dress as widows (*viudas*) of the outgoing year and go around asking for "funeral contributions" (aka a beer fund). This tradition has evolved in recent years, with men now dressing in full drag—a joy to witness in such a macho country. In the small coastal village of Manglaralto, on December 30 the men put on a full stage show as their female alter egos.

Día de los Difuntos (Day of the Deceased) on November 2 honors those who have passed away. All over the country, families visit cemeteries with flowers and food, traditionally *colada morada*, a purple corn drink, and *guaguas de pan*, sweet breads shaped as babies. On the coast, people prepare the favorite dishes of their departed loved ones and then call on their spirits to come and eat. They swear that the atmosphere changes when the ghosts arrive and that some of the food disappears. On this day, people go calling from house to house with the words *"Angeles somos, pan pedimos"* ("We are angels, we ask for bread") and are given a plate of food. Visitors are welcome to join this tradition.

Every town and village holds annual *fiestas patronales* in honor of their patron saint, which is usually a real religious effigy miraculously discovered somewhere local that gets paraded through the streets. As with every kind of Ecuadorian celebration, music, beauty pageants, and pyrotechnics play a key role. Fireworks are often attached to a tower (*el castillo*) or sometimes to a person in a cow costume (*la vaca loca*), who charges around shooting rockets into the crowd to frenetic music—a custom stemming from rituals asking for agricultural blessings. Amazingly, under the protective gaze of the patron saint no one gets hurt! The *fiestas* in Montañita take place in May and November, and it's a fun place to see a *vaca loca* (crazy cow).

A more private tradition takes place in the early hours of **Mother's Day** (Día de las Madres), when traveling bands individually serenade mothers and grandmothers, often with Julio Jaramillo's beautiful "Para Ti Madrecita."

a tendency to churn out the same old songs for visitors, such as "El Condor Pasa," a Peruvian tune made famous by Simon and Garfunkel in the 1960s, and, even worse, panpipe versions of ballads by Celine Dion and Lionel Richie. Flutes were considered holy by the Inca, who provided the original set of instruments and tunes for modern-day Andean music. The *quena,* a vertical flute once made from condor leg bones, is used to play the melody, along with panpipes such as the *rondador* and *zampoña.* Bass drums made from hollow logs or clay are used to keep the beat, with the help of various rattles and bells. Peguche, near Otavalo, is known for its workshops making traditional Andean instruments. The group Los Huayanay is an example of Ecuadorian Andean music.

The colonial Spanish tried their best to suppress indigenous music but only inspired the creation of a whole host of new sounds by introducing the *vihuela,* an ancestor of the guitar, the first stringed instrument seen on the continent. Offshoots include the 10-stringed *charango,* originally from Bolivia and made from armadillo shells, and the 15-stringed *bandolina.*

There are two key types of Afro-Ecuadorian music. Marimba, popular on the northern coast, is played on an instrument of the same name, a West-African wooden xylophone struck to a hypnotic beat. Banned for much of the early 20th century, marimba is seen as an expression of freedom by many Afro-Ecuadorians. *Marimba Esmeraldeña* was declared Intangible Cultural Heritage by UNESCO in 2015. An example is the album *Yo Soy El Hombre* by Don Naza y El Grupo Bambuco. The Chota Valley in the northern Sierra is the birthplace of another Afro-Ecuadorian type of music, *bomba,* which uses a wooden drum of the same name, usually accompanied by other drums and instruments of Spanish origin such as the guitar. Female *bomba* dancers sometimes balance a bottle on their head. *Bomba* bands to check out include Marabu and Mario Diego Congo y Las Chicas del Valle.

Caribbean-flavored *cumbia* from Colombia has indigenous, Afro, and Spanish influences. Ecuadorian *cumbia* began in the early 1990s with Grupo Coctel. In the last decade, one of the key Ecuadorian *cumbia* singers has been Manolo. *Technocumbia* fuses *cumbia* and electronic sounds, with recent Ecuadorian examples including María de los Angeles, Gerardo Morán, Veronica Bolaños, and Delfín Quishpe.

In the latter 20th century, salsa and merengue began to dominate, and they remain extremely popular across the generations. If you are in Ecuador for an extended period, consider taking classes, as dancing is very important at social occasions and a good way to meet people. Locals will be delighted to see you try. Etnia is a band from Esmeraldas who fuse salsa with Afro-Ecuadorian music.

International rock and pop are also very popular in Ecuador, and many top music acts come to Quito to perform. Heavy rock is particularly popular. Quito, and to a lesser extent Guayaquil, has a thriving *rockero* scene.

In the past 10 years, the booming beats of *reggaetón* have spilled out from the club scene and are heard blasting out just about everywhere in Ecuador. Originating in Puerto Rico in the 1990s and influenced by Caribbean music and hip hop, *reggaetón* burst onto the international scene in 2017 with *Despacito.* It's famous (or infamous) for its explicit lyrics, gyrating dance moves, and repetitive beat; you'll either love it or hate it. It is inexplicably popular at children's birthday parties, blasting out at earsplitting volume from speakers that are often bigger than the birthday boy or girl.

Literature

Most of the books listed have been translated into English.

Cumandá, a romantic drama set in the rainforest and written by Juan León Mera, is one of Ecuador's most famous books from the 19th century. Writers in the early 20th century mainly focused on realistic social themes of injustice and race. Jorge Icaza's *Huasipungo* (*The Villagers,* 1934) is considered one of

Ecuador's best novels, vividly portraying the hardships of everyday life in an indigenous village. The avant-garde movement in the 1930s was led by Pablo Palacios, who dealt with challenging subjects such as mental illness (of which he had personal experience). One of his most widely read works is *Un Hombre Muerto a Puntapiés* (*The Man Who Was Kicked to Death*). Adalberto Ortiz's *Juyungo* (1942) is a seminal novel on black life in Esmeraldas. Jorge Carrera Andrade, from Quito, was one of the most important Latin American poets of the century and can be read in Winds of Exile: The Poetry of Jorge Carrera Andrade.

The English-language compilation Contemporary Ecuadorian Short Stories, edited by Vladimiro Rivas Iturralde, is an easy toe in the water of Ecuadorian literature (and includes the English translation of *Un Hombre Muerto a Puntapiés*). *Fire from the Andes: Short Fiction by Women from Bolivia, Ecuador, and Peru* is another recommended anthology. In 2012, Abdón Ubidia, author of *Sueño de Lobos* (*Wolves' Dream*, 1986) and several other works was awarded the Eugenio Espejo Award, Ecuador's highest honor for its citizens who have made notable contributions to Ecuadorian culture. Santiago Páez has written several sci-fi novels, including *Profundo en la Galaxia* (*Deep in the Galaxy*) and *Shamanes y Reyes* (*Shamans and Kings*). His most recent book, *Ecuatox*, is an ecology-themed satire.

A voice for the Afro-Ecuadorian experience, Luz Argentina Chiriboga's novels explore race, gender, sexuality, class inequality, and the clash of cultures. *The Devil's Nose* (2015) is based on the true story of the Jamaicans who worked on Ecuador's railroads in the early 20th century. Gabriela Aleman, voted one of "Latin America's 40 most promising writers under 40," released the English version of her sci-fi political satire *Poso Wells* in 2018.

María Fernanda Ampuero's *Pelea de Gallos* was listed in the *New York Times*' top 10 publications of 2018, and Mónica Ojeda's *Mandibula* was ranked number 12 in the list of the year's best literary works in Spanish newspaper *El Pais*. At the time of writing, both books were only available in Spanish.

Essentials

Getting There

AIR

A number of airlines offer flights into Ecuador's two international airports: the **Mariscal Sucre International Airport,** located near the town of Tababela, about 12 kilometers (7.5 mi) east of Quito; and **José Joaquín de Olmedo International Airport** in Guayaquil. Both airports are new and efficient. For a list of airlines that fly into Ecuador, see the *Getting There and Around* sections of the *Quito* and *Guayaquil and the Southern Coast* chapters.

To find the best deals on flights, use a flight aggregator (www.

booking.com, www.skyscanner.com), be flexible with your dates if possible, and compare flights arriving to Quito and to Guayaquil, as there is often a significant price difference. Once in Ecuador, you can travel between the two cities easily by air or bus. It's a good idea to book well in advance if you want to travel during peak periods (Christmas and the summer holidays in the United States and Europe). If you're a student or under 26, check to see if **STA Travel** (www.statravel.com) has discounted air tickets.

BUS

International buses entering Ecuador will wait outside the immigration offices while passengers complete the formalities. Always check that your passport has been stamped upon arrival. It is fairly common for border officials to forget, and without a stamp you will be in the country illegally. This can cause enormous hassle when it comes to leaving Ecuador or extending a visa.

Pancontinental Buses

These buses traverse the continent and can transport you between Ecuador and Venezuela, Colombia, Peru, Argentina, and Chile. Be prepared for long journeys, though; from Buenos Aires in Argentina to Huaquillas in Ecuador, for example, is 84 hours (with stops en route for food). Departures are not daily, so check itineraries well in advance. Tickets can be bought online or at the bus company offices in Quito and Guayaquil and other departure cities.

Cruz del Sur (Quito: Av. Santa María 870 *y* 9 de Octubre, tel. 2/290-5823, and Quitumbe bus terminal, tel. 2/382-4791; Guayaquil: in the *terminal terrestre,* www.cruzdelsur.com.pe) is recommended and has a good website with itineraries and prices. Inquiries via Facebook and email are generally responded to within a day. Their routes start in Argentina and Chile and currently go no farther north than

Ecuador (at the time of writing, their services between Colombia and Ecuador had been discontinued but may restart in the future; check the website for information). Popular journeys include Lima to Quito (Tues., $110, 36 hours); Quito to Lima (Thurs., $110, 36 hours); Lima to Guayaquil (daily except Sun., $100, 28 hours); Guayaquil to Lima (daily except Tues., $100, 28 hours); Mancora to Guayaquil (daily except Mon. and Wed., $35, 8 hours); and Guayaquil to Mancora (daily except Tues. and Fri., $35, 8 hours).

Another good option is **Rutas de America** (Quito: Selva Alegre O1-72 *y* Av. 10 de Agosto, tel. 2/250-3611 or 2/254-8142; Guayaquil: La Garzota 3, Manzana 84 Villa 1, tel. 4/265-5373, https://rutasdeamerica.net), with routes between Venezuela and Peru. If you contact them on Facebook or online chat, you will be sent a link to a WhatsApp group and a staff member will respond to your query. The only route from Colombia is currently between Cúcuta and Guayaquil. Cúcuta to Guayaquil departs Tuesday and Thursday; Guayaquil to Cúcuta departs daily (50 hours, $115). Buses also run between Quito and Lima twice weekly (36 hours, $110) and between Guayaquil and Lima twice weekly (28 hours, $110).

Wanderbus (www.wanderbusecuador. com) offers a hop-on-hop off bus service that tours the country, taking in some of the major tourist destinations, including Quito, Montañita, Puerto Lopez, Cuenca, Quilotoa, Cotopaxi, Baños, Riobamba and Alausí. It's much more expensive than the regular bus, but prices include bilingual guides and stops at attractions en route. Tickets can be bought online.

From Colombia

The only recommended Colombia/Ecuador border crossing is 7 kilometers (4.3 mi) north of **Tulcán** in Ecuador and 13 kilometers (8 mi) south of **Ipiales** in Colombia. Situated on a

---

Previous: Kichwa vegetable vendors by the railway lines in Alausí.

bridge over the Río Carchi at **Rumichaca,** the crossing is open 24 hours. It's necessary to clear both countries' immigration stations, no matter which direction you're crossing, and there is just one line at each immigration station. At the time of writing, the influx of Venezuelans fleeing the humanitarian crisis has increased queues at the border from 15 minutes to several hours, so be prepared to wait. Direct any questions to the Ecuadorian immigration office (open 24 hours) located in the CENAF buildings at the bridge.

In Ipiales take a private taxi (13,000 pesos/$4) or a *colectivo* (1,700 pesos/$0.55) to the border and complete the formalities. Once you're in Ecuador, head to Tulcán ($4 by private taxi, $1 shared taxi, $0.75 microbus). Drivers accept pesos. Money changers in Tulcán's Parque Ayora are more trustworthy than at the border, with better rates. Official Ecuadorian changers should have photo IDs.

Tulcán has buses leaving for just about every major city in Ecuador, including Ibarra (2.5 hours, $3), Quito (5 hours, $5), Ambato (8 hours, $6), Lago Agrio (7 hours, $7), and Coca (9 hours, $7). There is even a bus to Huaquillas (18 hours, $22), if you want to bypass Ecuador altogether and go straight to Peru. See the *Northern Sierra* chapter for accommodation and restaurant suggestions in Tulcán.

From Peru

The most common way to enter from Peru is via the Ecuadorian town of **Huaquillas,** where the construction of new immigration offices a few kilometers outside the town center has made the crossing safe and convenient, with Ecuadorian and Peruvian border officials sitting side by side in the same building. Simply join the queue at the "Salida del Peru" desk, then queue up again to enter Ecuador at the "Ingreso al Ecuador" desk.

In addition to the pancontinental bus companies previously mentioned, **CIFA** (www. cifainternational.com) operates services from Peru that cross the border and wait for passengers while they complete the formalities. There are several buses per day between Tumbes and Guayaquil, and between Piura and Guayaquil. Both services go via Huaquillas and Machala. There is also one direct daily bus between Mancora and Montañita, leaving Mancora at 8:30pm and stopping in Tumbes, Huaquillas, Machala, and Guayaquil before arriving in Montañita at 7am.

Alternatively, to make the crossing independently, the immigration office is easily accessible via Tumbes in Peru ($10 or 33 soles by taxi). Once your passport has been stamped, Huaquillas is a $5 taxi ride away (the driver will accept soles).

Coming from Peru, it's best to get rid of Peruvian money before crossing into Ecuador, to avoid the dodgy money changers. Once in Ecuador, you can take out dollars at one of the ATMs in Huaquillas (there is a Banco Pichincha near the main plaza). Huaquillas is not a town you want to hang around for long, and luckily there are plenty of buses to shuttle you to more pleasant destinations. See the *Huaquillas* section of the *Guayaquil and the Southern Coast* chapter for onward travel information.

Huaquillas is not the only border crossing with Peru. If you're planning on exploring Ecuador's southern Sierra, or for a much more scenic experience, consider entering the country in the highlands south of Vilcabamba, either at **Zumba/La Balsa** (convenient if you're coming from the ruins at Chachapoyas or the Peruvian Amazon) or **Macará** (convenient if you're coming from the Peruvian coast or Lima). Both crossings are safe. **Nambija Internacional** (tel. 7/231-5177 or 7/303-9179, Facebook @coopnambija1987) has a couple of daily departures from **Jaén** in Peru to **Loja** in Ecuador (stopping in **Vilcabamba** en route), which wait while passengers complete the necessary formalities in Zumba/La Balsa. Between **Co-op Loja** (tel. 7/257-1861 or 7/272-9014) and **Union Cariamanga** (tel. 7/260-5613, Facebook @UnionCariamanga), there are three daily departures from **Piura** in Peru to **Loja** in Ecuador (8 hours, $14), which wait at the border while passengers complete formalities in Macará.

CAR OR MOTORCYCLE

To drive a vehicle into Ecuador from Colombia or Peru, you will need to obtain a **Carnet de Passages en Douane** (CPD, www.carnetde-passage.org) in your home country. A CPD is an internationally recognized customs document that allows you to temporarily "import" a car or motorbike into the country. It is valid for three months, with a further three-month extension possible. After that, there are hefty daily fines if you continue to use the vehicle. It is not legal to sell a car that has entered the country with a CPD. To permanently import a vehicle, you may end up paying more than its worth in tax and duty.

In addition to the CPD, you'll need your passport, your driver's license from your home state, and full registration papers. If the car isn't yours, bring a notarized letter signed by the owner authorizing you to use the vehicle. An international driver's license is also helpful.

Until the Pan-American Highway (Panamericana) penetrates the rainforests of the Darién Gap between Panama and Colombia, driving from Central to South America (and thus from North America to Ecuador) will remain impossible. Shipping companies in Panama City will transport your vehicle around the gap by ferry, and some go all the way to Ecuador.

Getting Around

CAR OR MOTORCYCLE

The bus service is so easy, extensive, and economical that few visitors choose to drive. The main roads are in good condition and, outside the heavily congested cities, there is generally little traffic. Out in the country, with the freedom to stop where you choose, driving can be a joy. However, the otherwise laid-back Ecuadorians tend to be rally drivers behind the wheel, and overtaking on blind bends seems to be a national pastime. Standards of driving can be extremely alarming, especially in cities, where driving is only recommended for the most confident of road users.

Cars drive on the right-hand side of the road. The legal driving age is 18 (although the required age for car rental is usually 25). In urban areas, the speed limit is 50 kph (about 32 mph). On highways, the speed limit is 90 kph (55 mph). Speeding may result in a hefty fine and three days in jail. It is technically a legal requirement for everyone in the car to wear a seatbelt, though this is only strictly enforced in the front seats (there are often no seatbelts in the back). Regular gasoline is known as *extra* ($1.90/gallon), and premium is *super* ($2.90/gallon).

Police and military checkpoints, especially in the Oriente, are common. Be prepared to stop and show your passport and documents, including the vehicle's registration, proof of insurance, and driver's license. An international driver's license is not required, but having one is a good idea.

It is illegal to bribe a public official, but if you are faced with unscrupulous traffic police (*transito*) looking to make an easy buck, handing over $20 may be considerably quicker and cheaper than the alternative paperwork and hassle. Asking whether a solution might be found (*"¿Es posible encontrar una solución?"*) might smooth things along.

In case of an accident, get a copy of the *denuncia* (report) for insurance and possible legal tangles. Remember that drivers are often assumed guilty until proven innocent, and there is a chance of being put in jail until things are sorted out.

Vehicle Rental

To rent a car, you need to present a passport, a valid driver's license, and an internationally recognized credit card. Minimum age is usually 25. A hefty deposit is charged on the card to ensure that the car is returned in one piece (21-25 years old might be able to negotiate rental upon payment of an even bigger deposit). Prices vary from $15/day or $105/week for a small car, rising to $100/day, $550/week for a larger 4WD vehicle. Check if the quoted rates include tax (IVA), unlimited mileage (*kilometraje libre*) and insurance (*seguro*). The deductible on the insurance is very high, usually between $1,000 and $3,500. Check the car carefully for any dings and scrapes before setting out.

Avoiding stressful city driving may be easier said than done, as car hire is rarely available outside the main hubs of Quito, Guayaquil, and Cuenca (although Quito's airport is outside the city, offering a relatively traffic-free escape). For details of rental agencies, see the *Getting There and Around* sections of these chapters.

In Quito, **Ecuador Freedom Bike Rentals** (www.freedombikerental.com) offers motorbike hire, which is also available at various agencies in Baños.

Taxis

Yellow taxis are readily available across most of the country. Some rural Amazonian and Sierran towns have a mix of conventional taxis and white pickup trucks (*camionetas*). Short taxi journeys are usually economical, often $1.50-2. In larger cities, drivers are supposed to use a meter, so insist that yours does ("*el taxi metro por favor*"). If the driver claims it is not working, consider using a different taxi, or negotiate the fare in advance. Where there are no meters, it's a good idea to ask a local person or your hotel what the approximate fare should be and suggest it to the driver, rather than asking him (or, very occasionally, her) how much it will be. Taxis at airports and bus terminals often have flat rates, which are nonnegotiable. Bear in mind that fares often increase at night in cities.

It is not uncommon for taxistas to play blaring music or to drive alarmingly. Feel free to ask them to turn the music down ("*¿Podria bajar la voluma por favor?*") or drive more slowly ("*¿Podria conducir mas despacio por favor?*") and to find a different taxi if the request is refused. Don't be put off: Many taxi drivers are extremely polite, helpful, a pleasure to talk to, and a great source of local information. Those learning Spanish can make the most of having a captive audience!

Throughout most of the country, taxis are a safe way to travel and it's generally fine to flag them down in the street. In cities at night, however, extra care should be taken. Guayaquil is the worst place in the country for "express kidnappings," where rogue taxi drivers briefly abduct passengers, relieve them of their valuables, and force them to take cash out of an ATM or hand over their PIN number. Victims are usually released unharmed, but these incidents are terrifying and can turn violent. This type of robbery is also fairly common in Quito, especially in La Mariscal. For more information, see the *Crime* section of this chapter.

Hiring a taxi by the day could cost anywhere between $50 and $100. Get a few quotes, as prices vary greatly. Using taxis for longer trips allows for tailor-made itineraries without the responsibility or stress of car rental. You'll find that some drivers are knowledgeable, friendly local guides.

Hitchhiking

While it shouldn't technically be recommended as a safe method of transport, it's fairly common for Ecuadorians to catch rides with passing motorists, especially in remote rural areas. Even though *ir al dedo* ("thumbing it") means the same in Latin America as it does elsewhere, here it's more common to wave down passing cars with a flap of the hand. It can be difficult to tell the difference between an unofficial taxi cruising for passengers and a friendly motorist offering a ride for free, so it's a good idea to clarify when you get in, by asking "*¿Cuanto seria?*" ("How much would that be?"), or to offer to pay when you get out "*¿Le debo algo?*" ("Do I owe you anything?"). Use your own judgment when deciding to get in. A good rule of thumb is to look for a car with a local woman driver or passenger(s).

BUS

Love it or hate it (and you'll probably experience both emotions), bus is the most common, recommended, and economical mode of transport, with journeys costing roughly $1-1.50 per hour of travel. The majority of Ecuadorians don't own cars and depend on the bus service, which is generally reliable. It's also incredibly comprehensive, covering even remote rural areas. Traveling by bus is a wonderful way to admire Ecuador's stunning scenery and travel with the locals.

There are downsides, however. Comfort levels vary widely, from bone-shaking rust buckets to ultramodern vehicles with air-conditioning, Wi-Fi, plug sockets, toilets, reclining seats, and attendants. Drivers often play music or movies at high volume, so take ear plugs if you're sensitive to noise. Inexplicably, the movies are usually ultra-violent and can be fairly sexually explicit, so bring a distraction if you're traveling with kids. Probably the most common way for visitors to fall victim to theft is to store their belongings in the overhead compartment on a bus; these are easy pickings for thieves. Don't leave any valuables in your main luggage, which will be stored under the bus. Keep anything of value in your day pack or handbag and hold it on your lap. If you put it on the floor in front of your seat, make sure that the person behind you can't access it. Putting it between your feet with a strap wound around your leg should do the trick.

Most journeys over 6 hours have departures during the day or overnight. Traveling by day means you can look out of the window and marvel at the rapid changes in landscape and vegetation, and you always get some unforgettable glimpses of everyday life as you pass by. Traveling at night is a good option for those who can sleep anywhere and are looking to save on a night in a hotel (though it may involve arriving to an unknown destination in the early hours, which can be unsettling).

Larger towns usually have a main bus terminal (*terminal terrestre*), where there is a row of ticket offices. It's often necessary to purchase a separate ticket ($0.25) to get out onto the platform, which goes toward the upkeep of the station. If there is no *terminal terrestre*, there is usually a park or intersection from which buses come and go. Some bus companies have their own office or terminal for arrivals and departures.

Adding to the wonderful flexibility of travel within Ecuador, many buses can be hailed from the roadside with a flap of the hand and will let you off upon request. On these buses, sometimes you pay the driver when you get on, other times when you get off. Most often, a conductor will come around and collect fares. Just watch what the locals do and follow their lead. To ask the driver to stop, say "*¡pare!*" (stop), "*a la esquina*" (at the corner), or simply "*¡gracias!*" (thanks). If you're not sure where to get off, ask the conductor to notify you when you get to your desired destination; they usually remember to do so.

If you prefer a faster, direct service with no unscheduled stops, buy a ticket for a *directo* at the terminal or bus company office. Tickets can be bought on the day of travel, though on public holidays and high season weekends (especially on beach routes), it's advisable to buy it the day before. Most tickets have allocated seat numbers, which may or may not be respected.

Long-distance buses stop for meals, and there is usually a toilet at the back, but you may have to ask the conductor for the key.

Even on short journeys, vendors climb aboard in most towns selling drinks, snacks, and fast food. In fact, Ecuador's buses are the livelihood of many thousands of vendors, selling everything from food to medical products. Although this can be an annoyance, remember that these people make a living from it, so perhaps giving a quarter for a few candies is not unreasonable. Many vendors have a set routine, and you'll be amazed at how much time and effort they put into their sales pitch. First they greet all the passengers, thank God for the beautiful day, and give a long apology for disturbing their journey. This may be followed by a tale of woe about their current economic situation. Then they give a detailed description of the product, its contents, benefits, and instructions for use. The vendor then walks through the bus handing a product to every passenger, emphasizing that this is by no means an indication of intent to purchase (you can refuse to take it or give it back later). The vendor will then try to surprise you with a very reasonable offer (most products are sold for $0.25-2) and then go back through the bus collecting sales. You'll notice that locals are very tolerant of the vendors and frequently make purchases.

Information about bus schedules can be unreliable on companies' websites, but many schedules can be checked online at Andes Transit (https://andestransit.com).

Police occasionally stop buses searching for contraband or criminals. All passengers will be asked to disembark. The men are patted down, everyone has their bag searched, and all are asked to present ID before getting back on the bus.

COLECTIVOS AND RANCHEROS

A *colectivo* is a shared form of transport on a set route, often a converted pickup truck with benches in the back, covered with a canvas awning. This can be an economical way to travel, though they usually only leave when they are full, so there may be a wait. *Chivas* or *rancheros* are open-sided buses with wooden bench seats, also common in rural areas.

METRO AND TROLLEY SYSTEMS

Quito's network of three electric trolley bus lines is cheap, well organized, and usually much faster than traveling by car, especially in heavy traffic. Overcrowding and pickpockets can be a problem, however. Flat fare for all services is $0.25. Guayaquil has a similar system, the Metrovía. At the time of writing, an overground metro system was being built in Cuenca. An underground metro system

is currently being built in Quito and is projected to be operational by July 2019 (delays not withstanding).

TRAIN

When it opened in the 1900s, Ecuador's railway was used to transport goods and passengers between Quito and Guayaquil. Crossing raging rivers, deep ravines, frosty Andean peaks, dense cloud forests, and rocky slopes, linking the Sierra and the coast was an impressive feat of engineering. The most famous section, just outside Alausí, was christened Nariz del Diablo (Devil's Nose), where a series of switchbacks are so tight the entire train has to back up to fit through, descending over 500 meters (over 1,600 ft) in just 12 kilometers (7.5 mi). With the new transport system, suddenly trade between the two regions was possible in hours rather than days, and, with three classes of ticket, rail travel was affordable for local people, boosting the economy along the whole route. Additional lines were added to Cuenca, Otavalo, and other cities and the railway flourished for decades, until the road system rendered it obsolete. The network fell into disrepair and was finally closed in the 1990s.

In 2008, Rafael Correa's government oversaw a multimillion-dollar renovation of the railways, and many sections have since been reopened. Rather than an everyday method of transport, however, a number of scenic journeys are available as tourist attractions, at prices that are out of reach for most Ecuadorians. As well as the Devil's Nose, several other routes are available, most of them round-trip one-day experiences with prices ranging $28-63. These leave from Otavalo, Ibarra, Riobamba, Ambato, and Quito in the Sierra, and Durán, just outside Guayaquil. There is also a three-day/four-night route from Quito to Durán for $1,650. For more information, see the **Tren Ecuador** website (http://trenecuador.com/en). Tickets can be bought online, by phone (800/873-637), or in person at the stations.

AIR

Flying within Ecuador is quick, convenient, and relatively inexpensive. From Quito, it's possible to fly in under an hour to Guayaquil, Esmeraldas, Manta, Portoviejo, Salinas, Machala, Santa Rosa, Tulcán, Cuenca, Loja, Coca, Lago Agrio, Macas, and the Galápagos (Baltra and San Cristóbal). Guayaquil has direct domestic connections to Quito and the Galápagos. With some exceptions, mainland flights are generally economical (from $40 one way). Flying to the Galápagos is much more expensive (at least $400 round-trip). To get the best deal, book in advance and be prepared to be flexible with dates. Some promotional deals only include hand luggage, so check carefully. Compare prices for all three domestic carriers: TAME, Avianca, and LAN.

TAME (www.tame.com.ec) is Ecuador's national carrier and covers the whole domestic network. **LAN** (www.latam.com) serves Quito, Guayaquil, Cuenca, and the Galápagos. **Avianca** (www.avianca.com) serves Quito, Guayaquil, Manta, Coca, and the Galápagos.

There are no roads in much of the Amazon region, which is only accessible via small plane or motorized canoe. Four-and six-seater planes leave from the airport at Shell near Puyo for destinations such as Sarayaku and Kapawi Ecolodge. **Aero Sarayaku** (tel. 3/279-5084 or 98/329-2734) offers charter flights in a six-seater plane for $330/hour.

CANOE

For the vast majority of Amazon communities, motorized canoe is the only form of transport, with most families owning their own boat. From docks in Coca, Misahuallí, and Lago Agrio, canoes and larger boats ferry passengers and cargo east down the Napo and Aguarico Rivers.

Visas and Officialdom

TOURIST VISAS

Travelers from the vast majority of countries do not require a visa to enter Ecuador and will be given a 90-day permit stamp upon arrival (exceptions are citizens of Afghanistan, Bangladesh, Cuba, Eritrea, Ethiopia, Kenya, Nepal, Nigeria, North Korea, Pakistan, Somalia, and Senegal, who require a visa). This 90-day permit is only issued once per year (i.e., if you are issued one on April 1, 2019, you cannot request another until April 1, 2020). Citizens of most Latin American countries are issued a 180-day visa upon arrival.

A passport with validity of at least six months is required. Border officials have the right to ask for proof of onward travel arrangements (a reservation for a bus ticket to Peru or Colombia is sufficient), though they often do not. If you are traveling from a country with a risk of yellow fever transmission, including Peru, Colombia, Brazil, Argentina, and Bolivia, you may be asked to show a vaccination certificate. Check with the World Health Organization for the current list of affected countries.

To enter the Galápagos, it is necessary to show a reservation for a Galápagos hotel or cruise boat, or a letter of invitation from a local resident of the islands. Foreign visitors must pay a fee to enter the Galápagos (Latin American citizens $50, the rest of the world $100) and complete an online form (www.gobiernogalapagos.gob.ec/pre-registro-tct-turistas). A health insurance requirement may be introduced. Check with your tour operator or hotel for the latest information.

If you enter or exit Ecuador via the border with Peru or Colombia, make sure you are given exit and entry stamps at the border showing the date. Officials are known to forget, and without a stamp, you're officially in the country illegally.

Since February 2018, overstaying a visa

involves a fine. At its most severe, the penalty is $772 and expulsion from the country.

If you know beforehand that you would like to stay in Ecuador beyond 90 days, consider applying for a longer visa with your local Ecuadorian embassy before your trip, to avoid formalities in Ecuador.

Alternatively, at the time of writing, the 90-day visa can be extended once, by a further 90 days, when you're in the country. Take your passport to any Migration office on the day your visa expires and you'll be asked to complete a form and pay $129 at a branch of Banco Pacifico. The extension will be granted on the same day. Migration offices can be found at the following locations: In Quito: Ministerio de Relaciones Exteriores, Carrión E1-76 at 10 de Agosto, 2/299-3200. In Guayaquil: Ministerio de Relaciones Exteriores y Movilidad Humana, Edif. Gobierno del Litoral, Avenida Francisco de Orellana y Justino Cornejo, tel. 4/206-8492. In Manta: Barrio el Murciélago, Avenida 23 y calle M3, tel. 5/262-8629. There are also smaller, regional offices in other towns across the country, as listed here: www.cancilleria.gob.ec/coordinaciones-zonales. Go early (8:30am) and be prepared to wait. After this extension it is possible to extend the visa for another 6 months by applying for a Visa Especial de Turismo at the Ministerio de Relaciones Exteriores, which costs $450. Visa rules and requirements change frequently. For up-to-date information, and to download the application form, see www.cancilleria.gob.ec (go to *Movilidad Humanos, Servicios,* and then *Visas*). For requirements in English, visit www.consuladovirtual.gob.ec/en.

If you have the resources, especially if you have limited Spanish or time, it is highly recommended to get some help navigating any kind of visa process. It's usually well worth paying a little extra to save an enormous amount of hassle. Lots of bilingual local people make a living assisting foreigners with these kinds of procedures, but make sure to get a recommendation, as there are some unscrupulous folks working in this area. On the coast, a recommended contact is Cecilia Lapellegrina (cecilialapellegrina@gmail.com). A recommended and economical lawyer is Joseph Guznay (josephguznay@gmail.com), who is based in Quito but works nationwide. Companies such as EcuaAssist (www.ecuaassist.com) can help with visas and a wide range of bureaucratic and legal procedures.

VISAS FOR LONGER STAYS

A wide range of visas exist for those wishing to stay longer in Ecuador, whether temporarily or as a resident. A list of visas and their requirements, in English, can be found here: www.consuladovirtual.gob.ec (select Visas from the Consular Services menu). You will certainly need to procure the services of a lawyer, such as Joseph Guznay (josephguznay@gmail.com) or a company such as EcuaAssist (www.ecuaassist.com), to negotiate this kind of red tape.

BRINGING PETS

If you're planning on bringing a four-legged friend, check the country-specific entry requirements here: www.pettravel.com. Have all paperwork on hand going through immigration and customs. The Agriculture Ministry is at customs and thoroughly checks all paperwork.

Sports and Recreation

MOUNTAINEERING

A variety of high-altitude climbing options in Ecuador will delight mountaineers, whether complete beginners or seasoned veterans. Options range from day climbs suitable for anyone with a reasonable degree of fitness, to highly technical snowy ascents, to seven-day expeditions through the wilderness.

With perhaps the exception of the "starter peak" of Fuya Fuya just outside Otavalo, it is not recommended to undertake any mountaineering expedition without a guide.

Since 2015, climbers of any glaciated mountain must be accompanied by an accredited, specialized guide and be registered by a licensed tour agency in the Biodiversity Information System (Sistema de Información de Biodiversidad, SIB). This system is strictly enforced. Any reputable agency will take care of this formality, so make sure that yours does. Recognized mountaineering clubs can apply for climbing permits with SIB (http://sib.ambiente.gob.ec). For more information, contact ASEGUIM, the **Ecuadorian Mountain Guide Association** (www.aseguim.org), or the **Ministry of the Environment** (tel. 2/398-7600, ext. 3001, mesadeayuda@ambiente.gob.ec).

Non-glaciated peaks should not be attempted without a guide either. Even trails that don't require technical knowledge are often poorly marked or nonexistent, and the weather can change rapidly, reducing visibility to near zero. It is very easy to get lost, and helicopter rescue teams are often sent out to search for overconfident tourists, especially Europeans who are accustomed to the Alps but unprepared for the Andes. With nighttime temperatures below freezing, fatalities from exposure have occurred. Don't underestimate the danger of attempting to strike out on your own. Aside from the safety benefit, hiring a local guide, directly or through an agency, is also a great way to learn about Ecuador while providing sustainable income for a fellow lover of the great outdoors.

Guided climbs typically include equipment, permits, transportation, meals, and overnight(s) in a refuge or camping. Check with your guide or tour agency about what you will need to bring: usually hiking shoes, warm clothes, and a waterproof jacket. Mountaineering gear is available at stores in Quito.

The central Sierra is the best region for mountaineering, home to the famous Avenue of the Volcanoes. Machachi and Latacunga both make good bases for the more northerly central peaks, including Corazón, the Ilinizas, Rumiñahui, and Cotopaxi. At 4,788 meters (15,709 ft), Volcán Corazón is a challenging day climb. Of the two Ilinizas, Iliniza Norte is known for being less difficult and, in good conditions, can be tackled by anyone with decent hiking and scrambling skills. In snow/ice conditions, however, it can be challenging, even for experienced climbers. Iliniza Sur has permanent snow cover and is more technical. Rumiñahui (4,712 m/15,459 ft) is a relatively straightforward climb, combining an uphill hike with a bit of scrambling; a rope and climbing protection are recommended for the more exposed stretches.

Two out of Ecuador's big three—Cotopaxi, Chimborazo, and Cayambe—are in the central Sierra. Cotopaxi (5,897 m/19,347 ft) is the country's most popular high-altitude climb because of its relative simplicity; it's mostly an uphill slog. However, less than half of those who attempt the summit actually succeed; climbers need to be in good physical condition, be fully acclimatized, and have a certain amount of luck with the conditions. Chimborazo (6,310 m/20,702 ft), the planet's closest point to the sun, is more challenging. Both require an overnight stay in a refuge. As part of guided tours of the national park, anyone with a decent level of fitness can climb to the snowy refuges on Cotopaxi and Chimborazo at 4,800 meters (15,750 ft) and 5,000 meters (16,400 ft), respectively. Both walks take a breathless 40 minutes from the parking lot.

The more southern central peaks are best accessed from Riobamba. Carihuairazo (5,020 m/16,470 ft) is usually climbed as practice for scaling its taller neighbor, Chimborazo. El Altar is considered the most technical ascent in the country, requiring four days. Sangay, one of the world's most active volcanoes, is the most inhospitable, requiring a seven-day expedition with the risk of being hit by falling rocks and breathing in sulfur gas near the summit. The highly active Tungurahua that looms over Baños can be climbed from nearby Pondoa, requiring an overnight stay in a refuge.

Near Quito, the two Pichincha volcanoes, Guagua and Rucu, can be climbed as day trips; the latter is easier and more accessible. To the south of the city, within the Pasochoa Protected Forest, it's possible to climb to the lip of Cerro Pasochoa's blasted volcanic crater in six hours. The Pichinchas and Cerro Pasochoa are good starters for acclimating and getting into shape. To the east of Quito, Antisana (5,704 m/18,714 ft) is Ecuador's fourth-highest peak and one of the least climbed. Its reputation for being difficult and dangerous is due in part to the presence of active glaciers and lack of a refuge. Reaching the summit requires a three-day expedition.

In the northern Sierra, Otavalo provides access to Fuya Fuya (4,262 m/13,983 ft), the only peak in the country that can safely be climbed without a guide, on a four-hour round-trip (do go with a companion, though). Tour operators in Otavalo offer day-trip climbs to Fuya Fuya and Cotacachi (4,939 m/16,204 ft). Cayambe (5,790 m/18,996 ft), Ecuador's third tallest peak, is for advanced climbers only due to an ever-changing network of crevasses, unusually high winds, strong snowstorms, and occasional avalanches. The volcanoes Imbabura (4,630 m/15,190 ft), and Cubilche (3,802 m/12,474 ft) can both be climbed as day trips from Esperanza near Ibarra.

In the southern Sierra, the cordillera is older and less volcanically active, without the soaring mountains that are found farther north, resulting in fewer climbing opportunities. One exception is a technical 2.2-kilometer (1.4-mi) climb to the summit of Cerro San Luis (4,264 m/13,990 ft) in El Cajas National Park just outside Cuenca.

The Amazon region is home to two of the country's least climbed volcanoes. Reventador (literally, "Exploder") isn't attempted often because of its muddy approach and constant volcanic activity. The two-day trek to the top crosses everything from jungle to lava-covered wasteland. Sumaco is not a technical climb, but it requires a three- to five-day expedition. Every mid-November, tourists can join a group of Kichwa shamans from Archidonia to climb the volcano and perform rituals at the top.

More information about all of these climbs can be found in the relevant destination chapters, along with recommended agencies and local guides. Guides can also be hired via the Ecuadorian Association of Mountain Guides (tel. 2/254-0599, www.aseguim.org). Its Members page lists the contact details of guides who speak English, German, French, and Italian.

A very helpful source of information for all things climbing is Wlady Ortiz, the bilingual local owner of Ecuador Eco Adventure (tel. 99/831-1282, www.ecuadorecoadventure. com) in Riobamba. As well as offering climbs of peaks nationwide, Wlady has opened Riobamba Base Camp, a hostel designed exclusively for hikers and climbers.

Wherever you climb, be prepared to deal with the effects of altitude. Even if you're fit, you might experience fatigue, headaches, and breathlessness. It is not uncommon to suffer some degree of **acute mountain sickness** (AMS), known locally as *soroche,* which feels like the world's worst hangover: headache, nausea, fatigue, insomnia, and loss of appetite. Your guide will know how to deal with this, and anyone suffering acutely will be accompanied back to a lower altitude. A couple of days walking around Quito (at 2,850 m/9,350 ft) is a good way to prepare for a climb. Drink plenty of fluids and avoid alcohol. Before tackling any of the highest peaks, ideally you should trek and sleep at around 4,000 meters (13,000 ft) for a couple of days or, even better, do a practice climb such as Iliniza Norte or Rumiñahui. All mountaineering tour agencies offer acclimatization climbs.

HIKING AND CAMPING

There are wonderful hikes in all regions of Ecuador, many of which can only be undertaken with a guide. There are also some areas with excellent trails for self-guided hikes, notably around Baños, Vilcabamba, Otavalo, Mindo, and Quilotoa. The two-day trek to the crater lake of the El Altar volcano, accessed via Riobamba, is one of the most beautiful in the country, though you'll need some hiking experience to undertake this independently.

Many national parks and private reserves also have well-marked trails for independent hiking, including to Los Frailes beach in Machalilla National Park; to the Laguna Voladero in El Ángel Ecological Reserve; to the Lagunas Llaviucu and Toreadora in El Cajas National Park; and to the Cascada Poderosa in Podocarpus National Park. Entrance to all national parks is free.

More details of all these hikes can be found in the relevant destination chapters, along with countless other self-guided and guided trails that are too numerous to mention here. Self-guided hikes are usually well marked, and maps are readily available from local hostels or online. Most are out of cell phone range, but if you have a smartphone you can download the application Maps.me (https://maps.me), which can be used offline to help guide your way. Serious hikers can request topographical maps from the Instituto Geográfico Militar (IGM, www.igm.gob.ec) in Quito, either in person or online (see *Servicios* on the IGM website).

Even when setting out for a popular,

well-marked, self-guided hike, it's sensible to take some precautions. It's not a good idea to go alone, in case of accident. Many hostels in popular hiking areas are good places to meet up with hiking buddies. Notify your hotel where you're going, your approximate route, and when you expect to be back; don't forget to confirm your safe return. Be prepared for rapid changes in weather, especially in the Sierra. Wear layers and take sunblock and sunglasses. Carry plenty of water; energy rich snacks such as dried fruit and nuts (chocolate is a godsend at altitude); a compass (or compass app on your phone); waterproof clothing (a thin plastic poncho is a good idea, as it folds up small and can also cover your day pack); and bandages in case of blisters.

Unless you're an outdoor survival expert, do not consider striking out on your own into the wilderness. Many trails are poorly marked or nonexistent, and the weather can change rapidly, reducing visibility to near zero if clouds descend. This book indicates wherever possible which hikes can be completed independently and which need a guide.

Several national parks have designated camping areas. Many hostels and lodges also have camping facilities for as little as $3 or $6 per night. Some even provide tents. It's best to bring your camping gear from home, including a water bottle that filters and purifies water. There are outdoors stores in Quito, but good-quality items are expensive. Tents are available for as little as $30 in most large supermarkets (such as Mi Comisariato), though they are only suitable for the kindest of weather (i.e., dry nights on the coast) or covered camping areas. In the Sierra, especially on the *páramo*, be prepared for sub-zero nighttime temperatures.

RAFTING AND KAYAKING

White-water sports are very popular in Ecuador, and the terrain is perfect, with rivers rushing down either side of the Andes to the coastal plains to the west and Amazon basin to the east. From half-day rafting and kayaking trips for complete beginners to weeklong advanced-level expeditions, the whole spectrum of activities is available, and the spectacular scenery through gorges, canyons, valleys, and jungles makes these trips as beautiful as they are exciting.

The main hubs for white-water sports are Quito, Baños, Tena, and the Quijos Valley. The Ministry of Tourism requires all rafting companies to be certified, so make sure that yours is. Most of the better companies have Class III certification or higher from the **International Rafting Federation** (IRF, www.internationalrafting.com). Trip leaders should have Wilderness Advanced First Aid qualifications.

Rivers

The **Río Blanco** and **Río Toachi** provide the nearest year-round white water to Quito, three hours from the capital. The Toachi (Class III-III+) is closest to the capital and is therefore Ecuador's most rafted river, though not its most pristine. It's navigable all year and is particularly good during the high-water season from January to the end of May. Much cleaner and more beautiful is the **Upper Río Blanco** (Class III), though the water can be too low to navigate June-December. Kayakers can take on **Río Mindo** (Class III-IV), **Río Saloya** (IV-V), **Río Pilatón** (IV-V), and the **Upper Río Toachi** (IV-V), depending on the time of year and their ability. A highly recommended company in Quito is **Torrent Duck** (tel. 99/867-9933, www.torrent-duck.com), which has excellent customer service and is environmentally conscious. **Rios Ecuador** (www.riosecuador.com) is the most well-established operator of white-water trips out of Quito, charging $87 for a rafting day trip to Ríos Toachi and Blanco, $299 for two days. Customized itineraries are possible, as are kayak rentals and courses.

Only a 90-minute drive from the capital, but more seasonal, is **Baeza** on the **Río Quijos** (Class III-IV), where there is excellent rafting and kayaking between October and February. Class III-V kayaking is also available on the nearby **Ríos Oyacachi** and **Cosanga,** with the Cosanga Gorge a highlight. Local family-run **Baeza Tours** (Facebook @BaezaToursEcuador) offers rafting and kayaking ($65-75 pp/day) and kayaking courses ranging from two days/one night ($180 pp) to four days/three nights ($360 pp), including accommodations. Companies in Quito also offer tours in the Baeza area.

Tena has developed into Ecuador's watersports capital, and there is excellent rafting and kayaking year-round, with a dozen rivers within an hour's drive. Half-day ($40 pp), full-day ($65-80 pp), and two-day trips (from $170 pp) are available. The most popular rafting trip is the **Jatunyacu** ("big water" in Kichwa), a Class III river also known as the Upper Napo, a major tributary of the Amazon. Its exciting rapids and verdant jungle scenery can be navigated year-round. Best rafted in the low-water season of mid-October to mid-March, the **Río Misahuallí** (Class IV) offers the country's most challenging rafting trip, including the single biggest rapid commonly rafted in all of Ecuador, called "the Land of the Giants." The **Río Jondachi** offers excellent kayaking for all levels. The Upper Jondachi (Class V) attracts experts from around the world to tackle its continuous rapids. The Middle Jondachi (Class IV) is more remote with more beautiful scenery and is usually paired with the Lower Jondachi and the Hollín Canyon for a six- seven-hour run. The Lower Jondachi to Hollín Canyon is the only section that is offered as a rafting trip—a beautiful 23-kilometer (14-mi) wilderness run suitable for intermediate paddlers (Class III+, then Class IV when it meets the Hollín). The **Río Piatua** is another favorite with kayakers, with excellent water quality and 12 kilometers (7.5 mi) of nearly continuous Class III rapids (occasionally reaching Class IV and V). Novice runs are found on the **Anzu, Napo, Pano,** and **Tena Rivers**. A highly recommended operator in Tena is **Torrent Duck** (www.torrent-duck. com), which is actively involved in conservation efforts to protect the Jatunyacu River from mining and deforestation. Other good options are **Caveman Adventures** (www.cavemanecuador.com) and Kichwa-owned **Raft Amazonia** (www.raftamazonia.com).

Baños is one of the more popular rafting destinations in Ecuador, despite the marginal water quality in the **Pastaza** and **Patate Rivers**. Expert kayakers generally opt to paddle the much cleaner side creeks and tributaries of the Pastaza, such as the **Ríos Verde Chico, Ulba, Verde, Topo, Zuñac**, and **Encanto**. It has been said that the **Río Topo** (Class V) is the best steep creek run in Ecuador. Half-day rafting in Baños costs $30, and full-day kayaking costs $90. A recommended operator is **Starline** (Facebook @ starlineexpeditions).

The southern Amazon town of **Macas** is the jumping-off point for rafting and kayaking in the **Upano** watershed, which offers superb white water for all skill levels in an area rarely explored by tourists. A highlight is the Namangosa Gorge of the **Río Upano** (Class IV).

Shiripuno Lodge (www.shiripunolodge.com) offers kayaking tours of **Yasuní National Park**, with camping in various riverside locations.

For something a bit different, try kayaking in the volcanic crater lake **Quilotoa**, offered by **Ecotrail** (https://ecotrail.com.ec, $25) in Latacunga. For some tropical kayaking, it's possible to paddle to the island of **Portete** from the northern coastal village of Mompiche. For further information on kayaking, www.kayakecuador.com is a useful website.

SURFING

Ecuador is an excellent destination for surfers of all levels, from complete novices to advanced wave riders, offering warm water and an incredible variety of breaks, most of them uncrowded and some world class. From point breaks to rock reefs, jetties, rivermouths, and endless beach breaks, there is a wave to suit everyone, whether goofy or natural.

The peak surf season is December to May, when the swell is from the north and winds are light or off-shore, generating epic, glassy conditions with up to 3-meter (10-ft) waves. During these months, Ecuador is a world-class surfing destination and one of the most consistent places for tropical waves during the Northern Hemisphere winter. Days on the coast are hot and sunny, with air temperatures around 30°C (86°F) and water temperatures only a couple of degrees lower. From June to November, the southern Humboldt Current dominates, circulating colder water up from Peru, creating more frequent overcast skies and onshore conditions (though mornings can still be glassy). Decent swells still arrive during this period, but with much less consistency. The vast majority of people do not require a wetsuit even in this cooler season.

There are no sharks to worry about off the mainland coast of Ecuador (though three surfers have been bitten in the leg by sharks in the Galápagos since 2007). Stingrays lurk in the shallows and can deliver a painful sting that will put you out of action for a day, so shuffle your feet when entering the water. Jellyfish can be an occasional annoyance but nothing more serious. More hazardous is the equatorial sun, which can be brutal in the high season between 10am and 4pm, especially sitting out on a board, with the rays glancing off the water. You will need a total sunblock, and if you have fair skin, it may be a good idea to invest in a peaked surfing cap to protect your head, eyes, and face.

Montañita is Ecuador's main surf destination, with a world-class right-hand point break that has hosted several international competitions. At the time of writing, two Montañita locals, Dominic "Mimi" Barona and Jonathan "El Gato" Chila, are currently the female and male surf champions of Latin America, respectively, with their sights set on the 2020 Olympics in Tokyo. Adjacent to the point break is a long beach break suitable for everyone, with classes readily available. The neighboring beaches have long, uncrowded breaks for surfers of all levels. Of these, Olón is probably the best place in the country to learn and has an excellent surf school. Surf shops in Montañita rent and sell boards (both new and secondhand). If you're heading to other destinations, it's best to take your own board. For information on other breaks in Ecuador, see *Surf's Up* in the *Explore* chapter, along with www.magicseaweed.com.

There are a couple of shapers in Montañita, including Cesar "Rasty" Moreira at **Balsa Surf Camp** (http://balsahouse.com), who makes beautiful, sustainably harvested balsa wood boards. Farther north, in Manta, René Burgos (reneburgos_surf@hotmail.com) is another highly recommended shaper, who makes tailor-made boards for around $400. His workshop can be found in front of the Oro Verde Hotel on the *malecón*.

BIRDING

Ecuador is indisputably one of the best birding destinations in the world. With almost 1,600 recorded species—twice as many as all of North America—incredibly, one-sixth of the planet's types of bird are found in this tiny country. Perhaps the most iconic is the hummingbird, present in every region from sea level to snowcapped mountains, including the world's second smallest, the Esmeraldas woodstar, or *estrellita Esmeraldeña*. At the other end of the scale is the Andean condor, the world's largest flying bird, with a wingspan of more than 3 meters (10 ft). Other avian stars include the blue-footed booby, the magnificent frigate bird, the long-wattled umbrella bird, the agami heron, the harpy eagle, the Andean cock-of-the-rock, and a variety of toucans, macaws, antpittas, and tanagers. For more details on Ecuador's birds, see the *Plants and Animals* section of the *Background* chapter.

Ecuador's premier bird-watching destination is Mindo. There is good birding to be had all over the country, but other especially notable locations include Cosanga, the world record holder in the Christmas Bird Count, with a total of 600 species recorded in one day; Limoncocha, with 470 total species; Podocarpus National Park, with over 600

species; and the cloud forests of Intag, where 40 percent of the bird and plant species are found nowhere else on the planet.

You don't have to be an avid birder to enjoy much of Ecuador's birdlife. Pretty much everyone will love watching countless hummingbirds buzzing around feeders in Mindo; spotting kingfishers and wading birds from a canoe on Laguna Limoncocha; or climbing a tower in Yasuní National Park to hear the jungle dawn chorus at canopy level.

The nonprofit **Jocotoco Foundation** (http://www.jocotoco.org) has a number of reserves that protect endemic and threatened bird species all over the country. They also have lodges and offer tours. **San Jorge** (www.eco-lodgesanjorge.com) owns eight private reserves and four ecolodges in birding hot spots. Specialized agencies such as **Neotropical** (www.neotropicalecuador.com) offer birding tours. Local bird guides are found all over the country and are more economical than an organized tour. Recommended local guides have been included throughout this book.

Robert Ridgely and Paul Greenfield's two-volume illustrated *The Birds of Ecuador: Field Guide* is considered the birding bible here.

OTHER RECREATION

See the *Adrenaline Rush* section of the *Explore* chapter for some of the best destinations for adventure sports in Ecuador.

SPECTATOR SPORTS

Soccer (*fútbol*) is Ecuador's national game, far more popular than all other sports combined. Informal matches pop up on makeshift fields everywhere—on a narrow strip of beach as the tide comes in, or on a patch of cleared rainforest with bamboo goalposts. Every village has its football pitch (*cancha de fútbol*) for more organized games. Antonio Valencia, an Ecuadorian from Lago Agrio who captains Manchester United, is a national hero.

The biggest teams in the country are from Guayaquil: **Emelec** (which plays at the Estadio Banco del Pacífico Capwell, also known as Estadio George Capwell) and

Barcelona (whose stadium is the Estadio Banco Pichincha or Estadio Monumental). Matches between the two rival clubs are known as El Clásico del Astillero. In Quito, the city's most successful club is the **Liga de Quito,** which plays at the Estadio Casa Blanca. Ticket prices range from around $5 for a seat behind the goal to $25 for a box seat at the main stand. Expect to pay at least $20 for El Clásico. The Ecuadorian national team plays at the Estadio Atahualpa in Quito at an elevation of 2,850 meters (9,350 ft), a huge advantage over teams from lower elevations. Check www.elnacional.ec for details of the next match. Tickets can be bought at the stadiums (*estadios*) and should be purchased ahead of time for popular matches (such as El Clásico).

Whenever there is a big match in Ecuador, men gather around televisions in stores and restaurants to watch. While football violence is known between rival fans in the cities, it is rare elsewhere in Ecuador.

Ecuavolley, the local version of volleyball, is another popular sport, both on the beach and on concrete courts. Big city parks, such as Quito's Parque La Carolina, are a good place to watch games, especially on Sundays.

Learning Spanish in Ecuador

Ecuador has many excellent Spanish schools, and it's worth shopping around to find one that fits your needs. Most provide 2-6 hours of instruction per day, either in groups ($5.50-6.50 per hour) or one on one ($7-13 per hour). An initial registration fee may be required ($20-35).

Most schools offer extra activities such as cooking, salsa classes, surf lessons, volunteering, cultural experiences, and group trips. Some will house you in private or shared accommodations (prices vary) or arrange for a homestay with a local family (typically $20-25 per day for full board, $17-20 for a room and two meals per day). You can make your own accommodation arrangements if you prefer.

SIERRA

The advantage of learning in the Sierra is that the people tend to speak more slowly and clearly than their coastal counterparts, making it easier to practice in public.

To give something back, consider the excellent nonprofit **Yanapuma Spanish School** (www.yanapumaspanish.org), which has locations in Quito and Cuenca. Proceeds go toward sustainable development projects in indigenous and marginalized communities and a scholarship fund for disadvantaged children. It's the only school using the Communicative Language Teaching methodology, which moves away from traditional grammar-based classes. Instead, students learn through interaction with the teacher and (if in a group class) other students. Prices start at $6/hour for group classes and $9/hour for private, individually tailored classes. Study & Travel programs combine classes with exploration of Ecuador with a teacher. Widely ranging volunteer opportunities are available.

In Quito, the following schools are also recommended: **Simon Bolivar Spanish School** (Mariscal Foch E9-20 *y* Av. 6 de Diciembre, tel. 2/254-4558, www.simon-bolivar.com); **Ailola Quito Spanish School** (Guayaquil N9-77 *y* Oriente, tel. 2/228-5657, www.ailolaquito. com); **Guayasamín Spanish School** (Calama E8-54 *cerca* 6 de Diciembre, tel. 2/254-4210, www.guayasaminschool.com); **Instituto Superior de Español** (Guayaquil N9-77 *y* Oriente, tel. 2/228-5657, www. superiorspanishschool.com); **La Lengua** (Av. Cristóbal Colón E6-12 *y* Rábida, Building Ave María, tel. 2/250-1271, www.la-lengua.com); and **South American Language Center** (Amazonas N26-59 *y* Santa María, tel. 99/520-2158, http://spanishschoolsouthamerican.

com). Of note is the **Cristóbal Colón Spanish School** (Colón 2088 y Versalles, tel./fax 2/250-6508, www.colonspanishschool. com), the most economical option for one-on-one classes at $7 per hour.

In Otavalo, **Mundo Andino Spanish School** (Bolívar y Abdón Calderón, 3rd floor, tel. 6/292-1864, www.mundoandino-spanishschool.com) and **Otavalo Learning & Adventure** (García Moreno y Atahualpa, tel. 99/700-8542) are recommended. Just north of Otavalo, the excellent **Pucará B&B & Spanish School** (tel. 99/521-6665, www. pucaraspanishschool.com) is in a beautiful rural setting. Ninety minutes west of Otavalo in the Intag region, the small village of Pucará is the location of an experimental "eco-pueblo," a new model for rural, low-income housing using sustainable energy technology, ecological design, and permaculture concepts (see http://casainteram.org/pucara). The **Intag Spanish School** (tel. 98/684-9950 or 6/301-5638, https://intagspanishschool. wordpress.com) provides the community with a sustainable source of income.

In Baños, recommended are **Centro de Idiomas Marco Polo** (Rocafuerte y Maldonado, tel. 9/499-5161, http:// languageschool-marcopolo.squarespace.com); **Baños Spanish Center** (Oriente y Cañar, tel. 8/704-5072, www.bspanishcenter.com); **Mayra's Spanish School** (Eduardo Tapia y Oriente, tel. 3/274-3019, www.mayraspanish-school.com), and **Raices Spanish School** (16 de Diciembre y Suárez, tel. 3/274-1921, www. spanishlessons.org).

In Cuenca, as well as the nonprofit **Yanapuma Spanish School** (www. yanapumaspanish.org) already mentioned, check out **Fundación Amauta** (Miguel y Córdova, tel. 7/284-6206, http:// amauta.edu.ec), which supports education for low-income children through scholarships, study materials, and other financial aid. The **Simon Bolivar Spanish School** (Mariscal Sucre 14-21, *entre* Estevez de Toral y Coronel Talbot, tel. 7/283-2052, www. bolivar2.com) receives consistently good reviews. **Spanish Institute Cuenca** (Calle Larga 2-92 y Tomás Ordóñez, tel. 7/282-4736, https://spanishinstitutecuenca.com) combines Spanish lessons with photography classes.

COAST

The advantage of learning on the coast is that surf classes are available as an extra activity! At the **Montañita Spanish School** (tel. 4/206-0116 www.montanitaspanishschool. com), individual and group Spanish lessons cost $170 and $240 for 20 hours per week, respectively. A "traveling classroom" option includes stays in Quito, Cuenca, Manta, Montañita, and the Amazon. In neighboring Olón, **Outdoor Ecuador** (Calle Othmar Stahelli, *frente a* Pacho's house, tel. 99/962-4398 or 95/940-0161, www.outdoorecuador. com) is a small, friendly Spanish school with al fresco classrooms. Classes cost $8/hour for group classes and $10/hour for individual classes. An intensive course of 15 hours per week costs $105 (group class) and $140 (individual).

Food and Drink

As with everything else, gastronomically Ecuador is a land of diversity, with many small towns and villages having their own specialty dishes. The most traditional food is sometimes made according to recipes passed down the generations. In some towns, you'll find unassuming little cafés where local women have been serving the same dish for 50 years, faithfully following their grandmother's secret formula. Most Ecuadorians are enthusiastic and knowledgeable about their cuisine and will happily point you in the direction of the best spots to try it. If you ask for restaurant recommendations, it may be assumed you're looking for international food and an expat hangout; for a more authentic experience, try asking where the locals eat ("*¿Donde comen los locales?*") or where you can try good local food ("*¿Donde puedo probar buena comida local?*").

Despite the abundance of delicious, economical fruit and vegetables, many Ecuadorians live primarily on a diet of carbohydrates, notably white rice (*arroz*), and meat, especially pork (*carne de chancho/cerdo*), chicken (*pollo*), and fish (*pescado*). Vegetable intake is often limited to a scrap of side salad and some truly delicious soups (*sopas*). Of particular note is *fanesca*, a traditional Easter soup containing salt cod to represent Jesus and 12 different kinds of beans and grains to represent the apostles. Traditional Ecuadorian food is known as *comida típica* (typical food), which is usually a blend of national staples and local dishes. Perhaps the most *típica* is *seco de pollo*, a slow-cooked chicken stew in a sauce of beer, naranjilla juice, onions, garlic, peppers, and tomatoes.

Often the best place to eat *comida típica* alongside the locals is the food court (*patio de comida*) at the central or municipal market (*mercado central/municipal*). If you're cooking for yourself, the markets are also the best source of fresh produce, usually much more flavorsome than at the supermarket. There are bound to be some weird and wonderful fruits you've never seen before. Local markets are also a great way to support small-scale local farmers and vendors.

As with anywhere, a restaurant filled with locals usually means the food is good. Ecuadorians commonly eat out for lunch (*almuerzo*), with many opting for a set meal (*menú del día*) at unfussy restaurants that are sometimes colloquially referred to as *huecos* (holes). These set meals, often available for around $3.50, offer the most economical and filling option for travelers, consisting of a juice or tea, a soup (*sopa*), and a main course (*segundo*). The main course is usually some sort of meat, chicken, or fish with rice and a side dish such as salad (*ensalada*), plantain (*platano*), manioc (yucca), or lentil stew (*menestra*). In the Sierra, hominy (*mote*) and avocado (*aguacate*) are popular sides. Occasionally there is a small dessert (*postre*). One o'clock is generally lunchtime. Dinner (*cena*) tends to be smaller and eaten from 7pm on, although many Ecuadorians will eat out as late as 10pm. A set evening meal is called a *merienda* and follows a similar format to lunch.

A number of Ecuadorian dishes tend to be eaten for breakfast (*desayuno*) but are available throughout the day, including *bolón* (a ball of plantain with cheese or ham, best served with fried eggs); *tigrillo* (mashed plantains with cheese and egg); *humitas* (ground corn mashed with cheese, onion, garlic, eggs, and cream and steamed in corn leaves); tamales (corn flour dough filled with pork, egg, and raisins, wrapped in leaves and steamed); *quimbolitos* (a sweet version of a tamale); and *mote pillo* (hominy scrambled with egg, onion, and herbs, available in the southern Sierra). Continental breakfasts (bread, jam, coffee and juice) and American breakfasts (the same, plus eggs) are available everywhere. A bowl of fruit, yogurt, and granola is another popular option.

An increasing number of vegetarian and vegan restaurants are popping up in Ecuador and have been featured in this book wherever they were found. A good online resource is www.happycow.com, which has a database of meat-free establishments searchable by town. Baños, Cuenca, Quito, Guayaquil, and Vilcabamba have an especially good range. Vegetarian options in restaurants are also improving, with some having a special section on the menu, most often with pasta or rice dishes. Most tourist towns have decent Italian restaurants, which always have veggie pizza and pasta. Even the least touristy midsized towns have Chinese restaurants, known as *chifas*, which reliably serve noodles with vegetables (*tallarines con verduras*) and rice with vegetables (*chaulafan con verduras*), which you can be sure will be meat-free. The servings at *chifas* are usually big, service is fast, and they are often the only option on Sunday, when many places are closed.

Off the beaten track, asking for vegetarian food (*comida vegetariana*) might result in a blank stare, but the situation is rarely hopeless; there are usually veggie options, it's just that they are not known as such. In the set lunch (*almuerzo*) places, the soup of the day (*sopa del día*, known as *crema* if it's smooth) might be of the vegetable variety, in which case you're in for a treat because Ecuadorian soups are generally very good. It's worth checking that it doesn't contain any animal products ("*¿Esto contiene productos de origen animal?*"). The same should be asked of *menestra* (lentil stew), which is widely available. Most places can rustle up a plate of rice, lentil stew, fried eggs (*huevos fritos*), and plantain fries (*patacones*). An omelet is another life saver for veggies, known as *tortilla de huevos*, especially good with vegetables (*con verduras*). Some street food options are meat-free, including *empanadas de queso* (pastry turnover with cheese) and *choclo* (corn on the cob).

In the Sierra, the *llapingachos* (fried potato patties) are delicious, but they are nearly always cooked in pork fat. Beans (*habas*), potatoes (*papas*), hominy (*mote*), and avocado (*aguacate*) are popular Sierran sides that can be put together to make a meal. *Locro de papa* (potato soup with avocado) is so filling it can make a meal in itself. In the Oriente—the most challenging region for vegetarians—you'll probably end up eating a lot of rice, yucca, and plantain. Wherever you go, the fruit salads (*ensalada de fruta*) are generally good, but the regular salads (*ensaladas*) are usually pitiful, consisting of iceberg lettuce, raw onion, and tomato. Vegetarians with access to a kitchen, the local market, and some cooking skills will be delighted by the cheap and plentiful abundance of vegetables, legumes, and grains.

Perhaps king of Ecuadorian street food is the empanada (pastry turnover filled with cheese or meat). Cheese empanadas, usually fried but sometimes baked, are often sprinkled with sugar.

Ecuador's tourist towns and larger cities have a wide range of international cuisine, most notably Baños, Cuenca, and Quito. For their size, Montañita, Olón, and Vilcabamba have a good range of international options.

Regional Specialties

Ceviche is the coast's most famous dish and consists of fish, shellfish, or shrimp marinated in lime juice, spiced with chili, and served with tomato sauce and toasted corn kernels or popcorn. When shrimp is used in ceviche,

it's cooked, but those made with raw *pescado* (fish) or *concha* (clams) may pose a health risk. If you prefer your food hot, then try *encebollado*, a tuna fish soup made with cassava root, tomatoes, onions, and cilantro. Local people swear it's the only hangover medicine you'll ever need. Central coast specialties include *cazuela*, a seafood broth made with plantains and flavored with peanuts; and *corviches*, deep fried balls of mashed green plantain and peanut, stuffed with fish. The north coast signature dish is *encocado*, seafood cooked in coconut milk.

The most popular fish on the coast are *corvina* (white sea bass), *dorado* (mahi-mahi), and albacore. It's usually available *frito* (fried), *apanada* (breaded and fried), *al vapor* (steamed), or *a la plancha* (filleted and baked). Shellfish include *camarones* (shrimp), *cangrejo* (crab), *calamare* (squid), *ostione* (oyster), and *langosta* (lobster or jumbo shrimp).

Patacones, fried plantain slices, are a popular coastal side dish and snack. They are made from *verde* (unripe green plantain), as is *tortilla de verde* (plantain patties stuffed with cheese). Mature yellow plantain (*maduro*) is baked or fried whole and often served with cheese.

The most famous specialty in the Sierra is *cuy* (guinea pig) roasted whole on a spit, though pork is much more commonly eaten. There is fierce competition among Sierran towns over which makes the best *hornado* (slow-roasted pork) and *fritada* (pork cooked in water and orange juice until the water is reduced and the meat is browned in its own fat). In Latacunga, the specialty is *chugchucara*, with chunks of pork, crispy skins, potatoes, plantains, and corn. The Cuencan pork dish is *mote pata* (corn soup with pork, sausage, bacon, and squash seeds), whereas in Loja it's *cecina* (thinly sliced sun-dried pork served with yucca).

Ambato's most famous specialty is *llapingachos*, crispy potato patties with cheese and onion, fried (sadly for veggies) in pork fat and accompanied with sausage, avocado, lettuce, and a fried egg. A wide variety of potatoes and corn are grown in the Andes, with the former being used to make the region's famous *locro de papa,* a thick soup served with avocado. Another Sierran soup is Loja's *repe*, made from green bananas.

The most typical Amazonian dish is *maito* (fish, grubs, or chicken grilled in a wrapped leaf). The fish is either tilapia, which is farmed, or various kinds of river fish, including *bagre*, a catfish. The grubs, known as *mayones,* are chonta palm worms. Farther south, the signature dish is *ayampaco* (chopped meat, chicken, or fish with palm hearts and onion, grilled in a wrapped *bijao* leaf). In Zamora, it's all about *ancas de rana* (frog legs). Throughout the region, popular accompaniments are yucca, *platano* (plantain), and *palmitos* (palm hearts).

Ecuadorians don't generally eat dessert, though in the southern Sierra meals are traditionally followed with *miel con quesillo* (honey with soft unsalted cheese). Cakes are popular for special occasions, including *tres leches* (three milks), made with evaporated milk, condensed milk, and cream. Wonderful fruit salads can be found all over the country, especially the coast. Regional sweet specialties include *helado de paila* (fruit sorbet originating in Ibarra); *helados de Salcedo* (ice cream on a stick made of layers of coconut, blackberry, mango, taxo, naranjilla, and milk flavors, originating in Salcedo); *cocadas* (balls of coconut with *panela*, or raw sugar, originating in Esmeraldas); and *bocadillos*, squares of raw sugar syrup and peanut that look like fudge, originating in Loja). The small town of Rocafuerte near Manta is known for its traditional sweets, including *alfajores* (shortbread cookies with a *dulce de leche* filling), *cocadas*, fruit and vegetable jellies, and meringues.

Drinks

One of the highlights of a trip to Ecuador is the vast range of fresh fruit available, which is made into *jugos* (pure juice or blended with water) or *batidos* (fruit blended with milk). They're often made very sweet, and you can ask for less sugar (*menos azúcar*). Especially popular are *mora* (blackberry), *maracuyá* (passion fruit), *naranjilla* (a tart Andean fruit), and *tomate de arbol* (tree tomato).

Ecuadorian coffee is among the best in the world, but sadly instant Nescafé is prevalent. The best high-altitude Arabica-growing regions include Loja, Zaruma, and Intag, though coffee is grown and processed all over the country. You're more likely to get a cup of real coffee in the Sierra; a bit more hunting is required on the coast and in the Oriente. Large supermarkets and small organic stores all over the country sell organic ground Ecuadorian coffee.

Tea, often referred to as *agua aromatica*, is widely available. The most common flavors are *manzanilla* (chamomile), *menta* (mint), *anis* (aniseed), *cedrón* (lemongrass), and *horchata,* a pink infusion of various medicinal herbs that originated in Loja. English breakfast tea is known as *té negro* (black tea), and you need to order milk separately, which often causes confusion. Brits might need to use two tea bags per cup to get it up to strength!

Sold by street vendors everywhere is *morocho,* a thick, sweet drink rather like rice pudding, made from *morocho* corn, milk, cinnamon, sugar, and raisins. Served hot, it's filling and comforting. *Avena polaca* is another thick milk-based drink, this time made with oats and served cold. Originating in Santo Domingo, it's wickedly creamy and sold by mobile vendors everywhere.

On the coast, you can't beat an ice-cold, fresh coconut (*coco helado*), which will be expertly macheted open before your eyes. Add a shot of rum to make it a *coco loco.* Afterwards, you can ask for the meat (*carne*) to take away and munch on.

A popular juice in the central Sierra is *borojó,* a fruit with energizing properties, laughingly referred to by the locals as the natural Viagra. The juices in the Riobamba market are special, made with ice mined by Baltazar Uscha, the only person who still maintains the tradition of mining ice by hand from Chimborazo and then hauling the blocks down by mule. The Guaranda market is famous for frozen drinks called *rompanucas,* literally "break necks," the colloquial term for brain freeze. A bit like liquid ice cream, the most popular flavor is *rosa y leche,* which is a violent shade of pink. In Cuenca, the nuns at the Monasterio del Carmen sell a health tonic, *agua de pitima,* from a hatch in the side of the convent. Made from flowers, especially carnations, and sweetened with honey, the pink drink is said to be good for the nervous system and sells like hotcakes with the locals. *Colada morada* is a thick, sweet drink made from ground purple corn and fruit, including pineapple. In the rest of the country, it's only available for the Day of the Dead celebrations on November 2, but in Ambato's Atocha neighborhood, you can buy it every day. In Baños and parts of the Amazon, freshly squeezed *jugo de caña* (sugarcane juice) is sold at roadside stalls.

Much of life in the Amazon revolves around *chicha,* a slightly alcoholic brew made commonly with yucca and water. Chewed by indigenous women as part of the preparation process, it is fermented by bacteria in their saliva. Another traditional drink from the Amazon is *guayusa,* a stimulant tea made from a rainforest relative of the holly bush. In the jungle, it's heated on the fire and drunk out of gourds at dawn as people analyze their dreams. In cities in the Oriente, it can be bought as teabags and is found on most menus, served either hot or cold.

A quick look in any store refrigerator will confirm the fact that 71 percent of Ecuador's drinks market is controlled by Cervecería Nacional (the national brewery) and Coca Cola. National beers include Pilsner and Club Verde, both of which will disappoint beer connoisseurs. Happily, craft beer is popping up everywhere and tends to be local. Ecuadorians often buy a big bottle of beer and share it among friends. Any alcohol imported from the United States or Europe is prohibitively expensive. Ecuadorian wine isn't very good (except for the sweet *vino de uva* in Patate), so Chilean is your best bet, but it's not cheap. Head to the big supermarkets for the best deals. The most popular brand is the boxed wine Clos, with the accompanying joke, "It's not wine but it's clos(e)," though the merlot is actually pretty good.

Rum is very popular in Ecuador, but the more traditional sugarcane liquor, known as *caña* or simply *trago,* is the alcohol of choice in most of rural Ecuador. Heated and mixed with cinnamon and sugar, the potent concoction is called *canelazo,* to which fruit is sometimes added. Also comforting on a chilly Sierran night is *vino hervido,* hot mulled wine, most commonly found in Quito. For a bewildering range of cocktails, head to Montañita's legendary Cocktail Alley. If you get too *borracho* (drunk) the night before, you may wake up *chuchaqui,* a Quechua word meaning "hungover" that proves even the Incas knew the perils of "the morning after."

Accommodations

The entire spectrum of overnight lodging is represented in Ecuador. Accommodations fall into the following categories, which the Ministry of Tourism is working to standardize according to the services offered: *hotel, hostal, casa de huespedes, hostería, hacienda, lodge, resort, refugio,* and *campamento.* In a hotel, all bathrooms are private and there should be a restaurant or café. A *hostal* (hostel) may have some dormitories and/or shared bathrooms and might not have a restaurant or café (though might have a shared kitchen). A *casa de huespedes* (guesthouse) sleeps a maximum of six people, usually in the converted home of the owner or manager. A *hostería* (inn) should have private rooms and/or cabins, gardens, green areas, and parking. These tend to be outside town and fairly swanky. *Haciendas* are even swankier, usually historical and out in the countryside. Many were converted into tourist lodging after the end of forced indigenous labor. They usually have expensive restaurants and activities such as horseback riding. Lodges will be out in nature, offering activities such as hiking and visiting local communities. A resort is a tourist complex with diverse facilities that offers recreational activities. A *refugio* (refuge) is usually found on mountains and in protected natural areas, offering basic accommodations for tourists engaged in activities such as trekking and climbing. *Campamentos* (campgrounds) provide a camping area, shared bathrooms, and outdoor areas for preparing food. Some provide tents, but most do not.

Not included in these categories are *centros de turismo comunitario* (community tourism centers, or CTCs), which are owned and run by communities, with the income distributed among members and going toward improvements in education and health care. These are usually fairly basic. An excellent resource on community tourism is the Federación Plurinacional de Turismo Comunitario del Ecuador (www.feptce.com, Facebook @ TurismoComunitarioEc). Homestays, where visitors lodge with local families, are another great way to experience community life. These can be arranged by most Spanish schools and many community tourism projects throughout the country, By stepping outside the normal world of hotels and restaurants, and branching out beyond the same conversations with fellow travelers, you can gain firsthand knowledge of the country as well as improve your Spanish.

Look for accommodations with sound environmental policies, which may include renewable energy, recycling, conservation of water and energy, ecological building methods, waste management practices (gray-water systems, composting), use of biodegradable cleaning products, support of local producers, organic gardens, and environmental education. These establishments are included in this guide wherever they were found.

Be aware that all over the country are "love motels" aimed at lovers rather than travelers, where rooms are rented by the hour. This is a necessary service in a country where most people live with their parents until they are married. These establishments, which are also popular for conducting extramarital affairs, can usually be identified by tacky names and hearts somewhere on the sign.

Some general tips on accommodations are as follows:

- Prices in this book have been given for dorm beds (where they exist), single rooms (s), and double rooms (d). Many of the places listed also offer private rooms for groups. Contact individual establishments for details and prices.

- Prices vary depending on the time of year, so be aware of national holidays and high season, when prices rise sharply, before planning your trip. New Year's, Carnival, and Easter are especially expensive.

- Prices are not usually fixed in cheaper hotels, so bargaining is possible, especially if you're staying a few nights.

- A 22 percent tax is levied in more expensive accommodations (included in the prices quoted in this book), along with a 10-20 percent surcharge for paying by credit card.

- Electric showers in less expensive places can be dangerous if improperly wired; *don't* touch the shower head with wet hands. Remember that C stands for *caliente* (hot) and F means *frio* (cold). If there are no letters, the left tap is usually hot. Many establishments have cranky hot water that may have a knack to it; the receptionist can usually help.

- The plumbing in Ecuador can't handle toilet paper, so be sure to throw it in the garbage instead of flushing it down the toilet.

Conduct and Customs

Ecuadorians are generally warmly welcoming of visitors and often lack the social reserve that prevents many Europeans from striking up a conversation with a stranger. While much leeway is given to the peculiar ways of foreigners, an effort to learn some of the local etiquette will be very much appreciated. It's also a basic way to show respect for your host country.

Keep your eyes open and you'll see that there is a lot to learn from Ecuadorian culture. Note that even though many people live in poverty, there are very few homeless people, a mark of the strong sense of community that has been lost from so many "developed" nations. Outside the cities, you will be met with incredulity if you mention that many people in your home country do not know their neighbors. Note how peaceful people are in public; this author has seen more fights in one night in the United Kingdom than in a decade of living in Ecuador. Note the respect that young people have for the elderly, or how all the generations socialize together.

GREETINGS AND GENERAL POLITENESS

Ecuadorians are renowned for their laid-back attitude and often smile through frustrations that can leave many gringos fuming. In other ways, the culture can be quite formal, such as the importance of greetings. Outside cities it is common to wish complete strangers "*buenos días/tardes/noches*" as you pass them in the street, and people entering a store or bus often announce "*¡Buenos días!*" to everyone inside. When meeting someone for the first time, shake their hand, say "*mucho gusto*" ("pleased to meet you"), and tell them your name. In informal situations among younger generations, people may introduce themselves with a kiss on the cheek. Two female friends will greet each other with a kiss on the cheek, as will a man and a woman. Two men usually shake hands or might embrace if they are close friends or family. If you're dining informally in a group, a new arrival will probably come around the table to kiss everyone's cheek in turn. If you approach a group and only know one person there, it is polite to introduce yourself to everyone. Ecuadorians often have social graces that can be hard to emulate for more awkward Brits such as this author!

Say "*buen provecho*" ("enjoy your meal") to your companions before a meal or to fellow diners when entering or leaving a restaurant. When arriving at someone's home, especially for the first time, it is polite to say "*permiso*" and wait for permission before stepping over the threshold. "*Permiso*" is also used as "excuse me" if you need to squeeze past someone or ask them to move out of the way. Yawning in public is considered rude, as is pointing or beckoning with a finger. Ecuadorians may point by puckering or pursing their lips or pointing with their chin, while beckoning is a downward flap of the hand.

Say What?

A lot of Ecuadorians have **nicknames,** and these often refer to their most obvious physical feature. It can be shocking for visitors from more politically correct countries to hear people referred to as *"El Gordo"* (fatty) or *"La Negra"* (dark skinned). Locals with Asian-looking eyes are almost invariably nicknamed *"Chino"* (Chinese); unusually light skinned people are *"Colorado"* (colored); and those with light eyes are usually *"El Gato"* (the cat). These terms are often suffixed with the colloquial *"ito"* or *"ita"*; e.g., *"La Flaca"* (skinny) becomes *"La Flaquita"* for a woman. While people rarely have any choice over their nickname (it seems unlikely that the guy with protuberant ears would relish being called "Dumbo" every day), these names are not meant offensively. As one local commented "I wouldn't call him Fatty if I didn't like him." Some of these words are also used as casual terms of address: *"¡Hola, Negra!"* or *"¡Hola, Flaquita!"* is a common way for a young person to casually address a close female friend of any skin color or size. The only word that is used in a derogatory way is *"indio"* to refer to an indigenous person. While some indigenous people believe in reclaiming the word (there is a hotel in Otavalo called El Indio, for example), visitors should avoid using it.

There are various terms of address in Ecuador. Greatly respected older people are known as *"Don"* or *"Doña"* and then their name (e.g., "Doña Elena"). Women who are well into middle age can safely be addressed as *"Señora,"* whereas young women are *"Señorita"*; if you're not sure, it's best to avoid any term of address. Men are referred to as *"Señor."* In more informal situations, you can't go far wrong addressing someone as "friend" (*"amigo"* or *"amiga"*). Even more informal are *"chico"* and *"chica,"* which roughly translate as "guy" and "girl." Young women will often greet each other with *"¡Hola, chica!"*

SOCIAL OCCASIONS

Note that if an Ecuadorian uses the word invite (*"te invito"*), this usually means that he or she will pay. Equally, if you invite someone, you will be expected to foot the bill. If your hosts want to pay, it's best to let them and then return the favor on another occasion.

Guests are not expected to be punctual for social gatherings and should arrive 30 minutes to an hour late. Parties probably won't get going until after midnight and the dancing will likely continue into the early hours. Many a gringo has missed out on a great party by going home too soon.

Often, Ecuadorians will order a big bottle of beer and pour a glass for everyone. It will be appreciated if you get the next bottle.

DRESS

Andean people are much more formal in dress than their coastal counterparts. Modest shorts with a T-shirt is fine, but skimpy clothes should be avoided. Even in sweltering Guayaquil, it's best for women to avoid plunging necklines and short shorts. On the beach, skimpy clothes are perfectly acceptable, even the tiniest of bikinis, but topless sunbathing is definitely not.

Ecuadorians generally dress smartly for any kind of official occasion. This might be tricky for backpackers, but it's a good idea to brush up as much as possible for visits to the immigration office, or anything but the most informal invitation to someone's home.

CHALLENGES

The famous lack of punctuality in Ecuador can be difficult for gringos. This fluidity with time keeping can even extend to simply not turning up. Ecuadorian bureaucracy can also be extremely frustrating, to the point of incredulity, but it's vital to maintain good humor; losing your temper will not get you anywhere. You will be required to present a dismayingly long list of documents, letters, references, and copies of ID (possibly notarized) to complete any kind of official business, such as visa extension. This author had to take six trips into the city to open a bank account. If you have good Spanish and plenty of time and patience, you may be able to handle "*tramites*" (the collective term for bureaucratic procedures) independently. Otherwise, it is highly recommended to take a local person with you who is used to navigating red tape.

There is a tolerance for noise in Ecuador that can be charming or challenging. For example, when this author's neighbors threw a party to baptize their twin girls, they closed the whole road, erected a marquee, and hired a band; the whole community salsa-danced until the early hours. Rather wonderfully, no one complained about the road closure or the music. On the other hand, it can be unbearable when someone decides to play thumping *reggaetón* all day from the back of their car, often so loud that it prevents any kind of thought, let alone conversation, nearby. This author has even visited some remote jungle communities where earsplitting *technocumbia* is played from dawn until dusk. The concept of "noise pollution" does not really exist in Ecuador, so, if you're sensitive to noise, bring good earplugs because they are hard to find locally. If you can afford it, noise-canceling headphones would be a good investment.

Queuing is not a popular pastime in Ecuador. Don't be pushy but be prepared to be firm.

Health and Safety

The information in this section is current at the time of writing. Before your trip, it's recommended to check for up-to-date information on the websites of the **U.S. Centers for Disease Control and Prevention** (www.cdc.gov/travel) and the U.K. government's **Travel Health Pro** (https://travelhealthpro.org.uk), both of which offer country-specific advice.

Most visitors to Ecuador suffer nothing more serious than some sunburn, a couple of altitude headaches, some itchy mosquito bites, and perhaps an upset stomach. Having said that, there are risks of much more significant health problems, many of which can be mitigated with basic precautions.

Before your trip, make sure you have adequate **travel insurance** that covers medical expenses and any activities that you are planning on undertaking (surfing, scuba diving, mountaineering, etc.). Stock up on any prescription medication you require (including oral contraceptives). Bring copies of prescriptions for eyewear, just in case.

VACCINATIONS

If possible, see a health professional at least 4-6 weeks before you leave for Ecuador. All visitors should make sure their routine immunizations are up to date, along with **hepatitis A** (a viral infection transmitted through contaminated food and water or by direct contact with an infectious person) and **tetanus** (often called lockjaw, a bacterial infection introduced through open wounds).

Those whose activities may put them at extra risk should also consider vaccinations against **hepatitis B** (a viral infection transmitted via infected blood or body fluids); **rabies** (a viral infection usually transmitted via the saliva of an infected animal); **typhoid** (a bacterial infection transmitted through contaminated food and water); and **tuberculosis** (a bacterial infection transmitted by inhaling respiratory droplets from an infectious person).

Yellow fever immunization is recommended for those traveling to the Amazon region and Esmeraldas province. When entering

Ecuador from a country with a risk of yellow fever transmission, including Peru, Colombia, Brazil, Argentina, and Bolivia, you may be asked for a vaccination certificate, which is valid for life. Check with the World Health Organization for the current list of affected countries.

DISEASES FROM BITING INSECTS OR TICKS

Ecuador is considered high risk for the **Zika virus,** which is usually mosquito-borne, though a few cases of sexual transmission have been reported. Zika only causes mild symptoms in most people, but there is scientific consensus that it can cause babies to be born with microcephaly (a small head and undeveloped brain) and other congenital anomalies. At the time of writing, the official advice is that pregnant women should postpone nonessential travel to Ecuador until after pregnancy. Women should avoid becoming pregnant while in Ecuador and for eight weeks after leaving. The risk can be reduced by visiting areas over 2,000 meters (6,500 ft) altitude, where the infected mosquitoes are unlikely to be present.

There is a low risk of **malaria** in most areas below 1,500 meters (5,000 ft), including the coastal provinces and Amazon basin. Bite avoidance is advised, rather than antimalarial medication.

More common is **dengue fever,** another mosquito-borne disease that causes flu-like symptoms. It can occasionally develop into a more serious life-threatening illness, but usually just means an unpleasant few days of fever, headaches, joint pain, and skin rash. The only treatments are rest and fluids. If you want to take pain relief, choose medication with acetaminophen and avoid aspirin. Medical attention is recommended, if only for diagnosis. The symptoms of **chikungunya,** which is also mosquito-borne and fairly common, are similar to dengue. Again, it is rarely serious and there is no treatment apart from rest and fluids.

Less common insect-borne diseases include **leishmaniasis** (an infection caused by the leishmania parasites, transmitted by the bite of infected phlebotomine sandfly) and American trypanosomiasis (also known as **Chagas disease,** an infection caused by the *Trypanosoma cruzi* parasites, transmitted by the bite of a triatomine insect. The most common form of leishmaniasis is cutaneous and starts with a red sore at the site of the sandfly bite, which may then develop into a lesion or ulcer. Common symptoms of Chagas disease are headaches, muscle aches, fever, and a rash. Both are potentially life threatening if not treated and are only prevented by bite avoidance.

It sounds obvious, but the best strategy for avoiding all these diseases is to reduce your likelihood of being bitten. If it's not too hot, wear long sleeves and pants, especially in the evenings. Light colors are less attractive to insects. Socks are a good idea, as ankles and feet are particularly prone to bites. This may not be practical on the beach, where repellent is a better strategy. DEET-based products are widely available. The higher the percentage of DEET, the more effective the repellent, but also the more toxic for your skin. Bring lemon eucalyptus or citronella oil from home if you're looking to avoid these harsh chemicals. Air-conditioning or a bedside fan can prevent nighttime bites. Mosquito nets are available in some general stores.

Most bites are nothing more than an itchy annoyance, but if a bite becomes infected or you start to feel unwell, seek medical assistance.

CONTAMINATED FOOD AND WATER

If you're going to get sick, it will probably be from contaminated water or food. As a tropical country, Ecuador is full of bacteria and parasites. The most common problem is **traveler's diarrhea,** which is unpleasant but not usually the sign of anything serious. Stay near a bathroom, drink plenty of water, and maybe get some oral rehydration solution such as Pedialyte, which is available in most pharmacies. Many travelers swear that a glass of flat cola and a banana is the best remedy. If symptoms persist or you have stomach pains, seek medical assistance. It may be a good idea to get tested for parasites, which are common and easily treated.

The precautions you take will depend on how sensitive your stomach is. In most of the country, water from the faucet is not drinkable, even by local people. If you have an easily upset stomach, use filtered water to brush your teeth and to wash fruits and vegetables. Many hostels provide free filtered drinking water in blue 20-liter bottles, which can be used to fill up your personal bottle. Most restaurants will also fill up small bottles upon request after a meal, to save on buying bottled water. Generally, ice cubes in Ecuador can be trusted. Other culprits are shellfish, pork, and undercooked or poorly prepared meats. Popular ceviche carts and seafood restaurants are usually fine, as they have a high turnover of produce, but less frequented places might reheat yesterday's shrimp. A place full of locals is a good sign. You might want to avoid food from street vendors, especially meat and fruit salads. Get in the habit of washing your hands several times a day. Many public restrooms do not have soap, so consider carrying hand sanitizer. Many travelers get away without taking any of these precautions and are just fine; you'll soon find out how careful you have to be!

HIV AND STDs

Human immunodeficiency virus (HIV) is transmitted by direct contact with the bodily fluids of an infected person, most often through sexual contact, intravenous injections, or blood transfusions. There is a high incidence of HIV in Ecuador, especially in coastal regions. This is due to a combination of poor sex education; the unpopularity of, or lack of access to, condoms; and the prevalence of men having extramarital sex, often at brothels. Sadly, there is such a stigma attached to HIV in Ecuador that many people are too ashamed or afraid to seek treatment or even diagnosis, leading to unnecessary deaths from AIDS. Preventing HIV is straightforward: Do not have unprotected sex or share needles.

For the same reasons, other types of **sexually transmitted diseases (STDs),** such as chlamydia, gonorrhea, syphilis, and herpes are also common. Prevention is the same: Use a condom.

OTHER CONCERNS
Contraception and Unwanted Pregnancy

Condoms (*condónes*) and **contraceptive pills** (*píldoras anticonceptivas*) are available at pharmacies (though not in some rural areas, so stock up when you're in a town or city). Condoms are of variable quality in Ecuador, so it's best to buy a recognized brand or bring them from home. The **morning after pill** (*el píldora del día después*) is also available and can be taken effectively up to 72 hours after unprotected sex (though the sooner it is taken, the more effective it is). Remember that the morning after pill does not protect from STDs.

Abortion is illegal in Ecuador, and as a result, unsafe abortion is a leading cause of injury for women and girls. Black market abortion drugs from Argentina are available, but many of them are fake and/or life threatening. Some private clinics do offer clandestine abortions in good faith for $800-1,000, but if something goes wrong, no one will take responsibility. If you find yourself in the difficult situation of an unwanted pregnancy in Ecuador and come from a country where abortion is legal, it is probably best to cut your trip short and head back home for the procedure. If you need to have an abortion in Ecuador, make discreet inquiries with as many local women as possible before making a decision about where to go. A new helpline set up by Salud Mujeres Ecuador 2.0 (Facebook @SaludMujeresEcuador 2.0) can also provide information (9/9830-1317, 5pm-10m daily).

Sunburn and Heatstroke

Never underestimate the power of the equatorial sun, even on a cloudy day, wherever you are in Ecuador. The coastal sun is more obviously brutal, whereas seemingly weaker Andean rays can be deceptively burning. A nasty **sunburn** can be very painful and seriously limit further outdoor activities. At the extreme end of the scale, **heatstroke** can be fatal. Limit your time in direct sunshine between 11am and 3pm, especially on the coast. Use high sun protection factor (SPF) sunscreen, sunglasses, and a hat. Drink plenty of water.

Altitude

Most people who visit Quito (at 2,850 m/9,350 ft above sea level) will notice the effects of being at **altitude,** especially breathlessness upon physical exertion. Also common are headaches, fatigue, appetite loss, nausea, a bloated stomach, and sleep disturbance. Take it easy for a couple of days, avoid alcohol, drink plenty of water, and you should acclimatize. Then, if you're planning on going higher, take it gradually if you can, increasing sleeping elevation by no more than 500 meters (1,600 ft) per day. Acetazolamide can be used to assist with acclimatization but should not replace gradual ascent.

The symptoms mentioned are signs of **acute mountain sickness** (AMS), the least serious of three altitude illnesses. The other two, **high-altitude cerebral edema** (HACE) and **high-altitude pulmonary edema** (HAPE), require immediate descent and emergency medical treatment. Signs of HACE include confusion, altered consciousness, and incoordination. Signs of HAPE include increasing breathlessness, breathlessness lying flat, cough (initially dry then wet), chest tightness, and blood-tinged sputum. These illnesses are just two of many reasons why you should only attempt very high altitude expeditions with a licensed guide, who will be trained in dealing with them.

PHARMACIES, DOCTORS, AND HOSPITALS

Provided you speak some Spanish, **pharmacies** in Ecuador can often be trusted to recommend treatments and medicines for minor ailments that require a prescription back home. However, if your problem is more serious, you need the expertise of a **doctor.** Ask around locally for a recommendation, as there are some charlatans out there. An appointment with a local private doctor might be $20; check beforehand to avoid any surprises. Take a Spanish speaker with you if you don't speak the language. The doctor will probably write you out a prescription for some kind of medication, which is usually economical, from the local pharmacy. Make sure to look everything up on the Internet before purchasing anything. This author was once prescribed a drug which, upon further investigation, turned out to be "licensed for veterinary use only in the majority of countries." If you're not sure, get a second opinion from another doctor.

If you think you are being prescribed too many drugs, you might be right. Some dodgy doctors are in cahoots with shady pharmacists to prescribe and sell unnecessary drugs and split the profits between them. If a doctor gives you a long prescription and then a "special offer" flyer for a specific pharmacy nearby, there is a good chance that something fishy is going on. This is why it's a good idea to ask around locally and get a few recommendations for the same doctor before making an appointment.

Health care at public hospitals is free for everyone, including visitors. Bear in mind that you may have a long wait to see a doctor, facilities are usually basic, and bedside manner is generally nonexistent. You (or a friend) will have to go to the closest pharmacy to purchase any medication that is not held in the hospital, but these items are usually inexpensive. In an emergency, consider taking a taxi to the closest private hospital or clinic, or at least the public hospital in the nearest big town. For any complex medical issue, it's best to go private. Good health care isn't cheap, which is why it's a good idea to have adequate insurance. Private hospitals will demand a credit card guarantee for admission. Be ready to pay up front, even if you have insurance coverage. Make sure to get a detailed, comprehensive receipt—in English, if possible—for making a claim.

Dental care is economical and generally good quality. If you're coming from a country where it's prohibitively expensive, consider making an appointment with a recommended dentist in Ecuador; you might save yourself hundreds or even thousands of dollars.

POST-TRAVEL REMINDERS

Pay close attention to your health for at least six months after your trip, since many exotic diseases have long incubation periods. Symptoms may resemble other illnesses, such as the flu, causing doctors unfamiliar with tropical medicine to misdiagnose. If you have any mysterious symptoms, tell your doctor where you've been—a fever in particular should call for a blood test.

CRIME

On the whole, Ecuador is a safe place to visit, and the majority of travelers experience no difficulties with security. Outside of the cities, violent crime is infrequent. It is, however, worth being aware of the risks and taking precautions to mitigate them. There are more thefts and assaults during public holidays (*feriados*), due to a lot of people moving around and high alcohol consumption, so be extra vigilant during these times.

The information in this section is current at the time of writing. Before your trip, especially if traveling to known areas of unrest (see *Danger Spots*), it's recommended to check for up-to-date security advice on the websites of the U.S. Department of State's **Bureau of Consular Affairs** (www.travel.state.gov) and the **British Foreign Office** (www.fco.

gov.uk/travel). U.S. citizens can register with the Department of State for free before taking a trip (http://travelregistration.state.gov), so that their information is on file in case of an emergency.

Theft and Robbery

Pickpocketing and **opportunistic theft** are by far the most common crimes against visitors, and the most preventable. Muggings also happen but are less frequent. Watch out for distraction techniques that allow pickpockets to go to work (e.g., spillages, staged fights, and pushing or shoving). Be especially alert in cities, on public transport, in crowded areas and at popular tourist attractions. In these places, especially on public transport, strap your backpack to your front. If you have valuables in there, don't keep them in easily accessible pockets, but at the bottom of the main section. Don't keep anything of value in your pockets. Don't wear expensive jewelry or a valuable watch (consider not bringing these to Ecuador). For any valuables that you do bring with you (cell phone, tablet, camera, MP3 player, etc.), write a list of the models and serial numbers and keep one copy with you and another back at home. Keep your cell phone out of sight. If you need to look at your phone (as this author constantly had to, for online maps), don't do it while walking along the street. Find somewhere to stop, have a careful look around, and then briefly consult your phone. In cities, you might be better off asking directions or having a printed map.

Don't carry large amounts of money. Have some emergency cash hidden away somewhere. It's a good idea to have a small purse with small denominations so that you don't reveal the whereabouts of your main wallet when paying small amounts like bus fares and snacks. If you have a debit card and a credit card, consider taking one out with you and leaving the other back at your hotel. Carry a color copy of your passport, including the visa entry stamp page, and keep the original safe. If your hostel or hotel has a security box (*caja fuerte* or *caja de seguridad*), you can leave valuables locked away while you explore. If there is no safe but your accommodations are secure and trustworthy, you may choose to leave valuables padlocked in your backpack and locked in your room.

Probably the most common way for visitors to fall victim to theft is to store their belongings in the overhead compartment on a bus; these are easy pickings for thieves. Don't leave any valuables in your main luggage, which will be stored under the bus. Keep anything of value in your day pack or handbag and hold it on your lap. If you put it on the floor in front of your seat, make sure that the person behind you can't access it. Putting it between your feet with a strap wound around your leg should do the trick.

Much more sinister are **"express kidnappings"** (*secuestro express*), where rogue taxi drivers briefly abduct passengers, relieve them of their valuables, and force them to take cash out of an ATM (or threaten them into revealing the PIN number and hold them while accomplices empty their account). Victims are usually released unharmed, but these incidents are terrifying and can turn violent. These robberies are fairly common in Guayaquil and Quito, especially at night, but rare outside these cities. To avoid this kind of incident, ask your hotel, restaurant, or bar to call you a radio (prebooked) taxi. If you have a cell phone, save the number of a reliable taxi company and call one yourself. If a radio taxi isn't available, airports, bus terminals, large supermarkets, and expensive hotels generally have taxi ranks with registered drivers. Look for the Transporte Seguro logo, meaning that video cameras, panic buttons, and GPS should be installed. Check for the cameras when you get in; there should be one on the right of the dashboard and one in the back. They are spherical with a ring of red lights that should be visible at night if the camera is working. The panic buttons are on either side of the car between the front and back seats. If they are activated, the video and audio footage from inside the taxi will be streamed to

the police and the GPS tracker activated. If you decide to flag down a city taxi at night and discover there is no camera, feel free to say *"no gracias, no tiene camera."* Other signs of a legitimate taxi include the municipality registration number sticker displayed on the windscreen and doors; the orange license plates; or the new white plates with an orange strip on the top. The driver should also have an ID, usually on the back of the driver's seat.

Also fairly common is the **use of drugs to subdue robbery victims.** This technique is usually employed in areas with bars and nightclubs. Don't accept anything from a stranger, including food, drinks, leaflets, perfume samples, telephone cards, or cigarettes, no matter how friendly or well-dressed they appear. These items may be covered with a substance known as *scopolamine,* which is absorbed through the skin and leaves victims in a subdued, compliant state. The most frequent targets of this kind of crime are young men on nights out. A number of local men died in 2018 as a result of these robberies.

Armed robbery is not unheard of, particularly in Quito, Guayaquil, and Manta. Robberies have also been reported at some remote hiking areas known to be frequented by tourists. If you are confronted by an armed robber, hand over your valuables without discussion or resistance. Aside from keeping valuables out of sight, the best defense is to walk confidently and stay alert. In cities at night, stay on the main, well-lit, populated streets in the center. Pay attention to your gut instincts: If something tells you to avoid a certain street or leave a certain area, do it.

The Ecuador District Attorney's Office (Fiscalia General) now has an English online tool for tourists to report robbery, theft, and loss of belongings and documents: www.fiscalia.gob.ec/denuncias-on-line-para-turistas.

Sexual Assault

Unwelcome attention in the street is common in Ecuador but rarely turns into anything more sinister. Sexual assaults and rape are not unheard of, however. Women should avoid walking on beaches late at night, even in pairs. Follow the rest of the advice in this section about staying safe in cities and taxis. Be especially alert around public holidays. Don't leave any drinks unattended or accept drinks from strangers. Canoa on the north coast is a hot spot for assaults against foreign women.

If the worst happens and you are attacked or raped, you may not receive much help from police. It is worth filing a report, however, especially if you can describe your attacker(s). Women's health clinics (*clínicas de la mujer*) in larger cities can provide specialized treatment and gather evidence for the police report. The morning after pill (*el píldora del día después*) is available from most pharmacies and should be taken as soon as possible in the case of rape.

Drugs

Most of the foreigners in jail in Ecuador are there for drug offenses, usually cocaine related. If you're caught with drugs, don't expect much support from your embassy or the Ecuadorian legal system. Jails are often hellholes, the judicial process can take years, and penalties are steep. Steer clear.

Danger Spots

Most of Ecuador can be roamed freely and relatively safely, taking the precautions already mentioned in this section. However, there are some areas which should be avoided, or should only be visited with the utmost precaution.

The northern part of Esmeraldas province is probably Ecuador's most dangerous region, and travelers are advised to completely avoid the area north of the city of Esmeraldas. The Colombian border zone has long been a hotbed for drug traffickers and FARC splinter groups (often one and the same) and was the setting for two car bomb attacks against military targets in early 2018, leaving four soldiers dead and 39 people wounded. In March 2018, two journalists from a leading newspaper who were investigating the attacks were kidnapped, along with their driver, by a dissident drug-trafficking faction. The three men were subsequently killed when the Ecuadorian government refused the kidnappers' demands to release imprisoned gang members and end anti-narcotics cooperation with Colombia. A month later, the same gang kidnapped and killed an Ecuadorian couple. While these events happened in or near the border town of San Lorenzo, the violence has also spread farther south. In April 2018 a homemade explosive was detonated in the town of Viche, 150 kilometers (90 mi) south of the border and only 50 kilometers (31 mi) from Esmeraldas city, on one of the main roads connecting the highlands to various popular beach destinations. In response to these incidents, President Moreno has boosted security for the region, sending 12,000 soldiers and police to combat drug gangs. Travelers are advised to completely avoid the area north of the city of Esmeraldas.

Other provinces that neighbor Colombia are Carchi and Sucumbíos, and the U.K. Foreign Office recommends avoiding the 20-kilometer (12-mi) strip of land that runs alongside the border, with the exception of the official crossing town of Tulcán, which is considered safe. However, there are destinations that fall within the exclusion zone that you may decide are worth the risk to visit. The general consensus in Ecuador is that the recommendation to avoid Lago Agrio, for example, is out of date. This author, a lone female traveler, felt safe enough to use it as a base from which to visit the surrounding Amazon communities, but was careful to not stray from the city center or to go out after 8pm. Similarly, the beautiful El Ángel Ecological Reserve in Carchi province falls within the exclusion zone but was a highlight of the northern Sierra region.

The situation in these provinces can change quickly, and travelers are advised to monitor the U.K. Foreign Office website (www.fco.gov.uk/travel) for the latest developments.

Drunken street violence, noticeably absent from the vast majority of the country, is present in Quito's La Mariscal and the northern coastal towns of Canoa and Atacames. All three are also high-risk areas for robbery and sexual assault.

Many midsized towns have very specific areas that are best avoided after dark, often around markets. These have been indicated in this book wherever local people indicated they exist. It's a good idea to ask your hotel about any places to avoid, especially if you're planning on exploring on foot.

If Something Happens

In an emergency, call 911 for police, ambulance, or the fire service. It's worth bearing in mind that Ecuadorian police do not provide the same safety net that those of us from many European countries are accustomed to. Some police are helpful and honest. The tourist police in Quito are a good example. There are reports that police in Guayaquil, too, are brushing up their act, responding quickly and in good faith to calls for assistance. However, generally speaking, corruption and inefficiency are rife. If you are in Ecuador for a while, it may be a good idea to have someone local to call in an event of an emergency, as the police may not show up. Choose someone who will answer their phone at any time of day or night.

If you are a victim of crime, head to the nearest police station to report it, even if just for insurance purposes. You may be redirected to the public prosecutor (*fiscalia*) to file a report (*denuncia*). If your bank cards have been stolen, call your bank immediately to block them. If your passport is lost or stolen, contact your embassy by phone or in person in Quito. Your embassy may also be able to help if you need emergency funds to get home or a lawyer. If the unthinkable happens and you are dealing with a fatality, embassies can also be extremely helpful in notifying the deceased's family back home and making other arrangements.

Natural Disasters

Ecuador is situated in an area of intense seismic activity. Aftershocks are still being felt following the April 2016 earthquake, which measured 7.8 on the Richter scale. In the event of a natural disaster, you should monitor the social media channels of the Ecuadorean National Geophysical Institute (www.igepn.edu.ec) and the National Service for Risk and Emergency Management (www.gestionderiesgos.gob.ec) (both Spanish only) and follow the advice of local authorities.

ROAD SAFETY

Ecuador has one of the highest rates of road accidents in Latin America, mainly due to careless driving, speeding, badly maintained vehicles, mobile phone use, and drunk driving. As with crime, road accidents are more frequent on public holidays. Apart from asking drivers to slow down ("*¿Es posible conducer mas despacio por favor?*"), there isn't a lot that visitors can do to mitigate this risk.

OCEAN SAFETY

People drown every year off Ecuador's beaches, many of which have strong currents and riptides. There is a lack of funding for lifeguards, so it's often local surfers who end up pulling people out of the water when they get into trouble. The main thing to remember is that a riptide is a narrow channel of water that is heading out to sea, so if you get stuck in one, swim parallel to the shore and you will quickly escape it. If there are red flags on the beach, don't go in the ocean.

TOILETS

There are public toilets in bus stations and in many tourist areas, often signposted SSHH (*servicios higiénicos*). You usually have to pay $0.15-0.25 to enter, which includes a handful of toilet paper from the attendant. In free public bathrooms and gas stations, there will probably be no toilet paper, so it's a good idea to carry your own at all times. This goes in the wastepaper bin, not flushed down the toilet. There may or may not be soap.

Travel Tips

TRAVELERS WITH DISABILITIES

After being shot in a 1998 robbery attempt, Ecuador's president, Lenín Moreno, is the world's only currently serving head of state to use a wheelchair. During his time as vice president (2007-2013), he increased the budget for people with disabilities more than fifty-fold and oversaw the initiation of some accessibility infrastructure. Despite these advances, however, Ecuador is still behind the times in making structural changes to address the needs of its own citizens with disabilities, not to mention visitors. Budget travelers especially may find themselves severely restricted. Many hotels and some tourist attractions with accessible facilities do exist in Ecuador, but getting around is a challenge.

In most cities, sidewalks are narrow, crowded, and uneven (sometimes cobbled). Public buses are not equipped to handle those in wheelchairs, with steep stairs that can be difficult to navigate for those with limited mobility. The Quito trolley system can handle wheelchair passengers, although its near-constant overcrowding makes this better in theory than in practice. Taxi drivers are often helpful, but there are no adapted taxis or rental cars. There are some wheelchair ramps and toilets in international airports, major bus stations, and some gas stations but their presence certainly cannot be relied upon.

A couple of options exist for those with the available budget, such as going with an organized tour. **South America for All** (www.southamericaforall.com) specializes in adapted tours and is recommended. If you prefer to travel independently, you could hire a driver or travel by taxi and take a companion without disabilities with you. **DisabledTravelers.com** (www.disabledtravelers.com) has a directory of companies offering trained, professional travel companions.

There are good online resources for disabled travelers. **Wheelchair Traveling** (http://wheelchairtraveling.com) has some excellent country-specific information about travel in Ecuador, so check there first. The government has created an online tourist guide for visitors with disabilities (http://turismoaccesible.ec) that is available in English. The translation leaves quite a bit to be desired, but there is information about the accessibility of various tourist attractions, plus a directory of accessible recreational activities, hotels, restaurants, and bars.

In addition to the hotels in the directory, the following have accessible facilities: **Hostería Mandála** (www.hosteriamandala.info) in Puerto López, **La Bicok** (Facebook @BicokLodge) in Mindo; and **Huasquila Amazon Lodge** (www.huasquila.com) outside Tena. The last even has a lift at the swimming pool and Jacuzzi, and off-road wheelchairs for jungle tours.

WOMEN TRAVELERS

Ecuador is generally a safe country for female travelers, but it is common practice for men to whistle and make comments at women in the street. Foreigners, especially blondes, are often singled out for extra attention. This can be annoying but rarely turns into anything more sinister. How you deal with this is up to you. Ignoring it is the safest strategy. This author sometimes stops and says loudly enough for all passersby to hear *"Señor, las mujeres solo quieren caminar en paz, sabe."* ("Sir, women just want to walk in peace, you know.")

If someone goes as far as to touch you, if there are other people around, the best strategy is probably to say loudly *"No me toques!"* ("Don't touch me!"). Ecuadorians generally want visitors to have a good time in their country and will be horrified at this kind of behavior.

Volunteering in Ecuador

Some organizations offer a range of nationwide volunteer placements, acting as middleman between visitors and the NGO or nonprofit that is seeking volunteers. One good example is the **Yanapuma Foundation** (www.yanapumaspanish.org), which charges a one-off fee of $85 to match volunteers with a variety of pre-screened placements, which includes an orientation in Quito, accompaniment to the placement, and ongoing support throughout. The fee goes toward Yanapuma's work in sustainable development among indigenous and marginalized communities. Another example is **Ecuador Volunteer** (www.ecuadorecovolunteer.org), a volunteer work agency set up by the owner of climbing tour company Ecuador Eco Adventure in Riobamba, who charges no fee for the service. Details of placements are on both organizations' websites.

All the following organizations accept volunteers directly. See the websites or contact them for more information about duties, length of placement, accommodations, food, and costs. Many other opportunities exist all over the country; this is just a small selection.

Both **Jatun Sacha** (www.jatunsacha.org) and **Jocotoco** (www.jocotoco.org) have a number of private nature reserves across the country that accept volunteers.

QUITO: The **Maquipucuna Reserve & Bear Lodge** (www.maquipucuna.org) is the best place in the world to see Andean bears and protects over 6,000 hectares (15,000 acres) of pristine rainforest in one of the earth's top five biodiversity hot spots. In the crater of the Pululahua volcano, the **Pululahua Hostal** (www.pululahuahostal.com) is an eco-hostel, organic farm, and restaurant that uses solar, wind, and biogas energy systems. Just west of the city center, the **Centro Tinku Escuela de Permacultura** (Facebook @centrotinku.escueladepermacultura) is a school that provides workshops on permaculture, bio-construction, agro-ecology, and related topics.

NORTHERN SIERRA: Intag, a mega biodiverse cloud-forested region where locals are battling against mega-mining, has a number of opportunities, including the community tourism project **Cabañas EcoJunín** (www.ecocabanas-junin.com); **Inter-American CASA** (http://casainteram.org/pucara), an experimental "eco-pueblo" with rural, low-income housing using sustainable energy technology, ecological design, and permaculture concepts; and **Finca San Antonio** (https://cloudforestadventure.com/en), an agro-ecological farm and ecotourism project. The neighboring **Los Cedros Biological Reserve** (www.reservaloscedros.org) protects nearly 7,000 hectares (17,300 acres) of tropical forest and cloud forest. Just outside Ibarra, the small Kichwa village of **San Clemente** (www.sclemente.com) shares the Caranqui way of life and has extensive organic gardens.

CENTRAL SIERRA: Opportunities around Baños include the **Fundación Arte del Mundo** (www.artedelmundoecuador.org), a nonprofit that provides a children's library and a free arts-based after-school program for children 6-12; the **Eco Zoológico San Martín**, a

Female travelers may find the central and northern coast more challenging than the south. From Manta and up, there is noticeably more unwelcome attention from men in the street. Women, especially those traveling alone if not accustomed to it, might consider heading to the beach destinations farther south. Montañita is considerably safer than Canoa, where sexual assaults are fairly common but unreported. Women should not walk on any beach late at night. While many genuine relationships occur between visitors and locals, it's wise to remember that the coastal area is home to some men who may not exactly be gigolos but do expect foreign women to pay for everything, from new surfboards to expensive holidays.

Wherever you go, take the usual precautions. Don't leave your drink unattended or accept drinks or anything else from strangers. Particular care needs to be taken around public holidays, due to the influx of people in tourist destinations and high alcohol consumption. See the *Crime* section for general information on staying safe in Ecuador.

Women should not be put off traveling

rehabilitation center for animals rescued from traffickers; and **Merazonia** (www.merazonia.org), a wildlife rescue and rehabilitation center outside town in the rainforest.

SOUTHERN SIERRA: Just outside Vilcabamba, **Pachamamita** (www.pachamamitaec. org) offers the opportunity to work on an agro-ecological farm and healing center. **APECAEL** (www.apecael.blogspot.com) is a community tourism project and association of organic coffee producers. Near Saraguro, **Yachay Kawsay** (www.yachaykawsay.org) is a small trilingual school (English, Spanish, and Kichwa) that accepts educationally focused volunteers, especially those interested in learning Kichwa.

ORIENTE: Just outside Puyo, the **YanaCocha Rescue Centre** (www.yanacocharescue. org) is a center for rescued wild animals. Nearby, **Los Yapas Holistic Center** (http://losyapas. org) is a permaculture project, botanical garden, ecolodge, and healing center. A sister permaculture project, **Amisacho** in Lago Agrio, has a laboratory where research is undertaken on bioremediation (the science of cleaning contamination with oil-munching mushrooms). Just outside Coca, **Sumak Allpa Island** (http://sumakallpa.org) is a primate rehabilitation center where volunteers can get involved with animal monitoring, environmental education classes, and reforestation programs. In Tena, contact Juan Tapuy of **Llaki Panka Adventours** (www.llaki-panka.de.rs) about a project in Shandia on the banks of the Jatunyacu River, where volunteers can teach English at the local school and/or get involved with organic agriculture. Volunteers pay $7/night including three meals. **Pachamamita** (www.pachamamitaec.org) offers the opportunity for teachers to work at a school in a remote Sápara community.

NORTH COAST: Rescate Animal Mompiche (Facebook @rescateanimalmompiche) is a shelter for stray dogs and cats on the beach in Mompiche. Just down the coast, **Playa Escondida** is a secluded ecolodge with 100 hectares (247 acres) of semitropical forest, where volunteers pay $10 per day for board and lodging, working six hours per day. In Puerto López, **Clara Luna** (www.claraluna.com.ec) leads community education projects, including afterschool programs, tutoring, English classes, and reading initiatives. In Ayampe, **La Cabaña de Jagannatha** (Facebook @yogapeeth) is a Hare Krishna temple and hostel offering yoga and meditation classes. Volunteers work in the gardens and grounds. Full-time volunteers stay for free; part-time volunteers pay $3 per day.

SOUTH COAST: Just outside Guayaquil, **Cerro Blanco** (http://bosquecerroblanco.org) is a protected forest with an award-winning reforestation program and an animal sanctuary. Near Playas, the **Centro Ecológico Turístico de Playas** (Facebook @cepvillamil) grows and sells organic fresh produce. Not far from Machala, **Happy Fruit** (www.fincahappyfruit.com) is an agro-ecological farm.

alone in Ecuador. As a blonde lone female traveler, I have been happily exploring Ecuador for nearly a decade, and I feel safe setting out alone for most destinations across the country (see the *Crime* section for any notable exceptions). It's one of reasons I love living here. Off the established tourist trail, I have often been the only visibly foreign person in a town and felt welcomed and comfortable. Walk confidently (even if you don't feel it) and you are much less likely to be a victim of any crime. Meet people with a friendly open manner and a smile, and you will usually get the same in return, which helps you to feel safer anywhere you go.

Lone female travelers should be prepared to respond to questions such as "Where is your husband?" and to be met with incredulity about traveling solo or not having children. How you respond is up to you. I usually take the opportunity to explain that, for me, motherhood and marriage are not the only valid choices for women and that I have opted to do other things with my life. If the questions make you feel uncomfortable, you could always say *"esa es una pregunta muy personal"* ("that is a very personal question"). If a combination of questions makes you feel unsafe (e.g., "Do you have a boyfriend?" "Where are you going?" and "Where exactly are you staying?"), it's probably best to invent a boyfriend, cut the conversation short, and go somewhere you feel secure (a busy restaurant, for example).

TRAVELING WITH CHILDREN

Ecuador is a great choice for traveling with children. It's safer and more compact than many other Latin American countries, offering the chance to experience coast, jungle, mountains, and Galápagos with minimal traveling time. If you're looking for resorts and theme parks, it's probably not the destination for you, but there's plenty of real-world excitement here, in terms of nature, wildlife, and adventure activities. There are lots of easily accessible opportunities to experience different indigenous nationalities as well, with world views very different to the western way of thinking. Many of these peoples live with few economic resources, but not in traumatizing poverty. A visit to Ecuador will provide your kids with plenty of food for thought and likely keep them thinking and questioning long after they return home.

People in Ecuador love children, so families traveling with youngsters will enjoy a warm welcome. If you're hoping to find other gringo families for your kids to play with, you may be out of luck. But, there is noticeably little bullying and social exclusion among Ecuadorian children, who will often play happily with visiting kids who speak no Spanish whatsoever. Outside cities and big towns, many Ecuadorians have the kind of childhood that many of us are nostalgic for: playing in the street with homemade toys, no parents in sight, no fear about "stranger danger" in small tightly knit communities. Older kids will enjoy picking up and learning a few words in Spanish and will be met with a kind audience upon which to practice.

Those with the budget for the Galápagos will find a wildlife paradise for kids, with lots of animals spotted with little hiking needed. Mindo is also a good destination, with hanging feeders thronged by hovering jewel-bright hummingbirds and a wonderful butterfly farm. Most of the beaches have fairly strong waves, not great for little ones, but Ayangue and Playa Escondida are notable exceptions.

A lack of safety regulations means you'll have to be extra vigilant about things like unexpected holes in the street and hazardous play equipment in parks. Safety seats are generally hard to come by in rental cars (be sure to arrange one ahead of time), and in taxis they're unheard of. Seatbelts in the back are also a rarity. This is, after all, a country where a family of four can blaze across town on a motorcycle with no helmets. Movies on buses are often very violent and/or sexually explicit. Drivers may or may not respond to pleas to put on something more child friendly.

Children pay full fare on buses if they occupy a seat, but they often ride for free if they sit on a parent's lap. The fare for children under 12 years is greatly reduced for domestic flights (perhaps half fare, and they get a seat), while infants under 2 cost around 10 percent of the fare (but they don't get a seat). Many tourist attractions have discounted tickets for children. Changing facilities are rare but sometimes exist in airports and newer bus terminals. Breastfeeding is accepted in public.

LGBTQ TRAVELERS

Although enormous progress has been made with LGBTQ rights in the last 20 years, Ecuador still has a largely conservative and macho culture, and gender queerness continues to be viewed negatively, especially by older generations. LGBTQ travelers are advised to keep a low profile and avoid public displays of affection.

There isn't much of an organized LGBTQ community in Ecuador. Quito has the most developed scene, with several gay clubs (see the *Quito* chapter for details). Younger people tend to frequent these, with the older generation preferring more discreet places like gay saunas. Quito has held a pride event every

June since 1998, and there is a gay film festival every November. Pride events now take place in other cities across the country, most notably Guayaquil (https://orgulloguayaquil.com). The most generally LGBTQ-friendly destination in the country is the coastal town of Montañita, the only place where it is common to see same-sex couples holding hands in the street. Some hotels specifically state that they are LGBTQ friendly, including Anahi Boutique Hotel (www.anahihotelquito.com/en) in Quito; the luxury ecological wellness retreat My Sachaji (www.mysachaji.com), just outside Otavalo; El Jardín de Playas (www.eljardindeplayas.com.ec) just outside Playas; and Hotel Ancora (www.hotelancoraec.com) in Puerto López.

The Nomadic Boys' website (https://nomadicboys.com) has an excellent section on the gay scene in Ecuador (especially Quito), and the Facebook pages @EcuadorGayPride and @OrgulloEcuador are good places to look for upcoming events.

See the *Gender and Sexuality* section of the *Background* chapter for information on LGBTQ rights in Ecuador.

SENIOR TRAVELERS

Age is respected in Ecuador, so senior travelers will generally be treated considerately. Those over 65 are entitled to discounts on bus travel and entrance to most museums and tourist attractions. Inquire in advance about the physical demands of tours, especially at altitude.

TRAVELING WITH PETS

If you're traveling with a really small "handbag-sized" dog, you probably won't encounter too many difficulties getting around, but anything bigger can be a challenge. Many bus companies have a No Pets policy or will insist that pets go in the luggage compartment, which is not option for anyone with the slightest bit of compassion for their animal. Some bus companies can be persuaded if you have a dog crate, offer to buy a ticket for it, and put it on the seat next to you. Buses in rural areas are more open to carrying pets. Taxi drivers might flat-out refuse to carry an animal or will try to insist that it goes in the trunk. Others will accept with no qualms or ask you to carry your pet on your lap. Check in advance whether hotels accepts pets, as policies vary widely.

To bring a pet into Ecuador, check the country-specific entry requirements here: www.pettravel.com. Have all paperwork on hand going through immigration and customs.

WHAT TO PACK

It can be a challenge packing for Ecuador, especially if you're planning on visiting the coast, jungle, and Andes. For the coast, bring beach and swimwear, shorts, etc. For the jungle, pack lightweight long pants (not jeans—leggings work well for women) and long-sleeved tops. If you are limited on space, you could buy cheap, basic jungle clothes once in Ecuador and give them away once you no longer need them. Rubber boots, essential for the Amazon, are readily available in Ecuador, though men with feet over U.S. men's size (women's size 12) or European size 43 should bring their own (or check ahead with the lodge or tour operator if they have your size). Large footwear of any kind is almost impossible to find in Ecuador. For the Sierra, bring layers, including warm sweaters. For high altitude towns and cities such as Quito and Cuenca, you will be glad of a warm jacket or coat in the evenings. You'll also need something waterproof. A lightweight plastic poncho is a good idea, as it can also cover your day pack (some are as thin as a garbage bag and roll up very small; they're very cheap and fine for moderate day hikes). Bring a comfortable pair of shoes or sneakers, and broken-in hiking boots if you plan to trek.

Anywhere you go, you will need sunglasses and sunblock (cheaper and better quality if brought from home). A hat or baseball cap is also a good idea; the midday sun can be brutal. Insect repellent is widely available in Ecuador, though bring lemon eucalyptus or citronella oil from home if you're looking to avoid DEET.

Bring a flashlight in case of power outages. A water bottle that filters and purifies water is an excellent investment and will enable you to safely drink water from the faucet, even rivers and streams. This will save you from buying water (and thus creating plastic waste) or constantly looking for places to fill your bottle. Ecuador can be noisy, so a few pairs of earplugs will probably save your sanity. If you have the budget, consider noise-canceling headphones. Remember power adaptors to charge your devices. These are available in airports, but expensive. A padlock for your main luggage (one for each zip) is also sensible.

Finally, bring small-denomination U.S. dollar bills. Leave room in your luggage for souvenirs if you like to visit markets.

CASH AND CARDS

The currency in Ecuador is the U.S. dollar. Outside the international airports, it's not easy to change money in Ecuador, so it's best to bring dollars with you or get money out of ATMs once in the country. If you are bringing cash from home, make sure to get small-denomination bills. It can be almost impossible to find a store that will accept a $50 or $100 bill. A lot of vendors will have trouble changing even a $20 when it comes to small purchases. There are ATMs in all cities and most towns that accept Visa and Mastercard. Most reliable for international cards are Banco Pichincha and Banco Internacional. Banco Guayaquil works for most cards but not all. The locations of these ATMs can be found on Google Maps, so check ahead of time if a destination has a cash machine, especially if you're headed to a small town or village. There are few ATMs on the Galápagos Islands. Many ATMs in smaller towns have a $100 withdrawal limit per transaction, so for $300 you may have to withdraw three lots of $100. If you need a large amount of cash, you may need to get it out over several days, due to withdrawal limits with your bank and/or the dispensing

(this author pays $2.50 per transaction). It is not uncommon for ATMs to be out of service, so it's a good idea to have enough cash on you for a couple of days, or you may end up having to make a quick dash to the nearest big town. Remember to tell your bank in advance that you are traveling, otherwise they may block your card if you try to use it abroad.

Outside major supermarkets and high-end stores, hotels, restaurants, and travel agencies, credit cards are not widely accepted in Ecuador, except to get cash out of ATMs. Just because an establishment sports a credit-card sticker doesn't mean it necessarily takes them; always ask. It's best to use cash wherever possible and have a credit card as a backup.

Money Transfers

Western Union is widely used all over Ecuador and there are branches everywhere. If you need to send money to someone, you will need their name exactly as it appears on their ID and the name of the town where they are located. Go into any Western Union branch, present your ID, and hand over the cash, plus the transfer fee (it costs around $6 to send $50). You will be given a code, which you send to the person receiving the money. They then take the code and their ID to a Western Union branch and withdraw the cash. Some jungle lodges and hotels (especially those requiring deposits to secure high-season bookings) may request advance payment via Western Union. Make sure to keep hold of the receipt in case of any issues.

Tipping

A *propina* (tip) isn't required or expected, but it doesn't take much out of your pocket and can make someone's day. Remember that most restaurant and bar staff earn minimum wage ($11/day) or even less if their employer has hired them informally (sadly, a situation faced by many Venezuelan immigrants). Any tip, even a dollar or two, will be appreciated. Some establishments have a tip jar at the cash register, which will get shared among the staff. Fancier restaurants add 10 percent for *servicio* (service) and the 12 percent IVA (value-added tax). It's not unheard of for the restaurant owner to pocket the service charge, so if your server has been particularly helpful, it will certainly be appreciated to leave an extra tip in cash. Airport and hotel porters should be tipped $0.50 or $1, as should the people who watch your car if you've parked in the street. Taxi drivers are often very patient about waiting outside a store, providing a wealth of local information, or helping load and unload bags, and will certainly appreciate a tip for these efforts. Guides are tipped depending on the cost and length of your stay or trip, from a couple of dollars to over ten in luxury jungle lodges and on Galápagos cruises.

Taxes

Shops, hotels, and restaurants must charge a 12 percent IVA (value-added tax), which should be noted separately on the *cuenta* (bill). When making reservations in advance for hostels and hotels, ask if the price quoted includes this charge, as many people receive a surprise when paying the bill. Wherever it was known, IVA has been included in the accommodation prices quoted in this book.

Receipts

When paying for things, especially in supermarkets, the cashier may ask you *"¿Con datos o consumidor final?"* If you would like your printed receipt to have your name and ID number on it say *"con datos"* ("with data"). Ecuadorians who are planning on submitting the receipt to the tax office will request this. For most visitor purposes, *"consumidor final"* is fine and quicker to process.

Budgeting

Ecuador is a comparatively inexpensive place to visit (with the exception of the Galápagos Islands). Serious budget travelers can get by for under $25 per day, staying in dorms, traveling by bus, and eating set meals. If you have $50 per day, you will be able to stay in a private room, eat at tourist restaurants, have a few drinks, and factor in some taxi travel.

Generally speaking, dormitory beds cost $8-10, though they are found only in the major tourist hubs. Decent single and double rooms are usually $15-25, occasionally as low as $10-12, some with shared bathrooms. Many hostels include breakfast and/or have kitchens so you can prepare your own food. Fresh produce from local markets is good quality and cheap. Most markets also have an economical food court (*patio de comida*) serving basic local fare. A basic breakfast (coffee, bread, jam, eggs) in a café might cost $3. Set lunches (*almuerzos*) in local restaurants are filling and economical ($2.50-3.50), usually consisting of a juice, a soup, and a main course (rice with chicken, fish, or meat, plus a side such as plantain or lentil stew). Less common are set dinners (*meriendas*), following a similar format. A main course in a tourist restaurant might cost $6-9. Cheap, filling street food is everywhere. Vegetarians traveling on a low budget should check *Tips for Vegetarians* in this chapter for meat-free local dishes to avoid more expensive tourist restaurants. Larger cities and tourist towns often have veggie restaurants with set lunches for $3.50-4. A large bottle of local beer is around $3.

The bus is an economical way to travel, with short local journeys usually costing $0.30 and longer distance trips around $1-1.50 per hour. Passing motorists will often offer a ride but may expect a small donation in return, so check in advance if you're very short on funds. A short taxi ride within a town might be $1.50-2.

Volunteering is often an economical way to experience Ecuador and give something back. Most programs cover expenses by charging to participate, but the cost is sometimes minimal. Check out *Volunteering in Ecuador* for some ideas.

COMMUNICATIONS AND MEDIA
Telecommunications

If you plan to bring your cell phone from home to use during your trip, you will need to first "unlock" it for international use. Once

Telephone Prefixes

Prefixes listed by province, with major cities in parentheses:

Prefix	Region
2	Pichincha (Quito), Santo Domingo de los Tsáchilas (Santo Domingo)
3	Bolívar (Guaranda), Cotopaxi (Latacunga), Chimborazo (Riobamba), Pastaza (Puyo), Tungurahua (Ambato, Baños)
4	Guayas (Guayaquil), Santa Elena (Salinas)
5	Los Ríos, Manabí (Manta, Portoviejo, Bahía de Caráquez), Galápagos (Puerto Ayora, Baquerizo Moreno)
6	Carchi (Tulcán), Esmeraldas (Atacames), Imbabura (Otavalo, Ibarra), Napo (Tena), Orellana (Coca), Sucumbíos (Lago Agrio)
7	Azuay (Cuenca), Cañar (Azogues), El Oro (Machala), Loja (Loja), Morona-Santiago (Macas), Zamora-Chinchipe (Zamora)
93, 95, 97, 98, 99	cell phones

you are in Ecuador you can buy a local SIM card (known locally as a *chip*) for around $5 with one of the local service providers. Of the two main companies, Claro and MoviStar, the former has better coverage and more branches nationwide. If you're arriving at the Quito airport, there is a Claro *chip* vending machine in the airport center across the road. With your SIM card you will be issued an Ecuadorian number and you can add credit (known as *saldo*) to your "account" in newsagents, pharmacies, and supermarkets everywhere. If you use a lot of data, consider creating an online account with Claro (https://miclaro.com.ec) and purchasing a data packet (e.g., 1GB for 30 days for $10). If the site doesn't accept your credit card, you can purchase credit with cash in a store and use your balance for online purchases. Another option is to buy a cheap local cell phone for about $40, but these only have capability for calls and text messages. WhatsApp is widely used in Ecuador. Some rural areas have no cell phone coverage.

If you don't have a cell phone, you can make national and international calls from pay phone booths known as *cabinas,* which are often part of Internet cafés. Per-minute local calls cost about $0.11, domestic calls $0.22. Calling an Ecuadorian cell phone costs $0.25 per minute, while calling North America costs from $0.20, Europe from $0.40, and Australia from $0.80. To make a call within Ecuador, dial 0 followed by the regional prefix code and the seven-digit phone number. In this book, the regional prefix codes come before the slash (/); e.g., if the number is written 6/239-1234, the regional code is 6. Cell phone numbers have a two-digit prefix starting with 9. To call Ecuador from abroad, the international dialing code is 593.

INTERNET

There are Internet cafés or *cybers* in every town and most villages. Many are open 8am-10pm daily and charge $1-1.50 per hour. Quality of equipment and Internet speed

Emergency Phone Numbers

- 911   General emergency number for ambulance, fire, or police
- 131   Ambulance
- 102   Fire
- 101   Police

vary widely. Most offer printing, copying, and scanning services. *Cybers* can get busy with local kids at school closing time (around 2:30pm). For the at sign (@), press Alt 64.

Wi-Fi is available in hotels, hostels, and restaurants all over the country but is often unreliable. Outside the main cities and tourist destinations, digital nomads may struggle to find decent connection (especially for video calls). If you need the Internet for work, it's a good idea to have a mobile device and purchase a data package to fall back on. In very rural areas, there may be no cell phone signal or Internet. Many buses claim to have Wi-Fi, but most do not. There is free Wi-Fi in some public places such as main squares; keep an eye out for signs. Monthly Internet is expensive in Ecuador ($40-50 for a basic service).

MAIL

Most people in Ecuador do not have a mailbox, house number, or street address. To send something within the country, head to a branch of the national postal service, **Correos Ecuador** (www.correosdelecuador.gob.ec) or the private courier company **Servientrega** (www.servientrega.com.ec). Items can be sent to another branch for collection by the recipient or to a nonresidential building that has an address (a large hotel or a lawyer's office, for example). Long-term visitors could rent a mailbox at the local branch of Correos Ecuador for an annual fee (around $25). To send something overseas, it's best to use an international courier such as FedEx, DHL, or UPS. Any packages that come in from abroad are routinely opened by customs and may be liable to customs fees. There is almost no online shopping in Ecuador (no Amazon deliveries, for example).

WEIGHTS AND MEASURES
Electricity

As in North America, electricity in Ecuador is 120 volts, 60 hertz alternating current, and plugs are type A (two flat prongs) and

type B (two flat prongs with a third grounding prong). Power outages are fairly common, even in major cities, and it's a good idea to bring a surge protector for expensive equipment.

Time

The Ecuadorian mainland is five hours earlier than UTC or Greenwich mean time, the same as North American eastern standard time. The Galápagos Islands are one hour earlier than the mainland. Because days and nights on the equator are almost the same duration year-round (with sunrise around 6am and sunset around 6:30pm), daylight saving time is not used in Ecuador.

Business Hours

Typical business hours are 8am or 9am to 5pm or 6pm Monday-Friday, with a lunch break 1pm-2pm. Banks usually open on Saturday mornings, but government offices and most tour agencies do not. Many small businesses keep fairly irregular opening hours.

TOURIST INFORMATION
Maps

Both **International Travel Maps** (www.itmb.com) and **Longitude Maps** (www.longitudemaps.com) offer a variety of Ecuador maps that can be ordered online. In Ecuador, the best resource is the **Instituto Geográfico Militar** (IGM, www.igm.gob.ec), where maps can be purchased at the office in Quito or online (see *Servicios* on the IGM website). Maps of city centers and popular attractions are available at tourist offices nationwide. If you have a smartphone you can download the application Maps.me (https://maps.me), which can be used offline and is a great tool for hikers.

Tourist Offices

Most towns and cities have official tourist offices, often called iTur. These are usually located in the municipal building on the main square or at major bus terminals. Most are only open Monday to Friday. Some are extremely helpful, with English-speaking staff and excellent websites with information about attractions, activities, accommodations, restaurants, tour agencies, etc. Others only really want to hand out maps. The Ministry of Tourism can be found online (www.ecuador.travel, www.turismo.gob.ec) and on Facebook (@MinisterioTurismoEcuador).

Resources

Glossary

aguardiente: sugarcane alcohol

aguas termales: hot springs

almuerzo: lunch

artesanías: handicrafts

cabaña: cabin

cabina: pay phone, often inside an Internet café

camioneta: pickup truck taxi, usually white

campesino: rural resident

canelazo: hot, sweet alcoholic drink made with sugarcane

cc or centro comercial: shopping center or mall

chicha: drink, often made from manioc, sometimes fermented with human saliva

chiva: open-sided bus with wooden seats, also known as a *ranchero*

colectivo: shared form of transport, often a converted pickup truck with seats in the bed

con datos: printed receipt with the name and ID number of the purchaser, for tax purposes

consumidor final: printed receipt without the name and ID number of the purchaser

cordillera: mountain range

criollo: originally a person of pure Spanish descent born in the colonies but now applied to anything traditional, especially food

curandero/a: medicinal healer

cyber: Internet café

denuncia: legal complaint or police report

ecuavolley: the local version of volleyball

feria: fair, usually selling artisanal goods or food

feriado: public holiday

gringo: term for North Americans, but applied to most white foreigners; not particularly derogatory

hacienda: farm or country estate

helado: literally means "iced"; can refer to ice cream, sorbet, or a cold coconut to drink (*coco helado*)

indígena: indigenous person (note that *indio* is considered insulting)

malecón: riverside or seaside promenade

merienda: supper, also used for cheap set-menu dinners

mestizo: person of mixed indigenous and European blood

minga: community voluntary work

mirador: viewpoint

municipio: town hall or city hall

obraje: textile workshop

Panamericana: Pan-American Highway

páramo: high-elevation grasslands

pasillo: Ecuador's national music

peña: bar with traditional live music

Oriente: the Amazon region

ranchero: open-sided bus with wooden seats, also known as a *chiva*

saldo: mobile phone credit

Sierra: Andean region

SS HH: sign for public restroom (*servicios higiénicos*)

terminal terrestre: bus terminal

tienda: shop

tramites: any kind of bureaucratic procedures; e.g., opening a bank account, obtaining visa extension

tsantsa: shrunken head

yucca: cassava or manioc

Spanish Phrasebook

PRONUNCIATION

Once you learn them, Spanish pronunciation rules—in contrast with English—don't change. There are 27 letters in the Spanish alphabet: the familiar English 26, plus ñ. Every letter is pronounced. The capitalized syllables below are stressed.

Vowels

a as 'ah' in "hah": *agua* AH-gwah (water), *pan* PAHN (bread), *casa* KAH-sah (house)

e as 'e' in "bet:" *mesa* MEH-sah (table), *tela* TEH-lah (cloth), *de* DEH (of, from)

i as 'ee' in "need": *diez* DEE-ehss (ten), *comida* ko-MEE-dah (meal), *fin* FEEN (end)

o two sounds: either the short "o" sound in British English "hot": *comer* KO-mare (eat); or like a longer "oh," as in *poco* POH-koh (a bit). *Ocho* has both sounds: O-choh (eight).

u as 'oo' in "cool": *uno* OO-noh (one) and *usted* oos-TEHD (you); when it follows a *q*, the u is silent; when it follows an *h* or has an umlaut (ü), it's pronounced like "w."

Consonants

b, f, k, l, m, n, p, q, s, r, t, w, x, y, z pronounced almost as in English; **h** is silent; **v** is pronounced the same as **b**

c as 'k' in "keep": *casa* KAH-sah (house); when it precedes *e* or *i*, c is pronounced as 's' in "sit": *cerveza* sayr-VAY-sah (beer), *encima* ehn-SEE-mah (on top of).

g as 'g' in "gift" when it precedes *a, o, u,* or a consonant: *gato* GAH-toh (cat), *hago* AH-goh (I do, make); otherwise, g is pronounced as 'h' in "hat": *giro* HEE-roh (money order), *gente* HEHN-tay (people)

j as 'h' in "has": *jueves* HOOAY-vays (Thursday), *mejor* meh-HOR (better)

ll as 'y' in "yes": *toalla* toh-AH-yah (towel), *ellos* AY-yohs (they, them), *llamas* YAH-mahs (llamas)

ñ as 'ny' in "canyon": *año* AH-nyo (year), *señor* SEH-nyor (Mr., sir)

rr like a Scottish rolled 'r.' This distinguishes *perro* (dog) from *pero* (but) and *carro* (car) from *caro* (expensive). Many foreigners have particular trouble with this sound. If you do, try to use a different word; e.g., *auto* for car.

Stressed Syllables

The rule for where to put the stress when pronouncing a word is simple: If a word ends in a vowel, an *n*, or an *s*, stress the next-to-last syllable; if not, stress the last syllable.

Pronounce *gracias* GRAH-seeahs (thank you), *orden* OHR-dayn (order), and *carretera* kah-ray-TAY-rah (highway) with stress on the next-to-last syllable.

Otherwise, accent the last syllable: *venir* veh-NEER (to come), *ferrocarril* feh-roh-cah-REEL (railroad), *edad* eh-DAHD (age).

Exceptions to the accent rule are always marked with an accent sign: (á, é, í, ó, or ú), such as *teléfono* teh-LAY-foh-noh (telephone), *jabón* hah-BON (soap), and *rápido* RAH-pee-doh (rapid).

BASIC AND COURTEOUS EXPRESSIONS

Most Spanish-speaking people consider formalities important. When approaching anyone for information or any other reason, do not forget the appropriate salutation—good morning, good evening, and so on.

Hello. *Hola.*

Good morning. *Buenos días.*

Good afternoon. *Buenas tardes.*

Good evening. *Buenas noches.*

How are you? *¿Cómo está?* (formal) *¿Cómo estás? ¿Qué tal?* (informal)

Very well, thank you. *Muy bien, gracias.*

OK; good. *Bien.*

So-so. *Más o menos.*

Not OK; bad. *Mal.*

And you? *¿Y usted?* (formal) *¿Y tu?* (informal)

Thank you. *Gracias.*

Thank you very much. *Muchas gracias.*

You're very kind. *Muy amable.*

You're welcome. *De nada.*

Good-bye. *Ciao* ("CHOW") or *Adios.*

See you later. *Hasta luego.*

please *por favor*

yes *sí*

no *no*

I don't know. *No sé.*

My name is . . . *Me llamo . . .*

What is your name? *¿Cómo se llama usted?*

Pleased to meet you. *Mucho gusto* or *Encantado* (more formal and stronger).

Just a moment, please. *Momentito, por favor.*

Excuse me, please (when you're trying to get attention). *Disculpe* or *Con permiso* (for moving past someone).

Sorry (when you've made an error). *Disculpe* or *Lo siento* (stronger and more formal).

Enjoy your meal. *Buen provecho.*

How do you say . . . in Spanish? *¿Cómo se dice . . . en español?*

Do you speak English? *¿Habla usted inglés?*

I don't speak Spanish well. *No hablo bien el español.*

I don't understand. *No entiendo.*

Could you speak more slowly please? *¿Podría hablar más despacio por favor?*

ECUADORIAN SLANG

Ecuadorians love slang (*jerga,* pronounced "yerga") and creative word play. Phrases come and go, some of them only used in a particular town or village. A few of the most popular, longstanding, non-offensive slang terms are listed below. Dropping these into casual conversation is a simple way to delight local people and make them laugh.

pana a close friend, a buddy

¡Tranquilo! Don't worry about it! (Use *¡Tranquila!* when talking to a woman.) Can be shortened to *¡Tranqui!*

bacán/chévere cool

buenazo awesome

The suffix *-azo* means "big" or "very"; e.g., *olazo* to refer to a big wave, *solazo* to mean "strong sun." The suffix *isimo* also means "very"; e.g., *riquisimo* (very delicious), *bacánsisimo/chéverisimo* (very cool). The suffix *-ita/-ito* is used to mean "little" or just to soften what you're saying; e.g., *animalito* (little animal), *panita* (affectionate way to say "buddy").

¡Que bestia! "How crazy!" or "That's wild!" (literally, "What a beast!")

¡Habla serio! Be serious! Used like "You must be kidding me!"

¡Chuta! Damn! Shoot! (Not be confused with "*¡Chucha!*" which is offensive and refers to female genitals)

¡Que huevada! ¡La misma huevada! What cr*p! The same old cr*p! (mildly offensive)

pendejo/a idiot (mildly offensive)

¡Qué asco! Gross!

Farra party; can also be used as a verb, "*farrear,*" meaning "to party"

Chupar to drink alcohol (literally "to suck")

chuchaqui hungover (from Quechua)

¡Dale! A bit like "hit it!" (when encouraging someone to catch a wave, for example). Used without emphasis, *dale* can be used to mean "ok, I agree."

¡De ley! ¡De una! Absolutely!

¡Pilas! A bit like "look sharp!" or "let's go!" Can also be used as an adjective; i.e., *Tengo que estar pilas mañana* (I have to be sharp tomorrow).

¡Ya sabe! You know it!

Perhaps the most Ecuadorian slang word is imported from English: *man* translates as "guy"; e.g., *el man* (the guy) or *estos manes* (these guys). It can also be used to refer to a woman; e.g., *la man* (the woman), and can be suffixed with *-ito/-ita,* as in *este mancito* (this little guy).

TERMS OF ADDRESS

When in doubt, use the formal *usted* (you) as a form of address.

I *yo*

you (formal) *usted*

you (familiar) *tu*

he/him *él*

she/her *ella*

we/us *nosotros*
you (plural) *ustedes*
they/them *ellos* (all males or mixed gender);
   ellas (all females)
Mr., sir *señor*
Mrs., Madam *señora*
Miss, young woman *señorita*
wife *esposa*
husband *esposo*
friend *amigo* (male); *amiga* (female)
boyfriend/girlfriend *novio/novia*
son/daughter *hijo/hija*
brother/sister *hermano/hermana*
father/mother *padre/madre*
grandfather/grandmother *abuelo/
   abuela*

GETTING AROUND

Where is . . . ? *¿Dónde está . . . ?*
How far is it to . . . ? *¿Que tan lejos está . . . ?*
(very) near/far *(muy) cerca/lejos*
How many blocks? *¿Cuántas cuadras?*
the bus station *la terminal terrestre*
the bus stop *la parada de bus*
the ticket office *la boletería*
I'd like a ticket to . . . *Quisiera un boleto
   a . . .* (*un ticket* is also common)
return *ida y vuelta*
Where is this bus going? *¿A dónde va este
   bús?*
What time does it leave? *¿A que hora
   sale?*
From which platform? *¿De que anden?*
Stop here, please. *Pare aquí, por favor.*
the taxi stand *la parada de taxis*
take me to . . . *llévame a . . .*
the boat *el barco/el bote/la lancha*
the airport *el aeropuerto*
reservation *reservación*
baggage *equipaje*
the entrance *la entrada*
the exit *la salida*
from . . . to . . . *de . . . a . . .*
by/through *por*
from *desde*
the right *la derecha*
the left *la izquierda*
straight ahead *derecho; recto*

in front *en frente*
beside *al lado*
behind *atrás*
the corner *la esquina*
the stoplight *el semáforo*
a turn *una vuelta*
here *aquí*
over here *por acá*
there *allí*
over there *por allá*
street/avenue *calle/avenida*
highway *carretera*
bridge *puente*
address *dirección*
north/south/east/west *norte/sur/este/
   oeste*

ACCOMMODATIONS

Do you have a room for tonight? *¿Tiene
   una habitación para esta noche?*
May I (may we) see it? *¿Puedo (podemos)
   verlo?*
What is the rate? *¿Cuál es el precio?*
Is that your best rate? *¿Es su mejor precio?*
Is there something cheaper? *¿Hay algo
   más económico?*
discount *descuento*
Does it include breakfast? *¿Incluye el
   desayuno?*
a single room *una habitación sencilla* or
   individual
a twin room *una habitación con dos camas*
a room with a double bed *una habitación
   matrimonial*
with private bath *con baño privado*
with shared bath *con baño compartido*
hot water *agua caliente*
shower *ducha*
towels *toallas*
soap *jabón*
toilet paper *papel higiénico*
blanket *corbija; manta*
sheets *sábanas*
air-conditioning *aire acondicionado*
fan *ventilador*
key *llave*
manager *gerente*

FOOD

I'm hungry/thirsty. *Tengo hambre/sed.*
breakfast *desayuno*
lunch *almuerzo*
daily lunch special *el menú del día*
dinner *cena*
It's really delicious! *¡Es muy rico!*
the bill *la cuenta*
menu *carta*
order *pedido*
glass *vaso*
fork *tenedor*
knife *cuchillo*
spoon *cuchara*
napkin *servilleta*
drink *bebida*
coffee *café*
tea *té* or *agua aromatica*
carbonated water *agua con gas*
noncarbonated water *agua sin gas*
beer *cerveza*
wine *vino*
milk *leche*
juice *jugo*
sugar *azúcar*
cheese *queso*
eggs *huevos*
bread *pan*
salad *ensalada*
fruit *fruta*
lime *limón*
fish *pescado*
shellfish *mariscos*
shrimp *camarones*
meat (without) *(sin) carne*
vegetarian *vegetarian/a*
vegan *vegano/a*
chicken *pollo*
pork *chancho*
beef/steak *res/bistec/lomo*
bacon/ham *tocino/jamón*

SHOPPING

money *dinero*
cash *efectivo*
Do you accept credit cards? *¿Aceptan tarjetas de crédito?*
How much does it cost? *¿Cuánto cuesta?*
Do you have any change? *¿Tiene cambio?*
expensive *caro*
cheap *barato; económico*
more *más*
less *menos*
a little *un poco*
too much *demasiado*

HEALTH

Help me, please. *Ayúdeme por favor.*
I am ill. *Estoy enfermo/a.*
Call a doctor. *Llame un doctor.*
Take me to . . . *Lléveme a . . .*
hospital *hospital; clínica*
drugstore *farmacia*
pain *dolor*
fever *fiebre*
headache *dolor de cabeza*
stomachache *dolor de estómago*
nausea *náusea*
to vomit *vomitar*
medicine *medicina*
antibiotics *antibióticos*
pill/tablet *pastilla*
ointment/cream *crema*
bandage *vendaje*
Band-Aid *curita*
sanitary napkins *toallas sanitarias*
tampons *tampones*
birth control pills *pastillas anticonceptivas*
morning after pill *píldora del día después*
pregnancy test *prueba de embarazo*
condoms *preservativos; condones*
dentist *dentista*
toothache *dolor de muelas*

COMMUNICATIONS

telephone call *llamada*
cell phone *celular*
SIM card *chip*
phone credit *saldo*
pay phones *cabinas*
I would like to call . . . *Quisiera llamar a . . .*
Internet café *cyber*
a computer, please *una maquina por favor*
@ sign *arroba*
copies *copias*
scan *escaneo*

print-out *impresión*
post office *Correos Ecuador*
letter *carta*
envelope *sobre*
stamp *sello de correo*
airmail *correo aereo*
delivery *entrega*
registered *registrado*
package/box *paquete/caja*

AT THE BORDER

border *frontera*
customs *aduana*
immigration in*migración*
passport *pasaporte*
identity card *cédula*
profession *profesión*
marital status *estado civil*
single *soltero/a*
married *casado/a*
divorced *divorciado/a*
widowed *viudado/a*
travel insurance *seguro de viaje*

VERBS

The infinitives of verbs have three possible endings: *ar, er,* and *ir. Many verbs are regular:*
to buy *comprar*
  I buy; you buy (formal); you buy (informal); we buy; they buy *yo compro; usted compra; tu compras; nosotros compramos; ellos/ellas compran*
to eat *comer*
  I eat; you eat (formal); you eat (informal); we eat; they eat *yo como; usted come; tu comras; nosotros comemos; ellos/ellas comen*
to climb *subir*
  I climb; you climb (formal); you climb (informal); we climb; they climb: *yo subo; usted sube; tu subes; nosotros subimos; ellos/ellas suben*
Some common verbs that can be conjugated using the pattern above for *ar, er,* and *ir* verbs are:
to pass, to spend (time), to happen *pasar*
to owe, must, should, ought to *deber*
to stay, remain *quedar*

to speak *hablar*
to carry, bring *llevar*
to arrive *llegar*
to leave, abandon, to let, allow *dejar*
to call, to name *llamar*
to take, drink *tomar*
to live *vivir*
to watch, look at *mirar*
to look for *buscar*
to wait for, to hope *esperar*
to love *amar*
to work *trabajar*
to need *necesitar*
to write *escribir*
to give *dar* (regular in the present tense except for *doy,* "I give")
to do or make *hacer* (regular in the present tense except for *hago,* "I do/make")
to tell or to say *decir* (regular in the present tense except for *digo,* "I tell/say")

Some of the most useful verbs are irregular:
to have *tener*
  I have; you have (formal); you have (informal); we have; they have *yo tengo; usted tiene; tu tienes; nosotros tenemos; ellos/ellas tienen*
to come *venir* (similarly irregular: *vengo, viene, vienes, venimos, vienen*)
to be able to *poder*
  I can; you can (formal); you can (informal); we can; they can *yo puedo; usted puede; tu puedes; nosotros podemos; ellos/ellas pueden*
to go *ir*
  I go; you go (formal); you go (informal); we go; they go *yo voy; usted va; tu vas; nosotros vamos; ellos/ellas van*
  Ir can be used to express the simplest future tense, the same as in English; i.e., "I am going to eat" would be *"Voy a comer"*; **"you are going to eat" would be** *"usted va a comer."*

Spanish has two forms of "to be." Use *estar* when speaking of location or a temporary state of being: *"Estoy en casa."* ("I am at home.") *"Estoy enfermo."* ("I'm sick.")

I am; you are (formal); you are (informal); we are; they are *yo estoy; usted está; tu estás; nosotros estámos; ellos/ ellas están*

Use *ser* for a permanent state of being: *"Soy doctora."* ("I am a doctor.")

I am; you are (formal); you are (informal); we are; they are *yo soy; usted es; tu eres; nosotros somos; ellos/ellas son*

NUMBERS

0 *cero*
1 *uno*
2 *dos*
3 *tres*
4 *cuatro*
5 *cinco*
6 *seis*
7 *siete*
8 *ocho*
9 *nueve*
10 *diez*
11 *once*
12 *doce*
13 *trece*
14 *catorce*
15 *quince*
16 *dieciseis*
17 *diecisiete*
18 *dieciocho*
19 *diecinueve*
20 *veinte*
21 *veinte y uno* or *veintiuno*
30 *treinta*
40 *cuarenta*
50 *cincuenta*
60 *sesenta*
70 *setenta*
80 *ochenta*
90 *noventa*
100 *ciento*
101 *ciento y uno* or *cientiuno*
200 *doscientos*
500 *quinientos*
1,000 *mil*
10,000 *diez mil*
100,000 *cien mil*
1,000,000 *millón*
half *medio* or *la mitad*
one-third *un tercio*
one-quarter *un cuarto*

TIME

What time is it? *¿Qué hora es?*
It's 1 o'clock. *Es la una.*
It's 3 in the afternoon. *Son las tres de la tarde.*
It's 4am *Son las cuatro de la mañana.*
6:30 *seis y media*
quarter to 11 *un cuarto para las once*
quarter past 5 *las cinco y cuarto*
midnight *medianoche*
midday *mediodía*
an hour *una hora*
a minute *un minuto*
a second *un segundo*
after *después*
before *antes*

DAYS, MONTHS, AND SEASONS

Monday *lunes*
Tuesday *martes*
Wednesday *miércoles*
Thursday *jueves*
Friday *viernes*
Saturday *sábado*
Sunday *domingo*
today *hoy*
tomorrow *mañana*
yesterday *ayer*
January *enero*
February *febrero*
March *marzo*
April *abril*
May *mayo*
June *junio*
July *julio*
August *agosto*
September *septiembre*
October *octubre*
November *noviembre*
December *diciembre*

a week *una semana*
a month *un mes*
spring *primavera*
summer *verano*
autumn *otoño*

Winter *invierno*

Courtesy of Bruce Whipperman, author of *Moon Pacific Mexico*. Amended for Ecuadorian usage by Bethany Pitts.

Suggested Reading

HISTORY AND POLITICS

Almeida Chávez, Mónica, and Ana Karina López Ramón. *El Séptimo Rafael.* Quito, Ecuador: Dinediciones, 2017. A deep journalistic investigation into Rafael Correa Delgado, president of Ecuador 2007-2017. In Spanish.

Barrett, Paul M. *Law of the Jungle: The $19 Billion Legal Battle Over Oil in the Rain Forest and the Lawyer Who'd Stop at Nothing to Win.* New York: Broadway Books, 2015. The true story of the legal battle against Chevron following the biggest environmental disaster in history.

Bassett, Carol Ann. *Galápagos at the Crossroads: Pirates, Biologists, Tourists and Creationists Battle for Darwin's Cradle of Evolution.* Washington, DC: National Geographic, 2009. Provocative analysis of the islands' environmental problems.

Becker, Marc. *The FBI in Latin America: The Ecuador Files (Radical Perspectives).* Durham, NC: Duke University Press, 2017. An examination of FBI documents that reveals the nature of U.S. imperial ambitions in the Americas.

Becker, Marc. *Pachakutik: Indigenous Movements & Electoral Politics in Ecuador.* Lanham, MD: Rowman & Littlefield, 2012. An overview of one of the Americas' most powerful social movements, the Confederation of Indigenous Nationalities of Ecuador (CONAIE).

Charbonneau, Steven J. *Valverde's Gold: The Royal Geographical Society Llanganati Papers.* Scotts Valley, CA: CreateSpace Independent Publishing Platform, 2012. A compilation of historical papers on the legendary lost Inca treasure.

De la Torre, Carlos. *The Ecuador Reader: History, Culture, and Politics.* Durham, NC: Duke University Press, 2009. An excellent collection of short, readable articles by Ecuadorian authors, politicians, and journalists on various topics such as agriculture, politics, women's rights, religion, etc.

Kane, Joe. *Savages.* New York: Vintage Departures, 1996. Eye-opening and very readable account of the Huaorani's fight against oil exploration.

Lavinas Picq, Manuela. *Vernacular Sovereignties: Indigenous Women Challenging World Politics.* Tucson, AZ: University of Arizona Press, 2018. Highlights the important, unrecognized role of indigenous women in politics, focused on Ecuador.

Perkins, John. *Confessions of an Economic Hitman.* London: Ebury Press, 2005. Explosive account of the economic pressure applied to South American governments by the United States. It claims that Ecuadorian president Jaime Roldós Aguilera was assassinated in a CIA conspiracy.

Sawyer, Suzana. *Crude Chronicles.* Durham, NC: Duke University Press, 2004.

Passionate account of indigenous resistance to oil exploration in the Ecuadorian Amazon.

FICTION

See the *Background* chapter for recommended literature by Ecuadorian authors.

Burroughs, William S. *Queer*. New York: Viking Penguin, 1996. A companion piece to Burroughs's first novel, *Junky* (1953), *Queer* describes a fictional addict's escapades during a pilgrimage from Mexico to Ecuador in search of ayahuasca.

Resau, Laura, and María Virginia Farinango. *The Queen of Water*. New York: Delacorte Books, 2011. A poignant novel for young adults based on a true story of an indigenous girl sold to a mestizo family as a servant.

Sepúlveda, Luis. *The Old Man Who Read Love Stories*. Boston, MA: Mariner Books, 1995. In the Ecuadorean jungle, an elderly widower who finds comfort in reading romance novels joins in the hunt for an enraged ocelot.

Vonnegut, Kurt Jr. *Galápagos*. New York: Delta, 1999. A novel about what would happen if the only people to survive a worldwide apocalypse were the passengers on a Galápagos cruise ship.

TRAVEL AND MEMOIRS

Angermeyer, Johanna. *My Father's Island: A Galápagos Quest*. New York: Viking, 1990. Angermeyer embarks on a search to discover what happened to her father, a refugee from Hitler, on the Galápagos Islands.

Bemelmans, Ludwig. *The Donkey Inside*. New York: Paragon House, 1990. Portrait of Quito and its people during World War II, by the French author of the famous *Madeline* children's series.

Honigsbaum, Mark. *Valverde's Gold*. London: Picador, 2005. True story of an expedition into the legend of the lost Inca gold in the Llanganates.

Lourie, Peter. *Sweat of the Sun, Tears of the Moon*. Lincoln: University of Nebraska Press, 1998. Firsthand account of an obsession with the treasure in the Llanganates.

Michaux, Henri. *Ecuador: A Travel Journal*. Evanston, IL: Marlboro Press/Northwestern, 2001. A short, quirky account of the Belgian-born author's travels in Ecuador in 1927.

Poole, Richard. *The Inca Smiled: The Growing Pains of an Aid Worker in Ecuador*. Oxford, UK: Oneworld Publications, 1997. The story of a British volunteer in Ecuador in the 1960s.

Quarrington, Paul. *The Boy on the Back of the Turtle: Seeking God, Quince Marmalade, and the Fabled Albatross on Darwin's Islands*. Vancouver, Canada: Greystone Books, 2003. A funny and observant story of a family cruise in the Galápagos.

Thomsen, Moritz. *Living Poor: A Peace Corps Chronicle*. Seattle: University of Washington Press, 1969. Describes two years on a farm in Esmeraldas in the 1960s. The narrative continues in *The Farm on the River of Emeralds* (Boston: Houghton Mifflin, 1978) and *The Saddest Pleasure: A Journey on Two Rivers* (St. Paul, MN: Graywolf Press, 1990).

Treherne, John E. *The Galápagos Affair*. New York: Pimlico, 2002. A notorious true story of murder and intrigue set on the island of Floreana.

von Däniken, Erich. *The Gold of the Gods*. London: Souvenir Press, 1973. The story of a 1969 expedition to Ecuador's Cueva de los Tayos and the discovery of ancient gold artifacts inside.

Wittmer, Margaret. *Floreana: A Woman's Pilgrimage to the Galápagos*. Wakefield, RI: Moyer Bell, 1990. Firsthand account of early Floreana settlers, including Margaret's account of the mysterious events of the 1930s.

CULTURE

Cuvi, Pablo. *Crafts of Ecuador*. Quito: Dinediciones, 1994. Beautifully photographed book on Ecuadorian crafts.

Miller, Tom. *The Panama Hat Trail: A Journey from South America*. Washington, DC: National Geographic Books, 2002. A book about the famous misnamed hat, as well as Ecuadorian history and culture.

Nikolovski, Goce. *Taste of Ecuadorian Cuisine (Latin American Cuisine Book 10)*. Morrisville, NC: Lulu Press, 2017. Collection of over 200 traditional Ecuadorian recipes.

Perkins, John, and Shakaim Mariano Shakai Ijisam Chumpi. *Spirit of the Shuar: Wisdom from the Last Unconquered People of the Amazon*. New York: Destiny Books, 2001. The cosmovision, history, and customs of the Shuar in their own words.

WILDLIFE & THE NATURAL WORLD

Castro, Isabel. *A Guide to the Birds of the Galápagos Islands*. Princeton, NJ: Princeton University Press, 1996. Presents every species to have been recorded within the archipelago, including accidentals and vagrants, with 32 color plates.

Fitter, Julian, Daniel Fitter, and David Hosking. *Wildlife of the Galápagos*. Princeton, NJ: Princeton University Press, 2016. 2nd edition. Over 400 species of wildlife most likely to be encountered on a trip to the islands.

Noboa, Andrés Vásquez. *Wildlife of Ecuador: A Photographic Field Guide to Birds, Mammals, Reptiles, and Amphibians*. Princeton, NJ: Princeton University Press, 2017. An all-in-one guide to mainland Ecuador's wildlife.

Ridgely, Robert, and Paul Greenfield. *The Birds of Ecuador: Field Guide*. Ithaca, NY: Comstock, 2001. The bible of birding in Ecuador, with 800 pages of color plates and descriptions of Ecuador's 1,600 species.

Weiner, Jonathan. *The Beak of the Finch: A Story of Evolution in Our Own Time*. New York: Vintage Books, 1995. Describes evolution happening before our eyes among the finches observed by Darwin on his *Beagle* voyage.

Internet Resources

GENERAL ECUADOR WEBSITES

EcuadorExplorer.com
www.ecuadorexplorer.com
Useful online guide.

Ecuador Travel
www.ecuador.travel
Ministry of Tourism site.

Andes Transit
www.andestransit.com
Useful site to check bus schedules.

QUITO

Quito Official Travel Information
www.quito.com.ec
City tourist office's website, with comprehensive information.

THE GALÁPAGOS ISLANDS

International Galápagos Tour Operators Association
www.igtoa.org

Charles Darwin Foundation
www.darwinfoundation.org
Information about the flora, fauna, and conservation of the Galápagos Islands.

Galápagos Conservation Trust
www.galapagosconservation.org.uk

NEWS AND MEDIA

BBC
www.bbc.com/travel/south-america/ecuador
BBC Travel page on Ecuador.

El Comercio
www.elcomercio.com
Quito-based national daily newspaper, in Spanish.

El Universo
www.eluniverso.com
Guayaquil-based national daily newspaper, in Spanish.

The Guardian
www.theguardian.com/world/ecuador
The Guardian offers the most comprehensive international coverage of Ecuador.

TRAVEL ADVICE

British Foreign Office Travel Advice
www.gov.uk/foreign-travel-advice/ecuador
Information on entry requirements, security, and health in Ecuador.

U.S. Department of State Ecuador Country Profile
http://travel.state.gov
Click on *Find International Travel Information* and then *Country Information*.

VOLCANOES AND NATURAL DISASTERS

Instituto Geofísico-Escuela Politécnica Nacional
www.igepn.edu.ec
Up-to-date information on volcanic and seismic activity, in Spanish.

Smithsonian Institution Global Volcanism Program
www.volcano.si.edu
Profiles on the world's volcanoes, searchable by country.

LANGUAGE

Cultures of the Andes
www.andes.org
Kichwa language links, songs, and pictures.

CONSERVATION

Acción Ecológica
www.accionecologica.org
Ecuador's most well respected environmental organization (in Spanish).

Amazon Frontlines
www.amazonfrontlines.org
NGO defending indigenous rights to land, life, and cultural survival in the Amazon.

DECOIN (Defense & Ecological Conservation of Intag)
www.decoin.org and http:// codelcoecuador.com
Information on the struggle to defend one of the world's most biodiverse regions from mining.

National System of Protected Areas
http://areasprotegidas.ambiente.gob. ec/en
Information on Ecuador's national parks and protected areas.

Protect Ecuador
http://protectecuador.org
Wealth of information on the horrors of mining in Ecuador, with some excellent maps.

HUMAN RIGHTS

Freedom House
https://freedomhouse.org/country/ ecuador
Profile on freedom of speech and democracy in Ecuador.

Human Rights Watch
www.hrw.org/americas
Information on human rights issues in Ecuador.

Index

INDEX

List of Maps

Photo Credits

All photos © Bethany Pitts except: page 1 © Maria Luisa Lopez Estivill | Dreamstime.com; page 6 © (top left) Efrain Velásquez-DIDEL-GAD Otavalo; (top right) © Barna Tanko | Dreamstime.com; (bottom) Markpittimages | Dreamstime.com; page 7 © (bottom right) Patricio Hidalgo | Dreamstime.com; page 8 © (top) Hans Heinz; page 9 © (top) Patricio Hidalgo | Dreamstime.com; (bottom left) Photosimo | Dreamstime.com; page 10 © Maria Luisa Lopez Estivill | Dreamstime.com; page 12 © Diego Grandi | Dreamstime.com; page 13 © (bottom) Max Bello; page 14 © (top) Mark Towner / Alamy Stock Photo; (bottom) Izanbar | Dreamstime.com; page 15 © Alanbrito | Dreamstime.com; page 16 © (top) Mauricebrand | Dreamstime.com; (bottom) Orionna | Dreamstime.com; page 17 © Jiri Hrebicek | Dreamstime.com; page 23 © (bottom) Diego Grandi | Dreamstime.com; page 26 © (bottom) Peter Joost; page 29 © (top) Erin Deo; page 30 © (bottom) Santiago Bancalari; page 32 © Diego Grandi | Dreamstime.com; page 33 © (top left) Hans Heinz; page 45 © (right middle) Museo de Arte Precolombino/Casa del Alabado; (bottom) F11photo | Dreamstime.com; page 49 © Museo Mindalae; page 63 © (bottom) Fundación Libera Ecuador; page 88 © Hans Heinz; page 90 © Efrain Velásquez-DIDEL-GAD Otavalo; page 99 © (top left) Pabloborca | Dreamstime.com; (top right) Barna Tanko | Dreamstime.com; (bottom left) Jo Merriam | Dreamstime.com; (bottom right) Thomas Wyness | Dreamstime.com; page 103 © Efrain Velásquez-DIDEL-GAD Otavalo; page 109 © (top left) Efrain Velásquez-DIDEL-GAD Otavalo; (top right) Patricio Hidalgo | Dreamstime.com; page 110 © Efrain Velásquez-DIDEL-GAD Otavalo; page 134 © Lou Jost; page 140 © (top) Barna Tanko | Dreamstime.com; (bottom) Kseniya Ragozina | Dreamstime.com; page 145 © (top right) Patricio Hidalgo | Dreamstime.com; (bottom) Patricio Hidalgo | Dreamstime.com; page 158 © Alfonso Toaquiza/Galeria Arte de Tigua Alfredo Toaquiza; page 163 © Ammit | Dreamstime.com; page 169 © (top left) Biathlonua | Dreamstime.com; (top right) Pabloborca | Dreamstime.com; (bottom) Jimmy Muñoz; page 192 © Burt Johnson | Dreamstime.com; page 193 © (top right) Kelly Kibbey | Dreamstime.com; page 203 © (top) Diego Grandi | Dreamstime.com; (left middle) Barna Tanko | Dreamstime.com; (right middle) Pablo Hidalgo | Dreamstime.com; (bottom) Irina Kurilovich | Dreamstime.com; page 208 © (top left) Omar Hidalgo; (top right) Artwork © Marco Medina; (bottom left) Siempreverde22 | Dreamstime.com; (bottom right) Patricio Hidalgo | Dreamstime.com; page 211 © (top) Diego Grandi | Dreamstime.com; (left middle) Jjjroy | Dreamstime.com; (right middle)Pablo Hidalgo | Dreamstime.com; (bottom) Kelly Kibbey | Dreamstime.com; page 219 © (top) Irina Kurilovich | Dreamstime.com; (bottom) Irina Kurilovich | Dreamstime.com; page 240 © Barna Tanko | Dreamstime.com; page 247 © (top right) Erin Deo; page 253 © (top left) Angela Perryman | Dreamstime.com; (top right) Javarman | Dreamstime.com; (bottom) Pablo Hidalgo | Dreamstime.com; page 258 © (top) Patricio Hidalgo | Dreamstime.com; page 265 © (top right) Erin Deo; (bottom) Erin Deo; page 274 © (top) Hans Heinz; (left middle) José Zambrano; page 287 © Selva Productions; page 293 © (top left) Mirian Calazacon; page 297 © Mirian Calazacon; page 303 © (top right) Pablo Hidalgo | Dreamstime.com; (bottom) Jarn Verdonk | Dreamstime.com; page 314 © Kelly Kibbey | Dreamstime.com; page 317 © Hugo Gozenbach; page 323 © (top) Sandra Plúa Albán; page 326 © (top) Julianaciendua | Dreamstime.com; (bottom) Pablo Hidalgo | Dreamstime.com; page 330 © (top right) Alanbrito | Dreamstime.com; page 337 © (top) Matyas Rehak | Dreamstime.com © (bottom) Emma Brown; page 355 © (bottom) Alejandro Miranda | Dreamstime.com; page 375 © Jorge Reina; page 378 © Scott Jones | Dreamstime.com; page 379 © (top left) Don Mammoser | Dreamstime.com; page 389 © (left middle)Donyanedomam | Dreamstime.com; (right middle) Pablo Hidalgo | Dreamstime.com; (bottom) Steven Cukrov | Dreamstime.com; page 393 © (bottom) Pablo Hidalgo | Dreamstime.com; page 399 © (top) Pablo Hidalgo | Dreamstime.com; (left middle)Don Mammoser | Dreamstime.com; (right middle)Patricio Hidalgo | Dreamstime.com; (bottom) Patricio Hidalgo | Dreamstime.com; page 407 © (top left) Maria Luisa Lopez Estivill | Dreamstime.com; (top right) Pablo Hidalgo | Dreamstime.com; (bottom left) Danflcreativo | Dreamstime.com; (bottom right) Pablo Hidalgo | Dreamstime.com; page 414 © (top) Maria Luisa Lopez Estivill | Dreamstime.com; (bottom) Bluesunphoto | Dreamstime.com; page 421 © (bottom) Martin Schneiter | Dreamstime.com; page 435 © (top right) Natursports | Dreamstime.com © (top) Mark Ray | Dreamstime.com; page 440 © (top) Donyanedomam | Dreamstime.com; (bottom) Jesse Kraft | Dreamstime.com; page 442 © Maria Luisa Lopez Estivill | Dreamstime.com; page 447 © (top left) Marie Lager; (top right) Marie Lager; (bottom) Carlos Zorilla; page 460 © (top right) BlueOrange Studio/123rf.com; page 467 © (top) Museum Carlos Zevallos Menéndez, Casa de Cultura Núcleo del Guayas; © (bottom) Museo de Arte Precolombino/Casa del Alabado; page 478 © Bryan Garces, Digital Lanceros - Comunication Confeniae; page 487 © Selva Productions.

Acknowledgments

The following people believed in and went out of their way to support this project, the first guidebook on Ecuador with a focus on ethical travel:

Carlos Sandoval, the pirate dreamers Tony and Collin, Fanny and Omar, Magaly and Edwin, Elba Villacis, Jimmy Muñoz, Tanya Romero, Jorge Reina, José Zambrano, Jorge Moran, Morongo García, Wlady Ortiz, Ivan Suarez, Ana María Falconí, Nelson Chanatasig, Peter Schramm, Gabriela Aguilar, Franco Terruzi, Gabriel Faidutti, Rosa Margarits, Hector Vargas, Fausto Valero, Juan Tapuy, Mateo Coellar, Lenín Vasonez, Gaby Espinoza, María Gabriela Albuja Izurieta, Don Marco Tulio Fiallo and Marco Fiallo, Cecilia La Pellegrina, Jorge Moran-Lopez, Paúl Rueda, Tamia Vercoutere, Pablo Hualinga, Hugo Gozenbach, Hans Heinz, Lexi Gropper, Colleen Geiss, Marie Lager, Karen Teran, Manuela Picq, and "El Teniente."And, for unstinting support, Mum and Dad, Mosh and Shwar.

Moon Travel Guides to the Caribbean

ARUBA

BAHAMAS
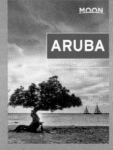

BERMUDA

CUBA
CHRISTOPHER P. BAKER

DOMINICAN REPUBLIC
LEBAWIT LILY GIRMA

JAMAICA

Central & South America Travel Guides

BELIZE

CARTAGENA & COLOMBIA'S CARIBBEAN COAST

COSTA RICA

ECUADOR & THE GALÁPAGOS ISLANDS
BETHANY PITTS

GALÁPAGOS ISLANDS

MACHU PICCHU

PATAGONIA
WAYNE BERNHARDSON

PERU
RYAN DUBE